NETWORKING

MCSA Guide to
Identity with
Windows Server® 2016

MCSE/MCSA

Exam #70-742

CENGAGE

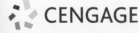
Australia • Brazil • Mexico • Singapore • United Kingdom • United States

Greg Tomsho

MCSA Guide to Identity with Windows Server 2016, Exam 70-742

Greg Tomsho

SVP, GM Skills: Jonathan Lau

Product Director: Lauren Murphy

Product Team Manager: Kristin McNary

Associate Product Manager: Amy Savino

Executive Director of Development: Marah Bellegarde

Senior Product Development Manager: Leigh Hefferon

Content Development Manager: Jill Gallagher

Senior Content Developer: Michelle Ruelos Cannistraci

Product Assistant: Jake Toth

Marketing Director: Michele McTighe

Production Director: Patty Stephan

Senior Content Project Manager: Brooke Greenhouse

Senior Designer: Diana Graham

Cover image: iStockPhoto.com/loops7

Production Service/Composition: SPi Global

For product information and technology assistance, contact us at
Cengage Customer & Sales Support, 1-800-354-9706
or support.cengage.com.

For permission to use material from this text or product, submit all requests online at **www.cengage.com/permissions.**

Library of Congress Control Number: 2017953117

Student Edition ISBN: 978-1-337-40089-3
Loose-leaf Edition ISBN: 978-1-337-68570-2

Cengage
20 Channel Street
Boston, MA 02210
USA

Cengage is a leading provider of customized learning solutions with employees residing in nearly 40 different countries and sales in more than 125 countries around the world. Find your local representative at: **www.cengage.com.**

Cengage products are represented in Canada by Nelson Education, Ltd.

To learn more about Cengage platforms and services, register or access your online learning solution, or purchase materials for your course, visit **www.cengage.com.**

Notice to the Reader

Printed in Mexico
Print Number: 08   Print Year: 2019

Brief Contents

Table of Contents

CHAPTER 7

CHAPTER 8

Implementing Active Directory Certificate Services 321

CHAPTER 9

Implementing Identity Solutions 359

Introduction

MCSA Guide to Identity with Windows Server® 2016, Exam 70-742, gives you in-depth coverage of the 70-742 certification exam objectives and focuses on the skills you need to configure identity services such as Active Directory, user and computer accounts, Group Policy, and Certificate Services with Windows Server 2016. With dozens of hands-on activities and skill-reinforcing case projects, you'll be well prepared for the certification exam and learn valuable skills to perform on the job.

After you finish this book, you'll have an in-depth knowledge of Windows Server 2016 identity management, including Active Directory OUs and accounts, Group Policy and preferences, domain controller and Active Directory management, Certificate Services, and advanced identity solutions such as Active Directory Federation Services (AD FS) and Active Directory Rights Management Services (AD RMS).

This book is written from a teaching and learning point of view, not simply as an exam study guide. The chapters guide readers through the technologies they need to master to perform on the job, not just to pass an exam.

Intended Audience

MCSA Guide to Identity with Windows Server® 2016, Exam 70-742, is intended for people who want to learn how to implement Windows Server 2016 identity solutions and earn the Microsoft Certified Solutions Associate (MCSA) certification. This book covers in full the objectives of Exam 70-742, one of three required for the MCSA: Windows Server 2016 certification. Exam 70-742 is also one of four exams needed for the MCSE: Cloud Platform and Infrastructure certification. This book serves as an excellent tool for classroom teaching, but self-paced learners will also find that the clear explanations, challenging activities, and case projects serve them equally well.

For those readers who start their study of Windows Server 2016 with this book (instead of the 70-740 book), Chapter 1 of the 70-740 book, which serves as an introduction to Windows Server 2016, is available as a free download from the Cengage website. That chapter introduces you to Windows Server 2016 core technologies such as Active Directory and the file system and provides a brief overview of new features found in Windows Server 2016 compared to earlier server versions.

What This Book Includes

- A lab setup guide is included in the "Before You Begin" section of this Introduction to help you configure a physical or virtual (recommended) lab environment for doing the hands-on activities.
- Step-by-step hands-on activities walk you through tasks ranging from installing Active Directory and configuring Group Policy to working with Active Directory Certificate Services. All activities have been tested by a technical editor.

- Extensive review and end-of-chapter materials reinforce your learning.
- Critical thinking case projects require you to apply the concepts and technologies learned throughout the book.
- Abundant screen captures and diagrams visually reinforce the text and hands-on activities.
- A list of 70-742 exam objectives is cross-referenced with chapters and sections that cover each objective (inside cover and Appendix A).

Note

This text does not include Windows Server 2016 software. However, 180-day evaluation versions of Windows Server 2016 are available at no cost from *https://www.microsoft.com/en-us/evalcenter/evaluate-windows-server-2016*. More specific instruction can be found in "Using an Evaluation Version of Windows Server 2016" in the "Before You Begin" section of this Introduction.

About Microsoft Certification: MCSA

This book prepares you to take one of three exams in the Microsoft Certified Solutions Associate (MCSA) Windows Server 2016 certification. The MCSA Windows Server 2016 certification is made up of three exams, which can be taken in any order:

- Exam 70-740: Installation, Storage, and Compute with Windows Server 2016
- Exam 70-741: Networking with Windows Server 2016
- Exam 70-742: Identity with Windows Server 2016

Note

This text focuses on Exam 70-742. Companion texts focus on Exam 740 and Exam 741, respectively: *MCSA Guide to Installation, Storage, and Compute with Windows Server 2016* (Cengage, 2018) and *MCSA Guide to Networking with Windows Server 2016* (Cengage, 2018).

Microsoft Certified Solutions Expert (MCSE): The Next Step

After achieving the MCSA Windows Server 2016 certification, you can move on to the MCSE certification. For the MCSE: Cloud Platform and Infrastructure certification, the MCSA Windows Server 2016 certification is a prerequisite. You then have the option of taking one of ten exams to complete the MCSE. To see the list of exams you can take to complete the MCSE, see *https://www.microsoft.com/en-us/learning/mcse-cloud-platform-infrastructure.aspx*.

Chapter Descriptions

This book is organized to cover the 70-742 exam objectives in a pedagogical sequence, not in the sequence presented by the list of 70-742 exam objectives. Chapter 1 starts you off with an introduction to Active Directory and Group Policy, the cornerstones of identity management on Windows Server 2016. It wraps up by discussing advanced identity solutions found in Windows Server 2016. The 70-742 exam objectives are covered throughout the book, and you can find a map of objectives and the chapters in which they're covered on the inside front cover with a more detailed mapping in Appendix A. The following list describes this book's chapters:

Note

Chapter 1 of the 70-740 book *MCSA Guide to Installation, Storage, and Compute with Windows Server® 2016* (Cengage, 2018) is available as a PDF for free download by students and instructors from the Cengage website. If you start studying Windows Server 2016 with this book, you might want to read Chapter 1 of the 70-740 book first because it provides an introduction to Windows Server 2016 and describes some of the core technologies you may need to understand while studying this book.

- **Chapter 1**, "Introducing Active Directory," begins by discussing the role of a directory service in a network followed by details on installing Active Directory. Next, it explains Active Directory components, such as the schema and Active Directory objects. You will also learn about the Active Directory structure using forests, trees, and domains followed by an introduction to Group Policy.
- **Chapter 2**, "Managing OUs and Active Directory Accounts," discusses GUI and command-line tools for creating and managing all aspects of Active Directory accounts. You also examine the use of several user account properties. Next, you learn about group account types and group scopes, including how to use groups to maintain secure access to resources. In addition, you learn the purpose of computer accounts and how to work with them. Finally, you explore some command-line tools that are useful for automating account management.
- **Chapter 3**, "User and Service Account Configuration," reviews user accounts and group policies so that you have a fresh context for learning how to configure account policies in a domain environment and on a local computer. Account policies help you maintain a secure authentication environment for your domain, but you need to find a balance between security and a system that works for all your users. You learn how to make exceptions in account policies so that you can designate more stringent or more lenient policies for groups of users as needed. This chapter also discusses how you can configure service authentication with a variety of methods, allowing you to choose which method fits each service you install.
- **Chapter 4**, "Configuring Group Policies," covers the architecture of group policies so that you can understand what a Group Policy Object (GPO) is and how and where it can be applied to your Active Directory structure. In addition, you learn about the myriad security settings and user and computer environment settings that can be configured through group policies. You also examine how to apply standard security settings throughout your network and work with Group Policy Preferences.
- **Chapter 5**, "Managing Group Policies," discusses GPO scope, precedence, and inheritance so that you can make sure that the appropriate objects are configured with the appropriate settings. In this chapter, you learn about these topics and see how to change the default group policy client processing.
- **Chapter 6**, "Domain Controller and Active Directory Management," discusses domain controllers (DCs), the main physical component of Active Directory. You learn how to deploy multiple DCs in both single-site and multi-site environments. You will also learn how to optimally deploy operations' master roles on your DCs and how to best configure your DCs for optimal replication.
- **Chapter 7**, "Configuring Advanced Active Directory," reviews the major components and operation of Active Directory and then describes when you might need to configure a multi-domain or multiforest network. You also learn how to configure trust relationships between domains and forests for efficient operation of Active Directory and to make using these complex environments easier for users. Finally, you learn about domain functional levels, the features that are supported in the different functional levels, and how to upgrade domains and forests to the latest functional level.

- **Chapter 8**, "Implementing Active Directory Certificate Services," describes how Microsoft Active Directory Certificate Services provides the infrastructure for issuing and validating digital certificates in a corporate environment. With digital certificates, users can provide proof of their identities to corporate resources and confirm the identity of resources that they can access. Active Directory Certificate Services is Microsoft's implementation of a public key infrastructure (PKI), which secures information transfer and identity management and verification. This chapter describes how a PKI works and defines the terms used to discuss a PKI and Active Directory Certificate Services. You learn how to install and configure the Active Directory Certificate Services role and how to configure and manage key elements of this role, such as certification authorities and certificate enrollments and revocations.
- **Chapter 9**, "Implementing Identity Solutions," discusses three server roles: Active Directory Federation Services, Active Directory Rights Management Services, and Web Application Proxy. These roles use or integrate with AD DS technology to give users flexible, secure access to applications and network resources.
- **Appendix A**, "MCSA 70-742 Exam Objectives," maps each 70-742 exam objective to the chapter and section where you can find information regarding that objective.

Features

This book includes the following learning features to help you master the topics in this book and the 70-742 exam objectives:

- *Chapter objectives*—Each chapter begins with a detailed list of the concepts to be mastered. This list is a quick reference to the chapter's contents and a useful study aid.
- *Hands-on activities*—Several dozen hands-on activities are incorporated into this book, giving you practice in setting up, configuring, and managing Windows Server 2016 identity solutions. Much of the learning about Windows Server 2016 comes from completing the hands-on activities, and much effort has been devoted to making the activities relevant and challenging.
- *Requirements for hands-on activities*—A table at the beginning of each chapter lists the hands-on activities and what you need for each activity.
- *Screen captures, illustrations, and tables*—Numerous screen captures and illustrations of concepts help you visualize theories and concepts and see how to use tools and desktop features. In addition, tables often are used to give you details and comparisons of practical and theoretical information and can be used for a quick review.
- *Chapter summary*—Each chapter ends with a summary of the concepts introduced in the chapter. These summaries provide a helpful way to recap and revisit the material covered in the chapter.
- *Key terms*—All terms in the chapter introduced in bold text are gathered together in the Key Terms list at the end of the chapter. This list gives you a way to check your understanding of all important terms. All key term definitions are listed in the Glossary at the end of the book.
- *Review questions*—The end-of-chapter assessment begins with review questions that reinforce the concepts and techniques covered in each chapter. Answering these questions helps to ensure that you have mastered important topics.
- *Critical thinking*—Each chapter closes with one or more case projects to provide critical thinking exercises. Many of the case projects build on one another.
- *Exam objectives*—Major sections in each chapter show the exam objective or objectives covered in that section, making it easier to find the material you need when studying for the MCSA exam.

Text and Graphics Conventions

Additional information and exercises have been added to this book to help you better understand what's being discussed in the chapter. Icons throughout the book alert you to these additional materials:

Tip

Tips offer extra information on resources, how to solve problems, and time-saving shortcuts.

Note 📎

Notes present additional helpful material related to the subject being discussed.

Caution ⚠

The Caution icon identifies important information about potential mistakes or hazards.

Activity

Each hands-on activity in this book is preceded by the Activity icon.

Critical Thinking

Critical Thinking icons mark the end-of-chapter case projects, which are scenario-based assignments that ask you to apply what you have learned in the chapter.

Q Certification

- Certification icons under chapter headings list exam objectives covered in that section.

Instructor Companion Site

Everything you need for your course in one place! This collection of book-specific lecture and class tools is available online via *www.cengage.com/login*. Access and download PowerPoint presentations, images, the Instructor's Manual, and more.

- *Electronic Instructor's Manual*—The Instructor's Manual that accompanies this book includes additional instructional material to assist in class preparation, including suggestions for classroom activities, discussion topics, and additional quiz questions.
- *Solutions Manual*—The instructor's resources include solutions to all end-of-chapter material, including review questions and case projects.
- *Cengage Testing Powered by Cognero*—This flexible, online system allows you to do the following:
  - Author, edit, and manage test bank content from multiple Cengage solutions.
  - Create multiple test versions in an instant.
  - Deliver tests from your LMS, your classroom, or anywhere you want.

- *PowerPoint presentations*—This book comes with Microsoft PowerPoint slides for each chapter. They're included as a teaching aid for classroom presentation, to make available to students on the network for chapter review, or to be printed for classroom distribution. Instructors, please feel free to add your own slides for additional topics that you introduce to the class.
- *Figure files*—All the figures and tables in the book are reproduced in bitmap format. Similar to the PowerPoint presentations, they're included as a teaching aid for classroom presentation, to make available to students for review, or to be printed for classroom distribution.

MindTap

MindTap for Tomsho / *MCSA Guide to Identity with Windows Server 2016, Exam 70-742*, is a personalized, fully online digital learning platform of content, assignments, and services that engages students and encourages them to think critically while allowing you to easily set your course through simple customization options.

MindTap is designed to help students master the skills they need in today's workforce. Research shows that employers need critical thinkers, troubleshooters, and creative problem solvers to stay relevant in our fast-paced, technology-driven world. MindTap helps you achieve this with assignments and activities that provide hands-on practice, real-life relevance, and certification test prep. Students are guided through assignments that help them master basic knowledge and understanding before moving on to more challenging problems.

The live virtual machine labs provide real-life application and practice. Based on the textbook's Hands-On Activities, the live virtual machine labs provide more advanced learning. Students work in a live environment via the Cloud with real servers and networks that they can explore. The IQ certification test prep engine allows students to quiz themselves on specific exam domains, and the pre- and post-course assessments are mock exams that measure exactly how much they have learned. Readings, labs, and whiteboard videos support lectures, and "In the News" assignments encourage students to stay current.

MindTap is designed around learning objectives and provides the analytics and reporting to easily see where the class stands in terms of progress, engagement, and completion rates. Use the content and learning path as is or pick and choose how our materials will wrap around yours. You control what the students see and when they see it.

Students can access eBook content in the MindTap Reader, which offers highlighting, note-taking, search, and audio (students can listen to text), as well as mobile access. Learn more at *http://www.cengage.com/mindtap/*.

Instant Access Code: 9781337400916
Printed Access Code: 9781337400923

Acknowledgments

I would like to thank Cengage Product Team Manager Kristin McNary and Associate Product Manager Amy Savino for their confidence in asking me to undertake this challenging project. In addition, thanks go out to Michelle Ruelos Cannistraci, Senior Content Developer, who assembled an outstanding team to support this project. A special word of gratitude goes to Deb Kaufmann, Development Editor, who took an unrefined product and turned it into a polished manuscript. Danielle Shaw, Technical Editor, tested chapter activities diligently to ensure that labs work as they were intended, and for that, I am grateful. I also want to include a shout-out to a former student, Shaun Stallard, who was instrumental in the creation of the end-of-chapter material including Chapter Summary, Key Terms, and Review Questions.

Finally, my family: my beautiful wife, Julie, lovely daughters Camille and Sophia, and son, Michael, deserve special thanks and praise for going husbandless and fatherless 7 days a week, 14 hours a day, for the better part of a year. Without their patience and understanding and happy greetings when I did make an appearance, I could not have accomplished this.

About the Author

Greg Tomsho has more than 30 years of computer and networking experience and has earned the CCNA, MCTS, MCSA, Network+, A+, Security+, and Linux+ certifications. Greg is the director of the Computer Networking Technology Department and Cisco Academy at Yavapai College in Prescott, Arizona. His other books include *MCSA Guide to Installation, Storage, and Compute with Windows Server 2016; Exam 70-740, MCSA Guide to Networking with Windows Server 2016; Exam 70-741, Guide to Operating Systems; MCSA Guide to Installing and Configuring Windows Server 2012/R2; Exam 70-410, MCSA Guide to Administering Windows Server 2012/R2; Exam 70-411, MCSA Guide to Configuring Advanced Windows Server 2012/R2 Services; Exam 70-412, MCTS Guide to Microsoft Windows Server 2008 Active Directory Configuration; MCTS Guide to Microsoft Windows Server 2008 Applications Infrastructure Configuration; Guide to Networking Essentials; Guide to Network Support and Troubleshooting;* and *A+ CoursePrep ExamGuide.*

Contact the Author

I would like to hear from you. Please email me at *w2k16@tomsho.com* with any problems, questions, suggestions, or corrections. I even accept compliments! Your comments and suggestions are invaluable for shaping the content of future books. You can also submit errata, lab suggestions, and comments via email. I have set up a website to support my books at *http://books.tomsho.com* where you'll find lab notes, errata, web links, and helpful hints for using my books. If you're an instructor, you can register on the site to contribute articles and comment on articles.

Before You Begin

Windows Server has become more complex as Microsoft strives to satisfy the needs of enterprise networks. In years past, you could learn what you needed to manage a Windows Server–based network and pass the Microsoft certification exams with a single server, some good lab instructions, and a network connection. Today, as you work with advanced technologies—such as highly available DHCP, IPAM, and RADIUS, just to name a few—your lab environment must be more complex, requiring several servers. Setting up this lab environment can be challenging, and this section was written to help you meet this challenge. Using virtual machines in Hyper-V on Windows 10 or Windows Server 2016 is highly recommended; other virtual environments work, too, but you'll want to choose one that allows nested virtualization, which means running a virtual machine within a virtual machine so you can do some of the Hyper-V activities that require it. Using virtual machines is also highly recommended because it allows you to easily change the storage and network configuration of your servers and allows you to revert your lab to its original state for each chapter.

 Note

The MindTap digital online learning platform for this text includes access to live virtual machine labs based on the textbook's hands-on activities without the need to set up your own lab environment.

Lab Setup Guide

 Note

If you can't set up a lab environment exactly as described in this section, you might be able to configure a partial lab with just one Windows Server 2016 server and still do many of the hands-on activities. Having two servers is even better, and having three enables you to do the majority of the book's activities. If you can't do an activity, it's important to read the activity steps to learn important information about Windows Server 2016.

Because of the flexibility and availability of using a virtual environment, the lab setup guide is designed with the assumption that virtualization is used, whether Hyper-V, VMware, VirtualBox, or some other product. The lab environment is designed so that the initial configuration of the virtual machines will take you through any chapter. Each chapter starts with an activity that instructs the reader to revert the virtual machines used in the chapter to the initial configuration using a saved snapshot/checkpoint.

A total of four virtual machines (VMs) with Windows Server 2016 installed are used throughout the book. However, they are not all used at the same time; some activities use as many as three VMs while some require only one or two. No client OS is used. This decision was made primarily on the basis that many readers will be using evaluation versions of Windows on their VMs and the evaluation period for Windows client OSs such as Windows 10 is very short compared to Windows Server 2016's evaluation period. In addition, Windows 10 is continually being upgraded and the upgrades may affect the outcome of some of the activities. Therefore, any activities that require a client will use a VM that has Windows Server 2016 installed. Readers should see little to no difference between using Windows Server 2016 as a client OS and using Windows 10.

The activities use four VMs running Windows Server 2016 in which one server is a domain controller (DC) and two servers are domain members. The fourth server is configured as a stand-alone server that is operating in workgroup mode. Some activities require your VMs to access the Internet. An easy way to accommodate this is to install the Remote Access role on your Hyper-V host (if you're using Hyper-V and Windows Server 2016 for your host computer) and configure NAT so your Hyper-V host can route packets to the physical network and the Internet. After installing the Remote Access role with the Routing role service, configure NAT and select the interface connected to the physical network as the public interface and the interface connected to the Hyper-V internal switch as the private interface. The interface connected to the Hyper-V internal switch should be configured with address 192.168.0.250/24. Figure 1 shows a diagram of this network.

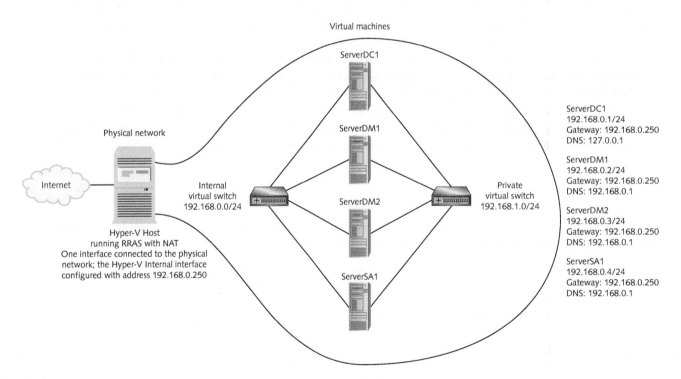

Figure 1   A diagram of the lab configuration used in this book

A few words about this diagram:
- The router address is an example; you can use a different address. You can complete most activities without a router to the Internet except those that require Internet access.
- ServerDC1 is a domain controller for domain MCSA2016.local and has both the Active Directory Domain Services (AD DS) and DNS server roles installed.
- Specific installation requirements for each server are explained in the following sections.

Host Computer Configuration

The following are recommendations for the host computer when you're using virtualization:
- Dual-core or quad-core CPU with Intel-VT-x/EPT support. You can see a list of supported Intel processors at *http://ark.intel.com/Search/Advanced*; click Processors and then select the "Intel-VT-x with Extended Page Tables (EPT)" filter.

Note

Most activities can be done without a CPU that supports EPT, but you can't install Hyper-V on a VM if the host doesn't support EPT for Intel CPUs.

- 8 GB RAM; more is better.
- 200 GB free disk space.
- Windows Server 2016 or Windows 10 if you're using Hyper-V.
- Windows 10 or Windows 8.1 if you're using VMware Workstation or VirtualBox.

Server Configuration Details

ServerDC1

This virtual machine should be configured as follows:
- Windows Server 2016 Datacenter—Desktop Experience
- Server name: ServerDC1
- Administrator password: Password01
- Memory: 2 GB or more
- Hard disk 1: 60 GB or more
- Ethernet connection—Connected to Internal Virtual Switch
  - IP address: 192.168.0.1/24
  - Default gateway: 192.168.0.250 (or an address supplied by the instructor)
  - DNS: 127.0.0.1
- Ethernet 2 connection—connected to Private Virtual Switch
  - IP address: 192.168.1.1/24
  - Default gateway: Not configured
  - DNS: Not configured
- Active Directory Domain Services and DNS installed:
  - Domain Name: MCSA2016.local
  - Create the following users in the Users folder: domuser1 and domuser2 with Password01; password does not expire. These two users are only members of the Domain Users group. Also create domadmin1 and domadmin2 with Password01; password does not expire. These two users are members of the Domain Admins group.
- Windows Update: Configured with most recent updates

- Power Setting: Never turn off display
- Internet Explorer Enhanced Security Configuration: Turned off for Administrator
- User Account Control: Lowest setting
- After Server DC1 is fully configured, create a checkpoint/snapshot named InitialConfig that will be applied at the beginning of each chapter's activities where this VM is used. Turn off the VM before you create a checkpoint/snapshot.

ServerDM1

This virtual machine should be configured as follows:

- Windows Server 2016 Datacenter—Desktop Experience
- Server name: ServerDM1
- Administrator password: Password01
- Memory: 2 GB or more
- Hard disk 1: 60 GB or more
- Hard disk 2: 20 GB
- Hard disk 3: 15 GB
- Hard disk 4: 10 GB
- Ethernet connection—connected to Internal Virtual Switch
  - IP address: 192.168.0.2/24
  - Default gateway: 192.168.0.250 (or an address supplied by the instructor)
  - DNS: 192.168.0.1 (the address of ServerDC1)
- Ethernet 2 connection—connected to Private Virtual Switch
  - IP address: 192.168.1.2/24
  - Default gateway: Not configured
  - DNS: Not configured
- Member of domain: MCSA2016.local
- Create the following local users: adminuser1 with Password01 and password doesn't expire. User is a member of the local Administrators group. Reguser1 with Password01 and password doesn't expire. User is only a member of the local Users group.
- Windows Update: Configured with most recent updates
- Power Setting: Never turn off display
- Internet Explorer Enhanced Security Configuration: Turned off for Administrator
- User Account Control: Lowest setting
- After Server DM1 is fully configured, create a Checkpoint/Snapshot named InitialConfig that will be applied at the beginning of each chapter's activities where this VM is used.

ServerDM2

This virtual machine should be configured as follows:

- Windows Server 2016 Datacenter—Server Core
- Server name: ServerDM2
- Administrator password: Password01
- Memory: 2 GB or more
- Hard disk 1: 60 GB or more
- Hard disk 2: 20 GB
- Hard disk 3: 15 GB
- Hard disk 4: 10 GB
- Ethernet connection—connected to Internal Virtual Switch
  - IP address: 192.168.0.3/24
  - Default gateway: 192.168.0.250 (or an address supplied by the instructor)
  - DNS: 192.168.0.1 (the address of ServerDC1)

- Ethernet 2 connection—connected to Private Virtual Switch
  - IP address: 192.168.1.3/24
  - Default gateway: Not configured
  - DNS: Not configured
- Member of domain: MCSA2016.local
- Windows Update: Configured with most recent updates
- Power Setting: Never turn off display
- Internet Explorer Enhanced Security Configuration: Turned off for Administrator
- User Account Control: Lowest setting
- After Server DM2 is fully configured, create a Checkpoint/Snapshot named InitialConfig that will be applied at the beginning of each chapter's activities where this VM is used.

ServerSA1

This virtual machine should be configured as follows:
- Windows Server 2016 Datacenter—Desktop Experience
- Server name: ServerSA1
- Administrator password: Password01
- Memory: 2 GB or more
- Hard disk 1: 60 GB or more
- Hard disk 2: 20 GB
- Hard disk 3: 15 GB
- Hard disk 4: 10 GB
- Ethernet connection—connected to Internal Virtual Switch
  - IP address: 192.168.0.4/24
  - Default gateway: 192.168.0.250 (or an address supplied by the instructor)
  - DNS: 192.168.0.1 (the address of ServerDC1)
- Ethernet 2 connection—connected to Private Virtual Switch
  - IP address: 192.168.1.4/24
  - Default gateway: Not configured
  - DNS: Not configured
- Workgroup: MCSA2016 (The workgroup name doesn't matter)
- Windows Update: Configured with most recent updates
- Power Setting: Never turn off display
- Internet Explorer Enhanced Security Configuration: Turned off for Administrator
- User Account Control: Lowest setting
- After Server SA1 is fully configured, create a checkpoint/snapshot named InitialConfig that will be applied at the beginning of each chapter's activities where this VM is used.

Using an Evaluation Version of Windows Server 2016

You can get a 180-day evaluation copy of Windows Server 2016 from the Microsoft Evaluation Center at *https://www.microsoft.com/en-us/evalcenter/evaluate-windows-server-2016/*. You will need to sign in with your Microsoft account or create a new account. You can download an ISO file that can then be attached to your virtual machine's DVD drive to install Windows Server 2016.

If your evaluation version of Windows Server 2016 gets close to expiration, you can extend the evaluation period (180 days) up to five times. To do so, follow these steps:

1. Open a command prompt window as Administrator.
2. Type **slmgr -xpr** and press **Enter** to see the current status of your license. It shows how many days are left in the evaluation. If it says you're in notification mode, you need to rearm the evaluation immediately.

3. To extend the evaluation for another 180 days, type **slmgr -rearm** and press **Enter**. You see a message telling you to restart the system for the changes to take effect. Click **OK** and restart the system.

4. After you have extended the evaluation period, you should take a new checkpoint/snapshot and replace the InitialConfig checkpoint/snapshot.

Where to Go for Help

Configuring a lab and keeping everything running correctly can be challenging. Even small configuration changes can prevent activities from running correctly. The author maintains a website that includes lab notes, suggestions, errata, and help articles that might be useful if you're having trouble, and you can contact the author at these addresses:

1. Website: *htttp://books.tomsho.com*
2. Email: *w2k16@tomsho.com*

CHAPTER 1

INTRODUCING ACTIVE DIRECTORY

After reading this chapter and completing the exercises, you will be able to:

Describe the role of a directory service

Install Active Directory

Describe objects found in Active Directory

Work with forests, trees, and domains

Configure group policies

Active Directory is the core component in a Windows domain environment. The Active Directory Domain Services role provides a single point of user identity and authentication, and client and server administration. To understand Active Directory and its role in a network, you need to know what a directory service is and how it's used to manage resources and access to resources on a network. Before administrators can use Active Directory to manage users, desktops, and servers in a network, they need a good understanding of Active Directory's structure and underlying components and objects, which are covered in this chapter. You also learn how to install Active Directory and work with forests, trees, and domains. Finally, you learn the basics of using the Group Policy tool to set consistent security, user, and desktop standards throughout your organization.

The Role of a Directory Service

Ⓠ Certification

- **70-742 – Install and configure Active Directory Domain Services (AD DS):**
  Install and configure domain controllers

Table 1-1 summarizes what you need for the hands-on activities in this chapter.

Table 1-1   Activity requirements

Activity	Requirements	Notes
Activity 1-1: Resetting Your Virtual Environment	ServerSA1	
Activity 1-2: Installing Active Directory Domain Services	ServerSA1	
Activity 1-3: Exploring Active Directory Container Objects	ServerSA1	
Activity 1-4: Viewing Default Leaf Objects	ServerSA1	
Activity 1-5: Creating Objects in Active Directory	ServerSA1	
Activity 1-6: Using the Command Line to Create Users	ServerSA1	
Activity 1-7: Locating Objects in Active Directory	ServerSA1	
Activity 1-8: Publishing a Shared Folder in Active Directory	ServerSA1	
Activity 1-9: Viewing the Operations Master Roles and Global Catalog Server	ServerSA1	
Activity 1-10: Exploring Default GPOs	ServerSA1	
Activity 1-11: Working with Group Policies	ServerSA1	

A network **directory service**, as the name suggests, stores information about a computer network and offers features for retrieving and managing that information. Essentially, it's a database composed of records or objects describing users and available network resources, such as servers, printers, and applications. Like a database for managing a company's inventory, a directory service includes functions to search for, add, modify, and delete information. Unlike an inventory database, a directory service can also manage how its stored resources can be used and by whom. For example, a directory service can be used to specify who has the right to sign in to a computer or restrict what software can be installed on a computer.

A directory service is often thought of as an administrator's tool, but users can use it, too. Users might need the directory service to locate network resources, such as printers or shared folders, by performing a search. They can even use the directory service as a phone book of sorts to look up information about other users, such as phone numbers, office locations, and email addresses.

Whether an organization consists of a single facility or has multiple locations, a directory service provides a centralized management tool for users and resources in all locations. This capability does add a certain amount of complexity, so making sure the directory service is structured and designed correctly before using it is critical.

Windows Active Directory

Active Directory is a directory service based on standards for defining, storing, and accessing directory service objects. X.500, a suite of protocols developed by the International Telecommunications Union (ITU), is the basis for its hierarchical structure and for how Active Directory objects are named and stored. **Lightweight Directory Access Protocol (LDAP)**, created by the Internet Engineering Task Force (IETF), is based on the X.500 Directory Access Protocol (DAP). DAP required the seldom-used, high-overhead Open Systems Interconnection (OSI) protocol stack for accessing directory objects. LDAP became a streamlined version of DAP, using the more efficient and widely used TCP/IP—hence the term "lightweight" in the protocol's name.

So why is knowledge of LDAP important? You run across references to LDAP periodically when reading about Active Directory, and as an administrator, you'll be using tools such as ADSI Edit that incorporate LDAP definitions and objects or running programs that use LDAP to integrate with Active Directory. In addition, integrating other OSs, such as Linux, into an Active Directory network requires using LDAP. In fact, you use a tool that incorporates LDAP terminology in this chapter when you run some command-line tools for working with Active Directory. LDAP and its syntax are covered in more detail when you work with command-line tools in Chapter 2. For now, you focus on Active Directory and its structure and features.

Windows Active Directory became part of the Windows family of server OSs starting with Windows 2000 Server. Before Windows 2000, Windows NT Server had a directory service that was little more than a user manager; it included centralized logon and grouped users and computers into logical security boundaries called domains. The Windows NT domain system was a flat database of users and computers with no way to organize users or resources by department, function, or location. This single, unstructured list made managing large numbers of users cumbersome.

Active Directory's hierarchical database enables administrators to organize users and network resources to reflect the organization of the environment in which it's used. For example, if a company identifies its users and resources mostly by department or location, Active Directory can be configured to mirror this structure. You can structure Active Directory and organize the objects representing users and resources in a way that makes the most sense. Active Directory offers the following features, among others, that make it a highly flexible directory service:

- *Hierarchical organization*—This structure makes management of network resources and administration of security policies easier.
- *Centralized but distributed database*—All network data is centrally located, but it can be distributed among many servers for fast, easy access to information from any location. Automatic replication of information also provides load balancing and fault tolerance. **Active Directory replication** is the transfer of information among all domain controllers to make sure they have consistent and up-to-date information.
- *Scalability*—Advanced indexing technology provides high-performance data access whether Active Directory consists of a few dozen or a few million objects.
- *Security*—Fine-grained access controls enable administrators to control access to each directory object and its properties. Active Directory also supports secure authentication protocols to maximize compatibility with Internet applications and other systems.
- *Flexibility*—Active Directory is installed with some predefined objects, such as user accounts and groups, but their properties can be modified, and new objects can be added for a customized solution.
- *Policy-based administration*—Administrators can define policies to ensure a secure and consistent environment for users yet maintain the flexibility to apply different rules for departments, locations, or user classes as needed.

Overview of the Active Directory Structure

As with most things, the best way to understand how Active Directory works is to install it and start using it, but knowing the terms used to describe its structure is helpful. There are two aspects of Active Directory's structure:

- Physical structure
- Logical structure

Active Directory's Physical Structure

The physical structure consists of sites and servers configured as domain controllers. An Active Directory **site** is nothing more than a physical location in which domain controllers communicate and replicate information periodically. Specifically, Microsoft defines a site as one or more IP subnets connected by high-speed LAN technology. A small business with no branch offices or other locations, for example, consists of a single site. However, a business with a branch office in another part of the city connected to the main office through a slow WAN link usually has two sites. Typically, each physical location with a domain controller operating in a common domain connected by a WAN constitutes a site. The main reasons for defining multiple sites are to control the frequency of Active Directory replication and to assign policies based on physical location.

Another component of the physical structure is a server configured as a **domain controller (DC)**, which is a computer running Windows Server 2016 with the Active Directory Domain Services role installed. Although an Active Directory domain can consist of many domain controllers, each domain controller can service only one domain. Each DC contains a full replica of the objects that make up the domain and is responsible for the following functions:

- Storing a copy of the domain data and replicating changes to that data to all other domain controllers throughout the domain
- Providing data search and retrieval functions for users attempting to locate objects in the directory
- Providing authentication and authorization services for users who sign in to the domain and attempt to access network resources

Active Directory's Logical Structure

The logical structure of Active Directory makes it possible to pattern the directory service's look and feel after the organization in which it runs. There are four organizing components of Active Directory:

- Organizational units
- Domains
- Trees
- Forests

These four components can be thought of as containers and are listed from most specific to broadest in terms of what they contain. To use a geographical analogy, an organizational unit represents a neighborhood, a domain is the city, a tree is the state, and a forest is the country.

An **organizational unit (OU)** is an Active Directory container used to organize a network's users and resources into logical administrative units. An OU contains Active Directory objects, such as user accounts, groups, computer accounts, printers, shared folders, applications, servers, and domain controllers. The OU structure often mimics a company's internal administrative structure, although this structure isn't required. For example, a corporation might create an OU for each department, but an educational

Figure 1-1   Active Directory organizational units

institution might create separate OUs for students, faculty, and administration or for campus locations. You can use a combination of structures, too, because OUs can be nested in as many levels as necessary. Besides being an organizational tool, OUs can represent policy boundaries, in which different sets of policies can be applied to objects in different OUs. Figure 1-1 shows OUs and the types of objects in them.

A **domain** is Active Directory's core structural unit. It contains OUs and represents administrative, security, and policy boundaries (see Figure 1-2). A small to medium company usually has one domain with a single IT administrative group. However, a large company or a company with several locations might benefit from having multiple domains to separate IT administration or accommodate widely differing network policies. For example, a company with major branches in the United States and the United Kingdom might want to divide administrative responsibilities into domains based on location, such as US.csmtech.local and UK.csmtech.local domains, each with a separate administrative group and set of policies. This arrangement addresses possible language and cultural barriers and takes advantage of the benefit of proximity.

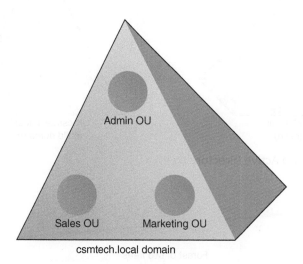

Figure 1-2   An Active Directory domain and OUs

An Active Directory **tree** is less a container than a grouping of domains that share a common naming structure. A tree consists of a parent domain and possibly one or more **child domains** (also called *subdomains*) that have the same second-level and top-level domain names as the parent domain. For example, US.csmtech.local and UK.csmtech.local are both child domains of the parent domain csmtech.local, and all three domains are part of the same tree. Furthermore, child domains can have child domains, as in phoenix.US.csmtech.local. Figure 1-3 depicts domains in an Active Directory tree.

An Active Directory **forest** is a collection of one or more trees. A forest can consist of a single tree with a single domain, or it can contain several trees, each with a hierarchy of parent and child domains. Each tree in a forest has a different naming structure, so although one tree might have csmtech.local as the parent, another tree in the forest might have csmpub.local as its parent domain. A forest's main purpose is to provide a common Active Directory environment in which all domains in all trees can communicate with one another and share information yet allow independent operation and administration of each domain. Figure 1-4 shows an Active Directory forest and the trees and domains it contains. Every forest has a forest root domain, which is the first domain created in a new forest. The forest root domain is discussed later in the section "The Role of Forests."

This section has given you an overview of Active Directory components. You learn more about Active Directory account objects in Chapter 2. To understand its features and structure, you install and work with Active Directory in the next section.

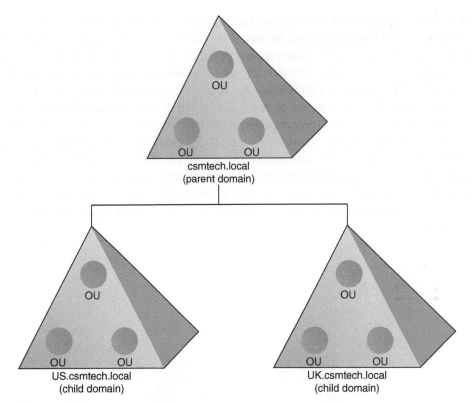

Figure 1-3   **An Active Directory tree**

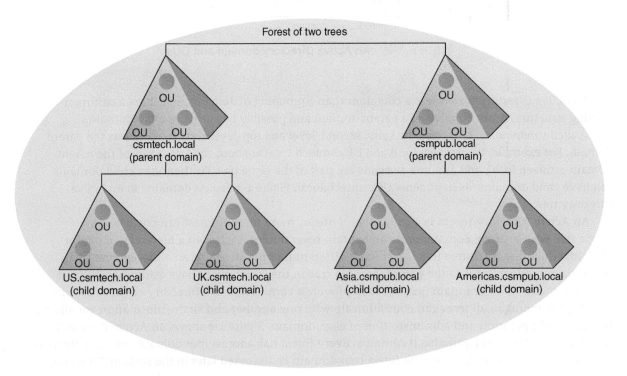

Figure 1-4   **An Active Directory forest**

Installing Active Directory

● 70-742 – Install and configure Active Directory Domain Services (AD DS):
  Install and configure domain controllers

The Windows Active Directory service is commonly referred to as *Active Directory Domain Services (AD DS)*. You must install this role for Active Directory to be part of your network. As with any server role, installing AD DS is fairly straightforward with the real work in the planning and postinstallation tasks.

To begin installing AD DS in Windows Server 2016 with Desktop Experience, you use Server Manager. Of course, you can also use PowerShell. After selecting the Active Directory Domain Services role to install, you add the necessary features, which include a variety of administration tools and PowerShell modules. The installation program states that you must install the DNS Server role if DNS isn't already installed on the network and informs you that a few other services needed for Active Directory replication must be installed. In the confirmation window, you have the option to export the Active Directory deployment configuration settings, which creates an XML file with the installation settings you selected. This file can be used to automate Active Directory installations on other servers. After the installation is finished, you must configure Active Directory. To get started, click the notifications flag in Server Manager and click *Promote this server to a domain controller (DC)*, which starts the Active Directory Domain Services Configuration Wizard.

> **Note** 📎
>
> In Windows Server 2008 and earlier, you needed to run the `dcpromo.exe` program to promote a server to a DC. `Dcpromo.exe` was deprecated starting with Windows Server 2012.

In the Deployment Configuration window, you select from these options: Add a domain controller to an existing domain, Add a new domain to an existing forest, and Add a new forest (see Figure 1-5). For the first DC in the network, you should choose the option to Add a new forest. Next, you're prompted for the **fully qualified domain name (FQDN)** for the new forest root domain. An FQDN is a domain name that includes all parts of the name, including the top-level domain.

> **Note** 📎
>
> The first domain in a new forest is also the name of the forest. The wizard checks to be sure the forest name doesn't already exist.

The next window is Domain Controller Options; it is where you choose the forest and domain functional levels (see Figure 1-6). Microsoft has expanded Active Directory's functionality with each server OS since Windows 2000. For the most advanced features and security, you should choose the most current functional level, which is Windows Server 2016. For the most backward compatibility with older DCs on the network, you should choose Windows 2008 for the forest functional level. You can't choose a forest functional level earlier than Windows Server 2008. If you choose the Windows Server 2016 forest functional level, you can't run DCs that have an OS version earlier than Windows Server 2016. You can, however, still run older servers as member servers.

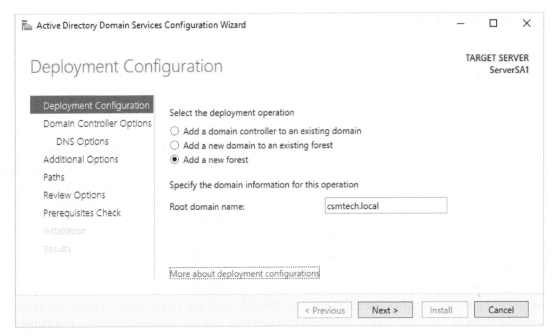

Figure 1-5   The Deployment Configuration window

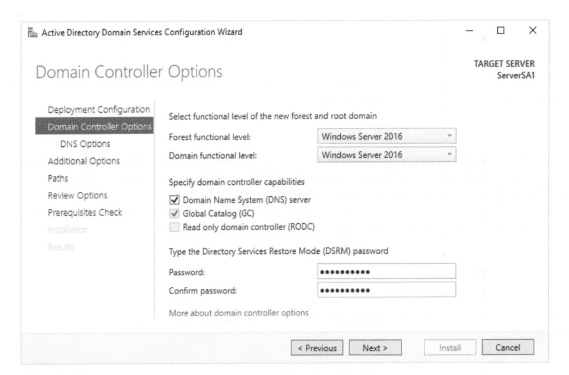

Figure 1-6   Choosing the forest and domain functional levels

You have three options to specify capabilities for the DC:

- *Domain Name System (DNS) server*—For the first DC in a new domain, DNS should be installed unless you will be using an existing DNS server for the domain.
- *Global Catalog (GC)*—For the first DC in a forest, this check box is selected and disabled because the first DC in a new forest must also be a global catalog server.

- *Read only domain controller (RODC)*—This check box isn't selected by default. This option is disabled for the first DC in the domain because it can't be an RODC.

At the bottom of the window, you enter a password for **Directory Services Restore Mode (DSRM)**. This boot mode is used to perform restore operations on Active Directory if it becomes corrupted or parts of it are deleted accidentally.

The next window, DNS Options, prompts you to create DNS delegation if an existing DNS server for the domain exists, allowing Windows to create the necessary records on the DNS server for the new domain. You must enter valid credentials for the DNS server. If you are installing DNS and there are no other DNS servers for the domain, this option is disabled.

In the next window, Additional Options, you specify a NetBIOS domain name, which is used for backward compatibility with systems that don't use DNS. A default name is entered, but you can change it, if needed. The default name is the first eight characters of the domain name.

In the Paths window, you specify the location of the Active Directory database, log files, and SYSVOL folder (see Figure 1-7). The **SYSVOL folder** is a shared folder containing file-based information that's replicated to other domain controllers. Storing the database and log files on separate disks, if possible, is best for optimal performance. Next, you review your selections in the Review Options window. You can also view and export a PowerShell script with your settings if you want to duplicate them for another Active Directory configuration.

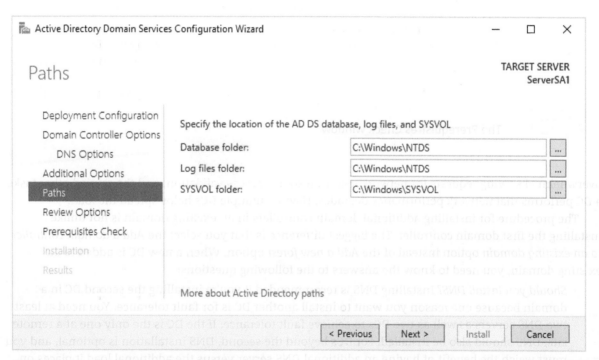

Figure 1-7   Specifying Active Directory paths

Windows then does a prerequisites check before starting the Active Directory installation and configuration (see Figure 1-8). This check notifies you of anything that could prevent successful installation and configuration of Active Directory. When the installation is finished, the server restarts. Server Manager then includes some new MMCs in the Tools menu for configuring and managing Active Directory.

Installing Additional Domain Controllers in a Domain

Microsoft recommends at least two domain controllers in every domain for fault tolerance and load balancing. Even the smallest domain should have two DCs because a domain controller can disrupt user access to network resources if no backup DC is available. In larger networks, a single DC can become so

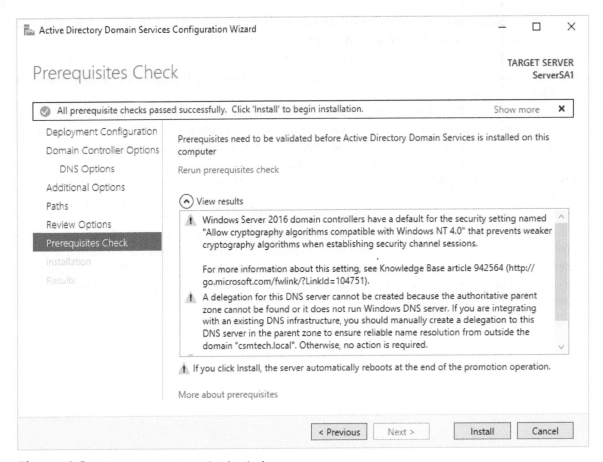

Figure 1-8   The Prerequisites Check window

overwhelmed serving requests for network logons, resource access validation, and the myriad other tasks a DC performs that network performance degrades. Having multiple DCs helps spread the load.

The procedure for installing additional domain controllers in an existing domain is not unlike installing the first domain controller. The biggest difference is that you select the *Add a domain controller to an existing domain* option instead of the *Add a new forest* option. When a new DC is added to an existing domain, you need to know the answers to the following questions:

- *Should you install DNS?* Installing DNS is recommended if you're installing the second DC in a domain because one reason you want to install another DC is for fault tolerance. You need at least two DNS servers as well as two DCs to achieve fault tolerance. If the DC is the only one at a remote site, DNS should also be installed. For DCs beyond the second, DNS installation is optional, and you must weigh the benefit of having an additional DNS server versus the additional load it places on the server.
- *Should the DC be a global catalog (GC) server?* The first DC is always configured as a GC server, but when you're installing additional DCs in a domain, this setting is optional. In most cases, it makes sense to make all your DCs global catalog servers as well, particularly in a single-domain forest. The global catalog and its importance in a network are discussed later in this chapter in the section "Working with Forests, Trees, and Domains."
- *Should this be a read only domain controller (RODC)?* An RODC is most often used in branch office situations in which ensuring the server's physical security is more difficult. An RODC doesn't store account credentials, so if an RODC is compromised, no passwords can be retrieved. If the DC isn't at a branch office, there's no substantial advantage in making it an RODC.
- *In which site should the DC be located?* If you have more than one site defined for your network, you can choose where you want the DC to be located.

When you are installing an additional DC in a domain, you have the option to use a feature called *Install from Media*, discussed later in the section "Installing a DC with Install from Media."

Installing a New Domain in an Existing Forest

Another reason to install a new DC is to add a domain to an existing forest. There are two variations to the procedure:

- *Add a child domain*—In this variation, you're adding a domain that shares at least the top-level and second-level domain name structure as an existing domain in the forest. For example, if your current domain is named csmtech.local and you add a branch office in Europe, your new domain might be named europe.csmtech.local. The new domain has a separate domain administrator, but the forest administrator has the authority to manage most aspects of both the child and parent domains. Figure 1-9 shows the window in the Active Directory installation where you choose to install a child domain. Notice that Child Domain is selected in the Select domain type list box. The other choice is Tree Domain, discussed next. The parent domain is the name of the existing domain for which you're creating a child domain. In the figure, the existing domain is csmtech.local. The new domain name is the name of the new child domain, which in this example is *europe*. The new domain has the FQDN europe.csmtech.local. You must have the right credentials (a user who's a member of Domain Admins) for the csmtech.local domain to perform the operation. The new DC must be able to contact a DC from the parent domain, so DNS must be configured correctly. All the other steps are the same as installing a DC in a new forest.

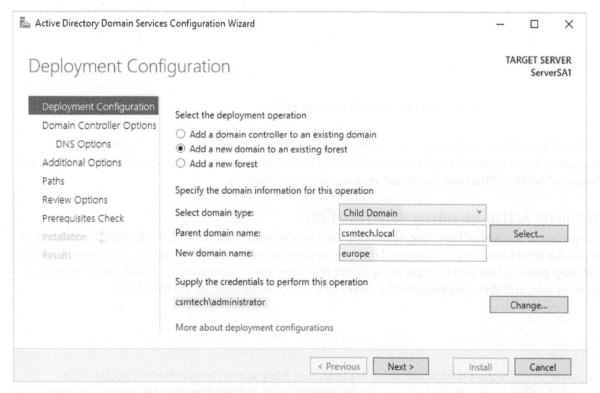

Figure 1-9   Adding a new child domain in an existing forest

- *Add a new tree*—In this variation, you're adding a new domain with a separate naming structure from any existing domains in the forest. So in a forest named csmtech.local, you can add a new domain (and, therefore, a new tree in the forest) named csmpub.local. Operationally, a new tree is the same as a child domain. Figure 1-10 shows the window in the Active Directory installation where you choose to install a new tree with Tree Domain selected as the domain type. You need to enter the name of the forest, which is always the name of the first domain installed when the forest was created (the forest root domain); in this example, it's csmtech.local. As when adding a child domain, you need credentials to add the domain to the forest, but in this case, you need a user who's a member of Enterprise Admins and Schema Admins. The administrator account for the forest root domain is a member of both groups.

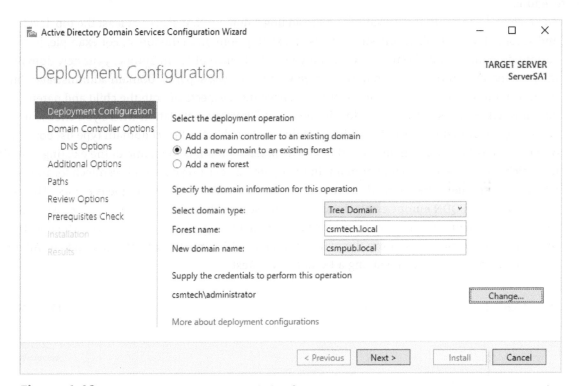

Figure 1-10   Adding a new tree in an existing forest

Working with multi-domain forests and multi-forest networks is an advanced topic. Some information you need to know is discussed later in this chapter in the "Working with Forests, Trees, and Domains" section. This topic is covered in more detail in Chapter 7.

Installing Active Directory in Server Core

The preferred method of installing Active Directory in a Windows Server 2016 Server Core installation is to use the PowerShell cmdlets designed for this purpose. Installing Active Directory with PowerShell is a two-step process, just as it is when using Server Manager. First, you install the Active Directory Domain Services role, and then you promote the server to a DC by configuring Active Directory.

> **Note**
>
> For server administrators familiar with using dcpromo.exe along with an answer file, this option is still available. Just be aware that dcpromo.exe is a deprecated command and it may not be available in future Windows versions.

Use the following command to install the Active Directory Domain Services role, like any other server role:

```
Add-WindowsFeature AD-Domain-Services
```

If you're using PowerShell in a Desktop Experience installation, you should probably include the `-IncludeManagementTools` parameter in this command. In a Server Core installation, however, you can't use the management tools. The preceding command prepares the server for promotion to a DC, but you must enter another command to start the promotion process. Which command you use depends on the type of installation you want:

- `Install-ADDSForest`—This command creates a new DC in a new forest. You must provide a domain name, which also serves as the forest name. So, for example, to create the csmtech.local domain in a new forest, use the following command:

```
Install-ADDSForest -DomainName "csmtech.local"
```

- `Install-ADDSDomainController`—This command adds a DC to an existing domain. You specify the name of the existing domain as shown:

```
Install-ADDSDomainController -DomainName "csmtech.local"
```

- `Install-ADDSDomain`—This command adds a new domain to an existing forest. You need to specify the new domain name, the parent domain, and the type of domain (`TreeDomain` or `ChildDomain`). The default is `ChildDomain`. To add a domain named *europe* to the existing forest named *csmtech.local*, use the following command:

```
Install-ADDSDomain -NewDomainName "europe" -ParentDomainName "csmtech.local"
 -DomainType ChildDomain
```

For the preceding commands, you need to specify credentials for an account with the necessary permissions to perform the installation. For each command, you can get detailed help in PowerShell with the `Get-Help` command, including examples of how to use the command. For instance, to get detailed help on using `Install-ADDSDomain`, including examples, use the following command:

```
Get-Help Install-ADDSDomain -detailed
```

If you want to see what a PowerShell cmdlet does without actually performing the operation, use the `-WhatIf` parameter. PowerShell displays the steps needed to perform the command, showing you the default settings and prompting you for other information the command requires.

Installing a DC with Install from Media

When you install a new DC in an existing domain, it must be updated with all existing data in the Active Directory database. Depending on the database's size and the new DC's location in relation to existing DCs, this process could take some time and use considerable bandwidth. If the new DC is the first in a branch office connected via a WAN, the time and bandwidth use might be a concern. Using the **Install from Media (IFM)** option during Active Directory configuration can substantially reduce the replication traffic needed to update the new DC. This utility copies the contents of an existing DC's Active Directory database (and optionally the SYSVOL folder) to disk. These contents are then used to populate the new DC's Active Directory database, thereby reducing the replication needed to bring the new DC's database up to date.

The procedure for using IFM is as follows:

1. Select a suitable DC from which you'll create the IFM data. If you're creating IFM data for a standard DC (a writeable DC, not an RODC), you must use a standard DC to create this data. If you're creating IFM data for an RODC, you can use an RODC or a standard DC.
2. On the selected DC, run the `ntdsutil` command-line program at an elevated command prompt. Ntdsutil is an interactive program, where you enter commands as shown in Figure 1-11 and explained in the following list:
   - ntdsutil: Starts the command-line program.
   - `activate instance ntds`: Sets the program focus on the Active Directory database.
   - `ifm`: Sets the program to IFM mode.

```
C:\Windows\system32>ntdsutil
ntdsutil: activate instance ntds
Active instance set to "ntds".
ntdsutil: ifm
ifm: create full c:\IFMdata
Creating snapshot...
Snapshot set {d4ff2365-d3c2-4a5a-a2e1-4d5b83ca6ca8} generated successfully.
Snapshot {910b49ba-bbe9-4e66-bba9-f5d00e844ab6} mounted as C:\$SNAP_201701281813_VOLUMEC$\
Snapshot {910b49ba-bbe9-4e66-bba9-f5d00e844ab6} is already mounted.
Initiating DEFRAGMENTATION mode...
     Source Database: C:\$SNAP_201701281813_VOLUMEC$\Windows\NTDS\ntds.dit
     Target Database: c:\IFMdata\Active Directory\ntds.dit

              Defragmentation  Status (% complete)

     0    10   20   30   40   50   60   70   80   90  100
     |----|----|----|----|----|----|----|----|----|----|
     ..................................................

Copying registry files...
Copying c:\IFMdata\registry\SYSTEM
Copying c:\IFMdata\registry\SECURITY
Snapshot {910b49ba-bbe9-4e66-bba9-f5d00e844ab6} unmounted.
IFM media created successfully in c:\IFMdata
ifm: _
```

Figure 1-11 Creating IFM data with `ntdsutil`

The next command creates the IFM data and has the following four variations. The `path` parameter specifies where to store IFM data and can be a local drive, a network share, or removable media. A network share is ideal so that the new DC has access to IFM data without having to copy data or transfer removable media. In addition, you can use the network share for multiple DC installations easily.

- `create full path`: Creates IFM data for a writeable DC.
- `create RODC path`: Creates IFM data for an RODC.
- `create Sysvol Full path`: Creates IFM data for a writeable DC and includes the SYSVOL folder.
- `create Sysvol RODC path`: Creates IFM data for an RODC and includes the SYSVOL folder.

3. Install the new DC and select the IFM option. If you're using Server Manager, click the Install from media check box in the Additional Options window (see Figure 1-12) of the Active Directory Domain Services Configuration Wizard, and specify the path to the media. If you're using Power-Shell, use the `-InstallationMediaPath` parameter and specify the path to the storage location.

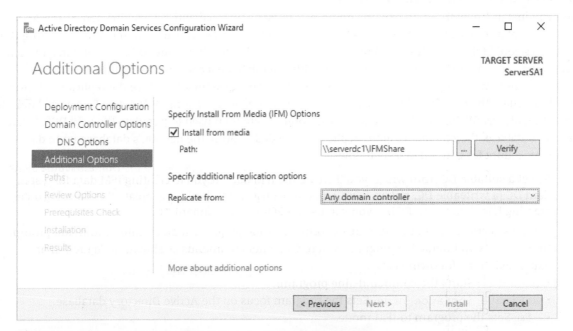

Figure 1-12 Selecting the IFM option during a DC installation

Activity 1-1: Resetting Your Virtual Environment

Time Required: 5 minutes
Objective: Reset your virtual environment by applying the InitialConfig checkpoint or snapshot.
Required Tools and Equipment: ServerSA1
Description: Apply the InitialConfig checkpoint or snapshot to ServerSA1.

1. Be sure ServerSA1 is shut down. In your virtualization program, apply the InitialConfig checkpoint or snapshot to ServerServerSA1.
2. When the snapshot or checkpoint has finished being applied, continue to the next activity.

Activity 1-2: Installing Active Directory Domain Services

Time Required: 15 minutes
Objective: Install AD DS as a new domain controller in a new forest.
Required Tools and Equipment: ServerSA1
Description: You're ready to start working with Active Directory. This server will be the first DC in a new forest. In addition, you install the DNS Server role as part of the installation because DNS is required for Active Directory to function.

1. Start ServerSA1 and sign in as **Administrator**, if necessary.
2. Because this computer will be a domain controller and DNS server, you want to first change the DNS server address so that it references itself. Open a PowerShell window and type **Set-DnsClientServerAddress -InterfaceAlias Ethernet -ServerAddresses 127.0.0.1** and press **Enter**. Close PowerShell.
3. In Server Manager, click **Manage**, **Add Roles and Features**. The Before You Begin window warns you to be sure the Administrator account has a strong password, your network settings are configured, and the latest security updates are installed. Click **Next**.
4. In the Installation Type window, click **Role-based or feature-based installation**, and then click **Next**.
5. In the Server Selection window, click **Next**.
6. In the Server Roles window, click the box next to **Active Directory Domain Services**. When you're prompted to add required features, click **Add Features**, and then click **Next**.
7. In the Features window, click **Next**. Read the information in the AD DS window, which explains that having two domain controllers is optimal and DNS must be installed on the network. Click **Next**.
8. In the Confirmation window, click **Install**.
9. The Results window shows the progress of the installation. When the installation is finished, click **Close**.
10. Click the **notifications flag**, and then click **Promote this server to a domain controller**. The Active Directory Services Configuration Wizard starts.
11. In the Deployment Configuration window, click the **Add a new forest** option button, type **TestDomain.local** in the Root domain name text box, and then click **Next**. You will use this domain only for the purposes of installing and testing some features of Active Directory, and it will not be used after this chapter.
12. In the Domain Controller Options window, verify that the forest and domain functional levels are set to **Windows Server 2016**. Under Specify domain controller capabilities, verify that the **Domain Name System (DNS)** server and **Global Catalog (GC)** check boxes are selected. The GC option is always selected for the first DC in a forest and cannot be changed. Notice that the read-only domain controller (RODC) option isn't available because the first DC in a new forest can't be an RODC.
13. In the Directory Services Restore Mode (DSRM) password section, type **Password01** in the Password and Confirm password text boxes. You can use a password different from the Administrator password, if you like, but for this activity, use the same password so that it's easier to remember. Click **Next**.
14. In the DNS Options window, the **Create DNS delegation** check box is disabled because there is no DNS server currently available for the domain. DNS will be installed as part of the AD DS installation. Click **Next**.

15. In the Additional Options window, leave the default NETBIOS domain name (it may take a few seconds before you see the name) and click **Next**.

16. In the Paths window, you can choose locations for the database folder, log files, and SYSVOL folder. Specifying different disks for the database and log files is ideal, but leave the defaults for now. Click **Next**.

17. Review your choices in the Review Options window, and go back and make changes if necessary. You can export your options to a Windows PowerShell script by clicking the View script button and saving the resulting text file with a `.ps1` extension; you can then run this file at a PowerShell prompt. To see the script that is created, click **View script**. The list of cmdlets is opened in a Notepad file. Review the script and then close Notepad. Click **Next**.

18. In the Prerequisites Check window, Windows verifies that all conditions for successfully installing Active Directory have been met. If all prerequisites have been met, a green circle with a check is displayed at the top of the window. If they haven't been met, Windows displays a list of problems you must correct before installing Active Directory. You may see some warnings, but these are likely okay. Click **Install**. Watch the messages under Progress to see the steps that Windows performs to install Active Directory. After the installation is finished, your computer restarts automatically.

19. After the server restarts, sign in as **Administrator**. (*Note*: You're now logging on to the *TestDomain.local* domain.) In Server Manager, click **Local Server** and verify the domain information shown under Computer name.

20. Click **Tools**. Note the new MMCs that have been added: Active Directory Administrative Center, Active Directory Domains and Trusts, Active Directory Module for Windows PowerShell, Active Directory Sites and Services, Active Directory Users and Computers, ADSI Edit, and DNS.

21. Stay signed in and continue to the next activity.

What's Inside Active Directory?

 **Certification**

- **70-742 – Install and configure Active Directory Domain Services (AD DS):**
  Create and manage Active Directory groups and organizational units (OUs)

After Active Directory is installed, you can explore it by using the Active Directory Administrative Center (ADAC) or Active Directory Users and Computers MMC; several PowerShell cmdlets are also available for working with Active Directory. The ADAC shown in Figure 1-13 is a central console for performing many Active Directory tasks, including creating and managing user, group, and computer accounts; managing OUs; and connecting to other domain controllers in the same or a different domain. You can also change the domain's functional level and enable the Active Directory Recycle Bin.

ADAC is built on PowerShell, so each command you use in ADAC issues a PowerShell command to perform the task. You can take advantage of this feature by using the Windows PowerShell History pane in ADAC (highlighted in Figure 1-14). This pane shows a list of commands generated by creating a new user named Test User1. These commands can be copied and edited to make a PowerShell script so that you can handle tasks such as creating users and adding users to groups by running a PowerShell script instead of using the GUI or typing PowerShell commands.

Active Directory Users and Computers (ADUC) is probably the most popular GUI tool among administrators. As shown in Figure 1-15, ADUC has two panes. In the left pane, the top node shows the server and domain being managed. The Saved Queries folder contains a list of Active Directory queries you can save to repeat Active Directory searches easily. The third node represents the domain and contains all the objects that make up the domain. In Figure 1-15, the domain being managed is

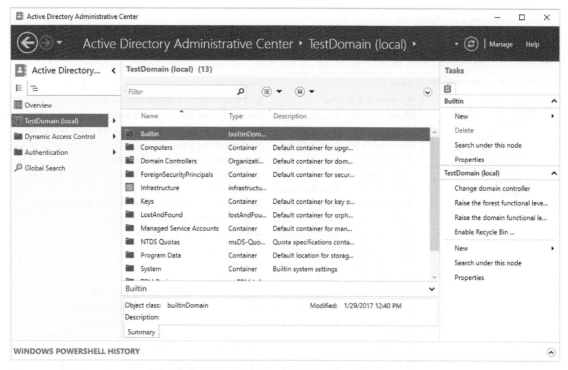

Figure 1-13 Active Directory Administrative Center

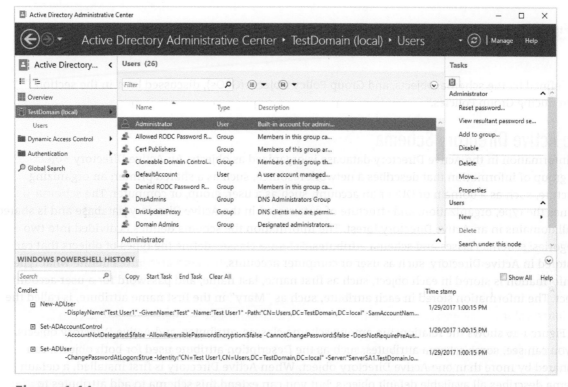

Figure 1-14 Viewing the PowerShell history

TestDomain.local. In this figure, the Users container is open, and objects in this container are displayed in the right pane.

Before you continue working with Active Directory, knowing something about the information you find in the database is helpful. Active Directory's contents and the functions it performs in your network

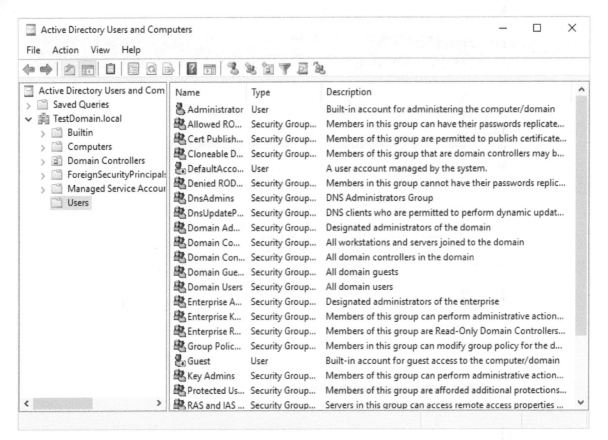

Figure 1-15   Active Directory Users and Computers

are defined by the schema, objects, and Group Policy Objects (GPOs), discussed later in the section "Introducing Group Policies."

The Active Directory Schema

All information in the Active Directory database is organized as objects. An Active Directory **object** is a group of information that describes a network resource, such as a shared printer; an organizing structure, such as a domain or OU; or an account, such as a user, group, or computer. The **schema** defines the type, organization, and structure of data stored in the Active Directory database and is shared by all domains in an Active Directory forest. The information the schema defines is divided into two categories: schema classes and schema attributes. **Schema classes** define the types of objects that can be stored in Active Directory, such as user or computer accounts. **Schema attributes** define what type of information is stored in each object, such as first name, last name, and password for a user account object. The information stored in each attribute, such as "Mary" in the first name attribute, is called the **attribute value**.

Figure 1-16 shows the relationship among schema classes, attributes, and Active Directory objects. As you can see, some schema attributes, such as the Description attribute used for both objects, can be shared by more than one Active Directory object. When Active Directory is first installed, a default schema describes all available default objects, but you can extend this schema to add attributes to existing object classes or create new object classes.

This discussion of Active Directory refers to several different object classes in Active Directory. Figure 1-17 shows object classes and their associated icons in Active Directory Users and Computers. Active Directory objects can be organized into two basic groups, discussed in the next sections regarding container objects and leaf objects. Similar icons are used in ADAC but are black and white.

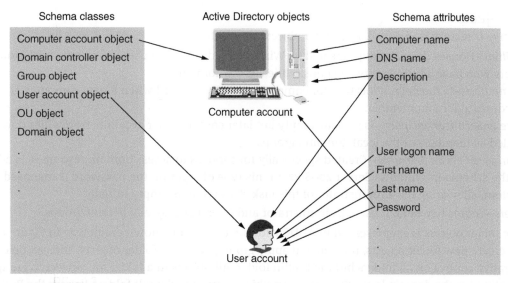

Figure 1-16   Schema classes, schema attributes, and Active Directory objects

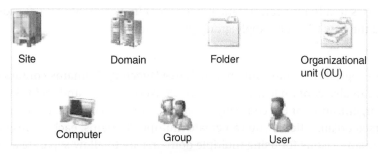

Figure 1-17   Icons used to represent Active Directory objects

Active Directory Container Objects

A container object, as the name implies, contains other objects. Container objects are used to organize and manage users and resources in a network. They can also act as administrative and security boundaries or a way to group objects for applying policies. Three container objects, explained in the following sections, are found in Active Directory: OU, folder, and domain.

Organizational Units

An OU is the primary container object for organizing and managing resources in a domain. Administrators can use OUs to organize objects into logical administrative groups, which makes it possible to apply policies to the OU that affect all objects in it. For example, you could apply a policy that prohibits access to Control Panel for all users in an OU. In addition, you can delegate administrative authority for an OU to a user, thereby allowing the user to manage objects in the OU without giving the user wider authority. Object types typically found in an OU include user accounts, group accounts, computer accounts, shared folders, shared printers, published applications, and other OUs. By nesting OUs, administrators can build a hierarchical Active Directory structure that mimics the corporate structure for easier object management.

In ADUCs, an OU is represented by a folder with a book inside as shown previously in Figure 1-17. When Active Directory is installed, a single OU, Domain Controllers, is created and contains a computer object representing the domain controller. When a new DC is installed in the domain, a new computer object representing it is placed in the Domain Controllers OU by default. A GPO is linked to the Domain Controllers OU and is used to set security and administrative policies that apply to all DCs in the domain.

Folder Objects

When Active Directory is installed, five folder objects are created:

- *Builtin*—Houses default groups created by Windows and is mainly used to assign permissions to users who have administrative responsibilities in the domain.
- *Computers*—Is the default location for computer accounts created when a new computer or server becomes a domain member.
- *ForeignSecurityPrincipals*—Is initially empty but later contains user accounts from other domains added as members of the local domain's groups.
- *Managed Service Accounts*—Created specifically for services to access domain resources, is added to the schema in Windows Server 2008 R2. In this type of account, the password is managed by the system, alleviating the administrator of this task. This folder is empty initially.
- *Users*—Stores two default users (Administrator and Guest) and several default groups.

These folder objects are represented in ADUC with the folder icon shown previously in Figure 1-17. You can't create new folder objects, nor can you apply group policies to folder objects. You can delegate administrative control on all folders but the Builtin folder. All objects in a folder are subject to group policies defined at the domain level. You can move objects from the default folders (except the Builtin folder) into OUs you have created. For example, because all computer accounts are created in the Computers folder by default, they're subject to the same policies defined at the domain level. If you want to apply different policies to different computers in your domain, you create one or more OUs, move the computer accounts to the new OUs, and apply group policies to these OUs.

Domain Objects

The domain is the core logical structure container in Active Directory. Domains contain OU and folder container objects but can also contain leaf objects, such as users, groups, and so forth. A domain typically reflects the organization of the company in which Active Directory is being used, but in large or geographically dispersed organizations, you can create multiple domains, each representing a business unit or location. The main reasons for using multiple domains are to allow separate administration and to define policy boundaries. Each domain object has a default GPO linked to it that can affect all objects in the domain. The domain object in ADUC is represented by an icon with three tower computers (refer to Figure 1-17).

Active Directory Leaf Objects

A **leaf object** doesn't contain other objects and usually represents a security account, network resource, or GPO. Security account objects include users, groups, and computers. Network resource objects include servers, domain controllers, file shares, printers, and so forth. GPOs aren't viewed as objects in the same way as other Active Directory objects are. In Windows Server 2016, GPOs are managed by the Group Policy Management MMC, discussed later. The following paragraphs explain some common leaf objects in Active Directory.

User Accounts

A user account object contains information about a network user. Typically, when a user account is created, the administrator enters at least the user's name, logon name, and password. However, the user account object contains much more information, such as group memberships, account restrictions (allowed logon hours and account expiration date, for example), profile path, and dial-in permissions. In addition, administrators can fill in descriptive fields, such as office location, job title, and department. The main purpose of a user account is to allow a user to sign in to a Windows computer or an Active Directory domain to access computer and domain resources. By supplying a user logon name and password, a user is authenticated on the computer or network. **Authentication** confirms a user's identity, and the account is then assigned permissions and rights that authorize the user to access resources and perform certain tasks on the computer or domain.

Windows Server 2016 defines three user account types: local user, domain user, and built-in user. A **local user account** is authorized to access resources only on that computer. Local user accounts are mainly used on standalone computers or in a workgroup network with computers that aren't part of an Active Directory domain. Local user accounts aren't defined on domain controllers but can be created on domain member computers. A **domain user account**, created in Active Directory, provides a single logon for users to access all resources in the domain to which they're authorized.

Windows creates two **built-in user accounts** automatically: Administrator and Guest. They can be local user accounts or domain user accounts, depending on the computer where they're created. On a workgroup or standalone Windows computer, these two accounts are created when Windows is installed, and they're local accounts that have access to resources only on the local computer. When Active Directory is installed on a Windows Server 2016 computer, these two accounts are converted from local user accounts to domain user accounts. User accounts are discussed in more detail in Chapter 2.

Groups

A group object represents a collection of users with common permissions or rights requirements on a computer or domain. **Permissions** define which resources users can access and what level of access they have. For example, a user might have permission to open and read a certain document but not to change it. A **right** specifies what types of actions a user can perform on a computer or network. For example, a user might have the right to sign in to and sign out of a computer but not shut the computer down. Groups are used to assign members permissions and rights. This method is more efficient than assigning permissions and rights to each user account separately because you have to perform the assignment task only once, and it applies to all accounts that are members of the group. For example, if all users in the Accounting Department need access to a shared folder, you can create a group containing all users in this department as members and assign permission to access the shared folder to the group as a whole. In addition, if a user leaves the department, you can remove his or her account as a group member, and the user loses all rights and permissions assigned to this group. Groups are explained in more detail in Chapter 2.

Computer Accounts

A computer account object represents a computer that's a domain controller or domain member and is used to identify, authenticate, and manage computers in the domain. Computer accounts are created automatically when Active Directory is installed on a server or when a server or workstation becomes a domain member. Administrators can also create computer accounts manually if they don't want to allow automatic account creation. By default, domain controller computer accounts are placed in the Domain Controllers OU, and domain member computer accounts are placed in the Computers folder.

The computer account object's name must match the name of the computer that the account represents. Like user accounts, computer accounts have a logon name and password, but a computer account password is managed by Active Directory instead of an administrator. A computer must have a computer account in Active Directory for users to sign in to it with their domain user accounts. You learn about managing computer accounts in Chapter 2.

Other Leaf Objects

The following list describes other leaf objects that are commonly created in Active Directory:

- *Contact*—Represents a person who is associated with the company but is not a network user. You can think of a contact object as simply being an entry in an address book used purely for informational purposes.
- *Printer*—Represents a shared printer in the domain. Printers shared on Windows computers that are domain members can be added to Active Directory automatically. If a printer is shared on a nondomain member, you must create the printer object manually and specify the path to the shared printer.
- *Shared folder*—Represents a shared folder on a computer in the network. Shared folder objects can be added to Active Directory manually or by using the publish option when creating a shared folder with the Shared Folders MMC snap-in.

Both printer and shared folder objects enable users to access shared printers and folders on any computer in the domain without knowing exactly which computer the resource was created on. Users can simply do a search in Active Directory to find the type of resource they want. In a large network, shared printers and folders could be located on any one of dozens or hundreds of servers. Publishing these resources in Active Directory makes access to them easier.

> **Note**
>
> There are other leaf objects, but the previous sections cover the most common leaf objects you find in Active Directory.

Recovering Objects with the Active Directory Recycle Bin

Working with Active Directory objects is usually straightforward, but what happens if you delete an object by mistake? There's no undo feature, as in word processors, image editors, and other tools you use to create, modify, and delete things. Before Windows Server 2008 R2, the procedure for recovering deleted objects in Active Directory was laborious and required cumbersome command-line syntax. Even worse, the domain controller the object was deleted from had to be taken offline. In Windows Server 2008 R2, Microsoft introduced the Active Directory Recycle Bin to allow easy restoration of deleted objects. Before you see this feature in action, you should be aware of the following:

- Active Directory Recycle Bin is disabled by default; it can be enabled in ADAC.
- After it's enabled, the Recycle Bin can't be disabled without reinstalling all domain controllers in the forest.
- To use the Recycle Bin, all DCs in the forest must be running Windows Server 2008 R2 or later, and the forest functional level must be at least Windows Server 2008 R2.

To enable the Recycle Bin, open ADAC, click the domain node in the left pane, and in the Tasks pane, click Enable Recycle Bin. Click OK in the warning message stating that the Recycle Bin can't be disabled after you enable it. You see a message stating that the Recycle Bin is being enabled and won't function reliably until all DCs are updated with the change. You need to refresh ADAC to see the new container added under the domain node Deleted Objects. The Recycle Bin can also be enabled using PowerShell. For example, to enable the Recycle Bin for the TestDomain.local domain, use the following cmdlet:

```
Enable-ADOptionalFeature -Identity 'CN=Recycle Bin Feature,CN=Optional
    Features,CN=Directory Service,CN=Windows NT, CN=Services, CN=Configuration,
    DC=TestDomain,DC=local' -Scope ForestOrConfigurationSet -Target
    'TestDomain.local'
```

To undelete an object using ADAC, double-click the Deleted Objects container. All objects that have been deleted because the Recycle Bin was enabled are listed. To restore an object, right-click it and choose one of these options from the menu: Restore (which restores the object to its original container if it's still available) or Restore To (which restores the object to a container you select). To restore a deleted object using PowerShell, you use a combination of the `Get-ADObject` and `Restore-Object` cmdlets. For example, if you want to restore a user object with the name TestUser, use the following cmdlet:

```
Get-ADObject -Filter {displayName -eq "TestUser"} -IncludeDeletedObjects |
    Restore-ADObject
```

Locating Active Directory Objects

In a large Active Directory environment with hundreds or thousands of users, groups, computers, and other domain objects, locating objects can be difficult for administrators and users alike. Luckily, ADUC has a search function for administrators, and File Explorer incorporates an Active Directory search function for users.

You search for Active Directory objects by first selecting the type of object you're searching for. For example, you can search for users, contacts, groups, computers, printers, shared folders, and so forth. In a multi-domain environment, you can search in a single domain or in the entire directory (all domains). You can also limit your search to a folder or an OU in a domain. The Find dialog box shown in Figure 1-18 is identical whether you're searching for objects with ADUC or File Explorer. However, not all objects are available to all users, depending on the object's security settings and its container.

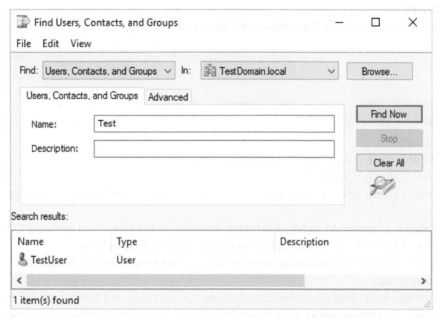

Figure 1-18   The Find Users, Contacts, and Groups dialog box

Now that you've gotten your feet wet using Active Directory, it's time to delve into some details of how Active Directory is structured and how it functions. The next section discusses working with forests, trees, and domains and describes how information from one DC is transferred (replicated) to another DC.

Activity 1-3: Exploring Active Directory Container Objects

Time Required: 10 minutes
Objective: Explore Active Directory container objects.
Required Tools and Equipment: ServerSA1
Description: After installing Active Directory, you want to view its structure by exploring the default container objects in ADUC.

1. Sign in to ServerSA1 as **Administrator**.
2. In Server Manager, open Active Directory Users and Computers by clicking **Tools, Active Directory Users and Computers** from the menu.
3. Click the domain object (**TestDomain.local**) in the left pane.
4. Right-click the **TestDomain.local** object and click **Properties**. Click the **General** tab, if necessary, and verify that both the domain and forest functional levels are Windows Server 2016.
5. Enter a description for the domain, such as **Windows Server 2016 Test Domain**, and then click **OK**.
6. Click to expand the domain node, if necessary. Click the **Builtin** folder in the left pane to view its contents, a list of group accounts created when Active Directory was installed, in the right pane.
7. Click the **Computers** folder in the left pane. This folder is empty. It will contain the computer accounts of computers that are joined to the domain.

8. Click the **Domain Controllers** OU. A computer object representing the domain controller is displayed in the right pane. The DC Type column displays GC, meaning the domain controller is a global catalog server. If more servers are added to the domain as domain controllers, the computer accounts will be added here.

9. Click the **Users** folder in the left pane. The right pane displays groups and the Administrator and Guest user accounts that are created by default. Notice that the Guest account has a down arrow, which means that the account is disabled. This folder also contains any user accounts that were created before the computer was promoted to a DC.

10. Leave Active Directory Users and Computers open for the next activity.

Activity 1-4: Viewing Default Leaf Objects

Time Required: 15 minutes
Objective: View the properties of a variety of leaf objects.
Required Tools and Equipment: ServerSA1
Description: You want to learn more about Active Directory objects, so you view the properties of several default leaf objects.

1. If necessary, sign in to ServerSA1 as **Administrator,** and open Active Directory Users and Computers.

2. In the left pane of Active Directory Users and Computers, click the **Builtin** folder.

3. In the right pane, right-click the **Administrators** group and click **Properties** (or double-click the **Administrators** group).

4. On the General tab, notice that the option buttons under Group scope and Group type are disabled because you can't change this information for built-in groups. (You learn more about group scope and group type in Chapter 2.)

5. Click the **Members** tab. You should see one user and two groups listed as members (see Figure 1-19). The Name column displays the name of the user or group member, and the Active Directory Domain Services Folder column displays the domain and folder or OU where the member is located. Groups can be nested as shown here; the Domain Admins and Enterprise Admins groups are members of the Administrators group.

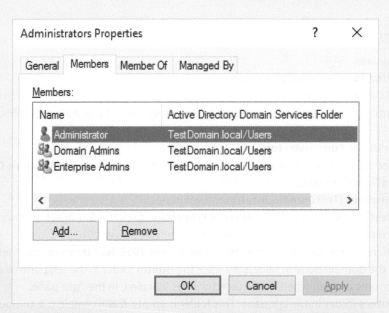

Figure 1-19   Viewing properties of the Administrators group

6. Click the **Member Of** tab. Because built-in groups can't be members of any other group, the Add and Remove buttons are disabled.

7. Click the **Managed By** tab. An administrator can specify another user or group that has the right to manage this group. Click **Cancel**.

8. In the left pane of Active Directory Users and Computers, click the **Domain Controllers** OU. Double-click the **ServerSA1** computer object in the right pane to open its Properties dialog box.

9. If necessary, click the **General** tab. Notice that only the Description text box can be changed for this object.

10. Click the **Operating System** tab, which displays the name, version, and service pack (if any) installed on the computer that this computer object represents.

11. Click the **Member Of** tab. Because this computer object represents a domain controller, it's a member of the Domain Controllers group. (If this computer object represented a domain member, it would be a member of the Domain Computers group.) Click **Cancel**.

12. In the left pane of Active Directory Users and Computers, click the **Users** folder. Double-click the **Administrator** user to open its Properties dialog box.

13. The information on the General tab is optional for user accounts but can be used as part of an employee directory. Type your first name and last name in the corresponding text boxes.

14. Click the **Account** tab. Here you can specify the user logon name, logon restrictions, and account options.

15. Click the **Member Of** tab. Note the groups to which the Administrator account belongs, and then click **OK**.

16. Find the Guest user, and notice the down arrow on its icon, indicating that it's disabled. Double-click the **Guest** user to open its Properties dialog box.

17. Click the **Account** tab. In the Account options list box, scroll down to view the available account options. You see that the *Account is disabled* option is checked. It's disabled by default because it's created with a blank password, which can pose a security risk. Click **Cancel**.

18. Leave Active Directory Users and Computers open for the next activity.

Activity 1-5: Creating Objects in Active Directory

Time Required: 15 minutes
Objective: Create an OU and add some objects to it.
Required Tools and Equipment: ServerSA1
Description: You want to learn more about Active Directory objects, so you create an OU and add a user object and a group object.

1. If necessary, sign in to ServerSA1 as **Administrator**, and open Active Directory Users and Computers.

2. Right-click the domain node, point to **New**, and click **Organizational Unit**. In the Name text box, type **TestOU1**. Click to clear the **Protect container from accidental deletion** check box, and then click **OK**.

3. Make sure **TestOU1** is selected in the left pane, and then right-click in the right pane, point to **New**, and click **User** to start the New Object - User Wizard.

4. In the First name text box, type **Test**, and in the Last name text box, type **User1**. Notice that the *Full name* text box is filled in automatically.

5. In the User logon name text box, type **testuser1**. The User logon name (pre-Windows 2000) text box is filled in automatically. (A user logon name longer than 20 characters is truncated to 20 characters in this text box.)

6. Click **Next**. In the Password text box, type **mypassword**, and type it again in the Confirm password text box. Click to clear the **User must change password at next logon** check box. Click **Next**, and then click **Finish**. You'll see an error message, but go on to the next step.

7. Read the error message carefully. By default, Windows Server 2016 requires a complex password, meaning one of a minimum length of 7 characters, with at least three of the characters of the following types: uppercase letters, lowercase letters, numbers, and special symbols (such as #, ?, and so forth). Click **OK**.

8. In the New Object - User window, click **Back**. In the Password text box, type **Password01**, making sure the P is capitalized and the last two characters are the numbers 0 and 1. Retype the password in the Confirm password text box. Click **Next**, and then click **Finish**.

9. Right-click in the right pane of Active Directory Users and Computers, point to **New**, and click **Group**.

10. Type **TestGroup1** in the Group name text box (see Figure 1-20). Verify that the Group scope setting is **Global** and the Group type setting is **Security**, and then click **OK**.

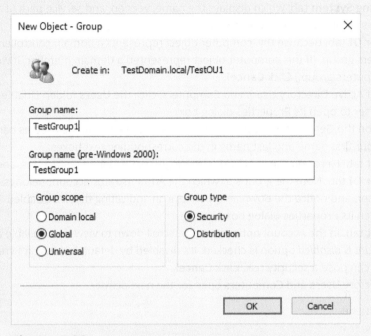

Figure 1-20   Creating a group

11. Double-click **Test User1** to open its Properties dialog box, and click the **Member Of** tab. This user account is already a member of the Domain Users group; all new users are members of this group by default.

12. Click the **Add** button to open the Select Groups dialog box. In the *Enter the object names to select* text box, type **TestGroup1**, and then click the **Check Names** button. Active Directory verifies that the group name you entered exists and underlines it if it does see it Figure 1-21. If the group doesn't exist, a Name Not Found message box is displayed where you can correct the group name. Click **OK**, and then click **OK** again.

Figure 1-21   The Select Groups dialog box

13. Double-click **TestGroup1** to open its Properties dialog box. Click the **Members** tab to verify that Test User1 has been added as a member. Users can be added to groups in the Member Of tab of the user account's Properties dialog box or the Members tab of the group's Properties dialog box. Click **Cancel**.

14. Close Active Directory Users and Computers, but stay signed in if you're continuing to the next activity.

Tip

Active Directory Users and Computers is a fairly straightforward, easy-to-use tool for managing Active Directory objects, but not every administrator wants to use a graphical utility to create and modify Active Directory objects. Sometimes using command-line tools is easier or even necessary. Although this topic is explored more thoroughly in Chapter 2, the following activity introduces you to the `dsadd` command-line tool for creating objects in Active Directory and `New-ADUser` PowerShell cmdlet.

Activity 1-6: Using the Command Line to Create Users

Time Required: 10 minutes

Objective: Create and modify user accounts with command-line tools.

Required Tools and Equipment: ServerSA1

Description: In this activity, you create and modify users using the `dsadd` and `dsmod` command-line tools and Power-Shell cmdlets.

1. Sign in to ServerSA1 as **Administrator**, if necessary, and open a command prompt window by right-clicking **Start** and clicking **Command Prompt**.

2. At the command prompt, type **dsadd user "cn=Test User2, ou=TestOU1, dc=TestDomain, dc=local"** and press **Enter**. This command creates a user named Test User2 and places the user in TestOU1. If you get a response other than "dsadd succeeded: cn=Test User2, ou=TestOU1, dc=TestDomain, dc=local," check the command for typos and try again.

3. The account you just created is disabled because no password was assigned. You could have assigned a password in the `dsadd` command, but you can also do it with the `dsmod` command. Type **dsmod user "cn=Test User2, ou=TestOU1,dc=TestDomain,dc=local" -pwd "Password01" -disabled no** and press **Enter**. This command sets the password and enables the account. You can use an asterisk (*) instead of the password and Windows will prompt you to enter a password.

4. To create a user using PowerShell, open a PowerShell window and type **New-ADUser TestUser3** and press **Enter**. This command creates a new user account and places it in the Users folder. To create a user and place it in the TestOU1 OU, type **New-ADUser TestUser4 -Path "OU=TestOU1, DC=TestDomain, DC=local"** and press **Enter**.

5. To set the password for TestUser3, type **Set-ADAccountPassword TestUser3** and press **Enter**. You are prompted to enter the current password so just press **Enter**. You are prompted for the new password so type **Password01** and press **Enter**. Type **Password01** again and press **Enter**.

6. To enable the TestUser3 account, type **Enable-ADAccount TestUser3** and press **Enter**.

7. Repeat Steps 5 and 6, substituting TestUser4 for TestUser3.

8. Close the command prompt and PowerShell windows. Leave Active Directory Users and Computers open for the next activity.

Note

These steps might seem like a lot of work to create a single user, but as you learn in Chapter 2, you can create several users at once quickly and easily with command-line tools and a text file.

Activity 1-7: Locating Objects in Active Directory

Time Required: 5 minutes

Objective: Search for user and group objects in Active Directory.

Required Tools and Equipment: ServerSA1

Description: In this activity, you use the search feature in Active Directory Users and Computers and then in File Explorer.

1. If necessary, sign in to ServerSA1 as **Administrator**, and open Active Directory Users and Computers.
2. Right-click the domain node in the left pane and click **Find**.
3. Click the **Find** list arrow and verify that **Users, Contacts, and Groups** is selected. In the In text box, make sure that TestDomain.local is selected. You could click Find Now, but if you do, all users, contacts, and groups in the entire domain are displayed. You want to narrow the choices first.
4. In the Name text box, type **test**. By specifying this name, all users, groups, and contacts starting with "test" are displayed. Click the **Find Now** button. You should see results similar to those in Figure 1-22.

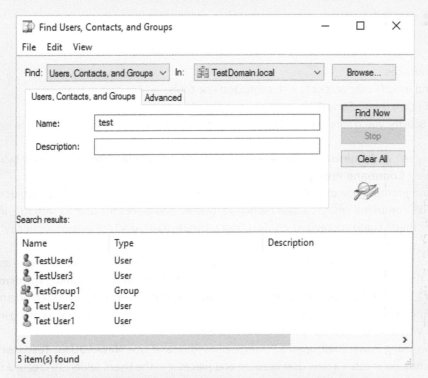

Figure 1-22   Results from an Active Directory find operation

5. In the Search results section, you can double-click any entry to access its properties. Close the Find dialog box and Active Directory Users and Computers.
6. Open File Explorer, and click **Network** in the left pane.
7. Click **Network,** and then click **Search Active Directory** to open the Find dialog box. It's the same as the one in Figure 1-22 shown previously. By default, Entire Directory is set as the search scope.

> **Tip** ⓘ
>
> If the Search Active Directory icon is disabled, it is because your network connection did not recognize that it is in a domain. To resolve the problem, open Network Connections, disable the Ethernet interface and re-enable it. It should show the network as TestDomain.local. Close File Explorer and open it again and try Step 7 again.

8.   In the Find drop-down list, click **Computers**. In the Role drop-down list, click **All Active Directory Domain Controllers** to specify that you want to search only for computers that are domain controllers.

9.   Click the **Find Now** button. You should see ServerSA1 in the search results.

10.   Close File Explorer and continue to the next activity.

Activity 1-8: Publishing a Shared Folder in Active Directory

Time Required: 25 minutes

Objective: Publish a shared folder in Active Directory and then find the folder.

Required Tools and Equipment: ServerSA1

Description: In this activity, you create a shared folder and then publish it in Active Directory. Then you use the find feature in File Explorer to locate the shared folder in Active Directory.

1.   Sign in to ServerSA1 as **Administrator**, if necessary.

2.   Open File Explorer. Create a folder in the root of the C: drive named **PubShare**.

3.   Share this folder with simple file sharing, giving the Everyone group **Read** permission and leaving the Administrator and Administrators accounts with the default permissions. Close File Explorer.

4.   Right-click **Start** and click **Computer Management**. Click to expand the **Shared Folders** node, and then click the **Shares** folder.

5.   In the right pane, double-click **PubShare** to open its Properties dialog box. Click the **Publish** tab, and then click the **Publish this share in Active Directory** check box (see Figure 1-23).

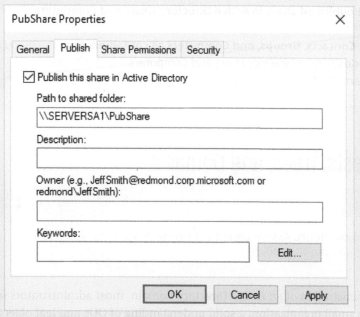

Figure 1-23   The Publish tab of a shared folder's Properties dialog box

6.   In the Description text box, type **A share to test publishing in Active Directory**.

7.   Click the **Edit** button. In the Edit Keywords dialog box, type **testing**, and then click **Add**. Click **OK** twice.

8.   Close Computer Management. Open File Explorer and click **Network**.

9.   Click **Network**, and then **Search Active Directory**.

10.   In the Find drop-down list, click **Shared Folders**. In the Keywords text box, type **test**, and then click **Find Now**.

11.   In the Search results section, right-click **PubShare** and click **Explore**. A File Explorer window opens, showing the contents of the PubShare shared folder (currently empty).

12. Close the File Explorer and Find Shared Folders windows. Open Active Directory Users and Computers.

13. When you publish a shared folder or printer, the published share appears as a child object of the server where the share is located. To view child objects of servers, click **View, Users, Contacts, Groups, and Computers as containers** from the menu.

14. Click to expand the **Domain Controllers** OU, and then click the server icon. You see the share you published in the right pane (see Figure 1-24).

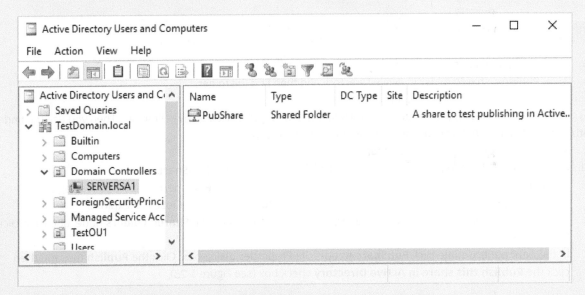

Figure 1-24   A published share in Active Directory Users and Computers

15. Click **View, Users, Contacts, Groups, and Computers as containers** from the menu again to disable this feature, and then close Active Directory Users and Computers.

16. Continue to the next activity.

Working with Forests, Trees, and Domains

 **Certification**

- 70-742 – Install and configure Active Directory Domain Services (AD DS):
  Install and configure domain controllers

In the day-to-day administration of an Active Directory domain, most administrators focus on OUs and their child objects. In a small organization, a solid understanding of OUs and leaf objects might be all that's needed to manage a Windows domain successfully. However, in large organizations, building an Active Directory structure composed of several domains, multiple trees, and even a few forests might be necessary.

When the first DC is installed in a network, the structure you see in Active Directory Users and Computers—a domain object and some folder and OU containers—isn't all that's created. In addition, a new tree and the root of a new forest are created along with elements that define a new site. As a business grows or converts an existing network structure to Active Directory, there might be reasons to add domains to the tree, create new trees or forests, and add sites to the Active Directory structure. This section starts by describing some helpful terms for understanding how Active Directory operates and is organized. Next, you learn the forest's role in Active Directory and how to use multiple forests in an Active Directory structure. Then you examine trust relationships and domains, particularly situations involving multiple domains and multiple trees.

Active Directory Terminology

A number of terms are used to describe Active Directory's structure and operations. In the following sections, you examine terms associated with replication, directory partitions, operations masters, and trust relationships. Although these terms are introduced in this chapter, many of them are explored in more depth in later chapters of this book.

Active Directory Replication

Replication is the process of maintaining a consistent database of information when the database is distributed among several locations. Active Directory contains several databases called *partitions* that are replicated between domain controllers by using intrasite replication or intersite replication. **Intrasite replication** takes place between domain controllers in the same site; **intersite replication** occurs between two or more sites. The replication process differs in these two types, but the goal is the same—to maintain a consistent set of domain directory partitions.

Active Directory uses **multimaster replication** for replicating Active Directory objects, such as user and computer accounts, which means that changes to these objects can occur on any DC and are propagated (replicated) to all other domain controllers. A process called the **Knowledge Consistency Checker (KCC)** runs on every DC to determine the replication topology, which defines the domain controller path through which Active Directory changes flow. This path is configured as a ring (or multiple rings if there are enough domain controllers) with each DC in the path constituting a hop. The KCC is designed to ensure that there are no more than three hops between any two domain controllers, which can result in multiple rings as shown in Figure 1-25.

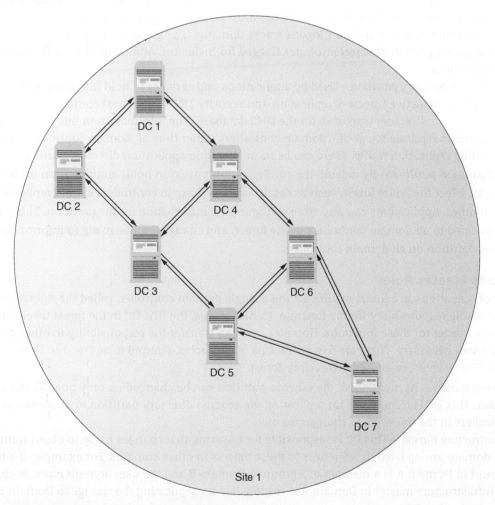

Figure 1-25 **Replication topology**

Intrasite replication occurs 15 seconds after a change is made on a domain controller with a 3-second delay between each replication partner. A **replication partner** is a pair of domain controllers configured to replicate with one another. The KCC also configures the topology for intersite replication, but it's different from intrasite replication's topology. Site replication and configuration is discussed more in Chapter 7.

Directory Partitions

An Active Directory database has many sections stored in the same file on a DC's hard drive. These sections must be managed by different processes and replicated to other domain controllers in an Active Directory network. Each section of an Active Directory database is referred to as a **directory partition**. There are five directory partition types in the Active Directory database:

- *Domain directory partition*—Contains all objects in a domain, including users, groups, computers, OUs, and so forth. There's one **domain directory partition** for each domain in the forest. Changes made to objects in domain directory partitions are replicated to each DC in the domain. Some object attributes are also replicated to global catalog servers (described later in "The Importance of the Global Catalog Server") in all domains. Changes to the domain directory partition can occur on any DC in the domain except read-only domain controllers.
- *Schema directory partition*—Contains information needed to define Active Directory objects and object attributes for all domains in the forest. The **schema directory partition** is replicated to all domain controllers in the forest. One domain controller in the forest is designated as the schema master domain controller (discussed in the next section) and holds the only writeable copy of the schema.
- *Global catalog partition*—The **global catalog partition** holds the global catalog, which is a partial replica of all objects in the forest. It stores the most commonly accessed object attributes to facilitate object searches and user logons across domains. The global catalog is built automatically by domain replication of object attributes flagged for inclusion. Administrators can't make changes to this partition.
- *Application directory partition*—Used by applications and services to hold information that benefits from automatic Active Directory replication and security. DNS is the most common service to use an **application directory partition** for the DNS database. The information in this partition can be configured to replicate to specific domain controllers rather than all domain controllers, thereby controlling replication traffic. There can be more than one application directory partition.
- *Configuration partition*—By default, the **configuration partition** holds configuration information that can affect the entire forest, such as details on how domain controllers should replicate with one another. Applications can also store configuration information in this partition. This partition is replicated to all domain controllers in the forest, and changes can be made to information stored in this partition on all domain controllers.

Operations Master Roles

A number of operations in a forest require having a single domain controller, called the **operations master**, with sole responsibility for the function. In most cases, the first DC in the forest takes on the role of operations master for these functions. However, you can transfer the responsibility to other domain controllers when necessary. There are five operations master roles, referred to as **Flexible Single Master Operation (FSMO) roles**, in an Active Directory forest:

- *Schema master*—As mentioned, the schema partition can be changed on only one DC, the schema master. This DC is responsible for replicating the schema directory partition to all other domain controllers in the forest when changes occur.
- *Infrastructure master*—This DC is responsible for ensuring that changes made to object names in one domain are updated in references to these objects in other domains. For example, if a user account in Domain A is a member of a group in Domain B and the user account name is changed, the infrastructure master in Domain A is responsible for replicating the change to Domain B. By default, the first DC in each domain is the infrastructure master for that domain.

- *Domain naming master*—This DC manages adding, removing, and renaming domains in the forest. There's only one domain naming master per forest, and the DC with this role must be available when domains are added, deleted, or renamed.
- *Relative identifier (RID) master*—All objects in a domain are identified internally by a **security identifier (SID)**. An object's SID is composed of a domain identifier, which is the same for all objects in the domain, and a **relative identifier (RID)**, which is unique for each object. Because objects can be created on any DC, there must be a mechanism that keeps two domain controllers from issuing the same RID, thereby duplicating an SID. The RID master is responsible for issuing unique pools of RIDs to each DC, thereby guaranteeing unique SIDs throughout the domain. The RID master must be available when adding a DC to an existing domain. There's one RID master per domain.
- *PDC emulator master*—The PDC emulator master manages password changes to help make sure user authentication occurs without lengthy delays. When a user account password is changed, the change is replicated to all domain controllers but can take several minutes. Meanwhile, the user whose password was changed might be authenticated by a DC that hasn't yet received the replication, so the authentication fails. To reduce this problem, password changes are replicated immediately to the PDC emulator master, and if authentication fails at one DC, the attempt is retried on the PDC emulator master. In addition, this role provides backward compatibility with Windows NT servers configured as Windows NT backup domain controllers or member servers, although it is unlikely you will see Windows NT still in operation in a network today.

Because domain controllers that manage FSMO role data are by definition single masters, special attention must be paid to them. When removing domain controllers from a forest, make sure that these roles aren't removed from the network accidentally. Domain administrators should keep track of which server holds each role and move the role to another DC if that machine is to be taken offline.

Using PowerShell to View FSMO Roles

You can use PowerShell commands to view the FSMO roles. To view the holder of the three domainwide roles, use the following PowerShell command:

```
Get-ADDomain
```

This command produces several lines of output (Figure 1-26). The highlighted lines show the three domainwide FSMO roles.

```
PS C:\Users\Administrator> Get-ADDomain

AllowedDNSSuffixes                 : {}
ChildDomains                       : {}
ComputersContainer                 : CN=Computers,DC=TestDomain,DC=local
DeletedObjectsContainer            : CN=Deleted Objects,DC=TestDomain,DC=local
DistinguishedName                  : DC=TestDomain,DC=local
DNSRoot                            : TestDomain.local
DomainControllersContainer         : OU=Domain Controllers,DC=TestDomain,DC=local
DomainMode                         : Windows2016Domain
Forest                             : TestDomain.local
InfrastructureMaster               : ServerSA1.TestDomain.local
LastLogonReplicationInterval       :
Name                               : TestDomain
NetBIOSName                        : TESTDOMAIN
ObjectClass                        : domainDNS
ObjectGUID                         : 2e76b4e4-d4a5-4d3b-8a1a-2e479a735c6c
ParentDomain                       :
PDCEmulator                        : ServerSA1.TestDomain.local
PublicKeyRequiredPasswordRolling   : True
QuotasContainer                    : CN=NTDS Quotas,DC=TestDomain,DC=local
ReadOnlyReplicaDirectoryServers    : {}
ReplicaDirectoryServers            : {ServerSA1.TestDomain.local}
RIDMaster                          : ServerSA1.TestDomain.local
UsersContainer                     : CN=Users,DC=TestDomain,DC=local
```

Figure 1-26   Output of `Get-ADDomain`

To view the folder of the two forestwide roles, use the following PowerShell command. Figure 1-27 shows its output.

```
Get-ADForest
```

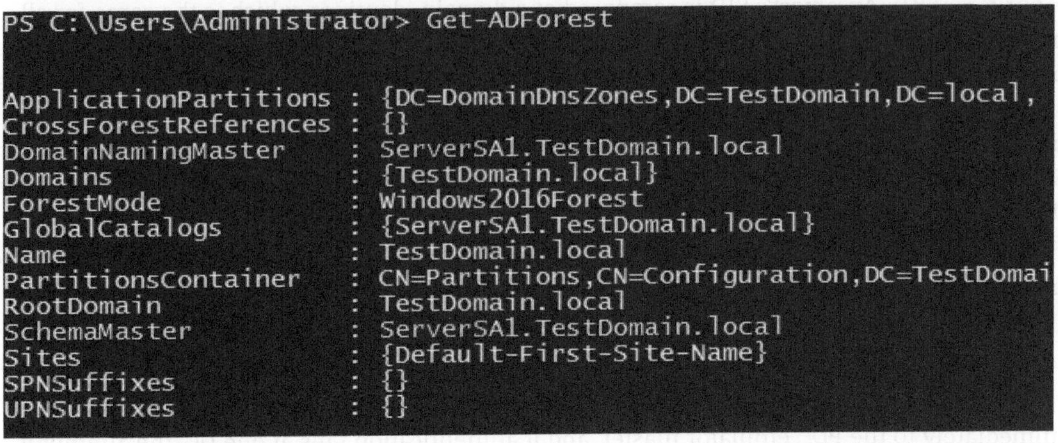

```
PS C:\Users\Administrator> Get-ADForest

ApplicationPartitions  : {DC=DomainDnsZones,DC=TestDomain,DC=local,
CrossForestReferences  : {}
DomainNamingMaster     : ServerSA1.TestDomain.local
Domains                : {TestDomain.local}
ForestMode             : Windows2016Forest
GlobalCatalogs         : {ServerSA1.TestDomain.local}
Name                   : TestDomain.local
PartitionsContainer    : CN=Partitions,CN=Configuration,DC=TestDomai
RootDomain             : TestDomain.local
SchemaMaster           : ServerSA1.TestDomain.local
Sites                  : {Default-First-Site-Name}
SPNSuffixes            : {}
UPNSuffixes            : {}
```

Figure 1-27　Output of `Get-ADForest`

Tip ⓘ

To list all of the FSMO role holders with a single command, type `netdom query fsmo` from a command prompt.

Trust Relationships

In Active Directory, a **trust relationship** defines whether and how security principals from one domain can access network resources in another domain. Trust relationships are established automatically between all domains in a forest. Therefore, when a user authenticates to one domain, the other domains in the forest accept, or trust, the authentication.

Don't confuse trusts with permissions. Permissions are still required to access resources even if a trust relationship exists. When there's no trust relationship between domains, however, no access across domains is possible. Because all domains in a forest have trust relationships with one another automatically, trusts must be configured only when your Active Directory environment includes two or more forests or when you want to integrate with other OSs. Trusts are discussed in more detail in Chapter 7.

The Role of Forests

The Active Directory forest is the broadest logical component of the Active Directory structure. Forests contain domains that can be organized into one or more trees. All domains in a forest share some common characteristics:

- *A single schema*—The schema defines Active Directory objects and their attributes and can be changed by an administrator or an application to best suit the organization's needs. All domains in a forest share the same schema, so a change to the schema affects objects in all domains. This shared schema is one reason that large organizations or conglomerates with diverse business units might want to operate as separate forests. With this structure, domains in different forests can still share information through trust relationships, but changes to the schema—perhaps from installing an Active Directory-integrated application, such as Microsoft Exchange—don't affect the schema of domains in a different forest.

- *Forestwide administrative accounts*—Each forest has two groups defined with unique rights to perform operations that can affect the entire forest: Schema Admins and Enterprise Admins. Members of Schema Admins are the only users who can make changes to the schema. Members of Enterprise Admins can add or remove domains from the forest and have administrative access to every domain in the forest. By default, only the Administrator account for the first domain created in the forest (the forest root domain) is a member of these two groups.
- *Operations masters*—As discussed, certain forestwide operations can be performed only by a DC designated as the operations master. Both the schema master and the domain naming master are forestwide operations masters, meaning that only one DC in the forest can perform these roles.
- *Global catalog*—There's only one global catalog per forest, but unlike operations masters, multiple domain controllers can be designated as global catalog servers. Because the global catalog contains information about all objects in the forest, it's used to speed searching for objects across domains in the forest and to allow users to sign in to any domain in the forest.
- *Trusts between domains*—These trusts allow users to sign in to their home domains (where their accounts are created) and access resources in domains throughout the forest without having to authenticate to each domain.
- *Replication between domains*—The forest structure facilitates replicating important information between all domain controllers throughout the forest. Forestwide replication includes information stored in the global catalog, schema directory, and configuration partitions.

The Importance of the Global Catalog Server

The first DC installed in a forest is always designated as a global catalog server, but you can use Active Directory Sites and Services to configure additional domain controllers as global catalog servers for redundancy. The following are some vital functions that the global catalog server performs:

- *Facilitates domain and forestwide searches*—As discussed, the global catalog is contacted to speed searches for resources across domains.
- *Facilitates logon across domains*—Users can sign in to computers in any domain by using their **user principal name (UPN)**. A UPN follows the format *username@domain*. Because the global catalog contains information about all objects in all domains, a global catalog server is contacted to resolve the UPN. Without a global catalog server, users could sign in only to computers that were members of the same domain as their user accounts.
- *Holds universal group membership information*—When a user logs on to the network, all the user's group memberships must be resolved to determine rights and permissions. Global catalog servers are the only domain controllers that hold universal group membership information, so they must be contacted when a user signs in. A universal group is the only type of group that can contain accounts from other domains, which is why this information must be stored in the global catalog.

Because of the critical functions a global catalog server performs, having at least one DC configured as a global catalog server in each location (such as a company's branch offices) is a good idea to speed logons and directory searches for users in all locations.

Forest Root Domain

As discussed, when the first domain is created in a Windows network, the forest root is also created. In fact, the first domain *is* the forest root and is referred to as the **forest root domain**. It has a number of important responsibilities and serves as an anchor for other trees and domains added to the forest. Certain functions that affect all domains in the forest are conducted only through the forest root domain, and if this domain becomes inoperable, the entire Active Directory structure ceases functioning. Figure 1-28 shows the forest root domain with multiple domains and trees. (Figure 1-4 showed the same structure, but for simplicity, it didn't show one of the domains as the forest root.)

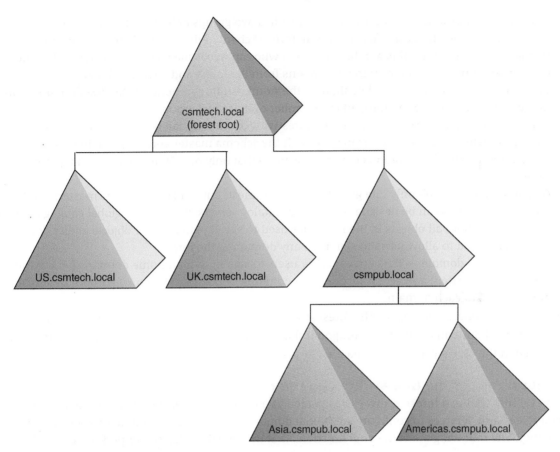

Figure 1-28   **The forest root domain**

What makes the forest root domain so important? It provides functions that facilitate and manage communication between all domains in the forest as well as between forests, if necessary. Some functions the forest root domain usually handles include the following:

- DNS server
- Global catalog server
- Forestwide administrative accounts
- Operations masters

The DNS server and global catalog server functions can be installed on other servers in other domains for fault tolerance. However, the forestwide operations masters and forestwide administrative accounts can reside only on a DC in the forest root domain. For these reasons, the forest root domain is a critical component of the Active Directory structure.

Understanding Domains and Trees

As discussed, an Active Directory tree is a group of domains sharing a common naming structure. A tree can consist of a single domain or a parent domain and one or more child domains, which can have child domains of their own. An Active Directory tree is said to have a contiguous namespace because all domains in the tree share at least the last two domain name components: the second-level domain name and the top-level domain name.

Organizations operating under a single name internally and to the public are probably best served by an Active Directory forest with only one tree. However, when two companies merge or a large company splits into separate business units that would benefit from having their own identities, a multiple tree structure makes sense. As you've learned, there's no major functional difference between domains in the same tree or domains in different trees as long as they're part of the same forest. The only operational difference is the necessity of maintaining multiple DNS zones.

Designing the Domain Structure

A domain is the primary identifying and administrative unit in Active Directory. A unique name is associated with each domain and used to access network resources. A domain administrator account has full control over objects in the domain, and certain security policies apply to all accounts in a domain. In addition, most replication traffic occurs between domain controllers in a domain. Any of these factors can influence your decision to use a single-domain or multi-domain design. Most small and medium businesses choose a single domain for reasons that include the following:

- *Simplicity*—The more complex something is, the easier it is for things to go wrong. Unless your organization needs multiple identities, separate administration, or differing account policies, keeping the structure simple with a single domain is the best choice.
- *Lower costs*—Every domain must have at least one DC and preferably two or more for fault tolerance. Each DC requires additional hardware and software resources, which increases costs.
- *Easier management*—Many management tasks are easier in a single-domain environment:
  - Having a single set of administrators and policies prevents conflicts caused by differing viewpoints on operational procedures and policies.
  - Object management is easier when personnel reorganizations or transfers occur. Moving user and computer accounts between different OUs is easier than moving them between different domains.
  - Managing access to resources is simplified when you don't need to consider security principals from other domains.
  - Placement of domain controllers and global catalog servers is simplified when your organization has multiple locations because you don't need to consider cross-domain replication.
- *Easier access to resources*—A single domain provides the easiest environment for users to find and access network resources. In a multi-domain environment, mobile users who visit branch offices with different domains must authenticate to their home domain. If their home domain isn't available for some reason, they can't sign in to the network.

Although a single-domain structure is usually easier and less expensive than a multi-domain structure, it's not always better. Using more than one domain makes sense or is even a necessity in the following circumstances:

- *Need for differing account policies*—Account policies that govern password and account lockout policies apply to all users in a domain. If you need to have differing policies for different business units, using separate domains is the best way to meet this requirement. The feature Passwords Settings Objects can be used to apply different password policies for users or groups in a domain, but this feature can be difficult to manage when many users are involved.
- *Need for different name identities*—Each domain has its own name that can represent a separate company or business unit. If each business unit must maintain its own identity, child domains can be created in which part of the name is shared or multiple trees with completely different namespaces can be created.
- *Replication control*—Replication in a large domain maintaining several thousand objects can generate substantial traffic. When multiple corporate locations are connected through a WAN, the amount of replication traffic could be unacceptable. Replication traffic can be reduced by creating separate domains for key locations because only global catalog replication is required between domains.
- *Need for internal versus external domains*—Companies that run public web servers often create a domain used only for publicly accessible resources and another domain for internal resources. In fact, Microsoft recommends that all companies have separate domain names for their public presence and their internal network.
- *Need for tight security*—With separate domains, stricter resource control and administrative permissions are easier. If a business unit prefers to have its own administrative staff, separate domains must be created.

Activity 1-9: Viewing the Operations Master Roles and Global Catalog Server

Time Required: 15 minutes

Objective: Discover where operations master roles and Global Catalog Server are configured.

Required Tools and Equipment: ServerSA1

Description: In this activity, you use Active Directory Users and Computers, Active Directory Domains and Trusts, and Active Directory Schema to view the FSMO roles. You also use PowerShell to view these roles. Then, you use Active Directory Sites and Services to see where to configure a DC as a Global Catalog Server.

1. Sign in to ServerSA1 as **Administrator**, if necessary, and open Active Directory Users and Computers.
2. In the left pane, right-click the top node **Active Directory Users and Computers [ServerSA1.TestDomain. local]**, point to **All Tasks**, and click **Operations Masters**.
3. The RID tab shows which DC performs the RID master role (see Figure 1-29). Click the **Change** button. The error message tells you that the DC you're connected to is the operations master, and you must first connect to the DC where you want to transfer the operations master role. You aren't going to transfer the role because there are no other DCs, so click **OK**.

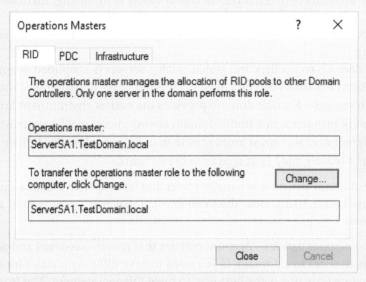

Figure 1-29 Viewing the RID master role

4. Click the **PDC** tab to view the DC that's the PDC emulator master, and then click the **Infrastructure** tab to view the DC that's the infrastructure master. Only one DC per domain performs the three operations master roles you just saw. Click **Close**.
5. Right-click **Active Directory Users and Computers [ServerSA1.410Server2016.local]** and click **Change Domain Controller**. If your domain has more than one DC, you could connect to any of them here and then change the operations master role to another DC. Click **Cancel**, and close Active Directory Users and Computers.
6. In Server Manager, click **Tools, Active Directory Domains and Trusts** from the menu.
7. Right-click **Active Directory Domains and Trusts [ServerSA1.410Server2016.local]** and click **Operations Master**. Here's where you can find which DC is the domain naming master. Note that only one DC in the entire forest performs this function. Click **Close**, and close Active Directory Domains and Trusts.
8. To view the schema master, you must use a different process because this role isn't shown in any standard MMC. Right-click **Start**, click **Run**, type **regsvr32 schmmgmt.dll** in the Open text box, and click **OK**. In the message box stating *DllRegisterServer in schmmgmt.dll succeeded*, click **OK**.

Note

The command in Step 8 is needed to register, or activate, certain commands that aren't normally available in Windows—in this case, the Active Directory Schema snap-in.

9. Right-click **Start**, click **Run**, type **MMC** in the Open text box, and click **OK**.

10. Click **File, Add/Remove Snap-in** from the MMC menu.

11. In the Available snap-ins list box, click **Active Directory Schema**. Click **Add**, and then click **OK**.

12. Click **Active Directory Schema** and then right-click **Active Directory Schema** and click **Operations Master**. As with the domain naming master, only one DC in the entire forest performs the schema master role. Click **Close**, and close the MMC. When prompted to save your console settings, click **No**.

13. Open a PowerShell window. Type **Get-ADDomain** and press **Enter**. You see a list of information about the domain. Look for the following lines : InfraStructureMaster, PDCEmulator, and RIDMaster. Because this is the only domain controller in the domain, it holds all the domainwide FSMO roles.

14. Type **Get-ADForest** and press **Enter**. You see information about the forest. Look for the following lines: DomainNamingMaster, and SchemaMaster. Because this is the only domain controller in the forest, it holds all the forestwide FSMO roles.

15. To see all the FSMO roles, type **netdom query fsmo** and press **Enter**. You see a list of all the FSMO roles and the server that holds them. This command can also be run from a command prompt.

16. Close the PowerShell window.

17. Now, you'll see where the Global Catalog Server can be configured. In Server Manager, click **Tools, Active Directory Sites and Services** from the menu.

18. Click to expand the **Sites** node. Click to expand **Default-First-Site-Name**, **Servers**, and then **ServerSA1**. Click **ServerSA1**. Your screen should look similar to the one in Figure 1-30.

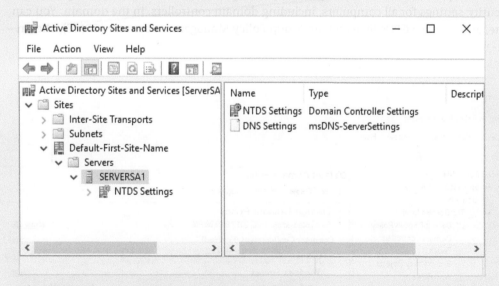

Figure 1-30 Active Directory Sites and Services

19. Right-click **NTDS Settings** under ServerSA1 and click **Properties**. When the Global Catalog check box is selected, the DC is a global catalog server. Because it's the only global catalog server in the forest, clearing the check box generates a warning message stating that users can't sign in if there's no global catalog server. Click **Cancel**.

20. Right-click **ServerSA1** and click **Properties**. Click the **General** tab, if necessary. Note that Global Catalog is specified in the DC Type text box. Click **Cancel**, and close Active Directory Sites and Services.

21. Continue to the next activity.

Introducing Group Policies

• **70-742 – Create and manage Group Policy:**
  Create and manage Group Policy Objects (GPOs)

A **Group Policy Object (GPO)** is a list of settings that administrators use to configure user and computer operating environments remotely. Group policies can specify security settings, deploy software, and configure a user's desktop among many other computer and network settings. They can be configured to affect an entire domain, a site, and, most commonly, users or computers in an OU. The **GPO scope** defines which objects a GPO affects.

Despite the name, GPOs don't apply to group objects. You can link GPOs to sites, domains, and OUs; GPOs linked to these containers affect only user or computer accounts in the containers. When Active Directory is installed, two GPOs are created and linked to two containers:

- *Default Domain Policy*—This GPO is linked to the domain object and specifies default settings that affect all users and computers in the domain. The settings in this policy are related mainly to account policies, such as password and logon requirements, and some network security policies.

- *Default Domain Controllers Policy*—This GPO is linked to the Domain Controllers OU and specifies default policy settings for all domain controllers in the domain (provided the computer objects representing domain controllers aren't moved from the Domain Controllers OU). The settings in this policy pertain mainly to user rights assignments, which specify the types of actions users can perform on a DC.

These default policies don't define any user-specific policies; instead, they're designed to provide default security settings for all computers, including domain controllers, in the domain. You can view, create, and manage GPOs by using the Group Policy Management console (GPMC), shown in Figure 1-31.

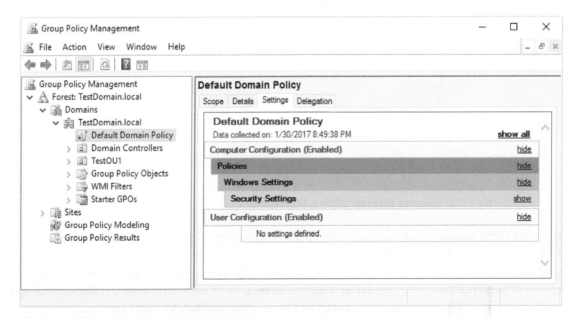

Figure 1-31   The Group Policy Management console

Each GPO has two main nodes in GPMC (shown in the right pane of Figure 1-31):

- *Computer Configuration*—Used to set policies that apply to computers within the GPO's scope. These policies are applied to a computer when the computer starts.
- *User Configuration*—Used to set policies that apply to all users within the GPO's scope. User policies are applied when a user signs in to any computer in the domain.

Each node contains a Policies folder and a Preferences folder. Settings configured in the Policies folder are applied to users or computers and can't be overridden by users. Settings in the Preferences folder are applied to users or computers but are just that: preferences. Therefore, users can change settings configured in the Preferences folder.

The Policies folder under both the Computer Configuration and User Configuration nodes contains three folders: Software Settings, Windows Settings, and Administrative Templates. They can store different information, depending on whether they're under Computer Configuration or User Configuration.

> **Note** 📎
>
> In GPMC, you see only folders containing configured settings. By default, there are no configured settings in the User Configuration node in the Default Domain Policy, which is why you don't see a Policies folder under User Configuration in Figure 1-31. Likewise, you don't see the Preferences folder in this figure because no preferences have been configured.

To change a GPO's settings, you use the Group Policy Management Editor (GPME, shown in Figure 1-32), which you open by right-clicking a GPO and clicking Edit.

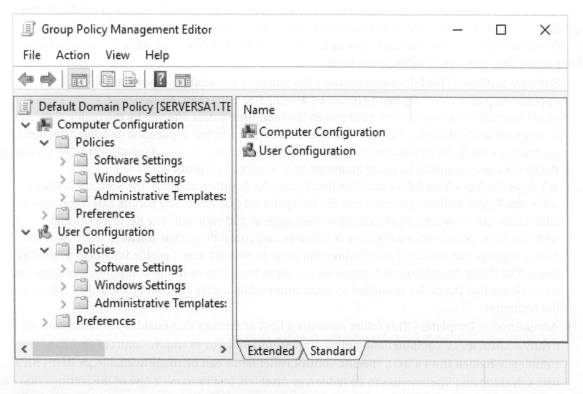

Figure 1-32 **The Group Policy Management Editor**

The Computer Configuration Node

In the Computer Configuration node, the three folders under the Policies folder contain the following information:

- *Software Settings*—This folder contains the item (**extension**) Software installation, which enables administrators to install and manage applications remotely. Application installation packages can be configured so that the next time a computer in the GPO's scope starts, the application is installed automatically. This feature is called "assigning" the application to the computer.
- *Windows Settings*—This folder contains the Name Resolution Policy node, Scripts extension, Security Settings node, and Policy-based QoS node. The Name Resolution Policy stores configuration settings for DNS security and DirectAccess. Administrators can use the Scripts extension to create scripts that run at computer startup or shutdown. The Security Settings node contains the lion's share of policies that affect computer security, including account policies, user rights, wireless network policies, Registry and file system permissions, and network communication policies among others. The Policy-based QoS node can be used to prioritize and control outgoing network traffic from a computer.
- *Administrative Templates*—This folder contains Control Panel, Network, Printers, System, and Windows Components folders. The settings in these folders affect computer settings that apply to all logged-on users. For example, the Network folder contains settings for configuring Windows Firewall, and Windows Components contains settings for configuring Windows Update. You can control hundreds of computer settings with the Administrative Templates folder.

Remember that policies configured in the Computer Configuration node affect all computers in the container (and child containers) to which the GPO is linked. So a policy set in the Computer Configuration node of a GPO linked to the domain object affects all computers in the domain, including all computers in the Domain Controllers OU and the Computers folder.

The User Configuration Node

In the User Configuration node, the Policies folder contains the same three folders as in the Computer Configuration node. However, the policies defined here affect domain users within the GPO's scope regardless of which computer the user signs in to. The following list describes other differences from folders under the Computer Configuration node:

- *Software Settings*—This folder also contains the Software installation extension. However, application packages configured here can be assigned or published. An **assigned application** is made available as an icon in the Start screen the next time a user affected by the policy signs in to a computer in the domain. The first time the user tries to run the application or open a document associated with it, the application is installed. A **published application** is made available via Group Policy for a user to install by using Programs and Features in Control Panel.
- *Windows Settings*—This folder contains four items: the Scripts extension, the Security Settings node, the Folder Redirection node, and the Policy-based QoS node. The Scripts extension enables administrators to create scripts that run at user sign-in and sign-out. The Security Settings node contains policies for configuring certificates and controlling what software users can run. Administrators can use the Folder Redirection node to redirect users' profile folders to a network share. The Policy-based QoS node provides the same functions as in the Computer Configuration node except that the policy is applied to a computer when a user affected by the policy signs in to the computer.
- *Administrative Templates*—This folder contains a host of settings that enables administrators to tightly control users' computer and network environments. For example, Control Panel can be completely hidden from a user, specific Control Panel items can be made available, or items on a user's desktop and Start menu can be hidden or disabled, just to name a few of the settings that can be configured here.

Group Policy is a powerful tool, but with this power comes complexity. This chapter serves as an introduction to group policies, and you learn more about working with their complexities in Chapter 4.

How Group Policies Are Applied

After reading about group policies and examining the two default policies, you might wonder how the Default Domain Policy can affect all computers in the domain when domain controllers have their own default policy. You might have noticed that the Default Domain Policy defines several account policies, such as password and account lockout settings, but no user rights assignment policies; the Default Domain Controllers Policy defines user rights assignment policies but no account policies. In addition, many policies are left undefined or not configured because GPOs, like Active Directory, work in a hierarchical structure.

GPOs can be applied in four places: local computer, site, domain, and OU. Policies are applied in this order, too. Policies that aren't defined or configured are not applied at all, and the last policy to be applied is the one that takes precedence. For example, a GPO linked to a domain affects all computers and users in the domain, but a GPO linked to an OU overrides the domain policies if there are conflicting settings.

Tip ⓘ

You can remember the order in which GPOs are applied with the acronym LSDOU: local computer, site, domain, and OU.

Activity 1-10: Exploring Default GPOs

Time Required: 30 minutes
Objective: Explore the two default GPOs in Active Directory.
Required Tools and Equipment: ServerSA1
Description: In this activity, you familiarize yourself with the default GPOs linked to the domain and the Domain Controllers OU.

1. Sign in to ServerSA1 as **Administrator**, if necessary.
2. Because GPMC uses Internet Explorer to display information, first you'll turn off **IE Enhanced Security Configuration** to avoid warning messages. In Server Manager, click Local Server and click the link next to **IE Enhanced Security Configuration** in the second column. Under Administrators, click **Off**, and then click **OK**. Click **Tools, Group Policy Management** from the menu.
3. In the left pane, click to expand the **Forest** and **Domains** nodes. Click to expand **TestDomain.local** under the Domains node.
4. Click **Default Domain Policy**. If a Group Policy Management console message is displayed, read the message, click the **Do not show this message again** check box, and then click **OK**.
5. In the right pane, click the **Scope** tab, if necessary (see Figure 1-33). The Links section shows you which container objects are linked to this GPO. In this case, your domain should be the only container linked. All objects in a container linked to the GPO are affected by that GPO.
6. Click the **Settings** tab. (The settings might take a few seconds to be displayed.) You can view GPO settings here, but you can't change them.
7. The two main nodes are highlighted: Computer Configuration and User Configuration. Click the **show all** link to expand the settings to see a screen similar to the one in Figure 1-34. Only nodes that have configured settings are shown.
8. Scroll through the settings for the Default Domain Policy, which pertain to user account settings, such as password policies, or security. Take some time to see how Windows initially configures security settings for the domain. Notice that no settings are displayed under the User Configuration node because no settings have been configured.

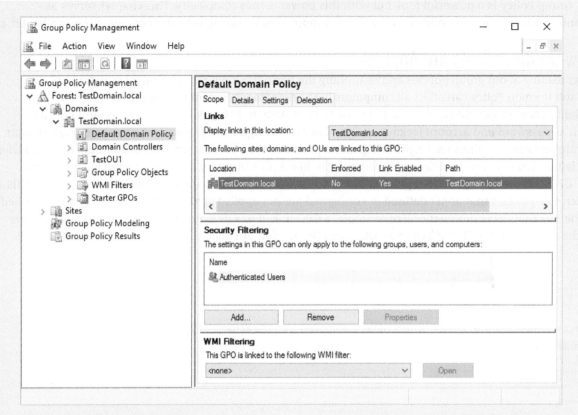

Figure 1-33   The Scope tab

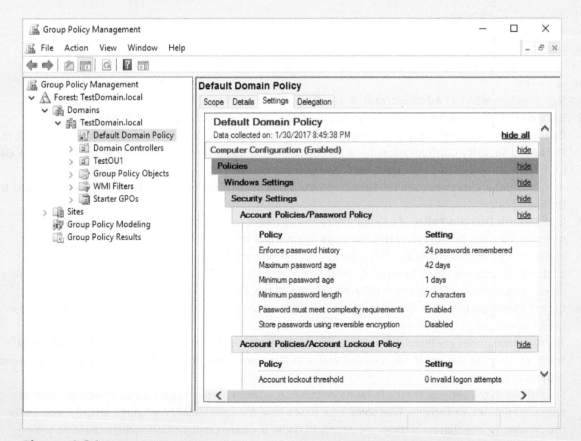

Figure 1-34   The Settings tab

9. Click to expand **Domain Controllers** in the left pane, and then click **Default Domain Controllers Policy**.

10. In the right pane, click the **Settings** tab, if necessary, and then click **show all**. Scroll through the settings for the Default Domain Controllers Policy. Most pertain to user rights assignments, such as which users are allowed to sign in to the computer locally or change the system time. Again, take some time to see how Windows initially configures security settings for domain controllers.

11. Right-click **Default Domain Policy** in the left pane and click **Edit** to open the Group Policy Management Editor.

12. If necessary, click to expand **Computer Configuration** and **User Configuration**. Under Computer Configuration, click to expand the **Policies** folder. You see the three folders described earlier.

13. Click to expand **Windows Settings** and then **Security Settings**. Click to expand the **Account Policies** node, and explore the settings in this node and the nodes under it. Figure 1-35 shows the settings in the Password Policy node. By default, account policies are defined only in the Default Domain Policy, and all domain users are subject to these settings.

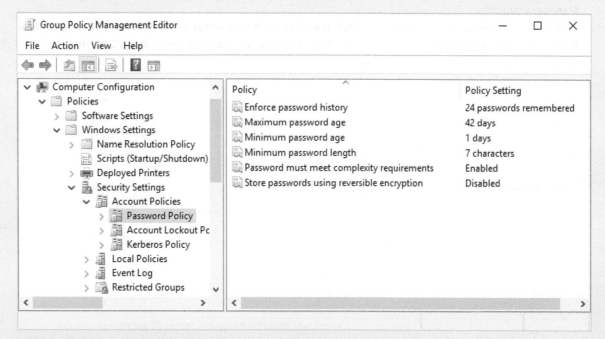

Figure 1-35   Password policies

14. Click to expand the **Local Policies** node, and explore the three nodes under it. Most settings in Local Policies are displayed as Not Defined. In fact, only three policies in the Local Policies node are defined. Can you find them?

15. Browse through some nodes in the Policies folder under User Configuration. No policies are configured in this node. Configuration of user policies is up to the server administrator.

16. Close the Group Policy Management Editor. In the Group Policy Management console, click to expand **Domain Controllers**, if necessary, and then right-click **Default Domain Controllers Policy** and click **Edit**.

17. Under the Computer Configuration node, click to expand the **Policies** folder, and then click to expand **Windows Settings** and then **Security Settings**. Click to expand **Account Policies** and **Local Policies**, and explore the settings in these nodes. Notice that no account policies are defined, but a number of user rights assignments are. Default settings that apply to domain controllers focus on what types of actions users can perform on domain controllers. Most actions are limited to members of the Administrators, Backup Operators, and Server Operators groups.

18. Take some time to explore the GPOs to familiarize yourself with what's available. Leave the Group Policy Management console open for the next activity.

Activity 1-11: Working with Group Policies

Time Required: 30 minutes

Objective: Create a GPO and see how the policies you configure affect user objects in the OU to which the GPO is linked.

Required Tools and Equipment: ServerSA1

Description: You want to see how some group policy settings affect users in your domain. You know that you want to restrict some users' access to Control Panel, so you decide to start with this policy. Because you want the policy to affect certain users, you configure it in the User Configuration node.

1. If necessary, sign in to ServerSA1 as **Administrator**, and open the Group Policy Management console.
2. Under the TestDomain.local node, right-click **TestOU1** (created earlier) and click **Create a GPO in this domain, and Link it here**. In the New GPO dialog box, type **GPO1** in the Name text box, and then click **OK**.
3. In the left pane, click to expand **TestOU1**, and then right-click **GPO1** and click **Edit** to open the Group Policy Management Editor.
4. Under User Configuration, click to expand **Policies** and then **Administrative Templates**. Click the **Control Panel** node. In the right pane, double-click the **Prohibit access to Control Panel and PC settings** policy to open the dialog box shown in Figure 1-36.

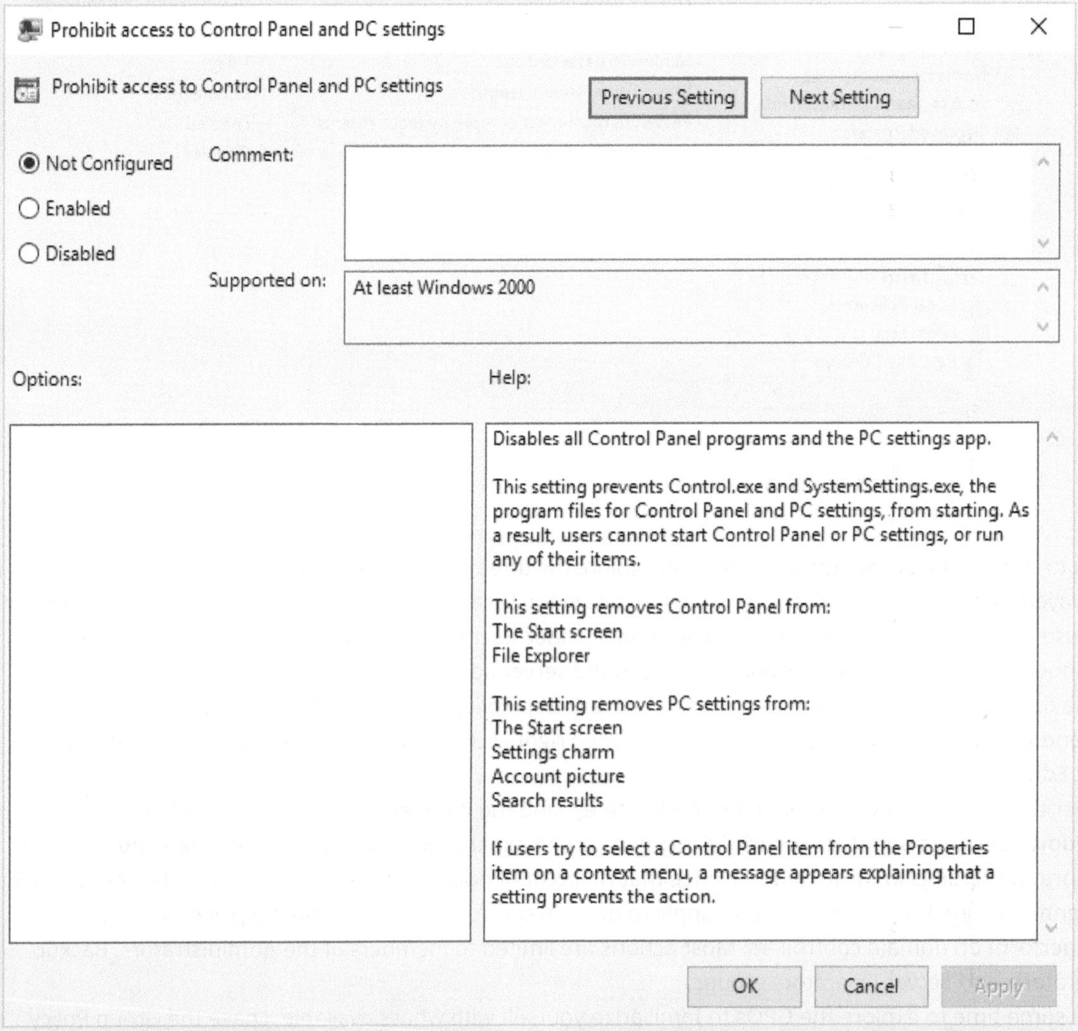

Figure 1-36 Configuring a policy setting

5. Read the description of the policy in the Help box, and then click the **Enabled** option button. Note that there are three possible settings: Enabled, Disabled, and Not Configured. If the policy is enabled, users affected by the policy are prohibited from accessing the Control Panel and PC settings. If the policy is disabled, users have normal access to Control Panel. If the policy is not configured, it has no effect on users' access to the Control Panel and PC settings. Click **OK**. Notice that the State column in the Group Policy Management Editor for the policy you changed then shows Enabled.

6. Close the Group Policy Management Editor and Group Policy Management console.

7. Sign out of ServerSA1 and sign back in as **testuser1** (which you created earlier). To do so, after you press **Ctrl+Alt+Delete**, click **Other user**. Type **testuser1** in the User name text box and **Password01** in the Password text box, and then press **Enter**. You see an error message, but continue to the next step.

8. You see a message stating that the sign-in method you're trying to use isn't allowed. This is because of a policy that prevents regular users from logging on locally to a domain controller. Click **OK**. You're going to fix this in the next series of steps.

9. Sign in as **Administrator**. Open the Group Policy Management MMC, and click to expand the **Domain Controllers** OU. Right-click **Default Domain Controllers Policy** and click **Edit** to open the Group Policy Management Editor.

10. Under Computer Configuration, click to expand **Policies, Windows Settings**, and then **Security Settings**. Click to expand **Local Policies**, and then click **User Rights Assignment**. You should see a list of User Rights Assignment policies in the right pane (see Figure 1-37).

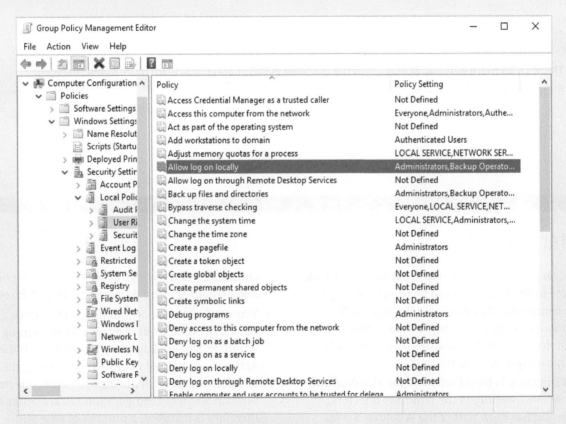

Figure 1-37   The User Rights Assignment node

11. In the right pane, double-click the **Allow log on locally** policy. Notice the list of groups that currently have this right. Click **Add User or Group**. In the Add User or Group dialog box, type **Domain Users**, and then click **OK** twice.

12. Sign out and sign back in as **testuser1**. If you still can't sign in, you might need to wait a few minutes and try again. Group policies take some time to take effect. It could take up to 5 minutes before the policy takes effect, so keep trying.

13. After you're signed in, right-click **Start** and click **Control Panel**. You see a message indicating that restrictions disallow the operation. In the Restrictions message box, click **OK**.

14. Right-click the desktop and click **Display Settings**. You may see a different message, but you will be unsuccessful trying to change display settings because it is a Control Panel operation. Click **OK**. Your policy has clearly taken effect.

15. Shut down ServerSA1.

Tip (i)

You might have noticed a delay between setting a policy and the policy taking effect. You can run the command-line program `gpupdate.exe`, which applies group policies immediately to the computer on which `gpupdate.exe` is running and to the currently logged-on user. This program is an invaluable tool for testing GPOs because it saves considerable time. As mentioned, computer policies are applied when a computer restarts, which can take some time, and user policies are applied when a user logs on. GPOs are also updated on domain controllers every 5 minutes and on workstations and servers every 90 minutes even if the computers don't restart.

Note 📎

There's a lot more to group policies than the overview in this chapter. You learn more about managing and configuring GPOs in Chapter 4.

Chapter Summary

- A directory service is a database that stores network resource information and can be used to manage users, computers, and resources throughout the network. A directory service provides network single sign-on for users and centralizes management in geographically dispersed networks.

- Active Directory is based on the X.500 standard and LDAP. Active Directory is the Windows directory service and has been part of the Windows Server family since Windows 2000 Server. Active Directory is a hierarchical, distributed database that's scalable, secure, and flexible. Active Directory's physical structure is composed of sites and domain controllers, and the logical structure is composed of organizational units, domains, trees, and forests.

- You use Server Manager to install the Active Directory Domain Services role. After running the wizard in Server Manager, you must finish the Active Directory installation by promoting the server to a domain controller using the Active Directory Domain Services Configuration Wizard. After Active Directory is installed, a number of new MMCs are added to the Administrative Tools folder. The main tools for managing an Active Directory domain are Active Directory Administrative Center and Active Directory Users and Computers.

- Installing the first DC in a network creates a new forest, and the domain is called the *forest root domain*. Adding additional domain controllers to a domain, or new domains in a forest are similar to creating a new forest. You can use Install from Media (IFM) to install subsequent DCs in a domain. Using IFM reduces the amount of initial replication traffic required to bring the new DC up to date.

- The data in Active Directory is organized as objects. Available objects and their structure are defined by the Active Directory schema, which is composed of schema classes and schema attributes. The data in a schema attribute is called an *attribute value*.

- There are two types of objects in Active Directory: container objects and leaf objects. Container objects contain other objects and include domains, folders, and OUs. OUs are the primary organizing container in Active Directory. Domains represent administrative, security, and policy boundaries. OUs are organizing and management containers mainly used to mimic a company's structure and apply group policies to collections of users or computers.

- Leaf objects generally represent security accounts, network resources, and GPOs. Security accounts include users, groups, and computers. There are three categories of user account objects: local user accounts, domain user accounts, and built-in user accounts. Groups are used to assign rights and permissions to collections of users. Computer account objects are used to identify computers that are domain members. Other leaf objects include contacts, printers, and shared folders.

- The AD Recycle Bin can be enabled in ADAC but once enabled cannot be disabled. The Recycle Bin feature requires a forest functional level of at least Windows Server 2008 R2.

- Active Directory objects can be located easily with search functions in Active Directory Users and Computers and Windows Explorer. Users can use the Active Directory search function to find network resources (such as shared printers and folders), other users, and contacts among many other items.

- Large organizations might require multiple domains, trees, and forests. Some terms for describing the Active Directory structure include directory partitions, operations master roles, Active Directory replication, and trust relationships.

- Directory partitions are sections of the Active Directory database that hold varied types of data and are managed by different processes. Directory partitions can be replicated from one domain controller to another. FSMO roles are functions carried out by a single domain controller per domain or forest and perform vital functions that affect Active Directory operations.

- The forest is the broadest logical Active Directory component. All domains in a forest share some common characteristics, such as a single schema, the global catalog, and trusts between domains. The global catalog facilitates several important functions, such as cross-domain logon and forestwide searching. The forest root domain is the first domain created in a forest.

- A domain is the primary identifying and administrative unit of Active Directory. Each domain has a unique name, and there's an administrative account with full control over objects in the domain. Some organizations can benefit by using multiple domains when different security or account policies are required among other reasons. A tree consists of one or more domains with a contiguous namespace. An Active Directory forest might require multiple trees when an organization is composed of companies with a noncontiguous namespace.

- GPOs are lists of settings that enable administrators to configure user and computer operating environments remotely. GPOs have two main nodes: Computer Configuration and User Configuration. Each node contains a Policies folder and a Preferences folder. Under the Policies folder are three additional folders: Software Settings, Windows Settings, and Administrative Templates.

- Policies defined in the Computer Configuration node affect all computers in the Active Directory container to which the GPO is linked. Policies defined in the User Configuration node affect all users in the Active Directory container to which the GPO is linked. Group objects aren't affected by GPOs. GPOs can be applied in these four places in order: local computer, site, domain, and OU. User policies are applied when a user signs in, and computer policies are applied when a computer restarts.

Key Terms

Active Directory	Flexible Single Master Operation	object
Active Directory replication	(FSMO) roles	operations master
application directory partition	forest	organizational unit (OU)
assigned application	forest root domain	permissions
attribute value	fully qualified domain name (FQDN)	published application
authentication	global catalog partition	relative identifier (RID)
built-in user account	GPO scope	replication partner
child domain	Group Policy Object (GPO)	right
configuration partition	Install from Media (IFM)	schema
directory partition	intersite replication	schema attribute
directory service	intrasite replication	schema class
Directory Services Restore	Knowledge Consistency	schema directory partition
Mode (DSRM)	Checker (KCC)	security identifier (SID)
domain	leaf object	site
domain controller (DC)	Lightweight Directory Access	SYSVOL folder
domain directory partition	Protocol (LDAP)	tree
domain user account	local user account	trust relationship
extension	multimaster replication	user principal name (UPN)

Review Questions

1. Which of the following best describes a directory service?
   a. A service similar to a list of information in a text file
   b. A service similar to a database program but with the capability to manage objects
   c. A program for managing the user interface on a server
   d. A program for managing folders, files, and permissions on a distributed server

2. The protocol for accessing Active Directory objects and services is based on which of the following standards?
   a. DNS   c. DHCP
   b. LDAP   d. ICMP

3. Which of the following is a feature of Active Directory? (Choose all that apply.)
   a. Has fine-grained access controls
   b. Can be distributed among many servers
   c. Can be installed on only one server per domain
   d. Has a fixed schema

4. Which of the following is a component of Active Directory's physical structure?
   a. Organizational units
   b. Domains
   c. Sites
   d. Folders

5. Which of the following is the responsibility of a domain controller? (Choose all that apply.)
   a. Storing a copy of the domain data
   b. Providing data search and retrieval functions
   c. Servicing multiple domains
   d. Providing authentication services

6. Which of the following is *not* associated with an Active Directory tree?
   a. A group of domains
   b. A container object that can be linked to a GPO
   c. A common naming structure
   d. Parent and child domains

7. Which of the following is *not* part of Active Directory's logical structure?
   a. Tree
   b. Forest
   c. DC
   d. OU

8. Which of the following is associated with an Active Directory forest? (Choose all that apply.)
   a. Can contain trees with different naming structures
   b. Allows independent domain administration
   c. Contains domains with different schemas
   d. Represents the broadest element in Active Directory

9. Which of the following is associated with installing the first domain controller in a forest?
   a. RODC
   b. Child domain
   c. Global catalog
   d. DHCP

10. When installing an additional DC in an existing domain, which of the following is an option for reducing replication traffic?
    a. New site   c. GC server
    b. Child domain   d. IFM

11. Which MMC is added after Active Directory installation? (Choose all that apply.)
    a. Active Directory Domains and Trusts
    b. Active Directory Groups and Sites
    c. ADSI Edit
    d. Active Directory Restoration Utility

12. Which of the following is the core logical structure container in Active Directory?
    a. Forest   c. Domain
    b. OU   d. Site

13. Which of the following defines the types of objects in Active Directory?
    a. GPOs
    b. Attribute values
    c. Schema attributes
    d. Schema classes

14. Which of the following defines the types of information stored in an Active Directory object?
    a. GPOs
    b. Attribute values
    c. Schema attributes
    d. Schema classes

15. Which of the following specifies what types of actions a user can perform on a computer or network?
    a. Attributes   c. Permissions
    b. Rights   d. Classes

16. Which of the following is considered a leaf object? (Choose all that apply.)
    a. Computer account
    b. Organizational unit
    c. Domain controller
    d. Shared folder

17. Which of the following is a default folder object created when Active Directory is installed?
    a. Computers
    b. Domain Controllers
    c. Groups
    d. Sites

18. Which type of account is *not* found in Active Directory?
    a. Domain user account
    b. Local user account
    c. Built-in user account
    d. Computer account

19. Which of the following is a directory partition? (Choose all that apply.)
    a. Domain directory partition
    b. Group policy partition
    c. Schema directory partition
    d. Configuration partition

20. Which is responsible for management of adding, removing, and renaming domains in a forest?
    a. Schema master
    b. Infrastructure master
    c. Domain naming master
    d. RID master

21. All domains in the same forest have which of the following in common? (Choose all that apply.)
    a. Domain name
    b. Schema
    c. Domain administrator
    d. Global catalog

22. You have an Active Directory forest of two trees and eight domains. You haven't changed any operations master domain controllers. On which domain controller is the schema master?
    a. All domain controllers
    b. The last domain controller installed
    c. The first domain controller in the forest root domain
    d. The first domain controller in each tree

23. To which of the following can a GPO be linked? (Choose all that apply.)
    a. Trees
    b. Domains
    c. Folders
    d. Sites

24. Which container has a default GPO linked to it?
    a. Users
    b. Printers
    c. Computers
    d. Domain

25. By default, when are policies set in the User Configuration node applied?
    a. Every 5 minutes
    b. Immediately
    c. At user logon
    d. At computer restart

Critical Thinking

The following activities give you critical thinking challenges. Case Projects offer a scenario with a problem to solve and for which you supply a written solution.

Case Project 1-1: Configuring Active Directory

When CSM Tech Publishing started its Windows network almost a year ago, the network was small enough that you simply used the default Users and Computers containers for the user account and computer account objects that you created. However, now that the company has grown to more than 50 users and computers, you decide that some structure is needed. You talk to the owner to understand how the business is organized and learn that there are four main departments: Executive, Marketing, Engineering, and Operations. Draw a diagram of the Active Directory structure based on this information, including the types of objects in each container. Include the objects you know about and where these objects should be located, and state whether you need to move any existing objects. Use triangles and circles to represent container objects in your diagram as shown in Figures 1-1 through 1-4.

Case Project 1-2: Explaining GPOs

The owner of CSM Tech Publishing has told you that she needs to lock down some desktops so that these users can't access certain Windows components, such as Control Panel. She also wants some standardization in the look of users' desktops, such as wallpaper and so forth. However, she's not sure how to make these changes without affecting all users and computers. Write a short explanation of how GPOs can be applied to achieve the owner's goals. Include information about how policies defined in one place can take precedence over policies defined elsewhere.

CHAPTER 2

MANAGING OUs AND ACTIVE DIRECTORY ACCOUNTS

After reading this chapter and completing the exercises, you will be able to:

Work with organizational units

Manage user accounts

Manage group accounts

Work with computer accounts

Automate account management

A directory service should be thought of as a tool to help administrators manage network resources. Like any tool, the better designed it is, the more useful it will be. In its default configuration, Active Directory is a useful directory service, but its real power is apparent when thought has been put into its design and configuration. An efficient Active Directory design that reflects how a business is organized improves the ease and efficiency of managing a Windows network. Likewise, correct configuration of Active Directory is paramount to a smoothly running and secure network. You learn more about organizational units, how to use them in a hierarchical design, and how to manage access to them.

A major task for an Active Directory domain administrator is managing user, group, and computer accounts. Users are hired, leave the company, change departments, and change their names. Passwords are forgotten and must be reset. New resources become available, and users or, more likely, groups of users must be given access to them. New computers are installed on the network and must be added to the domain. All these tasks, particularly in large networks, keep administrators busy.

This chapter discusses GUI and command-line tools for creating and managing all aspects of Active Directory accounts. You also examine the use of several user account properties. Next, you learn about group account types and group scopes, including how to use groups to maintain secure access to resources. In addition, you learn the purpose of computer accounts and how to work with them. Finally, you explore some command-line tools that are useful for automating account management.

Table 2-1 summarizes what you need for the hands-on activities in this chapter.

Table 2-1   Activity requirements

Activity	Requirements	Notes
Activity 2-1: Resetting Your Virtual Environment	ServerDC1, ServerSA1	
Activity 2-2: Working with OUs	ServerDC1	
Activity 2-3: Viewing Object Permissions	ServerDC1	
Activity 2-4: Creating User Accounts in Active Directory Users and Computers	ServerDC1	
Activity 2-5: Creating User Accounts in Active Directory Administrative Center	ServerDC1	
Activity 2-6: Creating a User Template	ServerDC1	
Activity 2-7: Editing Multiple Accounts	ServerDC1	
Activity 2-8: Creating Groups with Different Scopes	ServerDC1	
Activity 2-9: Working with Default Groups	ServerDC1	
Activity 2-10: Joining a Computer to the Domain	ServerDC1 and ServerSA1	
Activity 2-11: Creating a Batch File for the `dsadd` Command	ServerDC1	
Activity 2-12: Using Pipes	ServerDC1	
Activity 2-13: Using `csvde` to Create Users	ServerDC1	
Activity 2-14: Using `ldifde` to Create Users	ServerDC1	

Working with Organizational Units

 **Certification**

- 70-742 – Install and configure Active Directory Domain Services:
  Create and manage Active Directory groups and organizational units (OUs)

As you learned in Chapter 1, organizational units (OUs) are the building blocks of the Active Directory structure in a domain. Thoughtful planning of the OU structure eases managing users and computers and applying group policies and makes Active Directory easier for users and technical staff to work with. Here are some benefits of using OUs:

- You can create a familiar hierarchical structure based on the organizational chart that enables users and administrators to locate network users and resources quickly.
- You can delegate administration of network resources to other IT staff without assigning more comprehensive administrative permissions.
- You can change the OU structure easily to accommodate corporate reorganizations.
- You can group users and computers for the purposes of assigning administrative and security policies with the Group Policy tool.
- You can hide Active Directory objects for confidentiality or security reasons by configuring access permissions on OUs.

Note

An OU can't be used to assign permissions to objects it contains. Groups, not OUs, are the main Active Directory object for permission assignments and are discussed in detail later in the section "Managing Group Accounts."

OUs are containers holding objects such as user and computer accounts, but they can also contain other OUs. This ability to nest OUs gives you the flexibility to create a hierarchy with as many levels as needed for your organization. Take a look at a fictitious company, csmtech.local, which has about 40 employees and this top-level organizational structure:

- Administration
- Marketing
- Research and Development (R&D)
- Operations

This organization will likely have a single-level OU structure as shown on the left in Figure 2-1. Dividing R&D into the Engineering and Research departments and Marketing into Sales and Advertising creates the multilevel OU structure shown on the right in Figure 2-1.

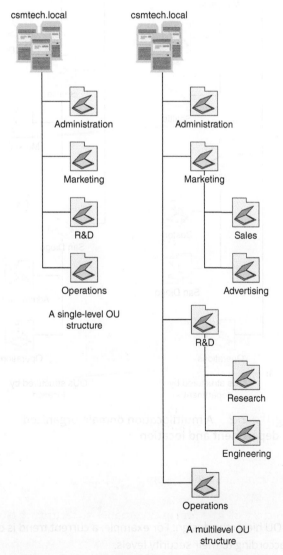

Figure 2-1   **Single-level and multilevel OU structures**

Now look at a larger organization with departments in different locations. If the company uses departments rather than locations for identification purposes, the OU structure could reflect that focus as shown on the left in Figure 2-2. The top-level structure remains intact, but under each department is an OU for each location. Conversely, if the business is organized mainly by location, the OU structure looks like the one on the right in Figure 2-2. Notice that some OUs have the same name, which is allowed as long as they're in different parts of the Active Directory hierarchy. For example, the R&D OU is under both the Boston and Seattle OUs.

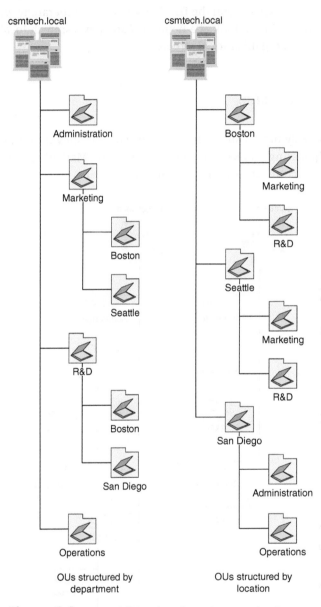

Figure 2-2   A multilocation domain organized by department and location

Tip ⓘ

There are other approaches to OU hierarchy design. For example, a current trend is designing OUs based on grouping users and resources according to their security levels.

OU Delegation of Control

As you've learned, one benefit of using OUs is that you can delegate administration of the OU and its contents to other users without giving them broader administrative capability. **Delegation of control**, in the context of Active Directory, means that a person with higher security privileges assigns authority to a person of lesser security privileges to perform certain tasks. Delegation of control of an OU is not an all-or-nothing proposition. You can assign specific tasks the user can perform on objects in that OU and even delegate other tasks to different users or groups. The following are the most common tasks that can be delegated:

- Create, delete, and manage user accounts
- Reset user passwords and force password change at next logon
- Read all user information
- Create, delete, and manage groups
- Modify the membership of a group
- Manage group policy links
- Generate Resultant Set of Policy (Planning)
- Generate Resultant Set of Policy (Logging)

Note

Three more predefined tasks can be delegated for the object class `inetOrgPerson`, which is a user and contact class defined in Active Directory for LDAP compatibility.

In addition to these tasks, you can define custom tasks, which allow fine-grained control over the management tasks a user can perform in an OU. When you create a custom task, you must fully understand the nature of objects, permissions, and permission inheritance. Even if you delegate control only by using predefined tasks, your understanding of how permissions and permission inheritance work is important. After all, the Delegation of Control Wizard does nothing more than assign permissions for Active Directory objects to selected users or groups.

After you have delegated control to a user, there's no clear indication that this change has been made. By default, the OU's properties don't show that another user has been delegated control. To verify who has been delegated control of an OU, you must view the OU's permissions, as explained in the following section.

Active Directory Object Permissions

Active Directory object permissions work almost identically to file and folder permissions. Three types of security principals can be assigned permission to an object: users, groups, and computers. An Active Directory object's security settings are composed of three components, collectively referred to as the object's *security descriptor*:

- Discretionary access control list (DACL)
- Object owner
- System access control list (SACL)

Like file system objects, every Active Directory object has a list of standard permissions and a list of special permissions that can be assigned to a security principal. For simplicity's sake, the term *users* is used when discussing permissions, but keep in mind that permissions can be assigned to any type of security principal: users, groups, and computers. Each permission can be set to Allow or Deny, and five standard permissions are available for most objects:

- *Read*—Users can view objects and their attributes and permissions.
- *Write*—Users can change an object's attributes.

- *Create all child objects*—Users can create new child objects in the parent object.
- *Delete all child objects*—Users can delete child objects in the parent object.
- *Full control*—Users can perform all actions granted by the previous four standard permissions, plus change permissions and take ownership of the object.

Different object types have other standard and special permissions. For example, a user object has the Reset password and Read logon information permissions; an OU object has the Create Account objects and Create Printer objects permissions.

Permission Inheritance in OUs

Permission inheritance in OUs works much the same way as it does in the file system. For example, an OU containing other objects is the parent object, and any objects contained in the OU, including other OUs, are considered child objects. All objects in Active Directory are child objects of the domain. By default, permissions applied to the parent OU with the Delegation of Control Wizard are inherited by all child objects of the parent OU. So, if a user has been given permissions to manage user accounts in an OU, these permissions apply to all existing and future user accounts in this OU, including user accounts created in child OUs. In the OU design structured by department in Figure 2-2, if a user is delegated control to create, delete, and manage user accounts in the R&D OU, this user could perform these actions on users in the R&D OU as well as the Boston and San Diego OUs.

Advanced Features Option in Active Directory Users and Computers

The default display settings in Active Directory Users and Computers hide some system folders and advanced features, but you can display them by enabling the Advanced Features option from the View menu. After selecting this option, five new folders are shown under the domain node:

- *LostAndFound*—Contains objects created at the same time their container is deleted, perhaps by another administrator on another domain controller
- *Program Data*—Initially empty; is available to store application-specific objects
- *System*—Used by Windows system services that are integrated with Active Directory
- *NTDS Quotas*—Stores NT Directory Service (NTDS) quota information that limits the number of Active Directory objects a user, group, computer, or service can create
- *TPM Devices*—Stores Trusted Platform Module (TPM) information about Windows 8 and later computer accounts; was new in Windows Server 2012

After Advanced Features is enabled, the Properties dialog box of domain, folder, and OU objects has three new tabs:

- *Object*—Used to view detailed information about a container object, such as the object class, created and modified dates, and sequence numbers for synchronizing replication. It also includes a check box you can select to protect an object from accidental deletion.
- *Security*—Used to view and modify an object's permissions.
- *Attribute Editor*—Used to view and edit an object's attributes, many of which aren't available in standard Properties dialog boxes.

For now, you're most interested in the Security tab of an OU's Properties dialog box (see Figure 2-3). The top section lists all accounts (user, group, and computer) that have an access control entry (ACE) in the DACL. The bottom section lists permission settings for each ACE. In Figure 2-3, the Domain Admins ACE is selected, and the bottom section shows the permissions granted to this group. To view details for this permission, you can click the Advanced button.

As you can see, permissions in Active Directory behave similarly to file system permissions, but there are some important differences. Active Directory permissions can become complex with the multitude of inheritance rules and options, so it's best to keep things as simple as possible without compromising security. Until you fully understand permissions in Active Directory, use the Delegation of Control Wizard to assign other users or groups the ability to perform specific functions in Active Directory containers.

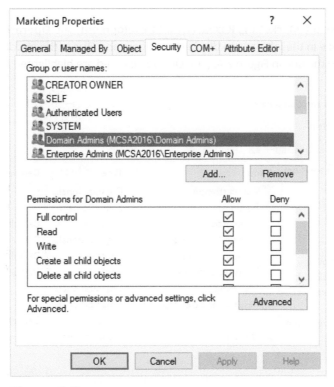

Figure 2-3   The Security tab of an OU's Properties dialog box

Activity 2-1: Resetting Your Virtual Environment

Time Required: 5 minutes

Objective: Reset your virtual environment by applying the InitialConfig checkpoint or snapshot.

Required Tools and Equipment: ServerDC1, ServerSA1

Description: Apply the InitialConfig checkpoint or snapshot to ServerDC1 and ServerSA1.

1. Be sure the servers are shut down. In your virtualization program, apply the InitialConfig checkpoint or snapshot to ServerDC1 and ServerSA1.
2. When the snapshot or checkpoint has finished being applied, continue to the next activity.

Activity 2-2: Working with OUs

Time Required: 10 minutes

Objective: Create OUs to reflect a company's departmental structure and then use the Delegation of Control Wizard.

Required Tools and Equipment: ServerDC1

Description: You have been asked to create the OU structure for a business with four main departments: Administration, Marketing, Research and Development, and Operations. You create a single-level OU structure based on these requirements, using Active Directory Users and Computers for this task.

1. Sign in to ServerDC1 as **Administrator**.
2. In Server Manager, click **Tools, Active Directory Users and Computers**.
3. In the left pane, right-click the domain node **MCSA2016.local**, point to **New**, and click **Organizational Unit**.
4. In the Name text box, type **Administration** and click **OK**.

5. Repeat Steps 3 and 4 to create the **Marketing, Research and Development**, and **Operations** OUs. When finished, click the domain node in the left pane to display the folders and OUs in the middle pane. Your OU structure should be similar to the one in Figure 2-4. (The OUs you created are highlighted in the figure.)

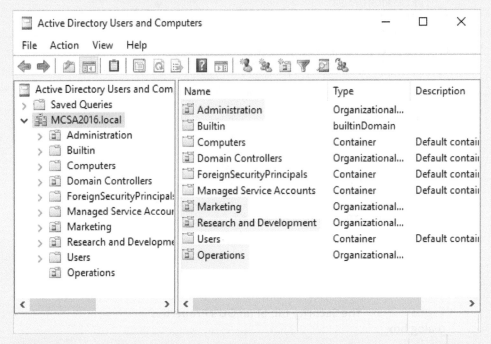

Figure 2-4   The Active Directory structure after creating OUs

6. Right-click the **Operations** OU, point to **New**, and click **User**.
7. Type **Joe** in the First name text box, **Tech1** in the Last name text box, and **jtech1** in the User logon name text box. Click **Next**.
8. Type **Password01** in the Password text box and again in the Confirm password text box. Click to clear the **User must change password at next logon** check box and click to select the **Password never expires** check box. Click **Next**, and then click **Finish**.
9. Right-click the **Marketing** OU and click **Delegate Control** to start the Delegation of Control Wizard. In the welcome window, click **Next**.
10. In the Users or Groups window, click **Add**. In the *Enter the object names to select* text box, type **jtech1**. Click **Check Names**, and then click **OK**. Click **Next**.
11. Click the **Create, delete, and manage user accounts** check box. Click **Next**, and then click **Finish**.
12. Leave Active Directory Users and Computers open and continue to the next activity.

Activity 2-3: Viewing Object Permissions

Time Required: 10 minutes
Objective: View object permissions in Active Directory.
Required Tools and Equipment: ServerDC1
Description: In this activity, you examine the results of delegating control on Active Directory object permissions. To view the settings, you need to enable the Advanced Features option in Active Directory Users and Computers.

1. If necessary, sign in to ServerDC1 as **Administrator**, and open Active Directory Users and Computers.
2. Right-click the **Marketing** OU and click **Properties**. Note the three tabs that are available now: General, Managed By, and COM+. (In the next step, you enable additional tabs.) Click **Cancel**.

3. Click **View, Advanced Features** from the menu. The display changes to include additional folders described previously.

4. Right-click the **Marketing** OU and click **Properties**. Click the **Object** tab, where you can find information that's useful in troubleshooting. In addition, when the *Protect object from accidental deletion* check box is selected, the object can't be moved or deleted unless this check box is cleared.

5. Click the **Security** tab. Scroll through the list of group and user names so that you know what ACEs are in the DACL. Click each ACE to view its permission settings at the bottom.

6. Click the **Joe Tech1** ACE, and notice in the Permission entries list that the Special permissions check box is selected. Click the **Advanced** button to open the Advanced Security Settings for Marketing dialog box (see Figure 2-5).

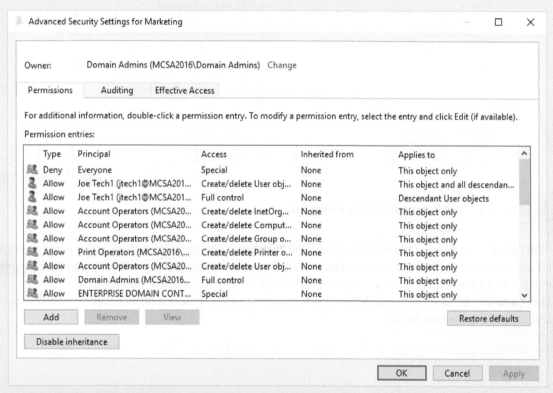

Figure 2-5 An OU's Advanced Security Settings dialog box

7. Double-click the first **Joe Tech1** entry to open the Permission Entry for Marketing dialog box (see Figure 2-6). Scroll down to see that the Create User objects and Delete User objects check boxes are selected, so Joe Tech1 has permission to create and delete users in the Marketing OU. Scroll back to the top of the window. The *This object and all descendant objects* option in the *Applies to* list means that Joe Tech1 can create and delete users in any OUs under Marketing.

Note

The term *descendant objects* means that all objects underneath the object are also affected by the permission settings.

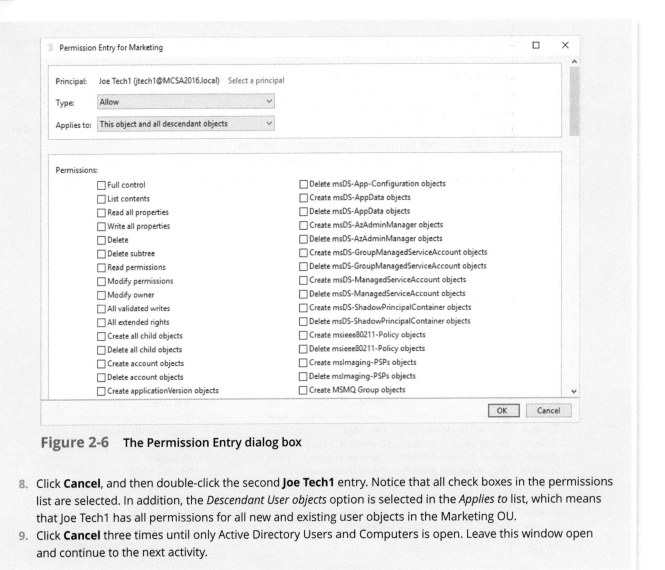

Figure 2-6 The Permission Entry dialog box

8. Click **Cancel**, and then double-click the second **Joe Tech1** entry. Notice that all check boxes in the permissions list are selected. In addition, the *Descendant User objects* option is selected in the *Applies to* list, which means that Joe Tech1 has all permissions for all new and existing user objects in the Marketing OU.

9. Click **Cancel** three times until only Active Directory Users and Computers is open. Leave this window open and continue to the next activity.

Managing User Accounts

- **70-742 – Install and configure Active Directory Domain Services:**
  Create and manage Active Directory Users and Computers

Working with user accounts is one of the most important Active Directory administrative tasks. User accounts are the main link between real people and network resources, so user account management requires not only technical expertise but also people skills. When users can't sign in to or access a needed resource, they usually turn to the IT department to solve the problem. Fortunately, an administrator's understanding of how user accounts work and how to best configure them can reduce the need to exercise people skills with frustrated users.

User accounts have two main functions in Active Directory:

- *Provide a method for user authentication to the network*—The user logon name and password serve as a secure method for users to sign in to the network to access resources. A user account can also contain account restrictions, such as when and where a user can sign in or an account expiration date.
- *Provide detailed information about a user*—For use in a company directory, user accounts can contain departments, office locations, addresses, and telephone information. You can modify the Active Directory schema to contain just about any user information a company wants to keep.

As you learned in Chapter 1, Windows OSs have three categories of user accounts: local, domain, and built-in. Local user accounts are found in Windows client OSs, such as Windows 10 as well as Windows Server OSs on systems that aren't configured as domain controllers. These accounts are stored in the **Security Accounts Manager (SAM) database** on local computers, and users can sign in to and access resources only on the computer where the account resides. A network running Active Directory should limit the use of local user accounts on client computers, however, because they can't be used to access domain resources. Local user accounts are mainly used in a peer-to-peer network where Active Directory isn't running. Administrators can also sign in to a computer with a local Administrator account for the purposes of joining the computer to a domain or troubleshooting access to the domain. Local user accounts are usually created in Control Panel's User Accounts applet or the Computer Management MMC's Local Users and Groups snap-in. Because these accounts don't participate in Active Directory, they can't be managed from Active Directory or be subject to group policies. The number of attributes in a local user account pales in comparison with those in Active Directory user accounts as shown in Figure 2-7.

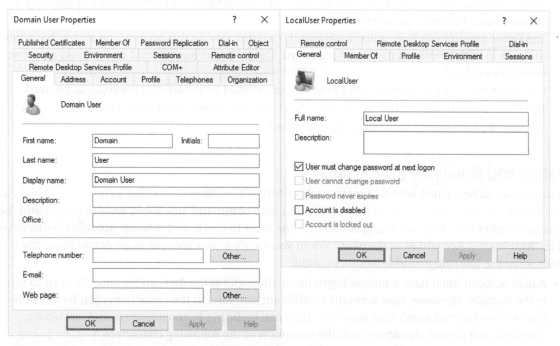

Figure 2-7   A domain user account (left) and local user account (right)

User accounts created in Active Directory are referred to as *domain user accounts*. Generally, these accounts enable users to sign in to any computer that's a domain member in the Active Directory forest. They also provide single sign-on access to domain resources in the forest and other trusted entities to which the account has permission. Domain user accounts can be managed by group policies and are subject to account policies linked to the domain.

Built-in user accounts include the Administrator and Guest accounts created during Windows installation. They can be local or domain user accounts, depending on whether they're stored in the computer's SAM database or in Active Directory. Built-in accounts have the same qualities as regular local or domain accounts except that they can't be deleted. When Active Directory is installed on a Windows Server 2016 computer, the Administrator and Guest accounts along with any other local accounts are converted from local user to domain user accounts. The Administrator and Guest accounts require special handling because of their unique role in being the two accounts on every Windows computer. The following guidelines apply to the built-in Administrator account:

- The local Administrator account has full access to all aspects of a computer, and the domain Administrator account has full access to all aspects of the domain.
- The domain Administrator account in the forest root domain has full access to all aspects of the forest. This administrator account is the only default member of the Enterprise Admins group, discussed later in the section "Managing Group Accounts."
- Because the Administrator account is created on every computer and domain, it should be renamed and given a very strong password to increase security. With these measures in place, a user attempting to gain unauthorized access has to guess not only the administrator's password but also the logon name.
- The Administrator account should be used to sign in to a computer or domain only when performing administrative operations is necessary. Network administrators should use a regular user account for signing in to perform nonadministrative tasks.
- The Administrator account can be renamed or disabled but can't be deleted.

The following guidelines apply to the built-in Guest account:

- After Windows installation, the Guest account is disabled by default and must be enabled by an administrator before it can be used to sign in.
- The Guest account can have a blank password, so if you enable this account, be aware that anybody can sign in with it without needing a password. The Guest account should be assigned a password before it's enabled.
- Like the Administrator account, the Guest account should be renamed if it's going to be used.
- The Guest account has limited access to a computer or domain, but it does have access to any resource for which the Everyone group has permission.

Creating and Modifying User Accounts

User accounts can be created with GUI tools, such as **Active Directory Users and Computers (ADUC)** and **Active Directory Administrative Center (ADAC)**, and with command-line tools, such as dsadd and the PowerShell cmdlet New-ADUser. Using command-line tools to create and manage accounts is discussed later in "Automating Account Management." When you create a user account in an Active Directory domain, keep the following considerations in mind:

- A user account must have a unique logon name throughout the domain because it's used to sign in to the domain. However, user accounts in different domains in the same forest can be the same.
- User account names aren't case sensitive. They can be from 1 to 20 characters and use letters, numbers, and special characters with the exception of the following characters: \ / " [ ] : ; < > ? * + @ | ^ =,. (Note that periods are allowed.)
- Devise a naming standard for user accounts, which makes creating users easier and can be convenient when using applications, such as email, that include the user name in the address. The downside of using a predictable naming standard is that attackers can guess user names easily to gain unauthorized access to the network. Common naming standards include a user's first initial plus last name (for example, kwilliams for Kelly Williams) or a user's first name and last name separated by a special character (such as Kelly.Williams or Kelly_Williams). In large companies where names are likely to be duplicated, adding a number after the user name is common.

- By default, a complex password is required as described in Chapter 1. Passwords are case sensitive.
- By default, only a logon name is required to create a user account. If a user is created without a password and the password policy requires a non-blank password, the user is created but disabled. Descriptive information, such as first and last name, should be included to facilitate Active Directory searches.

You have created a few users already, but take a closer look at the process, particularly some of the fields in ADUC and ADAC. Figure 2-8 shows the New Object - User dialog box in ADUC.

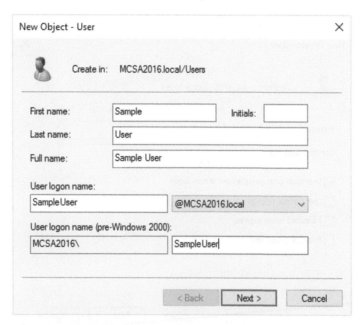

Figure 2-8   The New Object - User dialog box

As mentioned, the only field *required* for a valid user is a user logon name—or more specifically, only the User logon name (pre-Windows 2000) field shown in Figure 2-8. However, you can get away with skipping the other fields only when you're using command-line tools. When you use ADUC, you must enter a value for the following attributes:

- *Full name*—This field is normally a composite of the First name, Initials, and Last name fields, but you can enter a name that's different from what's in these three fields.
- *User logon name*—This field isn't actually required, but it's highly recommended. It's called the *user principal name* (UPN), and the UPN format is *logon name@domain*. The "@domain" part is the UPN suffix. You can fill in the logon name and select the domain in the drop-down list, which is set to the current domain controller's domain by default. By using the UPN, users can sign in to their home domains from a computer that's a member of a different domain or from a remote application. In ADAC, this field is called *User UPN logon*. If you omit this field and fill in only the User logon name (pre-Windows 2000) field, the user account is still valid. Windows creates an implicit UPN, using the User logon name (pre-Windows 2000) field and the domain name. Microsoft recommends making the UPN the same as the user's email address.
- *User logon name (pre-Windows 2000)*—This field is called the **downlevel user logon name** because of its backward compatibility with older applications and Windows versions. Generally, it's the same as the User logon name field but need not be. It consists of the domain name (without the top-level domain), a backslash, and the user logon name. Users running applications that don't recognize the UPN format can use this format to sign in: *domain\user*. Although the User logon name and User logon name (pre-Windows 2000) fields can be different, this is not recommended. This field is required when creating a user account. In ADAC, this field is called *User SamAccountName logon*.

- *Password and Confirm password*—These fields (see Figure 2-9) are required when creating a user in ADUC because account policies in a Windows Server 2016 domain don't allow blank passwords. The default password policy requires a minimum length of 7 characters and a maximum of 127, and the password must meet complexity requirements, meaning it must have at least three characters of the following types: uppercase letters, lowercase letters, numbers, and special characters. You can change this password policy by using Group Policy (discussed in Chapter 4). When creating users with ADAC, dsadd, or PowerShell, you have the option of leaving the password blank, but the account is disabled. You must set a suitable password before the account can be enabled.

Figure 2-9   Password fields

The four check boxes in Figure 2-9 are as follows:

- *User must change password at next logon*—This option, enabled by default, requires users to create a new password the next time they sign in. Typically, you use this option when users are assigned a generic password at account creation for logging on to the domain for the first time. After the first logon, the user is prompted to change the password so that it complies with the password policy. This option is also used when an existing user's password is reset.
- *User cannot change password*—This option is useful when multiple users sign in with the same user account, a practice common with part-time employees or guests who need access to the network. However, this option can't be set if *User must change password at next logon* is already selected. If you attempt to set both options, Windows displays a message stating that only one can be set.
- *Password never expires*—This option overrides the password policy that sets a maximum password age to force users to change their passwords periodically. It applies only to password expiration, not to account expiration, and can't be set when *User must change password at next logon* is already selected. Later in the section "Understanding Account Properties," you will see how to set an expiration date for a user account.
- *Account is disabled*—This option, which prevents using the user account, is sometimes set when user accounts are created before users need them, as when you've hired a new employee who hasn't started yet. You can also set this option on existing user accounts, as discussed in the following section.

Disabling User Accounts

You disable a user account to prevent someone from signing in with it. There are a number of reasons you might want to do this:

- *A user has left the company*—You disable the account instead of deleting it so that all the user's files are still accessible and all group memberships are maintained. If the user's position will be replaced, you can rename the account to match the new employee, and the new employee will have the previous user's rights and permissions. Even if a user isn't being replaced, you might want to disable rather than delete the account for auditing purposes.
- *The account is not ready to use*—You might want to create new accounts in anticipation of new hires. You can create these accounts in a disabled state, and when the users are ready to use the system, you enable the accounts for their first logons.
- *A user goes on extended leave*—For security reasons, it's best to disable an account that will be inactive for an extended period.

Aside from using ADUC and ADAC to enable and disable accounts, you can use the PowerShell cmdlets `Enable-ADAccount` and `Disable-ADAccount` as well as the `dsmod user` command.

Using User Templates

Creating users can be a repetitive task, especially when you're creating several users with similar group memberships, account options, and descriptive fields. Fortunately, you can reduce some of this repetition by using a **user template**, which is simply a user account that's copied to create users with common attributes. You can copy many user account attributes in this template to accounts you're creating, except for name, logon name, password, and some contact and descriptive fields (such as phone number and email address) that are generally unique for each user. You use ADUC to copy an account, and then the same wizard for creating a user starts so that you can fill in the name, logon name, password, and other unique fields. Here are some tips for creating user templates:

- Create one template account for each department or OU because users in the same department often have several common attributes.
- Disable the template account so that it doesn't pose a security risk.
- Add an underscore or other special character to the beginning of a template account's name so that it's easily recognizable as a template and is listed first in an alphabetical list of accounts.
- Fill in as many common attributes as you can so that after each account is created, less customizing is necessary.

User templates are useful for creating several users with a number of similar attributes. Unfortunately, some attributes, such as the Description, Office, Telephone number, Web page, and other fields, aren't copied to the new user account. In addition, if one of the attributes that's copied changes, quite a bit of manual configuration might be required. However, there's a way to work around these limitations, discussed in the following section.

Tip

You can use the Active Directory Schema snap-in to change whether an attribute is copied when the user is copied. Load the snap-in into an MMC, double-click the attribute, and click the *Attribute is copied when duplicating a user* check box.

Modifying Multiple Users

As mentioned, user templates don't copy all the common attributes you might want to set for multiple users, such as department members who have the same telephone number or office location. In addition, you might need to add several users to a group after the users are created. Fortunately, Active Directory

Users and Computers supports making changes to several accounts simultaneously. To select multiple accounts, hold down Ctrl and click each one separately. If the accounts are listed consecutively, click the first one, hold down Shift, and click the last account in the list, or drag over the accounts to select them. After making a selection, right-click it or click Action on the menu bar to perform the following actions on all selected accounts simultaneously:

- *Add to a group*—Adds the selected accounts to a group you specify
- *Disable Account*—Disables the selected accounts
- *Enable Account*—Enables the selected accounts
- *Move*—Moves the selected accounts to a new OU or folder
- *Send Mail*—Opens the configured email application and places each user's email address in the To field
- *Cut*—Cuts the selected accounts so that you can paste them into another OU or folder
- *Delete*—Deletes the selected accounts
- *Properties*—Opens the Properties for Multiple Items dialog box where you can edit certain attributes of the selected accounts

Editing multiple items isn't limited to user accounts, although it's most useful with these objects. You can edit multiple computer and group accounts and even objects of differing types, but the only attribute you can edit for these object types is the Description field.

Understanding Account Properties

After an account is created, your work as an administrator is just beginning. User account properties aren't static and require modification from time to time. Users might need their password changed, their group memberships altered, their logon restrictions modified, and other account changes. First you learn how to perform common actions on accounts such as resetting passwords and moving accounts to different containers:

- *Reset a password*—If users forget their passwords or are prohibited from changing them, administrators can reset a password by right-clicking the user account in ADUC and clicking Reset Password. In ADAC, the Overview window has a Reset Password check box so that you can quickly reset a password or unlock an account. To reset a user account password with PowerShell, enter the following command. You're prompted to enter and confirm the new password.

```
Set-ADAccountPassword LogonName -Reset
```

- *Rename an account*—The object name shown in the Name column of ADUC and ADAC is referred to as the *common name* (CN). A user account's CN is taken from the Full name field when the user is created. You can change the CN by right-clicking the account and clicking Rename in ADUC or by changing the Full name field in ADAC. In PowerShell, enter the following command. You need to specify the distinguished name of the object, the first part of which is the common name:

```
Rename-ADObject DistinguishedName -NewName "NewName"
```

Note

An object's distinguished name (DN) is used in some commands to identify Active Directory objects. It uses LDAP syntax. For example, `CN=Jr Admin,OU=Operations,DC=MCSA2016,DC=local` identifies a user named Jr Admin in the Operations OU in the MCSA2016.local domain. CN means common name, OU means organizational unit, and DC means domain component.

- *Move an account*—You can move a user account or any Active Directory object with any of the following methods:
  - Right-click the user and click Move. (You can also click Action, Move from the menu.) You're then prompted to select the container to which you're moving the object.
  - Right-click the user and click Cut. Then open a container object and paste the user into the container. This method works only in ADUC.
  - In ADUC, drag the user from one container to another.
  - Use the `Move-ADObject` cmdlet in PowerShell.

This chapter has covered only a small fraction of the many user account properties that can be configured. The following sections describe some other properties you might need to set on a user account. These sections are organized according to the tabs of an account's properties in ADUC. The same properties are available in ADAC but can be accessed in one place by scrolling down the Properties window.

The General Tab

The General tab of a user account's Properties dialog box contains descriptive information about the account, none of which affects a user account's logon, group memberships, rights, or permissions. However, some fields in the General tab do bear mentioning:

- *Display name*—The value in this field is taken from the Full name field during account creation and is usually the same as the CN. However, changing the display name doesn't change the CN, and changing the CN doesn't affect the display name. This field can be used in Active Directory searches.
- *E-mail*—You can use the value in this field to send an email to the user associated with the account. If you right-click the user account and click Send Mail, the default mail application starts, and the value in this field is entered in the email's To field.
- *Web page*—This field can contain a URL. If this field is configured, you can right-click the user account and click Open Home Page, and a web browser opens the specified webpage.

The remainder of the fields in the General tab can be used to locate an object with an Active Directory search.

Tip

If you want to see more account properties in ADUC, click View, Add/Remove Columns. In ADAC, right-click any column name and click the property you want to display.

The Account Tab

The Account tab (see Figure 2-10) contains the information that most affects a user's logon to the domain. Aside from a password reset, this tab is the best place to check when a user is having difficulty with the logon process.

- *User logon name* and *User logon name (pre-Windows 2000)*—These fields were described previously in "Creating and Modifying User Accounts."
- *Logon Hours*—Clicking this button opens a dialog box (see Figure 2-11) where administrators can restrict days and hours that users can sign in to the domain. By default, all days and all hours are permitted. To exclude hours, click the Logon Denied option button and select the boxes for the hours you want to exclude; each box represents one hour. You can drag over the hour boxes to select several days or hours at a time. In Figure 2-11, logging on is denied to the account every day from 12:00 a.m. to 3:00 a.m. The default behavior of this feature denies new attempts to sign in during denied hours but doesn't affect a user who's already logged on. However, you can set a group policy to force a user to be disconnected when logon hours are denied.

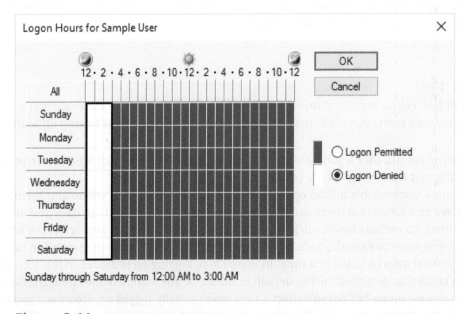

Figure 2-10 The Account tab

Figure 2-11 Setting logon hours

- *Log On To*—Click this button to specify by computer name which computers the user account can use to sign in to the domain. By default, a user can use all computers in the domain. However, you might want to limit accounts that have access to sensitive information to logging on only at designated computers (see Figure 2-12).

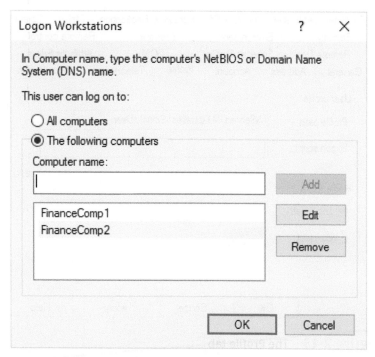

Figure 2-12   Setting logon workstations

- *Unlock account*—If a user's account is locked out due to too many incorrect sign-in attempts, there will be a message next to this checkbox indicating the account is currently locked out. The administrator must click to select the checkbox and click OK on the Account tab to unlock the user's account.
- *Account options*—Five of these options were described previously. Most account options pertain to the user's password and Kerberos authentication properties, but a few warrant more explanation:
  - Store password using reversible encryption: Allows applications to access an account's stored password for authentication purposes. Enabling this option poses a considerable security risk and should be used only when no other authentication method is available.
  - Smart card is required for interactive logon: Requires a smart card for the user to sign in to a domain member. When this option is enabled, the user's password is set to a random value and never expires.
  - Account is sensitive and cannot be delegated: Used to prevent a service from using an account's authentication credentials to access a network resource or another service. This option increases security and is most often set on administrator accounts.
- *Account expires*—An administrator uses this option to set a date after which the account can no longer sign in. You might set an expiration on a temporary or guest account.

The Profile Tab

The Profile tab (see Figure 2-13) is used to specify the location of files that make up a user's profile, a logon script, and the location of a home folder:

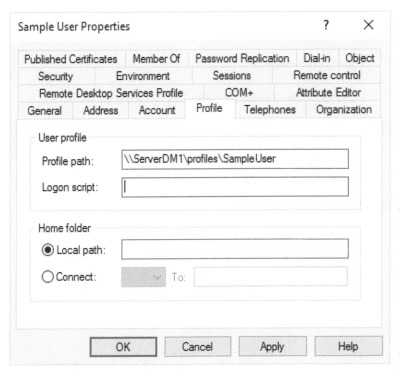

Figure 2-13   The Profile tab

- *Profile path*—Used to specify the path to a user's profile. By default, a user's profile is stored on the computer where the user is currently signed in. The profile is stored in the C:\Users*logonname* folder by default, and this field is blank. It needs to be filled in only if you want to change the profile path. It's most often used when creating roaming profiles where a user's profile is available from any station the user signs in to. When you're creating a user template, you can use the `%username%` variable instead of the actual logon name, and the variable is replaced automatically with the user logon name.
- *Logon script*—Used to specify a script that runs when the user signs in. The preferred method for specifying a logon script is with a group policy, so this field is rarely used with domain accounts, but it can be used with local accounts.
- *Local path*—Used to specify the path to a user's home folder. In general, the home folder has been replaced by the Documents folder. Some older applications use this field as the default location for storing user documents, however. You can also use it to specify the location on a terminal server where user documents are stored during Terminal Services sessions. The home folder can be a local path or a drive letter that points to a network share.
- *Connect*—Used to map a drive letter to a network share that's the user's home folder.

The Member Of Tab

The Member Of tab (see Figure 2-14) lists groups the user belongs to and can be used to change group memberships. Every new user is added to the Domain Users group automatically. You can remove a user from Domain Users, but it's not recommended because membership in this group is one way to give users default rights and permissions. The Set Primary Group button in this tab is needed only when a user is logging on to a Mac OS, UNIX, or Linux client computer.

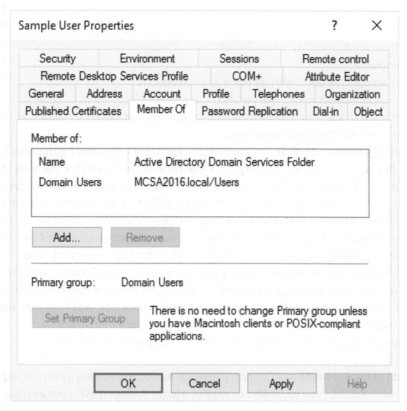

Figure 2-14   The Member Of tab

Using Contacts and Distribution Groups

User accounts are security principals, which means that permissions and rights can be assigned to them so that users can access network resources and perform certain operations on their computers. You can create two other user-related accounts that aren't security principals: contacts and distribution groups. A **contact** is an Active Directory object that usually represents a person for informational purposes only, much like an address book entry. Like a user account, a contact is created in Active Directory Users and Computers, but a contact isn't a security principal and, therefore, can't be assigned permissions or rights. The most common use of a contact is for integration into Microsoft Exchange's address book. The Full name field is the only information required to create a contact, but a contact's Properties dialog box has General, Address, Telephones, Organization, and Member Of tabs for adding detailed information about the contact. You use the Member Of tab to add a contact to a group or a distribution group.

A **distribution group** is created the same way as a group. The only real difference is the group type, which is distribution rather than security (explained later in "Managing Group Accounts"). Like a contact, a distribution group is used mostly with Microsoft Exchange for sending emails but to several people at once. Both regular user accounts and contacts can be added as members of a distribution group.

Note

You can't create contacts and distribution groups in ADAC.

Activity 2-4: Creating User Accounts in Active Directory Users and Computers

Time Required: 15 minutes

Objective: Create user accounts in ADUC with different account options.

Required Tools and Equipment: ServerDC1, ServerDM1

Description: You want to experiment with some user account options that can be set during account creation. In this activity, you use Active Directory Users and Computers.

1. Sign in to ServerDC1 as **Administrator**, and open Active Directory Users and Computers, if necessary.
2. Click to expand the domain node, if necessary. Click **Operations**, and then click the **New User** toolbar icon. (*Hint*: Hover your mouse pointer over toolbar icons to see their descriptions.) Type **testuser1** in the User logon name text box. The User logon name (pre-Windows 2000) text box is filled in automatically. However, the Next button is still disabled, which means you haven't filled in all the required fields. Type **Test** in the First name text box and **User1** in the Last name text box. Now the Full name text box is filled in automatically, and the Next button is enabled. (Alternatively, you could just fill in the full name.) Click **Next**.
3. In the Password text box, type **p@$$word**. Type **p@$$word** again in the Confirm password text box.
4. Click to select the **User cannot change password** check box. Read the warning message, and then click **OK**. Click to clear the **User must change password at next logon** check box, and then click **User cannot change password**. Click **Next**, and then click **Finish**. Read the error message that's displayed.
5. What can you do to change the password so that it meets complexity requirements? Click **OK**, and then click **Back**.
6. Type **p@$$word1** in the Password and Confirm password text boxes. Adding a number at the end meets complexity requirements, but you could also change one letter to uppercase, such as p@$$Word. Click **Next**, and then click **Finish**.
7. On **ServerDM1**, sign in as **testuser1** with the password you just set (p@$$word1).
8. Press **Ctrl+Alt+Delete**, and then click **Change a password**.
9. In the Old password text box, type **p@$$word1**. In the New password text box, type **p@$$word2**, and type it again in the Confirm password text box and press **Enter**. You see an *Access is denied* message because the account is prohibited from changing the password. Click **OK**, and then click **Cancel** and **Sign out**.
10. On ServerDC1, create a user in the Operations OU with the logon name **testuser2** and the first and last names **Test User2**. Enter an appropriate password, and then click **Account is disabled**. Click **Next**, and then click **Finish**.
11. In Active Directory Users and Computers, notice that Test User2's icon has a down arrow to indicate that the account is disabled. If you open the Users folder, you'll see that the Guest user has this icon, too, to indicate its disabled status. Close Active Directory Users and Computers, and stay signed in for the next activity.

Activity 2-5: Creating User Accounts in Active Directory Administrative Center

Time Required: 15 minutes

Objective: Create a user account in Active Directory Administrative Center.

Required Tools and Equipment: ServerDC1

Description: In this activity, you create a test user account with this Active Directory Administrative Center (ADAC). You also explore the Windows PowerShell History feature of ADAC that you first saw in Chapter 1.

1. On ServerDC1, open Active Directory Administrative Center.
2. Click **MCSA2016 (local)** in the left pane, if necessary. In the middle pane, right-click **Operations**, point to **New**, and click **User**.
3. In the Create User window, notice the two fields with asterisks next to them: Full name and User SamAccountName logon. In Active Directory Administrative Center, only these two fields are required to create a user. Type **Test User3** in the Full name box and **testuser3** in the User SamAccountName logon box (see Figure 2-15).

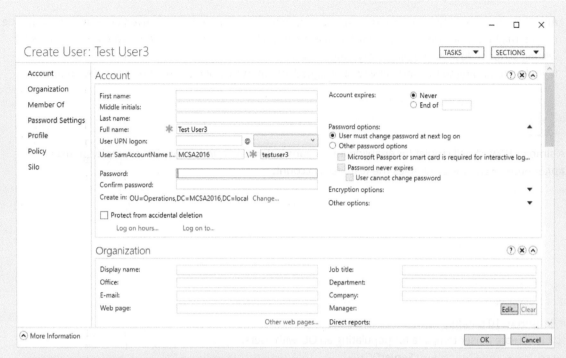

Figure 2-15   The Create User window (ADAC)

4. Click **OK**. In Active Directory Administrative Center, double-click **Operations** and notice that Test User3 is grayed out and has a down arrow icon to indicate the account is disabled. (If you don't see Test User3, refresh the view.) Right-click **Test User3** and click **Enable**. In the message stating that the password doesn't meet complexity requirements, click **OK**. You can't enable the account until a suitable password has been set.

5. Right-click **Test User3** and click **Reset password**. In the Reset Password dialog box, type **Password01** in the Password and Confirm password text boxes, and then click **OK**.

6. Right-click **Test User3** and click **Enable**. The account is enabled.

7. At the bottom of Active Directory Administrative Center, you see the Windows PowerShell History. Click the **up arrow** on the right side of the window to expand the Windows PowerShell History Viewer.

8. Scroll to the top of the history, if necessary, to see the New-ADUser command. Click to select **New-ADUser** and click **Copy** on the viewer's menu bar.

9. Open Notepad and paste the Clipboard into Notepad. You see the full PowerShell command that was generated when you created Test User3. Close Notepad without saving the file.

10. Scroll through the PowerShell history to see other commands that were generated for setting the password and other account properties. It isn't obvious which command enables the account. Find the last **Set-ADObject** command in the history. The userAccountControl=8389120 part of the command is what does the job. This parameter sets account properties that specify that the account is a normal user and the password must be changed at next logon.

Tip ⓘ

You can learn more about the userAccountControl parameter at *https://support.microsoft.com/kb/305144*.

11. Although the PowerShell commands generated by Active Directory Administrative Center aren't always the most straightforward way to accomplish a task, they can help you learn how to use these commands for writing scripts. Close Active Directory Administrative Center.

12. If you're continuing to the next activity, stay signed in; otherwise, sign out or shut down the computer.

> **Tip** ⓘ
>
> A simpler PowerShell cmdlet for enabling an account is `Enable-ADAccount`. For example, `Enable-ADAccount testuser3` enables the testuser3 account.

Activity 2-6: Creating a User Template

Time Required: 10 minutes
Objective: Create a user template for populating an OU with users.
Required Tools and Equipment: ServerDC1
Description: In this activity, you create a user template that will be used as a template for creating several users.

1. On ServerDC1, open Active Directory Users and Computers.

2. In the left pane, click the **Marketing** OU.

3. Click the **Group** icon on the tool bar to open the New Object - Group dialog box. In the Group name box, type **MarketingG**, and click **OK**.

4. Next, create a user with the full name **_Marketing Template**, the logon name **_MarketingTemplate**, and the password **Password01**. Make sure the **Account is disabled** check box is checked and the **User must change password at next logon** check box is not checked.

5. After you've created this user, right-click the **_Marketing Template** user and click **Properties**.

6. In the General tab, type **Marketing Template User Account** in the Description text box, **Building 1** in the Office text box, **555-5555** in the Telephone number text box, and **www.allaboutcomputernetworks.com** in the Web page text box.

7. Click the **Address** tab. Type **555 First St.** in the Street text box, **Metropolis** in the City text box, **AZ** in the State/province text box, and **12121** in the Zip/Postal Code text box. Click **United States** in the Country/region drop-down list.

8. Click the **Organization** tab. Type **Marketing Associate** in the Job Title text box, **Marketing** in the Department text box, and **All About Computer Networks** in the Company text box.

9. Click the **Member Of** tab. Add the account to the **MarketingG** group. Click **OK** until the Properties dialog box is closed.

10. In the right pane of Active Directory Users and Computers, right-click the **_Marketing Template** user and click **Copy**. Type **Marketing** in the First name text box, **Person1** in the Last name text box, and **marketing1** in the User logon name text box, and then click **Next**.

11. Type **Password01** in the Password and Confirm password text boxes. Notice that the Account is disabled check box is selected because you set this option for the _Marketing Template account. Click to clear the **Account is disabled** check box, and then click **Next**. Click **Finish**.

12. Right-click **Marketing Person1** and click **Properties**. Arrange the Properties dialog box so that you can see the _Marketing Template user in Active Directory Users and Computers. Right-click **_Marketing Template** and click **Properties**. Arrange the two Properties dialog boxes side by side so that you can compare them (see Figure 2-16). Make sure the General tab is visible in both.

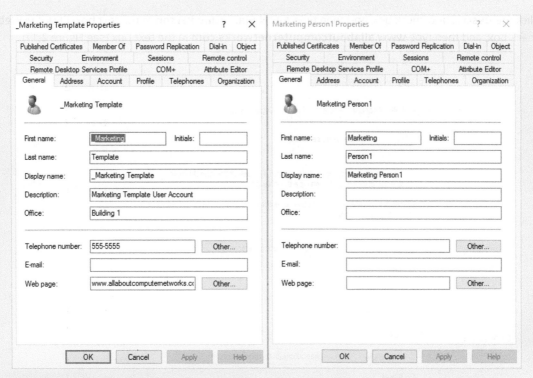

Figure 2-16   Comparing user properties

13. Notice that no fields in the template's General tab were copied to the Marketing Person1 user. Click the **Address** tab in both Properties dialog boxes, and notice that the Street field wasn't copied but the rest of the address was. Click the **Organization** tab, and notice that only the Job Title field wasn't copied.
14. Click the **Member Of** tab in both Properties dialog boxes, and notice that the group membership *was* copied.
15. Click **Cancel** to close both Properties dialog boxes, and leave Active Directory Users and Computers open if you're continuing to the next activity.

Activity 2-7: Editing Multiple Accounts

Time Required: 10 minutes
Objective: Create users and change attributes on several accounts simultaneously.
Required Tools and Equipment: ServerDC1
Description: You need to change some attributes on several users in your Marketing OU, so you decide to use the Properties for Multiple Items dialog box to make this task easier.

1. On ServerDC1, open Active Directory Users and Computers, if necessary.
2. Click the **Marketing** OU, if necessary.
3. Create two user accounts by using the _Marketing Template account. The accounts should have the first and last names **Marketing Person2** and **Marketing Person3** and logon names **marketing2** and **marketing3**. Use **Password01** for the password on both accounts. Leave the **Account is disabled** and the **User must change password at next logon** check boxes checked.
4. After you have created the two users, click **Marketing Person1**, and then hold down **Shift** and click **Marketing Person3** so that all three users are selected. Release **Shift**, and then click **Action, Properties** from the menu to open the Properties for Multiple Items dialog box.

5. Click the **Description** check box, and then type **AACN Marketing Person** in the text box. Click the **Web page** check box, and then type **www.allaboutcomputernetworks.com** in the text box (see Figure 2-17).

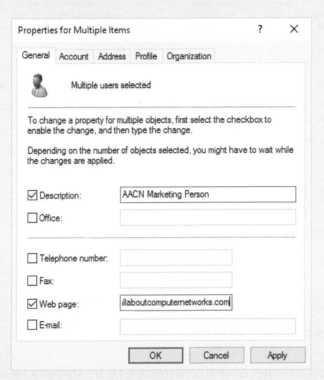

Figure 2-17   The Properties for Multiple Items dialog box

6. Click the **Account** tab. Scroll down in the Account options list box, and click to select the **Account is disabled** check box on the far left (see Figure 2-18). Click **Apply**.

Figure 2-18   Setting account properties for multiple items

7. Click the **Address** and **Profile** tabs to review which attributes you can change. Click the **Organization** tab. Click the **Job Title** check box, type **Marketing Associate** in the text box, and then click **OK**.

8. Open the Properties dialog box for each Marketing Person account to verify that the changes were made for all. When you're finished with each one, click **OK**.

9. Continue to the next activity.

Managing Group Accounts

• **70-742 – Install and configure Active Directory Domain Services:**
  Create and manage Active Directory groups and organizational units (OUs)

Active Directory group objects are the main security principal administrators use to grant rights and permissions to users. Using groups to assign user rights and permissions is preferable to using separate user accounts, mainly because groups are easier to manage. Users with similar access requirements to resources can be made members of a group, and instead of creating ACEs for each user in a network resource's DACL, you can make a single entry for the group. Furthermore, if a user changes departments or positions in the company, you can remove the user from one group and place the user in another group that meets his or her new access requirements. With a single administrative action, you can completely alter a user's access to resources. If permissions are assigned to a single user account, the administrator must find each resource for which the user has an ACE, make the necessary changes, and then add the user account to the DACL for each resource the new department or position requires. When an administrator creates a group in Active Directory Users and Computers, aside from assigning a name, there are two other settings, which are discussed in the following sections: "Group Types" and "Group Scope."

Group Types

There are two group types: security groups and distribution groups. As mentioned, a distribution group is used to group users together, mainly for sending emails to several people at once with an Active Directory-integrated email application, such as Microsoft Exchange. Distribution groups aren't security principals and, therefore, can't be used to assign rights and permissions to their members. A distribution group can have the following objects as members: user accounts, contacts, other distribution groups, security groups, and computers.

Because you can mix user accounts and contacts, you can build useful distribution groups that include people outside your organization. You can also nest groups, which makes organizing users and contacts more flexible. However, because distribution groups aren't used for security and are useful only with certain applications, their use in Active Directory is more limited than security groups.

Security groups are the main Active Directory object administrators use to manage network resource access and grant rights to users. Most discussions about groups focus on security groups rather than distribution groups, and in general, when the term *group* is used without a qualifier, a security group should be assumed. Security groups can contain the same types of objects as distribution groups. However, if a security group has a contact as a member and the security group is granted permission to a resource, the permission doesn't extend to the contact because a contact isn't a security principal. Security groups can also be used as distribution groups by applications such as Microsoft Exchange, so re-creating security groups as distribution groups isn't necessary for email purposes.

Converting Group Type

You can convert the group type from security to distribution and vice versa. However, only a security group can be added to a resource's DACL. If a security group is an entry in the DACL for a shared folder, for example, and the security group is converted to a distribution group, the group remains in the DACL but has no effect on access to the resource for any of its members.

The need to convert group type isn't all that common, but when it's necessary, usually a distribution group is converted to a security group. This conversion might be necessary when, for example, a group of users is assigned to collaborate on a project. Distribution groups composed of team members might be created for the purpose of email communication about the project, but later, it's determined that the project requires considerable network resources that team members need access to. The distribution group could be converted to a security group for the purpose of assigning rights and permissions, and the security group could still be used as an email distribution group.

Group Scope

The group scope determines the reach of a group's application in a domain or a forest: which security principals in a forest can be group members and to which forest resources a group can be assigned rights or permissions. Three group scope options are possible in a Windows forest: domain local, global, and universal. A fourth scope—local—applies only to groups created in the SAM database of a member computer or standalone computer. Local groups aren't part of Active Directory. For each group scope, Table 2-2 summarizes possible group members, which groups the scope can be a member of, and which resources permissions or rights can be assigned.

Table 2-2 Group scope membership and resource assignment

Group scope	Possible members	Can be a member of	Permissions and rights assignments
Domain local	User accounts, computer accounts, global groups from any domain in the forest, and universal groups Other domain local groups from the same domain User accounts, computer accounts, global groups, and universal groups from trusted domains in another forest	Domain local groups in the same domain Local groups on domain member computers; domain local groups in the Builtin folder can be members only of other domain local groups	Resources on any DC or member computer in the domain; domain local groups in the Builtin folder can be added to DACLs only on DCs, not on member computers
Global	User accounts, computer accounts, and other global groups in the same domain	Global groups in the same domain and universal groups Domain local groups or local groups on member computers in any domain in the forest or trusted domains in another forest	Resources on any DC or member computer in any domain in the forest or trusted domains in another forest
Universal	User accounts, computer accounts, global groups from any domain in the forest, and other universal groups	Universal groups from any domain in the forest Domain local groups or local groups on member computers in any domain in the forest or trusted domains in another forest	Resources on any DC or member computer in any domain in the forest or trusted domains in another forest

Domain Local Groups

A **domain local group** is the main security principal recommended for assigning rights and permissions to domain resources. Although both global and universal groups can also be used for this purpose, Microsoft best practices recommend using these groups to aggregate users with similar access or rights requirements. Global and universal groups should then be added as members of domain local groups, which are added to a resource's DACL to assign permissions. The process can be summarized with the mnemonics *AGDLP* and *AGGUDLP*. In single-domain environments or when users from only one domain are assigned access to a resource, use AGDLP:

- **A**ccounts are made members of
- **G**lobal groups, which are made members of
- **D**omain **L**ocal groups, which are assigned
- **P**ermissions to resources

In multi-domain environments where users from different domains are assigned access to a resource, use AGGUDLP:

- **A**ccounts are made members of
- **G**lobal groups, which when necessary are nested in other
- **G**lobal groups, which are made members of
- **U**niversal groups, which are then made members of
- **D**omain **L**ocal groups, which are assigned
- **P**ermissions to resources

The repeating theme is that permissions should be assigned to as few different security principals as possible, namely domain local groups. Using this method to assign permissions keeps the list of ACEs short, making resource access management considerably easier. This rule isn't hard and fast because there are circumstances in which other group scopes and individual user accounts should be assigned permissions. Whenever possible, however, these rules should be followed.

Some administrators create a domain local group for each level of access to each shared resource. For example, you have a shared folder called SalesDocs that requires two levels of access by different groups: Read access and Modify access. You could create two domain local groups, SalesDocs-Read-DL with Read permission and SalesDocs-Mod-DL with Modify permission. By using this group-naming standard, you have identified the resource, access level, and group scope. Next, you need only add the global or universal groups containing users to the correct domain local group. Keep in mind that the "local" in domain local refers to where resources this group scope is assigned to can be located. You can't, for example, give a domain local group from Domain A permission to a resource in Domain B.

Global Groups

As mentioned, a **global group** is used mainly to group users from the same domain with similar access or rights requirements. A global group's members can be user accounts, computer accounts, and other global groups from the same domain. However, a global group is considered global because it can be made a member of a domain local group in any domain in the forest or trusted domains in other forests. Global groups can also be assigned permissions to resources in any domain in the forest or trusted domains in other forests.

A common use of global groups is creating one for each department, location, or both. In a single-domain environment, global groups are added to domain local groups for assigning resource permissions. You might wonder why user accounts aren't simply added directly to a domain local group, bypassing global groups altogether. In a single-domain environment, you can do this, but this approach has some drawbacks:

- Domain local group memberships can become large and unwieldy, particularly for resources to which many users from several departments must have access. Examine Figure 2-19 and think about which group you would rather manage.

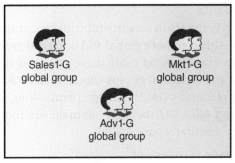

MktDocs-Mod-DL
(domain local group)

Figure 2-19   Global groups nested inside a domain local group

- If the company ever adds a domain, you need to redesign group memberships to grant permissions to cross-domain resources. This task is necessary because a domain local group can't be a member of a group or assigned permission to a resource in another domain.

In multi-domain environments where departments are represented in more than one domain, departmental global groups from each domain can be aggregated into a universal group, which is then made a member of a domain local group for resource access. For example, in Figure 2-20, both the U.S. and U.K. csmtech.local domains have a global group called Sales. These global groups are added to the universal group Sales-U in the csmtech.local parent domain; Sales-U is then made a member of the domain local group assigned permissions to the shared folder. Keep in mind that the shared resource could be located in any of the three domains as long as the domain local group is in the same domain as the shared resource. The universal group in this example can be added to a domain local group in any domain in the forest as well as trusted domains in other forests.

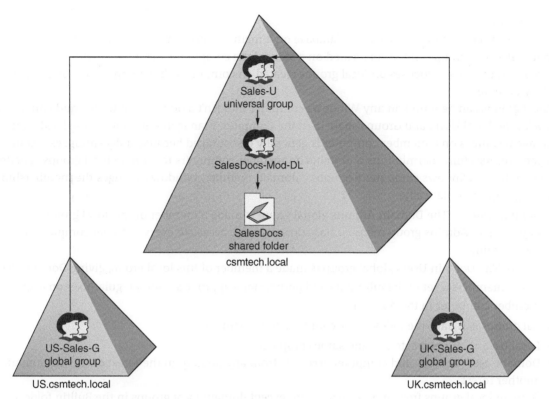

Figure 2-20   Using global and universal groups

Universal Groups

A **universal group** is special in a couple of ways. First, a universal group's membership information is stored only on domain controllers configured as global catalog servers. Second, they are the only type of group with a truly universal nature:

- User accounts, computer accounts, global groups, and universal groups from any domain in the forest can be a member.
- They can be a member of other universal groups or domain local groups from any domain in the forest.
- They can be assigned permissions to resources in any domain in the forest.

Because universal groups' membership information is stored only on global catalog servers, you need to plan the placement of domain controllers configured as global catalog servers in multi-domain networks carefully. When users sign in, a global catalog server must be available to determine their memberships in any universal groups. For that reason, a remote office with many users should have at least one domain controller configured as a global catalog server to reduce WAN traffic during user logons.

An alternative to having a global catalog server at each site is to enable **universal group membership caching** on a remote office's domain controller. With caching enabled, a domain controller queries a global catalog server to determine universal group membership and then keeps a local copy of this information to use for future logons.

Universal group membership changes require replication to all global catalog servers. If you're operating a WAN with global catalog servers in remote locations, extra bandwidth is required to replicate universal group membership changes. Plan your Active Directory group design carefully so that changes to universal groups don't happen often.

Local Groups

A local group is created in the local SAM database on a member server, workstation, or standalone computer. Because groups and users created on a standalone computer can't interact with Active Directory, this discussion focuses on local groups created on computers that are members of an Active Directory domain.

Local groups can be found on any Windows computer that isn't a domain controller, and you manage them with the Local Users and Groups snap-in in the Computer Management MMC. Using local groups to manage resources on a member computer is generally discouraged because it decentralizes resource management. Assigning permissions and rights on member computers to domain local groups is better. However, when a Windows computer becomes a domain member, Windows changes the membership of two local groups automatically:

- *Administrators*—The Domain Admins global group is made a member of this local group, so any Domain Admins group member has administrative access to every member computer in the domain.
- *Users*—The Domain Users global group is made a member of this local group, giving Domain Users group members a set of default rights and permissions appropriate for a regular user on every member computer in the domain.

Local groups can have the following account types as members:

- Local user accounts created on the same computer
- Domain user accounts and computer accounts from any domain in the forest or trusted domains in another forest
- Domain local groups from the same domain (except domain local groups in the Builtin folder)
- Global or universal groups from any domain in the forest or trusted domains in another forest

Local groups can be assigned permissions only to resources on the local computer. The most common use of local groups, except for the Administrators and Users local groups, is in a workgroup environment on non-domain computers. However, when a member computer's user requires considerable autonomy for managing local computer resources, you can grant the user enough rights on the local computer for this autonomy.

Nesting Groups

Nesting groups is exactly what it sounds like: making one group a member of another group. There are few restrictions on group nesting as long as you follow the group scope's membership rules. Group nesting is often used to group users who have similar roles but work in different departments. For example, you can create a global group for supervisors in each department and place users in each department with a supervisory role in this group. Next, create a SuperAll global group and place the department supervisor groups in this group (see Figure 2-21). In this way, all department supervisors can easily be assigned the rights and permissions their role specifies. Furthermore, in a multi-domain environment, a similar group configuration can be developed for each domain. The SuperAll global groups from each domain can then be added to a universal supervisors group for assigning permissions and rights throughout the forest. This example follows the AGGUDLP rule described earlier.

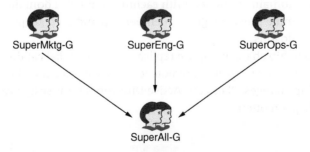

Figure 2-21 Nesting global groups

Although there are few restrictions on group nesting, the complexity of tracking and troubleshooting permissions increases as the number of levels of nested groups increases. Like OUs, groups can be nested an unlimited number of levels, but that doesn't mean you should. In most circumstances, one level of nesting groups of the same type is enough as shown in Figure 2-21. An additional level, such as aggregating nested global groups into a universal group, should work for most designs. The last step is to put your group of groups, whether global or universal, into a domain local group for resource access.

Converting Group Scope

When you create a group, the default setting is a security group with global scope. However, just as you can convert group type from security to distribution and vice versa, you can convert the group scope with some restrictions as explained in the following list:

- *Universal to domain local*—Provided the original universal group isn't a member of another universal group because you would have a domain local group as a member of a universal group, which isn't allowed.
- *Universal to global*—Provided no universal group is a member of the universal group because universal groups can't be members of global groups.
- *Global to universal*—Provided the global group isn't a member of another global group because universal groups can't be members of global groups.
- *Domain local to universal*—Provided no domain local group is a member because domain local groups can't be members of universal groups.

Group scope conversions not mentioned in this list aren't allowed. Even though you can't do certain group scope conversions directly, however, you can do some conversions with two steps. For example, to convert from domain local to global, first convert the domain local group to universal and then convert the universal group to global.

Default Groups in a Windows Domain

When an Active Directory domain is created, some default groups are created automatically to establish a framework for assigning users rights and permissions to perform common tasks and access default resources. Windows assigns default groups a variety of rights and permissions so that users can carry out certain tasks simply by being added to the appropriate group. For example, the default Backup Operators group is assigned the right to back up all files and directories on all computers in the Domain Controllers OU. To give users this capability, simply add them as members of the Backup Operators group.

There are three categories of default groups in a Windows domain: groups in the Builtin folder, groups in the Users folder, and special identity groups that don't appear in Active Directory management tools and can't be managed. A fourth category, the default local groups in the SAM database on member computers, corresponds roughly to groups in the Builtin folder.

Default Groups in the Builtin Folder

All default groups in the Builtin folder are domain local groups used for assigning rights and permissions in the local domain. Neither the group scope nor type can be converted. Each group in this folder has a brief description in ADUC or ADAC. Table 2-3 describes the most prominent of these groups in more detail.

Table 2-3	Default groups in the Builtin folder
Group	**Description**
Account Operators	Members can administer domain user, group, and computer accounts except for computers in the Domain Controllers OU and the Administrators, Domain Admins, Enterprise Admins, Schema Admins, and Read-Only Domain Controllers groups. Members can sign in locally and shut down domain controllers in the domain. There are no default members.
Administrators	Members have full control of all DCs in the domain and can perform almost all operations on DCs. Default members are Domain Admins, Enterprise Admins, and the Administrator user account.
Backup Operators	Members can back up and restore all files and directories on DCs in the domain with an Active Directory-aware backup program. Members' ability to access all files and folders doesn't extend beyond their use of backup software. Members can sign in locally to and shut down DCs. There are no default members.
Event Log Readers	Members can read event logs on the local machine. This default group is helpful because you want a technician to be able to read event logs without having broader administrative capabilities. There are no default members.
Guests	This group has no default rights or permissions. The Domain Guests group and Guest user account are default members.
Hyper-V Administrators	Members have full access to all Hyper-V features. A virtualization specialist can be added to this group without giving the user broader administrative capabilities on the server. There are no default members.
IIS_IUSRS	Internet Information Services uses this group to allow anonymous access to web resources.
Network Configuration Operators	Members can change TCP/IP settings and release and renew DHCP-assigned addresses on DCs. There are no default members.
Print Operators	Members can manage all aspects of print jobs and printers connected to DCs. Members can sign in locally to and shut down DCs in the domain. There are no default members.
Remote Desktop Users	Members can sign in remotely to DCs with the Remote Desktop client. There are no default members.
Server Operators	Members can sign in locally to DCs, manage some services, manage shared resources, backup and restore files, shut down DCs, format hard drives, and change the system time. There are no default members.
Users	Members can run applications and use local printers on member computers, among other common tasks. Members of this group can't, by default, sign in locally to DCs. Domain Users and the special identity Authenticated Users and Interactive groups are members of the Users group by default. Because all user accounts created in a domain are automatically members of the Domain Users global group, all domain users become members of this group as well.

Default Groups in the Users Folder

The default groups in the Users folder are combinations of domain local, global, and, in the forest root domain, universal scope. User accounts are generally added to global and universal groups in this folder for assigning permissions and rights in the domain and forest. Table 2-4 describes several groups in the Users folder.

Table 2-4   Default groups in the Users folder

Group/scope	Description
Allowed RODC Password Replication Group/ domain local	Members can have their passwords replicated to RODCs. There are no default members.
Denied RODC Password Replication Group/ domain local	Members can't have their passwords replicated to RODCs, so this group is a security measure to ensure that passwords for sensitive accounts don't get stored on RODCs. Default members include Domain Admins, Enterprise Admins, and Schema Admins.
DnsAdmins/domain local	This group is created when DNS is installed in the domain. Members have administrative control over the DNS Server service. There are no default members.
Domain Admins/global	Members have full control over domain-wide functions. This group is a member of all domain local and local Administrators groups. The domain Administrator account is a member by default.
Domain Computers/global	All computers that are domain members (excluding DCs) are added to this group by default.
Domain Controllers/global	All DCs are members of this group by default.
Domain Users/global	All user accounts in the domain are added to this group automatically. This group is used to assign rights or permissions to all users in the domain, but it has no specific rights by default. This group is a member of the Users domain local group by default.
Enterprise Admins/universal	This universal group is found only on DCs in the forest root domain. Members have full control over forest-wide operations. This group is a member of the Administrators group on all DCs. The Administrator account for the forest root domain is a member by default.
Group Policy Creator Owners/global	Members can create and modify group policies throughout the domain.
Read-only Domain Controllers/global	RODCs are members by default.
Schema Admins/universal	This universal group is found only on DCs in the forest root domain. Members can modify the Active Directory schema. The Administrator account for the forest root domain is a member by default.

Special Identity Groups

Special identity groups, some of which are described in Table 2-5, don't appear as objects in ADUC or ADAC, but they can be assigned permissions by adding them to resources' DACLs. Membership in these groups is controlled dynamically by Windows, can't be viewed or changed manually, and depends on how an account accesses the OS. For example, membership in the Authenticated Users group is assigned to a user account automatically when the user logs on to a computer or domain. No group scope is associated with special identity groups, and users can be members of more than one special identity group at a time. For example, anyone who authenticates to a Windows computer is a member of the Authenticated Users group. In addition, users who sign in remotely with Remote Desktop are members of both the Interactive group and the Remote Interactive Logon group. Special identity groups are also called *well-known groups*. You can view all your group memberships, including current membership in special identity groups, by entering `whoami /groups` at a command prompt.

Tip ⓘ

For more information on using the `whoami` command, enter `whoami /?` at a command prompt.

Table 2-5 Special identity groups

Group	Description
Anonymous Logon	Users and services that access domain resources without using an account name or a password. Typically used when a user accesses an FTP server that doesn't require user account logon.
Authenticated Users	Members include any user account (except Guest) logging on to a computer or domain with a valid user name and password. Often used to specify all users in a forest.
Creator Owner	A user becomes a member automatically for a resource (such as a folder) that he or she created or took ownership of. Often assigned Full control permission for subfolders and files only on the root of a drive so that a user who creates a file or folder on the drive has full control of the object automatically.
Dial-up	A user logged on through a dial-up connection is a member.
Everyone	Refers to all users who access the system. Similar to the Authenticated Users group but includes the Guest user.
Interactive	Members are users logged on to a computer locally or through Remote Desktop. Used to specify that only a user sitting at the computer's console is allowed to access a resource on that computer.
Local	Includes all users who have signed in locally.
Network	Members are users signed in to a computer through a network connection. Used to specify that only a user who's trying to access a resource through the network can do so.
Remote Interactive Logon	Members include users who sign in to a computer remotely through Remote Desktop.
Owner Rights	Represents the current owner of a folder or file. Permissions set on this group can be used to override implicit permissions granted to the owner of a file, such as Change Permissions and Take Ownership.
Service	Any security principal logged on as a service is a member.
System	Refers to the Windows OS.
Self	Refers to the object whose permissions are being set. If this group is an ACE in the object's DACL, the object can access itself with the specified permissions.

Activity 2-8: Creating Groups with Different Scopes

Time Required: 20 minutes

Objective: Create groups with different scopes.

Required Tools and Equipment: ServerDC1

Description: In this activity, you work with groups and see how nesting groups and converting group scope work.

1. On ServerDC1, open Active Directory Users and Computers.
2. Create a new OU named **TestOU1**. Click **TestOU1**, and create the following security groups with the indicated scope: **Group1-G** (global), **Group2-G** (global), **Group1-DL** (domain local), **Group2-DL** (domain local), **Group1-U** (universal), and **Group2-U** (universal).

3. In the right pane of Active Directory Users and Computers, double-click **Group1-G** to open its Properties dialog box. In the Group scope section, notice that the Domain local option is disabled because converting from global to domain local isn't allowed.

4. Click the **Members** tab, and then click **Add**. Type **Group2-G**, click **Check Names**, and then click **OK**.

5. Click **Add**. Type **Group1-DL** and click **Check Names**. The Name Not Found message box is displayed because domain local groups can't be members of global groups. Click **Cancel**.

6. Click **Advanced**, and then click **Find Now**. Active Directory displays only valid objects that can be made a group member, so no domain local or universal groups are listed. Click **Cancel** twice, and then click **OK**.

7. Double-click **Group2-G** to open its Properties dialog box. In the Group scope section, click the **Universal** option button, and then click **OK**. You should get an error message stating that a global group can't have a universal group as a member. Because Group2-G is a member of Group1-G, attempting to convert it to universal violates that rule. Click **OK**, and then click **Cancel**.

8. Double-click **Group1-DL** to open its Properties dialog box. In the Group scope section, the Global option is disabled because you can't convert a domain local group to a global group.

9. Click the **Members** tab and add **Group1-G** as a member. Adding a global group as a member of a domain local group is in line with the AGDLP best practice. Click **OK** twice.

10. Double-click **Group1-U** to open its Properties dialog box. Add **Group2-U** as a member, and then click **OK** twice. Double-click **Group2-U** to open its Properties dialog box. In the Group scope section, click **Domain local**, and then click **OK**. You get an error message, which reinforces the rule that universal groups can be converted to domain local groups only if they're not already a member of another universal group. Click **OK**, and then click **Cancel**.

11. Double-click **Group1-U** to open its Properties dialog box. Try to add **Group1-DL** as a member. Nesting domain local groups in universal groups isn't permitted. Add **Group1-G** as a member. Success! Global groups can be members of universal groups. Close all open dialog boxes.

12. Leave Active Directory Users and Computers open for the next activity.

Activity 2-9: Working with Default Groups

Time Required: 15 minutes
Objective: View properties of default groups.
Required Tools and Equipment: ServerDC1
Description: In this activity, you examine the properties of default groups to see their scope and default membership.

1. On ServerDC1, open Active Directory Users and Computers, if necessary.

2. Click the **Builtin** folder. Double-click the **Administrators** group to open its Properties dialog box. The options in the Group scope and Group type sections are disabled because you can't change the scope or type of groups in the Builtin folder. Notice that the selected scope is Builtin local. These groups are considered domain local, but there are some differences between Builtin local and other domain local groups, as you'll see.

3. Click the **Members** tab to see this group's members, and then click **Cancel**.

4. Next, view the membership of the **Guests** and **Users** groups. Notice that the Users group has two special identities as members: Authenticated Users and Interactive. In addition, Domain Users is a member. Close both Properties dialog boxes.

5. Click the **Users** folder. Double-click **Domain Admins** to open its Properties dialog box. Notice that you can't change this group's scope or type. Click the **Members** tab to view the group membership, and then click **Cancel**.

6. Next, view the membership of the **Domain Users** group. Notice that all the users you have created became members of this group automatically. Close this Properties dialog box.

7. View the membership of the **Domain Computers** group. Currently, ServerDM1 and ServerDM2 are both members. When a computer is joined to the domain, the computer account is added to this group.

8. To see the groups your currently logged-on account is a member of, open a command prompt window. Type **whoami /groups** and press **Enter**. You see a long list of groups the domain administrator is a member of, including several special identity groups, such as Everyone, Interactive, Authenticated Users, and Local. In the output, these groups are identified as well-known groups. Close the command prompt window.

9. Continue to the next activity.

Working with Computer Accounts

 **Certification**

- **70-742 – Install and configure Active Directory Domain Services:**
  Create and manage Active Directory Users and Computers

Computer accounts are created in Active Directory when a client computer becomes a member of the domain. Like a user account, a computer account is a security principal with an SID and a password and must authenticate to the domain. Unlike a user account, an administrator can't manage a computer account's password. The Windows OS changes it automatically every 30 days as long as it can contact a domain controller.

Don't confuse logging on to a computer connected to a computer account in Active Directory with a user's ability to access domain resources. A user can sign in to a workgroup computer with any Windows version installed and still access domain resources. For example, if users sign in to a Windows 10 computer that isn't a domain member, they can access domain resources in the usual way by using the UNC path. However, they must sign in to each domain resource they want to access in the format *domain\username*. Just the same, from an administrator standpoint, having users sign in to computers that are domain members has these advantages:

- *Single sign-on*—Users who sign in from domain member computers have access to any permitted resources throughout the forest without needing to authenticate again.
- *Active Directory search*—Users of domain member computers can search Active Directory for objects and resources throughout the forest.
- *Group policies*—Administrators can manage aspects of member computers by using group policies, including security settings and use restrictions.
- *Remote management*—Administrators can right-click a computer object and click Manage to run the Computer Management MMC for member computers.

Creating Computer Accounts

Computer accounts are created in Active Directory in two ways:

- A user changes the computer membership from Workgroup to Domain in the System Properties dialog box of a computer, thereby joining the domain and creating the computer account automatically.
- An administrator creates the account manually in Active Directory.

Usually, computer accounts are created when a computer joins the domain. When a computer account is created in this way, the account is placed in the Computers folder by default. This behavior applies to both client OS computers, such as Windows 10 computers, and server OS computers running a version of Windows Server.

By default, the Authenticated Users group is granted the *Add workstations to domain* right so that users need only a valid user name and password to join their computers to the domain if the computer account doesn't already exist. This right permits users to join computers to the domain and create up to 10 computer accounts in the domain. If administrators don't want users to have this right, they can change it through group policies. Other groups that can add workstations to a domain are Domain Admins, Account Operators, and Enterprise Admins.

You can also create computer accounts manually before a computer joins a domain. When a computer attempts to join a domain, Active Directory attempts to find a computer account matching the computer name. If it finds the account, the user is prompted for domain credentials. The computer is joined to the domain if the user has correct credentials. When a computer account is created manually, the administrator chooses which users or groups can join a computer with that account name to the domain. By default, the Domain Admins group has that right (see Figure 2-22). Using this method for creating computer accounts means more work for an administrator but more control over which computers can join the domain.

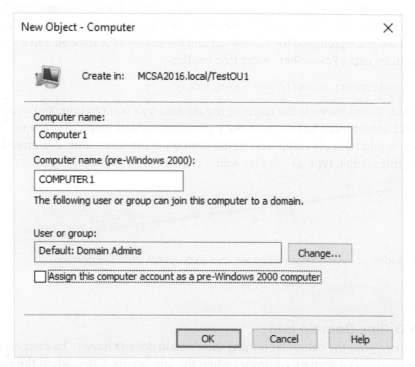

Figure 2-22   Creating a computer account

Changing the Default Computer Account Location

To gain the full benefit of computer accounts, move them to an OU you have created because the Computers folder can't have a group policy linked to it. Furthermore, because you usually require different policies for servers and user computers, you can move server computer accounts and user computer accounts to separate OUs and link different group policies to these OUs.

You can change the default location for computer accounts that are created automatically when they join the domain by using the `redircmp.exe` command-line program. You might want to do this so that computers joined to the domain are immediately subject to group policies and you don't have to remember to move them later. For example, to change the default location for computer accounts to the MemberComputers OU in the csmtech.local domain, type the following command on a domain controller:

```
redircmp ou=MemberComputers,dc=csmtech,dc=local
```

Joining a Domain

The process for joining a domain is straightforward: On the computer joining the domain, go to the Computer Name tab in the System Properties dialog box, click Change, click the Domain option button, and type the name of the domain you want the computer to join. You're prompted for credentials for a domain user account and then prompted to restart the computer to finish the operation. If the computer account doesn't already exist, it's created automatically if the domain user account has the *Add workstations to the domain* right. If the computer account already exists, the user account must have been granted the right to join the computer to the domain when the computer account was created.

As with most tasks you perform in the GUI, a command-line program is available to perform the same task. These commands are particularly useful when you're joining a Server Core computer to the domain. To join a domain, enter this command:

```
netdom join ComputerName /Domain:DomainName /UserD:UserName
  /PasswordD:Password
```

In this command, `ComputerName` is the name of the computer you want to join to the domain, and `DomainName` is the name of the domain. `UserName` is the logon name of a user account that has the right to join the computer to the domain. `Password` is the password for `UserName`. You can use * instead of specifying the password so that users are prompted for a password and the password is masked when they type it.

To join a domain by using PowerShell, enter this cmdlet:

```
Add-Computer -DomainName DomainName -Restart
```

In this command, `DomainName` is the name of the domain you want to join. You're prompted for credentials for a user account that has the necessary permissions, and then the computer restarts. You can use this cmdlet to join multiple computers to the domain at the same time. For more information and examples on using this cmdlet, type `get-help Add-Computer -detailed`

Tip ⓘ

Use the PowerShell cmdlet `Remove-Computer` to remove a computer from the domain.

Performing an Offline Domain Join

With an **offline domain join**, the computer joining the domain doesn't have to be connected to the network or be able to contact a domain controller when the join occurs. Later, when the computer does communicate with a DC in the domain where the offline join occurred, the computer is authenticated to the domain.

Offline domain joins are useful for large deployments of virtual machines or for mobile device deployments where network connectivity might not be available when the VM or device is deployed. It can also be useful as part of an unattended Windows installation and during setup of branch offices when DC and WAN connectivity hasn't been established. In addition, offline domain joins can be done when regular domain joins can't be performed reliably, as with some WAN connections.

Note 🖉

Offline domain joins can be done on a running computer or an offline virtual hard drive (VHD or VHDX) image.

To perform an offline domain join, you use the `djoin.exe` command. There are two phases to the process. In the first phase, you run the `djoin.exe` command to create the computer account in the domain and create a file with metadata that's used with the `djoin.exe` command on the computer you're joining. This file is called a *blob file*. The syntax for this command in the first phase is as follows:

```
djoin /provision /domain DomainName /machine ComputerName
 /savefile filename.txt
```

In this command, the `/provision` option creates the computer account in Active Directory. *DomainName* is the name of the domain you're joining, and *ComputerName* is the computer account name of the computer joining the domain. *Filename.txt* is the name of the blob file where metadata is saved. You transfer this file to the computer joining the domain. The next phase is done on the computer joining the domain or an offline image. The following is the syntax for a running computer:

```
djoin /requestODJ /loadfile filename.txt /windowspath %systemroot% /localos
```

In this command, the `/requestODJ` option requests an offline domain join at the next system start. *Filename.txt* is the name of the blob file created in the first phase. The `/windowspath` option specifies the path to the Windows directory of an offline image. If the `/localos` option is used, the path to the local Windows directory is specified by using `%systemroot%` or `%windir%`. Djoin.exe has a number of other optional parameters. To learn more about using them, type `djoin /?` at an elevated command prompt.

> **Caution** ⚠
>
> The metadata file created with the `djoin.exe` command contains very sensitive information, such as the computer account password and the domain's security ID. Take precautions when transferring this file.

Managing Computer Accounts

Computer account objects are, for the most part, a set-it-and-forget-it proposition. After creating them and possibly moving them to another OU, you might not need to do anything with these objects. However, sometimes administrators must attend to computer accounts—usually when something has gone wrong.

As mentioned, a computer account has an associated password and must sign in to the domain. The computer changes this password automatically every 30 days by default. If the password becomes unsynchronized between the computer and the computer account in Active Directory, the computer can no longer access the domain. Sometimes the password can become unsynchronized if a computer has been turned off or is otherwise unable to contact a domain controller for an extended period and, therefore, can't change its password. In effect, the password expires, and the only solution is to reset the computer account by right-clicking the computer object in Active Directory Users and Computers and clicking Reset Account. After resetting, the computer must leave the domain (by joining a workgroup) and then join it again. You can also use the `netdom` command on member servers with an unsynchronized account. This command resets the password on the local server and the corresponding computer account, so the server doesn't have to leave and rejoin the domain.

> **Tip** ⓘ
>
> If the computer does become unsynchronized with its account in Active Directory, users get a message stating that the trust relationship between the workstation and the domain failed.

Another reason for an administrator to access a computer account is to run the Computer Management MMC remotely on a member computer. As mentioned, clicking Manage in the right-click menu of a computer account opens Computer Management on that computer. The Computer Management MMC includes the Task Scheduler, Event Viewer, Shared Folders, Local Users and Groups, Reliability and Performance, Device Manager, Disk Management, and Services and Applications snap-ins—quite a bit of management capability available at a click.

Disabling Computer Accounts

Computer accounts can be deleted or disabled just as user accounts can be. You might need to delete a computer account if it's no longer a permanent domain member or if resetting the account doesn't solve the problem of a computer not being able to sign in to the domain. In these cases, you can delete the account and re-create it. The computer must also leave and rejoin the domain.

When a computer leaves the domain, its associated computer account is disabled automatically. If the same computer rejoins the domain, the account is enabled again. You might need to disable a computer account manually if the computer (a laptop, for example) won't be in contact with the domain for an extended period. When the computer needs access to the domain again, you can re-enable the computer account. You enable, disable, and reset a computer account by right-clicking it and choosing the option from the shortcut menu in ADUC or ADAC.

You might wonder why you would want to place computer accounts into groups. A common reason for creating groups for computer accounts is to use group policy filtering to configure exceptions for a group of users or computers that would normally be affected by a policy. Group policy filtering is discussed in Chapter 8.

Activity 2-10: Joining a Computer to the Domain

Time Required: 20 minutes

Objective: Join a computer to a domain using the GUI and PowerShell.

Required Tools and Equipment: ServerDC1 and ServerSA1

Description: In this activity, you join the ServerSA1 computer to the domain using the GUI. Then, you remove the computer from the domain and join it again using PowerShell. Finally, you remove the computer from the domain again.

1. Ensure that ServerDC1 is running. Sign in to ServerSA1. ServerSA1's DNS configuration must point to ServerDC1. Verify that ServerSA1's DNS server is 192.168.0.1 and if it isn't, change it.
2. On ServerSA1, right-click **Start** and click **System**. In the System control panel, click **Change settings** next to Computer name. The System Properties dialog box opens. In the Computer Name tab, click **Change**.
3. Click the **Domain** option button, type **MCSA2016.local**, and then click **OK**. You're prompted for credentials.
4. Type **jtech1** (you created jtech1 earlier, in Activity 2-2) in the User name text box and **Password01** in the Password text box. Click **OK**. You see a message welcoming you to the domain. Click **OK**. In the message stating that you need to restart the computer to apply the changes, click **OK** and then click **Close**.
5. When prompted to restart your computer, click **Restart Now**. While ServerSA1 is restarting, sign in to ServerDC1, and open Active Directory Users and Computers.
6. Click the **Computers** folder, and you see a computer object named ServerSA1. It was created automatically when you joined ServerSA1 to the domain. (If you don't see the object, click the **Refresh** icon in Active Directory Users and Computers.)
7. When ServerSA1 restarts, click **Other user** on the sign in screen and sign in to the domain as **mcsa2016\ administrator**. (*Note:* When you sign in to the domain as administrator from a member server, you must preface the user name with the domain name as in mcsa2016\administrator; to sign in to the domain as any other user, you do not need to enter the domain name.)
8. On ServerSA1 in Server Manager, click **Local Computer**. Under Computer name, it now says Domain instead of Workgroup.

9. Open a PowerShell window. Type **systeminfo** and press **Enter**. Information about the computer is displayed, including the domain membership and which DC logged you on (see Figure 2-23). Type **Get-ADDomain** and press **Enter** to list information about the domain the computer is a member of.

```
PS C:\Users\administrator.MCSA2016> systeminfo

Host Name:                 SERVERSA1
OS Name:                   Microsoft Windows Server 2016 Datacenter Evaluation
OS Version:                10.0.14393 N/A Build 14393
OS Manufacturer:           Microsoft Corporation
OS Configuration:          Member Server
OS Build Type:             Multiprocessor Free
Registered Owner:          Windows User
Registered Organization:
Product ID:                00377-10000-00000-AA360
Original Install Date:     2/19/2017, 12:36:15 PM
System Boot Time:          2/19/2017, 1:36:42 PM
System Manufacturer:       Microsoft Corporation
System Model:              Virtual Machine
System Type:               x64-based PC
Processor(s):              1 Processor(s) Installed.
                           [01]: Intel64 Family 6 Model 44 Stepping 2 GenuineIntel ~2533 Mhz
BIOS Version:              Microsoft Corporation Hyper-V UEFI Release v1.0, 11/26/2012
Windows Directory:         C:\Windows
System Directory:          C:\Windows\system32
Boot Device:               \Device\HarddiskVolume2
System Locale:             en-us;English (United States)
Input Locale:              en-us;English (United States)
Time Zone:                 (UTC-07:00) Arizona
Total Physical Memory:     1,179 MB
Available Physical Memory: 373 MB
Virtual Memory: Max Size:  2,331 MB
Virtual Memory: Available: 1,329 MB
Virtual Memory: In Use:    1,002 MB
Page File Location(s):     C:\pagefile.sys
Domain:                    MCSA2016.local
Logon Server:              \\SERVERDC1
Hotfix(s):                 3 Hotfix(s) Installed.
```

Figure 2-23   Output from the systeminfo command

10. Next, you'll remove the computer from the domain. Type **Remove-Computer** and press **Enter**. Press **Enter** to confirm. Note that the changes take effect only after you restart the computer. Type **Restart-Computer** and press **Enter**.

11. When ServerSA1 restarts, sign in as the local administrator. Open a PowerShell window and type **systeminfo** and press **Enter**. Notice that the Logon Server is now \\SERVERSA1.

12. On ServerDC1, in ADUC, click the **Computers** folder. Click the **Refresh** icon and you should see that the ServerSA1 computer account has a down arrow, which means that it's disabled. Right-click **ServerSA1**, click **Delete**, and then click **Yes** to confirm. Click **Yes** again.

13. Right-click in the **Computers** OU, point to **New**, and click **Computer**. In the New Object - Computer dialog box, type **ServerSA1** in the Computer name box. Notice that the default setting in User or group is Domain Admins, which means that only members of that group can join the computer to the domain. Click **OK**.

14. On ServerSA1, in the PowerShell window, type **Add-Computer MCSA2016.local -Restart** and press **Enter**. When prompted for credentials, type **jtech1** and **Password01** and click **OK**. You see a message stating that the computer failed to join the domain because access was denied. That's because when you created the computer account, you specified that only Domain Admins had the right to join the computer to the domain and jrtech1 is not a member of Domain Admins.

15. Type **Add-Computer MCSA2016.local -Restart** and press **Enter**. When prompted for credentials, type **administrator** and **Password01** and click **OK**. The computer restarts.

16. When ServerSA1 restarts, click **Other user** and sign in as **mcsa2016\administrator**.

17. Open a PowerShell window, type **Remove-Computer** and press **Enter**. Press **Enter** to confirm. Type **Stop-Computer** and press **Enter** to shut down ServerSA1.

18. Leave ServerDC1 running for the next activity.

Automating Account Management

- 70-742 – Install and configure Active Directory Domain Services:
  Create and manage Active Directory Users and Computers

Account management has been discussed mostly from the standpoint of using ADUC and ADAC. When only a few accounts require action, using a GUI tool is convenient. When many accounts require action or certain tasks must be repeated many times, however, a command-line program is often the most efficient tool for the job. Administrators can take advantage of batch files to handle lengthy and cumbersome command-line syntax. A **batch file** is a text file with the .bat extension that's used to enter a command or series of commands normally typed at the command prompt. Batch files can take arguments to replace variables in the command. PowerShell is a more powerful scripting tool than batch files. Administrators can create complex PowerShell scripts to aid in account management. Bulk import/export programs also make account management faster and easier. These programs can read an input file (import) to create several Active Directory objects at once or produce an output file (export) from Active Directory objects. In the following sections, examples and activities walk you through using command-line tools and bulk import/export programs to manage accounts.

Command-Line Tools for Managing Active Directory Objects

The GUI interfaces of ADUC and ADAC are convenient for creating a few accounts or making changes to a few objects. Even with the help of a template, however, quite a bit of manual entry is still required to create a user. Many administrators prefer a command-line tool, often used with a batch file, to create or change accounts. The following commands are used at a command prompt or in a batch file for managing accounts:

- dsadd—Adds objects to Active Directory. Used mainly for adding account objects but can also be used to create OUs and contacts.
- dsget—Displays an object's properties onscreen by default, but the output can be redirected to a file.
- dsmod—Modifies existing Active Directory objects.
- dsmove—Moves objects in a domain to another folder or OU or renames the object.
- dsquery—Finds and displays objects in Active Directory that meet specified criteria. The output can be displayed onscreen or sent (piped) to other commands. For example, dsquery could find and display a list of all users in an OU, and this list could be piped to a dsmod command that adds the users to a group.
- dsrm—Removes, or deletes, objects from Active Directory.

You can type a command followed by /? to get help on syntax and use. For example, if you need to know more about the dsadd command, type dsadd /? at the command prompt.

You used dsadd in Chapter 1 to create a user. Now take a closer look at its syntax and see how you can use it in a batch file to make account creation easier. The syntax for using dsadd to create objects is as follows:

```
dsadd ObjectType ObjectDN [options]
```

- *ObjectType* is the type of object you want to create, such as a user or group.
- *ObjectDN* is the object's distinguished name (DN), which includes the full path in Active Directory where the object should be created. The path is specified by starting with the object name followed by each parent container object up to the top-level domain name. Each component of the path is separated by a comma. A DN's components are as follows:
  - CN (common name): The name of the object as shown in Active Directory.
  - CN (common name): The CN component can be repeated if the object is in a folder, such as the Users or Computers folder, rather than an OU.

- OU (organizational unit): Use this component if the object is in an OU. It's repeated for as many levels as necessary, starting with the lowest OU level.
- DC (domain component): Each part of the domain name is specified separately until the top-level domain name is reached.

For example, to create a user account named BSmith in the Sales OU, which is in the Marketing parent OU in the csmtech.local domain, the command is as follows:

```
dsadd user CN=BSmith,OU=Sales,OU=Marketing,DC=csmtech,DC=local
```

To create a computer account named New Computer in the Computers folder in the same domain, the command is as follows:

```
dsadd computer "CN=New Computer,CN=Computers,DC=csmtech,DC=local"
```

The quotation marks around the distinguished name path are required if the path contains any spaces, including after commas. Following the DN, a command can include options specified with this syntax:

```
-OptionName OptionValues
```

For example, if you want to add BSmith and include the first name and last name attributes, the command uses the -fn and -ln options as shown:

```
dsadd user CN=BSmith,OU=Sales,OU=Marketing,DC=csmtech,DC=local-fn Bill -ln Smith
```

The dsadd command's syntax is somewhat intimidating, and if you had to type this entire command over and over, you might start to wonder how useful it is. The command's usefulness is apparent, however, when you have to create several accounts with similar properties except a few that are unique for each user. You can construct the command once in a batch file with a placeholder for the unique information that varies each time the command is used. For example, you could type the following command in a text file saved as uadd.bat:

```
dsadd user "CN=%1,OU=Sales,OU=Marketing,DC=csmtech,DC=local"
  -fn %2 -ln %3 -pwd Password01 -memberof Sales-G -mustchpwd yes
```

Tip

The distinguished name path in the preceding commands isn't case sensitive, so you can use "ou" and "dc" instead of "OU" and "DC." The capitalization just makes the commands easier to read.

This command creates a user in the specified container and domain, assigns the password Password01, places the user in the Sales-G group, and requires that the user change the password at next logon. The %1, %2, and %3 are variables replaced with user name, first name, and last name. For example, to run the uadd.bat batch file to create a user named Susan Martin with the user name SMartin, you enter the following:

```
uadd SMartin Susan Martin
```

For each user you need to create, you have to specify only the user name, first name, and last name. If you have several users with similar properties to create, you could perform the task much faster than in Active Directory Users and Computers, even if you used a user template.

Piping Output

A benefit of some command-line programs is that you can use one command's output as input to another, which is called **piping**. You can use piping with the dsquery and dsmod commands, but it's not unique to directory service commands. It's also used extensively with PowerShell commands. One of the most common uses of piping is sending the output of any command producing more than one screen of information to the more command. You can try it by displaying the help information for a command:

```
dsmod user /? | more
```

The vertical bar, called a *pipe*, specifies sending the output of dsmod user /? to the more command, which simply paginates information it receives so that you can view one page of output at a time. In the Activity 2-11, you use dsquery to find and display Active Directory information and then use a pipe to dsmod to add users to a group.

Another feature of many command-line programs is redirecting output to a file instead of displaying it onscreen. The syntax to redirect output is as follows:

```
command > outputfile
```

For example, you could use the dsquery command from the previous activity to send the results to a file named MktgUsers.txt:

```
dsquery user OU=Marketing,DC=csmtech,DC=local > MktgUsers.txt
```

Commands such as dsadd work well when you have many objects to create, especially when used with a batch file. Dsquery is also useful for displaying a list of objects based on particular criteria or piping data to commands such as dsmod for further processing. What if you already have a database or spreadsheet of possibly hundreds of users to create, however? When you have a file with Active Directory objects to create, two command-line tools can import that information into Active Directory: csvde and ldifde.

Bulk Import and Export with csvde and ldifde

The csvde and ldifde commands can import or export Active Directory data in bulk; the difference between them is mainly the format of files they use. csvde uses the comma-separated values (CSV) format common in database and spreadsheet programs. ldifde uses LDAP Directory Interchange Format (LDIF), which isn't as common but is useful when you're working with LDAP applications. Another difference is that csvde can create objects only in Active Directory, and ldifde can create or modify objects.

Neither command-line program has a simple method for importing a list of people directly from a database or spreadsheet, but with a little database or spreadsheet programming know-how, you can do it without too much trouble. The easiest way to get an idea of the file format these programs use is to use their export functions to create an output file. In csvde, the following command creates a file called MktUsers.csv that can be opened in Notepad as shown in Figure 2-24:

```
csvde -m -f mktusers.csv -d "ou=marketing,dc=mcsa2016,dc=local"
  -r (objectClass=user)
```

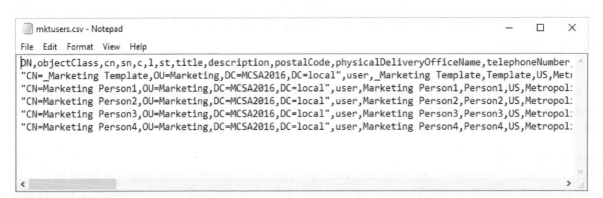

Figure 2-24   An export file created by csvde

To see the same output in `ldifde` format (see Figure 2-25), use the following command:

```
ldifde -f MktUsers -d "ou=Marketing,dc=MCSA2016,dc=local"
  -r (objectClass=user)
```

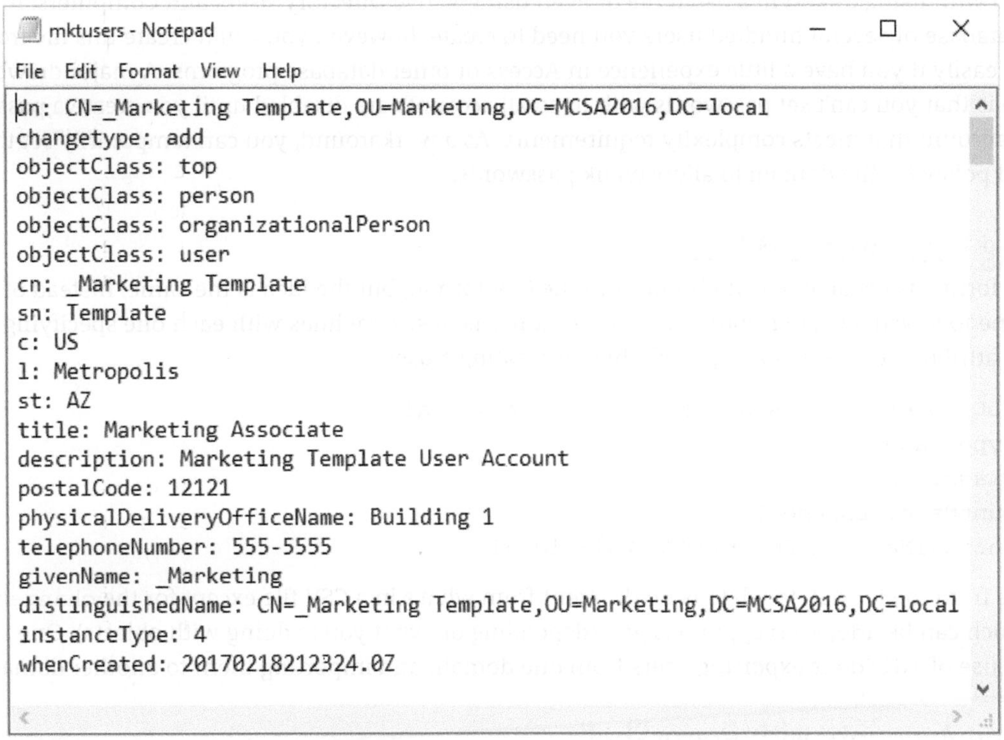

```
mktusers - Notepad                                    —    □    ×
File  Edit  Format  View  Help
dn: CN=_Marketing Template,OU=Marketing,DC=MCSA2016,DC=local
changetype: add
objectClass: top
objectClass: person
objectClass: organizationalPerson
objectClass: user
cn: _Marketing Template
sn: Template
c: US
l: Metropolis
st: AZ
title: Marketing Associate
description: Marketing Template User Account
postalCode: 12121
physicalDeliveryOfficeName: Building 1
telephoneNumber: 555-5555
givenName: _Marketing
distinguishedName: CN=_Marketing Template,OU=Marketing,DC=MCSA2016,DC=local
instanceType: 4
whenCreated: 20170218212324.0Z
```

Figure 2-25   An export file created by `ldifde`

As mentioned, `ldifde` is more powerful because of its capability to modify Active Directory objects. One method is exporting the objects you want to modify, making changes to the attributes you're modifying, and importing the file. Each object in the exported file has an associated action specified by the `changetype` line (the second line of output in Figure 2-25). To modify objects, change the action in this line to `modify`. The `ldifde` command is also useful for moving a bulk of users from one domain to another.

Creating Users with `csvde`

You can use a regular text file to import users (and other objects) into Active Directory with `csvde`, but the file must be formatted correctly. A CSV file must have a header record (the first line of a file) listing attributes of the object to be imported. For a user, it normally includes at minimum the distinguished name, the SAM account name, the UPN, and the object class attribute. Here's an example of a header record:

```
dn,SamAccountName,userPrincipalName,objectClass
```

Tip ⓘ

To find a list of any object's attributes, open the Attribute Editor tab of its Properties dialog box. To see this tab, you must enable Advanced Features on Active Directory Users and Computer's View menu.

A data record for this CSV file looks like this:

```
"cn=New User,ou=TestOU,dc=MCSA2016,dc=local",NewUser,
  NewUser@MCSA2016.local,user
```

You add a data record for each user you need to create. Creating this file manually is no time saver compared with using dsadd in a batch file or even using Active Directory Users and Computers. If you have a database of several hundred users you need to create, however, you could create this file from the database easily if you have a little experience in Access or other database programs. A major drawback of csvde is that you can't set passwords with it, so all accounts are disabled until you create a password for each account that meets complexity requirements. As a workaround, you can temporarily set the password policy for the domain to allow blank passwords.

Creating Users with `ldifde`
The LDIF format is considerably different from the CSV format, but the idea is the same. Instead of a header line followed by data records, each object consists of several lines with each one specifying an action or attribute. Here's an example of a file for creating a user:

```
dn: cn=LDF User1,ou=TestOU1,dc=MCSA2016,dc=local
changetype: add
ObjectClass: user
SamAccountName: LDFUser1
UserPrincipalName: LDFUser1@MCSA2016.local
```

Aside from the format, the data is no different from what's in a CSV file except for the changetype entry, which can be add, modify, or delete (depending on what you're doing with objects). One common use of ldifde is exporting users from one domain and importing them to another domain.

Managing Accounts with PowerShell
There are numerous PowerShell cmdlets you can use to manage Active Directory accounts and just about every other aspect of Active Directory. Table 2-6 lists some commands that work with user, group, and computer accounts. As always, to see how to use any of these commands, type get-help *cmdlet* at a PowerShell prompt (replacing *cmdlet* with the name of the command). To see an entire list of Active Directory PowerShell commands, type the following at a PowerShell prompt:

```
Get-Command -module ActiveDirectory
```

As with the commands described previously, you can use pipes with PowerShell commands. For example, to get a list of disabled user accounts, use this command:

```
Search-ADAccount -AccountDisabled
```

To enable all accounts that are disabled, you can use the following command:

```
Search-ADAccount -AccountDisabled | Set-ADUser -Enabled $true
```

When using PowerShell commands that might produce results you're not entirely sure of, you can add the -whatif parameter to the command. PowerShell shows the results of the command without actually performing it.

Some of the real power of PowerShell comes when using filters to list Active Directory objects that have particular properties. Say you want to get a list of all computer accounts that haven't logged on for one month. They might be considered inactive accounts. First, you need to construct a variable representing the current date minus 30 days. Then use the Get-ADComputer cmdlet to produce the list of computers meeting the criteria:

```
$InactiveDate=$(get-date).AddDays(-30)
Get-ADComputer -Properties * -Filter 'LastLogonDate -lt $InactiveDate'
```

Table 2-6	PowerShell cmdlets for account management

Cmdlet	Description
`New-ADUser`	Creates a user account
`Remove-ADUser`	Deletes a user account
`Set-ADUser`	Changes user account properties
`Get-ADUser`	Gets information about user accounts
`New-ADGroup`	Creates a group account
`Remove-ADGroup`	Deletes a group account
`Set-ADGroup`	Changes group account properties
`Get-ADGroup`	Gets information about group accounts
`New-ADComputer`	Creates a computer account
`Remove-ADComputer`	Deletes a computer account
`Set-ADComputer`	Changes computer account properties
`Get-ADComputer`	Gets information about computer accounts
`Disable-ADAccount`	Disables a user or computer account
`Enable-ADAccount`	Enables a user or computer account
`Search-ADAccount`	Searches for accounts that match specific properties
`Unlock-ADAccount`	Unlocks a locked user account
`Set-ADAccountPassword`	Resets a user account password
`Add-ADGroupMember`	Adds one or more users to a group

Resetting Passwords Using PowerShell

To reset a user's password with Powershell, use the following cmdlet:

```
Set-ADAccountPassword -Identity username -Reset -NewPassword
  (ConvertTo- SecureString -AsPlainText "NewP@ssWord1" -Force)
```

In this cmdlet, change *username* to the user's logon name. Next, you will want to set the user account so the user has to change the password at next logon:

```
Set-ADUser -Identity username -ChangePasswordAtLogon $true
```

To automate the process, you can create a PowerShell script (a text file with .ps1 as the extension) using the following command:

```
$user = Read-Host -Prompt "Enter the user logon name:"
Set-ADAccountPassword -Identity $user -Reset -NewPassword
  (ConvertTo- SecureString -AsPlainText "NewP@ssWord1" -Force)
Set-ADUser -Identity $user -ChangePasswordAtLogon $true
```

Save the script file as ChPass.ps1, for example, and you can run the PowerShell script whenever you need to reset a user's password. You will be prompted for the user logon name and the string you type will be saved to the variable $user, which is used in place of the logon name in both cmdlets.

Managing Group Membership with PowerShell

Let's suppose you have just created a bunch of users in the Marketing OU and you need to add them to the Marketing group. You can create a PowerShell script to perform this task as follows:

```
$users = get-aduser -filter * -searchbase "ou=marketing,dc=mcsa2016,dc=local"
ForEach ($SamAccountName in $users)
{
      Add-ADGroupMember MarketingG2 -member $SamAccountName
}
```

The preceding example can, of course, be changed so that you can specify different user attributes to select users based on their properties. And you can get user input for the group name and so forth.

Activity 2-11: Creating a Batch File for the `dsadd` Command

Time Required: 15 minutes

Objective: Create a batch file for the `dsadd` command.

Required Tools and Equipment: ServerDC1

Description: In this activity, you create a batch file for the `dsadd` command. First you create a new group in the Administration OU, and then you create the batch file to allow you to easily create users and add them to the group.

1. If necessary, sign in to ServerDC1 as **Administrator**, and open a command prompt window.
2. To create a security group called **AdvertG** with global scope, type **dsadd group "CN=AdminG,OU=Administration,DC=MCSA2016,DC=Local"** and press **Enter**. If you typed it correctly, you'll see a message starting with "dsadd succeeded." You don't need to specify the scope because global is the default.
3. Open Notepad by typing **notepad** and pressing **Enter**.
4. In Notepad, type the following on one line: **dsadd user "CN=%1,OU=Advertising,OU=Marketing,DC=MCSA2016,DC=local" -fn %2 -ln %3 -upn %1@MCSA2016.local -pwd Password01 -memberof "CN=AdminG, OU=Administration, DC=MCSA2016, DC=local" -mustchpwd yes -disabled yes.**
5. Save the file as **"C:\uadd.bat"**. Because Notepad adds the `.txt` extension automatically, enclose the filename in quotation marks to preserve the `.bat` extension. Exit Notepad.
6. At the command prompt, type **C:\uadd AdminUser1 Administration User1** and press **Enter**. The last line of the command output should start with "dsadd succeeded." If `dsadd` failed, check the syntax in the `uadd.bat` file. Make sure there's a space between the option name and the option value; for example, make sure there's a space between `-fn` and `%2`.
7. Refresh the view in Active Directory Users and Computers by clicking **Action, Refresh** from the menu or clicking the **Refresh** toolbar icon. The user you just created should appear in the Administration OU and be a member of the AdminG group.
8. Create two more users named **AdminUser2** and **AdminUser3** using the batch file (with first names and last names in the format shown in Step 6). Leave Active Directory Users and Computers and the command prompt window open and continue to the next activity.

Activity 2-12: Using Pipes

Time Required: 10 minutes

Objective: Use pipes in the command prompt and PowerShell.

Required Tools and Equipment: ServerDC1

Description: In this activity, you use `dsquery` and `dsmod` to assign group memberships. Then, you use PowerShell to find disabled users and use a pipe to enable those users.

1. First, you'll create a new group in the Marketing OU. On ServerDC1, at the command prompt, type **dsadd group "CN=SalesG, OU=Marketing, DC=MCSA2016, DC=local"** and press **Enter**.

2. Type **dsquery user "OU=Marketing,DC=MCSA2016,DC=local"** and press **Enter**. The output should be a list of all users, shown in DN format, in the Marketing OU. This data is what's piped to the dsmod command in the next step. (*Note*: If there were OUs nested under the Marketing OU, users in those OUs would also be listed.)

3. Type **dsquery user "OU=Marketing,DC=MCSA2016,DC=local" | dsmod group "CN=SalesG,OU=Marketing ,DC=MCSA2016,DC=local" -addmbr** and press **Enter**.

4. If you get a message indicating that dsmod was successful, open Active Directory Users and Computers, if necessary. If you get an error, check the syntax and spelling, and make sure there are no spaces between DN components.

5. In Active Directory Users and Computers, double-click the **SalesG** group in the Marketing OU. (You might need to refresh the view before you can see this group.) Click the **Members** tab. You should see all the users the dsquery command displayed in Step 3. Close the Properties dialog box.

6. At some point, the passwords of some users you have created will expire. To set their passwords to never expire, type **dsquery user | dsmod user -pwdneverexpires yes** and press **Enter**.

7. Next, you'll use PowerShell to work with users. Close the command prompt and open a PowerShell window.

8. Find all accounts that are disabled. Type **Search-ADAccount -AccountDisabled** and press **Enter**. You see a number of accounts in the list, including the Guest account and some other accounts you probably don't want to enable.

9. To narrow the search to just those users in the Administration OU, type **Search-ADAccount Account-Disabled -SearchBase "OU=Administration,DC=MCSA2016,DC=local"** and press **Enter**. You see the list of users you created in the previous activity.

10. To enable the disabled accounts, press the up arrow to repeat the previous command and at the end of the command, type **| Set-ADUser -Enabled $true** and press **Enter**. Press the up arrow twice to repeat the command from Step 9 and press **Enter**. You should not see any output since none of the accounts is disabled now.

11. Continue to the next activity.

Activity 2-13: Using csvde to Create Users

Time Required: 10 minutes
Objective: Create a text file to use with csvde to import users.
Required Tools and Equipment: ServerDC1
Description: In this activity, you use the csvde command to bulk create users. You will manually add users to the input file, but in practice, you would export users from a database program to create the file.

1. Start Notepad and type the following, pressing **Enter** after each line:

   dn,SamAccountName,userPrincipalName,objectClass
   "cn=CSV User1,ou=TestOU1,dc=MCSA2016,dc=local",CSVUser1, CSVUser1@MCSA2016.local,user
   "cn=CSV User2,ou=TestOU1,dc=MCSA2016,dc=local ",CSVUser2, CSVUser2@MCSA2016.local,user

2. Click **File, Save As** from the menu. In the File name text box, type **"C:\csvusers.csv"**, and then click **Save**. Exit Notepad.

3. Open a command prompt window. Type **cd ** and press **Enter** to move to the root of the C drive where you saved the file. Type **csvde -i -f csvusers.csv** and press **Enter**. You should see a message stating that two entries were modified successfully and the command was successful.

4. Close the command prompt window, and open Active Directory Users and Computers. Click the **TestOU1** OU and verify that the users were created. You'll see that the accounts are disabled.

5. Continue to the next activity.

Activity 2-14: Using `ldifde` to Create Users

Time Required: 10 minutes

Objective: Create a text file to use with `ldifde` to import users.

Required Tools and Equipment: ServerDC1

Description: In this activity, you use the `ldifde` command to bulk create users. You will manually add users to the input file, but in practice, you would export users from a database program to create the file.

1. Start Notepad and type the following, pressing **Enter** after each line:

   ```
   dn: cn=LDF User1,ou=TestOU1,dc=MCSA2016,dc=local
   changetype: add
   ObjectClass: user
   SamAccountName: LDFUser1
   UserPrincipalName: LDFUser1@MCSA2016.local
   ```

2. Click **File**, **Save As** from the menu. In the File name text box, type **"C:\ldfusers.ldf"**, and then click **Save**. Exit Notepad.

3. Open a command prompt window. Type **cd ** and press **Enter**. Type **ldifde -i -f ldfusers.ldf** and press **Enter**. You should see a message stating that the command was successful.

4. Close the command prompt window, and open Active Directory Users and Computers, if necessary. Click the **TestOU1** OU and verify that LDFUser1 was created. If necessary, refresh the view so that you can see this user.

5. Sign out or shut down ServerDC1.

Chapter Summary

- OUs, the building blocks of the Active Directory structure in a domain, can be designed to mirror a company's organizational chart. Delegation of control can be used to give certain users some management authority in an OU. You need to be familiar with OU permissions and permission inheritance to understand delegation of control.

- OU permissions and permission inheritance work much the same way as they do in the file system. You must enable the Advanced Features option in Active Directory Users and Computers (ADUC) to view an object's Security tab and other folders and tabs.

- User accounts provide a way for users to authenticate to the network and contain user information that can be used in a company directory. There are three categories of users in Windows: local, domain, and built-in. The two built-in accounts are Administrator and Guest.

- Active Directory Users and Computers (ADUC) and Active Directory Administrative Center (ADAC) are GUI tools for creating and maintaining user accounts. User account names must be unique in

a domain, not be case sensitive, and must be 20 or fewer characters. A complex password is required by default. A naming standard should be devised before creating user accounts. At the very least, the user's full name, logon name, and password are required to create a user account in ADUC.

- User templates facilitate creating users who have some attributes in common, such as group memberships. Administrators can use the multiple edit feature of ADUC to edit certain fields for several users at once.

- This chapter covers the user account properties in the General, Account, Profile, and Member Of tabs. The Account tab contains information that controls many aspects of logging on to the domain, such as logon name, logon hours, logon locations, account lockout, and account expiration. The Profile tab contains information about where a user's profile data is stored and can specify a logon script. The Member Of tab lists groups the user belongs to and can be used to change group memberships. Every new user is added to the Domain Users group automatically.

- Groups are the main security principal used to grant rights and permissions. The two group types are security and distribution, but only security groups are used to assign permissions and rights. The group type can be converted from security to distribution and vice versa.

- The group scope determines the reach of a group's application in a domain or a forest: which security principals in a forest can be group members and to which forest resources a group can be assigned rights or permissions.

- There are three group scopes in Active Directory: domain local, global, and universal. (Local groups are found on domain member computers and standalone computers.) The recommended use of groups can be summarized with the acronyms AGDLP and AGGUDLP. Groups can be nested as long as the rules for group membership are followed. Group scope can be converted with some restrictions. There are default groups in the Builtin and Users folders, and there are special identity groups with dynamic membership that can't be managed.

- Computers that are domain members have computer accounts in Active Directory. Domain users logging on to member computers can use single sign-on forest-wide and perform Active Directory searches. Computers can be managed by using group policies and remote MMCs.

- Computer accounts are created manually by an administrator or automatically when a computer joins a domain. By default, computer accounts are created in the Computers folder, but to use group policies, they must be moved to an OU that has a group policy linked to it.

- Computer accounts can be deleted or disabled, just as user accounts can be. When a computer leaves the domain, its associated computer account is disabled automatically. If the same computer rejoins the domain, the account is enabled again. When the computer needs access to the domain again, you can re-enable the computer account.

- You can automate account management by using command-line tools, such as dsadd and dsmod, or PowerShell cmdlets. There are also the bulk import/export command-line programs csvde and ldifde. Command-line tools can be simplified by using batch files and piping.

Key Terms

Active Directory Administrative Center (ADAC)	domain local group	Security Accounts Manager (SAM) database
Active Directory Users and Computers (ADUC)	downlevel user logon name	security group
	global group	special identity group
batch file	group scope	universal group
contact	group type	universal group membership caching
delegation of control	local group	user template
distribution group	offline domain join	
	piping	

Review Questions

1. Which of the following are true about organizational units? (Choose all that apply.)
   a. OUs can be added to an object's DACL.
   b. OUs can be nested.
   c. A group policy can be linked to an OU.
   d. Only members of Domain Administrators can work with OUs.

2. You want to see the permissions set on an OU, so you open Active Directory Users and Computers, right-click the OU, and click Properties. After clicking all the available tabs, you can't seem to find where permissions are set in the Properties dialog box. What should you do?
   a. Log on as a member of Enterprise Admins and try again.
   b. In the Properties dialog box, click the Advanced button.
   c. Right-click the OU and click Security.
   d. In Active Directory Users and Computers, click View, Advanced Features.

3. You have hired a new junior administrator and created an account for her with the logon name JrAdmin. You want her to be able to reset user accounts and modify group memberships for users in the Operations department whose accounts are in the Operations OU. You want to do this with the least effort and without giving JrAdmin broader capabilities. What should you do?

   a. In the Active Directory Administrative Center, right-click the Operations OU, click Properties, and click Managed By.

   b. In Active Directory Users and Computers, right-click the Operations OU and click Delegate Control.

   c. Open the Operations Security tab and add JrAdmin to the DACL.

   d. Add JrAdmin to the Password Managers domain local group.

4. Which of the following components are collectively grouped together and referred to as the object's security descriptor? (Choose all that apply.)

   a. DACL   c. SACL

   b. Object owner   d. OUs

5. An account named SrAdmin created an OU named QandA under the Operations OU. Which of the following is true by default?

   a. Domain Admins is the owner of the QandA OU.

   b. SrAdmin is the owner of the QandA OU and all objects created inside it.

   c. SrAdmin has all standard permissions except Full control for the QandA OU.

   d. The Everyone group has Read permission to the QandA OU.

6. Which of the following are user account categories? (Choose all that apply.)

   a. Local

   b. Global

   c. Domain

   d. Universal

7. Which of the following are built-in user accounts? (Choose all that apply.)

   a. Administrator

   b. Operator

   c. Anonymous

   d. Guest

8. Which of the following is *not* a valid Windows Server 2016 user account name?

   a. Sam$Snead1

   b. Sam*Snead35

   c. SamSnead!24

   d. Sam23Snead

9. Which of the following are true about user accounts in a Windows Server 2016 domain? (Choose all that apply.)

   a. The name can be from 1 to 20 characters.

   b. The name is case sensitive.

   c. The name can't be duplicated in the domain.

   d. Using default settings, PASSWORD123 is a valid password.

10. Which of the following account options can't be set together? (Choose all that apply.)

    a. User must change password at next logon.

    b. Store password using reversible encryption.

    c. Password never expires.

    d. Account is disabled.

11. Which of the following members can belong to the global group? (Choose all that apply.)

    a. Computer accounts

    b. Global groups from any domain

    c. User accounts

    d. Universal groups

12. Jane has left the company. Her user account is a member of several groups and has permissions and rights to a number of forest-wide resources. Jane's replacement will arrive in a couple of weeks and needs access to the same resources. What's the best course of action?

    a. Find all groups Jane is a member of and make a note of them. Delete Jane's user account and create a new account for the new employee. Add the new account to all the groups Jane was a member of.

    b. Copy Jane's user account and give the copy another name.

    c. Disable Jane's account. When the new employee arrives, rename Jane's account, assign it a new password, and enable it again.

    d. Export Jane's account and then import it when the new employee arrives. Rename the account and assign it a new password.

13. Over the past several months, Tom, who has access to sensitive company information, has signed in to computers in other departments and left them without signing out. You have discussed the matter with him, but the problem continues to occur. You're concerned that someone could access these sensitive resources easily. What's the best way to solve this problem?

    a. Ensure that all computers Tom is signing in to have screen savers set to lock the computer after 15 minutes of inactivity.

b. Specify which computers Tom can sign in to in the domain by using the "Log On To" option in his account's properties.

c. Move Tom's account and computer to another domain, thereby making it impossible for him to sign in to computers that are members of different domains.

d. Disable local logon for Tom's account on all computers except Tom's.

14. You have noticed the inappropriate use of computers for gaming and Internet downloads by some employees who come in after hours and on weekends. These employees don't have valid work assignments during these times. You have been asked to devise a solution for these employees that doesn't affect other employees or these employees' computers during working hours. What's the best solution?

a. Install personal firewall software on their computers in an attempt to block the gaming and Internet traffic.

b. Request that the Maintenance Department change the locks on their office doors so that they can enter only during prescribed hours.

c. Set the Logon Hours options for their user accounts.

d. Before you leave each evening and before the weekend, disable these employees' accounts and re-enable them the next working day.

15. You have decided to follow Microsoft's best practices to create a group scope that will allow you to aggregate users with similar rights requirements. Which group scope should you initially create?

a. Global

b. Domain local

c. Local

d. Universal

16. Which of the following are considered security principals? (Choose all that apply.)

a. Contacts

b. Computer accounts

c. User accounts

d. Distribution groups

17. Which of the following is a valid group scope? (Choose all that apply.)

a. Global

b. Domain local

c. Forest

d. Domain global

18. What happens if a security group that's an ACE in a shared folder is converted to a distribution group?

a. A security group can't be converted to a distribution group if it has already been assigned permissions.

b. The group is removed from the DACL automatically.

c. The group remains in the DACL, but the ACE has no effect on members' access to the resource.

d. The group remains in the DACL, and permissions assigned to the group affect access to the resource as though it were still a security group.

19. Which of the following can be a member of a universal group? (Choose all that apply.)

a. User accounts from the local domain only

b. Global groups from any domain in the forest

c. Other universal groups

d. Domain local groups from the local domain only

20. Which direct group scope conversion is allowed?

a. Domain local to universal provided no domain local group is already a member

b. Global to domain local without restriction

c. Domain local to global provided no domain local group is already a member

d. Universal to global without restriction

21. Which of the following is true about the Users domain local group?

a. It's in the Users folder.

b. It can be converted to a global group.

c. Domain Users is a member.

d. Its members can log on locally to a domain controller.

22. A domain user logging on to the domain becomes a member of which special identity group?

a. Creator Owner

b. System

c. Authenticated Users

d. Anonymous Logon

23. Which of the following creates a file named disabled.txt containing a list of disabled Active Directory accounts?

a. net accounts /show disabled

b. ldifde -accounts -property=enabled -value=false

c. Query-Account -Disable=True | disabled.txt

d. Search-ADAccount -AccountDisabled > disabled.txt

24. A user is having trouble signing in to the domain from a computer that has been out of service for several months, and nobody else can seem to sign in from the computer. What should you try first to solve the problem?

    a. Reinstall Windows on the workstation and create a new computer account in the domain.

    b. Rename the computer and create a new computer account with the new name.

     c. Reset the computer account, remove the computer from the domain, and rejoin it to the domain.

    d. Disable the computer account, remove the computer from the domain, and rejoin it to the domain.

25. Which commands can you use together to change attributes of several users at once?

    a. dsget and dsadd

    b. dsget and dsmod

    c. dsquery and dsmod

    d. dsquery and dsget

Critical Thinking

The following activities give you critical thinking challenges. Case Projects offer a scenario with a problem to solve and for which you supply a written solution.

Case Project 2-1: Adding User Accounts

CSM Tech Publishing has added a branch office with about 50 users. The HR Department has given you a spreadsheet with the employee information that includes the employee name, office location, department, title, and so forth. Describe at least two different methods you can use to add these user accounts to Active Directory that don't involve manual creation of each account from scratch.

Case Project 2-2: Enabling Disabled Accounts

You have created about 50 users for a new branch office of the csmtech.local domain that will be opening soon. The accounts are in the BranchOff OU and are currently disabled. You want to enable them when the branch office opens next week. Construct a `dsquery` command that pipes to a `dsmod` command that will enable all accounts that are disabled.

CHAPTER 3

USER AND SERVICE ACCOUNT CONFIGURATION

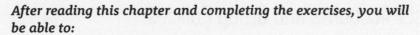

After reading this chapter and completing the exercises, you will be able to:

Configure user accounts and group policies

Configure account policies

Create password settings objects

Work with service accounts

This chapter reviews user accounts and group policies so that you have a fresh context for learning how to configure account policies in a domain environment and on a local computer. Account policies help you maintain a secure authentication environment for your domain, but you need to find a balance between security and a system that works for all your users. You learn how to make exceptions in account policies so that you can designate more stringent or more lenient policies for groups of users as needed.

Services that run on your computer must also be authenticated to the network, and traditional methods for configuring service authentication have posed challenges in security, manageability, or both. This chapter discusses how you can configure service authentication with a variety of methods, allowing you to choose which method fits each service you install.

Table 3-1 describes what you need for the hands-on activities in this chapter.

Table 3-1	Activity requirements		
Activity	**Requirements**		**Notes**
Activity 3-1: Resetting Your Virtual Environment	ServerDC1, ServerDM1, ServerDM2, ServerSA1		
Activity 3-2: Working with Domain Password Policies	ServerDC1		
Activity 3-3: Applying Account Policies to an OU	ServerDC1		
Activity 3-4: Working with Account Lockout Policy	ServerDC1, ServerDM1		
Activity 3-5: Creating a Password Settings Object	ServerDC1, ServerDM1		

Overview of User Accounts and Group Policies

You learned about creating, configuring, and managing user accounts in Chapter 2. However, because you're learning about another aspect of user accounts—account policies—this section serves as a review of user accounts and their role in a domain. User accounts have two main functions:

- *Provide a method for user authentication to the network*—The user name and password serve as a secure method for users to sign in to the network to access resources. A user account can also contain account restrictions, such as when and where a user can sign in and an account expiration date.
- *Provide detailed information about a user*—User accounts can contain information about departments, office locations, addresses, and telephone information. You can modify the Active Directory schema to contain just about any user information a company wants to keep, such as for use in a company directory.

Of these two functions, this chapter focuses on account policies and how they affect a user's ability to authenticate to the network or a local computer. Recall that on local computers, user accounts are stored in the Security Accounts Manager (SAM) database, and users can sign in to and access resources only on the computer where the account resides. A network running Active Directory should limit the use of local user accounts on client computers, however, because local accounts can't be used to access domain resources. Local user accounts are mainly used in a peer-to-peer network in which Active Directory isn't running. Administrators can also sign in to a computer with a local Administrator account for the purposes of joining the computer to a domain or troubleshooting access to the domain. Local user accounts are usually created in Control Panel's User Accounts applet or the Computer Management MMC's Local Users and Groups snap-in. Because these accounts don't participate in Active Directory, they can't be managed from Active Directory or be subject to group policies.

User accounts created in Active Directory are referred to as *domain user accounts*. Generally, these accounts enable users to sign in to any computer that's a domain member in the Active Directory forest. They also provide single sign-on access to domain resources in the forest and other trusted entities for which the account has permission. Domain user accounts can be managed by group policies and are subject to account policies linked to the domain.

Creating and Configuring Group Policies

A Group Policy Object (GPO) is a list of settings that administrators use to configure user and computer operating environments remotely. Group policies can specify security settings, deploy software, and configure a user's desktop among many other computer and network settings. They can be configured to affect an entire domain, a site, and, most commonly, users or computers in an organizational unit (OU). The **GPO scope** defines which objects a GPO affects.

You can link GPOs to sites, domains, and OUs, and GPOs linked to these containers affect only the user or computer accounts in the containers. When Active Directory is installed, two GPOs are created and linked to two containers:

- *Default Domain Policy*—This GPO is linked to the domain object and specifies default settings that affect all users and computers in the domain. The settings in this policy are related mainly to account policies, such as password and logon requirements, and some network security policies.
- *Default Domain Controllers Policy*—This GPO is linked to the Domain Controllers OU and specifies default policy settings for all domain controllers in the domain (as long as the computer objects representing domain controllers aren't moved from the Domain Controllers OU). The settings in this policy pertain mainly to user rights assignments, which specify the types of actions users can perform on a domain controller (DC).

Recall that you view, create, and manage GPOs by using the Group Policy Management console (GPMC). Each GPO has two main nodes in GPMC:

- *Computer Configuration*—Used to set policies that apply to computers in the GPO's scope. These policies are applied to a computer when the computer starts. Account policies are configured in this node.
- *User Configuration*—Used to set policies that apply to all users in the GPO's scope. User policies are applied when a user logs on to any computer in the domain.

The GPMC is used to create GPOs, view a GPO's settings, link and unlink GPOs with containers, and manage the inheritance settings of GPOs. To configure policy settings, you right-click a GPO in GPMC and click Edit to start the Group Policy Management Editor (GPME). When you change settings in a GPO that's linked to an Active Directory container, the change takes place as soon as the policy is downloaded to a computer. Computer Configuration policies are downloaded when a computer boots and about every 90 minutes on a running computer. User Configuration policies are downloaded when a user signs in and every 90 minutes for a signed-in user. You can also initiate a group policy update for both users and computers by entering gpupdate at a command prompt.

You learn more about working with GPOs in Chapters 4, 5, and 6; in this chapter, you focus on user account policies.

> **Note**
>
> The gpupdate command, when run with no arguments, updates changes to group policies. If you use gpupdate /force, the result is the same, but all group policies are downloaded whether they have changed or not. In a small network with few policies to download, using the /force option isn't a problem, but in a large network with many group policies, it can create a substantial processing burden on DCs and cause unnecessary network traffic. In a production network, use the /force option only if you suspect a problem with group policy processing.

Configuring Account Policies

 Certification

- **70-742 – Manage and maintain AD DS:**
  Configure service authentication and account policies

Account policies control settings related to user authentication and logon. They're found in a GPO in the path Computer Configuration, Policies, Windows Settings, Security Settings, Account Policies. It seems strange that account policies should be under the Computer Configuration node because they affect user accounts. The key is that account policies affect user accounts on the computer where the account is located. For example, domain user accounts are stored on domain controllers, so account policies applied to domain controllers affect all user accounts in the domain. Local user accounts are stored in the SAM database where the user account was created, so account policies applied to member computers affect the user accounts stored on these computers.

An important point to remember about account policies for domain user accounts is that they're effective only if the GPO where they're configured is linked to the domain. In other words, if you configure account policies on a GPO and link it to an OU, these policies don't affect domain users. However, the settings affect local user accounts on computers in the GPO's scope. Having said that, configuring settings only at the domain level is recommended so that both domain and local accounts are subject to the same policies. The Default Domain Policy GPO contains settings for many account policies so that a domain has secure settings defined when it's created. You can edit the Default Domain Policy GPO if you want to change the default settings, or you can create a GPO and link it to the domain to override the Default Domain Policy settings. Creating a GPO is recommended instead of editing the Default Domain Policy so that you can revert to the original settings easily.

There are three subnodes under Account Policies. These subnodes and their settings are described in the following list. If the setting is configured in Default Domain Policy, the default setting value is given.

- *Password Policy*—Contains the following policies that control password properties. You can't enable a user account that has a password that doesn't meet the policy, and users can't change their passwords to one that doesn't meet the policy (see Figure 3-1).

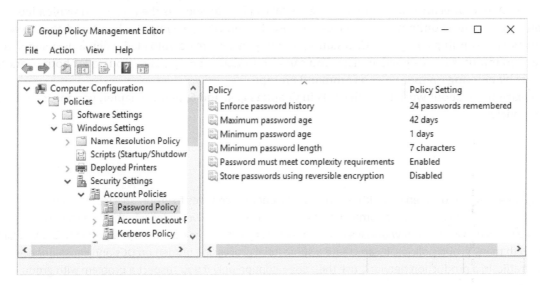

Figure 3-1 Password Policy default settings configured in the Default Domain Policy GPO

- Enforce password history: Contains a value between 0 and 24, which indicates how many passwords Windows remembers before a user can reuse a password. The Default Domain Policy sets it to 24 by default. A value of 0 means that Windows doesn't keep a password history. To keep users from changing their passwords many times in succession to skirt this policy, you should set the *Minimum password age* policy.
- Maximum password age: A value between 0 and 999 indicates how many days a user can use a password before having to change it. If a user doesn't change his or her password within the required number of days, the password expires, and the user can't sign in until the password is changed. A value of 0 means that the password never expires. The default is 42 days.

- Minimum password age: A value between 0 and 998 indicates how many days must elapse between successive password changes. A value of 0 means that users can change their passwords as often as they want. The default is 1 day.
- Minimum password length: A value between 0 and 14 indicates the minimum number of characters a user's password must be. A 0 means that blank passwords are allowed. The default is 7.
- Password must meet complexity requirements: If enabled (the default setting), a user's password must meet certain requirements: at least six characters (or meeting the *Minimum password length* policy, whichever is longer); doesn't contain more than two consecutive characters found in the user's account name or full name; and must contain characters from three of these categories: uppercase letters, lowercase letters, numbers, and symbols ($, @, !, #, and so on).
- Store passwords using reversible encryption: If enabled, passwords are stored with a method that's essentially plaintext and not secure. This policy should be set only if a critical application requires access to user passwords for authentication purposes. The default is disabled.
- *Account Lockout Policy*—Contains the following policies that control user account lockout. If a user account is locked, the user can't sign in until the account is unlocked (see Figure 3-2):

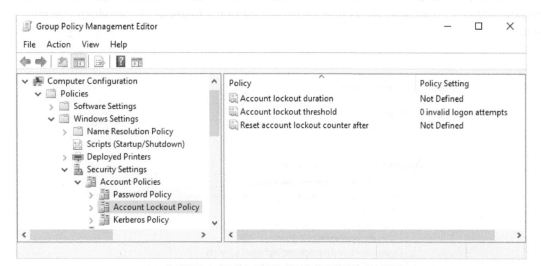

Figure 3-2   Account Lockout Policy default settings configured in the Default Domain Policy GPO

- Account lockout duration: Contains a value between 0 and 99999 that indicates how many minutes a user's account is locked and, therefore, unable to be used for sign-in if the *Account lockout threshold* setting is exceeded. The account is unlocked automatically after this number of minutes passes. A value of 0 means that the account remains locked until an administrator unlocks it. The default is *Not defined* because this setting has meaning only when the *Account lockout threshold* is defined and isn't 0. After the *Account lockout threshold* has a value other than 0 defined, the suggested setting for *Account lockout duration* is 30.
- Account lockout threshold: Contains a value between 0 and 999 that determines how many times a user's password can be entered incorrectly before the account is locked out. The default is 0, which means that accounts are never locked.
- Reset account lockout counter after: Contains a value between 1 and 99999 that indicates the number of minutes that must elapse between failed logon attempts before the failed logon attempt counter is reset to 0. The default is *Not defined* because this setting has meaning only when the *Account lockout threshold* is defined and isn't 0. When *Account lockout threshold* has a value other than 0 defined, the suggested setting for *Reset account lockout counter after* is 30.

- *Kerberos Policy*—Administrators can use this suite of policies to fine-tune parameters for Kerberos, the default authentication protocol in a Windows domain. The policies deal mostly with the length of time Kerberos authentication tickets are active. Shortening the active time increases security but increases authentication overhead. In most cases, the default values shouldn't be changed. The Kerberos policy settings are discussed more in the section "Kerberos Policy Settings."

Delegating Password Settings Management

Working with user passwords and password settings is a common task for server administrators. It can be useful for administrators to be able to delegate the ability to manage user password tasks to junior IT personnel. Common tasks such as resetting a user's password or forcing a password change at next logon can be easily delegated using the Delegation of Control Wizard in Active Directory. You can delegate control of these tasks by right-clicking a folder or OU in Active Directory Users and Computers and clicking Delegate Control. In the Delegation of Control Wizard, you select users or groups to which you wish to delegate control and then select the tasks to delegate (see Figure 3-3). The delegation affects only the accounts that are contained in the folder or OU on which you ran the wizard.

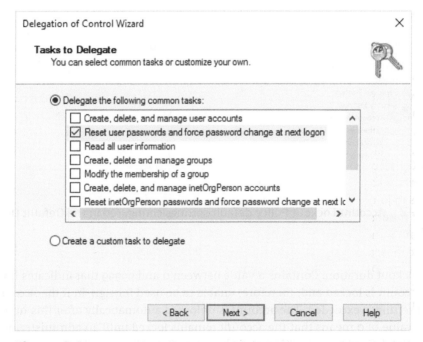

Figure 3-3   Using the Delegation of Control Wizard to delegate user password tasks

You can delegate password settings management by delegating permissions to GPOs. For example, if you create a new GPO in which all the password settings are configured, you could delegate control of that GPO to another user. That user will then be able to change settings in the GPO. For example, create a GPO named PasswordPolicies, select the GPO in Group Policy Management, and click the Delegation tab (see Figure 3-4). Click the Add button and type a group or user account you want to have access to the GPO. You can give the user *Edit settings* or *Edit settings, delete, modify security* permissions to the GPO depending on your requirements.

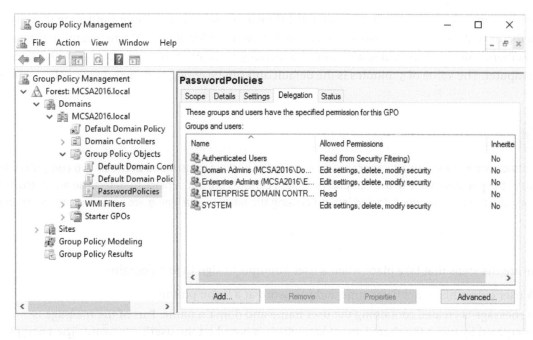

Figure 3-4   The Delegation tab for a GPO

Local Account Policies

As mentioned, account policies set in GPOs linked to an OU containing computer accounts affect only local user accounts defined in the computer's SAM database. Account policies set in GPOs linked to OUs take precedence over policies set at the domain level unless the GPO linked to the domain has the Enforced setting enabled. Policies that aren't defined in a GPO linked to an OU use the policy setting defined in the domain-linked GPO, but if a policy is defined in both, the OU-linked policy is used.

Account policies are set in the Local Security Policy MMC on computers that aren't domain members because only domain members are affected by group policies. You can use the Local Security Policy MMC on domain members to view policy settings, but you can change only the ones that aren't defined by a group policy.

Kerberos Policy Settings

Kerberos is the authentication protocol used in a Windows domain environment to authenticate logons and grant accounts access to domain resources. An account can be a user or a computer because computers must also authenticate to the domain. Kerberos provides mutual authentication between a client and server or between two servers. **Mutual authentication** means that the identity of both parties is verified. Kerberos is also the basis for authorization to network resources in a Windows domain.

Kerberos uses shared secret key encryption to ensure privacy, and passwords are never sent across the network. Kerberos authentication and authorization uses the following components:

- *Key Distribution Center*—Every domain controller is a **Key Distribution Center (KDC)**, which uses the Active Directory database to store keys for encrypting and decrypting data in the authentication process. The keys are based on an account's encrypted password.
- *Ticket-granting tickets*—When an account successfully authenticates with a domain controller (a KDC), the account is issued a **ticket-granting ticket (TGT)**. A TGT grants an account access to the domain controller and is used to request a service ticket without having to authenticate again.
- *Service tickets*—A **service ticket** is requested by an account when it wants to access a network resource, such as a shared folder. It contains the account's access information, such as group memberships. A service ticket is sometimes called a *session ticket*.

- *Timestamps*—A **timestamp** is a record of the time a message is sent. Timestamps are used in Kerberos to determine a message's validity and prevent replay attacks. When a computer receives a Kerberos message, the timestamp must be within 5 minutes of the current time on the receiving computer. The value of 5 minutes is the default and can be configured in Kerberos policy settings.

> **Note** 📎
>
> A replay attack occurs when an attacker captures a stream of packets transmitted between two computers and later replays the packets to one of the computers. Unless controls are put in place to detect the attack (such as a timestamp), the target computer is fooled into processing the packets as a legitimate communication session.

Here are the steps that take place when a user attempts to sign in to a domain:

1. A user enters his or her user name and password at a logon prompt.
2. A message is created containing the user name and domain name. Part of the message is encrypted by using the shared secret key, which is based on the user's password. The encrypted message includes a timestamp.
3. A domain controller (a KDC) receives the message and retrieves the password from the Active Directory database for the user name in the message. It then decrypts the message's encrypted part by using the user's password. If the message is decrypted successfully, the user's identity is verified. The timestamp is also decrypted. The time on it must be within the value specified in the Kerberos Policy setting *Maximum tolerance for computer clock synchronization* (5 minutes by default) for the server's current time. If the user's identity is verified and the timestamp is valid, the user is authenticated.
4. The domain controller sends the user a TGT, which includes a timestamp that authorizes the user to access the domain controller and request service tickets. The timestamp is again checked for validity. The user account caches the TGT information for future communication with the domain controller. A TGT is valid until it expires or the user signs out. By default, it's valid for 10 hours.

After an account has a TGT, it can request a service ticket to access a domain resource. For example, a user has just signed in to the domain and wants to access a shared folder on a file server. For this example, the KDC is DC1, and the file server is FS1. All messages include a timestamp, which is validated.

1. The user attempts to open a shared folder on FS1. The client computer sends a service ticket request to DC1 that includes the original TGT issued when the user authenticated and the name of the requested resource.
2. DC1 validates the request and sends a service ticket to the client, which contains the user's access information, including group memberships.
3. The client sends the service ticket to FS1, which validates the ticket and then checks the user's permissions based on the access information in the ticket.
4. If the user has permissions to the resource, the user is granted access, and the service ticket is cached on the client computer. Future requests to access FS1 are sent directly to FS1, using the cached service ticket. A service ticket is valid until it expires or the user signs out. By default, it's valid for 10 hours.

The steps for Kerberos authentication and authorization left out some details about encryption and message contents, but they contain enough information for you to understand the purpose of these Kerberos policy settings (see Figure 3-5):

- *Enforce user logon restrictions*—If this setting is enabled (the default), the KDC validates every request for service tickets against the rights granted to the requesting account. This process takes extra time, and although it's somewhat more secure, it might slow access to network resources so that it can be disabled if needed.

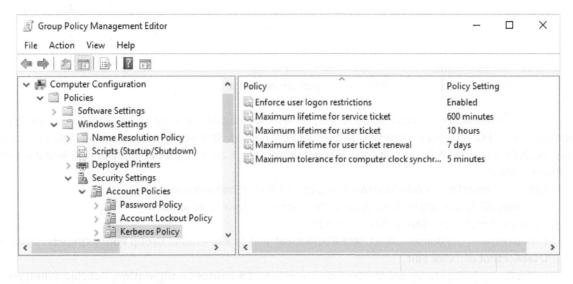

Figure 3-5   Kerberos Policy default settings configured in the Default Domain Policy GPO

- *Maximum lifetime for service ticket*—This setting specifies in minutes how long a service ticket can be used before a new ticket must be requested to access the resource for which the ticket was granted. The default is 600 minutes or 10 hours. The minimum allowed value is 10 minutes, and the maximum value is equal to the *Maximum lifetime for user ticket* setting.
- *Maximum lifetime for user ticket*—This setting is the maximum amount of time in hours that a TGT can be used before it must be renewed or a new one must be requested. The default value is 10 hours.
- *Maximum lifetime for user ticket renewal*—This setting, specified in days, is the maximum period during which a TGT can be renewed. The default setting is 7 days. In this period, a TGT can be renewed without having to go through the full authentication process. After this period has expired (or the account logs off), a new TGT must be requested.
- *Maximum tolerance for computer clock synchronization*—This setting determines the maximum time difference allowed between a Kerberos message timestamp and the receiving computer's current time. If the time difference falls outside this limit, the message is considered invalid. The default is 5 minutes. Timestamp messages are corrected for time zone, so it's important to have the correct time zone set on all computers in the domain and have the domain controller clocks synchronized with a reliable source. By default, member computers are synchronized with the DC's clock.

Activity 3-1: Resetting Your Virtual Environment

Time Required: 5 minutes
Objective: Reset your virtual environment by applying the InitialConfig checkpoint or snapshot.
Required Tools and Equipment: ServerDC1, ServerDM1, ServerDM2, ServerSA1
Description: Apply the InitialConfig checkpoint or snapshot to ServerDC1, ServerDM1, ServerDM2, and ServerSA1.

1. Be sure the servers are is shut down. In your virtualization program, apply the InitialConfig checkpoint or snapshot to ServerDC1, ServerDM1, ServerDM2, and ServerSA1.
2. When the snapshot or checkpoint has finished being applied, continue to the next activity.

Activity 3-2: Working with Domain Password Policies

Time Required: 15 minutes
Objective: Change and test password policies for domain accounts.
Required Tools and Equipment: ServerDC1
Description: In this activity, you change password policies from their default settings. Rather than edit the Default Domain Policy GPO, you create a new GPO and link it to the domain. The settings in the new GPO take precedence over the Default Domain Policy so that you can revert to the default account policies easily by unlinking the new GPO from the domain.

1. Sign in to ServerDC1 as **Administrator**, and open a PowerShell window.
2. Type **New-GPO UserAcctPol** and press **Enter**. Close the PowerShell window.
3. Open the Group Policy Management console.
4. Click to expand the domain object, **MCSA2016.local**, and click to expand **Group Policy Objects**. Right-click **UserAcctPol** and click **Edit**.
5. In the Group Policy Management Editor, click to expand **Computer Configuration, Policies, Windows Settings, Security Settings**, and **Account Policies**, and then click **Password Policy**. In the right pane, double-click **Enforce password history**. Click the **Define this policy setting** check box, leave the passwords remembered value at **0**, and then click **OK**.

Tip ⓘ

To see a detailed description of any account policy, double-click the policy, and click the Explain tab in its Properties dialog box.

6. Double-click **Minimum password age**. Click the **Define this policy setting** check box, set the value to **0** days so that passwords can be changed immediately, and then click **OK**. Windows provides a suggested value for Maximum password age because this policy must be defined if Minimum password age is defined. Click **OK** to accept the suggested value. Close the Group Policy Management Editor. Settings that you didn't define, such as Minimum password length, are still set because the Default Domain Policy defines them.
7. Before you test this policy, see how it works with the current policy in place. The default value for the Enforce password history policy you changed is 24, which means you shouldn't be able to change your password to the same value. Press **Ctrl+Alt+Del**, and then click **Change a password**. In the Old password text box, type your current password. In the New password and Confirm password text boxes, type your current password and press **Enter**. You see a message stating that Windows is unable to update the password. This is because Enforce password history is set to 24, which means that you can't reuse the same password until you have used 24 different passwords. Click **OK**, and then click **Cancel** and **Cancel** again to return to the desktop.
8. In the Group Policy Management console, link UserAcctPol to the domain by right-clicking **MCSA2016.local** and clicking **Link an Existing GPO**. In the Select GPO dialog box, click **UserAcctPol** (see Figure 3-6) and click **OK**.
9. Click **MCSA2016.local**, and in the right pane, click **Linked Group Policy Objects**. The current link order causes the Default Domain Policy to take precedence over UserAcctPol. You want UserAcctPol to have precedence, so click **UserAcctPol** and click the **up arrow** to change UserAcctPol's link order to **1** (see Figure 3-7).

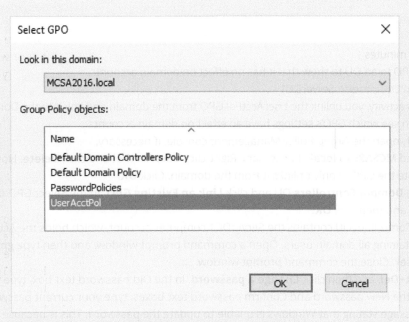

Figure 3-6   Selecting a GPO to link to the domain

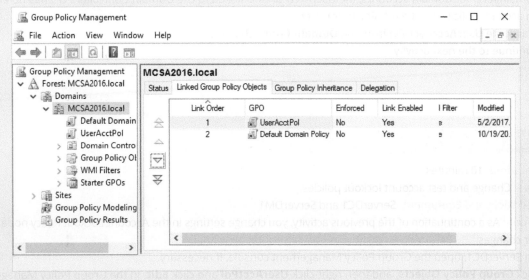

Figure 3-7   Changing a GPO's link order

10. Open a command prompt window, and then type **gpupdate /force** and press **Enter**. When the command finishes running, try to change your password again following the instructions in Step 7, using the same password for both the old and new passwords. You should be successful. Click **OK**. Close the command prompt window.

11. Continue to the next activity.

Activity 3-3: Applying Account Policies to an OU

Time Required: 10 minutes

Objective: Link a GPO to an OU to show that it has no effect on domain accounts.

Required Tools and Equipment: ServerDC1

Description: In this activity, you unlink the UserAcctPol GPO from the domain and link it to the Domain Controllers OU. Next, you test to see which GPO's settings have an effect on domain accounts.

1. On ServerDC1, open the Group Policy Management console, if necessary.
2. Click to expand **MCSA2016.local**, if necessary. Right-click **UserAcctPol** and click **Delete**. Note that this action does not delete the GPO; it only unlinks it from the domain. Click **OK**.
3. Right-click the **Domain Controllers** OU and click **Link an Existing GPO**. In the Select GPO dialog box, click **UserAcctPol**, and then click **OK**.
4. The Domain Controllers OU contains the ServerDC1 computer account, which holds the Active Directory database containing all domain users. Open a command prompt window, and then type **gpupdate /force** and press **Enter**. Close the command prompt window.
5. Press **Ctrl+Alt+Del**, and then click **Change a password**. In the Old password text box, type your current password. In the New password and Confirm password text boxes, type your current password.
6. You see a message stating that Windows is unable to update the password. This is because the Default Domain Policy is in effect. Enforce password history is set to 24 in the Default Domain Policy, so you can't change your password to the same value you used before. Because account policies can be set only at the domain level for domain accounts, the UserAcctPol GPO linked to the Domain Controllers OU has no effect on account policies for the Administrator user.
7. Unlink the **UserAcctPol** GPO from the **Domain Controllers** OU.
8. Continue to the next activity.

Activity 3-4: Working with Account Lockout Policy

Time Required: 10 minutes

Objective: Change and test account lockout policies.

Required Tools and Equipment: ServerDC1 and ServerDM1

Description: As a continuation of the previous activity, you change settings in the Account Lockout Policy node and test your changes.

1. On ServerDC1, open the Group Policy Management console, if necessary.
2. Click **Group Policy Objects**, and then right-click **UserAcctPol** and click **Edit**. In the Group Policy Management Editor, click to expand **Computer Configuration, Policies, Windows Settings, Security Settings**, and **Account Policies**, and then click **Account Lockout Policy**. Double-click **Account lockout threshold**. Click the **Define this policy setting** check box, change the invalid logon attempts value to **2**, and then click **OK**.
3. The Suggested Value Changes dialog box suggests values for *Account lockout duration* and *Reset account lockout counter after*. Click **OK** to accept these settings, and close the Group Policy Management Editor.
4. Link **UserAcctPol** to the domain node, and make sure it's first in the link order.
5. Open a command prompt window, and then type **gpupdate /force** and press **Enter**. (Password policies that affect domain users are stored on domain controllers, not member computers, so the policy must be updated on the domain controller even though you will sign in from ServerDM1.) Close the command prompt window.

6. Open Active Directory Users and Computers and create a user in the Users folder with the following properties:

   Full name: **Test User1**
   User logon name: **testuser1**
   Password: **Password01**
   User must change password at next logon: **Unchecked**

   Repeat this step to create another user with Full Name **Test User2** and User logon name **testuser2** with the same password and password properties.

7. Start ServerDM1 if necessary and attempt to sign in twice as **testuser1** with an incorrect password. Attempt to sign in a third time with the correct password (Password01). You should get a message stating that the account is currently locked out. Click **OK**.

8. On ServerDC1, open Active Directory Users and Computers. Open the Properties dialog box for **Test User1** and click the **Account** tab. Under the Logon Hours button is a message stating that the account is locked out. Click the **Unlock account** check box to unlock the account manually (see Figure 3-8), but be aware that the account unlocks automatically after the number of minutes in the Account lockout duration setting expires if it hasn't been unlocked manually. Click **OK**.

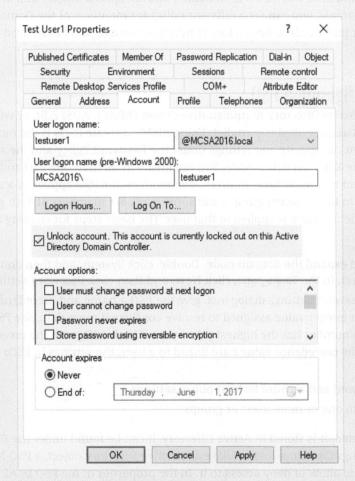

Figure 3-8   Unlocking a user account

9. Attempt to sign in as **testuser1** from ServerDM1 again. You should be successful.

10. Sign out of ServerDM1, but stay signed in to ServerDC1 and continue to the next activity.

Configuring Password Settings Objects

 Certification

- **70-742 – Manage and maintain AD DS:**
  Configure service authentication and account policies

A **password settings object (PSO)** is an Active Directory object that enables an administrator to configure password settings for users or groups that are different from those defined in a GPO linked to the domain.

Another term for PSOs is *fine-grained password policies*. Whichever term you use, PSOs allow you to configure multiple password and account lockout policies for different sets of user accounts in the same domain. Recall that GPOs containing account policies are linked to the domain object, so all users in the domain are subject to the same account policies. Before PSOs, the only way to have different account policies affect different users was to have more than one domain to which you could apply the policies. PSOs have the effect of overriding account policies set at the domain level, but they aren't configured like a GPO and linked to an OU or domain. PSOs are special objects that are assigned to users or groups. For example, you can set a different policy for members of the Domain Admins group, perhaps requiring their passwords to have a longer minimum length and be changed more often than other users' passwords.

Creating and Configuring a PSO

PSOs are created with Active Directory Administrative Center (ADAC), ADSI Edit, or with the PowerShell `New-ADFineGrainedPasswordPolicy` cmdlet. Using ADAC to create PSOs is the most convenient method. With PSOs, you can specify any settings under the Password Policy and the Account Lockout Policy nodes but not the Kerberos Policy node. You can create more than one PSO and configure different settings and assign them to different sets of users. If more than one PSO applies to a user (for example, two PSOs are assigned to two different groups, and some users are members of both groups), the PSO with the highest precedence value is applied to that user. The basic steps for creating and using a PSO are as follows:

1. Open ADAC, and expand the domain node. Double-click System, and then double-click Password Settings Container. In the Tasks pane, click **New**, and then click Password Settings.
2. In the Create Password Settings dialog box, give the PSO a name and precedence. The precedence is an integer value assigned to resolve conflicts if more than one PSO applies to a user. The lowest number has the highest priority. So if both PSO1 with the precedence value 1 and PSO2 with the precedence value 2 are linked to a user, the settings in PSO1 are applied to the user.
3. Configure password and account lockout policy settings.
4. Assign the PSO to one or more users or groups.

When a PSO is created, it is stored in Active Directory. It can be found under the Domain node in the System\Password Settings Container folder. Like every Active Directory object, a PSO has security settings that you can configure to allow or deny access to it. In the properties of the PSO in ADAC, simply scroll down to see the security settings. By default, the local Administrators group can make changes to a PSO, and both Domain Admins and Enterprise Admins have full control of a PSO. If you want other users or groups to manage a PSO, you can add them to the discretionary access control list (DACL) and give them read and write permissions.

Activity 3-5: Creating a Password Settings Object

Time Required: 15 minutes

Objective: Create a password settings object linked to a group.

Required Tools and Equipment: ServerDC1, ServerDM1

Description: In this activity, you first create a group to link to a new PSO. Then, you create a new PSO, define password settings, and link it to a group. Finally, you test the settings.

1. First, you'll create a new group to link the PSO to and add a user to it. On ServerDC1, open a PowerShell window. Type **New-ADGroup PSO-Group -GroupScope Global** and press **Enter**. Next add testuser1 to the group by typing **Add-ADGroupMember PSO-Group testuser1** and press **Enter**. Close the PowerShell window.

2. Open Active Directory Administrative Center. Click **MCSA2016 (local)** to see the folders and OUs in the middle pane. Double-click **System** and then **Password Settings Container**. In the Tasks pane, click **New**, and then click **Password Settings**.

3. In the Create Password Settings dialog box, type **PSO1** in the Name text box and **5** in the Precedence text box. The Precedence value doesn't mean much until you have more than one PSO defined.

4. In the Minimum password length (characters) text box, type **4**, and in the Number of passwords remembered text box, type **5**. Click to clear the **Password must meet complexity requirements**, **Enforce minimum password age**, and **Enforce maximum password age** check boxes. Leave the **Enforce account lockout policy** at the default so that accounts are never locked out. Click to clear **Protect from accidental deletion** because you're deleting this PSO at the end of this activity.

5. Click the **Add** button, and type **PSO-Group**. Click **Check Names** and then **OK**. The settings should look like Figure 3-9. Click **OK**.

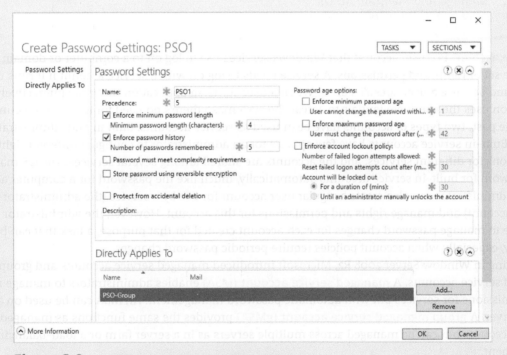

Figure 3-9   Creating a password settings object

6. In Active Directory Administrative Center, click **MCSA2016 (local)** in the left pane, and then double-click **Users** in the middle pane. Click to select **Test User1**. In the Tasks pane, click **Reset password**. Type **pass1** in the Password and Confirm password text boxes, and click to clear **User must change password at next log on**. Click **OK**. The new password is accepted. Recall that the password policy defined in the Default Domain Policy requires a complex password of at least 7 characters.

7. Click to select **Test User2**. In the Tasks pane, click **Reset password**. Type **pass1** in the Password and Confirm password text boxes, and then click **OK**. You see a message stating that the password doesn't meet complexity requirements. Click **OK** and then **Cancel**. The PSO you created applies only to members of the PSO-Group of which Test User2 is not a member.

8. On ServerDM1, try to sign in as **testuser1** with an incorrect password three times. Recall that the domain policy is set to lockout accounts after two incorrect attempts to log on. Now, try to sign in with **pass1**. You're successful because the PSO applied to PSO-Group disables account lockout. Sign out of ServerDM1.

9. Next, return account policies to their default values. On ServerDC1, open the Group Policy Management console. Expand the domain node so that you can see the two policies linked to it. Right-click **UserAcctPol** and click **Delete**. Click **OK** to confirm the deletion. That's it! No need to remember which policies to undo; by using a second GPO linked to the domain, you can simply link it or unlink it, depending on your policy requirements. In Active Directory Administrative Center, browse to the Password Settings Container, and then right-click **PSO1** and click **Delete**. Click **Yes** to confirm.

10. Shut down all servers.

Managing Service Accounts

Certification

- **70-742 – Manage and maintain AD DS:**
  Configure service authentication and account policies

A **service account** is a user account that Windows services use to log on to a computer or domain with a specific set of rights and permissions. A service needs to log on with a service account if it runs in the background because a user doesn't start it. When a user starts an application that runs interactively, the application uses the user's credentials to access the system, so there's no need for a service account.

In the past, two types of accounts have been used as service accounts: built in and administrator created. Built-in service accounts have few options for an administrator to configure different rights and permissions for different services, and the accounts are shared among several services. The OS manages the password for built-in service accounts automatically, much like the password for a computer account.

An administrator can also create a regular user account for use by a service (the administrator-created account) and manage rights and permissions for this account. However, the administrator would also have to manage password changes for each account created for that purpose, a task that can become unwieldy, especially when account policies require periodic password changes.

Starting in Window Server 2008 R2, Microsoft introduced managed service accounts and group managed service accounts. A **managed service account (MSA)** enables administrators to manage rights and permissions for services but with automatic password management. An MSA can be used on a single server. A **group managed service account (gMSA)** provides the same functions as managed service accounts but can be managed across multiple servers as in a server farm or a load-balancing arrangement.

Note 🖉

In this context, a service includes applications that run in the background, such as database or mail server applications.

Working with Service Accounts

There are three built-in service accounts, each with its own rights and permissions:

- *Local Service*—Intended primarily for services and background applications that need few rights and privileges. This account runs as a member of the local Users group or the Domain Users group in a domain environment. If network access is needed, Local Service runs as an anonymous user.
- *Network Service*—Intended primarily for services that need local and network access. This account runs as a member of the Users or Domain Users group and accesses the network as an Authenticated User member, which provides more privileges than for an anonymous user.
- *Local System*—This account should be used with caution because it has privileges that are in some ways more extensive than the Administrator account when accessing local resources. When accessing network resources, the Local System account uses the local computer account's credentials.

The advantage of using a built-in service account is that no management is needed, and the password is managed automatically. However, if a service requires more privileges than the Local Service or Network Service accounts have, you might need to use the Local System account, which in all likelihood offers more privileges than the service needs. The Services MMC (see Figure 3-10) shows services using all three types of built-in service accounts.

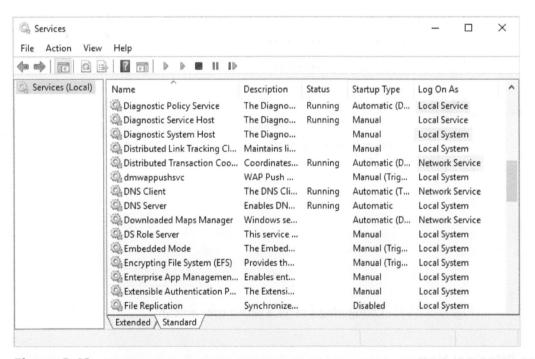

Figure 3-10   Viewing the Log On As setting in the Services MMC

Using Administrator-Created Service Accounts

An administrator-created service account is simply a regular user account that you create for the purpose of assigning a logon account to a service. By using a regular user account, you can assign the service's logon account only the rights and permissions it needs to run correctly. Here are some guidelines to keep in mind when you use a regular user account as a service account:

- Assign only the rights and permissions that the service needs.
- Use a very complex password because a user doesn't use this account to sign in.
- Remove the account from the Users or Domain Users group if it doesn't need that group's rights and permissions.

- Set the password to never expire. If you leave the account subject to regular password policies, the service stops working if you fail to change the password when it expires. However, setting this option creates a security risk, which is why using managed service accounts, discussed next, is better.
- Never use the account to log on interactively.
- Use one account per service.

To configure a service with a logon account, open the Services MMC, double-click the service, and click the Log On tab. When you configure a service with a user account, you must enter and confirm the password, and then Windows automatically assigns the Log On As A Service right (see Figure 3-11).

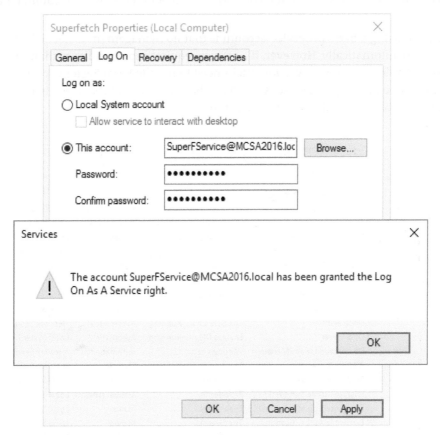

Figure 3-11   Configuring a service with a user account

Service Principal Names

A **service principal name (SPN)** is a name that uniquely identifies a service instance to a client. Multiple instances of a service can be installed in a Windows Active Directory forest, and each instance must have a unique SPN. A service instance can also have multiple SPNs if clients can use different names to access it. An SPN is required for Kerberos authentication, and although administrators had to manage SPNs in the past, they're managed automatically for managed service accounts in a Windows Server 2008 R2 or later domain functional level.

When a client wants to connect to a service, it finds the service based on the SPN, which consists of the following elements:

- *Service type*—The service type is usually something like LDAP, MSSQLSvc, or HTTP.
- *Instance name*—This element is usually the hostname or IP address of the host running the service.

- *Port number*—The port number, such as 80 for HTTP or 389 for LDAP. If the service uses the standard port number, you don't need to specify this element.
- *Service name*—This element is usually the DNS name of the host providing the service. The service name and instance name are often the same, in which case the service name isn't needed.

The SPN is specified with the following syntax:

```
service type/instance name:port number/service name
```

As mentioned, the service name can be omitted if it's the same as the instance name, and the port number can be omitted if it's the standard port number for a well-known service. So, an SPN that provides web services on the host www.csmtech.local, using the standard port, can be specified as follows:

```
HTTP/www.csmtech.local
```

If you're using user accounts rather than managed service accounts, you might need to manage SPNs, but in most cases, they're created automatically. However, if you do have to change an SPN because, for example, a computer name changes or you need clients to be able to connect with a different name, you can do so with the `setspn.exe` command:

```
setspn.exe -s service/instance name ServiceAccount
```

For example, if you want to set the SPN for a service named LDAP on a server named ldsServ1.cmstech.local, using port 2300 and a service account called LDAPsvc, use the following command:

```
setspn.exe -s LDAP/ldsServ1.csmtech.local:2300 LDAPsvc
```

Working with Managed Service Accounts

An MSA is a new type of object in Active Directory with the following attributes:

- Has a system-managed password
- Has automatic SPN support
- Is tied to a specific computer
- Can be assigned rights and permissions
- Can't be used for interactive logon
- Can't be locked out

The requirements for using an MSA include the following:

- It must be created in an Active Directory domain.
- The computer on which the MSA is used must be Windows 2008 R2 or Windows 7 or later.
- The Active Directory module for PowerShell must be installed.
- For automatic SPN support, you must be using a domain functional level of Windows Server 2008 R2 or later.

You create and manage MSAs with PowerShell; there's no GUI tool for working with them. Follow these steps to use MSAs:

1. Create an MSA in Active Directory in the Managed Service Accounts folder (which can be seen in Active Directory Users and Computers if you enable Advanced Features on the View menu). You can also set one or more SPNs on the account when you create it by using the `-ServicePrincipalNames` option. To create an MSA named LDAPsvc, use the following PowerShell cmdlet on a DC:

   ```
   New-ADServiceAccount -Name LDAPsvc
   ```

2. Associate the MSA with a member computer that will use the MSA. To allow a computer named ldsServ1 to use the service account, run this cmdlet on a DC:

   ```
   Add-ADComputerServiceAccount -Identity ldsServ1 -ServiceAccount LDAPsvc
   ```

3. Install the MSA on the target computer by using the following cmdlet on the computer running the service. If the computer isn't a domain controller, you need to install the Active Directory module for Windows PowerShell.

```
Install-ADServiceAccount -Identity LDAPsvc
```

4. Configure the service on the target computer using the MSA. On the computer running the service, open the Services MMC, open the service's properties, and click the Log On tab. Specify the name of the account in the format *domain\MSAname*, or click Browse to select the account. Clear the password fields because the password is managed by the OS, and then stop and start the service.

Other PowerShell cmdlets you can use to work with MSAs include the following:

- `Set-ADServiceAccount`—Change an existing MSA's settings.
- `Get-ADServiceAccount`—Show an MSA's properties.
- `Remove-ADServiceAccount`—Delete an MSA.
- `Reset-ADServiceAccountPassword`—Reset the MSA's password on the computer where the account is installed.
- `UninstallADServiceAccount`—Uninstall the account on the computer where the account is installed.
- `Test-ADServiceAccount`—Test the account to be sure that it can access the domain with its current credentials or can be installed on a member computer.

Working with Group Managed Service Accounts

Managed service accounts can be used on only a single server. If a service is running on multiple servers, as in a server farm or load-balancing configuration, you can use a group managed service account (gMSA) and still get all the benefits of an MSA. gMSAs can be used only on computers running Windows Server 2012 or later with a domain functional level of Windows Server 2012.

gMSAs aren't actually different types of accounts from regular MSAs, but when you create them, you must use an additional option to specify which servers can use the account. You can specify server names or a group in which the servers are members. To create a gMSA named LDAPsvc that's available to ldServ1, ldsServ2, and ldsServ3 (all members of the ldsServers global group), use the following cmdlet:

```
New-ADServiceAccount -Name LDAPsvc
  -PrincipalsAllowedToRetrieveManagedPassword ldsServers
```

> **Tip** ⓘ
>
> You can also specify which servers can use the account after it's created by using the `Set-ADServiceAccount` cmdlet.

After the account is created, you need to go to each server using the account and run the `Install-ADServiceAccount` cmdlet using the same syntax described in the preceding section.

Virtual Accounts

Virtual accounts, introduced in Windows Server 2008 R2, are the simplest service accounts to use because you don't need to create, delete, or manage them in any way. Microsoft refers to them as "managed local accounts." To use them, you simply configure the service to log on as NT Service*ServiceName* with no password (as shown in Figure 3-12) because Windows manages the password. The service name isn't necessarily the name displayed in the Services MMC. You can find the service name in the General tab of the service's Properties dialog box.

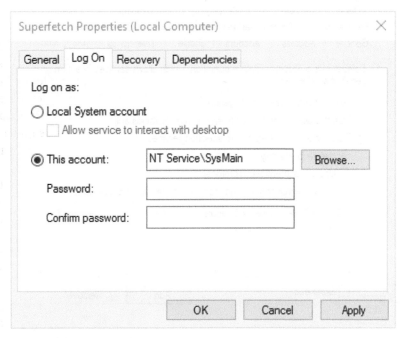

Figure 3-12   Configuring a service to use a virtual account

Virtual accounts access the network with the credentials of the computer account where they're used. If the service needs to access network resources, you give permission for that resource to *ComputerName$* (replacing *ComputerName* with the name of the computer). In most cases, it's better to use MSAs than virtual accounts if the service must access network resources because giving the computer account permission can be a security risk. For purely local services, however, virtual accounts are simple to use and effective.

Kerberos Delegation

Kerberos delegation is a feature of the Kerberos authentication protocol that allows a service to "impersonate" a client, relieving the client from having to authenticate to more than one service. In other words, if a client has authenticated to a service successfully, the service can then use the user's credentials to authenticate to another service on the client's behalf. For example, say that a user signs in to an Outlook Web Access account. The user authenticates with the Outlook Web Access service, but the user's actual mailbox is on another server. Without delegation, the user would then have to authenticate to the server where the mailbox is located. With Kerberos delegation, the Outlook Web Access service can perform the authentication on the user's behalf.

Kerberos delegation is available when you use a domain account as a service account and the account has been assigned an SPN. The Delegation tab is added to the account's Properties dialog box; this tab isn't available for a regular user account that hasn't been assigned an SPN. Figure 3-13 shows the properties of the krbtgt user account being used as a service account.

The Delegation tab has three main options:

- *Do not trust this user for delegation*—The account can't use Kerberos delegation.
- *Trust this user for delegation to any service (Kerberos only)*—The account can be used for delegation to any service but only by using the Kerberos authentication protocol.

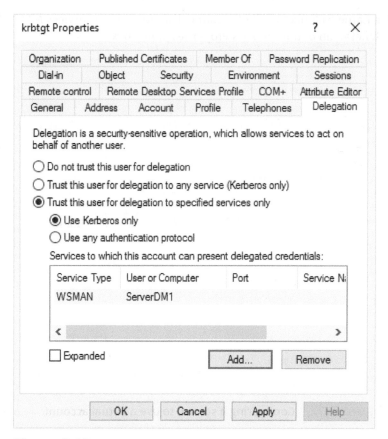

Figure 3-13 The Delegation tab for a service account

- *Trust this user for delegation to specified services only*—This option is called **constrained delegation** because it limits the delegation to specific services running on specific computers. Constrained delegation can be limited to the Kerberos protocol, or you can specify using any authentication protocol.

Kerberos delegation is a convenient feature, especially when using multitiered applications where users connect only to a front-end interface, such as a web server. It relieves administrators of having to find a way for users to authenticate to servers that might not be directly accessible to them.

Chapter Summary

- User accounts have two main functions: providing a method for user authentication to the network and providing detailed information about a user. On local computers, user accounts are stored in the SAM database, and users can sign in to and access resources only on the computer where the account resides. User accounts created in Active Directory are referred to as domain user accounts. Generally, these accounts enable users to sign in to any computer that's a domain member in the Active Directory forest.

- A GPO is a list of settings that administrators use to configure user and computer operating environments remotely. Group policies can specify security settings, deploy software, and configure a user's desktop, among many other computer and network settings.

- Account policies control settings related to user authentication and logon. They're found in a GPO under Computer Configuration, Policies, Windows Settings, Security Settings, Account Policies. Account policies affect user accounts on the computer where the account is located. Account policies for domain user accounts are effective only if the GPO in which they're configured is linked to the domain.

- Account policies set in GPOs linked to an OU containing computer accounts affect only local user accounts defined in the computer's SAM database.

- Kerberos is the authentication protocol used in a Windows domain environment to authenticate logons and grant account access to domain resources. Kerberos is also the basis for authorization to network resources in a Windows domain. Kerberos authentication and authorization use the following components: Key Distribution Center, ticket-granting tickets, service tickets, and timestamps.

- A password settings object is an Active Directory object that enables an administrator to configure password settings for users or groups that are different from those defined in a GPO linked to the domain. Another term for PSOs *is fine-grained password policies.*

- PSOs are created with Active Directory Administrative Center (ADAC), ADSI Edit, or with the PowerShell New-ADFineGrainedPasswordPolicy cmdlet. You can create more than one PSO and configure different settings and assign them to different sets of users.

- A service account is a user account that Windows services use to log on with a specific set of rights and permissions. A service needs to log on with a service account if it runs in the background because a user doesn't start it.

- A managed service account enables administrators to manage rights and permissions for services with automatic password management. A group managed

- service account (gMSA) provides the same functions but can be managed across multiple servers.

- There are three built-in service accounts, each with its own rights and permissions: Local Service, Network Service, and Local System. The advantage of using a built-in service account is that no management is needed, and the password is managed automatically.

- A service principal name is a name that uniquely identifies a service instance to a client. Multiple instances of a service can be installed in a Windows Active Directory forest, and each instance must have a unique SPN.

- An MSA is a new type of object in Active Directory that has the following attributes: system-managed password, automatic SPN support, can be assigned rights and permissions, cannot be used for interactive logon, cannot be locked out, and is tied to a specific computer.

- Virtual accounts are the simplest service accounts to use because you don't need to create, delete, or manage them in any way. Microsoft refers to them as "managed local accounts." They access the network with the credentials of the computer account where they're used.

- Kerberos delegation is a feature of the Kerberos authentication protocol that allows a service to impersonate a client, relieving the client from having to authenticate to more than one service. Kerberos delegation is available when you use a domain account as a service account, and the account has been assigned an SPN.

Key Terms

constrained delegation	Key Distribution Center	service account
GPO scope	(KDC)	service principal name (SPN)
group managed service account	managed service account	service ticket
(gMSA)	(MSA)	ticket-granting ticket (TGT)
Kerberos	mutual authentication	timestamp
Kerberos delegation	password settings object (PSO)	virtual account

Review Questions

1. Which of the following are the main functions of user accounts? (Choose all that apply.)
   a. User authentication
   b. Biometric identity
   c. Autonomous access
   d. Detailed information

2. Where are user accounts stored on a standalone computer?
   a. SQL database
   b. SAM database
   c. Active Directory
   d. A flat file

3. Which of the following GPOs are created by default when Active Directory is installed? (Choose all that apply.)
   a. Default Domain Controllers Policy
   b. Default Group Policy
   c. Default Active Directory Domain Policy
   d. Default Domain Policy

4. Which of the following is true about GPOs?
   a. They affect all groups in their scope.
   b. Account policies are under the User Configuration node
   c. The Default Domain Policy affects only user accounts.
   d. Account policies are under the Computer Configuration node.

5. Which of the following is included in account policies for a GPO? (Choose all that apply.)
   a. Password Policy
   b. Authorization Policy
   c. Account Lockout Policy
   d. Kerberos Policy

6. Which of the following best describes the Account lockout threshold setting?
   a. Specifies how many minutes a user's account is locked
   b. Defines the number of times a user can enter an incorrect user name
   c. Specifies the number of minutes that must elapse between failed logon attempts
   d. Defines the number of times a user's password can be entered incorrectly

7. A junior administrator is configuring settings for the Password Policy of a new GPO he created and sets the minimum password length to 4. He links the GPO to the EngUsers OU containing the user and group accounts for the Engineering Department. A user in the Engineering Department calls and says she's trying to change the password on his domain user account to A$c1, but the system isn't taking the new password. What's the problem?
   a. The user doesn't belong to the Engineering group.
   b. The user's computer account isn't in the EngUsers OU.
   c. Password policies can be set only at the domain level.
   d. The user can't use the $ symbol in the password.

8. Which of the following can be used by a Windows Server 2016 administrator to create a PSO? (Choose all that apply.)
   a. ADAC
   b. Server Manager
   c. ADSI Edit
   d. PowerShell

9. You discovered that a user changed his password 10 times in one day. When you ask why he did this, he replied that the system required him to change his password. He wanted to use his favorite password, but the system wouldn't accept it until he changed it 10 times. What should you do to prevent this user from reusing the same password for at least 60 days?
   a. Change the value for the Enforce password history setting.
   b. Change the value for the Maximum password age setting.
   c. Change the value for the Minimum password age setting.
   d. Enable the *Password must meet complexity requirements* setting.

10. A user is signed in to a Windows Server 2016 domain from a Windows 10 computer and requests access to a shared folder. What must the user account request before the shared folder can be accessed?
    a. A service ticket
    b. A TGT
    c. A KDC
    d. An access code

11. You're the network administrator for several Windows Server 2016 servers in New York. Your company just opened an office in California, and you sent one of the servers to the new office. The server was up and running within 2 days after you sent it. Now you're having authentication problems between the server in California and the domain controllers in New York. There's nothing wrong with the WAN connection, and you never had problems with the California server before, which seems to operate okay in every other way. What's a possible cause of this problem?
    a. The California server's hard drive was damaged in the move.
    b. The time zone on the California server needs to be changed.
    c. The computer account needs to be reset.
    d. The authentication protocol is incorrect.

12. A group of users in the Research Department has access to sensitive company information, so you want to be sure that the group members' passwords are strong with a minimum length of 12 characters and a requirement to change their passwords every 30 days. The current password policy requires passwords with a minimum length of 7 characters that users must change every 120 days. You don't want to inconvenience other users in the domain by making their password policies more stringent. What can you do?

   a. Create a GPO, configure the password policy for the Research Department, and link it to the domain. Block inheritance on all other OUs in the domain.

   b. Create a GPO, configure the password policy for the Research Department, and link it to the domain. Configure a security filter for the Research group.

   c. Create a PSO in ADAC, configure the password policy, and apply it to the Research Department group.

   d. Create a PSO in ADAC, configure the password policy, and link it to the Research Department OU.

13. Which of the following service accounts can be managed across multiple servers?

   a. AD managed service account

   b. Group managed service account

   c. Multi-managed service account

   d. Managed service account

14. Which of the following are built-in service accounts? (Choose all that apply.)

   a. Anonymous Logon

   b. Local system

   c. Network Service

   d. Authenticated Users

15. Which of the following are advantages of using a managed service account instead of a regular user account for service logon? (Choose all that apply.)

   a. The system manages passwords.

   b. You can assign rights and permissions precisely.

   c. You can use the account to log on interactively.

   d. You can't be locked out.

16. Which of the following is used to uniquely identify a service instance to a client?

   a. SPN   c. Service ticket

   b. KDC   d. TGT

17. You have created an MSA on DC1 to run a service on the ldsServ1 server. What's the last thing you should do before using the Services MMC to configure the service to use the new MSA?

   a. On DC1, run the `Install-ADServiceAccount` cmdlet.

   b. On ldsServ1, run the `Install-ADServiceAccount` cmdlet.

   c. On DC1, run the `Add-ADComputerServiceAccount` cmdlet.

   d. On ldsServ1, run the `Add-ADComputerServiceAccount` cmdlet.

18. You have four servers running a service in a load-balancing configuration, and you want the services on all four servers to use the same service account. What should you do?

   a. Create a group and add the servers' computer accounts to it. Run the `New-ADServiceAccount` cmdlet.

   b. Run the `New-ADServiceAccount` cmdlet and configure constrained Kerberos delegation.

   c. Run the `New-gMSAServiceAccount` cmdlet and specify the four servers in the SPN.

   d. Move the four servers' computer accounts to the Managed Service Accounts folder in Active Directory.

19. In your Windows Server 2016 domain, you have a member server also running Windows Server 2016. You want to install the LocSvc service, which will be accessing only local resources. You need to configure authentication for this service but don't want to use one of the built-in service accounts and want to do this with the least administrative effort. What should you do?

   a. Create a local user on the server, and configure the service to log on as that user.

   b. Create an MSA with PowerShell, and configure the service to log on as the MSA.

   c. Create a domain user, and in the Delegation tab, select LocSvc.

   d. Configure the service to log on as NT Service\ LocSvc.

20. You're configuring a web-based intranet application on the WebApp server, which is a domain member. Users authenticate to the web-based application, but the application needs to connect to a back-end database server, BEdata, on behalf of users. What should you configure?

    a. On the WebApp server, create a local user account, and grant it permission to BEdata.

    b. On the BEdata server, assign the Authenticate Users permission to the database files.

    c. On a domain controller, configure constrained delegation on the service account.

    d. Create an MSA on WebApp, and run `Add-ADComputerServiceAccount` with BEdata as the target.

Critical Thinking

The following activities give you critical thinking challenges. Case Projects offer a scenario with a problem to solve and for which you supply a written solution.

Case Project 3-1: Solving a Password Policy Problem

You've been called in to solve a problem for CSM Tech Publishing, which is running Windows Server 2016 servers in a domain environment. Strict account policies that require password changes every 20 days, a password history of 24, complex passwords, and an account lockout threshold of 2 are in place because five high-level managers have access to information about future projects that must be kept secret. The problem is that the support team is constantly fielding calls to unlock accounts and reset passwords because users forget them. Worse, many users have taken to writing their passwords on notes stuck to their desks or monitors. What can you suggest to maintain a strict password policy for the five managers but loosen requirements for the remaining staff? What steps would you take?

Case Project 3-2: Working with Service Accounts

You're installing six new servers as members of a Windows Server 2016 domain. All existing servers are also running Windows Server 2016. Server 1 is running the NetServ1 network service, Server 2 is running the LocServ2 local service, and Servers 3 through 6 are server farms, each running the LBServ service. Security policies forbid using built-in service accounts for configuring authentication on new services. You don't want to have to manage service account passwords, and you want to perform this task with the least administrative effort. Describe what type of service account you should use for each server, and explain your reasons.

CHAPTER 4

CONFIGURING GROUP POLICIES

After reading this chapter and completing the exercises, you will be able to:

Describe the architecture and processing of group policies

Configure group policy settings

Configure group policy security settings

Configure and manage administrative templates

Work with security templates

Configure Group Policy preferences

Group Policy is a powerful tool for network administrators to manage domain controllers, member servers, member computers, and users. It allows administrators to manage most aspects of computer and user environments centrally through Active Directory. An administrator's solid understanding of how to get the most out of group policies can relieve some of the burden of user and computer management. Even more important, designing and applying group policies correctly result in a more secure network.

This chapter covers the architecture of group policies so that you can understand what a Group Policy Object (GPO) is and how and where GPOs can be applied to your Active Directory structure. In addition, you learn about the myriad security settings and user and computer environment settings that can be configured through group policies. You also examine how to apply standard security settings throughout your network and work with Group Policy preferences.

Table 4-1 describes what you need to do the hands-on activities in this chapter.

Table 4-1	Activity requirements	
Activity	**Requirements**	**Notes**
Activity 4-1: Resetting Your Virtual Environment	ServerDC1, ServerDM1, ServerDM2, ServerSA1	
Activity 4-2: Working with Local GPOs	ServerDC1, ServerDM1	
Activity 4-3: Browsing GPTs and GPCs	ServerDC1	
Activity 4-4: Creating, Linking, and Unlinking GPOs	ServerDC1	
Activity 4-5: Configuring and Testing a GPO	ServerDC1, ServerDM1	
Activity 4-6: Creating and Using Starter GPOs	ServerDC1	
Activity 4-7: Deploying a Shutdown Script to a Computer	ServerDC1, ServerDM1	
Activity 4-8: Configuring a Folder Redirection Policy	ServerDC1, ServerDM1	
Activity 4-9: Reviewing User Rights Assignment and Security Options Settings	ServerDC1	
Activity 4-10: Working with Computer Administrative Template Settings	ServerDC1, ServerDM1	
Activity 4-11: Working with User Administrative Template Settings	ServerDC1, ServerDM1	
Activity 4-12: Viewing Policy Settings with Filter Options	ServerDC1	
Activity 4-13: Configuring and Testing Preferences	ServerDC1, ServerDM1	
Activity 4-14: Configuring Item-Level Targeting	ServerDC1, ServerDM1	

Group Policy Objects

 **Certification**

- **70-742 – Create and manage Group Policy:**
  Create and manage Group Policy Objects (GPOs)

The processes of centrally maintaining lists of computer and user settings, replicating these settings to all domain controllers (DCs), and applying these settings to users and computers are complex. The architecture of group policies is equally complex, at least when you're trying to envision the architecture as a whole. When broken down into their constituent parts, however, the architecture is easier to grasp. Group policy architecture and functions involve the following components:

- *GPOs*—A GPO is an object containing policy settings that affect user and computer operating environments and security. GPOs can be local (stored on users' computers), or they can be Active Directory objects linked to sites, domains, and organizational units (OUs).
- *Replication*—Replication of Active Directory–based GPOs ensures that all DCs have a current copy of each GPO. Changes to GPOs can be made on any DC and are replicated to all other DCs.
- *Creating and linking*—GPOs are created in the Group Policy Management console and can then be linked to one or more Active Directory containers. Multiple GPOs can be linked to the same container. This chapter discusses the basics of creating and linking GPOs, and Chapter 5 discusses linking GPOs to different Active Directory containers and managing GPO links.

- *Scope and inheritance*—The scope of a group policy defines which users and computers are affected by its settings. The scope can be a single computer (in the case of a local GPO) or an OU, a domain, or a site. Like permissions, policy settings applied to users and computers are inherited from parent containers, and like permission inheritance, an administrator can override the default behavior of group policy inheritance. Group Policy scope and inheritance is discussed in detail in Chapter 5.

Local and Domain Group Policy Objects

A GPO, the main component of group policies, contains policy settings for managing many aspects of domain controllers, member servers, member computers, and user accounts. There are two main types of GPOs: local GPOs and domain GPOs.

Local GPOs

Local GPOs are stored on local computers and can be edited with the Group Policy Object Editor snap-in (see Figure 4-1). To use this tool, you add the Group Policy Editor snap-in to a custom management console (MMC) or enter `gpedit.msc` at the command line to open an already configured MMC called Local Group Policy Editor. You use one of these tools to manually edit local GPOs on workgroup computers. The policy settings on domain member computers can be affected by domain GPOs linked to the site, domain, or OU in Active Directory. Settings in local GPOs that are inherited from domain GPOs can't be changed on the local computer; only settings that are undefined or not configured by domain GPOs can be edited locally.

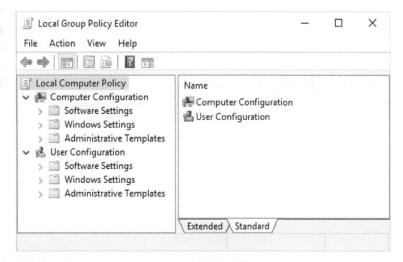

Figure 4-1   The Local Group Policy Editor

When you run `gpedit.msc`, you open a local GPO named Local Computer Policy containing Computer Configuration and User Configuration nodes. When configured on nondomain member computers, the policies defined in this GPO apply by default to all users who sign in to the computer. For example, a computer used in a public environment, such as a kiosk, might have policies that severely restrict what users can do on the computer.

Note

Windows has a preconfigured MMC called Local Security Policy that enables you to edit policies in just the Security Settings node of the local GPO. You access this MMC via Administrative Tools in Control Panel or by entering `secpol.msc` at the command line.

In addition to the Local Computer Policy GPO, there are local GPOs, described in the following list, that allow different policy settings depending on who signs in to the computer. The policies in these GPOs aren't configured, so they have no effect on users until they're configured. In addition, these GPOs have only a User Configuration node, so policies are limited to user-related settings:

- *Local Administrators GPO*—Members of the local Administrators group are affected by settings in this GPO. The default membership includes the local Administrator account and the Domain Admins global group when the computer is a domain member.
- *Local Non-Administrators GPO*—All users, including domain users when the computer is a domain member, who sign in to the computer who aren't members of the local Administrators group are affected by settings in this GPO.
- *User-specific GPO*—A user-specific GPO is created for each account (except Guest) created in the local Security Accounts Manager (SAM) database.

To access these GPOs, first add the Group Policy Object Editor snap-in to an MMC. Instead of accepting the default Local Computer Policy when asked to select a GPO, click Browse to open the dialog box shown in Figure 4-2, click the Users tab, and select one of the GPOs. Local GPOs are intended to be configured on nondomain computers because domain GPOs take precedence over local GPOs, and administration is centralized by using domain GPOs. Configuring the domain-based group policy *Turn off Local Group Policy objects processing* causes member computers to ignore local GPOs. Doing so is a good idea to ensure that all policies are controlled from the domain.

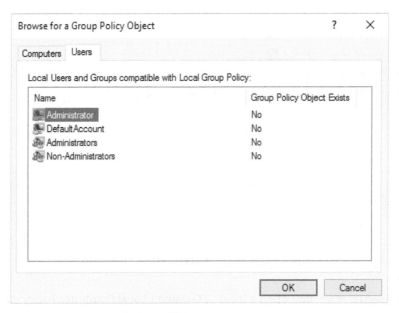

Figure 4-2   Viewing local GPOs

Three of the four local GPOs can contain settings that affect a particular user signing into a Windows computer. The Local Computer Policy object is processed first for all users and is the only local GPO that affects the computer configuration. If configured, the local Administrators or local Non-Administrators GPO is processed next and the user-specific GPO is processed last. Any conflicting settings are resolved in the same order. In other words, the last configured policy setting that's applied takes precedence.

Here's an example: User MSmith has an account on a computer that's not a domain member. The Local Computer Policy is configured to prohibit access to Control Panel, and the Control Panel policy isn't configured in the Non-Administrators GPO. MSmith has a user-specific GPO that enables access to Control Panel. When MSmith signs in, the Local Computer Policy is processed first, which disables access to Control Panel; next, the Non-Administrators policy is processed, which has no effect on the Control

Panel policy because it's not configured. Finally, the user-specific MSmith GPO is processed, which allows Control Panel access, so MSmith has Control Panel access.

Note

Local GPOs (except for the Local Computer Policy) were introduced in Windows Server 2008 and Vista, so they aren't available in Windows XP and earlier.

Domain GPOs

Domain GPOs are stored in Active Directory on domain controllers. They can be linked to a site, a domain, or an OU and affect users and computers whose accounts are stored in these containers. A domain GPO is represented by an Active Directory object, but it's composed of two separate parts: a Group Policy Template (GPT) and a Group Policy Container (GPC). The GPT and GPC have different functions and hold very different information, but they do have these things in common:

- *Naming structure*—Each GPO is assigned a globally unique identifier (GUID), a 128-bit value represented by 32 hexadecimal digits that Windows uses to ensure unique object IDs. The GPT and GPC associated with a GPO are stored in a folder with the same name as the GPO's GUID. This naming structure makes associating each GPO with its GPT and GPC easier.
- *Folder structure*—Each GPT and GPC has two subfolders: Machine and User. The Machine folder stores information related to a GPO's Computer Configuration node, and the User folder stores information about the User Configuration node.

One reason administrators must understand the structure of GPOs is so that they know where to look when problems happen, particularly with replication of GPOs (covered later in this chapter in "Group Policy Replication"). To that end, you examine GPT and GPC components more closely in the following sections.

Group Policy Templates

A **Group Policy Template (GPT)** isn't stored in Active Directory but in a folder in the SYSVOL share on a domain controller. It contains all the policy settings that make up a GPO as well as related files, such as scripts. Every GPO has a GPT associated with it. The local path to GPT folders on a domain controller is *%systemroot%*\SYSVOL\sysvol*domain*\Policies; *%systemroot%* represents the drive letter and folder name where the Windows OS is stored, usually C:\Windows, and *domain* is the domain name. Each GPT is actually a series of folders and files, but the root folder has the name of the GPO's GUID. Figure 4-3 shows the Policies folder with four GPT folders.

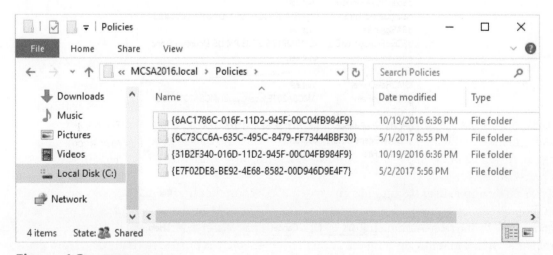

Figure 4-3   GPT folders

The names of GPT folders look random, but two folders have the same name on every domain controller. The folder starting with 6AC1 is the GPT for the Default Domain Controllers Policy, and the folder starting with 31B2 is the 0 GPT for the Default Domain Policy. The other folders are for GPOs created by the administrator.

When a GPO is created, files and subfolders are created under the root folder. The number of files and subfolders in each GPT folder varies depending on which policies have been configured, but each one has at least these three items:

- GPT.ini—This file contains the version number used to determine when a GPO has been modified. Every time a GPO changes, its version number is updated. When GPO replication occurs, DCs use this version number to determine whether the local copy of the GPO is up to date.
- *Machine*—This folder contains subfolders that store policy settings related to the Computer Configuration node.
- *User*—This folder contains subfolders that store policy settings related to the User Configuration node.

A GPO with few policy settings defined or configured has only a few other subfolders and files under the root folder. For example, only a few policies are configured on the Default Domain Controllers GPO, which is in the folder starting with 6AC1. If you browse the Machine folder, you'll likely find only one additional file, GptTmpl.inf. This file contains settings configured in the Security Settings node under Computer Configuration. If you browse the User folder, you won't find any files because no policy settings are configured in the User Configuration node of the Default Domain Controllers GPO.

Group Policy Containers

A **Group Policy Container (GPC)** is an Active Directory object stored in the System\Policies folder and can be viewed in Active Directory Users and Computers with the Advanced Features option enabled. A GPC stores GPO properties and status information but no actual policy settings. Like a GPT, the folder name of each GPC is the same as the GPO's GUID.

A GPC is composed of several attributes you can view in the Attribute Editor tab of its Properties dialog box as shown in Figure 4-4. Although deciphering the purpose of each attribute isn't always easy, some information the GPC provides includes the following:

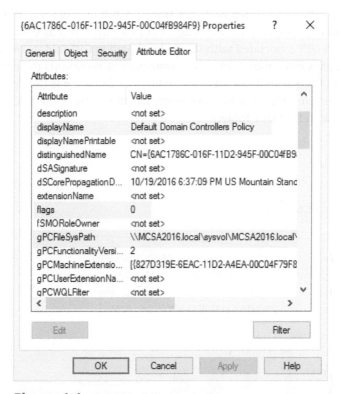

Figure 4-4   Viewing GPC attributes

- *Name of the GPO*—The displayName attribute tells you the name of the GPO with which the GPC is associated.
- *File path to GPT*—The gPCFileSysPath attribute specifies the Universal Naming Convention (UNC) path to the related GPT folder.
- *Version*—The versionNumber attribute (not shown in Figure 4-4) should have the same version number as the GPT.ini file in the GPT folder.
- *Status*—The flags attribute contains a value that indicates the GPO's status. In Figure 4-4, it has the value 0, which indicates that the GPO is enabled. The value 3 means the GPO is disabled.

A GPC might seem less interesting than a GPT, but it's just as important. This Active Directory object links the GPO to Active Directory, which is critical for GPO replication to all domain controllers.

Group Policy Replication

Because the two components of a GPO are stored in different places on a DC, different methods are required to replicate GPOs to all domain controllers. GPCs, which are Active Directory objects, are replicated during normal Active Directory replication. GPTs, which are located in the SYSVOL share, are replicated by using one of these methods:

- *File Replication Service (FRS)*—FRS is used if you have DCs in your domain that are running versions of Windows Server earlier than Windows Server 2008.
- *Distributed File System Replication (DFSR)*—DFSR is used when all DCs are running Windows Server 2008 or later.

Of these two replication methods, DFSR is the more efficient and reliable. It's efficient because it uses an algorithm called remote differential compression (RDC) in which only data blocks that have changed are compressed and transferred across the network. DFSR is more reliable because of improvements in handling unexpected service shutdowns that could corrupt data and because it uses a multimaster replication scheme.

Because GPCs and GPTs use different replication methods, they can become out of sync. As mentioned, GPCs are replicated when Active Directory replication occurs. Between DCs in the same site, this interval is about 15 seconds after a change occurs. Between DCs in different sites, the interval is usually much longer—minutes or even hours. DFSR of the SYSVOL share (and, therefore, the GPT) occurs immediately after a change is made. Strange and unpredictable results could occur when a client computer attempts to apply a GPO when the GPC and GPT aren't synchronized. However, starting with Windows XP, the client computer checks the version number of both components before applying GPO settings.

As long as replication services are running correctly, the most likely problem with GPO replication is a delay in clients receiving changes in policy settings. This problem usually occurs when multiple sites are involved. When you open Group Policy Management Console and click the domain node in the left pane and the Status tab in the right pane, you see a summary of Active Directory and SYSVOL replication. Click Detect Now to gather replication information to see a report similar to the one in Figure 4-5.

Creating and Linking GPOs

Chapter 1 introduced you to the Default Domain Policy and Default Domain Controllers Policy, and in Chapter 3, you worked with account policies, but as you work with Active Directory, you'll need to create additional GPOs, configure settings, and link them to Active Directory containers. As discussed in Chapter 3, creating new GPOs and linking them to containers is recommended instead of editing the default GPOs.

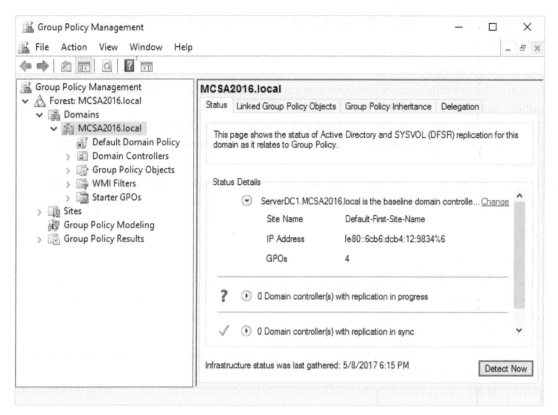

Figure 4-5 Viewing replication status in GPMC

As you have learned, the main tools for managing, creating, and editing GPOs are the Group Policy Management console (GPMC) and the Group Policy Management Editor (GPME), both of which you used in earlier chapters. The purpose of using these tools is to carry out changes to the security and/or working environment for users or computers. There are several ways to go about this task:

- Edit an existing GPO that's linked to an Active Directory container.
- Link an existing GPO to an Active Directory container.
- Create a new GPO for an Active Directory container.
- Create a new GPO in the Group Policy Objects folder, which isn't linked to an Active Directory object.
- Create a new GPO by using a Starter GPO.

If you edit an existing GPO that's already linked to an Active Directory container, keep in mind that changes in policy settings take effect as soon as client computers download them. In other words, there's no Save option in the GPME; changes are saved immediately. By default, computer policies download GPOs when the computer is started, and user policies are downloaded at the next logon. Therefore, the best practice is usually creating GPOs in the Group Policy Objects folder, and then linking them to the target Active Directory container after all changes have been made and tested. When you're changing several policy settings at once or are unsure of the effect policy changes will have, you should test policies before enabling them by using the following method:

1. Set up at least one test computer per OS used in the organization.
2. Join test computers to the domain and place their accounts in a test OU.
3. Create one or more test user accounts in the test OU.
4. Create the new GPO in the Group Policy Objects folder and set the policies you want.
5. Link the GPO to the test OU.
6. Restart and sign in to the test computers with the test user accounts to observe the policy effects.

7. Make changes to the GPO, if necessary, and repeat Step 6 until the policy has the desired effect.

8. Unlink the policy from the test OU, and link it to the target Active Directory container.

Editing an Existing GPO

To edit an existing GPO, right-click it in the GPMC and click Edit, which opens the GPO in the GPME. In the GPMC, all GPOs are stored in the Group Policy Objects folder, and you can also find GPOs linked to an Active Directory container displayed as shortcut objects in the container to which they're linked. Checking whether and where a GPO is linked is a good idea before editing. To do this, select the GPO in the left pane of the GPMC and view the Scope tab in the right pane (see Figure 4-6). All Active Directory objects the GPO is linked to are listed for the selected location. In this figure, the domain is selected as the location, and you can also select Entire forest or All sites in the Display links in this location list box.

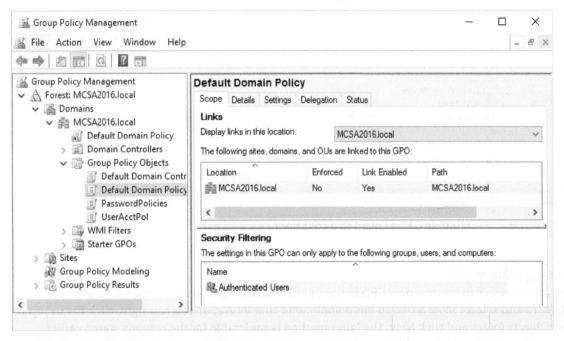

Figure 4-6   The Scope tab for a GPO

As mentioned, editing the two default GPOs is not advisable. One reason is that you can't test the GPO adequately because it's already linked to the domain or the Domain Controllers OU. Another reason is that you might want to revert to the default settings, and you could have difficulty determining what was changed. The recommended method for making changes to domain policies is creating a new GPO and linking it to the domain. Remember: you can have multiple GPOs linked to the same container. The steps for making policy changes that affect the whole domain are as follows, assuming you already have the test computers, users, and OU set up as described previously:

1. Create the new GPO in the Group Policy Objects folder, and set the policies you want.

2. Link the GPO to the test OU, making sure to unlink any GPOs that are linked there from previous tests.

3. Test your policies by restarting and signing in to the test computers with the test user accounts to observe the policy effects.

4. Make changes to the GPO, if necessary, and repeat testing until the policy has the effect you want.

5. Unlink the policy from the test OU, and link it to the domain.

You might wonder how this procedure tests domainwide settings. Because a GPO can be linked to multiple containers, you could have linked the Default Domain Policy to the test OU as well. However, by default, policy settings are inherited by child objects, so settings in the Default Domain Policy affect objects in all Active Directory containers in the domain, including containers with another GPO linked. If you have two or more GPOs linked to the domain, as in Figure 4-7, GPOs are applied to objects in reverse of the specified link order. In this example, the TestGPO policy is applied, and then the Default Domain Policy is applied. If any settings conflict, the last setting applied takes precedence. GPO processing and inheritance are discussed in Chapter 5.

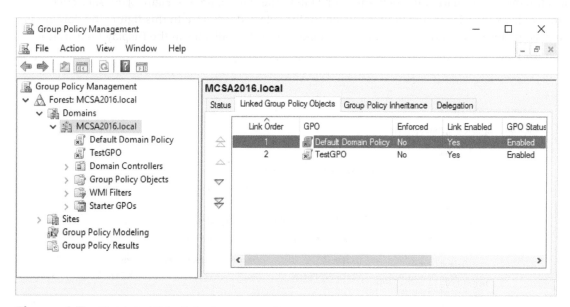

Figure 4-7   Multiple GPOs linked to a container

Creating a New GPO

There are two ways to create a new GPO in the GPMC. You can right-click the container you're linking the GPO to and select *Create a GPO in this domain, and Link it here*, or you can right-click the Group Policy Objects folder and click New. The latter method is preferable for the reasons stated earlier. After creating a GPO, you can edit it and link it to an Active Directory container, if necessary. Because several GPOs can be linked to the same container, the best practice is to create GPOs that set policies narrowly focused on a category of settings and then name the GPO accordingly. For example, if you need to configure policy settings related to the Network node under Computer Configuration, create a GPO named CompNetwork. If this policy will apply only to a certain container, you could include the container name in the GPO name—for example, CompNetwork-TestGPO. Creating and naming GPOs in this manner make it easier to identify the GPO that sets a particular policy and to troubleshoot GPO processing problems.

Using Starter GPOs

A **Starter GPO** is a GPO template, for lack of a better word, and is not to be confused with the GPTs discussed earlier. An administrator creates a Starter GPO to be used as a baseline for new GPOs, much like the user account templates discussed in Chapter 2.

When you create a GPO, the New GPO Wizard includes an option to use a Starter GPO. Starter GPOs are stored in the Starter GPOs folder in GPMC. As discussed, creating GPOs that focus on a narrow category of settings is a best practice. Starter GPOs can be used to specify a baseline for certain setting categories and then modified when the Starter GPO is used to create the new GPO.

To use a Starter GPO to create a new GPO, select one in the Source Starter GPO list box in the New GPO Wizard, or right-click a Starter GPO in the Starter GPOs folder and click New GPO From Starter GPO. To create a Starter GPO, right-click the Starter GPOs folder and click New. After creating a Starter GPO, you can edit it just like any GPO. However, Starter GPOs don't contain all the nodes of a regular GPO; only the Administrative Templates folder in both Computer Configuration and User Configuration is included.

Starter GPOs can be useful for making sure your policies are consistent throughout the domain by defining a baseline for group policy setting categories. You can change the baseline settings as needed in the GPO created from the Starter GPO. However, after a new GPO is created from a Starter GPO, changes to the Starter GPO aren't propagated to existing GPOs created from it.

Starter GPOs can also be shared with other administrators by placing them in cabinet (CAB) files. If you click the Starter GPOs folder in GPMC (see Figure 4-8), all Starter GPOs are listed in the right pane. You can use the Load Cabinet and Save as Cabinet buttons to load a Starter GPO from a CAB file or save a Starter GPO as a CAB file. The two Starter GPOs you see in Figure 4-8 come pre-installed on Windows Server 2016.

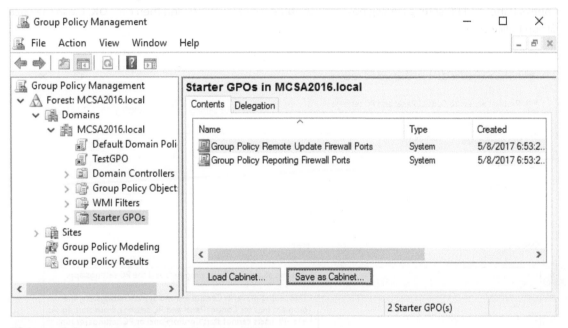

Figure 4-8   Saving Starter GPOs as CAB files

Activity 4-1: Resetting Your Virtual Environment

Time Required: 5 minutes
Objective: Reset your virtual environment by applying the InitialConfig checkpoint or snapshot.
Required Tools and Equipment: ServerDC1, ServerDM1, ServerDM2, ServerSA1
Description: Apply the InitialConfig checkpoint or snapshot to ServerDC1, ServerDM1, ServerDM2, and ServerSA1.

1. Be sure the servers are shut down. In your virtualization program, apply the InitialConfig checkpoint or snapshot to ServerDC1, ServerDM1, ServerDM2, and ServerSA1.
2. When the snapshot or checkpoint has finished being applied, continue to the next activity.

Activity 4-2: Working with Local GPOs

Time Required: 20 minutes

Objective: Configure local GPOs.

Required Tools and Equipment: ServerDC1, ServerDM1

Description: In this activity, you sign in to ServerDM1 with the *local* Administrator account, configure some local GPOs, and create a local user account. Then you see how local GPOs can affect different users.

1. Sign in to **ServerDM1** with the adminuser1 account. To do so, on the sign in screen, click **Other user**, and then type **serverdm1\adminuser1** in the User name box and **Password01** in the Password box. You must specify that you are signing in to the local computer instead of the domain by prefacing the user name with the name of the computer unless you are signing in as Administrator.

2. Right-click **Start** and click **Control Panel** to verify you have access to it, and then close Control Panel. Right-click **Start**, click **Run**, type **gpedit.msc** in the Open text box, and press **Enter** to open the Local Group Policy Editor for the Local Computer Policy GPO.

3. Click to expand **User Configuration, Administrative Templates**, and then click the **Control Panel** node.

4. In the right pane, double-click **Prohibit access to Control Panel and PC settings**. In the Prohibit access to Control Panel and PC settings dialog box, click **Enabled** (see Figure 4-9) and then click **OK**. Close the Local Group Policy Editor.

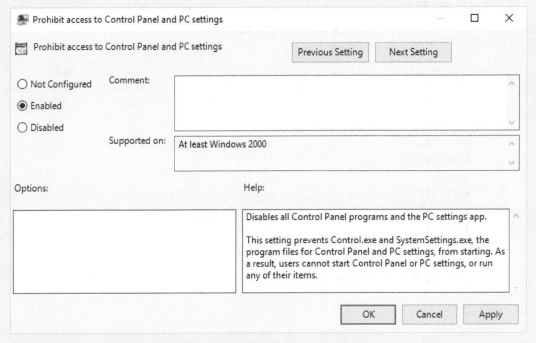

Figure 4-9 Prohibit access to Control Panel

5. Right-click **Start** and click **Control Panel**. You see a message indicating that the action has been canceled because of restrictions in effect on the computer so click **OK**. Close Local Group Policy Editor.

6. Right-click **Start**, click **Run**, type **mmc** in the Open text box, and press **Enter**.

7. In the MMC window, click **File**, **Add/Remove Snap-in** from the menu. In the Available snap-ins list box, click **Group Policy Object Editor**, and then click **Add**. The Group Policy Wizard starts.

8. In the Select Group Policy Object window, click **Browse**. In the Browse for a Group Policy Object dialog box, click the **Users** tab. Click **Administrators** (make sure you click the Administrators group, not the Administrator user account), and then click **OK**. Click **Finish** and then **OK**.

9. Click to expand **Local Computer\Administrators Policy**. Click to expand **User Configuration** and **Administrative Templates**, and then click the **Control Panel** node. (*Hint*: You might want to click the Standard tab at the bottom so that you can see the policy setting descriptions better.)

10. In the right pane, double-click **Prohibit access to Control Panel and PC settings**. In the dialog box for configuring the policy, click **Disabled**, and then click **OK**. Close the MMC window and click No when prompted to save the console settings.

11. Right-click **Start** and click **Control Panel**, which opens. The Administrators local GPO overrode the Local Computer Policy (because you're signed in as adminuser1, which is a member of the Administrators group). Close Control Panel.

12. Sign out of ServerDM1 and sign back in as **reguser1** with **Password01**. Be sure to enter the user name as **serverdm1\reguser1** so that Windows knows you're signing in to the local computer.

13. Right-click **Start** and click **Control Panel**. You see the same message as you did in Step 5. Click **OK**. Because reguser1 isn't an administrator and doesn't have a user-specific GPO configured, the default Local Computer Policy, which prohibits access to Control Panel, takes effect.

14. Sign out of ServerDM1, and sign in to the domain as **domuser1** using password **Password01**.

15. Right-click **Start** and click **Control Panel**. You see the same message as you did in Steps 5 and 13; it demonstrates that the Local Computer Policy affects domain users as well as local users. The only local GPO that doesn't affect domain users is the user-specific GPO. Click **OK**.

16. Sign out and sign in to ServerDM1 as **adminuser1**. (Remember to sign in as ServerDM1\adminuser1.) Open the Group Policy Object Editor for the Local Computer Policy (gpedit.msc). Change the Prohibit access to the Control Panel policy back to **Not Configured**, and then click **OK**. Close the Local Group Policy Editor. Sign out of ServerDM1.

17. Continue to the next activity.

Activity 4-3: Browsing GPTs and GPCs

Time Required: 15 minutes
Objective: Browse subfolders and files in a GPT folder.
Required Tools and Equipment: ServerDC1
Description: In this activity, you explore the folders where the GPT component of GPOs is located and then you investigate the GPC component in Active Directory.

1. On ServerDC1, open File Explorer, and navigate to **C:\Windows\SYSVOL\sysvol\MCSA2016.local\Policies**, where you should see a list of folders similar to those in Figure 4-3 shown previously.

2. Double-click the folder starting with **6AC1**, which is the Default Domain Controllers Policy GPT. Double-click the **GPT.ini** file to open it in Notepad. Notice the version number, which changes each time the GPO is modified. Exit Notepad.

3. Click to expand the **MACHINE\Microsoft\Windows NT\SecEdit** folder, and double-click the **GptTmpl.inf** file to open it in Notepad. Knowing the details of what's in this and other GPT files isn't important; you just need to know that they exist and how to find them. Exit Notepad.

4. Open Active Directory Users and Computers. Click **View** on the menu bar and click **Advanced Features** to enable the advanced features option for Active Directory Users and Computers. You'll see a few more folders.

5. Click to expand the **System** folder and then click the **Policies** folder to see the list of GPC folders shown in Figure 4-10.

6. In the right pane, right-click the GPC folder associated with the Default Domain Controllers GPO (the one that starts with **6AC1**) and click **Properties**. In the Properties dialog box, click the **Attribute Editor** tab. Scroll down to view some attributes of the GPC; attributes are listed in alphabetical order. Although you can edit attributes here, it isn't recommended unless you're sure of the results.

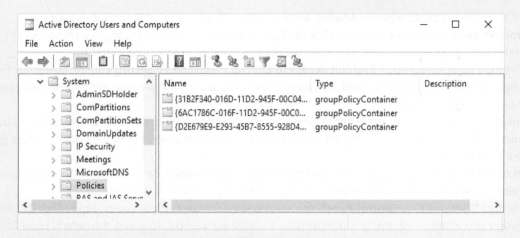

Figure 4-10 GPC folders in Active Directory

7. Find the **versionNumber** attribute. It should have the same value you noted for the `GPT.ini` file in Step 2.
8. Find the **flags** attribute. Its value should be 0, indicating that the GPO is enabled. Click **Cancel**.
9. Open the Group Policy Management console from the **Tools** menu in Server Manager. In the left pane, navigate to the **Group Policy Objects folder**. Right-click the **Group Policy Objects** folder and click **New**.
10. In the New GPO dialog box, type **TestGPO** in the Name box and click **OK**.
11. Click **TestGPO** in the left pane, and in the right pane, click the **Details** tab.
12. Click the **GPO Status** list arrow, click **All settings disabled** (see Figure 4-11), and then click **OK**.

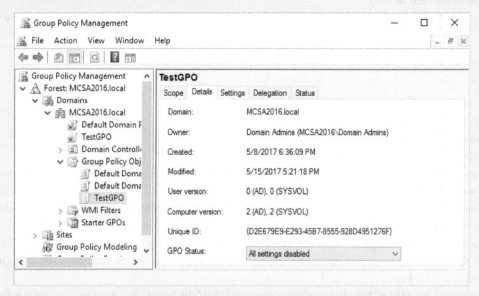

Figure 4-11 The Details tab for a GPO

In Active Directory Users and Computers, click the **Refresh** icon to see that a new folder has been added under Policies. Open the Properties dialog box of the GPC folder associated with TestGPO (the folder that does *not* start with 6AC1 or 31B2). Click the **Attribute Editor** tab and then view the value of the flags attribute. It's 3, indicating that the GPO is disabled.
13. Click the **flags** attribute and click the Edit button. Type **0**, and then click **OK** twice. Close Active Directory Users and Computers.
14. In the Group Policy Management console, click the **Refresh** icon. The GPO status changes to Enabled because you changed the flag's attribute to 0. Close the Group Policy Management console.
15. Continue to the next activity.

Activity 4-4: Creating, Linking, and Unlinking GPOs

Time Required: 15 minutes
Objective: Create, link, and unlink GPOs.
Required Tools and Equipment: ServerDC1
Description: In this activity, you create an OU and GPO and work with GPO links.

1. On ServerDC1, open Active Directory Users and Computers, and create an OU named **TestOU1** under the domain node.
2. Open the Group Policy Management console. Right-click **TestOU1** and click **Create a GPO in this domain, and Link it here**. In the New GPO dialog box, type **GPO1** in the Name text box, and then click **OK**.
3. In the right pane, notice that GPO1 is listed as Enabled. Changes you make to GPO1 affect any user or computer accounts that might be in TestOU1. Right-click **GPO1** and click **Delete**. Click **OK**. This action deletes only the link to the GPO, not the GPO itself.
4. Click the **Group Policy Objects** folder to see all your GPOs, including the default GPOs.
5. Right-click **GPO1** and point to **GPO Status**. You can enable or disable a GPO or just disable the Computer Configuration or User Configuration settings.
6. Right-click the **TestOU1** OU and click **Link an Existing GPO**. In the Select GPO dialog box, click **GPO1**, and then click **OK**.
7. To link another GPO to test **TestOU1**, right-click **TestOU1** and click **Link an Existing GPO**. Click **TestGPO** and then click **OK**.
8. Click **TestOU1**. Notice that both GPO1 and TestGPO are linked to TestOU1. If both GPOs had the same policy setting configured but with different values, the value of the policy setting in GPO1 would take precedence because it would be applied last.
9. Click **TestGPO** in the right pane and click the **up arrow** to the left of the Link Order column. TestGPO now has link order 1, and GPO1 has link order 2, so TestGPO takes precedence if any settings conflict.
10. Right-click **TestGPO** and click **Delete**. Click **OK** in the message box asking you to confirm the deletion. Next, right-click **GPO1** and click **Delete**, and then click **OK**. No policies should be linked to TestOU1 now.
11. Continue to the next activity.

Activity 4-5: Configuring and Testing a GPO

Time Required: 25 minutes
Objective: Configure and test a GPO.
Required Tools and Equipment: ServerDC1 and ServerDM1
Description: In this activity, you move the ServerDM1 computer account to TestOU1 and test some computer settings by configuring GPO1.

1. Start ServerDM1. On ServerDC1, open Active Directory Users and Computers, if necessary.
2. Click the **Computers** folder, and drag the **ServerDM1** computer account to the **TestOU1** OU. If necessary, click **Yes** in the warning message about moving Active Directory objects.
3. Open the Group Policy Management console, if necessary. Right-click **TestOU1** and click **Link an Existing GPO**. Click **GPO1** and then click **OK**. Right-click **GPO1** and click **Edit** to open it in the Group Policy Management Editor.
4. Click to expand **Computer Configuration, Policies, Windows Settings, Security Settings**, and **Local Policies**, and then click **User Rights Assignment**.
5. In the right pane, double-click **Allow log on locally** to open its Properties dialog box. Notice that the policy setting is currently not defined. Click the **Define these policy settings** check box, and then click **Add User or Group**. In the Add User or Group dialog box, click **Browse**. Type **Administrators** in the *Enter the object names to select* text box and click **Check Names**. Click **OK** three times.

6. On ServerDM1, sign in to the domain as **Administrator**. To update the policies on ServerDM1, open a command prompt and type **gpupdate** and press **Enter**. Close the command prompt.

> **Tip** ⓘ
>
> In this chapter's activities, if `gpupdate.exe` doesn't seem to update policies on the local computer, try using `gpupdate /force`, which reapplies all policy settings, even those that haven't changed.

7. Right-click **Start**, click **Run**, type **secpol.msc** in the Open dialog box, and press **Enter** to open the Local Security Policy console. The Local Security Policy console contains only the security settings for the local computer.

8. Click to expand **Local Policies**, and then click **User Rights Assignment**. Notice in Figure 4-12 that the icon next to the *Allow log on locally* policy looks like two towers and a scroll instead of the torn-paper icon next to the other policies. This icon indicates that the policy is defined by a domain GPO.

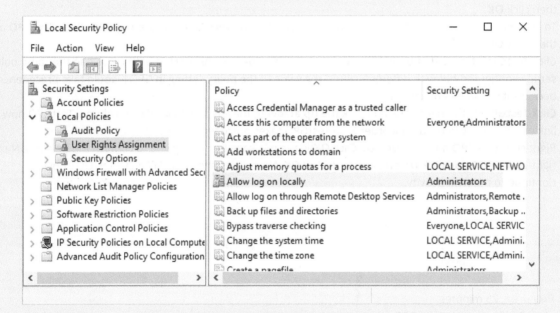

Figure 4-12   The Local Security Policy MMC with a policy set by a domain GPO

9. In the right pane, double-click **Allow log on locally**. In the list box of users and groups, click **Administrators**. Neither the Add User or Group nor the Remove button is active because no users, not even administrators, can override domain polices on the local computer. Click **Cancel**.

10. Sign out of ServerDM1, and then try to sign back in as **domuser1** using **Password01**. Because you have restricted local logon to Administrators only, you'll see the following message: "The sign-in method you're trying to use isn't allowed. For more info, contact your network administrator." The sign-in method referred to in the message is interactive logon or local logon. Click **OK**.

11. On ServerDC1, change the **Allow log on locally** policy on GPO1 to Not Defined by clearing the **Define these policy settings** check box, and then click **OK**. Close the Group Policy Management Editor.

12. On ServerDM1, try again to sign in as **domuser1**. You'll probably get the same message about not being able to sign in because the policy hasn't been updated yet. Click **OK**. Sign in as administrator, run **gpupdate** at a command prompt, and sign out again.

13. Sign in to ServerDM1 as **domuser1**. Only an administrator can run the Local Security Policy MMC, but there's a workaround if you start it from an elevated command prompt. Right-click **Start** and click **Command Prompt (Admin)**. When prompted, type the Administrator account credentials and click **Yes**.

14. At the command prompt, type **secpol.msc** and press **Enter**.

15. In the Local Security Policy console, click to expand **Local Policies** and **User Rights Assignment**. In the right pane, double-click **Allow log on locally** to view the list of users and groups assigned this permission. Notice that this right is now assigned from a local GPO rather than a domain GPO, so you can make changes if needed. Click **Cancel**.

16. On ServerDC1, from the Group Policy Management console, unlink GPO1 from TestOU1 by right-clicking **GPO1** under TestOU1 and clicking **Delete**. Click **OK**.

17. Sign out of ServerDM1. Continue to the next activity.

Activity 4-6: Creating and Using Starter GPOs

Time Required: 20 minutes

Objective: Create Starter GPOs to be used to create new GPOs.

Required Tools and Equipment: ServerDC1

Description: In this activity, you create some Starter GPOs for creating new GPOs. You create two: one in the Computer Configuration node for configuring printers and one in the User Configuration node for configuring Start menu options.

1. On ServerDC1, open the Group Policy Management console. Right-click the **Starter GPOs** folder and click **New**.

2. In the New Starter GPO dialog box, type **StartPrintersC** in the Name text box. (*Start* stands for Starter GPO, *Printers* refers to the Printers node, and *C* refers to the Computer Configuration node of the GPO.) In the Comment text box, type **Starter GPO for the Printers node of Computer Configuration**, and then click **OK**.

3. Right-click the **StartPrintersC** GPO and click **Edit**. In the Group Policy Starter GPO Editor, click to expand **Computer Configuration** and **Administrative Templates**, and then click **Printers**.

4. In the right pane, double-click **Automatically publish new printers in Active Directory**. In the Properties dialog box, click **Enabled**. Read the explanation of this policy setting, and then click **OK**.

5. Double-click **Always render print jobs on the server**. In the Properties dialog box, click **Enabled**. Read the explanation of this policy setting, and then click **OK**.

 Tip

> To list the policy settings in alphabetical order so you can find them easier, click the Setting column header in Group Policy Management Editor.

6. Close the Group Policy Starter GPO Editor. In the Group Policy Management console, right-click the **Group Policy Objects** folder and click **New**. In the New GPO dialog box, type **PrintConfigGPO** in the Name text box, click **StartPrintersC** in the Source Starter GPO list box, and then click **OK**.

7. Right-click **PrintConfigGPO** and click **Edit**. In the Group Policy Management Editor, expand and navigate to the **Computer Configuration, Policies, Administrative Templates, Printers** to verify that your Starter GPO settings are there. Now you can link this new GPO to a container with computer accounts that have print servers installed, and the printer policies will be in effect on these servers. Close the Group Policy Management Editor.

8. To see the other method of using Starter GPOs to create new GPOs, click the **Starter GPOs** folder in the Group Policy Management console. Right-click **StartPrintersC** and click **New GPO From Starter GPO**. The New GPO Wizard starts. Click **Cancel**.

9. Create another Starter GPO named **StartU**, which is used as a baseline for Start screen options in a later activity.

10. Right-click the **StartU** GPO and click **Edit**. In the Group Policy Management Editor, click to expand **User Configuration** and **Administrative Templates**, and then click **Start Menu and Taskbar**.

11. Configure the following policies as shown:
    - Lock the Taskbar: **Enabled**
    - Remove the networking icon: **Enabled**

12. Continue to the next activity.

Group Policy Settings

- **70-742 – Create and manage Group Policy:**
  Configure Group Policy settings

As you have learned, GPOs have a Computer Configuration node that affects all computer accounts in a GPO's scope and a User Configuration node that affects all user accounts in a GPO's scope. Computer Configuration policies are downloaded by a computer when the OS starts, and User Configuration policies are downloaded when a user signs in to a domain. All policies are updated every 90 minutes thereafter. Although many policies take effect when the GPO is updated, some might require a computer restart. Most policies in these two nodes affect different aspects of the working environment, but a few policies are the same. If the same policy is configured in both nodes and the settings conflict (for example, one disables a policy and the other enables it), the setting in Computer Configuration takes precedence.

Both nodes have a Policies folder and a Preferences folder. Under the Policies folder are these three folders: Software Settings, Windows Settings, and Administrative Templates. The Software Settings and Windows Settings folders include items called extensions because they extend the functionality of Group Policy beyond what was available in Windows 2000. The Administrative Templates folder contains categorized folders or nodes with settings that affect users' or computers' working environments, mainly by changing Registry settings.

Policy settings can be managed or unmanaged. A **managed policy setting** is applied to a user or computer when the object is in the scope of the GPO containing the setting. When the object is no longer in the GPO's scope or the policy is set to Not configured, however, the setting on the user or computer reverts to its original state. An **unmanaged policy setting** is persistent, meaning that it remains even after the computer or user object falls out of the GPO's scope until it is changed by another policy or manually. The policies already loaded in Active Directory are managed policies, but you can customize Group Policy by adding your own policies, which are unmanaged.

You learned about user account policies in Chapter 3. Administrative Templates are discussed later in "Working with Administrative Templates." The following sections focus on these categories of settings:

- *Software installation*—In the Software Settings folder under both the Computer Configuration and User Configuration nodes.
- *Scripts*—In the Windows Settings folder under both the Computer Configuration and User Configuration nodes.
- *Folder redirection*—In the Windows Settings folder under the User Configuration node.

Software Installation Policies

The Software installation extension (see Figure 4-13) is used to install software packages remotely on member computers. If it's configured under the Computer Configuration node, the software package is installed regardless of who signs in to the targeted computers. When it's configured under User Configuration, the software package is available to targeted users when they sign into any domain computer.

Applications are deployed with the Windows Installer service, which uses installation packages called *MSI files*. A **Microsoft Software Installation (MSI) file** is a collection of files gathered into a package with an `.msi` extension that contains the instructions that Windows Installer needs to install an application.

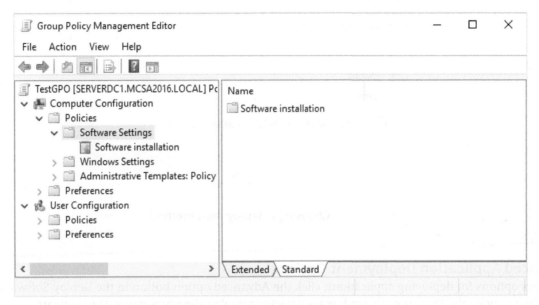

Figure 4-13   The Software installation extension

 Note

You might want to install a software package that's available only as an executable (`.exe`) file. Depending on the software developer, an `.exe` file might contain an MSI file that you can extract with the command `filename.exe /extract` (replacing `filename` with the `.exe` file's name). If that's not possible, you might need to convert the `.exe` to an MSI file. Although there's no Windows utility for this purpose, third-party programs, such as Advanced Installer (*www.advancedinstaller.com*) and Exe to MSI Converter Pro (*www.exetomsi.com*), are available.

Configuring Software Installation for Computers

In the Computer Configuration node, software packages are assigned to target computers, meaning that installation of the software is mandatory and assigned packages are installed the next time the computer starts. To assign a software package to a computer, you must create a shared folder on a server that gives the computer the Read & execute permission. Typically, you do this by assigning the necessary permissions to the Authenticated Users special identity group. If you're deploying several applications through Group Policy, you can create a separate folder in the share for each package.

After creating the shared folder and copying the installation package to it, you can create the deployment policy by using the Software installation extension. To do so, follow these steps from the Group Policy Management Editor:

1. Right-click Software installation, point to New and click Package.

2. Browse to and select the application installation file using the UNC path of the shared folder.

3. Select the deployment method (see Figure 4-14). If you choose Assigned, the application will be deployed the next time any computer in the scope of the policy restarts. If you choose Advanced, you can choose additional deployment options as discussed in the following section.

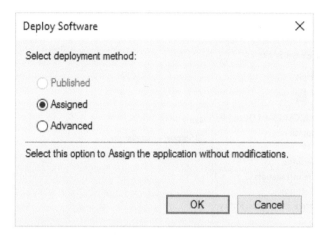

Figure 4-14   Choosing a deployment method

Advanced Application Deployment Options

To access options for deploying applications, click the Advanced option button in the Deploy Software dialog box or open the Properties dialog box for a package you've already added to the Software installation node. The Properties dialog box has several tabs with options for changing how the application is deployed:

- *General*—This tab contains information about a package, including the name, version, language, publisher, and hardware platform. You can change the package name here.
- *Deployment*—You can select whether a package is published or assigned. In the Computer Configuration node, software packages can only be assigned, so the Published option is disabled (see Figure 4-15). The Deployment type selection determines what's available in the Deployment options section, including when and how an application is deployed. For example, an application can be installed at user logon or when a document used by the application is opened. Another deployment option uninstalls the application automatically if the user or computer falls out of the GPO's scope. In the Computer Configuration node, the only two deployment options are Auto-install and Uninstall. At the bottom of this tab, you can choose user interface options (Basic or Maximum), but this option is available only in the User Configuration node. Clicking the Advanced button shows options for ignoring the language when deploying the package and making a 32-bit application available on 64-bit machines (enabled by default).
- *Upgrades*—You can deploy a package upgrade by specifying which existing packages should be upgraded by the new package and which packages can upgrade the current package.
- *Categories*—You use this tab to associate a published package with a category. Control Panel's Programs applet lists available applications under the specified categories. This option is used only for packages published in the User Configuration node.

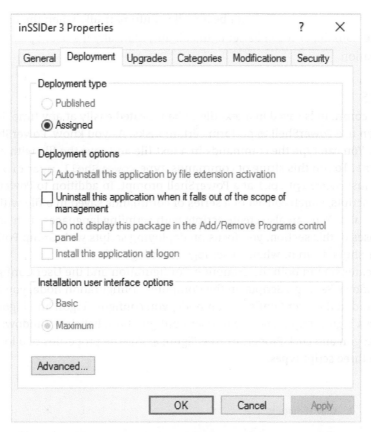

Figure 4-15   Settings for installing a software package

- *Modifications*—You can use this tab to customize a package installation by using a transform file (`.mst` extension). Select transform files for customizing the installation of an MSI file. A transform file contains information about features and components that can be used to customize an application installation. For example, if you're installing Microsoft Office, you can use the Office Resource Kit to create a transform file that overrides the default installation path or specifies which Office components should be installed.
- *Security*—A standard permissions dialog box for the package object. By default, Authenticated Users have Read permission, and Domain Admins have Full control.

After a package is deployed to a computer, by default it's not installed again. However, if changes have been made to the original package, right-click the package in the Software installation extension, click All Tasks, and then click Redeploy application. This action re-installs the package on target computers. To remove a deployed package, right-click the package, click All Tasks, and then click Remove. You have the option to uninstall the software immediately or simply prevent new installations yet allow users to use already deployed packages.

Configuring Software Installation for Users

The Software installation extension performs the same function in the User Configuration node as in the Computer Configuration node—deploying software to remote destinations—but has important differences in options and execution. A software package can be assigned only to a computer, but there are two options for deploying software to users:

- *Published*—A **published application** isn't installed automatically; instead, a link to install the application is available in Control Panel's Programs and Features by clicking the *Install a program from the network* link. Published applications can also be configured to install when the user opens a file type associated with the application.

- *Assigned*—An **assigned application** can be installed automatically when the user logs on to a computer in the domain, or it can be set to install automatically if a user opens a file associated with the application.

Deploying Scripts

A **script** is a series of commands saved in a text file to be repeated easily at any time. For example, suppose that you often use PowerShell to perform certain tasks. As you know, PowerShell commands can be long and complex. You can type the commands in a text file and save the file with a `.ps1` extension, such as `myscript.ps1`. To run this string of commands, type `PowerShell myscript.ps1` at a command prompt or just `myscript.ps1` at a PowerShell prompt. In addition to PowerShell scripts, you can create command scripts, which consist of a series of commands saved in a file with a `.bat` extension, also known as a **batch file**. You can also create scripts with scripting languages such as VBScript and JScript. For the purposes of this section, you focus on deploying scripts with Group Policy that run when a computer starts up or shuts down or when a user logs on or logs off.

There's a Scripts extension in both the Computer Configuration and the User Configuration nodes in the path Policies, Windows Settings, Scripts. In the Computer Configuration node, you configure startup or shutdown scripts and in the User Configuration node, you configure logon and logoff scripts. For example, to configure a logon script, navigate to User Configuration, Policies, Windows Settings, Scripts, and then right-click Logon and click Properties (see Figure 4-16). The properties of a logon script are the same as for the other three script types.

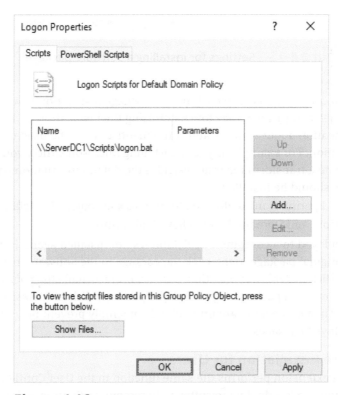

Figure 4-16 The properties of a logon script

This dialog box has two tabs:

- *Scripts*—This tab is used for command scripts (batch files) and scripts that can be run by Windows Scripting Host (WSH). WSH is used to run VBScript and JScript files.
- *PowerShell Scripts*—To run PowerShell scripts, the target computer must be running Windows 7 or later.

To add a script in the Scripts or PowerShell Scripts tabs, click the Add button. You can type the UNC path to a share where the script file is located or click Browse to search for the file. By default, Windows looks in the SYSVOL share on the DC in the folder containing the GPO where you're creating the script. The advantage of using the SYSVOL share is that scripts are replicated automatically and can be retrieved by clients from a DC in the domain. If you use a regular shared folder, the server hosting the share must always be available, and the script might have to run across a WAN link if the server is in a remote site.

If you want to store scripts in the SYSVOL folder with your GPO, you need the GUID of the GPO to locate the correct folder. You can find the GUID by looking in the System\Policies folder in Active Directory Users and Computers.

Folder Redirection

Folder redirection enables an administrator to set policies that redirect folders in a user's profile directory. This feature is useful when you want users to store documents on a server for centralized backup, but you don't want to change the way they access their document folders. It's also quite useful when roaming profiles are used because it decreases the network bandwidth needed to upload and download a user's roaming profile.

Folder redirection applies strictly to user accounts and is found only under the User Configuration node in Policies, Windows Settings, Folder Redirection. There are 13 folders you can redirect as shown in Figure 4-17.

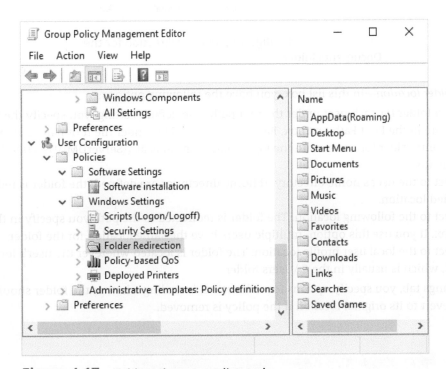

Figure 4-17 Folders that can redirected

To redirect a folder, right-click it in the Folder Redirection node and click Properties. In the Target tab of a folder's Properties dialog box, you have the following options (see Figure 4-18):

- *Setting*—In this list box, you have the following options:
  - Not configured: This default option means that folder redirection isn't enabled for the folder.
  - Basic: Redirect everyone's folder to the same location: This option redirects the selected folder to the same location for all user accounts in the GPO's scope.
  - Advanced: Specify locations for various user groups: With this option, you can redirect folders to different locations based on group membership.

Figure 4-18 Configuring folder redirection for the Documents folder

- *Target folder location*—In this list box, you have the following options:
  - Create a folder for each user under the root path: The default setting; you specify the UNC path to a share in the Root Path text box. Each user has a folder under the root path. For example, the Documents folder for a user with the logon name jsmith is at \\ServerDM1\UserDocs\jsmith\ Documents.
  - Redirect to the user's home directory: If home directories are defined, the folder is redirected to the specified location.
  - Redirect to the following location: The folder is redirected to the path you specify in the Root Path text box. If you use this option, multiple users have the same location for the folder.
  - Redirect to the local user profile location: The folder is located wherever the user's local profile is stored, which is usually in the C:\Users folder.

In the Settings tab, you specify options for redirection, including whether the folder should remain redirected or revert to its original location if the policy is removed.

Activity 4-7: Deploying a Shutdown Script to a Computer

Time Required: 15 minutes
Objective: Create and deploy a shutdown script.
Required Tools and Equipment: ServerDC1, ServerDM1
Description: In this activity, you write a shutdown script that deletes all files with a `.temp` extension, and deploy this script using group policies.

1. On ServerDC1, start Notepad and type **del /F /S c:*.temp**. The `/F` option forces the deletion of read-only files, and the `/S` option deletes the file in the current directory and all subdirectories.
2. Click **File, Save As** from the menu. Choose the desktop as the location for saving your file. In the Save as type list box, click **All Files (*.*)**. Type **deltemp.bat** in the File name text box and click **Save**. Exit Notepad.

3. Right-click **deltemp.bat** on your desktop and click **Copy**. (You paste the script into the SYSVOL share in a later step.)

4. Open the Group Policy Management console. Click the **Group Policy Objects** folder and create a GPO named **Scripts**.

5. Right-click the **Scripts** GPO and click **Edit.** In the Group Policy Management Editor, click to expand **Computer Configuration, Policies,** and **Windows Settings,** and then click **Scripts (Startup/Shutdown).** Right-click **Shutdown** in the right pane and click **Properties**. In the Shutdown Properties dialog box, click **Show Files**. In the File Explorer window that opens, right-click the right pane and click **Paste**. Note the path where the script is stored—a folder in the SYSVOL share on your DC. Close the File Explorer window.

6. In the Shutdown Properties dialog box, click **Add**. In the Add a Script dialog box, click **Browse.** Click **deltemp**, and then click **Open**. Click **OK** twice.

7. Close the Group Policy Management Editor. Link **Scripts** to the **TestOU1** OU, which is where you moved the ServerDM1 account to earlier.

8. Sign in to ServerDM1 as **domadmin1**. You're going to create a few files on your desktop that have the `.temp` extension. Open a command prompt window, then type **cd desktop**, and press **Enter**. Type **copy nul > file1.temp** and press **Enter** to create an empty file. Repeat the command two more times, changing **file1** to **file2** and then **file3**. You see the files on your desktop (you may have to minimize Server Manager and the command prompt to see the files).

> **Note** 🖉
>
> In the `copy nul > file1.temp` command, `nul` is a system device that's just an empty file, and the `>` redirects the empty file to a new file named `file1.temp`.

9. Type **gpupdate** and press **Enter.** After `gpupdate` is finished, restart ServerDM1. (If you don't run `gpupdate`, you have to restart the computer to load the policy and then shut it down again to make the shutdown script run.) The shutdown process will probably take a little longer than usual because the script has to run.

10. Sign in to ServerDM1 as **domadmin1** again, and verify that the `.temp` files have been deleted. Sign out of ServerDM1.

11. On ServerDC1, unlink the **Scripts** GPO from the **TestOU1** OU. Continue to the next activity.

Activity 4-8: Configuring a Folder Redirection Policy

Time Required: 15 minutes
Objective: Redirect the Documents folder.
Required Tools and Equipment: ServerDC1 and ServerDM1
Description: In this activity, you configure a folder redirection policy for the Documents folder and apply it to ServerDM1.

1. On ServerDC1, open File Explorer and create a folder named **Redirected** in the **C** volume. Share the folder, giving the **Everyone** group **Read/Write** sharing permission, and leave the remaining permissions at their default settings. Close File Explorer.

2. Open the Group Policy Management console and create a GPO named **FolderRedir** in the Group Policy Objects folder. Open **FolderRedir** in the Group Policy Management Editor. Expand **User Configuration, Policies, Windows Settings,** and **Folder Redirection**. Right-click the **Documents** folder and click **Properties**.

3. In the Documents Properties dialog box, click **Basic - Redirect everyone's folder to the same location** in the Setting drop-down list. Click the **Target folder location** list arrow to view the available options, and then, if necessary, click **Create a folder for each user under the root path** in the list. In the Root Path text box, type **\\ServerDC1\Redirected**.

4. Click the **Settings** tab and review the available options. Click to clear the **Grant the user exclusive rights to Documents** check box. Click **Redirect the folder back to the local userprofile location when policy is removed,** click **OK,** and in the warning message box, click **Yes.** Close the Group Policy Management Editor.

5. In the Group Policy Management console, link the **FolderRedir** GPO to **TestOU1.**

6. Open Active Directory Users and Computers and move the user **domadmin1** (located in the Users folder) to TestOU1 by dragging and dropping the user account.

7. On ServerDM1, sign in as **domadmin1** and run **gpupdate** from a command prompt. Then sign out of ServerDM1 and sign in again as **domadmin1.** You might see a message indicating that folder redirection is occurring.

8. On ServerDC1, open File Explorer and navigate to C:\redirected. You see a folder there named domadmin1 and in that folder is folder named Documents.

9. Unlink the **FolderRedir** GPO from **TestOU1.** Continue to the next activity.

Security Settings

 Certification

- **70-742 – Create and manage Group Policy:**
  Configure Group Policy settings

- **70-742 – Install and configure Active Directory Domain Services:**
  Create and manage Active Directory Users and computers

- **70-742 – Install and configure Active Directory Domain Services:**
  Create and manage Active Directory groups and organizational units (OUs)

There are well over 100 policies under Security Settings. Some of the most important are under Account Policies and Local Policies because they contain baseline security options for your computers. The following list describes the types of policies found under Security Settings, and some are covered in more detail in the next sections:

Note 📎

Except where noted, the following security settings are primarily found only under the Computer Configuration node; the User Configuration node has far fewer Security Settings policies.

- *Account Policies*—Contains settings that affect user authentication and logon. A GPO with settings configured in Account Policies must be linked to the domain for these policies to have any effect on domain logons. If a GPO linked to an OU has settings configured in Account Policies, they only affect the account policy settings on local computer accounts within the scope of the GPO, which pertains only to local user accounts. The Default Domain Policy is configured with default account policies settings. These policies were discussed in detail in Chapter 3.

- *Local Policies*—Sets security options applied to computers and what users can and can't do on the local computer to which they sign in. Because these policies affect computers, they're defined in GPOs linked to OUs containing computer accounts, such as the Default Domain Controllers Policy. There are three subnodes under Local Policies: Audit Policy, User Rights Assignment, and Security Options.
- *Event Log*—Controls parameters of the main logs in Event Viewer on target computers. Policies include log file sizes and retention parameters.
- *Restricted Groups*—Controls group membership for both domain groups and local SAM groups. After the policy is applied, existing members of the target group are deleted and replaced with the membership specified in the policy.
- *System Services*—Manages the startup mode and security settings of services on target computers.
- *Registry*—Sets NTFS permissions on Registry keys on target computers.
- *File System*—Sets NTFS permissions and controls auditing and inheritance on files and folders on target computers.
- *Wired Network (IEEE 802.3) Policies*—Controls a variety of authentication parameters on computers with wired connections to the network.
- *Windows Firewall with Advanced Security*—Controls firewall settings on Windows Vista and Server 2008 and later computers.
- *Network List Manager Policies*—Controls aspects of the networks identified by Windows such as the location type (public, private, domain), the network name, and whether users can change this information.
- *Wireless Network (IEEE 802.11) Policies*—Controls how wireless clients can connect to wireless networks, including network type (ad hoc or infrastructure), service set identifier (SSID), authentication, and encryption protocols.
- *Public Key Policies*—Controls parameters associated with Public Key Infrastructure, including EFS and certificate handling. This set of policies is found under both Computer Configuration and User Configuration.
- *Software Restriction Policies*—Controls which software can run on a computer. This set of policies is found under both Computer Configuration and User Configuration.
- *Application Control Policies*—Contains the subnode AppLocker, which extends the function of Software Restriction Policies. This policy can be used only on computers running Windows 7/Windows 2008 R2 and later.
- *IP Security Policies on Active Directory*—Controls IPsec policies on target computers. IPsec is a network protocol that provides secure, encrypted communication between computers.
- *Advanced Audit Policy Configuration*—Provides detailed control over audit policies.

Local Policies: Audit Policy

An administrator can audit events occurring on a computer, including logon and logoff, file and folder access, Active Directory access, and system and process events (see Figure 4-19). Auditing can be enabled for successful events, failed events, or both. For example, you can audit a user's successful access to a file, attempted accesses that fail, or both. Auditing file and folder access should be used sparingly and for only short periods because of the system overhead that it creates when monitoring objects and writing events to the Security log when access occurs. By default, no audit policies are defined on either default GPO. However, certain events, such as logons and directory service access, are audited by default and can be changed only by using the command-line tool `auditpol.exe`. Events created by auditing are listed in the Security log, which you can view with Event Viewer.

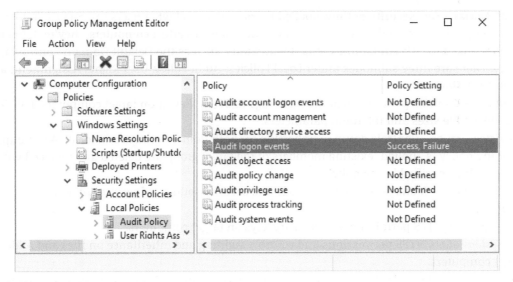

Figure 4-19 Auditing policies

Auditing Object Access

Auditing, particularly auditing access to file system objects, requires additional explanation. There are two steps for auditing objects:

- Enable the *Audit object access* policy for success, failure, or both.
- Enable auditing on target objects for success, failure, or both.

After object access auditing is enabled in Group Policy, you need to enable auditing on the target object, such as a file or folder. You do this by changing the system access control list (SACL) for the object in the Auditing tab of the Advanced Security Settings dialog box for the object (see Figure 4-20). By default, there are no entries in the Auditing tab. Figure 4-20 shows an entry in which the Users group is being audited for successful write access to the C:\InstallApps folder. As you can see in the figure, there are inheritance considerations with auditing, too. By default, when you audit a folder, the auditing extends to subfolders and files, but like permissions inheritance, you can change this setting.

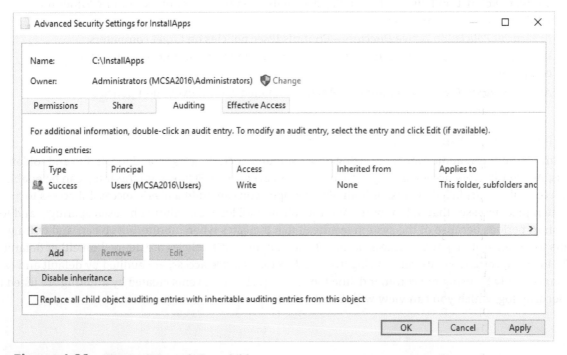

Figure 4-20 The Auditing tab for a folder

A single object access, such as opening a file, can create several log entries. For this reason, auditing objects should be done for only brief periods or when an object is accessed infrequently. In highly secure environments, however, auditing access to sensitive data on an ongoing basis can be useful. Because auditing writes events to the Security log, it makes little sense to enable auditing unless logs are checked regularly.

Changing Default Auditing

As mentioned, Windows logs successful logon events and certain other events by default, even though auditing isn't enabled in Group Policy. If you check the Security log, you'll see quite a few events logged there, most pertaining to computer accounts logging on and off. Each category of audit events shown previously in Figure 4-19 has a number of subcategories, which give you more control over the types of events that are audited. Unfortunately, these subcategories can't be managed with the GPME; you must use the `auditpol.exe` command-line tool. As mentioned, some subcategories are enabled by default, such as logon and logoff events, and these subcategories take precedence over policies set in GPOs.

To clear all audit policy subcategories so that auditing is controlled only by Group Policy, type `auditpol /clear` at a command prompt. This command stops all auditing on the computer where you run it unless auditing is enabled in the local policy or a GPO in the computer's scope.

Tip

For more information on `auditpol.exe`, see *http://support.microsoft.com/kb/921469/*.

Local Policies: User Rights Assignment

User rights define the actions users can take on a computer, such as shutting down the system, logging on locally, and changing the system time. More than 40 user rights policies can be assigned (see Figure 4-21), and for each policy, you can add users or groups. The Default Domain Controllers Policy specifies User Rights Assignment policies that define the default actions users can take on domain controllers. It's a good idea to spend some time examining the policies you can define in this node so that you know what types of rights you can enable and disable for users.

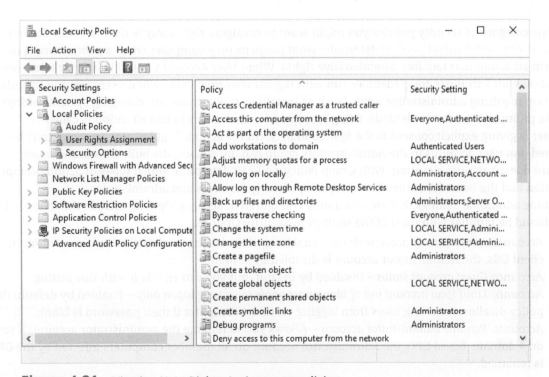

Figure 4-21   Viewing User Rights Assignment policies

Local Policies: Security Options

This subnode includes almost 100 settings; only a small percentage are shown in Figure 4-22. Available policies are organized into 15 categories, such as Accounts, Interactive logon, Network access, and User Account Control. Only a handful of the policies are defined in Default Domain Policy and Default Domain Controllers Policy. Most of these policies are configured with a simple Enable or Disable setting. For example, if *Interactive logon: Do not display last user name* is enabled, the account name of the last user to log on isn't displayed in the logon window.

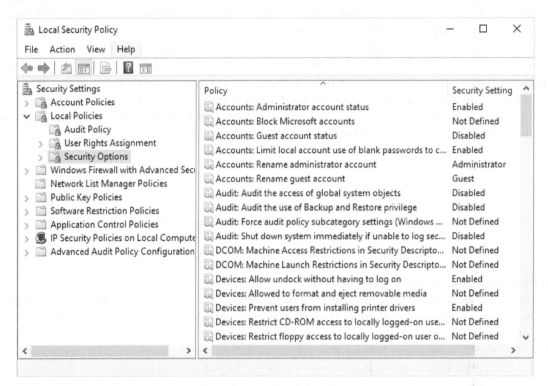

Figure 4-22   Viewing Security Options policies

One category of security policies you might want to configure right away is User Account Control. The **User Account Control policies** determine what happens on a computer when a user attempts to perform an action that requires administrative rights. When User Account Control is fully enabled, users logged on with administrator credentials run with regular user privileges. When users attempt to perform an action requiring administrative rights (such as installing applications and changing system settings), they're prompted to enter credentials. Being prompted for credentials in this situation is called **elevation**; the user is giving explicit consent to the system to perform the action. Regular user accounts can't be elevated, but user accounts in the Administrators group can. By default, the built-in Administrator account doesn't require elevation. With Group Policy, you can determine which types of action prompt for elevation and the behavior of the elevation prompt for regular users and administrators.

Some additional settings that are commonly configured in Security Options include the following, but you should be familiar with most of the settings in Security Options:

- *Accounts: Administrator account status*—Enables or disables the local Administrator account. In client OSs, the Administrator account is disabled by default.
- *Accounts: Guest account status*—Disabled by default, but you can enable it with this setting.
- *Accounts: Limit local account use of blank passwords to console logon only*—Enabled by default; this policy disallows network users from logging on to the computer if their password is blank.
- *Accounts: Rename administrator account*—Allows you to rename the administrator account; if set on a domain-based GPO, the Administrator account on all member computers affected by the GPO is renamed.

- *Accounts: Rename guest account*—Similar to the *Rename administrator account* setting.
- *Interactive logon: Do not display last user name*—Prevents the logon screen from showing the username of the last logged on user; disabled by default.
- *Interactive logon: Do not require CTRL+ALT+DEL*—If this setting is enabled, users don't have to press Ctrl+Alt+Del to log on to the local computer.
- *Interactive logon: Message text for users attempting to log on*—Allows the administrator to define a message that users see on the logon screen.
- *Interactive logon: Number of previous logons to cache*—Allows the computer to locally cache logon information so that users can log on to the computer if no domain controller is available. By default, 10 logons are cached. If it's set to 0, a DC must be available for a user to log on to the local computer.
- *Microsoft network server: Disconnect clients when logon hours expire*—Enabled by default, if user accounts have restricted logon hours, their sessions are disconnected from file shares if they're connected outside valid logon hours. If it's disabled, users can continue to work after logon hours expire if they're already logged on.

Tip

To see a detailed explanation of any user rights assignment or security option policy setting, double-click the policy setting and click the Explain tab.

Restricted Groups

The Restricted Groups policy allows an administrator to control the membership of both domain groups and local groups on member computers. By default, this node is empty; you configure it by adding groups that you want to restrict. This policy is typically used on groups that require especially high security, perhaps because the group has been assigned powerful rights or permissions to sensitive data. You can control both the *Members of this group* and *This group is a member of* properties of a group (see Figure 4-23). The *Members of this group* property controls which accounts can be members of the group. Current members of the target group not on the list are removed (unless the Administrator account is among them), and those in the list that aren't already members of the target group are added. In Figure 4-23, the domuser1 account will be added to the Backup Operators group.

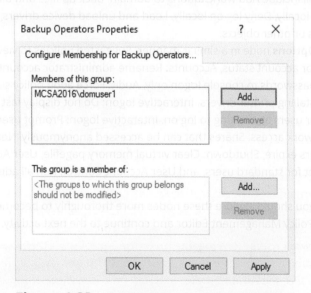

Figure 4-23   Configuring a restricted group

The *This group is a member of* property operates somewhat differently. It adds the target group to groups on the list that it isn't already a member of, but it doesn't remove the target group from existing memberships. If the GPO in which this policy is configured is linked to the domain because Backup Operators is a group in both the domain and on local computers, domuser1 is added to the group on all domain members and domain controllers in the domain. Furthermore, any existing members of Backup Operators are removed, and domuser1 is the sole member. Because there are no entries in the *This group is a member of* list, the groups Backup Operators is a member of are unchanged.

File System

The File System node enables an administrator to configure permissions and auditing on files and folders on any computers that fall in the scope of the GPO on which the policy is configured. Similar to Restricted Groups, there are no File System policies defined by default, so you need to add a folder or file and then configure the settings as you would configure permissions and auditing on any file or folder. When you're done, the file system settings are transmitted to the file system of target computers. If the file or folder doesn't exist on a computer within the GPO's scope, the policy has no effect. For example, say you configure a File System policy for a folder named *scripts* on the C drive, giving the Administrators group Full control and the Users group Read permissions. Any computer that falls in the scope of the GPO that has a folder named *scripts* on the C drive receives these permissions. Any existing permissions are replaced.

Activity 4-9: Reviewing User Rights Assignment and Security Options Settings

Time Required: 20 minutes
Objective: Review several User Rights Assignment and Security Options settings.
Required Tools and Equipment: ServerDC1
Description: In this activity, you open the Group Policy Management Editor and explore the User Rights Assignment and Security Options policies.

1. On ServerDC1, open the Group Policy Management console, and then open **GPO1** in the Group Policy Management Editor.
2. Click to expand **Computer Configuration**, **Policies**, **Windows Settings**, **Security Settings**, and **Local Policies**, and then click **User Rights Assignment**. Browse the list of policies, and double-click any that look interesting or that aren't self-explanatory. Click the **Explain** tab and read the detailed description. Suggested policies to view in detail include Add workstations to domain, Back up files and directories, Bypass traverse checking, Allow log on locally, Deny log on locally, Load and unload device drivers, Shut down the system, and Take ownership of files or other objects.
3. Browse the **Security Options** node in a similar manner. Suggested policies to view in detail include Accounts: Administrator account status, Accounts: Rename administrator account, Accounts: Limit local account use of blank passwords to console logon only, Audit: Force audit policy subcategory settings, Devices: Prevent users from installing printer drivers, Interactive logon: Do not display last user name, Interactive logon: Message text for users attempting to log on, Interactive logon: Prompt user to change password before expiration, Network access: Shares that can be accessed anonymously, Network security: Force logoff when logon hours expire, Shutdown: Clear virtual memory pagefile, User Account Control: Behavior of the elevation prompt for standard users, and User Account Control: Run all administrators in Admin Approval Mode.
4. When you have time, you should explore these nodes more thoroughly to become more familiar with the settings. Close Group Policy Management Editor and continue to the next activity.

Working with Administrative Templates

Q Certification

- **70-742 – Create and manage Group Policy:**
  Create and manage Group Policy Objects (GPOs)

- **70-742 – Create and manage Group Policy:**
  Configure Group Policy settings

Both the Computer Configuration and User Configuration nodes have an Administrative Templates folder. In the Computer Configuration node, the settings in Administrative Templates affect the HKEY_LOCAL_MACHINE Registry key. Settings in the User Configuration node affect the HKEY_LOCAL_USER Registry key.

Hundreds of settings are defined in the Administrative Templates nodes, and many more can be added through customization. The Administrative Templates folder uses policy definition files, called **administrative template files**, in XML format (with an `.admx` extension), which makes creating your own policies fairly easy if you need to control a setting not provided by default. The following sections cover these topics related to administrative templates:

- Computer Configuration settings
- User Configuration settings
- The ADMX central store
- Administrative Templates property filters
- Custom administrative templates
- Migrating administrative template files

Computer Configuration Settings

This section doesn't attempt to cover all the settings in Administrative Templates, but it gives you a brief explanation of the types of settings in each folder under Administrative Templates. You're encouraged to spend some time browsing through the settings with the Group Policy Management Editor so that you have a good idea where to look when you need to configure a particular type of policy setting. To see an explanation of a setting, double-click it and read the Help section of the dialog box for the policy's settings (see Figure 4-24).

Administrative Templates in the Computer Configuration node, where many aspects of the computer working environment are controlled, contains the following folders (see Figure 4-25), most with additional subfolders:

- *Control Panel*—This folder has three subfolders: Personalization, Regional and Language Options, and User Accounts. Personalization has settings that affect the look of Windows, in particular the lock screen and background. Settings in Regional and Language Options allow administrators to set and restrict the language in the Control Panel user interface. The single policy in User Accounts configures a default user logon picture for all users on target computers.
- *Network*—There are 20 subfolders where you can control a host of network settings on target computers, including but not limited to Background Intelligent Transfer Service (BITS) parameters, DNS client settings, network connection settings, offline files configuration, and TCP/IP settings.

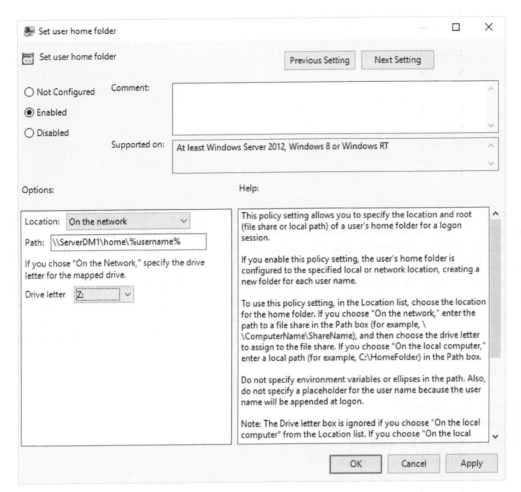

Figure 4-24 Configuring settings for a policy

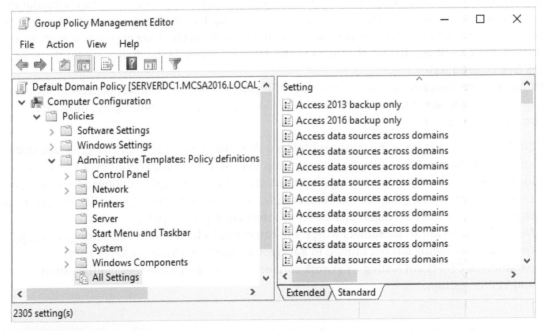

Figure 4-25 The Administrative Templates folders under Computer Configuration

- *Printers*—Settings in this folder control how computers interact with network printers, including automatic printer publishing in Active Directory, printer browsing, and Internet printing parameters.
- *Server*—Settings in this folder control options for backing up a computer.
- *Start Menu and Taskbar*—Settings in this folder allow you to specify a Start screen layout and pin apps to the Start screen.
- *System*—This folder contains more than 35 subfolders with settings for controlling general computer system operation. Some computer functions that can be controlled include disk quotas, the file system, group policy processing, logon and shutdown, power management, and user profiles.
- *Windows Components*—This folder contains more than 50 subfolders with settings for configuring specific Windows components, such as app deployment, Event Viewer, File Explorer, Internet Explorer, Windows PowerShell, Windows Update, Work Folders, and many others. Some settings in this folder have an identical counterpart in the User Configuration node. When a conflict exists, the setting in Computer Configuration takes precedence.

Tip

An additional node under Administrative Templates called All Settings displays all Administrative Template settings and can be sorted in alphabetical order. You can select View, Filter Options from the GPME menu to list policies by certain criteria or keywords.

User Configuration Settings

Most of the previous information about Administrative Templates in the Computer Configuration node also applies to the User Configuration node. Administrative Templates in User Configuration also contain the Control Panel, Network, Start Menu and Taskbar, System, and Windows Components subfolders, although most of the settings are different because they apply to specific users rather than all users who log on to a computer. With Administrative Templates in the User Configuration node, you can customize many aspects of a user's working environment. Policies in this node add the following subfolders to the previous list for the Computer Configuration node:

- *Desktop*—Controls the look of users' desktops, determines which icons are available, and can limit actions users can take on the desktop.
- *Shared Folders*—Controls whether a user can publish shared folders and Distributed File System (DFS) root folders in Active Directory.

The ADMX Central Store

Administrative templates are collections of policy definition files in XML format. These XML files, referred to as "ADMX files" because of their .admx extension, specify Registry entries that should be controlled and the type of data the entries take. The **ADMX central store** is a centralized location for maintaining ADMX files so that when an ADMX file is modified from one domain controller, all DCs receive the updated file. You can also create custom ADMX files that are available to all administrators to use without having to copy the files from one location to another.

The default location of ADMX files is in the *%systemroot%*\PolicyDefinitions folder. Without a central store, any ADMX file you customize or create would have to be copied manually to all other systems where group policies are being configured and managed. In a large network with many people working with group policies, ADMX files would get out of sync rapidly without a central store.

To create a central store, simply create a folder named PolicyDefinitions in the *%systemroot%*\SYSVOL\sysvol*domain*\Policies folder (the same folder where GPTs are stored). In the PolicyDefinitions folder, create a language-specific folder that uses the two-character ISO standard for worldwide languages. Variations of some languages use an additional two characters to specify the country. For example,

English is en-US for U.S. English or en-GB for Great Britain English. In a network with multiple domain controllers, the central store should be created on the DC that controls the PDC emulator role.

After creating folders for the central store, you just need to copy the ADMX files from their current location to the central store location. If you're managing ADMX files from a computer other than where you created the central store, the process is easy—simply copy the ADMX files to the SYSVOL share (*server*\SYSVOL*domain*\Policies\PolicyDefinitions). Because the SYSVOL share is replicated, the files and folders in the PolicyDefinitions folder are too.

Working with Filters

The number of settings in the Administrative Templates section of a GPO can be daunting when you're trying to find a particular policy to configure. There are several hundred policy settings under both Computer Configuration and User Configuration. If you know the name of the setting you need to configure or at least know the first word of the name, you can sort the settings alphabetically under All Settings and find it that way. However, if you don't know the name and perhaps know only the policy's general function, you could be searching for a while. Thankfully, you can narrow the search by using a filter in the Group Policy Management Editor:

1. Open a GPO in the GPME and click Policies, Administrative Templates under Computer Configuration or User Configuration. You see the filter icon on the toolbar.

2. Click Action, Filter Options from the menu to open the Filter Options dialog box (see Figure 4-26).

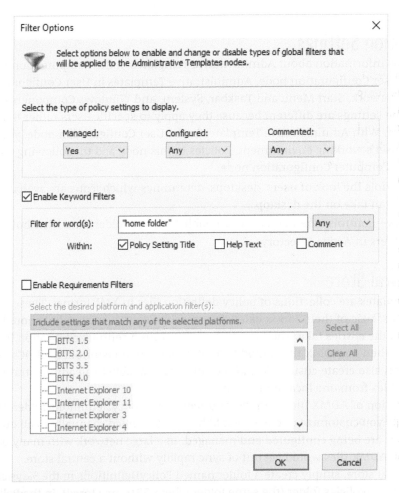

Figure 4-26 Configuring an Administrative Templates filter

3. You can configure a filter with the following criteria:

- Managed: Select Any, Yes, or No. If you select Any, both managed and unmanaged policies are included in the filter criteria. If you select Yes, only managed policies are included, and if you select No, only unmanaged policies are included.
- Configured: Select Any, Yes, or No to see only configured policies, unconfigured policies, or both.
- Commented: You can add a comment to any policy setting in Administrative Templates by double-clicking it and typing a comment in the Comment text box. This filter option allows you to view only policy settings with a comment, those without a comment, or both. By default, policy settings don't have a comment.
- Enable Keyword Filters: Select this check box, if needed, and in the Filter for word(s) text box, type one or more words that are part of the policy setting's title, help text, or comment field. You can specify how the words match by selecting Exact, All, or Any.
- Enable Requirements Filters: Narrow the search by OS or application platform. For example, you might want to see only policy settings that work with Windows Server 2016.

Note

Filters work only with settings in the Administrative Templates folders; you can't filter settings in the Software Settings or Windows Settings folders.

After you have configured filter options, you apply the filter by clicking Action, Filter On from the menu or clicking the Filter toolbar icon. Only policies matching the criteria are displayed in the GPME.

Using Custom Administrative Templates

As mentioned earlier, an Administrative template is a collection of policy definition files in XML format that use the .admx extension. Many software vendors provide administrative template files for controlling their applications' settings through group policies. For example, Microsoft offers administrative template files for the Microsoft Office suite.

Windows versions before Vista and Server 2008 used .adm files. This format can still be used on the same system as ADMX files, but you can create and edit ADMX files only on Windows Vista or later computers. ADMX files can also have an .adml extension, which provides a language-specific user interface in the Group Policy Management Editor. You can find all ADMX and ADML files under %systemroot%\PolicyDefinitions and open them in Notepad or an XML editor. However, you don't usually edit the standard ADMX files that ship with Windows.

Adding a Custom Administrative Template to Group Policy

If you create your own ADMX file or download one for configuring settings on an installed application, you can simply add the ADMX file to the %systemroot%\PolicyDefinitions folder. The next time you open the GPME, the file is loaded. Any language-specific files (.adml) should be placed in the corresponding language folder. For example, if there's a U.S. English file, place it in the en-US folder under the PolicyDefinitions folder.

If you have created a central store for policy definition files, place your custom ADMX files in this location so that they're replicated to all domain controllers. It's a folder named PolicyDefinitions on the SYSVOL share of a DC that makes sure all policy definitions are replicated to other DCs.

Tip

Creating custom ADMX files is beyond the scope of this book, but you can read about the basics at http://technet.microsoft.com/en-us/library/cc770905(v=ws.10).aspx.

Working with Older Administrative Templates

If you're using older ADM administrative templates that were used in Windows Server 2008 and earlier, you can add them manually by following these steps:

1. In the GPMC, open a GPO in the GPME. Right-click the Administrative Templates folder under Computer Configuration or User Configuration and click Add/Remove Templates.
2. In the Add/Remove Templates dialog box, click Add.
3. In the Policy Templates File Explorer window, browse to the ADM file's location. Select the ADM file and click Add.
4. In the Add/Remove Templates dialog box, click Close.

Migrating Administrative Templates

If you're running a Windows Server 2008 or later domain but still have to support clients older than Vista or are running older applications that use ADM files, you might want to migrate the older ADM files to ADMX format so that you can make use of the central store. As mentioned, the central store ensures that all policy definitions are replicated to other DCs. Because the central store can't work with ADM files, you need to convert the ADM files to ADMX files with ADMX Migrator, a snap-in tool available free from the Microsoft Download Center. To use this tool, follow these steps:

1. Download ADMX Migrator from the Microsoft Download Center.
2. Install ADMX Migrator on the computer with the ADM files; in most cases, it's a domain controller.
3. Navigate to the folder where you installed ADMX Migrator, and double-click the `faAdmxEditor.msc` file. An MMC opens with the ADMX Migrator snap-in.
4. Click Generate ADMX from ADM.
5. After the ADMX file is generated, move it to the %*windir*%\PolicyDefinitions folder or the central store.

Activity 4-10: Working with Computer Administrative Template Settings

Time Required: 15 minutes
Objective: Become familiar with Administrative Template settings in Computer Configuration.
Required Tools and Equipment: ServerDC1, ServerDM1
Description: In this activity, you explore Administrative Templates settings under Computer Configuration and configure some settings to see the effect they have on the computer operating environment.

1. On ServerDC1, open **GPO1** in the Group Policy Management Editor.
2. Under Computer Configuration, click to expand **Policies** and **Administrative Templates**. Browse through the folders under Administrative Templates to see the settings and subfolders under each one. Take your time to get a good feel for the types of settings available in each main folder.
3. Click the **All Settings** folder to see the full list of settings in Administrative Templates. The settings are arranged in alphabetic order by default. Click the **State** column to view the settings according to their state, which is Not configured, Enabled, or Disabled. Because GPO1 has no configured settings, the view doesn't change.
4. In the left pane, click to expand the **System** folder, and then click **Logon**. In the right pane, click the **Setting** column header to arrange the setting in alphabetical order and then double-click **Run these programs at user logon**. This policy can be used in place of a logon script if you want more programs to run when any user logs on to certain computers.
5. In the Run these programs at user logon window, click **Enabled**, and then click **Show**. In the first row of the Show Contents dialog box, type **explorer.exe**, and in the second row, type **notepad.exe** (see Figure 4-27). Now all target computers run File Explorer and Notepad when a user logs on. Click **OK** twice, and close the Group Policy Management Editor.

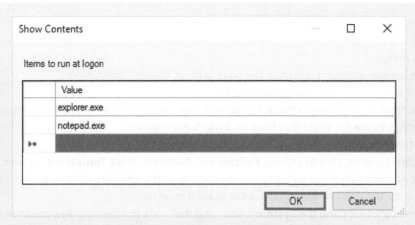

Figure 4-27   Configuring programs to run at user logon

6. Link **GPO1** to the **TestOU1** OU.

7. On ServerDM1, sign in as **domadmin1** and run **gpupdate**. Then sign out of ServerDM1, and sign in again as **domadmin1**. After a few moments, File Explorer and Notepad open. Close File Explorer and Notepad.

8. On ServerDC1, unlink **GPO1** from **TestOU1** and link it to the domain node. Open **GPO1** in the Group Policy Management Editor. Navigate to the **Run these programs at user logon policy** and set it to **Not Configured**.

9. Navigate to **Computer Configuration**, **Policies**, **Administrative Templates**, and **Windows Components**, and click **Windows Logon Options**. In the right pane, double-click **Display information about previous logons during user logon**. Read the Help information about this policy setting. Click **Enabled,** and then click **OK**.

10. On ServerDM1, run **gpupdate**, and then sign out and sign in again as **domadmin1**. You see a message stating that it's the first time you have signed in to the account. That's because this is the first time you have signed in since the policy was enabled. Click **OK**.

11. Sign out of ServerDM1, and then try to sign in again, but with an incorrect password. Then sign in with the correct password. A window opens showing the last successful sign-in and an unsuccessful sign-in attempt (see Figure 4-28). This information is intended to let users know whether somebody has been trying to use their accounts to log on. Click **OK**.

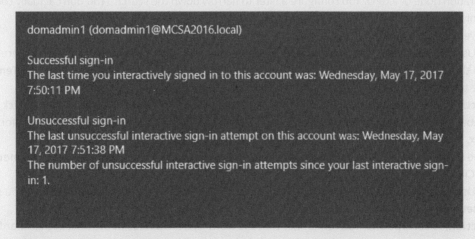

Figure 4-28   Showing information about previous sign-ins

12. Sign out of ServerDM1. On ServerDC1, in Group Policy Management Editor, set the **Display information about previous logons during user logon** policy to **Not Configured**. Unlink GPO1 from the domain node.

13. Continue to the next activity.

Activity 4-11: Working with User Administrative Template Settings

Time Required: 10 minutes

Objective: Become familiar with Administrative Template settings in User Configuration.

Required Tools and Equipment: ServerDC1, ServerDM1

Description: In this activity, you explore Administrative Templates settings under User Configuration, and then configure some settings to see the effect they have on a user's environment.

1. On ServerDC1, open **GPO1** in the Group Policy Management Editor.
2. Under User Configuration, click to expand **Policies** and **Administrative Templates**. Browse through the folders under Administrative Templates to see the settings and subfolders under each one. Take your time to get a good feel for the types of settings available in each main folder.
3. In the left pane, click to expand the **System** folder, and then click to select the **System** folder. In the right pane, double-click **Prevent access to the command prompt**.
4. Read the policy help information. Click **Enabled**, and then click **OK**. Close the Group Policy Management Editor.
5. In Group Policy Management, link **GPO1** to **TestOU1**.
6. On ServerDM1, sign in as **domadmin1**. Right-click **Start** and click **Command Prompt**. A command prompt window opens, but you see a message stating that the administrator has disabled it. Press any key to close the command prompt window.
7. On ServerDC1, unlink **GPO1** from **TestOU1**.
8. Sign off ServerDM1. Continue to the next activity.

Activity 4-12: Viewing Policy Settings with Filter Options

Time Required: 10 minutes

Objective: Configure filter options to find a policy setting in Administrative Templates.

Required Tools and Equipment: ServerDC1

Description: In this activity, you want to configure the setting that displays the desktop instead of the Start screen when users sign in to Windows 8 computers. You can't remember the exact setting name, but you know it's in the User Configuration node of a GPO. You configure a filter to narrow down the search. (You don't actually configure the policy; you only use the filter option to find the policy.)

1. On ServerDC1, open **GPO1** in the Group Policy Management Editor.
2. Under User Configuration, click to expand **Policies**, and click **Windows Settings**. Notice that there's no Filter icon on the toolbar because you can't filter settings in Windows Settings. Click **Administrative Templates**. You see the Filter icon now.
3. Click **Action**, **Filter Options**. In the Filter Options window, click the **Enable Keyword Filters** check box. You remember that the policy setting title has the word "desktop" in it, so type **desktop** in the Filter for words(s) text box. If necessary, click **Any** in the list box next to the Filter for words(s) text box.
4. Click the **Policy Setting Title** check box, and if necessary, click to clear the **Help Text** and **Comment** check boxes. Click **OK**. You see a filter icon on the Administrative Templates folder.
5. Under User Configuration, click to expand **Administrative Templates**, and click **All Settings**. You see a list of policy settings with the word *desktop* in the title. That's still quite a few settings to sift through.
6. Click **Action**, **Filter Options**. You remember that the word "start" was also in the title. In the Filter for words(s) text box, type the word *start* next to "desktop," making sure to leave a space between them. In the list box, click **All** so that the filter shows only policy settings with both words in them. Click **OK**.
7. Now you see only one policy setting, and it's the one you are looking for. Click the filter icon on the toolbar to remove the filter. You see all settings again. Close the Group Policy Management Editor.
8. Continue to the next activity.

Working with Security Templates

Certification

- **70-742 – Create and manage Group Policy:**
  Configure Group Policy settings

Security templates are text files with an `.inf` extension that contain information for defining policy settings in the Computer Configuration\Policies\Windows Settings\Security Settings node of a local or domain GPO. You can use them to create and deploy security settings to a local or domain GPO and to verify the current security settings on a computer against the settings in a template. There are two tools for working with security templates that are discussed in the following sections: "The Security Templates Snap-in" and "The Security Configuration and Analysis Snap-in."

The Security Templates Snap-in

You use the Security Templates snap-in to create and edit security templates. You can create templates for computers with differing security requirements, such as servers with different roles installed or different physical locations. Servers in branch offices that don't have tight physical security, for example, might require stronger security settings than servers in a secure location. Computers used by employees who have access to sensitive information often require tighter security than computers used by employees with limited access on the network.

Figure 4-29 shows the Security Templates snap-in with a new security template named LowSecurityWS. Notice that only a subset of the policies in a GPO are available in the template. When a user creates a new template, it's stored in the user's Documents folder in Security\Templates. After the template is created, it can be imported into a local or domain GPO or be used by the Security Configuration and Analysis snap-in. If you configure account policies in your template to import into a GPO, remember that settings in the Account Policies node are used only when linked to a domain or applied to a local GPO.

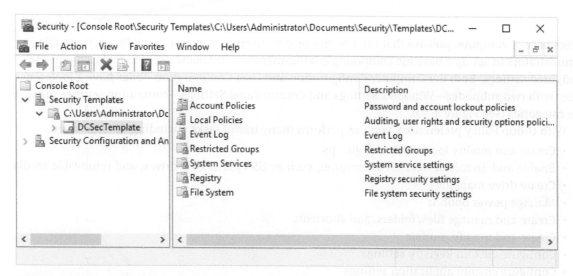

Figure 4-29   The Security Templates snap-in with an imported template

You create a security template in one of two ways:

- *Use the existing security settings on a computer*—If you want to create a security template using a baseline of settings from an existing desktop computer or server, open `secpol.msc`, and then right-click the Security Settings node and click Export policy. By default, policies are exported to the user's Documents folder in Security\Templates. Then you open the exported policy with the Security Templates snap-in, make changes as necessary, and save the template.

- *Create a security template from scratch*—Open the Security Templates snap-in in an MMC, and then right-click the folder under the Security Templates node and click New Template. This method creates a template with no defined settings.

The Security Configuration and Analysis Snap-in

The Security Configuration and Analysis snap-in is useful for checking a computer's existing security settings against the known settings in security template files that have been imported into a security database. You can also use this snap-in to apply a security template to a computer. Windows doesn't supply a configured MMC, so you have to add this snap-in to an MMC. If you'll be working with security templates quite a bit, you can create a custom MMC containing the Security Templates and Security Configuration and Analysis snap-ins.

When you analyze a template against the current security settings on a computer, a report is generated. For each policy setting, there are five possible results:

- An X in a red circle indicates that the template policy and current computer policy don't match.
- A check mark in a green circle indicates that the template policy and computer policy are the same.
- A question mark in a white circle indicates that the policy wasn't defined in the template or the user running the analysis didn't have permission to access the policy.
- An exclamation point in a white circle indicates that the policy doesn't exist on the computer.
- No indicator indicates that the policy wasn't defined in the template.

Configuring Group Policy Preferences

 **Certification**

- **70-742 – Create and manage Group Policy:**
  Configure Group Policy preferences

Unlike user or computer policies that can't be changed by users, **Group Policy preferences** enable administrators to set up a baseline computing environment yet still allow users to make changes to configured settings. Both the Computer Configuration and User Configuration nodes have a Preferences folder with two subnodes—Windows Settings and Control Panel Settings—containing settings organized into categories (see Figure 4-30).

With Group Policy preferences, you can perform many useful tasks, including the following:

- Create and modify local users and groups
- Enable and disable devices on a computer, such as USB ports, DVD drives, and removable media
- Create drive mappings
- Manage power options
- Create and manage files, folders, and shortcuts
- Create and modify printers
- Configure custom Registry settings
- Configure custom application settings
- Configure Control Panel settings
- Configure Internet settings

Many of these tasks were managed by complex logon scripts in the past, but using Group Policy preferences should reduce the need for scripts substantially. In addition, new preferences can be created. For example, software vendors can create ADMX files for managing settings in their applications.

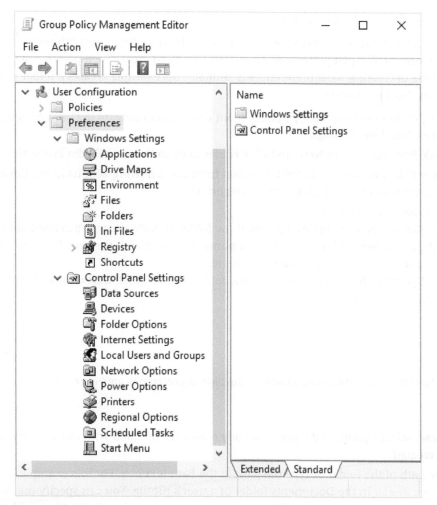

Figure 4-30   Categories for preference settings

Computers need the Group Policy Preferences Client Side Extensions (GPP CSE) package installed to recognize and download settings in the Preferences folder when processing group policies. This package is already installed in Windows Server 2008 and later. For older clients (such as Windows XP, Windows Vista, and Windows Server 2003), you can download the client-side extensions package by going to *www.microsoft.com/download* and searching for "client-side extensions."

How Group Policy Preferences Are Applied

As mentioned, Group Policy preferences are simply preferences, which means that users can usually change the settings configured here as long as they have the permission to do so. However, preferences are refreshed on the same schedule as policies by default. This means that Computer Configuration preferences are refreshed when the computer restarts and every 90 minutes thereafter, and User Configuration preferences are refreshed when the user signs in and then every 90 minutes. You can change this behavior by setting preferences to be applied only once. That way, preferences are used as a baseline configuration for the settings they affect, but users can still change them. Another difference between policies and preferences is management. If a managed policy setting is removed, unconfigured, or disabled, the original setting is restored on target users or computers. With preferences, the settings aren't restored by default, but you can change this behavior to make preferences act more like managed policies.

Creating Group Policy Preferences

There aren't hundreds of built-in preference settings to configure as there are with policies. In fact, there aren't any preferences at all—just preference categories. You must create each preference you want to deploy. The process of creating most preferences is similar. This example creates a folder preference under the User Configuration node:

1. Open the GPO in the Group Policy Management Editor, and navigate to User Configuration, Preferences, Windows Settings.

2. Right-click Folders, point to New, and click Folder to open the New Folder Properties dialog box.

3. In the New Folder Properties dialog box, select from the following actions in the General tab (which are common to most preferences categories):

   - Create: Creates a new folder.
   - Replace: Deletes and re-creates a folder. If the folder already exists, it's deleted along with its contents, and a new folder with the same name is created with the specified attributes. If the folder doesn't already exist, a new folder is created.
   - Update: Updates a folder's properties. If the folder doesn't exist, a new folder is created.
   - Delete: Deletes a folder.

> **Note**
>
> The General tab has different settings depending on the type of preference you're creating.

4. In this case, select Update. If the folder already exists, it's updated with any changes; otherwise, the folder is created.

5. Select the path of the folder or type the path in the Path text box. For this example, create a file named `TestPrefs` in the Documents folder of a user's profile. You can specify the %UserProfile% variable in the path. For example, if the user is testuser1, the %UserProfile% variable has the value C:\Users\testuser1, so the full path is %UserProfile%\Documents\TestPrefs (see Figure 4-31).

Figure 4-31   Creating a folder preference

6. Select attributes for the folder. You can choose from Read-only, Hidden, and Archive (the default setting).

7. If you choose Delete or Replace, you have additional options for deleting the folder. When the action is Create or Update, the delete options are grayed out.

8. Click the Common tab to see additional properties that are common to all preferences (see Figure 4-32):

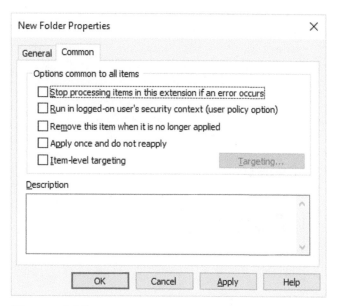

Figure 4-32   Common preferences properties

- Stop processing items in this extension if an error occurs: If there's more than one preference in the extension (for example, you create two folder preferences) and this option is selected, no additional preferences are processed in the extension if there's an error.
- Run in logged-on user's security context (user policy option): By default, preferences are processed with the SYSTEM account security context. Enable this option to have preference processing use the logged-on user's security context. This option ensures availability of resources that the user has permission to and makes sure environment variables are set for the logged-on user.
- Remove this item when it is no longer applied: Select this option if you want preferences to be restored to their original values when the user or computer account falls out of the GPO's scope. For example, if you select this option and the user account falls out of the GPO's scope, the folder is removed. This option isn't available when the action in the General tab is set to Delete.
- Apply once and do not reapply: By default, preferences are applied on the same schedule as policies. Enable this option if you want users to be able to change the preference setting without their changes being overridden by the next Group Policy refresh.
- Item-level targeting: **Item-level targeting** enables you to target specific users or computers based on criteria, as described next in "Item-Level Targeting."

There are too many preference types to cover all of them thoroughly in one chapter, but some of the activities in this chapter walk you through creating a few types of preferences. You should explore the Preferences folders and try creating different preferences in a lab environment to get a good idea of what you can do with them.

Item-Level Targeting

Preferences operate the same way as policies for default inheritance and scope. However, you can target users or computers for each preference based on certain criteria. For example, you can specify that only portable computers that are docked have a preference applied. Select the *Item-level targeting* option in the Common tab of the preference's Properties dialog box, and then click the Targeting button to define criteria that a computer or user must meet before the preference is applied. Figure 4-33 lists the properties that can be selected to define criteria.

Criteria can be combined with the AND and OR operators. For example, if you want to target only mobile computers running Windows 10, you can create an item-level targeting statement that effectively says "If the operating system is Windows 10 AND a battery is present, apply this preference" (see Figure 4-34).

Figure 4-33   List of criteria for item-level targeting

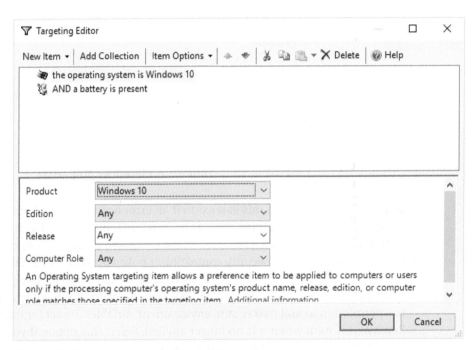

Figure 4-34   Configuring item-level targeting

Activity 4-13: Configuring and Testing Preferences

Time Required: 20 minutes

Objective: Configure and test preferences.

Required Tools and Equipment: ServerDC1 and ServerDM1

Description: In this activity, you configure a number of Group Policy preferences. You create a file preference, deploy a VPN connection, and configure local groups.

1. To create a file preference in which a folder with files is distributed to all computers, first you create a share for the files to be copied in a preference. On ServerDC1, open **File Explorer**.

2. Create a folder named **PandP** on the **C:** volume. Share this folder, and give the **Everyone** group **Read** permission.

3. In the PandP folder, create two text files: Name the first file **Policy.txt** and the second one **Procedure.txt**. Close File Explorer.

4. Open the Group Policy Management console, if necessary. Create a GPO named **Prefs** in the Group Policy Objects folder, and open it in the Group Policy Management Editor.

5. Under User Configuration, click to expand **Preferences** and **Windows Settings**. Right-click **Files**, point to **New**, and click **File**.

6. In the Action list box, click **Create**.

7. In the Source file(s) text box, type **\\ServerDC1\PandP*.***. Using a wildcard copies all files in the PandP folder. In the Destination folder text box, type **%UserProfile%\Documents\PandP**. The PandP folder is created automatically when the policy is applied. Leave the default **Archive** attribute selected (see Figure 4-35).

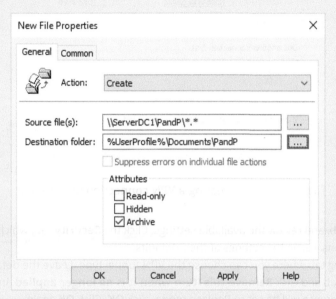

Figure 4-35   Creating a file preference

8. Click the **Common** tab. Review the available options, and then click **OK**. Note that you can change the processing order of preferences, so if you need one preference to be processed before another, you can arrange them in the order you want. Close the Group Policy Management Editor.

9. In the Group Policy Management console, link the **Prefs** GPO to the domain object.

10. Sign in to ServerDM1 as **domadmin**. Open File Explorer, and in the left pane, click **Documents** under This PC. Double-click the **PandP** folder, and you should see the two files you created. Sign out of ServerDM1.

11. Next, you'll create a Control Panel preference in which you deploy a VPN connection. On ServerDC1, open the **Prefs** GPO in the Group Policy Management Editor. Under Computer Configuration, click to expand **Preferences** and **Control Panel Settings**. Right-click **Network Options**, point to **New**, and click **VPN Connection**.

12. In the Action drop-down list, leave the default setting **Update**. Click the **All users connection** option button so that all users logging on to target computers have access to the connection. In the Connection name text box, type **WorkVPN**. In the IP Address text box, type **192.168.0.1** (see Figure 4-36).

Tip ⓘ

If the VPN connection was already created on the server, you could select it by clicking the browse button, and the preferences settings would be populated from the existing connection.

Figure 4-36 Creating a VPN connection preference

13. Click the **Options** tab, and review the available settings. Click the **Security** tab, which is where you set authentication options. Leave the settings at their defaults.

14. Click the **Networking** tab where you can choose the VPN tunnel type. Leave the default setting **Automatic**.

15. Click the **Common** tab and click **Remove this item when it is no longer applied**. In the warning message stating that the preference will be set to Replace mode, click **OK**. Click **OK** again.

16. Link the **Prefs** GPO to the **Desktops** OU. Sign in to ServerDM1 as **domadmin1**. Because it's a Computer Configuration policy, you have to restart the computer or run `gpupdate` for it to be applied. Open a command prompt window, and then type **gpupdate** and press **Enter**.

17. Right-click **Start** and click **Network Connections**. You see the WorkVPN connection.

18. Because you selected the *Remove this item when it is no longer applied* option, you should test that functionality. On ServerDC1, unlink **Prefs** from the domain. On ServerDM1, run **gpupdate** again.

19. Look in the Network Connections window to verify that the VPN connection has been removed. Sign out of ServerDM1.

20. Next, you'll create a preference that configures local groups on member computers. On ServerDC1, open Active Directory Users and Computers. Click the **Users** folder, and then create a global security group named **Local_Admins** in this folder. Add **domuser1** to this group.

21. Open the Group Policy Management console, and open the **Prefs** GPO in the Group Policy Management Editor. Delete the **Network Options** preference under the Computer Configuration\Control Panel Settings.

22. Next, right-click **Local Users and Groups**, point to **New**, and click **Local Group.**

23. Make sure **Update** is the selected action. Click the **Group name** list arrow, and click **Administrators (built-in)** in the list.

24. Click the **Add** button, and then click the browse button next to the Name text box. In the Select User, Computer, or Group dialog box, type **Local_Admins**, click **Check Names**, and then click **OK**. Make sure the action is **Add to this group**, and then click **OK** twice. Close Group Policy Management Editor.

25. Link the **Prefs** GPO to the **TestOU1** OU.

26. Sign in to the domain from ServerDM1 as **domadmin1**. Open a command prompt window, type **gpupdate**, and press **Enter**. Close the command prompt window.

27. Right-click **Start** and click **Computer Management**. Click to expand **Local Users and Groups**, click **Groups**, and then double-click **Administrators** to open the Properties dialog box. You should see Local_Admins in the Members text box. Click **OK**. Now any domain user you add to the Local_Admins group has local administrator access to all computers in the scope of the Prefs GPO. Sign out of ServerDM1.

28. On ServerDC1, unlink the **Prefs** GPO from the **TestOU1** OU. Continue to the next activity.

Activity 4-14: Configuring Item-Level Targeting

Time Required: 10 minutes
Objective: Configure a preference with item-level targeting.
Required Tools and Equipment: ServerDC1 and ServerDM1
Description: In this activity, you configure item-level targeting for the file preference so that you can still have the policy linked to the domain, and other preferences affect all users.

1. On ServerDC1, open the **Prefs** GPO in the Group Policy Management Editor. Under User Configuration, expand **Preferences** and **Windows Settings**, and then click **Files**.
2. Double-click the **PandP** file preference in the right pane. In the Properties dialog box, click the **Common** tab.
3. Click the **Item-level targeting** check box, and then click the **Targeting** button.
4. In the Targeting Editor window, click **New Item**, and then click **Organizational Unit**.
5. In the Organizational Unit text box, click the browse button, click **TestOU1**, and then click **OK**. Click **OK** twice to get back to the Group Policy Management Editor. This will limit the preference to only users in the TestOU1 organization unit, which in this case is only domadmin1.
6. Close Group Policy Management Editor. Link the **Prefs** GPO to the domain.
7. Sign in to ServerDM1 as **domadmin1**. Open File Explorer, click **Documents** in the left pane, and delete the **PandP** folder. Sign out of ServerDM1.
8. Sign in again to ServerDM1 as **domadmin1**, and verify that the PandP folder and the two files were created again.
9. Sign out of ServerDM1, and sign in as **domuser1**, (This user account is in the Users folder in Active Directory.) Open File Explorer, and in the left pane, click **Documents** under This PC. You don't see the PandP folder because item-level targeting limited this preference to user accounts in TestOU1. Sign out of ServerDM1.
10. On ServerDC1, unlink the **Prefs** GPO from the domain.

Chapter Summary

- Group Policy is a powerful tool for network administrators to manage domain controllers, member servers, member computers, and users. It allows administrators to manage most aspects of computer and user environments centrally through Active Directory.

- Group policy architecture and function involves these components: GPOs, replication, scope and inheritance, and creating and linking GPOs. The main component of group policies contains policy settings for managing many aspects of domain controllers, member servers, member computers, and user accounts. GPOs can be local or domain.

- GPO replication is handled by Active Directory replication for GPCs and by FRS or DFSR for GPTs. DFSR is used only when all DCs are running Windows Server 2008 and later.

- You use the Group Policy Management console to create, link, and manage GPOs and the Group Policy Management Editor to edit GPOs.

- GPOs can be linked to sites, domains, and OUs. Policies are applied in this order, and the last policy setting applied takes precedence when conflicts exist. Local policies are applied before domain policies, so when conflicts exist, domain policies take precedence over local policies.

- Starter GPOs are like template files for GPOs. You can create a new GPO by using a Starter GPO as a baseline. Starter GPOs contain only the Administrative Templates folder in the Computer Configuration and User Configuration nodes.

- A script is a series of commands saved in a text file to be repeated easily at any time. There's a Scripts extension in both the Computer Configuration and the User Configuration nodes in the path Policies, Windows Settings, Scripts. In the Computer Configuration node, you configure startup or shutdown scripts, and in the User Configuration node, you configure logon and logoff scripts.

- Folder redirection enables administrators to set policies that redirect folders in a user's profile directory. This feature is useful when you want users to store documents on a server for centralized backup, but you don't want to change the way they access their document folders.

- There are over 100 policies under Security Settings. Some of the most important are under Account Policies and Local Policies because they contain baseline security options for your computers.

- An administrator can audit events occurring on a computer, including logon and logoff, file and folder access, Active Directory access, and system and process events. Auditing can be enabled for successful events, failed events, or both.

- Both the Computer Configuration and User Configuration nodes have an Administrative Templates folder. In the Computer Configuration

node, the settings in Administrative Templates affect the HKEY_LOCAL_MACHINE Registry key. Settings in the User Configuration node affect the HKEY_LOCAL_USER Registry key.

- Administrative templates are a collection of policy definition files in XML format. These XML files, referred to as ADMX files because of their `.admx` extension, specify Registry entries that should be controlled and the type of data the entries take.

- The ADMX central store can be created to ensure that ADMX files are synchronized among all computers where group policies are managed.

- The number of settings in the Administrative Templates section of a GPO can be daunting when you're trying to find a policy to configure. You can narrow the search by using a filter in the Group Policy Management Editor.

- If you're running a Windows Server 2008 or later domain but still must support clients older than Vista or are running older applications that use ADM files, you might want to migrate the older ADM files to ADMX format so that you can make use of the central store.

- Security templates are text files with an `.inf` extension that contain information for defining policy settings in the Computer Configuration, Policies, Windows Settings, and Security Settings node of a local or domain GPO. The Security Configuration and Analysis snap-in is useful for checking a computer's existing security settings against the known settings in security template files.

- Unlike user or computer policies that can't be changed by users, Group Policy preferences enable administrators to set up a baseline computing environment yet still allow users to make changes to configured settings. You must create each preference you want to deploy.

- Preferences operate the same way as policies for default inheritance and scope. However, you can target users or computers for each preference based on a set of criteria, a feature called *item-level targeting*.

Key Terms

administrative template file
ADMX central store
assigned application
batch file
domain GPO
elevation
folder redirection
Group Policy Container (GPC)

Group Policy preferences
Group Policy Template
  (GPT)
item-level targeting
local GPO
managed policy setting
Microsoft Software Installation
  (MSI) file

published application
script
security template
Starter GPO
unmanaged policy setting
User Account Control policies

Review Questions

1. Which of the following are local GPOs on a Windows 10 computer? (Choose all that apply.)
   a. Local Administrators
   b. Local Default User
   c. Local Default Domain
   d. Local Non-Administrators

2. Which of the following are true about GPOs? (Choose all that apply.)
   a. Local GPOs override domain GPOs.
   b. Domain GPOs are stored on member servers.
   c. Domain GPOs can be linked to Active Directory sites.
   d. The gpedit.msc tool can be used to edit local GPOs.

3. Where is a GPT stored?
   a. In a folder named the same as the GPO in the SYSVOL share
   b. In a folder named the same as the GUID of the GPO in Active Directory
   c. In a folder named the same as the GUID of the GPO in the SYSVOL share
   d. In a folder named the same as the GPO in Active Directory

4. You're having replication problems with your GPOs and suspect that the version numbers have somehow gotten out of sync between the GPT and the GPC. What can you do to verify the version numbers on a GPO?
   a. Check the versionNumber attribute of the GPC and open the GPT.ini file.
   b. Check the versionNumber attribute of the GPT and open the GPC.ini file.
   c. Right-click the GPO in the Group Policy Management console, click Properties, and view the version in the General tab.
   d. Right-click the GPO in the Group Policy Management Editor, click Properties, and view the version in the General tab.

5. Which of the following are methods for creating a GPO? (Choose all that apply.)
   a. Use Active Directory Users and Computers.
   b. Link it to a container.
   c. Use the Group Policy Objects folder of the Group Policy Management console.
   d. Use an XML editor.

6. You have configured a policy setting in the User Configuration node of a domain GPO and linked the GPO to OU-X. Later, you discover that you linked it to the wrong OU, so you unlink it from OU-X and link it to OU-Y, which is correct. A few days later, you find that users in OU-X still have the policy setting applied to their accounts. What's the most likely cause of the problem?
   a. Group policy settings haven't been refreshed.
   b. The policy setting is unmanaged.
   c. Users in OU-X have an item-level target filter configured.
   d. The GPO is disabled.

7. All your domain controllers are running Windows Server 2016. You're noticing problems with GPT replication. What should you do?
   a. Verify that Active Directory replication is working correctly.
   b. Verify that FRS is operating correctly.
   c. Verify that DFSR is operating correctly.
   d. Check the GPOReplication flag for the GPT in the Attribute Editor.

8. You want to deploy a software package that's available to all users in the domain if they want to use it, but you don't want the package to be installed unless a user needs it. How should you configure the software installation policy?
   a. Publish the package under the Computer Configuration node.
   b. Assign the package under the Computer Configuration node.
   c. Publish the package under the User Configuration node.
   d. Assign the package under the User Configuration node.

9. You want to deploy a logon script by using Group Policy. You have several sites connected via a WAN with a DC at each site. You want to make sure the script is always available when users log on from any computer at any location. What should you do?
   a. Create a share on the fastest DC in the network and save the script there.
   b. Send the script via email to all users and have them save it locally.
   c. Save the script in the SYSVOL share.
   d. Copy the script to cloud storage.

10. You want to centrally back up the files that users store in the Documents folder in their user profiles, but you don't want users to have to change the way they access their files. What's the best way to go about this?
    a. Deploy a script that copies files from the Documents folder to a share on a server.
    b. Configure folder redirection in the User Configuration node of a GPO.
    c. Deploy a Mapped Drive preference, and tell users to save their files to the mapped drive.
    d. Configure a backup policy in the Computer Configuration node of a GPO.

11. Which of the following is best described as policy definition files saved in XML format?
    a. Administrative templates
    b. Security templates
    c. Group Policy objects
    d. Group Policy templates

12. Which of the following is a subfolder in the User Configuration node but not the Computer Configuration node of a GPO?
    a. Network
    b. Windows Components
    c. System
    d. Desktop

13. You have been working with ADMX files to modify existing Administrative Templates and create new templates. You work on different domain controllers depending on your location. Despite a concerted effort, your ADMX files are getting out of sync. How can you solve this problem?
    a. Remove group policy management tools from all but one domain controller so that policies can be managed from only one computer.
    b. Create an ADMX store in the SYSVOL share and copy the ADMX files to the ADMX store.
    c. Create an ADMX store in Active Directory and move all your ADMX files to Active Directory.
    d. Share the %systemroot%\PolicyDefinitions folder on all your domain controllers and set up Task Scheduler to copy ADMX files automatically from one system to all other systems.

14. You need to find a policy related to an application that was installed a couple years ago. You know that the policy is persistent when the computer that it's applied to falls out of scope, but you can't remember its name. You remember a word or two that might be in the policy name or comments. What can you do to find this policy quickly?
    a. In the Group Policy Management console, create a policy search term; set Persistent to Any, and enable Full Text search.

b. In the Group Policy Management Editor, configure a filter; set Managed to No, and enable Keyword Filters.
    c. In the Group Policy Management console, configure a search script; set Managed to Yes, and enable Requirements Filters.
    d. In the Group Policy Management Editor, configure a policy screen; set Persistent to Yes, and enable Title and Comments.

15. You have created a custom administrative template. You want this template to be available to all DCs so that policies can be configured with it from any DC. Where should you save it?
    a. In %systemroot%\PolicyDefinitions
    b. In the central store
    c. In the root of the C: drive
    d. In ADUC

16. You have installed an application that can be configured with Group Policy. The application came with a custom ADM file that must be replicated to all DCs. What should you do first?
    a. Copy the file to %windir%\PolicyDefinitions.
    b. Open the file with an XML editor and save it.
    c. Open the file with ADMX Migrator.
    d. Change the extension to .inf.

17. You're concerned that some domain controllers and workstations don't meet security requirements. What should you do to verify security settings on a computer against a list of known settings?
    a. Run Security Configuration and Analysis on the computer to compare its security settings against a security database.
    b. Open the Group Policy Management console on the computer, click the Security node, and run Group Policy Results.
    c. Run secpol.msc on the computer and use Group Policy Modeling.
    d. Use secedit /configure on the computer and read the report that's generated.

18. You want to set a Group Policy preference that affects only computers with a CPU speed of at least 4.0 GHz. What's the best way to do this?
    a. Configure item-level targeting.
    b. Move all computers meeting the criteria to a separate OU.
    c. Configure the group policy client on each computer with this type of CPU.
    d. Create a WMI filter with the Group Policy Management Editor.

19. You have configured a group policy preference that creates a VPN connection for all computers in the GPO's scope. One user says the connection was there yesterday, but it's no longer showing in his Network Connections window. You suspect he might have deleted the connection accidentally. What can you do to make sure that the VPN connection is re-created even if a user deletes it?
a. Disable the *Remove this item when it is no longer valid* option.
b. Configure the Read-only option.
c. Configure item-level targeting.
d. Disable the *Apply once and do not reapply* option.

20. You want all users to have the company home page and two other websites loaded in tabs when they start Internet Explorer, but you want them to be able to change their home pages if they like. What should you do?
a. Configure an IE policy and set it to unmanaged.
b. Configure an Internet Options preference and accept the default options in the Common tab.
c. Configure an IE policy and enable the *Allow user changes* option.
d. Configure an Internet Options preference and change the defaults in the Common tab.

Critical Thinking

The following activities give you critical thinking challenges. Case Projects offer a scenario with a problem to solve and for which you supply a written solution.

Case Project 4-1: Configuring Users' Working Environments
You have been told that all users in the Marketing Department must have a computer working environment that meets certain criteria. Marketing Department users don't always sign in to the same computer every day, so these requirements should apply wherever they sign in. You have a Windows Server 2016 domain, and all computers are domain members. All Marketing Department user and computer accounts are in the Marketing OU. All desktops run Windows 10. The criteria follow:

- Marketing users must be able to access documents they save in the Documents folder in their profiles from any computer they sign in to.
- A company marketing application must be installed automatically when users sign in if it's not already installed.
- The marketing application they run leaves behind temporary files named `mktapp.tmpX` in the C:\MktApp folder (with the X representing a number). These files contain sensitive information and must be deleted when the user signs out.

How can you make sure all these criteria are met? What should you configure to meet each criterion? Be specific about any options that should be enabled or disabled and how the configuration should be applied.

Case Project 4-2: Configuring Preferences
Users in the Engineering Department need a higher level of access on their local computers than other users do. In addition, you want to set power options on mobile computers that Engineering users use. All Engineering Department user and computer accounts are in the Engineering OU. What should you configure to meet the following criteria?
- When an Engineering user signs in to a computer, the user account is added to the local Administrators group on that computer.
- Enable the hibernation power mode but only if the user's computer is identified as a portable computer. Set the power scheme to hibernate mode if the laptop's lid is closed or the power button is pressed.

CHAPTER 5

MANAGING GROUP POLICIES

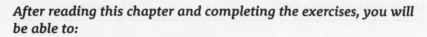

After reading this chapter and completing the exercises, you will be able to:

Configure group policy processing

Configure group policy client processing

Configure the Group Policy Results and Group Policy Modeling tools

Manage GPOs

Aside from understanding how to configure policy and preference settings in a Group Policy Object (GPO), it's important to understand GPO scope, precedence, and inheritance so that you can make sure that the appropriate objects are configured with the right settings. In this chapter, you learn about these topics and see how to change the default group policy client processing.

Sometimes you need to confirm that the settings you think are being set are actually being set on the target accounts. The Group Policy Results tool can show you the actual results of group policy processing, and the Group Policy Modeling tool enables you to create "what-if" scenarios so that you know what policies will be applied if you move an account to an Active Directory container or change an account's group memberships. Finally, you learn how to back up, restore, copy, and migrate GPOs.

Table 5-1 summarizes what you need for the hands-on activities in this chapter.

Table 5-1   Activity requirements

Activity	Requirements	Notes
Activity 5-1: Resetting Your Virtual Environment	ServerDC1, ServerDM1	
Activity 5-2 Working with GPO Inheritance Blocking and Enforcement	ServerDC1, ServerDM1	
Activity 5-3: Using GPO Security Filtering	ServerDC1, ServerDM1	
Activity 5-4: Using GPO Security Filtering for a Computer Account	ServerDC1, ServerDM1	
Activity 5-5: Configuring Loopback Policy Processing	ServerDC1, ServerDM1	
Activity 5-6: Using Remote Group Policy Updates	ServerDC1, ServerDM1	
Activity 5-7: Using Group Policy Results and Group Policy Modeling	ServerDC1, ServerDM1	
Activity 5-8: Backing Up and Restoring a GPO	ServerDC1	

Configuring Group Policy Processing

 **Certification**

- **70-742 – Create and manage Group Policy:**
  Configure Group Policy processing

Group policy processing can be confusing because there are so many exceptions to normal processing and inheritance behavior. When you configure and link a GPO to an Active Directory container, you need to be aware of how that GPO affects objects in the container and subcontainers. To do so, you need to have a solid understanding of how GPOs are processed, how settings are inherited, and the exceptions to normal processing and inheritance. This section discusses the following topics related to group policy processing:

- *GPO scope and precedence*—Defines which objects are affected by settings in a GPO and which settings take precedence if conflicts exist
- *GPO inheritance*—Defines how settings are applied to objects in subcontainers
- *GPO filtering*—Creates exceptions to the normal scope by using security and Windows Management Instrumentation (WMI) filtering
- *Loopback processing*—Changes how settings in the User Configuration node are applied

GPO Scope and Precedence

GPO scope defines which objects are affected by settings in a GPO. As you've learned, policies and preferences defined in a GPO's Computer Configuration node affect computer accounts, and policies and preferences in the User Configuration node affect user accounts. In addition, GPOs are applied in the following order:

1. Local policies
2. Site-linked GPOs
3. Domain-linked GPOs
4. OU-linked GPOs

Policies that aren't defined or configured are not applied at all, and the last policy applied is the one that takes precedence. For example, a GPO linked to a domain affects all computers and users in the domain, but settings in a GPO linked to an organizational unit (OU) override the settings in a GPO linked to the domain if there are conflicts.

When OUs are nested, the GPO linked to the OU nested the most deeply takes precedence over all other GPOs. When a policy setting isn't configured, its status is Not defined or Not configured. When a GPO is applied to an object, only the configured settings have any effect on that object. If two GPOs are applied to an object and a certain setting is configured on one GPO but not the other, the configured setting is applied.

Understanding Site-Linked GPOs

GPOs linked to a site object affect all users and computers physically located at that site. Because sites are based on IP address, GPO processing determines where a user is signing in and from what computer based on that computer's IP address. So users who sign in to computers at different sites might have different policies applied to their accounts. In addition, mobile computers can have different policies applied, depending on the site where the computer connects to the network. Keep in mind that if a site contains computers and domain controllers from multiple domains, a site-linked GPO affects objects from multiple domains. For simplicity, when you have only one site and one domain, domain GPOs should be used rather than site-linked GPOs. As you might imagine, using site-linked GPOs can be confusing for users, particularly if there is a lot of user mobility between sites, so site-linked GPOs should be used with caution and only when there are valid reasons for different sites to have different policies.

Understanding Domain-Linked GPOs

GPOs set at the domain level should contain settings that you want to apply to all objects in the domain. The Default Domain Policy is configured and linked to the domain object by default and mostly defines user account policies. Account policies that affect domain logons can be defined only at the domain level as you learned in Chapter 3. Default account policies are configured in the Default Domain Policy, but you can change them by creating a new GPO, configuring account policies, and linking the GPO to the domain object.

Active Directory folders, such as Computers and Users, are not OUs, and therefore can't have a GPO linked to them. Only domain-linked GPOs and site-linked GPOs affect objects in these folders. If you need to manage objects in these folders with group policies, moving the objects to OUs is recommended instead of configuring domain or site GPOs to manage them.

It might be tempting to define most group policy settings at the domain level and define exceptions at the OU level, but in a large Active Directory structure, this strategy could become unwieldy. Best practices suggest setting account policies and a few critical security policies at the domain level and setting the remaining policies on GPOs linked to OUs.

Understanding OU-Linked GPOs

Most fine-tuning of group policies, particularly user policies, should be done at the OU level. Because OU-linked policies are applied last, they take precedence over site and domain policies (with the exception of account policies, which can be applied only at the domain level). Because the majority of policies are defined at the OU level, a well-thought-out OU design is paramount in your overall Active Directory design. Users and computers with similar policy requirements should be located in the same OU or have a common parent OU when possible.

Because OUs can be nested, so can the GPOs applied to them. When possible, your OU structure should be designed so that policies defined in GPOs linked to the top-level OU apply to all objects in that OU. GPOs applied to nested OUs should be used for exceptions to policies set at the higher-level OU or when certain computers or users require more restrictive policies. For example, suppose that you have a scenario in which all full-time employees in the Engineering Department need complete access to Control Panel, but part-time employees should be restricted from using it. You can configure a policy allowing Control Panel access in a GPO linked to the Engineering OU. Then you create an OU under the Engineering OU that contains part-time employees' accounts and link a GPO to it that restricts use of Control Panel.

Group Policy Inheritance

By default, GPO inheritance is enabled and settings linked to a parent object are applied to all child objects. Therefore, settings in a GPO linked to the domain object are inherited by all OUs and their child objects in the domain. Settings in a GPO linked to the site are inherited by all objects in that site. To see which policies affect a domain or OU and where the policies are inherited from, select a container in the left pane of the Group Policy Management console (GPMC) and click the Group Policy Inheritance tab in the right pane. There are two main ways to change default GPO inheritance:

- Blocking inheritance
- GPO enforcement

Blocking Inheritance

Although the default inheritance behavior is suitable for most situations as with file permissions inheritance, sometimes you need an exception to the default. One method is blocking inheritance, which prevents GPOs linked to parent containers from affecting child containers. To block inheritance, in the GPMC, right-click the child domain or OU and click Block Inheritance (see Figure 5-1). You can enable this setting on a domain or an OU. On a domain object, this setting blocks GPO inheritance from a site, and on an OU, it blocks inheritance from parent OUs (if any), the domain, and the site. If inheritance blocking is enabled, the OU or domain object is displayed with an exclamation point in a blue circle. Inheritance blocking should be used sparingly; if you find that you need to block GPO inheritance frequently, this is an indication that your OU design is probably flawed and should be reexamined.

What happens if you have a nested OU and want to block GPO inheritance from its parent OU, but you still want domain- and site-linked GPOs to apply? This is where GPO enforcement, discussed next, comes in.

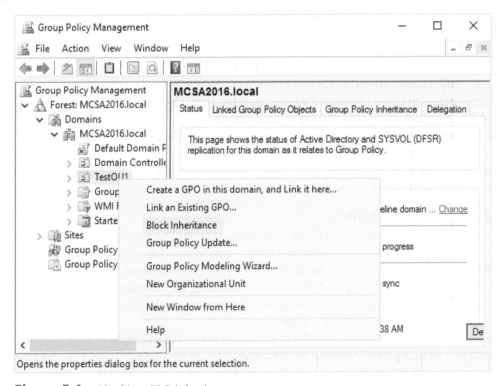

Figure 5-1 Blocking GPO inheritance

GPO Enforcement

GPO enforcement forces inheritance of settings on all child objects in the GPO's scope, even if a GPO with conflicting settings is linked to a container at a deeper level. In other words, a GPO that's enforced has the strongest precedence of all GPOs in its scope. If multiple GPOs have the Enforced option set, the GPO that's highest in the Active Directory hierarchy has the strongest precedence. For example, if both a GPO linked to an OU and a GPO linked to a domain have the Enforced option set, the GPO linked to the domain has stronger precedence. GPO enforcement also overrides GPO inheritance blocking, so using inheritance blocking will not block inheritance of settings in a GPO that has enforcement configured.

Tip (i)

Remember that the Block Inheritance option is set on a domain or OU, and the Enforced option is set on a GPO that is linked to a site, domain, or OU.

GPO enforcement is configured on the GPO, not the Active Directory container. To configure enforcement in the GPMC, right-click the shortcut to a linked GPO and click Enforced (see Figure 5-2).

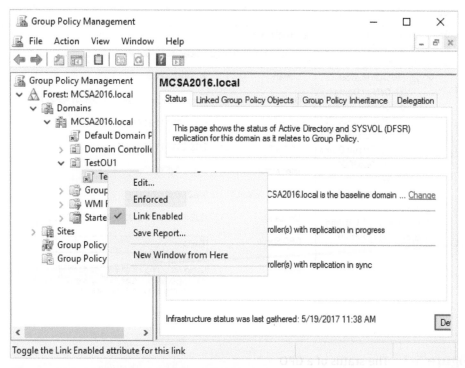

Figure 5-2 Configuring GPO enforcement

Managing GPO Status and Link Status

After a GPO is created, it can be in one of the following states:

- *Link status: unlinked*—The GPO is in the Group Policy Objects folder but hasn't been linked to any container objects.
- *Link status: Enabled*—The GPO is listed under the container object, and the link is enabled. This status is set by right-clicking a container, clicking Link an Existing GPO, and choosing a GPO from the Group Policy Objects folder or by right-clicking a container and clicking *Create a GPO in this domain, and Link it here.*
- *Link status: Disabled*—The GPO is listed under the container object and the link is disabled. Link status can be toggled between enabled and disabled by right-clicking a GPO linked to a container and clicking Link Enabled.
- *GPO status: Enabled*—The GPO is fully functional. In the Group Policy Objects folder, right-click a GPO, point to GPO Status, and click Enabled.
- *GPO status: User configuration settings disabled*—The User Configuration node isn't processed by computers running the group policy client. In the Group Policy Objects folder, right-click a GPO, point to GPO Status, and click User configuration settings disabled.

- *GPO status: Computer configuration settings disabled*—The Computer Configuration node isn't processed by computers running the group policy client. In the Group Policy Objects folder, right-click a GPO, point to GPO Status, and click Computer configuration settings disabled.
- *GPO status: All settings disabled*—The GPO is disabled. In the Group Policy Objects folder, right-click a GPO, point to GPO Status, and click All settings disabled.

You can view and modify the GPO status by clicking the GPO in the left pane of Group Policy Management and clicking the Details tab (see Figure 5-3).

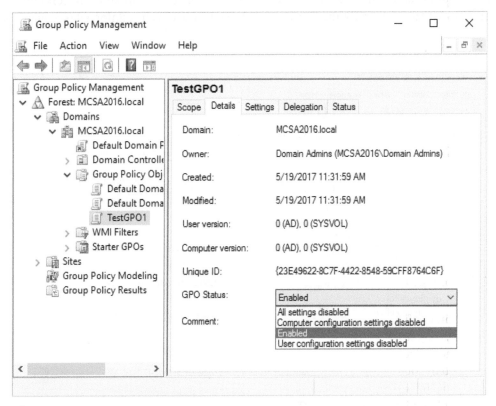

Figure 5-3   The status of a GPO

GPO Filtering

Blocking inheritance excludes all objects in an OU from inheriting GPO settings (unless they're enforced), but what if you want to exclude only some objects in the OU? This is where GPO filtering comes into play. There are two types of **GPO filtering**: security filtering and WMI filtering.

Security filtering uses permissions to restrict objects from accessing a GPO. Like any object in Active Directory, a GPO has a discretionary access control list (DACL) that contains lists of security principals with assigned permissions to the GPO. User and computer accounts must have the Read and Apply Group Policy permissions for a GPO to apply to them. By default, the Authenticated Users special identity is granted these permissions to every GPO; Authenticated Users applies to both logged-on users and computers. You can see a GPO's DACL in Active Directory Users and Computers in the System\Policies folder and in the Delegation tab in the GPMC, but for basic GPO filtering, you can use the Scope tab in the GPMC. To view the current security filtering settings, click a GPO in the GPMC and click the Scope tab on the right (see Figure 5-4).

You use the Security Filtering dialog box in the GPMC to add or remove security principals from the GPO access list. For example, if you want a GPO to apply to all users except a few in a domain or OU, follow these steps:

1. Create a security group in Active Directory Users and Computers.
2. Add all users who should be subject to the GPO as members of the new group.

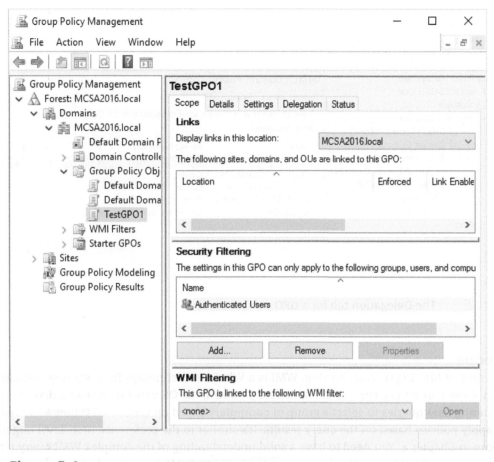

Figure 5-4   Viewing security filtering settings

3. In the GPMC, click the GPO, and click the Scope tab in the right pane.
4. Use the Security Filtering dialog box to add the new group to this GPO.
5. In the Security Filtering dialog box, remove the Authenticated Users special identity from this GPO.

Remember that computer accounts are also affected by GPOs. So if the GPO you're filtering contains computer settings, you must add a group containing the computer accounts that should be subject to the GPO's policies.

Another way to use security filtering is to edit the GPO's DACL directly. This method is often easier when the GPO must be applied to many users or computers with just a few exceptions. In the GPMC, click the GPO in the Group Policy Objects folder, and click the Delegation tab in the right pane to see the complete list of access control entries (ACEs) for the GPO as in Figure 5-5. You can add security principals to the DACL or click the Advanced button to open the Advanced Security Settings dialog box.

By using the Advanced Security Settings dialog box, you can assign Deny permissions as well as Allow permissions. Assigning the Deny Read permission, for example, enables you to create exceptions to normal GPO processing. You can add a single user or computer account or a group to the DACL and prevent these security principals from being affected by the GPO.

For example, suppose you have a GPO that has some Internet Explorer settings in the Computer Configuration node that restrict access to advanced features. You have more than 500 computer accounts in different OUs, so you want to link the GPO to the domain so that it affects all computers in the domain. However, you have a dozen or so power users whose computers you want to exempt from these policies. You can create a group, add the power users' computers as members, add the group to the GPO's DACL, and then configure Deny Read permission.

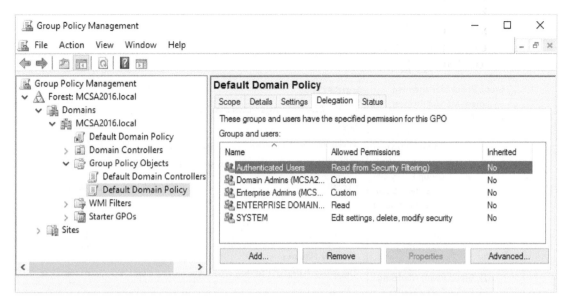

Figure 5-5 The Delegation tab for a GPO

WMI Filtering

The second type of filtering is **WMI filtering**. WMI is a Windows technology for gathering management information about computers, such as the hardware platform, the OS version, available disk space, and so on. WMI filtering uses queries to select a group of computers based on certain attributes and then applies or doesn't apply policies based on the query results. It's similar to the preference item-level targeting you learned about in Chapter 4. You need to have a solid understanding of the complex WMI query language before you can create WMI filters. Here's an example of using a WMI query to select only computers running Windows 10 Enterprise:

```
Select * from Win32_OperatingSystem where Caption =
  "Microsoft Windows 10 Enterprise"
```

This next example uses the OS version number. Windows 8.1 and Windows Server 2012 R2 have version numbers beginning with 6.3, and Windows 10 and Windows Server 2016 have version numbers beginning with 10. This command selects computers running an OS with a version number beginning with 10:

```
Select * from Win32_OperatingSystem where Version
  like "10%"
```

The next example uses `Version` and `ProductType`. `ProductType` differentiates client and server OSs. A client OS, such as Windows 10, has a `ProductType` of 1, and a server OS, such as Windows Server 2016, has a `ProductType` of 3. This example selects Windows 10 systems:

```
Select * from Win32_OperatingSystem where Version
  like "10%" and ProductType = "1"
```

Suppose you want a policy that installs a large application on target machines with at least 20 GB of disk space available. You can use the following command:

```
Select * from Win32_LogicalDisk where
  FreeSpace > 20000000000
```

This example targets computers from a specific manufacturer and model:

```
Select * from Win32_ComputerSystem where
  Manufacturer = "Dell" and Model = "Optiplex 960"
```

You create WMI filters in the WMI Filters node of the GPMC. Right-click in the right pane and click New to open the New WMI Filter dialog box. You assign a name and an optional description to the WMI filter and then click Add to create a new query (see Figure 5-6). After creating a WMI filter, select it in the Scope tab of a GPO (see Figure 5-7). Only one WMI filter can be selected per GPO, but you can use the same WMI filter in multiple GPOs.

Tip (i)

To learn more about WMI and WMI filtering, search the Microsoft TechNet website at *http://technet.microsoft.com*.

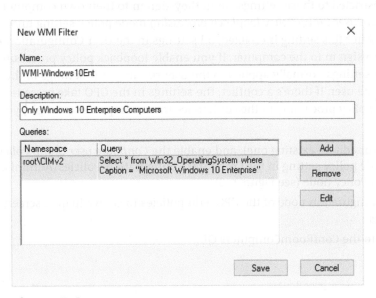

Figure 5-6   Creating a new WMI filter

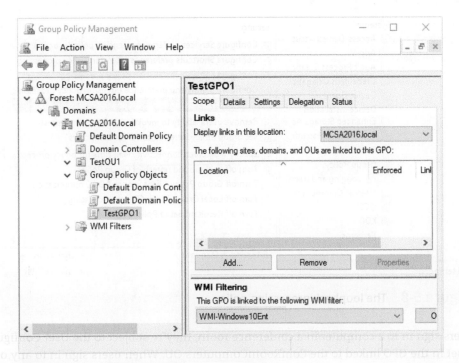

Figure 5-7   Linking a WMI filter to a GPO

Loopback Policy Processing

By default, users are affected by policies in the User Configuration node, and computers are affected by policies in the Computer Configuration node. Furthermore, users are affected by GPOs whose scope they fall within, and the same goes for computers.

Normally, the policies that affect user settings follow users to whatever computer they sign in to. However, you might want user policy settings to be based on the GPO within whose scope the computer object falls. To do this, you can use **loopback policy processing**. For example, suppose you have an OU named ConfRoomComputers containing all computer accounts of computers in conference rooms. Perhaps you want standardized desktop settings, such as wallpaper, screen savers, Start screen, and so forth, so that these computers have a consistent look for visitors. All these settings are in the User Configuration node, however, so they can't apply to computer accounts. You don't want all users in the organization to be restricted to these settings when they sign in to their own computers. The solution is to enable the *Configure user Group Policy loopback processing mode* policy setting under the Computer Configuration node. After this setting is enabled, all settings in the User Configuration node of the GPO apply to all users who sign in to the computer. If you enable loopback policy processing, you have the option to replace the settings normally applied to the user or merge the settings in the GPO with settings normally applied to the user. If there's a conflict, the settings in the GPO take precedence.

To use loopback policy processing in the conference room computers example, you take the following steps:

1. Create a GPO (or edit an existing one), and enable the *Configure user Group Policy loopback processing mode* policy setting in the Computer Configuration\Policies\Administrative Templates\System\Group Policy node (see Figure 5-8).

2. In the User Configuration node of the GPO, edit policies to set wallpaper, screen saver, and Start screen options.

3. Link the GPO to the ConfRoomComputers OU.

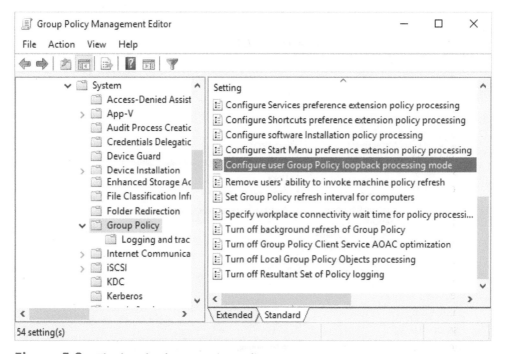

Figure 5-8   The loopback processing policy

When users sign in to a computer in a conference room, they're subject to the User Configuration policies you set in the GPO linked to the ConfRoomComputers OU. When users sign in to any other computer, they're subject to whatever policies normally affect their user accounts.

Activity 5-1: Resetting Your Virtual Environment

Time Required: 5 minutes
Objective: Reset your virtual environment by applying the InitialConfig checkpoint or snapshot.
Required Tools and Equipment: ServerDC1, ServerDM1
Description: Apply the InitialConfig checkpoint or snapshot to ServerDC1 and ServerDM1.

1. Be sure the servers are shut down. In your virtualization program, apply the InitialConfig checkpoint or snapshot to ServerDC1 and ServerDM1.
2. When the snapshot or checkpoint has finished being applied, continue to the next activity.

Activity 5-2: Working with GPO Inheritance Blocking and Enforcement

Time Required: 20 minutes
Objective: Use the Block Inheritance option on an OU and the Enforcement option on a GPO.
Required Tools and Equipment: ServerDC1, ServerDM1
Description: In this activity, you configure a policy to prohibit access to Control Panel. Then you block inheritance to see that the policy doesn't affect objects below where inheritance blocking is enabled. Then, you configure the enforcement option on the GPO to see that GPO enforcement option overrides the block inheritance option.

1. Sign in to ServerDC1 as **Administrator**, and open the Group Policy Management console.
2. Create a GPO named **GPO1** in the Group Policy Objects folder. Open GPO1 in the Group Policy Management Editor (GPME).
3. Navigate to **User Configuration\Policies\Administrative Templates\Control Panel**. In the right pane, double-click the **Prohibit access to Control Panel and PC settings** policy. Click **Enabled** to enable the policy. Read the Help information so that you know what the policy does. Click **OK**. Close GPME.
4. Link GPO1 to the domain by right-clicking **MCSA2016.local** and clicking **Link an Existing GPO**. Click **GPO1** and click **OK**.
5. Open Active Directory Users and Computers. Right-click **MCSA2016.local**, point to **New**, and click **Organizational Unit**. Type **TestOU1** and click **OK**.
6. Click the **Users** folder and then drag and drop **domuser1** to **TestOU1**. Click **Yes** to confirm. Close Active Directory Users and Computers.
7. On ServerDM1, sign in as **domuser1**. Right-click **Start** and click **Control Panel**. You should see a message that the operation has been canceled due to restrictions (see Figure 5-9). Click **OK**. As you can see, domuser1 is restricted from using Control Panel. Sign out of ServerDM1.

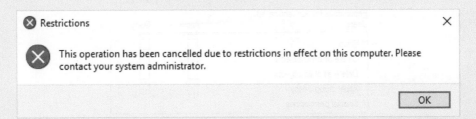

Figure 5-9 The message indicating the Control Panel is restricted

8. On ServerDC1, in Group Policy Management, right-click **TestOU1** and click **Block Inheritance**. You see a blue circle with a white exclamation point indicating that inheritance is blocked. Now users in TestOU1 aren't affected by GPOs linked to the domain.

9. On ServerDM1, sign in again as **domuser1**. Right-click **Start** and click **Control Panel**. Control Panel opens normally because the policy setting in GPO1 is being blocked. Sign out of ServerDM1.

10. On ServerDC1 in Group Policy Management, right-click **GPO1** under the domain node and click **Enforced**.

11. Sign in to ServerDM1 as **domuser1**. Right-click **Start** and **click Control Panel**. You should see the message that the operation has been canceled due to restrictions. Click **OK**. As you can see, domuser1 is once again restricted from using the Control Panel because enforcement overrides block inheritance. Sign out of ServerDM1.

12. On ServerDC1, right-click **GPO1** under the domain node and click to uncheck **Enforced**. Right-click **TestOU1** and click to uncheck **Block Inheritance**.

13. Continue to the next activity.

Activity 5-3: Using GPO Security Filtering

Time Required: 15 minutes

Objective: Change the default security filtering on a GPO and examine the results.

Required Tools and Equipment: ServerDC1, ServerDM1

Description: In this activity, you use GPO filtering to change the default inheritance behavior of GPO processing.

1. On ServerDC1, in the Group Policy Management console, click to expand the **Group Policy Objects** folder, and then click **GPO1**. In the right pane, click the **Scope** tab, if necessary.

2. In the Security Filtering dialog box in the right pane, click the **Add** button. Type **domuser2,** click **Check Names**, and then click **OK**.

3. Click the **Delegation** tab. Click **Advanced**. In the top pane of the GPO1 Security Settings dialog box, click **Authenticated Users**. In the bottom pane, scroll down and click to clear **Apply group policy** (see Figure 5-10). Click **OK**.

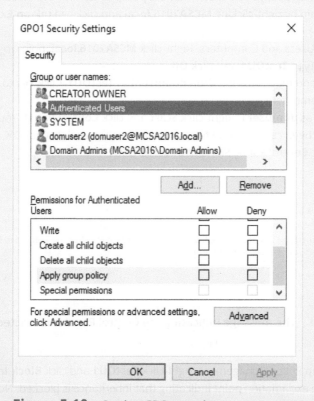

Figure 5-10   Setting GPO security

4. Click the **Scope** tab again. Now domuser2 is the only security principal with Read and Apply Group Policy permissions for GPO1.

Note 📎

Authenticated Users must have the Read permission in order for other users to access a GPO. This is unexpected but a known issue.

---

5. GPO1 is still linked to the domain object, so there's no need to link it to a container. On ServerDM1, sign in as **domuser1**. Right-click **Start** and click **Control Panel**. Control Panel opens normally because only domuser2 has permission to read the GPO1 Group Policy object that restricts access to Control Panel.

6. Sign off ServerDM1 and sign in as **domuser2**. Right-click **Start** and click **Control Panel**. You should see the message that the operation has been canceled due to restrictions because domuser2 has permission to read the GPO that restricts access to Control Panel. Sign out of ServerDM1.

7. On ServerDC1, click to select **GPO1**, if necessary, and click the **Scope** tab, if necessary. Click **Add,** type **Authenticated Users,** and click **Check Names**. Click **OK**. Click **domuser2,**click **Remove,** and click **OK**.

8. Right-click **GPO1** under the domain node and click **Delete** to unlink it.

9. Continue to the next activity.

Activity 5-4: Using GPO Security Filtering for a Computer Account

Time Required: 15 minutes
Objective: Change the default security filtering on a GPO and examine the results.
Required Tools and Equipment: ServerDC1, ServerDM1
Description: In this activity, you change the security filtering on a GPO for a computer account.

1. On ServerDC1, open the Group Policy Management console, if necessary. Right-click the **Group Policy Objects** folder and click **New**. Type **GPO2** in the Name text box and click **OK**.

2. Click **GPO2** in the left pane. In the right pane, click the **Scope** tab, if necessary.

3. In the Security Filtering dialog box in the right pane, click the **Add** button. Click the **Object Types** button. By default, computer accounts aren't recognized in this dialog box. In the Object Types dialog box, click to select **Computers**. Click **OK**.

4. Type **ServerDM1**, click **Check Names**, and click **OK**.

5. Click the **Delegation** tab and then click **Advanced**. In the top pane of the GPO2 Security Settings dialog box, click **Authenticated Users**. In the bottom pane, scroll down and click to clear **Apply group policy**. Click **OK**. ServerDM1 is now the only security principal with Read and Apply Group Policy permissions for GPO2.

6. Open GPO2 in Group Policy Management Editor. Navigate to **Computer Configuration\Policies\Windows Settings\Security Settings\Local Policies\Security Options**.

7. Find and double-click **Interactive logon: Message text for users attempting to log on**. Click **Define this policy setting in the template**. In the text box, type **Authorized users only may attempt to sign in to this computer!** Click **OK**.

8. Double-click **Interactive logon: Message title for users attempting to log on**. Click **Define this policy setting** and then type **Sign in Warning** in the text box. Click **OK**.

9. Close Group Policy Management Editor. Link GPO2 to the domain.

10. Sign in to ServerDM1 as domuser1. Since the policy you configured is a Computer policy, it is only applied when the computer restarts or if you run gpupdate. Open a command prompt and run **gpupdate**, then sign out of ServerDM1.

11. Attempt to sign in again to ServerDM1 (you usually need to press Ctrl+Alt+Delete to sign in; with a virtual machine, you probably need to press the Ctrl+Alt+Delete toolbar icon or alternate key sequence). You see the sign-in warning you just created. Click **OK**. You don't need to sign in right now.

12. On ServerDC1, run **gpupdate**. Because you linked the policy to the domain, it would normally affect ServerDC1 as well as ServerDM1. Sign out of ServerDC1, and try to sign in again as **Administrator**. You don't see the warning message because only ServerDM1 has permission to read and apply GPO2. Sign in to ServerDC1.

13. On ServerDC1, open Group Policy Management. Navigate to the **Group Policy Objects** folder and click **GPO2** in the left pane. Under Security Filtering, click **Add**. Type **Authenticate Users**, click **Check Names**, and click **OK**. Click **ServerDM1$ (MCSA2016\ServerDM1$)**, click **Remove**, and click **OK** to set Security Filtering back to the default.

14. Continue to the next activity.

Activity 5-5: Configuring Loopback Policy Processing

Time Required: 20 minutes

Objective: Configure loopback policy processing.

Required Tools and Equipment: ServerDC1, ServerDM1

Description: In this activity, you configure loopback policy processing.

1. On ServerDC1, open Active Directory Users and Computers. Create an OU under the domain node named **MemberServers**. Click the **Computers** folder and drag and drop **ServerDM1** to the **MemberServers** OU. Click **Yes** to confirm. Close Active Directory Users and Computers.

2. Open the Group Policy Management console, if necessary. Create a GPO named **GPO3**, and open it in the Group Policy Management Editor.

3. Expand **User Configuration**, **Policies**, and **Administrative Templates**, and configure the following settings:
   - Desktop\Remove Recycle Bin icon from desktop: **Enabled**
   - Desktop\Desktop\DesktopWallpaper: **Enabled**
   - Wallpaper Name: **C:\windows\web\wallpaper\theme2\img7.jpg** (or another image file if you don't have img7.jpg)
   - Wallpaper Style: **Fill**

4. Link **GPO3** to the **MemberServers** OU. (If you don't see the MemberServers OU, click the **Refresh** icon.) Remember that these settings are User Configuration settings, so they don't normally have an effect on computer accounts, which is the only type of account in MemberServers.

5. Sign in to ServerDM1 as **domuser1**. Run **gpupdate**, sign out, and sign in again. The changes you made in GPO3 don't have any effect. The Recycle Bin is still on the desktop, and the wallpaper hasn't changed. Stay signed in to ServerDM1.

6. On ServerDC1, open **GPO3** in the Group Policy Management Editor, if necessary.

7. Expand **Computer Configuration**, **Policies**, **Administrative Templates**, **System**, and **Group Policy**. Double-click **Configure user Group Policy loopback processing mode**. Click **Enabled**, and in the Mode drop-down list box, click **Merge**. This option allows existing user settings that are normally applied to be applied as long as there's no conflict. Click **OK**.

8. On ServerDM1, run **gpupdate**. Sign out, and sign in again as **domuser1**. The settings made in the User Configuration node of GPO3 should now be applied. The wallpaper has changed, and the Recycle Bin is no longer on the desktop. Sign out of ServerDM1.

9. On ServerDC1, unlink **GPO3** from the **MemberServers** OU. Close Group Policy Management Editor.

10. Continue to the next activity.

Configuring Group Policy Client Processing

- **70-742 – Create and manage Group Policy:**
  Configure Group Policy processing

Group Policy is a client/server system. Each Windows OS has a Group Policy client that contacts a domain controller to see whether any GPOs that apply to the computer or user have changed since the last time the client contacted the DC. When Group Policy determines that a GPO should be downloaded, the client activates client-side extensions. A **client-side extension (CSE)** is an extension to the standard Group Policy client that applies specific types of group policy settings to the client computer. For example, the Security CSE applies policy settings defined in a GPO's Security node, and the Software Installation CSE applies policies defined in the Software Installation node. CSEs are also used to apply Group Policy preferences.

As you have learned, group policies are processed when Windows boots and when a user signs in. Group policies are processed at these times by using **foreground processing**. Certain policies, such as Software Installation, are processed only during foreground processing. After Windows has booted and a user has signed in, most group policy settings are refreshed periodically with **background processing**.

Group policies are processed only if the client detects that a policy has changed. In addition, some policies aren't processed if the client detects that the network connection is slow. For many policies, you can change the way the client behaves by default. Settings for group policy processing behavior are found in Policies\Administrative Templates\System\Group Policy under both the Computer Configuration and User Configuration nodes. There are three main ways to change the default processing of certain types of policies discussed in the following sections:

- Slow link processing
- Background processing
- Process even if the Group Policy objects haven't changed

Configuring Slow Link Processing

Processing certain policies across a slow wide area network (WAN) connection might not be desirable. For example, a software installation policy can use quite a lot of bandwidth if a large software package is being downloaded. A slow network link is by default a network connection that's less than 500 kilobits per second (Kbps).

Slow link detection is a function of the Network Location Awareness (NLA) feature. Slow link estimates occur when a Group Policy client authenticates to a domain controller and determines the network name.

Many types of policies aren't processed across a slow network link by default, including the following:
- Disk quota
- Folder redirection
- Internet Explorer maintenance
- Scripts
- Software installation
- Wireless network policies
- Wired network policies
- Most preferences

> **Note** 📎
>
> Administrative Templates policies are always applied because they control slow link processing and other client behavior. Security Settings policies are always applied to ensure that security settings are always in effect.

You might want to change the default behavior of slow link processing. You can do this in a couple of ways:

• *Configure the slow link detection policy*—You can configure the threshold value of what's considered a slow link. The range is between 0 and 4,294,967,200 Kbps; 0 indicates that no links are to be considered slow. If you set the value to 0, all policies are processed without attempting to detect whether the link is slow. The default value is 500 Kbps. You can also specify that wireless WAN (WWAN) connections are always considered slow. A WWAN is a 3G wireless link. To configure slow link detection, go to Policies\Administrative Templates\System\Group Policy, and enable the *Configure Group Policy slow link detection* policy (see Figure 5-11). This policy is under both Computer Configuration and User Configuration and affects policy settings configured in these sections of a GPO.

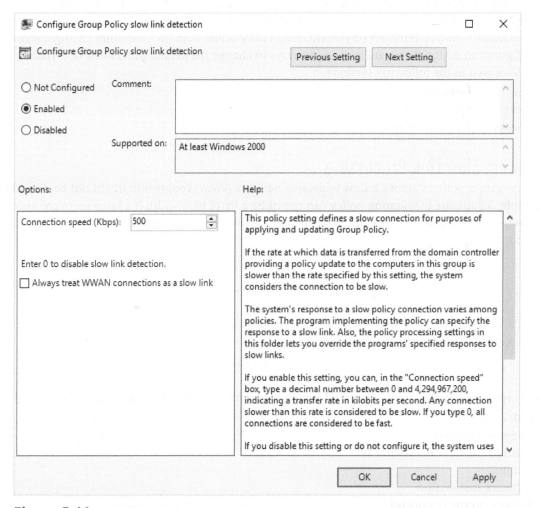

Figure 5-11   Configuring slow link detection

- *Allow slow link processing for selected policies*—The policies that aren't processed by default when a slow link is detected can be configured to allow processing. For example, if you want scripts to be processed even when a slow link is detected, enable the *Configure scripts policy processing* policy found in Policies\Administrative Templates\System\Group Policy\ (see Figure 5-12).

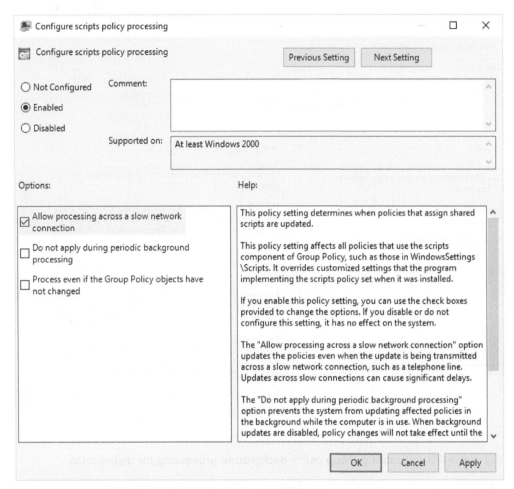

Figure 5-12   Configuring scripts policy processing

Changing Background Processing

After Windows is started, the Computer Configuration node of GPOs affecting the client is refreshed every 90 minutes with a random offset between 0 and 30 minutes. The random offset prevents all computers that were turned on at the same time from refreshing policies simultaneously. In some cases, changes occur immediately while the computer is running, and in other cases, the policy setting is applied, but the system doesn't reflect the change until the next restart. Likewise, after a user signs in, the User Configuration node is refreshed every 90 minutes with the same random offset period. These settings work for most situations, but you might want certain policies to be applied only when a computer restarts or a user signs in, forgoing the periodic refresh. For example, you might not want a policy change that affects a user's working environment while the user is actively using the system.

Note 📎

For domain controllers, the refresh period is 5 minutes with no random offset.

You have the option to turn off background processing for several types of policies and preferences, including but not limited to the following (see Figure 5-13):

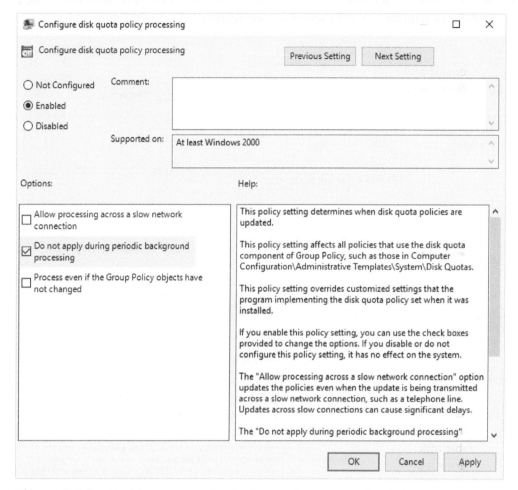

Figure 5-13 Disabling group policy background processing for disk quotas

- Application preference
- Devices preference
- Disk quota policy
- Files and folders preference
- Internet Explorer maintenance policy
- Internet settings preference
- Local users and groups preference
- Network options preference
- Scripts processing
- Wired and wireless policy

For the full list of policies and preferences that can have background processing disabled, look in the Computer Configuration\Policies\Administrative Templates\System\Group Policy node.

Note

Some policies, such as software installation and folder redirection, are never processed in the background. For example, it might be quite surprising to a user if an application is updated or installed while it's in use.

You can also change the background processing interval for computers, domain controllers, and users. The *Set Group Policy refresh interval for computers* policy (see Figure 5-14) lets you set the refresh interval for computers from 0 to 44640 minutes and the random offset from 0 to 1440 minutes. There's a similar policy for domain controllers and users.

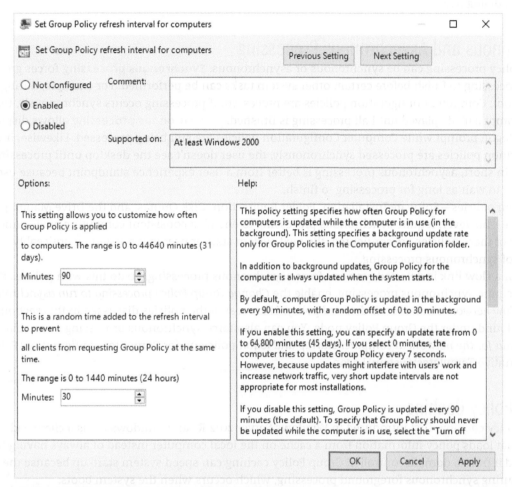

Figure 5-14   Setting the group policy refresh interval

Note

You can turn off all background processing for all computers, domain controllers, and users in the scope of the GPO by enabling *Turn off background refresh of Group Policy*. If this policy is enabled, policies are updated only when the computer starts and when the user signs in.

Processing Unchanged Policies

By default, the Group Policy client downloads and processes only policies that have changed. You can force policies and preferences to be processed even if they haven't changed since the last time they were processed. To do so, select the *Process even if the Group Policy objects have not changed* check box (shown earlier in Figure 5-13). This option isn't usually necessary because most settings configured by Group Policy can't be changed by regular users. However, if some users are signing in with administrative rights, they can change some policy settings. By enabling this setting, such as for security policies, you ensure that any settings the user changes are reapplied at the next refresh interval or system start. This setting can also be enabled for software installation policies, so if a user uninstalls an application, it's reinstalled the next time the computer restarts or the user signs in. If this option is set as a preference, it overrides the *Apply once and do not reapply* option in the Common tab of the preference's Properties dialog box.

Synchronous and Asynchronous Processing

Group policy processing can be synchronous or asynchronous. **Synchronous processing** forces group policy processing to finish before certain other system tasks can be performed. For example, during system boot, Computer Configuration policies are processed. If processing occurs synchronously, the user logon prompt isn't displayed until all processing is finished. **Asynchronous processing** allows displaying the user logon prompt while Computer Configuration policies are still being processed. Likewise, if User Configuration policies are processed synchronously, the user doesn't see the desktop until processing is finished. In short, asynchronous processing is better from a user experience standpoint because users don't have to wait as long for processing to finish.

Certain policies—Software Installation, Folder Redirection, Disk Quotas, and the Drive Mapping preference—however, require synchronous processing to ensure a consistent computing environment. After any of these policies are configured, the next system start or user logon might be noticeably slower because of synchronous processing.

When a slow link is detected, you can force asynchronous processing. To do this with policies that usually require synchronous processing, enable the *Change Group Policy processing to run asynchronously when a slow network connection is detected* policy. Like most of the policies discussed in this section, this policy is found under the Group Policy node. You can also force synchronous processing by enabling the *Always wait for the network at computer startup and logon* policy under Computer Configuration\Policies\ Administrative Templates\System\Logon.

Group Policy Caching

Group Policy caching, first introduced in Windows Server 2012 R2 and Windows 8.1, is a client-side feature that loads policy information from a cache on the local computer instead of always having to download it from a domain controller. Group Policy caching can speed system start-up because the cache is used during synchronous foreground processing, which occurs when the system boots.

Group Policy caching is enabled by default on Windows Server 2012 R2 and Windows 8.1 computers and higher. A policy setting, Configure Group Policy Caching, in the Computer Configuration\ Administrative Templates\System\Group Policy path allows you to disable caching and configure some parameters (see Figure 5-15).

Group Policy settings are cached each time background processing takes place. Note that the cache is used only when the system boots, not during background processing, and only GPOs that have caching enabled are saved. Figure 5-15 shows the Configure Group Policy Caching setting. If you enable caching (which is enabled by default, you need to enable it only if you want to change these parameters or override a higher-precedence GPO that disables it), you can change two timing parameters:

- *Slow link value*—This value specifies the threshold for the response time from a domain controller to consider a link slow. When the Group Policy cache is read, the client contacts a DC and measures the response time. If the response time is slower than the specified value, the link is considered slow. In this case, only policies with slow link processing enabled are cached.
- *Timeout value*—This value is the maximum time that the Group Policy client waits for a response from a DC before determining that there's no network connection to the DC. If a timeout occurs, group policy processing stops until a connection is established.

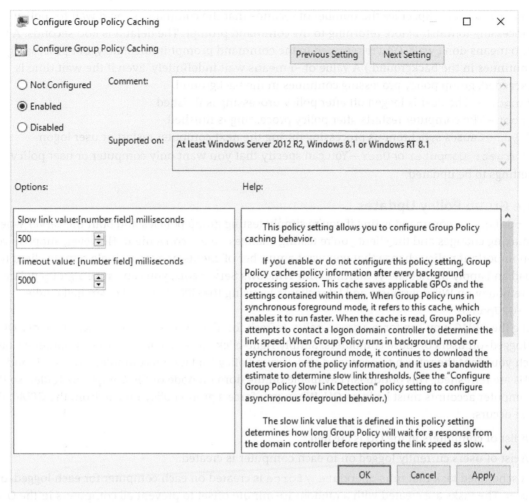

Figure 5-15   Configuring Group Policy caching

 Note

The Group Policy cache is on the local computer at *%systemroot%*\System32\GroupPolicy\Datastore on Windows client OSs only.

Forcing Group Policy Updates

As you know, you don't need to wait for a system reboot, user logon, or refresh interval to update group policies on a client computer. By now, you're quite familiar with the gpupdate.exe command that you run on the client at a command prompt. However, additional options available with the gpupdate.exe command haven't been discussed yet. The following list describes this command and its options:

- *No options*—If you just type gpupdate and press Enter, the command's default behavior takes place: The Group Policy client contacts a DC and then downloads and applies only changed policies for both the Computer Configuration and User Configuration nodes of all GPOs applicable to the computer and user account.
- /force—All settings from all applicable GPOs are reapplied even if they haven't changed.

- /wait: *value*—Specifies the number of seconds that the command should wait for policy processing to finish before returning to the command prompt. The default is 600 seconds. A value of 0 means don't wait. (You're returned to the command prompt immediately, but processing continues in the background.) A value of –1 means wait indefinitely. Even if the wait time is exceeded, group policy processing continues in the background.
- /logoff—The user is logged off after policy processing is finished.
- /boot—The computer restarts after policy processing is finished.
- /sync—Causes synchronous processing during the next computer restart or user logon.
- /target: Computer *or* User—You can specify that you want only computer or user policy settings to be updated.

Remote Group Policy Updates

The gpupdate.exe command is fine if you're simply testing group policies and both the server where you're making changes and the client you're testing changes on are convenient. However, suppose you make an important policy change that you want a number of clients or even a single remote client to download and apply immediately? Starting with Windows Server 2012, you can cause a group policy refresh remotely on Windows Vista and later clients by using the GPMC or the PowerShell cmdlet Invoke-GPUpdate.

Using the GPMC, you can force a group policy refresh for all computers in an Active Directory OU and all logged-on users of those computers. Simply right-click an OU containing the computer accounts on which you want the refresh to occur and click Group Policy Update. All computers in the OU and child OUs are refreshed. This option isn't available on the domain node or the Computers folder, so the target computer accounts must be in an OU. When you force a group policy update from the GPMC, the following occurs:

1. A list of computers in the OU is created.
2. A list of users currently logged on to each computer is created.
3. A scheduled task that runs gpupdate /force is created on each computer for each logged-on user. The tasks are created with a random 10-minute offset to prevent all computers in the OU from initiating the update at the same time.
4. After the random delay period, users who are logged on see a command prompt open, and the gpupdate /force command runs.

The Invoke-GPUpdate PowerShell cmdlet performs similarly except that you specify a computer rather than an OU to update. By default, only changed policies are applied, but you can use the -force option to reapply all settings. In addition, you can cause the update to occur immediately or after a random delay specified in minutes. By using a pipe with the Get-ADComputer command, you can update several computers at once, including those in the Computers folder. The following two commands show examples of using Invoke-GPUpdate. The first command updates a single computer, and the second one forces updates on all computers in the Computers folder:

```
Invoke-GPUpdate -Computer ServerDM1

Get-ADComputer -filter * -Searchbase "cn=computers,
  dc=411Dom1,dc=local" | foreach{ Invoke-GPUpdate
  -computer $_.name -force}
```

Configuring the Firewall for Remote Group Policy Updates

Target client computers must have the following inbound firewall rules enabled on the domain profile for a remote group policy update to be successful:

- Remote Scheduled Tasks Management (RPC)
- Remote Scheduled Tasks Management (RPC-EPMAP)
- Windows Management Instrumentations (WMI-In)

You can configure the firewall with the Group Policy tool or on the client computer. If you use Group Policy, a Starter GPO named *Group Policy Remote Update Firewall Ports* that already has the firewall settings configured correctly is available.

Activity 5-6: Using Remote Group Policy Updates

Time Required: 10 minutes

Objective: Configure the firewall and perform a remote group policy update.

Required Tools and Equipment: ServerDC1, ServerDM1

Description: Configure the firewall for a remote group policy update on ServerDM1.

1. On ServerDM1, sign in as the domain **Administrator**. Open the Network and Sharing Center, and click **Windows Firewall** at the lower left.

2. In the Windows Firewall window, click **Advanced settings**. In the Windows Firewall with Advanced Security window, click **Inbound Rules**.

3. In the Actions pane, click **Filter by Profile** and click to select **Filter by Domain Profile**. Right-click the following settings and click **Enable Rule** for each one: **Remote Scheduled Tasks Management (RPC)**, **Remote Scheduled Tasks Management (RPC-EPMAP)**, and **Windows Management Instrumentations (WMI-In)**. Close Windows Firewall with Advanced Security and Windows Firewall.

4. On ServerDC1, open the Group Policy Management console, if necessary. Right-click the **MemberServers** OU and click **Group Policy Update**. You'll see a message indicating that one computer will be updated because the ServerDM1 account is in the MemberServers OU. Click **Yes**.

5. In the Remote Group Policy update results window, you should see ServerDM1 in the list of computers (see Figure 5-16). Click **Close**. On ServerDM1, a command prompt window opens after a while, and the gpupdate command runs.

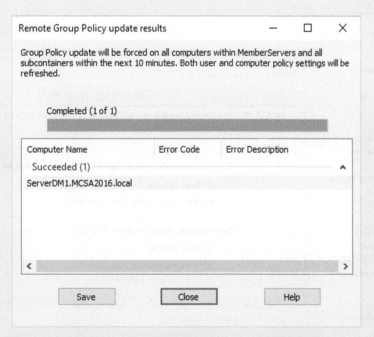

Figure 5-16   Results of a remote group policy update

6. To perform a remote Group Policy update using PowerShell, open a PowerShell prompt on ServerDC1. Type **Invoke-GPUpdate -Computer ServerDM1 RandomDelayInMinutes 0** and press **Enter**. A command prompt window opens immediately on ServerDM1. On ServerDC1, close the PowerShell prompt.

7. Sign out of ServerDM1 but stay signed in to ServerDC1 and continue to the next activity.

Group Policy Results and Modeling

- **70-742 – Create and manage Group Policy:**
  Configure Group Policy processing

No matter how well you understand group policy processing and inheritance, determining exactly what GPOs and policy settings are applied to an object can be difficult. Windows includes the following tools to help you determine which policies are applied to a user or computer and which GPO supplied the policy. The information supplied by these tools can help you troubleshoot group policy processing:

- *Group Policy Results*—This wizard built into the GPMC creates a report to show administrators which policy settings apply to a user, computer, or both. To use this wizard, right-click the Group Policy Results node in the GPMC and click Group Policy Results Wizard. You have the option to display policy results for the current computer or another computer, and you can select which user to report on from a list of users who have signed in to the target computer. The wizard can show results only of policies that have already been applied to the computer or user. After the wizard finishes, the report has three tabs:

  - Summary: Shows information about when the computer and user polices were last refreshed and whether any errors were detected. In addition, the report shows whether a fast or slow link was detected (see Figure 5-17). You can right-click this window and click Print or Save Report (which saves it in an HTML or XML file).

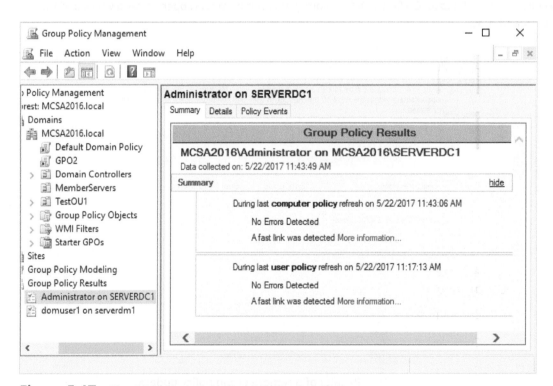

Figure 5-17   The Summary tab in Group Policy Results

- Details: Displays information about the computer and user configuration Group Policy components, including when policies were last processed. All defined settings that were applied to the computer and user are listed. The Winning GPO column shows which GPO the setting came from (not shown in Figure 5-18). You also see a list of GPOs that were denied, why they were denied, and the results of WMI filters. As with the Summary tab, you can right-click to print or save the report.

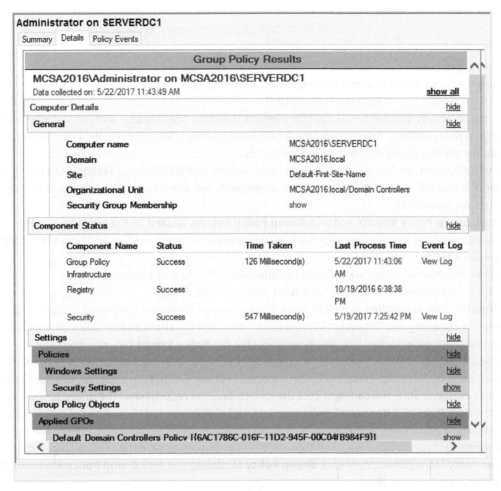

Figure 5-18   The Details tab in Group Policy Results

- Policy Events: Displays all events that are generated by group policies in Event Viewer. To see the events on a remote computer, all three Remote Event Log Management rules must be enabled for inbound connections on the remote computer.
- gpresult.exe—This command-line version of the Group Policy Results Wizard outputs a report onscreen, or you can specify the name of a file with an .html extension. To produce a summary report for the ServerDM1 computer and the testuser1 user, enter the following at a command prompt:

```
gpresult /s ServerDM1 /user testuser1 /r
```

- *Group Policy Modeling*—This is a what-if tool for group policies. Like Group Policy Results, it's a wizard built into the GPMC that shows administrators which policy settings would apply to a computer and/or user account if it were moved to a different container. Essentially, the report shows which policy settings are in effect for a user whose account is placed in a particular OU and whose computer is placed in a particular OU. You can select user and computer membership in security groups so that GPO filtering is taken into account. In addition, you can select options for slow link processing and loopback processing and specify WMI filters. Group Policy Modeling produces a report similar to Group Policy Results with Summary and Details tabs. Instead of a Policy Events tab, the third tab, Query, summarizes the what-if choices that were made to produce the report.
- *Resultant Set of Policy (RSoP) snap-in*—This MMC snap-in functions much like Group Policy Results and Group Policy Modeling. RSoP has two modes: logging and planning. Logging mode produces a database of policy results that you browse similarly to using the Group Policy Management Editor. Planning mode is similar to Group Policy Modeling, producing a database of what-if results based on the same criteria you can choose from the Group Policy Modeling Wizard.

Activity 5-7: Using Group Policy Results and Group Policy Modeling

Time Required: 25 minutes
Objective: Use the Group Policy Results and Group Policy Modeling tools.
Required Tools and Equipment: ServerDC1, ServerDM1
Description: In this activity, you use the Group Policy Results Wizard to see how user and computer accounts are affected by group policy settings. Then you use the Group Policy Modeling Wizard to create a what-if scenario to see how accounts are affected if they're moved to a different OU.

1. On ServerDC1, open the Group Policy Management console. Link **GPO3** to the **TestOU1** OU (this is where domuser1 is located). On ServerDM1, sign in as **domuser1**. This ensures that the latest policies are applied to domuser1 on ServerDM1.
2. Right-click **Group Policy Results** and click **Group Policy Results Wizard**. In the welcome window, click **Next**.
3. In the Computer Selection window, click the **Another computer** option button, and type **ServerDM1** in the text box. Click **Next**.
4. In the User Selection window, click **MCSA2016\domuser1**, and then click **Next**.
5. In the Summary of Selections window, click **Next**, and then click **Finish**.
6. Click **domuser1 on serverdm1** in the left pane, if necessary. In the report generated in the right pane, examine the Summary and Details tabs. In the Details tab, click the **show all** link to see all applied settings. Pay particular attention to the User Details section. Click the **Policy Events** tab. You won't see the events unless you enable all three Remote Event Log Management rules in Windows Firewall on ServerDM1.
7. In the left pane of the Group Policy Management console under Group Policy Results, you see the icon domuser1 on serverdm1. You can right-click the icon to save the report, rerun the query, and see an advanced view. Right-click **domuser1 on serverdm1** and click **Advanced View**. The policy information opens in the Resultant Set of Policy (RSoP) snap-in. You can browse through the policies to see all the policies that are currently configured. Close the RSoP console. When prompted to save the console, click **No**.
8. In Group Policy Management, right-click **Group Policy Modeling** and click **Group Policy Modeling Wizard**. In the welcome window, click **Next**.
9. In the Domain Controller Selection window, click the **This domain controller** option button, and then click **Next**.
10. In the User and Computer Selection window, click the **User** option button and type **mcsa2016\domuser1**. Click the **Computer** option button, type **mcsa2016\serverdm1** (see Figure 5-19), and click **Next**.

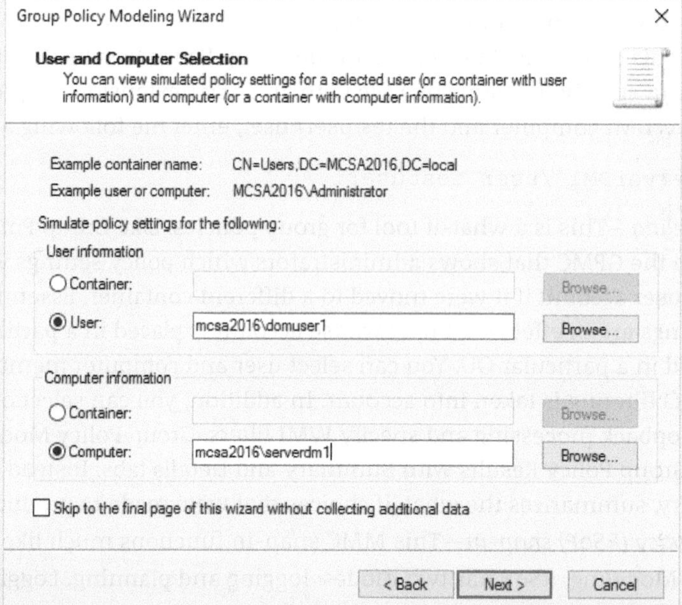

Figure 5-19 Selecting the user and computer for Group Policy Modeling

11. In the Advanced Simulated Options window, accept the defaults, and click **Next**.
12. In the Alternate Active Directory Paths window in the User location text box, change TestOU1 to **MemberServers**. This change simulates the policies that would be applied to domuser1 if the user were in the MemberServers OU. Click **Next**.
13. Click **Next** in the User Security Groups window, the Computer Security Groups window, the WMI Filters for Users window, and the WMI Filters for Computers window.
14. In the Summary of Selections window, click **Next**, and then click **Finish**.
15. The report is displayed in the right pane. Click the **Details** tab, and scroll down until you see User Details. Under the General section, notice that the User container shows mcsa2016.local/MemberServers to indicate that the results are based on domuser1 being located in MemberServers. Also notice that GPO3 is not shown as an applied GPO as it was in the Group Policy Results report. That's because GPO3 would not be applied to the user account if the user was in the MemberServers OU.
16. Continue to the next activity.

Managing GPOs

 **Certification**

- **70-742 – Create and manage Group Policy:**
  Create and manage Group Policy Objects (GPOs)

You know how to create and link GPOs with the GPMC, and you have learned about group policy processing and inheritance. The following sections discuss GPO backup and restore, GPO migration, GPO delegation, and GPO import and copy.

GPO Backup and Restore

In a large, complex network with many different policy needs for users, servers, and workstations, configuring and testing GPOs often takes many hours. Thankfully, Windows has a solution for backing up and restoring GPOs in case disaster strikes: GPO backups. GPO backups are also helpful if you need to revert to an older version of a GPO or if you delete a GPO accidentally. For example, if many changes are made to a GPO and the changes cause unexpected problems, you might save time by restoring an older version instead of trying to undo the changes.

When you back up a GPO, the policy settings are backed up, and so are the security filtering settings, delegation settings, and WMI filter links. What's not backed up are the WMI filter files associated with the WMI links, IPsec policies, and GPO container links. Backing up a GPO is a simple three-step process:

1. In the GPMC, right-click the GPO in the Group Policy Objects folder (because you can't back up a GPO from the shortcut link to an Active Directory container) and click Back Up.
2. Select (or create) a folder where the GPO should be stored.
3. Enter a description of the GPO if you want, and click Back Up.

Multiple GPO backups can be stored in the same folder, so you don't need to create a folder each time you back up a GPO. The folder where you store GPO backups should be secure and backed up by a regular system backup routine. You can also right-click the Group Policy Objects folder and select options to back up all GPOs and manage backups.

The procedure for restoring a GPO varies, as follows:

- *Restore a previous version*—If the settings of a backed-up GPO have been changed and you need to revert to an older version, right-click the GPO in the Group Policy Objects folder and click Restore from Backup. All policy and security settings in the current GPO are replaced by the backup GPO's settings.

- *Restore a deleted GPO*—Right-click the Group Policy Objects folder and click Manage Backups to open the Manage Backups dialog box (see Figure 5-20). You can select which GPO you want to restore, view a backed-up GPO's settings, or delete a backed-up GPO. Multiple versions of backed-up GPOs are listed by default, or you can specify seeing only the latest version of each GPO.

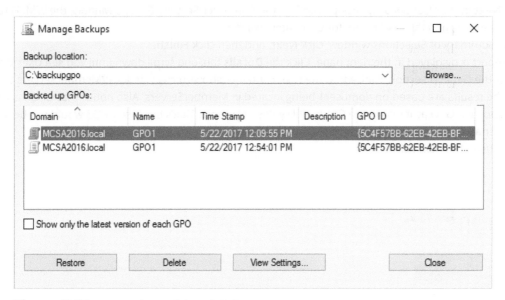

Figure 5-20   Restoring a deleted GPO

- *Import settings*—You can import settings from a backed-up GPO to an existing GPO by right-clicking the GPO and clicking Import Settings. This action is similar to restoring a GPO except that the existing GPO need not be the same GPO as the backed-up GPO. As with a GPO restore, all existing settings in the current GPO are deleted.

GPO Copy and Paste

If you simply want to copy the settings of a GPO into a new GPO, you can do so using the following steps from GPMC:

1. Right-click a GPO in the Group Policy Objects folder and click Copy.
2. Right-click the Group Policy Objects folder.
3. Click Paste. You're asked whether to use the default permissions for the new GPO or preserve the existing permissions of the copied GPO. Make your choice and click OK.
4. Click OK in the progress dialog box after the copy is finished. The new GPO is named Copy of *OriginalGPOName*. For example, if you copied GPO1, the new GPO is named "Copy of GPO1."
5. Rename the copied GPO by right-clicking it and clicking Rename.

Resetting Default GPOs

Making changes to the two default GPOs (Default Domain Policy and Default Domain Controller Policy) isn't recommended. However, if you do make changes and need to revert to the original settings, you can do so without using a backup and restore operation. You can use the command-line program `dcgpofix.exe` to reset settings for either or both default GPOs. This command also resets permissions and any existing security or WMI filters:

- `dcgpofix`—Resets both the Default Domain Policy and the Default Domain Controllers Policy
- `dcgpofix /target:DC`—Resets the Default Domain Controllers Policy
- `dcgpofix /target:domain`—Resets the Default Domain Policy

GPO Migration

You might need to migrate GPOs from one domain to another for a variety of reasons. For example, you have a multidomain environment, and two domains have similar policy requirements. After perfecting the GPOs in one domain, you can migrate them to be used in the other domain. Migration is also useful when you have set up a test environment that's similar to one of your production domains. You can configure and test a GPO in the test environment thoroughly and then migrate it to the production domain.

GPOs can be migrated across domains in the same or different forests by adding the domain to the GPMC. To add a domain in the same forest, right-click the Domains node in the left pane of the GPMC and click Show Domains to open the dialog box shown in Figure 5-21. Then select the domains that you want to add to the GPMC.

Figure 5-21   Selecting domains to add to the GPMC

To add a domain from a different forest, right-click the Group Policy Management node in the left pane of the GPMC and click Add Forest. Then enter the name of the domain in the forest that you want to add.

When you have multiple domains in the GPMC, you can simply copy and paste a GPO from the source domain's Group Policy Objects folder to the target domain's Group Policy Objects folder. When you click Paste in the target folder, the Cross-Domain Copying Wizard starts. It gives you the option to use default permissions or preserve existing permissions on the GPO and translates any security principals or Universal Naming Convention (UNC) paths in the GPO. Recall that security principals are assigned in policies such as User Rights Assignment and Restricted Groups, and UNC paths are used in policies such as Folder Redirection, Software installation, and Scripts. This information must be modified or translated during the migration process.

A second method for migrating GPOs uses the backup and import procedure. The biggest difference between these two methods is that the copy-and-paste method creates a new GPO and the backup and import procedure overwrites settings in an existing GPO in the target domain.

Configuring a Migration Table

If you're migrating several GPOs from one domain to another, you might want to use a migration table to map security principals and UNC paths. A **migration table** is a list of security principals and UNC paths in a GPO that can be mapped to the security principals and UNC paths in the destination domain (see Figure 5-22). The migration table can then be used when copying a GPO from one domain to another.

You create a migration table by right-clicking the Domains node in the GPMC and clicking Open Migration Table Editor or using the Cross-Domain Copying Wizard. In the Migration Table Editor, click Tools, and then choose Populate from GPO or Populate from Backup. All security principals and UNC

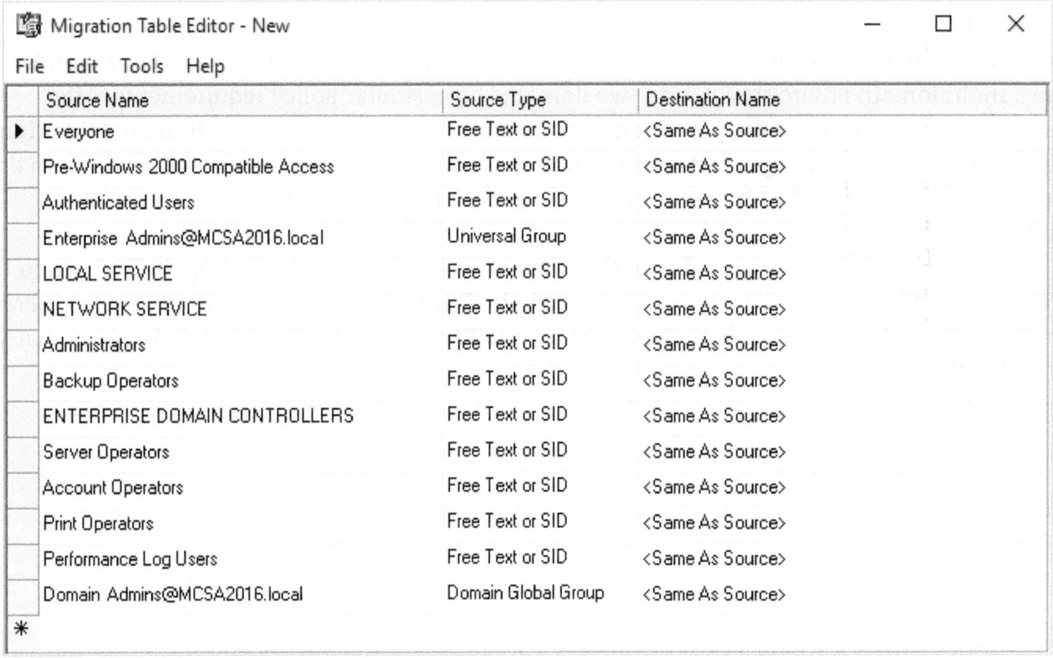

Source Name	Source Type	Destination Name
Everyone	Free Text or SID	<Same As Source>
Pre-Windows 2000 Compatible Access	Free Text or SID	<Same As Source>
Authenticated Users	Free Text or SID	<Same As Source>
Enterprise Admins@MCSA2016.local	Universal Group	<Same As Source>
LOCAL SERVICE	Free Text or SID	<Same As Source>
NETWORK SERVICE	Free Text or SID	<Same As Source>
Administrators	Free Text or SID	<Same As Source>
Backup Operators	Free Text or SID	<Same As Source>
ENTERPRISE DOMAIN CONTROLLERS	Free Text or SID	<Same As Source>
Server Operators	Free Text or SID	<Same As Source>
Account Operators	Free Text or SID	<Same As Source>
Print Operators	Free Text or SID	<Same As Source>
Performance Log Users	Free Text or SID	<Same As Source>
Domain Admins@MCSA2016.local	Domain Global Group	<Same As Source>

Figure 5-22 **The Migration Table Editor**

paths used in the selected GPO are listed as shown in Figure 5-22. By default, the Destination Name column is set to <Same As Source>. You change this column to translate information to the appropriate security principals or UNC paths in the destination domain. Special identities and built-in groups don't need to be translated.

GPO Management Delegation

The possible permissions for GPO delegation depend on whether you're working with the GPO or the target to which the GPO is linked. Eight possible permissions can be applied to GPOs and the container objects they're linked to through delegation:

- *Create GPOs*—This permission applies only to the Group Policy Objects folder where you can find all GPOs in the GPMC. When you click the Group Policy Objects folder and click the Delegation tab in the right pane, you can view, add, and remove security principals who are allowed to create GPOs in the domain (see Figure 5-23). By default, Domain Admins, Group Policy Creator Owners, and the SYSTEM special identity have this permission.
- *Link GPOs*—This permission can be set on sites, domains, and OUs and determines who can link or unlink a GPO to or from the container. Administrators, Domain Admins, Enterprise Admins, and the SYSTEM special identity are granted this permission by default.
- *Perform Group Policy Modeling analyses*—This permission is set on domains and OUs and determines who can run the GPO Modeling Wizard (discussed in "Group Policy Results and Modeling" earlier in this chapter) on the specified container. The default users are the same as for the Link GPOs permission.
- *Read Group Policy Results data*—This permission is set on domains and OUs and determines who can run the Group Policy Results Wizard (also discussed in "Group Policy Results and Modeling") on users and/or computers. The default users are the same as for the Link GPOs permission.
- *Read*—This permission is set on GPOs; users with this permission can view settings and back up a GPO. By default, the Enterprise Domain Controllers universal group has this permission for all GPOs.
- *Read (from Security Filtering)*—This permission is used in group policy filtering. By default, the Authenticated Users group has this permission for all GPOs. It includes both the Read and Apply Group Policy permission and is generally set in the Scope tab of a GPO's Properties dialog box.

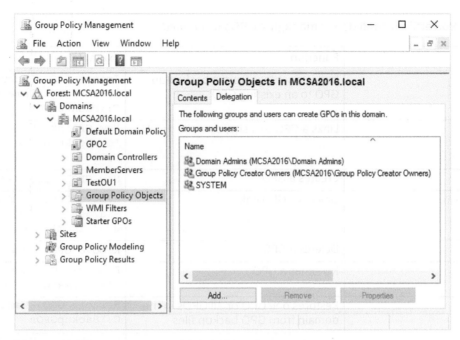

Figure 5-23   Delegating GPO creation

- *Edit settings, delete, modify security*—This permission is set on GPOs and determines who can edit, change status on, back up, delete, and change security on a GPO. By default, Domain Admins, Enterprise Admins, and the SYSTEM special identity are granted this permission.
- *Edit Settings*—With this permission, security principals can change existing settings, import settings, and enable or disable a GPO. No users are granted this permission by default.

To configure delegation on a GPO, click the GPO in the GPMC and click the Delegation tab. You can add users and groups from the Delegation tab or click the Advanced button to add specific Allow and Deny permissions. The Advanced button opens the familiar DACL you have used to configure file and folder permissions.

PowerShell Cmdlets for Managing GPOs

A number of PowerShell cmdlets, described in Table 5-2, are available for managing GPOs. As with all PowerShell cmdlets, to find more information on using a cmdlet, type `Get-Help cmdletName -detailed` at a PowerShell prompt (replacing *cmdletName* with the name of the cmdlet).

Table 5-2   PowerShell cmdlets for managing GPOs

Cmdlet	Function	Example
Backup-GPO	Backs up one GPO or all the GPOs in a domain	`Backup-GPO -All -Path C:\BackupGPOs`
Copy-GPO	Copies the settings from an existing GPO and creates a new GPO with those settings	`Copy-GPO -SourceName GPO1 -TargetName NewGPO1`
Get-GPO	Gets information about one GPO or all GPOs in the domain	`Get-GPO -All`
Get-GPResultantSetOfPolicy	Gets the RSoP information for a user, computer, or both and saves it to a file	`Get-GPResultantSetOfPolicy -ReportType xml -Path C:\GPReports\RSoPReport.xml`

(continues)

Table 5-2   PowerShell cmdlets for managing GPOs *(continued)*

Cmdlet	Function	Example
`Import-GPO`	Imports settings from a backed-up GPO to an existing GPO	`Import-GPO -BackupGPOName GPO1 -TargetName GPO2 -Path C:\BackupGPOs`
`New-GPLink`	Links a GPO to a site, domain, or OU	`New-GPLink -Name GPO1 -Target "ou=Desktops,dc=411Dom1,dc=Local"`
`New-GPO`	Creates a GPO	`New-GPO -Name GPO5`
`Remove-GPLink`	Deletes a GPO link	`Remove-GPLink -Name GPO1 -Target "ou=Desktops, dc=411Dom1,dc=Local"`
`Remove-GPO`	Deletes a GPO	`Remove-GPO -Name GPO5`
`Rename-GPO`	Renames a GPO	`Rename-GPO -Name TestGPO -TargetName ScriptsGPO`
`Restore-GPO`	Restores one GPO or all GPOs in the domain from GPO backup files	`Restore-GPO -Name GPO1 -Path C:\BackupGPOs`
`Set-GPLink`	Sets GPO link properties, such as enabled, disabled, enforced, and precedence order	`Set-GPLink -Name GPO1 -Target "ou=Desktops,dc=411Dom1,dc=Local" -Enforced Yes`
`Set-GPPermission`	Sets permissions for a security principal to a GPO or to all GPOs	`Set-GPPermission -Name GPO1 -TargetName "Domain Users" -TargetType Group -PermissionLevel GpoRead`
`Get-Command -module GroupPolicy`	Displays a list of all group policy–related cmdlets	

Activity 5-8: Backing Up and Restoring a GPO

Time Required: 10 minutes
Objective: Back up and restore a GPO.
Required Tools and Equipment: ServerDC1
Description: In this activity, you use PowerShell cmdlets to back up and restore a GPO.

1. On ServerDC1, create a directory named **C:\backupgpo** to store backed-up GPOs.
2. Open a PowerShell prompt. Type **Backup-GPO -Name GPO1 -Path C:\backupgpo** and press **Enter**.
3. In the Group Policy Management console, open **GPO1** in the Group Policy Management Editor.
4. Expand **Computer Configuration**, **Policies**, **Windows Settings**, **Security Settings**, **Local Policies**, and **User Rights Assignment**. Double-click the **Add workstations to domain** policy.
5. Click **Define these policy settings**. Click the **Add User or Group** button, and type **Domain Users** in the User or group names text box. Click **OK** twice, and close the Group Policy Management Editor.
6. In the PowerShell window, type **Restore-GPO -Name GPO1 -Path C:\backupgpo** and press **Enter**.
7. In the Group Policy Management console, open **GPO1** in the Group Policy Management Editor.
8. Expand **Computer Configuration**, **Policies**, **Windows Settings**, **Security Settings**, **Local Policies**, and **User Rights Assignment**. Double-click the **Add workstations to domain** policy.
9. Verify the policy has been restored to its original setting, Not Defined.
10. Shut down all servers.

Chapter Summary

- Group policy processing can be confusing because there are so many exceptions to normal processing and inheritance behavior. When you configure and link a Group Policy Object (GPO) to an Active Directory container, you need to be aware of how that GPO will affect the objects in the container and subcontainers.

- GPO scope defines which objects are affected by the settings in a GPO. GPOs are applied in this order: local computer, site, domain, and OU. When OUs are nested, the GPO linked to the OU nested most deeply takes precedence over all other GPOs.

- There are two main ways to change default GPO inheritance: blocking inheritance and using GPO enforcement.

- After a GPO is created, it can be in a specific state. You can view and modify the GPO status by clicking the GPO in the left pane of Group Policy Management and clicking the Details tab.

- There are two types of GPO filtering: security filtering and WMI filtering. Security filtering uses permissions to restrict objects from accessing a GPO. WMI filtering uses queries to select a group of computers based on certain attributes and then applies or doesn't apply policies based on the query's results.

- If you enable loopback policy processing, all settings in the User Configuration node of the GPO apply to all users who sign in to the computer.

- Group Policy is a client/server system. Each Windows OS has a Group Policy client that contacts a domain controller to see whether any GPOs that apply to the computer or user have changed since the last time the client contacted the DC.

- After Windows is started, the Computer Configuration node of GPOs affecting the client is refreshed every 90 minutes with a random offset between 0 and 30 minutes.

- Group policy processing can be synchronous or asynchronous. Synchronous processing forces group policy processing to finish before certain other system tasks can be performed. Asynchronous processing allows displaying the user logon prompt while Computer Configuration policies are still being processed.

- Group Policy caching is a client-side feature that loads policy information from a cache on the local computer instead of always having to download it from a domain controller.

- Using the GPMC, you can force a group policy refresh for all computers in an Active Directory OU and all logged-on users of those computers.

- Group Policy Results is a wizard built into the GPMC that creates a report to show administrators which policy settings apply to a user, a computer, or both. Group Policy Modeling is a what-if tool for group policies.

- When you back up a GPO, the policy settings are backed up and so are the security filtering settings, delegation settings, and WMI filter links. What's not backed up are the WMI filter files associated with the WMI links, IPsec policies, and GPO container links.

- You might need to migrate GPOs from one domain to another for a variety of reasons. After perfecting GPOs in one domain, you can migrate them to be used in another domain.

- The possible permissions for GPO delegation depend on whether you're working with the GPO or the target to which the GPO is linked. Eight possible permissions can be applied to GPOs and the container objects they're linked to through delegation.

Key Terms

asynchronous processing	GPO filtering	security filtering
background processing	GPO scope	synchronous processing
client-side extension (CSE)	Group Policy caching	WMI filtering
foreground processing	loopback policy processing	
GPO enforcement	migration table	

Review Questions

1. Which of the following represents the correct order in which GPOs are applied to an object that falls within the GPO's scope?
   a. Site, domain, OU, local GPOs
   b. Local GPOs, domain, site, OU
   c. Domain, site, OU, local GPOs
   d. Local GPOs, site, domain, OU

2. After a GPO is created, which of the following are possible states for the new GPO? (Choose all that apply.)
   a. GPO status: Enabled
   b. GPO status: Unlinked
   c. Link status: Enabled
   d. GPO status: All settings disabled

3. You have created a GPO named RestrictU and linked it to the Operations OU (containing 30 users) with link order 3. RestrictU sets several policies in the User Configuration node. After a few days, you realize the Operations OU has three users who should be exempt from the restrictions in this GPO. You need to make sure these three users are exempt from RestrictU's settings, but all other policy settings are still in effect for them. What's the best way to proceed?
   a. Move the three users to a new OU. Create a GPO with settings suitable for the three users, and link it to the new OU.
   b. Create an OU under Operations, and move the three users to this new OU. Create a GPO and link it to this new OU. Configure the new OU to block inheritance of the RestrictU GPO.
   c. Create a global group and add the three users as members. Configure GPO security filtering so that the global group is denied access to the GPO.
   d. Set the Enforced option on RestrictU with a WMI filter that excludes the three user accounts.

4. None of the computers in an OU seem to be getting computer policies from the GPO linked to the OU, but users in the OU are getting user policies from this GPO. Which of the following are possible reasons that computer policies in the GPO aren't affecting the computers? (Choose all that apply.)

   a. The GPO link is disabled.
   b. The Computer Configuration settings are disabled.
   c. The computer accounts have Deny Read permission.
   d. The OU has the Block Inheritance option set.

5. You need to move some user and computer accounts in Active Directory, but before you do, you want to know how these accounts will be affected by the new group policies they'll be subject to. What can you do?
   a. Run `secedit.exe` with the planning option.
   b. Run Group Policy Modeling.
   c. Run Group Policy Results.
   d. Run RSoP in logging mode.

6. You don't have policies that force settings for the look of users' computer desktops. Each user's chosen desktop settings are applied from his or her roaming profile to any computer he or she signs in to. You think it's important for users to have this choice, but you'd like a consistent look for computers used for product demonstrations to customers. What's the best way to do this without affecting users when they sign in to other computers?
   a. Configure desktop policies in the Computer Configuration node of a GPO and link this GPO to the OU containing the demonstration computers.
   b. Configure loopback policy processing in Computer Configuration. Configure the desktop settings in User Configuration and link the GPO to the OU containing the demonstration computers.
   c. Create a user named Demo. Configure Demo's desktop settings and use only this user account to sign in to demonstration computers.
   d. Create a GPO with a startup script that configures desktop settings suitable for demonstration computers when these computers are started. Link the GPO to the OU containing the demonstration computers. Instruct users to restart demonstration computers before using them.

7. You want to create policies in a new GPO that affect only computers with Windows 8 installed. You don't want to reorganize your computer accounts to do this, and you want computers that are upgraded to Windows 10 to fall out of the GPO's scope automatically. What can you do?
   a. For each policy, use selective application to specify Windows 8 as the OS.
   b. Create a new OU, place all computer accounts representing computers with Windows 8 installed in this OU, and link the GPO to this OU.
   c. Create a group called Win8Computers. Place all computer accounts representing computers with Windows 8 installed in this group and use this group in a security filter on the GPO. Link the GPO to the domain.
   d. Configure a WMI filter on the GPO that specifies Windows 8 as the OS. Link the GPO to the domain.

8. An administrator has just backed up a GPO to save specific policy settings. Which of the following additional settings and information were also backed up in this procedure? (Choose all that apply.)
   a. Delegation settings
   b. Security filtering settings
   c. Network Policy Updates
   d. WMI filter links

9. An OU structure in your domain has one OU per department, and all the computer and user accounts are in their respective OUs. You have configured several GPOs defining computer and user policies and linked the GPOs to the domain. A group of managers in the Marketing Department need policies that differ from those of the rest of the Marketing Department users and computers, but you don't want to change the top-level OU structure. Which of the following GPO processing features are you most likely to use?
   a. Block inheritance
   b. GPO enforcement
   c. WMI filtering
   d. Loopback processing

10. You have created a GPO that sets certain security settings on computers. You need to make sure that these settings are applied to all computers in the domain. Which of the following GPO processing features are you most likely to use?
    a. Block inheritance
    b. GPO enforcement
    c. WMI filtering
    d. Loopback processing

11. You have a branch office connected to the main office with a sometimes unreliable and slow WAN link. Users are complaining about long logon times. Which Group Policy client feature are you most likely to configure to solve the problem?
    a. Synchronous processing
    b. Background processing
    c. Slow link processing
    d. Remote update processing

12. You have just made changes to a GPO that you want to take effect as soon as possible on several user and computer accounts in the Sales OU. Most of the users in this OU are currently signed in to their computers. There are about 50 accounts. What's the best way to update these accounts with the new policies as soon as possible?
    a. Configure a script preference that runs `gpupdate` the next time the user signs out.
    b. Configure the GPO to perform foreground processing immediately.
    c. Run the `Get-ADComputer` and `Invoke-GPUpdate` PowerShell cmdlets.
    d. Use the `gpupdate /target:Sales /force` command.

13. You have just finished configuring a GPO that modifies several settings on computers in the Operations OU and linked the GPO to the OU. You right-click the Operations OU and click group Policy Update. You check on a few computers in the Operations department and find that the policies haven't been applied. On one computer, you run `gpupdate` and find that the policies are applied correctly. What's a likely reason the policies weren't applied to all computers when you tried to update them remotely?
    a. The Computer Configuration node of the GPO is disabled.
    b. A security filter that blocks the computer accounts has been set.
    c. The Operations OU has Block Inheritance set.
    d. You need to configure the firewall on the computers.

14. You want to create an HTML report that shows which policies and GPOs are applied to a particular user and computer. Which command should you use?

    a. gpupdate   c. rsop

    b. gpresult   d. Invoke-GPReport

15. An administrator would like to configure a computer to load policy information that is stored locally to speed system startup. What client-side feature should the administrator select?

    a. Locals processing

    b. WMI filtering

    c. Group Policy caching

    d. Network Location Awareness

16. A junior administrator deleted a GPO accidentally, but you had backed it up. What should you do to restore the deleted GPO?

    a. Right-click the GPO backup file in File Explorer and click Restore.

    b. Open the Active Directory Recycle Bin, right-click the GPO object, and click Restore.

    c. Right-click the Group Policy Objects folder and click Manage Backups.

    d. Create a GPO, right-click the new GPO, and click Restore from Backup.

17. You were hired to fix problems with group policies at a company. You open the GPMC to look at the default GPOs and see that extensive changes have been made to both. You want to restore settings to a baseline so that you know where to start. What should you do?

    a. Delete the default GPOs and create new GPOs with the same names.

    b. Run gpofix.

    c. Create a domain and use GPO migration.

    d. Run gpupdate /revert.

18. You manage a multidomain forest with domains named DomainA and DomainB. You want to use the GPOs from DomainA in DomainB without having to reconfigure all GPOs. What do you need to configure?

    a. Migration table

    b. GPO backup and restore

    c. Delegation

    d. RSoP

19. What kind of group policy processing always occurs when a user is logged on to the computer at the time a group policy refresh occurs?

    a. Foreground processing

    b. Slow link processing

    c. Background processing

    d. Selective processing

20. Users who sign in from a branch office connected to the DC via a slow WAN link are complaining of slow logon times when you assign applications via group policies. What can you do to speed their logons?

    a. Perform a remote group policy update.

    b. Disable Group Policy caching.

    c. Configure synchronous processing when a slow link is detected.

    d. Configure asynchronous processing when a slow link is detected.

Critical Thinking

The following activities give you critical thinking challenges. Case Projects offer a scenario with a problem to solve and for which you supply a written solution.

Case Project 5-1: Dealing with Group Policies at a Branch Office

You have set up a branch office with 50 computers. The office is connected via a slow 256 Kbps WAN connection to the main office where all the DCs are located. When you return to the main office, you run Group Policy Results on several users and computers in the branch office. You discover that several policies aren't being applied, including some software installation policies and folder redirection. What's the likely problem, and how can you solve it without incurring additional costs?

Case Project 5-2: Working with Power Users

You have several users who have local administrative access to their computers. Some of these users are changing certain policies that shouldn't be changed for security reasons. You don't want to take away their local administrative access, but you want to be sure that these important policies are reapplied to computers if a user changes them. What can you do?

CHAPTER 6

DOMAIN CONTROLLER AND ACTIVE DIRECTORY MANAGEMENT

After reading this chapter and completing the exercises, you will be able to:

Describe Active Directory key concepts and components

Clone a virtual domain controller

Configure a read only domain controller

Configure sites

Work with operations master roles

Maintain Active Directory

Domain controllers are the main physical component of Active Directory and must be used strategically to get the best performance and reliability from your domain. A single DC is rarely enough, even for a small domain. To provide fault tolerance and load balancing of the functions that DCs provide, inevitably you need to install two or more DCs in your network. To facilitate creating DCs, you can use virtual domain controller cloning. In a multisite domain, you might want to use read only domain controllers (RODCs). If you have multiple sites, it's important to understand how replication works between sites. When new DCs are deployed or DCs are taken offline, you need to be aware of the function and placement of DCs that hold operations master roles. This chapter covers all these topics so that you can manage DCs safely and efficiently in a variety of domains.

Although the Active Directory database is usually reliable, problems can occur because of accidental deletion of Active Directory objects as well as hardware and software failures. This chapter discusses how to back up and restore the Active Directory database and restore objects as needed.

Table 6-1 summarizes the requirements for the hands-on activities in this chapter.

Table 6-1   Activity requirements

Activity	Requirements	Notes
Activity 6-1: Resetting Your Virtual Environment	ServerDC1, ServerDM1, ServerSA1	
Activity 6-2: Installing an RODC with Staging	ServerDC1, ServerSA1	
Activity 6-3: Configuring the Password Replication Policy	ServerDC1, ServerSA1	
Activity 6-4: Creating a Subnet in Active Directory Sites and Services	ServerDC1	
Activity 6-5: Viewing Site Properties	ServerDC1	
Activity 6-6: Changing an RODC to a Standard DC	ServerDC1, ServerSA1	
Activity 6-7: Transferring FSMO Roles	ServerDC1, ServerSA1	
Activity 6-8: Creating a System State Backup	ServerDC1, ServerSA1	
Activity 6-9: Restoring Active Directory from a System State Backup	ServerDC1, ServerSA1	
Activity 6-10: Restoring Deleted Objects from the Active Directory Recycle Bin	ServerDC1, ServerSA1	
Activity 6-11: Compacting the Active Directory Database	ServerDC1, ServerSA1	

Active Directory Review

As you have learned, domain controllers (DCs) are the heart of the physical structure of a Windows Active Directory domain. The other physical component of Active Directory is a site. The logical components of Active Directory are forests, domains, and organizational units (OUs). Before you learn about new topics related to DCs and Active Directory, review the following list of key points to keep in mind:

- DCs are servers that have a Windows Server OS installed with the Active Directory Domain Services server role installed and configured.
- DCs depend on Domain Name System (DNS) as part of the Active Directory infrastructure, and there must be at least one DNS server in a domain.
- One DC per domain is required, but having two DCs for each domain is recommended for reliability and availability. A DC can support only a single domain.
- DCs maintain data consistency in Active Directory with other DCs in the domain by using multimaster replication.
- A **read only domain controller (RODC)** is a DC that stores a read-only copy of the Active Directory database but no password information. Changes to the domain must be made on a writeable DC and then replicated to an RODC, which is called *unidirectional replication*.
- Some functions related to maintaining the Active Directory infrastructure are stored in certain DCs referred to as *operations masters*. These DCs are assigned the Flexible Single Master Operation (FSMO) role, which uses single master replication.
- A **global catalog (GC) server** is a DC configured to hold the global catalog. Every forest must have at least one GC server. GC servers facilitate domain-wide and forest-wide searches and logons across domains, and they hold universal group membership information. Each site should have at least one GC server to speed logons and directory searches.
- Active Directory is based on the Lightweight Directory Access Protocol (LDAP) standard for accessing directory objects.
- An Active Directory tree is made up of one or more domains that share a common top-level and second-level domain name.
- An Active Directory forest consists of one or more trees with domains that share a common trust relationship and schema yet allow independent policies and administration.

- An Active Directory site is a physical location in which DCs communicate and replicate information frequently. A site is composed of one or more IP subnets connected by high-speed local-area network (LAN) technology. Replication between DCs in separate sites can be configured according to the available bandwidth.

Now that you've reviewed the basics of DCs and Active Directory, turn your attention to a couple of new topics in the following sections: cloning a virtual domain controller and configuring RODCs.

Cloning a Virtual Domain Controller

- **70-742 – Install and configure Active Directory Domain Services:**
  Install and configure domain controllers

Because of the benefits of virtualization, implementing DCs as virtual machines in Hyper-V is a common practice. Starting with Windows Server 2012, DCs running as VMs in Hyper-V are virtualization aware, and there are built-in safeguards to prevent the Active Directory database from being adversely affected when the VM is rolled back in time by applying a checkpoint.

These safeguards not only allow checkpoints to be used with DCs but also permit cloning virtual DCs safely, saving administrators from having to install the OS and configure Active Directory on each DC to be deployed. A **DC clone** is a replica of an existing DC and has the following benefits:

- Fast deployment of new DCs in a new or existing domain
- Fast DC restoration during disaster recovery
- Easy deployment of new branch office DCs

Domain Controller Cloning Prerequisites

To clone a DC, you need to verify the following prerequisites:

- The hypervisor must support virtual machine generation identifiers. Currently, this includes Hyper-V running on Windows Server 2012 and later, Microsoft Hyper-V Server 2012 and later, and VMWare vSphere 5.0 Update 2 and later.
- The DC to be cloned must be running Windows Server 2012 or later.
- The PDC emulator FSMO role must be running Windows Server 2012 or later.
- A GC server must be available.
- The following server roles must not be installed on the source DC: DHCP, Active Directory Certificate Services (AD CS), and Active Directory Lightweight Directory Services (AD LDS).

Steps for Cloning a Domain Controller

After you have verified the prerequisites, you clone a DC by following these steps:

1. Authorize the source DC for cloning by adding the DC's computer account to the Cloneable Domain Controllers group in the Users folder in Active Directory.

2. Run the PowerShell cmdlet `Get-ADDCCloningExcludedApplicationList` on the source DC to be sure it's not running any services that are incompatible with cloning. If any unsupported server roles are listed, they must be uninstalled. Other services or applications that are listed must be verified with the software vendor to determine whether they will be affected by a computer name or security identifier (SID) change. Listed software that's determined to be compatible must be added to the compatible list of programs by running the same command with the `-GenerateXml` option.

3. Run the PowerShell cmdlet `New-ADDCCloneConfigFile` on the source DC. This command creates an `.xml` file named `DCCloneConfig.xml` in the *%windir%*\NTDS folder. With this command, you can specify the computer name and IP address settings for the target DC.

4. Shut down the source DC.

5. Export the source DC virtual machine. You can export the VM to a share or a local drive by using the Hyper-V console or the `Export-VM` PowerShell cmdlet. If you export to a local drive, you must first copy the exported folder to a location where the other Hyper-V server can access it. Before you export the VM, make sure to delete all checkpoints first.

6. Import the virtual machine into Hyper-V. You can use the Hyper-V console or the `Import-VM` PowerShell cmdlet. If you're using the Hyper-V console, be sure to select *the Copy the virtual machine (create a new unique ID)* option, and when using PowerShell, make sure you use the `-GenerateNewId` option to create a `VM-Generation-ID` on the new DC. Rename the VM.

7. Start the source DC and then the new DC. The cloned DC processes the `DCCloneConfig.xml` file created on the source DC because it was copied during the export/import process.

8. Both the source DC and the cloned DC are members of the Cloneable Domain Controllers group at this point. Best practices suggest removing both accounts and leaving the group empty until you're ready to clone again.

When you import the source DC, you can use the exported files in place or copy the exported files so that the original files can be used to create another DC. You can import the new DC to the same Hyper-V server or another Hyper-V server. The latter option is more common because having the DCs operate on two different Hyper-V hosts provides another level of fault tolerance. Try walking through this example of cloning a DC named DC1 on a server named HyperV-S1 to a new DC named DC2 running on HyperV-S2, all running Windows Server 2016:

1. On DC1, add the DC1 computer account to the Cloneable Domain Controllers group.

2. On DC1, open an elevated PowerShell prompt and enter the `Get -ADDCCloningExcludedApplicationList` cmdlet. In this example, no incompatible applications or services are found.

3. Next, specify the new DC's configuration by using this cmdlet at the PowerShell prompt:

```
New-ADDCCloneConfigFile -CloneComputerName "DC2" -Static
    IPv4Address "192.168.0.102" -IPv4DNSResolver "192.168.0.101"
    -IPv4SubnetMask "255.255.255.0" -IPv4DefaultGateway "192.168.0.250"
```

If the new DC should be placed in a different Active Directory site, you can use the `-SiteName` option to specify a site.

4. Shut down DC1.

5. Export the DC1 VM. In this example, you use PowerShell to export it to a share named VMExports on a server named Server1:

```
Export-VM -Name DC1 -Path \\Server1\VMExports
```

The VM is copied to a subfolder of the specified path named DC1\Virtual Machines.

6. Import the DC1 VM. On HyperV-S2, issue the following command:

```
$vm = Import-VM -Path \\Server1\VMExports\DC1\Virtual Machines
    -Copy -GenerateNewID
```

The `$vm` parameter captures the name of the imported VM, which is the name of the exported VM plus a time stamp. This parameter is used in the next step. If you use the exported VM to create additional DCs, you also need to specify paths for the configuration file, virtual hard disk (VHD) files, snapshot files, and the smart paging folder.

7. Rename the imported VM on HyperV-S2 with this cmdlet:

```
Rename-VM -VM $vm -NewName "DC2"
```

8. Start DC1 and DC2. The new DC reads the `DCCloneConfig.xml` file and configures itself with the parameters specified in this file.

9. Remove DC1 and DC2 from the Cloneable Domain Controllers group.

Note

It's not necessary to use PowerShell for exporting, importing, and renaming the VM. You can perform these tasks in the Hyper-V Manager console. However, you do need PowerShell to check for compatible software and create the clone configuration file.

Configuring Read Only Domain Controllers

Certification

- **70-742 – Install and configure Active Directory Domain Services:**
  Install and configure domain controllers

An RODC is simply an installation option of a server role you're already familiar with: Active Directory Domain Services. The RODC role was developed to address the need to have a domain controller in a branch office where server expertise and physical security are often lacking. An RODC performs many of the same tasks as a regular DC, but changes to Active Directory objects can't be made on an RODC. An RODC maintains a current copy of Active Directory information through replication. However, there are some important differences in the information an RODC keeps that make it more secure than writeable DCs. These differences are discussed later in the section "RODC Replication." In addition, you should be aware of some factors before installing an RODC in your network. This section discusses the following aspects of using RODCs in a Windows network:

- RODC installation
- RODC replication
- The Password Replication Policy
- Read only DNS

RODC Installation

Before you can install an RODC, you must meet these prerequisites:

- A writeable DC running Windows Server 2008 or later must be operating in the domain. RODCs were introduced in Windows Server 2008, and they can't replicate with DCs running earlier versions of Windows Server.
- The forest functional level must be at least Windows Server 2003.
- In Windows Server 2008/R2, you must use the `adprep /rodcprep` command before installing the RODC if the forest functional level isn't Windows Server 2008 or later. This command is run automatically during Active Directory installation on a Windows Server 2012 and newer server.

Installing an RODC isn't too much different from installing a regular DC. You still install the Active Directory Domain Services role and run the Active Directory configuration wizard. In the Domain Controller Options window (see Figure 6-1), you select the *Read only domain controller (RODC)* check box.

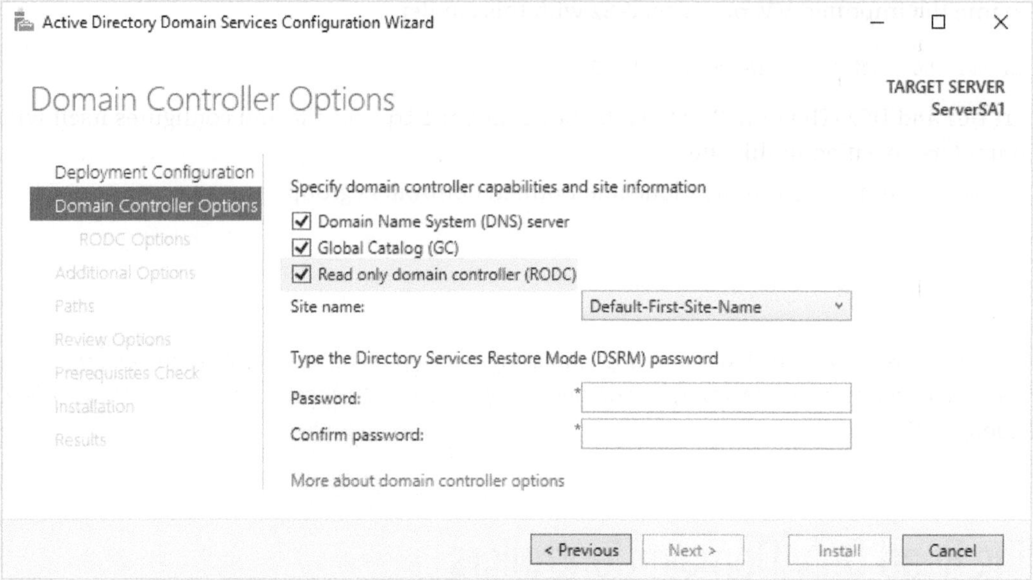

Figure 6-1   The Domain Controller Options window

If you select the RODC option, you move to the RODC Options window (shown in Figure 6-2), where you can select a **delegated administrator account**. This account has local administrative rights and permissions to the RODC, similar to members of the local Administrators group on a member computer or standalone computer. A delegated administrator account for an RODC doesn't have domain administrative rights and permissions, so the scope of the delegated permissions is limited to just the RODC computer. Delegated administration is useful if you need someone in a branch office to perform tasks on an RODC that require administrative capability without giving that user broader domain authority. Delegated administrators çan perform tasks such as installing drivers and software updates, managing disk drives, installing devices, and starting and stopping Active Directory Domain Services.

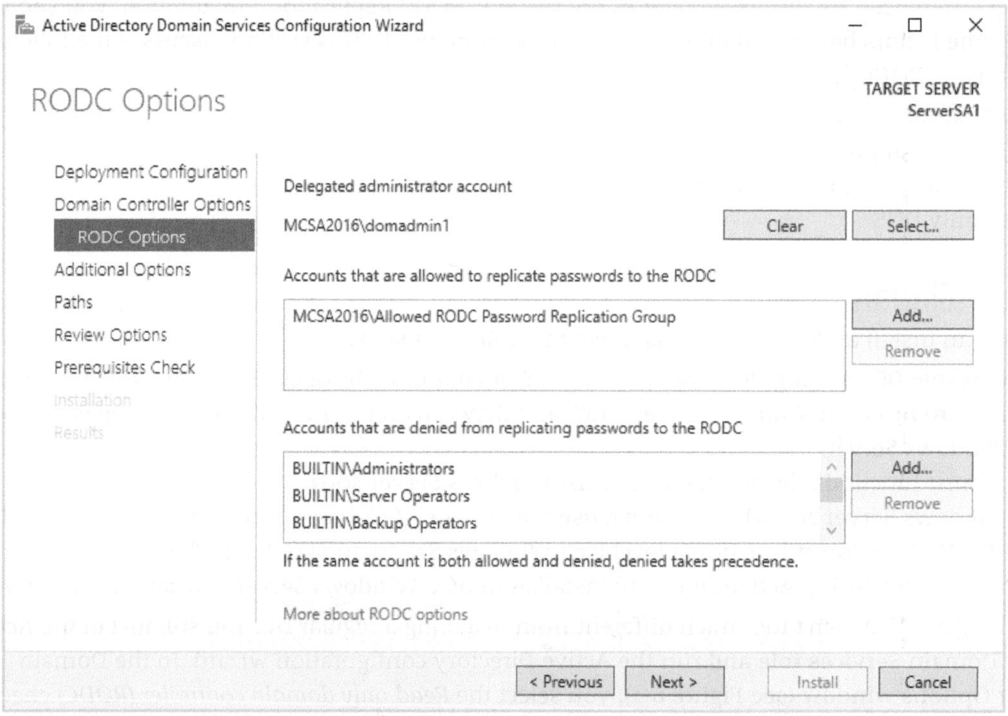

Figure 6-2   The RODC Options window

In Figure 6-2, notice the two boxes listing group accounts:

- *Accounts that are allowed to replicate passwords to the RODC*—Contains the Allowed RODC Password Replication group, which has no members by default. You add accounts to this box or the Allowed RODC Password Replication group if you want account passwords to be replicated to the RODC.
- *Accounts that are denied from replicating passwords to the RODC*—You add accounts to this box or the Denied RODC Password Replication group to specifically deny replication of account passwords.

Password replication is discussed more in the section "Password Replication Policy."

Staged RODC Installation

Another option for installing an RODC that isn't available with a regular DC is a **staged installation** or *delegated installation*, as it was called in Windows Server 2008. With staged installation, a domain administrator creates the RODC computer account in Active Directory, and then a regular user can perform the installation at a later time. To use this feature, you create a computer account for the server performing the RODC role in the Domain Controllers OU before installing the RODC. To do so, in Active Directory Administrative Center (ADAC) click the Domain Controllers OU and click *Pre-create a Read-only domain controller account* in the Tasks pane to start the Active Directory Domain Services Installation Wizard (see Figure 6-3).

Figure 6-3   The Active Directory Domain Services Installation Wizard

In the next window, you enter credentials if you aren't already signed in as an administrator. In the Specify the Computer Name window, you enter the name of the new RODC computer account (see Figure 6-4). The target server must not be a domain member before you install Active Directory Domain Services on it.

Next, you select a site for the new RODC. The target server must have an IP address configuration that's suitable for the site. The next window looks much like Figure 6-1, where you specify whether the RODC should also be a DNS server or GC server. The *Read only domain controller (RODC)* option is selected and grayed out. In the Delegation of RODC Installation and Administration window, you specify the user or group who can perform the RODC installation (see Figure 6-5). This account should represent a user or users who are physically at the place where the RODC is to be installed. Administration of the RODC is also delegated to this account.

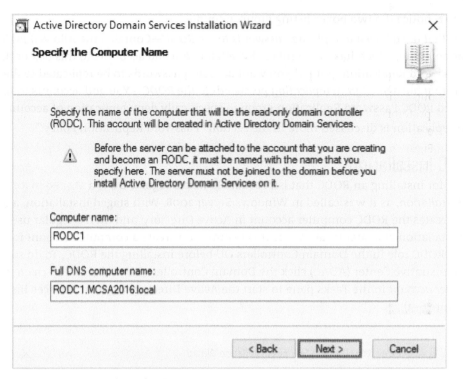

Figure 6-4   Specifying the computer name

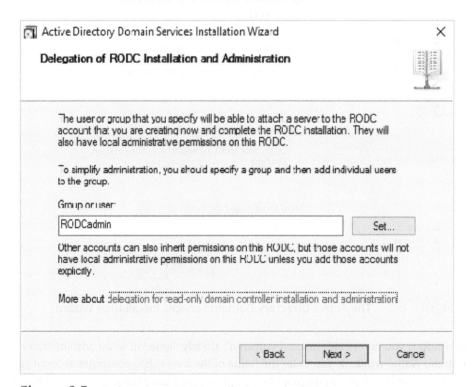

Figure 6-5   Delegating RODC installation and administration

Finally, you review your selections and finish the wizard. A computer account is created in the Domain Controllers OU, and ADAC shows the Domain Controller Type as Unoccupied Domain Controller until the RODC installation is finished. The rest of the process is performed on the target server that will be the RODC. Make sure that the target server's computer name is the name specified in the wizard and the server isn't currently a domain member.

Note

The procedure for staging RODC installation can also be done in Active Directory Users and Computers by right-clicking the Domain Controllers OU and clicking *Pre-create Read-only Domain Controller account.*

Staged RODC Installation with PowerShell

As you might expect, the procedure for staging an RODC installation can be done with a PowerShell cmdlet. At an elevated PowerShell prompt, use the following command to create an RODC computer account named RODC1 in the csmtech.local domain in a site named BranchOffice with a group named BranchOff-G as the delegated administrator account:

```
Add-ADDSReadOnlyDomainControllerAccount
    -DomainControllerAccountName RODC1 -DomainName
    csmtech.local -SiteName BranchOffice
    -DelegatedAdministratorAccountName BranchOff-G
```

Tip

Some PowerShell commands are lengthy. Remember that you can type them more easily by using the Tab key shortcut. Type a few letters of the command (enough letters to make it unique) and press the Tab key. PowerShell finishes the command for you. This method also works for options in the command. For example, you could type `Add-ADDSR <Tab> -DomainC <Tab>` for the first part of the preceding command.

Staged RODC Installation on the Target Server

To install the RODC on the target server, follow these steps:

1. Sign in to the server as a local administrator.
2. Change the computer name to match the RODC account name, if necessary.
3. Install the Active Directory Domain Services role.
4. To configure the Active Directory Domain Services role, start the Active Directory Domain Services Installation Wizard by clicking the Alert flag and clicking *Promote this server to a domain controller.*
5. Next, click *Add a domain controller to an existing domain*. In this window, you specify the domain name and the credentials of an account that can perform the operation. Use the account credentials for an account that was delegated installation and administration for the RODC.
6. In the Domain Controller Options window, you see a message stating that a pre-created RODC account exists. The options are grayed out because they were specified when the computer account was created. However, you must supply a Directory Services Restore Mode (DSRM) password. The *Reinstall this domain controller* option can be used if a DC is being replaced by another server because of hardware failure.

The remainder of the installation is the same as installing a regular DC or RODC. To use PowerShell to complete the staged RODC installation, first install the AD DS server role. Then type the following command at an elevated PowerShell prompt to configure RODC1 as an RODC in the csmtech.local domain, using credentials from BranchUser1:

```
Install-ADDSDomainController -DomainName csmtech.local
    -UseExistingAccount -credential (get-credential)
```

After you enter this command, you're prompted for the user name and password of the delegated account and for the DSRM password.

> **Note**
>
> Because an RODC is meant to address the needs of a branch office, administrators can combine the RODC installation with another one that's designed for branch office installation: Server Core. This configuration often goes together because both optimize security and are meant for remote management.

RODC Replication

Replication on an RODC is unidirectional, meaning that the Active Directory database is replicated from a writeable DC to an RODC, but data is never replicated from an RODC to another DC. RODCs can replicate only with Windows Server 2008 and later writeable DCs. Unidirectional replication provides an extra level of security for networks with branch office locations. Even if a server is compromised and someone is able to make malicious changes to Active Directory on the RODC, the changes can't be propagated to DCs in the rest of the network.

You have already learned that you can limit which accounts' passwords are replicated to an RODC. To increase security of the Active Directory data stored on an RODC, administrators can configure a filtered attribute set, which specifies domain objects that aren't replicated to RODCs. The type of data to filter usually includes credential information that might be used by applications using Active Directory as a data store. Any data that might be considered security sensitive can be filtered except objects required for system operation. Filtered attribute sets are configured on the schema master.

RODC placement in your site topology is important to ensure that replication occurs between an RODC and a writeable DC. A writeable DC is usually placed in the site nearest in the replication topology to the RODC's site. The nearest site is defined as the site with the lowest cost site link. If this placement isn't possible, you must create a site link bridge between the RODC site and a site with a writeable DC. Site links and site link bridges are discussed later in this chapter in "Understanding and Configuring Sites."

Password Replication Policy

As discussed, by default, both user and computer account passwords are not stored on an RODC. This arrangement makes the RODC more secure should an attacker try to crack locally stored passwords. However, this policy also negates some advantages of having a domain controller on the local network. If the RODC stores no passwords, each user and computer authentication must be referred to a writeable DC, most likely located across a wide area network (WAN) link. To prevent this problem, as you learned, you can specify accounts for which passwords will be replicated. When an account password is replicated, its password is retrieved from a writeable DC the first time the account logs on, and thereafter, the password is retrieved from the RODC.

> **Note**
>
> Password replication is also known as *credential caching*.

Password replication is controlled by the Password Replication Policy (PRP), accessed in the Properties dialog box of the RODC computer account (see Figure 6-6). A PRP lists users and groups along with a setting of Allow or Deny. Account Operators, Administrators, Backup Operators, and Server Operators are built-in domain local groups added to the PRP with the Deny setting by default. Passwords of these groups' members aren't stored on the RODC.

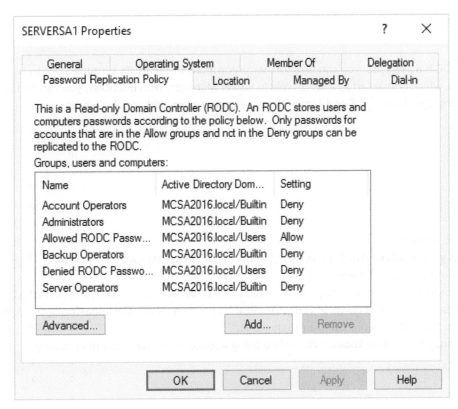

Figure 6-6   Viewing the Password Replication Policy

The PRP also contains groups named Allowed RODC Password Replication group and Denied RODC Password Replication group. These two groups are added to the PRP of all RODCs. These groups have no members at first, but administrators can add users or groups to these groups to centrally control password caching on all RODCs. If a user is a member of a group with the Allow setting and a group with the Deny setting, the Deny setting takes precedence. Generally, groups or users with permission to sensitive information should be added to the Denied RODC Password Replication group. Users who often visit where RODCs are used might be candidates for membership in the Allowed RODC Password Replication group.

In addition to the default groups added to the PRP for all RODCs, an administrator can customize each RODC's PRP. For example, a group can be created for all users located at a branch office, and this group can be added to the PRP of the RODC at the branch office with an Allow setting. In addition, you can create a group for the computer accounts in the branch office and add this group to the PRP. Adding computer accounts to the PRP speeds up computer boot times and other actions that require the computer account to authenticate to the domain.

Read Only DNS

If you install DNS on an RODC, all Active Directory-integrated DNS zones are read only on the RODC. This is a departure from standard terminology because the zone is still considered a primary zone, even though it is read only. Zone information is replicated from other DNS servers, but zone changes can't be made on the RODC. Client workstations can still make name resolution queries to the RODC, but workstations in the branch office using Dynamic DNS can't create or update their DNS records on the RODC. Instead, the RODC sends a referral record to the client with the address of a DNS server that can handle the update. To maintain a current DNS database, the RODC requests a single-record replication from the DNS server that updated the client record. Note that if you attempt to create a new DNS zone on an RODC, you can create only a standard primary, secondary, or stub zone. You can't create a new Active Directory-integrated zone on an RODC.

> **Tip** ⓘ
>
> If theft of an RODC is a likely risk, you can take further precautions to secure its sensitive data by using BitLocker Drive Encryption, which is installed as a server role in Server Manager. With BitLocker, you can secure data on the volume containing the Windows OS and Active Directory as well as on additional volumes.

Activity 6-1: Resetting Your Virtual Environment

Time Required: 5 minutes

Objective: Reset your virtual environment by applying the InitialConfig checkpoint or snapshot.

Required Tools and Equipment: ServerDC1, ServerDM1, ServerSA1

Description: Apply the InitialConfig checkpoint or snapshot to ServerDC1, ServerDM1, and ServerSA1.

1. Be sure all servers are shut down. In your virtualization program, apply the InitialConfig checkpoint or snapshot to ServerDC1, ServerDM1, and ServerSA1.
2. When the snapshot or checkpoint has finished being applied, continue to the next activity.

Activity 6-2: Installing an RODC with Staging

Time Required: 20 minutes

Objective: Install a RODC with staging.

Required Tools and Equipment: ServerDC1, ServerSA1

Description: In this activity, you use RODC staging using PowerShell, so first you create a group and an account you delegate administration to. ServerSA1 will be the RODC.

1. Start ServerDC1 and ServerSA1, and sign in to both as **Administrator.**
2. On ServerDC1, open Active Directory Users and Computers. Create a new OU under the domain node named **BranchOffice**. In the BranchOffice OU, create a global group named **BranchOff-G** and a user named **BranchUser1** with **Password01**. Make sure to set the password to never expire. Make BranchUser1 a member of the BranchOff-G group.
3. Right-click the **Domain Controllers** OU. Notice the option to "Pre-create" an RODC account. You can use this wizard to stage the RODC account, but you're using PowerShell.
4. On ServerDC1, open a PowerShell window. Type **Add-ADDSReadOnlyDomainControllerAccount -DomainControllerAccountName ServerSA1 -DomainName mcsa2016.local -SiteName Default-First-Site-Name -DelegatedAdministratorAccountName BranchOff-G** and press **Enter**. You might see a warning message about default security settings, which you can ignore. The last part of the output should say "Operation completed successfully."
5. In Active Directory Users and Computers, make sure the **Domain Controllers** OU is selected and click the **Refresh** button. You should see ServerSA1 in the middle pane with the DC Type showing Unoccupied DC Account (see Figure 6-7).
6. On ServerSA1, open a PowerShell prompt. First you need to install the Active Directory server role. Type **Install-WindowsFeature AD-Domain-Services -IncludeManagementTools** and press **Enter**. This installation takes some time.
7. At the PowerShell prompt, type **Install-ADDSDomainController -DomainName mcsa2016.local -UseExistingAccount -credential (get-credential)** and press **Enter**.

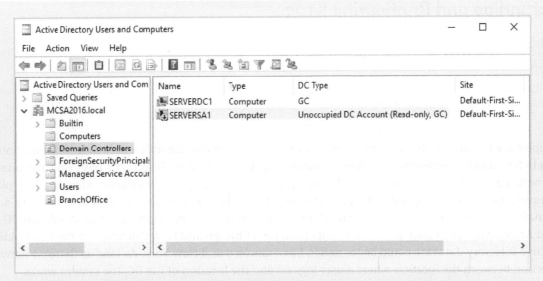

Figure 6-7   The staged RODC account in Active Directory Users and Computers

8. In the credentials dialog box, type **mcsa2016\BranchUser1** in the User name text box and **Password01** in the Password text box, and then click **OK**.

9. When you're prompted for the SafeModeAdministratorPassword (which is the DSRM password), type **Password01**, press **Enter**, type it again, and press **Enter**.

10. When you're prompted to continue with the operation, press **Enter**.

11. The installation takes a while. When it's finished, you see a message stating that you'll be signed out. Click **Close** or just wait for Windows to restart.

12. While ServerSA1 is restarting, refresh the screen in Active Directory Users and Computers on ServerDC1 to see that ServerSA1 is now listed as a read-only, global catalog domain controller.

13. Continue to the next activity.

Activity 6-3: Configuring the Password Replication Policy

Time Required: 15 minutes

Objective: Add a group to the PRP of the ServerSA1 computer account.

Required Tools and Equipment: ServerDC1, ServerSA1

Description: In this activity, you create a group and add it to the Allowed RODC Password Replication group.

1. On ServerDC1, open Active Directory Users and Computers, click **Domain Controllers** in the left pane, and in the middle pane, double-click **ServerSA1** to open its Properties dialog box. Click the **Password Replication Policy** tab.

2. Click the **Advanced** button. The Advanced Password Replication Policy for ServerSA1 dialog box shows you which account passwords are stored on the RODC. By default, the RODC computer account is replicated as is a special account used by the Kerberos authentication process. Click **Close** and then **Cancel**.

3. Open a PowerShell prompt. Add the BranchOff-G group to the Allowed RODC Password Replication Group by typing **Add-ADGroupMember "Allowed RODC Password Replication Group" BranchOff-G** and pressing **Enter**.

4. Sign in to ServerSA1 as **BranchUser1**.

5. On ServerDC1, open the Properties dialog box for the ServerSA1 account again, and click the **Password Replication Policy** tab. Click **Advanced** to see that BranchUser1 is now among the accounts whose passwords are stored on the RODC. Click **Close** and then **Cancel**.

6. Sign out of ServerSA1. Continue to the next activity.

Understanding and Configuring Sites

 **Certification**

- **70-742 – Install and configure Active Directory Domain Services:**
  Install and configure domain controllers

In Chapter 1, you learned what an Active Directory site is and some of the differences in how replication occurs between DCs in different sites. As you know, a site is one of Active Directory's physical components along with a domain controller. An Active Directory site represents a physical location where DCs are placed and group policies can be applied. When you're designing the logical components of Active Directory, such as domains and OUs, you don't need to consider the physical location of objects. In other words, an OU named Accounting could contain user accounts from both Chicago and New Orleans, and the DCs holding the Active Directory database could be located in San Francisco and New York. As long as there's a network connection between the location where a user logs on and the location of the DC, the system works.

Having said that, locating a DC near the accounts using it makes sense. Authentication and resource access usually work fine across a reliable WAN link, but if a company location contains several users, placing DCs in that location is more efficient. Performance and reliability are less predictable on slower WAN links than on LAN links. So the productivity gained from faster, more reliable network access can outweigh the extra cost of additional DCs.

When the first DC of a forest is installed, a site named Default-First-Site-Name is created, but you can rename the site as something more descriptive. Any additional DCs installed in the forest are assigned to this site until additional sites are created. Figure 6-8 shows a single-site domain in two locations at the top and the same domain defined as two sites at the bottom.

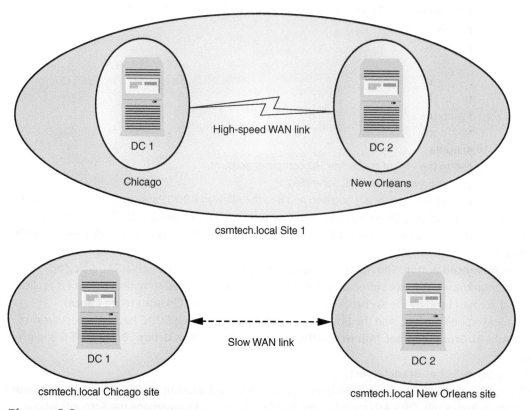

Figure 6-8   Active Directory sites

There are three main reasons for establishing multiple sites:

- *Authentication efficiency*—When a user logs on to a domain, the client computer always tries to authenticate to a DC in the same site to ensure that logon traffic is kept in the same site and off slower WAN links.
- *Replication efficiency*—A DC in every branch office facilitates faster and more reliable network access, but DCs must communicate with one another to replicate the Active Directory database. Using the default replication schedule, however, can create considerable replication traffic. Replication between DCs occurs within 15 seconds after a change is made and once per hour when no changes have occurred. In databases with several thousand objects, this schedule can take a toll on available bandwidth for other network operations. With multiple sites, intersite replication can be scheduled to occur during off-peak hours and at a frequency that makes most sense. For example, a small branch office site with a limited bandwidth connection to the main office can be configured to replicate less often than a larger branch office that requires more timely updates.
- *Application efficiency*—Some distributed applications, such as Exchange Server (an email and collaboration application) and Distributed File System (DFS), use sites to improve efficiency. These applications ensure that client computers always try to access data in the same site before attempting to access services in remote sites by using the WAN link.

Sites are created by using Active Directory Sites and Services. A site is linked to an IP subnet that reflects the IP addressing scheme used at the physical location the site represents. A site can encompass one or more IP subnets, but each site must be linked to at least one IP subnet that doesn't overlap with another site. When a DC is created and assigned an IP address, it's assigned to a site based on its address automatically. Figure 6-9 shows the relationship between sites and IP subnets.

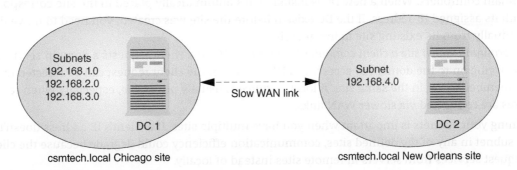

Figure 6-9   The relationship between sites and subnets

Site Components

Sites and connections between sites are defined by several components that can be created and configured in Active Directory Sites and Services. They include subnets, site links, and bridgehead servers discussed in the following sections.

Subnets

As discussed, each site is associated with one or more IP subnets. An IP subnet is a range of IP addresses in which the network ID is the same. All computers assigned an address in the subnet can communicate with one another without requiring a router. By default, no subnets are created in Active Directory Sites and Services. When a new site is created, all subnets used by the default site should be created and associated with the default site. Then the subnets for the new site should be created and associated with the new site. Figure 6-10 shows Active Directory Sites and Services with the Default-First-Site-Name Properties dialog box open.

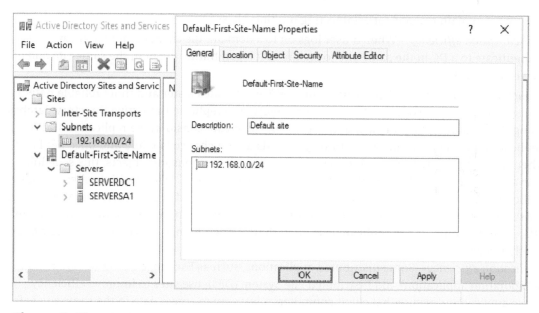

Figure 6-10   Viewing Site properties

After creating a site, you must associate one or more subnets with it. Active Directory uses this information in two important ways:

- *Placing new domain controllers in the correct site*—Correct placement is necessary to determine the optimum intrasite and intersite replication topology and to associate clients with the nearest domain controllers. When a new DC is installed, it's automatically placed in the site corresponding with its assigned IP address. If the DC existed before the site was created, you need to move the DC manually from its existing site to the new site.
- *Determining which site a client computer belongs to*—When a client requests a domain service, such as logging on to the domain or accessing a DFS resource, the client request can be directed to a DC or member server in the same site. A local resource is usually preferable, especially when remote sites are connected via slower WAN links.

Defining your subnets is important when you have multiple sites. If a client's IP address doesn't match a subnet in any of the defined sites, communication efficiency could degrade because the client might request services from servers in remote sites instead of locally.

Site Links

A **site link** is needed to connect two or more sites for replication purposes. When Active Directory is installed, a default site link called DEFAULTIPSITELINK is created. Until new site links are created, all sites that are added use this site link. Site links determine the replication schedule and frequency between two sites. If all locations in an organization are connected through the same WAN link or WAN links of equal bandwidth, one site link might be suitable. If the locations use different WAN connections at differing speeds, however, additional links can be created to configure differing replication schedules. You access the properties of a site link in Active Directory Sites and Services by expanding Sites and Inter-Site Transports and then clicking IP. Site links have three configuration options, as shown in Figure 6-11.

The Cost field is an administrator-assigned value that represents the bandwidth of the connection between sites. The default value is 100. An administrator can alter this value to influence which path is chosen when more than one path exists between two sites. As shown in Figure 6-12, Site A replicates with Site B and Site C through the corresponding site links, but Site A has two options for replicating with Site D: the link with Site B or the link with Site C. The site link cost determines that Site A will use the link with Site B. Site link costs are additive, so the total cost for Site A to replicate with Site D through Site C is 400; the total cost to replicate with Site D via Site B is only 300. When you have more than one path option between two sites, the lower cost path is always used unless links in the path become unavailable.

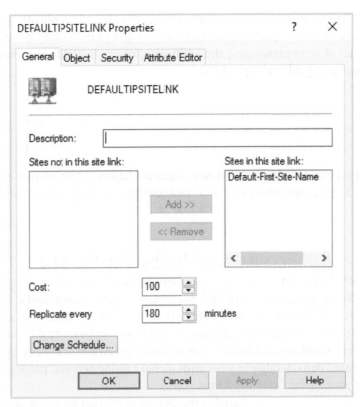

Figure 6-11   The Properties dialog box for DEFAULTIPSITELINK

In this case, the replication process reconfigures itself to use the next lower cost path, if available. Site links are transitive by default, which means that Site A can replicate directly with Site D and Site C can replicate directly with Site B without creating an explicit link between the two sites.

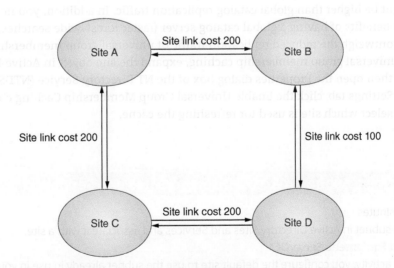

Figure 6-12   Site replication topology

Bridgehead Servers

Intrasite replication occurs among several domain controllers after the Knowledge Consistency Checker (KCC) creates the topology. Intersite replication occurs between bridgehead servers. When the KCC detects that replication must occur between sites, one DC in each site is designated as the Inter-Site Topology

Generator (ISTG). The ISTG then designates a bridgehead server to handle replication for each directory partition. Because bridgehead servers perform such a vital function in multisite networks, and this function can consume a lot of server resources, the administrator can override automatic assignment of a bridgehead server and assign the role to a specific DC.

> **Note**
>
> Configuration of sites and site components is discussed in detail in Chapter 7. This chapter covers just enough so that you understand what a site is, particularly in relation to Active Directory replication and the global catalog.

The Global Catalog and Universal Group Membership Caching

As you've learned, the global catalog is a critical component for many Active Directory operations. It's the only place where universal group membership information is maintained, and it contains a partial replica of all domain objects. Access to a global catalog server must be considered when designing sites and configuring site replication. Having a global catalog server used to be critical in sites with more than a few users because it speeded logons and forest-wide searches for Active Directory objects. However, replication traffic is increased considerably in sites with global catalog servers, particularly if there are several large domains in your Active Directory forest.

Universal group membership caching handles the potential conflict between faster logons and increased replication traffic. When this feature is enabled, the first time a user logs on to a domain in the site with no global catalog server, the user's universal group membership information is retrieved from a global catalog server in a different site. Thereafter, the information is cached locally on every DC in the site and updated every 8 hours, so there's no need to contact a global catalog server. Having this feature available, however, doesn't mean that a global catalog server should never be placed in a site. Microsoft recommends placing a global catalog server in the site when the number of accounts (user and computer) exceeds 500 and the number of DCs exceeds 2. With 500 cached accounts, the traffic created by refreshing every 8 hours might be higher than global catalog replication traffic. In addition, you need to determine whether the other benefits of having a global catalog server (faster forest-wide searches, faster updates of universal groups) outweigh the reduced replication traffic of universal group membership caching.

To configure universal group membership caching, expand the site object in Active Directory Sites and Services, and then open the Properties dialog box of the NT Directory Service (NTDS) Site Settings object. In the Site Settings tab, click the Enable Universal Group Membership Caching check box. In addition, you can select which site is used for refreshing the cache.

Activity 6-4: Creating a Subnet in Active Directory Sites and Services

Time Required: 5 minutes

Objective: Create a subnet in Active Directory Sites and Services and associate it with a site.

Required Tools and Equipment: ServerDC1

Description: In this activity, you configure the default site to use the subnet already in use in your network. In addition, you rename the default site.

1. On ServerDC1, in Server Manager, click **Tools, Active Directory Sites and Services** from the menu.
2. Double-click to expand **Sites**, if necessary. Right-click **Subnets**, point to **New**, and click **Subnet**.
3. In the Prefix text box, type **192.168.0.0/24** (assuming that you're following the IP address scheme used in this book; otherwise, ask your instructor what to enter).
4. In the Select a site object for this prefix list box, click **Default-First-Site-Name**, and then click **OK**.

5. In the left pane, click **Subnets**. Right-click **192.168.0.0/24** and click **Properties**. In the General tab, you can give the subnet a description and change the site with which the subnet is associated. For now, leave it as is. Click **Cancel**.

6. In the left pane, right-click **Default-First-Site-Name** and click **Rename**. Type **Site0** and press **Enter**. You're using the third octet of the IP address as part of the site name.

7. In the left pane, right-click **Site0** and click **Properties**. In the Description text box, type **Site for the 192.168.0.0/24 subnet**, and then click **OK**.

8. Continue to the next activity.

Activity 6-5: Viewing Site Properties

Time Required: 10 minutes
Objective: View site properties.
Required Tools and Equipment: ServerDC1
Description: In this activity, you explore the properties of NTDS site settings, server NTDS settings, and connection objects.

1. On ServerDC1, open Active Directory Sites and Services, if necessary. Click to expand **Sites**, **Site0**, **Servers**, and **ServerDC1**. Under ServerDC1 in the left pane, right-click **NTDS Settings** and click **Properties**.

2. In the General tab, you can select or clear the Global Catalog option to configure whether the server is a global catalog server. Click the **Connections** tab. You see ServerSA1 in the Replicate To list box (see Figure 6-13). Click **Cancel**.

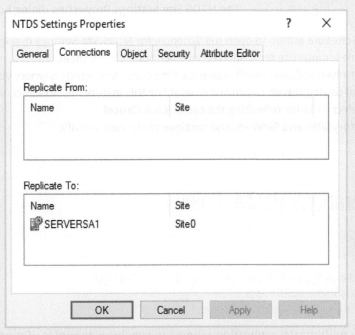

Figure 6-13   NTDS settings for ServerDC1

3. In the left pane, click **Site0**. In the right pane, right-click **NTDS Site Settings** and click **Properties** to open the dialog box shown in Figure 6-14. There are NTDS settings associated with server objects and NTDS site settings associated with site objects.

Figure 6-14   The NTDS Site Settings Properties dialog box

4. Click the **Change Schedule** button to open the Schedule for NTDS Site Settings dialog box. As you can see, the regular schedule for intersite replication is once per hour. Click **Cancel**.
5. Notice the Enable Universal Group Membership Caching check box, which is where you enable this feature if the DC isn't a global catalog server. Because it is, enabling this feature has no effect. In the *Refresh cache from* list box, you can select a site for refreshing the cache. Click **Cancel**.
6. Close Active Directory Sites and Services, and continue to the next activity.

Working with Operations Master Roles

 **Certification**

- **70-742 – Install and configure Active Directory Domain Services:**
  Install and configure domain controllers

Active Directory uses a multimaster replication scheme to synchronize copies of most information in the Active Directory database. However, some critical information is subject to a single master replication scheme to avoid any possibility of the information becoming unsynchronized. The servers that keep this critical information are assigned a **Flexible Single Master Operation (FSMO) role**. FSMO roles can be summarized as follows:

- *Forest-wide FSMO roles*—Only one DC per forest performs these roles: domain naming master and schema master.

- *Domain-wide FSMO roles*—Only one DC per domain performs these roles: PDC emulator, RID master, and infrastructure master.

This section discusses best practices for locating these DCs in your network for optimal reliability and replication efficiency and explains how to transfer and seize FSMO roles when you need to assign a role to a different DC.

Operations Master Best Practices

The decision of where to place an FSMO role holder is part of your overall Active Directory design strategy. If you build a new forest, the first DC installed performs all five FSMO roles. When a new domain is created in the forest, the first DC performs all three domain-wide FSMO roles for that domain, and a DC in the forest root domain handles the forest-wide roles. In a smaller network, having all these critical roles on a single server can work, but in a large network with multiple domains and sites, you might need to transfer some roles to different servers. Placement of the DCs functioning in these roles can affect replication and the capability to recover from a server failure. In addition, being able to restore the functioning of FSMO roles quickly after a server failure is critical. However, not all FSMOs have equal importance; some roles must be functioning almost continuously for correct domain operation, but other roles can be offline for a while with little disturbance to the network. Here are some common rules for operations masters:

- Unless your domain is very small, transfer some operations master roles from the first DC installed in the forest to other DCs because some FSMO roles require a lot of resources.
- Place the servers performing these roles where network availability is high.
- Designate an alternate DC for all roles. The alternate assumes the role if the original server fails, and it should be a direct replication partner with the original FSMO role holder. Document your plan to make sure alternate DCs aren't burdened with other services that could impede their performance as an FSMO role holder.

The following sections explain best practices with FSMO roles in more detail.

Domain Naming Master

The **domain naming master** manages adding, removing, and renaming domains in the forest. There's only one domain naming master per forest, and the DC with this role must be available when domains are added, deleted, or renamed. In most cases, neither users nor administrators notice its absence until one of these operations is attempted. If the DC performing this role goes offline, you should probably wait until it comes back online before attempting to add or remove a domain or DC. The exception, of course, is if you need to add a domain to the network immediately. If you decide to install this role on another DC, the original domain naming master server must not be put back into service unless you uninstall Active Directory.

When possible, the domain naming master should be a direct replication partner with another DC that's also a global catalog server in the same site. Ideally, the domain naming master should also be a global catalog server. If the role must be moved, the direct replication partner is the preferred choice because it should be most fully replicated with the original FSMO. The domain naming master and the other forest-wide FSMO role, the schema master, can be on the same server but need not be.

Schema Master

The **schema master** is responsible for replicating the schema directory partition to all other domain controllers in the forest when changes occur. It is needed when the Active Directory schema is changed, including raising the forest functional level. Its absence isn't apparent to users or administrators unless a schema change is attempted. Generally, the schema master should be transferred to another server only when you're certain the original server will be down permanently.

Primary Domain Controller (PDC) Emulator

The **PDC emulator** processes password changes for older Windows clients (Windows 9x and NT) and is used during sign-in authentication. The DC performing this role should be centrally located where there's a high concentration of users to facilitate logons. The PDC emulator is the most heavily used of the FSMO roles and should be placed on a suitable DC. Unless your forest configuration has all DCs configured as

GC servers, the PDC emulator should be on a DC that's not a global catalog server because global catalog servers are also used heavily. If the PDC emulator role fails, you might want to move the role to another server immediately. After the original server returns to service, the role can be transferred back to it. As mentioned earlier in "Domain Controller Cloning Prerequisites," the PDC emulator must be running Windows Server 2012 or later to perform DC cloning.

RID Master

All objects in a domain are identified internally by a security identifier (SID). An object's SID is composed of a domain identifier, which is the same for all objects in the domain, and a relative identifier (RID), which is unique for each object. Because objects can be created on any DC except RODCs, there must be a mechanism that keeps two DCs from issuing the same RID, thereby duplicating an SID. The RID master is responsible for issuing unique pools of RIDs to each DC, thereby guaranteeing unique SIDs throughout the domain. The RID master must be available when adding a DC to an existing domain and should be placed in an area where Active Directory objects are created most often, such as near the server administrator's office. This FSMO role must be highly available to other DCs and is ideally placed with the PDC emulator because the PDC emulator uses the RID master's services frequently. Because the RID master doles out RIDs to DCs in blocks of 500, temporary downtime might not be noticed. However, if a DC has exhausted its pool of RIDs and the RID master isn't available, new objects can't be created. If the RID master fails, moving this role to another server should be considered only if the original RID master is down permanently.

Infrastructure Master

This DC is responsible for ensuring that changes made to object names in one domain are updated in references to these objects in other domains. A temporary interruption of this role's services probably won't be noticed. This role is most needed when many objects have been moved or renamed in a multidomain environment. The infrastructure master role shouldn't be performed by a DC that's also a global catalog server unless all servers in the forest have been configured as global catalog servers or there's only one domain in the forest. However, a global catalog server should be in the same site as the infrastructure master because there's frequent communication between these two roles. If an infrastructure master fails, the role can be moved to another DC, if necessary, and returned to the original server when it's back in service.

> **Caution** ⚠
>
> The only times the infrastructure master and global catalog can be on the same DC is when there's only one domain in the forest or all DCs are configured as global catalog servers. If neither is the case and the infrastructure master is also a global catalog server, the infrastructure master never finds out-of-date data, so it never replicates changes to other DCs in the domain.

Managing Operations Master Roles

Because of the critical nature of the functions that FSMO role holders perform, administrators should be familiar with two important FSMO management operations: transferring and seizing. These two functions enable administrators to change the DC performing the FSMO role to make the Active Directory design more efficient and to recover from server failure. Of course, system backups should always be part of managing disaster recovery.

Transferring Operations Master Roles

Transferring an operations master role means moving the role's function from one DC to another while the original DC is still in operation. This transfer is generally done for one of the following reasons:

- The DC performing the role was the first DC in the forest or domain and, therefore, holds all domain-wide or domain- and forest-wide roles. Unless you have only one DC, distributing these roles to other servers is suggested.

- The DC performing the role is being moved to a location that isn't well suited for the role.
- The current DC's performance is inadequate because of the resources the FSMO role requires.
- The current DC is being taken out of service temporarily or permanently.

There is one restriction when transferring FSMO roles: An RODC can't be an FSMO role holder. Table 6-2 lists each FSMO role and its corresponding scope, the MMC used to work with the role, and the PowerShell command used to transfer the role to another DC.

Table 6-2   The MMCs and PowerShell cmdlets for transferring FSMO roles

FSMO role/scope	MMC	PowerShell cmdlet
Schema master/forest	Active Directory Schema	`Move-ADDirectoryServerOperationMasterRole -Identity "TargetDC" -OperationMasterRole SchemaMaster`
Domain naming master/forest	Active Directory Domains and Trusts	`Move-ADDirectoryServerOperationMasterRole -Identity "TargetDC" -OperationMasterRole DomainNamingMaster`
RID master/domain	Active Directory Users and Computers	`Move-ADDirectoryServerOperationMasterRole -Identity "TargetDC" -OperationMasterRole RIDMaster`
PDC emulator master/domain	Active Directory Users and Computers	`Move-ADDirectoryServerOperationMasterRole -Identity "TargetDC" -OperationMasterRole PDCEmulator`
Infrastructure master/domain	Active Directory Users and Computers	`Move-ADDirectoryServerOperationMasterRole -Identity "TargetDC" -OperationMasterRole InfrastructureMaster`

In Table 6-2, you can replace the role name with a number to shorten the PowerShell command, as shown in the following list:

- PDC emulator: 0
- RID master: 1
- Infrastructure master: 2
- Schema master: 3
- Domain naming master: 4

Note

To seize the role by using PowerShell, add the `-Force` parameter to the command.

You can also use PowerShell to see which servers carry the FSMO roles:

- `Get-ADForest`—Shows which servers carry forest-wide roles and other forest information
- `Get-ADDomain`—Shows which servers carry domain-wide roles and other domain information

Before you begin to work with FSMO roles, you need another writeable DC. In the next activity, you demote your RODC to a member server and then promote it again to a standard DC.

Tip

To see which servers hold the FSMO roles with a single command, use `netdom /query fsmo` from a command prompt.

Seizing Operations Master Roles

An operations master role is seized when the current role holder is no longer online because of some type of failure. Seizing should never be done when the current role holder is accessible and should usually be done only when it's unlikely that the original server can be restored to service. If a DC is scheduled to be decommissioned, you should transfer the role while the DC is still online. If the operations master DC becomes inaccessible because of network failure or a temporary hardware failure, you should wait until this server is back online rather than seize the operations master role.

An exception might be the PDC emulator role, which can affect user logons, or the RID master, which might be needed to create Active Directory objects. If either role holder is going to be offline for an extended period, seizing the role and then transferring it to the original DC when it's back online might be best for continued Active Directory operation. You can't use MMCs to seize a role. You must use the PowerShell cmdlets discussed previously with the `-Force` option or use `ntdsutil` from the command line, as shown in these steps:

1. Open a command prompt window, type `ntdsutil`, and press Enter.
2. Type `roles` and press Enter to get the FSMO Maintenance prompt.
3. Type `connections` and press Enter to get the Server Connections prompt.
4. Type `connect to server` *DCName*, replacing *DCName* with the domain controller where you're transferring the FSMO role.
5. Type `quit` to get back to the FSMO Maintenance prompt.
6. Type `seize` *RoleName* and press Enter, replacing *RoleName* with the name of the role you want to seize. Possible role names are domain naming master, schema master, PDC emulator, RID master, and infrastructure master.
7. Windows attempts to transfer the role first, and if a transfer fails, the role is seized. Type `quit` and press Enter to exit `ntdsutil`.

Activity 6-6: Changing an RODC to a Standard DC

Time Required: 20 minutes

Objective: Change an RODC to a standard writeable DC.

Required Tools and Equipment: ServerDC1, ServerSA1

Description: You want to transfer some FSMO roles from ServerDC1 to ServerSA1, but first you must change ServerSA1 from an RODC to a standard DC. You use PowerShell for this task.

1. Sign in to ServerSA1 as **Administrator**. On ServerSA1, open a PowerShell prompt. First, uninstall DNS because it's also read only. Type **Remove-WindowsFeature DNS -Restart** and press **Enter**. DNS is removed, and the server restarts.
2. Next, uninstall the domain controller function. This command doesn't remove the role; it just demotes ServerSA1 to being a member server. From a PowerShell window, type **Uninstall-ADDSDomainController** and press **Enter**.
3. When you're prompted for the local administrator password (which you need to sign in to the server when it's no longer a DC), type **Password01**, press **Enter**, type **Password01** to confirm, and press **Enter**.
4. A message states that the server restarts automatically. When you're prompted to continue, press **Enter**. When the operation is finished, ServerSA1 restarts.
5. Sign in to ServerSA1 as **Administrator**. When you installed Active Directory and DNS, the DNS server address in the IP address configuration was set to 127.0.0.1 because this server was a DNS server. You need to set it back to the address of ServerDC1. Open a PowerShell window and type **Set-DnsClientServerAddress -InterfaceAlias Ethernet -ServerAddresses 192.168.0.1** and press **Enter**.
6. Sign in to ServerSA1 as **mcsa2016\Administrator**, and open a PowerShell prompt. Type **Install-ADDSDomainController -DomainName mcsa2016.local -credential (get-credential)** and press **Enter**. When you're prompted for credentials, type **mcsa2016\administrator** and **Password01**.

7. When you're prompted for the safe mode administrator password, type **Password01**, press **Enter**, type **Password01** to confirm, and press **Enter**. Press **Enter** to confirm. The rest of the settings are the defaults for new DCs, which include installing DNS and configuring the paths to C:\Windows. The site is chosen based on the server's IP address, or if no subnets are defined, the default site is used.

8. You see warning messages about default security settings, dynamic IP addresses, and DNS delegation, which you can ignore. When the configuration is finished, the server restarts. Continue to the next activity.

Activity 6-7: Transferring FSMO Roles

Time Required: 15 minutes

Objective: Transfer the schema master and infrastructure master roles.

Required Tools and Equipment: ServerDC1, ServerSA1

Description: In this activity, you transfer the schema master and infrastructure master roles to ServerSA1 using PowerShell.

1. On ServerDC1, open a PowerShell prompt. Type **Get-ADForest** and press **Enter**. Find the output lines listing DomainNamingMaster and SchemaMaster. Both indicate that ServerDC1 is the FSMO role holder for the two forest-wide roles.

2. Type **Get-ADDomain** and press **Enter**. Find the FSMO roles and verify that ServerDC1 is shown as the FSMO role holder for all three domain-wide roles.

3. To see what roles, if any, a server holds, type **Get-ADDomainController** and press **Enter**. Look for the output line OperationMasterRoles, which lists the roles held by the current DC.

4. Now move the schema master role to ServerSA1 by typing **Move-ADDirectoryServerOperationMasterRole -Identity ServerSA1 -OperationMasterRole 3** and pressing **Enter**. The number 3 is the role number for the schema master.

5. When prompted to confirm, press **Enter**. When the operation is finished (no confirmation message, but the PowerShell prompt returns), type **Get-ADForest** and press **Enter**. Verify that the schema master role is now held by ServerSA1. Another way to confirm is to type **Get-ADDomainController -Server ServerSA1** and press **Enter**. It might take a while to display the results.

6. Next, transfer the infrastructure master role by typing **Move-ADDirectoryServerOperationMasterRole -Identity ServerSA1 -OperationMasterRole 2** and pressing **Enter**.

7. Press **Enter** to confirm. To view the domainwide FSMO role holders in an easier-to-read format, type **Get-ADDomain | Format -Table PDCEmulator, RIDMaster, InfrastructureMaster** and press **Enter**. This command displays information about only these three items.

8. You'll need the schema master back on ServerDC1 to enable the Active Directory Recycle Bin in a future activity, so transfer it back by typing **Move-ADDirectoryServerOperationMasterRole -Identity ServerDC1 -OperationMasterRole 3** and pressing **Enter**. Press **Enter** to confirm.

9. Continue to the next activity.

Maintaining Active Directory

 **Certification**

- **70-742 – Manage and maintain AD DS:**
  Maintain Active Directory

You have learned how to configure Active Directory, install writeable and read only domain controllers, and work with FSMO roles. In the following sections, you learn how to maintain Active Directory whether you need to recover from accidental object deletion or recover Active Directory from catastrophic failure.

You also learn how to optimize the Active Directory database, clean up metadata after DCs or domains are removed, and configure Active Directory snapshots.

Before getting into the details of how to maintain Active Directory, examine the two folders that hold most of the components of Active Directory:

- *NTDS*—By default, this folder is located in *%systemroot%* (usually C:\Windows). It contains the following files:
  - `ntds.dit`: The main Active Directory database.
  - `edb.log`: Holds a log of Active Directory transactions (changes). If Active Directory is shut down unexpectedly, changes that were not fully written to the database can be redone by using the data in this file to commit the changes. This file can grow to a maximum of 10 MB, and then new log files named `edb00001.log, edb00002.log`, and so forth are created.
  - `edb.chk`: Stores information about the last committed transaction; used with `edb.log` to determine which transactions still need to be written to the database.
  - `edbres00001.jrs`: A placeholder file that simply takes up disk space. If the volume on which `ntds.dit` is stored fills up, this file and another named `edbres00002.jrs` are deleted to free disk space so that pending transactions can be committed to the database. After the changes are made, the DC is shut down, and the administrator must make disk space available before Active Directory can operate again.
- *SYSVOL*—By default, this folder is located in *%systemroot%*. It contains group policy templates, logon/logoff scripts, and DFS synchronization data.

During Active Directory installation, you can change the default location for these folders rather than accept the default *%systemroot%*. If you do, you don't have to do anything special to back them up because Windows recognizes the new location as part of the Windows system state. The Windows system state on a DC is composed of the same elements as on a non-DC plus the SYSVOL folder and the `ntds.dit` file.

Active Directory Backup

Active Directory is backed up when you perform a full backup of a DC, when you back up the volumes containing system recovery information, and when you perform a system state backup. Backups can be created with one of three methods included with Windows Server 2016:

- *Windows Server Backup*—A GUI backup tool that guides you through creating a number of backup types, including system state backups. This tool isn't installed by default. You install it with the Add Roles and Features Wizard or the `Add-WindowsFeature` PowerShell cmdlet.
- `wbadmin.exe`—A command-line tool for automating aspects of a backup. The Windows Server Backup tool must be installed for this command to work.
- *PowerShell*—The `Start-WBBackup` cmdlet has many of the same capabilities as `wbadmin.exe`. The Windows Server Backup tool must be installed for this cmdlet to work.

Although having a disaster recovery plan for all your servers that includes regular backups is a good idea, this chapter focuses on backing up Active Directory with system state backups.

System State Backup

A system state backup on a DC includes the Registry, boot files, the Active Directory database, the SYSVOL folder, some system files, and other files, depending on roles installed on the server. A system state backup doesn't include user files and installed applications. To perform a system state backup, you can run the Windows Server Backup tool or the `wbadmin` commands described here:

- *Recover the system state*—To start a system state recovery, including the Active Directory database, use the `wbadmin start systemstaterecovery` command.
- *Delete a system state backup*—The `wbadmin delete systemstatebackup` command deletes one or more system state backups.

- *Restore or delete a backup catalog*—A backup catalog is generated each time a backup is performed. The catalog stores details about each backup and must be available when a recovery procedure is attempted. If the catalog becomes corrupt or deleted, it must be restored before backups can be accessed. To restore a catalog, use the `wbadmin restore catalog` command. To delete a catalog, use the `wbadmin delete catalog` command.

To perform most tasks with the `wbadmin` command, you must be a member of the Backup Operators or Administrators group. You must also open a command prompt window with elevated privileges by right-clicking Start and clicking Command Prompt (Admin) if you aren't signed in with the Administrator account.

Active Directory Restorations

An Active Directory restoration can be nonauthoritative or authoritative. A **nonauthoritative restore** restores the Active Directory database or portions of it and allows it to be updated through replication by other domain controllers. An **authoritative restore** ensures that restored objects aren't overwritten by changes from other domain controllers through replication. The restored objects are replicated to other domain controllers.

Nonauthoritative Active Directory Restore

A nonauthoritative restore of Active Directory is usually done when the Active Directory database is corrupt or when you're doing a full server recovery. For this restore, you can stop Active Directory Domain Services or restart the DC in Directory Services Restore Mode (DSRM) before restoring from backup. The first option is preferable because it doesn't require a server restart. To stop Active Directory Domain Services, use one of the following methods:

- In the Services MMC, right-click the Active Directory Domain Services service and click Stop.
- At a command prompt, type `net stop ntds` and press Enter.
- At a PowerShell prompt, type `Stop-Service ntds` and press Enter.

To restart the DC in DSRM, press F8 when the server begins to boot to access the Advanced Boot Options menu. This method doesn't always work with virtual machines or if you are accessing the server remotely via Remote Desktop Protocol (RDP). Another option is to run `msconfig.exe` and click to select Safe boot and then select Active Directory repair (see Figure 6-15). The next time the server boots, it will boot into Directory Services Repair mode. You will need to set the boot options back to the default settings after you have finished restoring Active Directory.

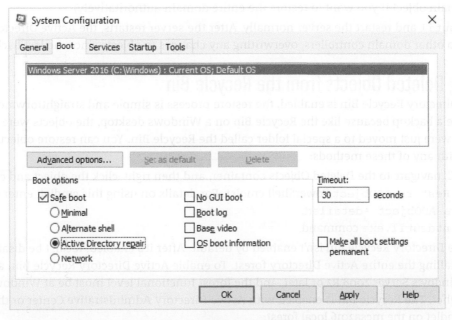

Figure 6-15   Configuring the Active Directory repair boot option

After you have stopped Active Directory Domain Services or have booted into DSRM, run `wbadmin` to restore from a system state backup or from a backup that includes all critical volumes. After the restoration, restart the service or restart the server normally, and Active Directory replication updates the DC with any objects changed since the backup was created. If you have only one DC, any changes to Active Directory since the last backup are lost.

Authoritative Restore

With an authoritative restore, you can select specific Active Directory objects to be restored, or you can choose one or more containers and their contents, including the domain container. You can also choose to restore the SYSVOL folder authoritatively. A complete restore of an Active Directory domain should be a rare occurrence and a last-ditch effort to solve a major Active Directory problem because any changes made to objects on other DCs in the domain since the last backup will be lost. To perform an authoritative restore, follow these steps:

1. Boot the DC into DSRM.
2. Restore from the last system state backup by using the Recovery Wizard in Windows Server Backup or the `wbadmin` command.
3. Run `ntdsutil` to mark one or more objects as authoritative.
4. Restart the DC.

If you want the SYSVOL folder to be restored authoritatively, you have two options. If you're using the Recovery Wizard in Windows Server Backup, select the *Perform an authoritative restore of Active Directory files* option in the Select Location for System State Recovery window. If you're using `wbadmin`, include the `-authsysvol` parameter in the command.

After you have restored the system state from backup, you must use `ntdsutil` to mark one or more objects as authoritative before restarting the server. To mark an object or subtree as authoritative, enter these commands:

- `ntdsutil`
- `activate instance ntds`
- `authoritative restore`
- `restore object DistinguishedName` (to restore a single object)
- `restore subtree DistinguishedName` (to restore an entire OU and its child objects or specify the domain object if you want to restore the entire domain authoritatively)

Quit `ntdsutil` and restart the server normally. After the server restarts, the Active Directory database is replicated to other domain controllers, overwriting any changes to objects since the last backup.

Recovering Deleted Objects from the Recycle Bin

If the Active Directory Recycle Bin is enabled, the restore process is simple and straightforward and doesn't require a backup because like the Recycle Bin on a Windows desktop, the objects were never really deleted. They were just moved to a special folder called the Recycle Bin. You can restore objects from the Recycle Bin with any of these methods:

- In ADAC, navigate to the Deleted Objects container, and then right-click the object and click Restore.
- Use the `Restore-ADObject` PowerShell cmdlet. For details on using this cmdlet, enter `Get-Help Restore-ADObject -detailed`.
- Use the `ntdsutil.exe` command.

The Active Directory Recycle Bin isn't enabled by default. After it's enabled, it can't be disabled without reinstalling the entire Active Directory forest. To enable Active Directory Recycle Bin, all DCs must be running Windows Server 2008 R2 or later, and the forest functional level must be at Windows Server 2008 R2 or higher. The Recycle Bin is enabled with Active Directory Administrative Center or the following PowerShell cmdlet on the mcsa2016.local forest:

```
Enable-ADOptionalFeature -Identity "cn=Recycle Bin
  Feature,cn=Optional Features,cn=Windows NT,
  cn=Services,cn=Configuration,dc=mcsa2016,dc=local"
  -Scope ForestOrConfigurationSet -Target "mcsa2016.local"
```

Active Directory Defragmentation

To maintain performance and efficiency, the Active Directory database requires periodic maintenance in the form of defragmentation and compaction. There are two methods of Active Directory defragmentation: online and offline. **Online defragmentation** occurs automatically when Active Directory removes deleted objects and frees space in the database but doesn't compact the database (performs garbage collection). Garbage collection runs every 12 hours on a DC and removes objects that have been deleted for more than 180 days. Objects that have been deleted but not removed are referred to as *tombstoned*. When an Active Directory object is deleted, it's not actually removed from the database, much as a deleted file isn't physically erased from the file system. Instead, the object is marked for deletion and left in the database for a period called the **tombstone lifetime**, which by default is 180 days. During garbage collection, tombstoned objects older than the tombstone lifetime are removed from the database.

The tombstone lifetime has important implications for Active Directory backups. Suppose that the tombstone lifetime is set to its default 180 days, and the Active Directory database is backed up on Day 1. A user account, Julie, is deleted purposefully on Day 3. On Day 15, the database on a DC becomes corrupted and must be restored from backup with a nonauthoritative restore. The backup from Day 1 is used for the restore, which is before the Julie account was deleted. However, because other DCs still have a record of the Julie account as being deleted, replication deletes the Julie account on the DC being restored. This is the result you want.

Now suppose that the tombstone period is only 10 days. In the same situation, the Julie account is removed from the database during garbage collection on Day 13. When the database is restored, the Julie account is restored with it, but the other DCs have no record of the Julie account being deleted, so the account remains, which isn't the result you want. Because of this potential database inconsistency, an Active Directory backup is considered invalid if it's older than the tombstone lifetime. The tombstone lifetime applies to the entire forest and can be changed by using Attribute Editor on the ForestRootDomain object. (Attribute Editor is a tab in the Properties dialog box of an Active Directory object.)

Online defragmentation removes deleted objects and frees up space in the database, but it doesn't compact the database to close up gaps that deleted objects create in the database. **Offline defragmentation** is necessary to keep the database lean and efficient. In Windows Server versions before Windows Server 2008, you had to restart the DC in DSRM to perform offline defragmentation, which interrupts other services running on the DC. Starting with Windows Server 2008, offline maintenance is possible because the Active Directory service can be stopped for performing maintenance and then restarted. Microsoft refers to this feature as **restartable Active Directory**. Use of this feature doesn't require a server restart. However, another DC must be online before you can stop the Active Directory service so that users can continue to sign in. While Active Directory is stopped, DNS on that DC stops servicing queries, so client computers should have the address of an alternate DNS server configured, too.

Like a file system, a database becomes fragmented over time because of object deletion and creation. Gaps in the database are created where deleted objects once were, which makes the database less efficient in performance. Compacting the database removes the gaps, much as defragmenting a hard drive does for the file system.

Active Directory compaction is done with the `ntdsutil` command. The database can't be compacted in place, so a copy is made to a location you specify. After compaction is finished, the compacted database is copied to the original location.

Active Directory Metadata Cleanup

Active Directory metadata describes the Active Directory database, not the actual Active Directory data. Metadata can be left over if a DC had to be removed forcibly from the domain, which can occur if the DC stops communicating correctly with other DCs, perhaps because of Active Directory corruption or hardware failure. The metadata is information about the failed DC that stays in the Active Directory database on the remaining DCs in the domain. Metadata might also have to be cleaned up if an attempt to install a new DC in the domain fails after a partial installation.

Metadata that's not cleaned up can have varying and unpredictable effects on the domain—some unnoticeable and some that cause replication and other functions to malfunction. In addition, any attempts to install a DC with the same name as the failed one will be unsuccessful until the metadata is cleaned up. Even after successful removal of a DC, it's a good idea to check for leftover metadata. There are three main methods for cleaning up metadata: Active Directory Users and Computers, Active Directory Sites and Services, and `ntdsutil`.

Using Active Directory Users and Computers is the simplest cleanup method. Locate the computer account of the failed DC in the Domain Controllers OU and delete it. You're asked to confirm the deletion, and then you see a message stating that you should try to remove the DC with the Remove Roles and Features Wizard. Select the *Delete this Domain Controller anyway* check box, and then click Delete. If the server is a GC server, you're prompted again to continue with the deletion. If the server is an FSMO role holder, you're asked to confirm moving the roles to another DC. This procedure should clean up all remaining metadata for the selected DC.

To use Active Directory Sites and Services, you expand the site name, the Servers folder, and then the failed DC. Right-click NTDS Settings and click Delete, and then click Yes to confirm. After the NTDS Settings node is deleted, right-click the computer object and delete it.

To clean up metadata with `ntdsutil`, follow these steps:

1. Open a command prompt window and type the following commands, pressing Enter after each one:

   ```
   ntdsutil
   metadata cleanup
   remove selected server DomainController
   ```

2. In the warning message, click Yes to confirm the removal.

3. Type `quit` and press Enter twice to exit `ntdsutil`.

4. Open Active Directory Sites and Services and delete the computer object, if necessary.

> **Note**
>
> There are times when metadata cleanup can be fully accomplished using only `ntdsutil`. Depending on your Active Directory configuration, you may need to remove domain and site information as well.

Working with Active Directory Snapshots

An **Active Directory snapshot** is just what it sounds like: an exact replica of the Active Directory database at a specific moment. It's similar to a snapshot (or *checkpoint*, as it's called in Hyper-V) of a virtual machine. You can browse through Active Directory snapshots to view Active Directory's state at different times. You can also export Active Directory objects from a snapshot and import them with `ldifde`. The basic procedure for working with snapshots is as follows:

1. Create and mount the snapshot with `ntdsutil`.

2. Activate the snapshot with `dsamain`.

3. Browse the snapshot with Active Directory Users and Computers or another LDAP tool.

4. Dismount the snapshot.

Creating and Mounting Snapshots

To use a snapshot, create one first and then mount it with `ntdsutil`, using the following procedure (shown in Figure 6-16):

1. Open a command prompt window, and type `ntdsutil` and press Enter.

2. Type `snapshot` and press Enter.

3. Type `activate instance ntds` and press Enter.

4. Type `create` and press Enter.

5. `Ntdsutil` names the snapshot by using a globally unique ID (GUID). You need the GUID, so instead of having to type it, use your mouse to highlight the number between the braces and press Ctrl+C to copy it.

6. Type `mount` and press the spacebar. Press Ctrl+V to paste the GUID.

7. Copy the part of the output starting with `C:\$SNAP` and ending with `VOLUMEC$\` because you need it in the command in the following section to activate a snapshot. It's the path to the snapshot, which includes a time stamp. If you open File Explorer, you see a volume mounted in the root of the C drive with that name.

8. Type `quit` and press Enter twice to exit `ntdsutil`.

```
C:\Windows\system32>ntdsutil
ntdsutil: snapshot
snapshot: activate instance ntds
Active instance set to "ntds".
snapshot: create
Creating snapshot...
Snapshot set {b9869340-a167-41b7-a664-5e90dad659b9} generated successfully.
snapshot: mount
Error parsing Input - Invalid Syntax.
snapshot: mount b9869340-a167-41b7-a664-5e90dad659b9
Snapshot {d1635857-c873-472e-8d0e-2cd188827e22} mounted as C:\$SNAP_201705231941_VOLUMEC$\
snapshot: quit
ntdsutil: quit
```

Figure 6-16   Creating an Active Directory snapshot

Activating a Snapshot

After you've created a snapshot, you need to let the Active Directory service know about it by using the following steps:

1. At a command prompt, type `dsamain /dbpath SnapshotPath\windows\ntds\ntds.dit /ldapport 20000` and press Enter. The `SnapshotPath` is the output you copied in the previous section, and `ldapport` is the port number you use when browsing the snapshot.

2. When you see the line beginning with `EVENTLOG` and ending with `1000`, the process is finished. Leave the command prompt window open.

3. To browse the snapshot, open Active Directory Users and Computers, and then right-click the domain object and click Change Domain Controller. In the Change Directory Server dialog box, click "<Type a Directory Server name[:port] here>," type `DCName:20000`, and press Enter (replacing `DCName` with the name of the domain controller), which results in Figure 6-17. Click OK.

You can browse the snapshot of Active Directory in Active Directory Users and Computers. Just realize that if you make any changes, they're made to the snapshot, not to the live Active Directory database.

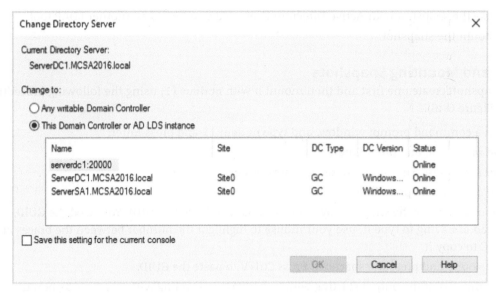

Figure 6-17 Opening a snapshot in Active Directory Users and Computers

Exporting a Snapshot

You can export Active Directory objects from the snapshot by using `ldifde` and import them into another instance of Active Directory. To export the users in the TestOU1 OU to the `testOU1users.txt` file, enter the following command at a command prompt:

```
ldifde -t 20000 -f testOU1users.txt -d
  "ou=TestOU1,dc=mcsa2016,dc=local" -r (ObjectClass=user)
```

Unmounting and Deleting a Snapshot

When you use `dsamain` to activate a snapshot, you leave the command prompt window open until you're finished with the snapshot. To stop `dsamain` and unmount the snapshot, use the following steps:

1. In the command prompt window where dsamain is running, press Ctrl+C.
2. Type the following commands, pressing Enter after each:

   ```
   ntdsutil
   snapshot
   unmount SnapshotGUID
   quit
   quit
   ```

In these commands, *SnapshotGUID* is the GUID that was generated when you mounted the snapshot. If you need to see the GUID, type `list all` in `ntdsutil` while in snapshot mode. Unmounting the snapshot doesn't delete it. To delete the snapshot, type `delete SnapshotGUID` after you enter snapshot mode.

Activity 6-8: Creating a System State Backup

Time Required: 25 minutes or longer
Objective: Create a system state backup.
Required Tools and Equipment: ServerDC1, ServerSA1
Description: In this activity, you create a system state backup, but first you need to install the Windows Server Backup tool. You will store backups on a separate volume from Windows, so you create a new volume on Disk 1 on ServerSA1 for this purpose. Then you create some objects in Active Directory and create the system state backup.

1. On ServerSA1, open Disk Management. Create a 15 GB NTFS volume named **Backup** and assign it drive letter **B** (the backup should take about 12 GB of space). Use the defaults for all other options. Close Disk Management.
2. Open Active Directory Users and Computers. First, you create some objects that you delete in a later activity to test the backup. Right-click the domain object, point to **New**, and click **Organizational Unit**. Type **TestOU1** in the Name text box. Click to clear the **Protect container from accidental deletion** check box. Click **OK**.
3. Create a user in TestOU1 with the full name **Test User1**, the logon name **testuser1**, and the password **Password01**. Set the password to never expire.
4. Open a PowerShell prompt. Type **Install-WindowsFeature Windows-Server-Backup** and press **Enter**.
5. Even though wbadmin isn't a PowerShell cmdlet, you can still run it from PowerShell. Type **wbadmin start systemstatebackup -backuptarget:B:** and press **Enter** to start a system state backup on the B drive.
6. When you're prompted to start the backup operation, type **y** and press **Enter**.
7. The backup must first identify all system state files, and you see progress displays as wbadmin finds the files. When the files have been found, the backup begins. (It might take several minutes.) Progress lines are displayed periodically to show the percentage complete. When the backup is finished, a log of files backed up successfully is created in the C:\Windows\Logs\WindowsServerBackup folder. Close the PowerShell window.
8. To view files in the backup, open File Explorer and navigate to **B:\WindowsImageBackup\ServerSA1**. You see a folder named Backup *DateAndTime* where the backup you created is stored. You also see a folder named Catalog that holds the files composing the catalog of backups.
9. Close File Explorer, but stay signed in for the next activity.

Activity 6-9: Restoring Active Directory from a System State Backup

Time Required: 30 minutes or longer
Objective: Restore Active Directory from a backup.
Required Tools and Equipment: ServerDC1, ServerSA1
Description: In this activity, you delete an OU from Active Directory and then perform an authoritative restore on the deleted object.

1. On ServerSA1, open Active Directory Users and Computers. Click **TestOU1** and press **Delete**. When prompted to confirm the deletion, click **Yes**.
2. In the Confirm Subtree Deletion message box, click the **Use Delete Subtree server control** check box so that protected objects can be deleted, and then click **Yes**.
3. Now, you'll restore the objects using the backup. To do so, you need to restart ServerSA1 in Directory Services repair mode. Right-click **Start**, click **Run**, type **msconfig**, and press **Enter** to start System Configuration.
4. Click the **Boot** tab. Click the **Safe boot** check box and click **Active Directory repair**. Click **OK**.
5. Click **Restart** to restart ServerSA1 in Safe Mode.
6. Sign in to ServerSA1 using the local administrator account and the DSRM password, which is **Password01**. It might take a while before you see the desktop. "Safe Mode" is displayed in the corners of the desktop.
7. Open a command prompt window. You must get a list of the available backups before you can restore the system state. Type **wbadmin get versions -backuptarget:B:** and press **Enter**. After a short wait, a list of backups is displayed. Make a note of the version identifier of the most recent backup, which is the system state backup you created in the previous activity.
8. To begin the recovery, type **wbadmin start systemstaterecovery -version:***Version* **-backuptarget:B:** (replacing `Version` with the version identifier you noted in Step 7) and press **Enter**. When prompted to start the recovery operation, type **y** and press **Enter**. You see a warning about replicated content causing latency or outage issues and are prompted to continue. Type **y** and press **Enter**.

9. The restoration will probably take several minutes. When it's finished, you're prompted to restart. However, don't restart the server because you must first mark deleted objects as authoritative. The prompt doesn't give you the option to enter "n" to prevent a restart, so press **Ctrl+C** to quit wbadmin. If this server were the only writeable DC, the next step isn't necessary, but ServerDC1 is also writeable. With a nonauthoritative restore, you would simply restart the server to finish the restoration.

10. Type **ntdsutil** and press **Enter**. Type **activate instance ntds** and press **Enter** to make the Active Directory database the focus of the command. Type **authoritative restore** and press **Enter**. At the authoritative restore prompt, type **restore subtree ou=TestOU1,dc=mcsa2016,dc=local** and press **Enter**. When the Authoritative Restore Confirmation Dialog message box opens, click **Yes**. Type **quit** and press **Enter**, and then type **quit** again and press **Enter**. The restore command specifies the object to restore authoritatively. The rest of the Active Directory database is stored nonauthoritatively.

11. Change the boot setting so that ServerSA1 boots normally. Right-click **Start**, click **Run**, type **msconfig**, and press **Enter** to start System Configuration. Click the **Boot** tab. Click to clear the **Safe boot** check box. Click **OK**. Click **Restart** to restart the server.

12. Sign in to ServerSA1 as the domain administrator. The system state recovery performs some final tasks, opens a command prompt window, and displays a "Completed successfully" message. Press **Enter** to continue when prompted.

13. Open Active Directory Users and Computers and click **TestOU1** to verify that the objects have been restored.

14. Close Active Directory Users and Computers and continue to the next activity.

Activity 6-10: Restoring Deleted Objects from the Active Directory Recycle Bin

Time Required: 20 minutes

Objective: Restore deleted objects from the Active Directory Recycle Bin.

Required Tools and Equipment: ServerDC1, ServerSA1

Description: You have seen that recovering deleted objects can involve quite a bit of time if the Active Directory Recycle Bin isn't enabled. To make the process easier, you enable and test this feature.

1. On ServerDC1, open Active Directory Administrative Center, and click **MCSA2016 (local)** in the left pane.

2. In the right pane, click **Enable Recycle Bin**. You see a message explaining that the Recycle Bin can't be disabled after it's enabled. Click **OK**. You see a message telling you to refresh the Active Directory Administrative Center now. Click **OK**.

3. Click the **Refresh** icon to refresh Active Directory Administrative Center. You see a new folder named Deleted Objects. Sign in to ServerSA1 as administrator, if necessary. Open Active Directory Administrative Center and click the domain object to verify that the Deleted Objects folder is there. If it is, the Recycle Bin is enabled on both DCs.

4. Now delete some objects. Right-click **TestOU1** and click **Delete**. Click **Yes** to confirm. Click **Use delete subtree server control** and click **Yes**.

5. On ServerDC1, refresh Active Directory Administrative Center and verify that **TestOU1** has been deleted. Double-click the **Deleted Objects** folder. You see TestOU1 and Test User1.

6. To restore both objects, click **Test User1**, hold down the **Ctrl** key, and click **TestOU1** so that both objects are highlighted and then release the **Ctrl** key. In the right pane, click **Restore**.

7. In the left pane, click **MCSA2016 (local)**. Double-click **TestOU1** and verify that Test User1 is also restored.

8. Next, you see how to restore an object with PowerShell. First you need a deleted object, so delete **Test User1** from TestOU1, but don't delete TestOU1 this time.

9. Open a PowerShell prompt. Type **Get-ADObject -Filter {DisplayName -eq "Test User1"} -IncludeDeletedObjects | Restore-ADObject** and press **Enter**.

10. Refresh Active Directory Administrative Center, and you'll see that Test User1 is restored.

11. Close the PowerShell window and Active Directory Administrative Center. Continue to the next activity.

Activity 6-11: Compacting the Active Directory Database

Time Required: 15 minutes

Objective: Compact the Active Directory database.

Required Tools and Equipment: ServerDC1, ServerSA1

Description: In this activity, you compact the Active Directory database. You create folders to hold temporary copies of the database, stop the Active Directory service, and then compact the database with one of the folders you created as the destination. First, you make a copy of the original database in case a problem occurs with compaction, and then you must delete the Active Directory log files and copy the compacted database to replace the original database.

1. On ServerDC1, set the alternate DNS server address in the network connection IP address settings to the address of ServerSA1 (192.168.0.2). This step is done as a precaution. Because DNS doesn't respond to DNS queries while Active Directory is stopped, ServerDC1 might need to contact a DNS server if you have to sign in after Active Directory is stopped. This can happen, for example, if your screen saver comes on and requires a password to access the desktop. When you have finished changing the alternate DNS server address, close any open dialog boxes.

2. Create two folders in the root of the C drive: **tempAD** and **backupAD**.

3. Open a command prompt window. Type **net stop ntds** and press **Enter** to stop the Active Directory service. When prompted to continue, type **y** and press **Enter**.

4. Type the following commands, pressing **Enter** after each one (see Figure 6-18):

   ntdsutil, activate instance ntds
   files
   compact to c:\tempAD

```
C:\Users\Administrator>ntdsutil
ntdsutil: activate instance ntds
Active instance set to "ntds".
ntdsutil: files
file maintenance: compact to c:\tempAD
Initiating DEFRAGMENTATION mode...
      Source Database: C:\Windows\NTDS\ntds.dit
      Target Database: c:\tempAD\ntds.dit

              Defragmentation  Status (% complete)

       0    10   20   30   40   50   60   70   80   90  100
       |----|----|----|----|----|----|----|----|----|----|
       ..................................................

It is recommended that you immediately perform a full backup
of this database. If you restore a backup made before the
defragmentation, the database will be rolled back to the state
it was in at the time of that backup.

Compaction is successful. You need to:
    copy "c:\tempAD\ntds.dit" "C:\Windows\NTDS\ntds.dit"
and delete the old log files:
    del C:\Windows\NTDS\*.log

file maintenance:
```

Figure 6-18   Compacting the database with `ntdsutil`

5. The Defragmentation Status display shows the progress of compaction. When you see a message stating that you need to copy the new file over the old file and delete the log files, type **quit** and press **Enter**, and then type **quit** and press **Enter** again.

6. To copy the original database file to the backup folder you created, type **copy c:\windows\ntds\ntds.dit c:\backupAD** and press **Enter**.

7. To delete the log files, type **del c:\windows\ntds*.log** and press **Enter**.

8. To copy the compacted database over the original database, type **copy c:\tempAD\ntds.dit c:\windows\ntds\ntds.dit** and press **Enter**. Type **y** and press **Enter** to confirm the copy.

9. Next, to verify the integrity of the new database, type the following commands, pressing **Enter** after each one:

   ntdsutil

   activate instance ntds

   files

   integrity

10. Assuming the integrity check was successful, type **quit** and press **Enter**. If it wasn't successful, copy the backup from C:\backupAD to C:\Windows\Ntds, and attempt the compaction process again, starting with Step 4.

11. To check the semantic database integrity (which is recommended), type **semantic database analysis** and press **Enter**, then type **go fixup**, and press **Enter**. Type **quit** and press **Enter**, and then type **quit** and press **Enter** again.

12. To restart Active Directory, type **net start ntds** and press **Enter**. You can verify a successful startup by checking the most recent events in the event log. Shortly after the service starts, a new event with ID 1000 should be created in the Directory Service log under Applications and Services Logs in Event Viewer, indicating a successful Active Directory start.

13. Close all open windows, and shut down both servers.

Chapter Summary

- DCs and sites are the physical components of Active Directory, and forest, domains, and OUs are the logical components. DCs use multimaster replication, but read only domain controllers (RODCs) use unidirectional replication.

- A global catalog (GC) server is a DC configured to hold the global catalog. Every forest must have at least one GC server. GC servers facilitate domain-wide and forest-wide searches, enable logons across domains, and hold universal group membership information. Each site should have at least one GC server to speed logons and directory searches.

- Because of the benefits of virtualization, implementing DCs as virtual machines in Hyper-V is common practice. Starting with Windows Server 2012, DCs running on Hyper-V are virtualization aware, and there are built-in safeguards to prevent the Active Directory database from being adversely affected when the VM is rolled back in time by applying a checkpoint.

- To clone a domain controller, you need to verify that the hypervisor supports virtual machine generation identifiers, the PDC emulator FSMO role

is running Windows Server 2012 or later, a GC server is available, and only supported roles are installed on the DC to be cloned.

- RODCs were developed to provide secure Active Directory support in branch office installations where physical server security is lax and there are no on-site server administrators. Before installing an RODC, make sure there's a writeable Windows Server 2008 DC or later to which the RODC can replicate. The forest functional level must be at least Windows Server 2003, and you must use `adprep /rodcprep` if the functional level isn't Windows Server 2008.

- Replication on an RODC is unidirectional, and user passwords aren't stored on the RODC by default. You can configure credential caching if you want the RODC to store passwords of selected users locally.

- With staged RODC installation, a domain administrator creates the RODC computer account in Active Directory, and a regular user can then perform the installation.

- An Active Directory site represents a physical location where domain controllers reside. Multiple sites are used for authentication efficiency,

- replication efficiency, and application efficiency. Site components include subnets, site links, and bridgehead servers.
- Universal group membership caching handles the potential conflict between faster logons and additional replication traffic.
- Deciding where to place the FSMO role holder is part of the overall Active Directory design strategy. Two important operations for managing FSMOs are transferring and seizing operations master roles.
- Active Directory is composed of two important folders: *%systemroot%\NTDS* and *%systemroot%\SYSVOL*. When you back up the system state, both folders are included in the backup. A system state backup on a domain controller includes the Registry, boot files, the Active Directory database, the SYSVOL folder, some system files, and other files, depending on roles installed on the server.
- You can restore Active Directory by using a nonauthoritative restore or an authoritative restore. A nonauthoritative restore restores the Active Directory database, or portions of it, and allows it to be updated through replication by other DCs. An authoritative restore ensures that restored objects aren't overwritten by changes from other DCs through replication.

- The Active Directory Recycle Bin isn't enabled by default, and after it's enabled, it can't be disabled without reinstalling the entire Active Directory forest. It's enabled in ADAC, and objects that are deleted can be restored from the Deleted Folders container.
- The Active Directory database becomes fragmented over time. Online defragmentation simply deletes deleted objects that have been deleted longer than the tombstone lifetime, a process called garbage collection. You can't restore a backup that's older than the tombstone lifetime. Offline defragmentation compacts the database for more efficient operation. Offline defragmentation can be performed by stopping the Active Directory service without having to restart the server.
- Active Directory metadata is data that describes the Active Directory database, not the actual Active Directory data. Metadata can be left over if a DC has to be forcibly removed from the domain. Metadata that isn't cleaned up can have varying and unpredictable effects on the domain.
- An Active Directory snapshot is an exact replica of the Active Directory service at a specific moment. Active Directory snapshots can be browsed to view the state of Active Directory when the snapshot was taken. You can export objects from a snapshot by using `ldifde`.

Key Terms

Active Directory metadata	global catalog (GC) server	RID master
Active Directory snapshot	infrastructure master	schema master
authoritative restore	nonauthoritative restore	security identifier (SID)
bridgehead server	offline defragmentation	site link
DC clone	online defragmentation	staged installation
delegated administrator account	PDC emulator	tombstone lifetime
domain naming master	read only domain controller (RODC)	unidirectional replication
filtered attribute set	relative identifier (RID)	universal group membership caching
Flexible Single Master Operation (FSMO) role	restartable Active Directory	

Review Questions

1. Which of the following is *not* a function of the global catalog?
   a. Facilitating forest-wide searches
   b. Keeping universal group memberships
   c. Facilitating intersite replication
   d. Facilitating forest-wide logons

2. You have an Active Directory forest of two trees and eight domains. You haven't changed any of the operations master domain controllers. On which domain controller is the schema master?
   a. All domain controllers
   b. The last domain controller installed
   c. The first domain controller in the forest root domain
   d. The first domain controller in each tree

3. Which of the following are reasons for establishing multiple sites? (Choose all that apply.)
   a. Improving authentication efficiency
   b. Enabling more frequent replication
   c. Reducing traffic on the WAN
   d. Having only one IP subnet

4. Users of a new network subnet have been complaining that logons and other services are taking much longer than they did before being moved to the new subnet. You discover that many logons and requests for DFS resources from clients in the new subnet are being handled by domain controllers in a remote site instead of local domain controllers. What should you do to solve this problem?
   a. Create a new site and add the clients and new GC server to the new site.
   b. Change the IP addresses of the clients to correspond to the network of the DCs that are handling the logons.
   c. Compact the Active Directory database because fragmentation must be causing latency.
   d. Create a new subnet and add the subnet to the site that maps to the physical location of the clients.

5. You want to decrease users' logon time at SiteA but not increase replication traffic drastically. You have 50 users at this site with one domain controller. Overall, your network contains 3000 user and computer accounts. What solution can decrease logon times with the least impact on replication traffic?
   a. Configure the domain controller as a domain naming master.

   b. Configure the domain controller as a global catalog server.
   c. Configure multiple connection objects between the domain controller in SiteA and a remote global catalog server.
   d. Enable universal group membership caching.

6. Which of the following configurations should you avoid?
   a. Domain naming master and schema master on the same domain controller
   b. PDC emulator and RID master on the same computer
   c. Infrastructure master configured as a global catalog server
   d. Schema master configured as a global catalog server

7. User authentications are taking a long time. The domain controller performing which FSMO role will most likely decrease authentication times if it's upgraded?
   a. RID master
   b. PDC emulator
   c. Infrastructure master
   d. Domain naming master

8. You're taking an older server performing the RID master role out of service and will be replacing it with a new server configured as a domain controller. What should you do to ensure the smoothest transition?
   a. Transfer the RID master role to the new domain controller and then shut down the old server.
   b. Shut down the current RID master and seize the RID master role from the new domain controller.
   c. Back up the domain controller that's currently the RID master, restore it to the new domain controller, and then shut down the old RID master.
   d. Shut down the current RID master, and then transfer the RID master role to the new domain controller.

9. Which of the following is true about an RODC installation?
   a. A Windows server running at least Windows Server 2012 is required.
   b. The forest functional level must be at least Windows Server 2003.
   c. `Adprep /rodcprep` must be run in Windows Server 2008 forests.
   d. Another RODC must be available as a replication partner.

10. You need to install an RODC in a new branch office and want to use an existing workgroup server running Windows Server 2016. The office is a plane flight away and is connected via a WAN. You want an employee at the branch office, Michael, to do the RODC installation because he's good at working with computers and following directions. What should you do?

    a. Add Michael to the Domain Admins group and give him directions on how to install the RODC.

    b. Add Michael's domain account to the Administrators group on the server and give him directions on how to install the RODC.

    c. Create the computer account for the RODC in the Domain Controllers OU and specify Michael's account as one that can join the computer to the domain.

    d. Create a group policy specifying that Michael's account can join RODCs to the domain and then use the Delegation of Control Wizard on the Domain Controllers OU.

11. You have an application integrated with AD DS that maintains Active Directory objects containing credential information, and there are serious security implications if these objects are compromised. An RODC at one branch office isn't physically secure, and theft is a risk. How can you best protect this application's sensitive data?

    a. Configure the PRP for the RODC and specify a Deny setting for the application object.

    b. Configure a filtered attribute set and specify the application-related objects.

    c. Use EFS to encrypt the files storing the sensitive objects.

    d. Turn off all password replication on the RODC.

12. You maintain an RODC running Windows Server 2016 at a branch office, and you want Juanita, who has solid computer knowledge, to perform administrative tasks, such as driver and software updates and device management. How can you do this without giving her broader domain rights?

    a. Assign Juanita's account as a delegated administrator in the RODC's computer account settings.

    b. Create a local user on the RODC for Juanita and add it to the Administrators group. Have Juanita log on with this account when necessary.

    c. Create a script that adds Juanita to the Domain Admins group each day at a certain time, and then removes her from the group 1 hour later. Tell Juanita to log on and perform the necessary tasks during the specified period.

    d. Send Juanita for extensive Windows Server 2016 training and then add her to the Domain Admins group.

13. Users usually notice a failure of the domain naming master immediately. True or False?

14. You have installed an RODC at a branch office that also runs the DNS Server role. All DNS zones are Active Directory integrated. What happens when a client computer attempts to register its name with the DNS service on the RODC?

    a. The DNS service rejects the registration. The client must be configured with a static DNS entry.

    b. The DNS service passes the request to another DNS server. After registration is completed, the DNS server that performed the registration sends the record to the DNS service on the RODC.

    c. The DNS service creates a temporary record in a dynamically configured primary zone. The record is replicated to other DNS servers and then deleted on the RODC.

    d. The DNS service sends a referral to the client. The client registers its name with the referred DNS server.

15. You have four users who travel to four branch offices often and need to log on to the RODCs at these offices. The branch offices are connected to the main office with slow WAN links. You don't want domain controllers at the main office to authenticate these four users when they log on at the branch offices. What should you do that requires the least administrative effort yet adheres to best practices?

    a. Create a new global group named AllBranches, add the four users to this group, and add the AllBranches group to the Allowed RODC Password Replication group.

    b. Add the four users to a local group on each RODC and add the local groups to the PRP on each RODC with an Allow setting.

    c. Add each user to the PRP on each RODC with an Allow setting.

    d. Create a group policy, set the "Allow credential caching on RODCs" policy to Enabled, add the four users to the policy, and link the policy to the Domain Controllers OU.

16. Which of the following is the term for a DC in a site that handles replication of a directory partition for that site?

    a. Inter-Site Topology Generator

    b. Knowledge Consistency Checker

    c. Bridgehead server

    d. Global catalog server

17. Where would you find files related to logon and logoff scripts in an Active Directory environment?
    a. C:\Windows\NTDS
    b. %*systemroot*%\SYSVOL
    c. %*Windir*%\ntds.dit
    d. C:\Windows\edb.log

18. Which of the following commands backs up the Registry, boot files, the Active Directory database, and the SYSVOL folder to the B drive?
    a. `robocopy C:\Windows /r /destination:B:`
    b. `wbadmin start systemstatebackup -backuptarget:B:`
    c. `backup %systemroot% -selectsystemstate > B:`
    d. `ntdsutil create snapshot -source C:\Windows\ntds -dest B:`

19. Which command must you use to restore deleted Active Directory objects in a domain with two or more writeable DCs if the Active Directory Recycle Bin isn't enabled?
    a. `wbadmin` with the `-authsysvol` option
    b. `wbadmin` with the `-restoreobject` option
    c. `ntdsutil` with the `authoritative restore` command
    d. `ntdsutil` with the `create snapshot` command

20. What's the term for removing deleted objects in Active Directory?
    a. Tombstoning
    b. Offline defragmentation
    c. Recycling objects
    d. Garbage collection

21. Which of the following is the period between an object being deleted and being removed from the Active Directory database?
    a. Tombstone lifetime
    b. Defragmentation limit
    c. Object expiration
    d. Restoration period

22. Your Active Directory database has been operating for several years and undergone many object creations and deletions. You want to make sure it's running at peak efficiency, so you want to defragment and compact the database. What procedure should you use that will be least disruptive to your network?
    a. Create a temporary folder to hold a copy of the database. Restart the server in DSRM. Run `ntdsutil` and compact the database in the temporary folder. Copy the `ntds.dit` file from the temporary folder to its original location. Verify the integrity of the new database and restart the server normally.
    b. Create a temporary folder and a backup folder. Stop the Active Directory service. Run `ntdsutil` and compact the database in the temporary folder. Copy the original database to the backup folder and delete the `ntds` log files. Copy the `ntds.dit` file from the temporary folder to its original location. Verify the integrity of the new database and restart the server.
    c. Create a temporary folder and a backup folder. Restart the server in DSRM. Run `ntdsutil` and compact the database in the temporary folder. Copy the original database to the backup folder, and delete the `ntds` log files. Copy the `ntds.dit` file from the temporary folder to its original location. Verify the integrity of the new database and restart the Active Directory service.
    d. Create a temporary folder and a backup folder. Stop the Active Directory service. Run `ntdsutil` and compact the database in the temporary folder. Copy the original database to the backup folder, and delete the `ntds` log files. Copy the `ntds.dit` file from the temporary folder to its original location. Verify the integrity of the new database and restart the Active Directory service.

23. You have four DCs in your domain. Active Directory appears to be corrupted on one of the DCs, and you suspect a failing hard drive. You attempt to remove it from the domain, but the procedure fails. You take the DC offline permanently and will replace it with another DC of the same name. What must you do before you can replace the DC?
    a. Restore the system state.
    b. Perform metadata cleanup.
    c. Back up SYSVOL.
    d. Transfer the FSMO roles.

24. Your company has had a major reorganization, and you need to transfer several hundred user accounts to another domain. Which of the following can help with this task?
    a. Create a system state backup and restore `ntds.dit` to the new domain.
    b. In Active Directory Users and Computers, select each account and export it.
    c. Create a snapshot and export the accounts with `ldifde`.
    d. Use the `Export-ADUser` PowerShell cmdlet.

Critical Thinking

The following activities give you critical thinking challenges. Case Projects offer a scenario with a problem to solve and for which you supply a written solution.

Case Project 6-1: Devising a DC Strategy

This project is suitable for group or individual work. You're the administrator of a network of 500 users and three Windows Server 2016 DCs. All users and DCs are in a single building. Your company is adding three satellite locations that will be connected to the main site via a WAN link. Each satellite location will house between 30 and 50 users. One location has a dedicated server room where you can house a server and ensure physical security. The other two locations don't have a dedicated room for network equipment. The WAN links are of moderate to low bandwidth. Design an Active Directory structure taking into account global catalog servers, FSMO roles, sites, and domain controllers. What features of DCs and Active Directory discussed in this chapter might you use in your design?

Case Project 6-2: Recovering from Accidental Deletion

A junior administrator accidentally deleted the Sales OU, which contained 25 user accounts and 4 group accounts. You have five DCs in your network: two running Windows Server 2016, two running Windows Server 2008 R2, and one running Windows Server 2008. Explain what you need and the procedure for recovering the deleted objects.

CHAPTER 7

CONFIGURING ADVANCED ACTIVE DIRECTORY

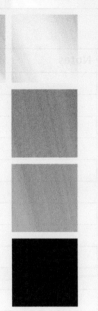

After reading this chapter and completing the exercises, you will be able to:

Configure a multidomain environment

Configure a multiforest environment

Describe Active Directory trusts

Configure Active Directory trusts

Upgrade domains and forests

Configure Active Directory sites

Manage Active Directory replication

The majority of day-to-day work in an Active Directory environment involves managing objects in a domain. With a single-domain, single-forest environment, administrators rarely need to use other tools besides Active Directory Users and Computers and Active Directory Administrative Center. However, multidomain and multiforest environments require configuring the Active Directory infrastructure in addition to user, group, and computer objects. For example, multiple forests or forests with several domains and trees might require trust configuration. In addition, a Windows network often has a mix of server OSs that must be integrated into the forest. If your network has older Windows versions, you might need to upgrade a domain or forest. Understanding domain and forest functional levels is critical to maintain this environment.

In this chapter, you review the major components and operation of Active Directory and then learn when you might need to configure a multidomain or multiforest network. You also learn how to configure trust relationships between domains and forests for efficient operation of Active Directory and to make using these complex environments easier for users. Then, you learn about domain functional levels, what features are supported in the different functional levels, and how to upgrade domains and forests to the latest functional level.

The larger your network becomes, the more you need to be concerned with Active Directory features, such as replication and site configuration. A network with many subnets and domain controllers (DCs) might require additional configuration to ensure efficient replication between DCs. A multisite network requires a solid understanding of site configuration and how domain controllers at different sites replicate with one another. This chapter discusses how to create new sites and configure them for optimal domain operation and replication. Replication between DCs is critical to a well-functioning domain. This chapter explains how to configure replication within a site for both Active Directory and the SYSVOL share, which holds vital files related to group policies and user logon. You also learn how to manage and monitor replication.

Table 7-1 summarizes the requirements for the hands-on activities in this chapter.

Table 7-1   Activity requirements

Activity	Requirements	Notes
Activity 7-1: Resetting Your Virtual Environment	ServerDC1, ServerSA1	
Activity 7-2: Installing a Subdomain	ServerDC1, ServerSA1	
Activity 7-3: Removing a Subdomain and Creating a New Tree	ServerDC1, ServerSA1	
Activity 7-4: Creating a New Forest	ServerDC1, ServerSA1	
Activity 7-5: Testing Cross-Forest Access Without a Trust	ServerDC1, ServerSA1	
Activity 7-6: Creating and Testing a Forest Trust	ServerDC1, ServerSA1	
Activity 7-7: Creating a Subnet and a Site	ServerDC1, ServerSA1	
Activity 7-8: Adding a DC to the MCSA2016 Domain	ServerDC1, ServerSA1	
Activity 7-9: Working with Connection Objects	ServerDC1, ServerSA1	
Activity 7-10: Creating a Site Link	ServerDC1, ServerSA1	
Activity 7-11: Managing Replication	ServerDC1, ServerSA1	

Configuring Multidomain Environments

 **Certification**

- **70-742 – Manage and maintain AD DS:**
  Configure Active Directory in a complex enterprise environment

In the day-to-day administration of an Active Directory domain, most administrators focus on organizational units (OUs) and their child objects along with Group Policy. In a small organization, a solid understanding of OUs, leaf objects, and Group Policy might be all that's needed to manage a Windows domain successfully. However, in large organizations, building an Active Directory structure composed of several domains, multiple trees, and even a few forests might be necessary.

Reasons for a Single-Domain Environment

A domain is the primary identifying and administrative unit in Active Directory. A unique name is associated with each domain and used to access network resources. A domain administrator account has full control over objects in the domain, and certain security policies apply to all accounts in a domain.

Additionally, most replication traffic occurs between DCs in a domain. Any of these factors can influence your decision to use a single-domain or multidomain design. Most small and medium businesses choose a single domain for reasons that include the following:

- *Simplicity*—The more complex something is, the easier it is for things to go wrong. Unless your organization needs multiple identities, separate administration, or different account policies, keeping the structure simple with a single domain is the best choice.
- *Lower costs*—Every domain must have at least one DC and preferably two or more for fault tolerance. Each DC requires additional hardware and software resources, which increase costs.
- *Easier management*—Many management tasks are easier in a single-domain environment:
  - Having a single set of administrators and policies prevents conflicts caused by differing viewpoints on operational procedures and policies.
  - Object management is easier when personnel reorganizations or transfers occur. Moving user and computer accounts between different OUs is easier than moving them between different domains.
  - Managing access to resources is simplified when you don't need to consider security principals from other domains.
  - Placement of DCs and global catalog servers is simplified when your organization has multiple locations because you don't need to consider cross-domain replication.
- *Easier access to resources*—A single domain provides the easiest environment for users to find and access network resources. In a multidomain environment, mobile users who visit branch offices with different domains must authenticate to their home domain. If their home domain isn't available for some reason, they can't log on to the network.

Reasons for a Multidomain Environment

Although a single-domain structure is usually easier and less expensive than a multidomain structure, it's not always better. Using more than one domain makes sense or is even a necessity in the following circumstances:

- *Need for different account policies*—Account policies that govern passwords and account lockouts apply to all users in a domain. If you need different policies for different business units, using separate domains is the best way to meet this requirement. Although you can use a password settings object (PSO) to apply different password policies for users or groups in a domain, this feature can be difficult to manage when many users are involved.
- *Need for different name identities*—Each domain has its own name that can represent a separate company or business unit. If each business unit must maintain its own identity, child domains in which part of the name is shared can be created, or multiple trees with completely different namespaces can be created.
- *Replication control*—Replication in a large domain maintaining several thousand objects can generate substantial traffic. In addition, when multiple business locations are connected through a WAN, the amount of replication traffic could be unacceptable. Replication traffic can be reduced by creating separate domains for key locations because only global catalog replication is required between domains.
- *Need for internal versus external domains*—Companies that run public web servers often create a domain used only for publicly accessible resources and another domain for internal resources.
- *Need for tight security*—With separate domains, stricter resource control and administrative permissions are easier, especially when dealing with hundreds or thousands of users in multiple business units. If a business unit prefers to have its own administrative staff, separate domains must be created.

The following sections discuss several aspects of multidomain environments, including adding subdomains, adding a tree to an existing forest, and configuring user accounts in multidomain environments.

Adding a Subdomain

Adding a subdomain is a common reason for expanding an Active Directory forest. A subdomain maintains a common naming structure with the forest root, so the top-level and second-level domain names remain the same. What makes a subdomain name different from the forest root's name is the third-level domain name. For example, if the forest root domain is csmtech.local, you might create subdomains named US.csmtech.local and Europe.csmtech.local to represent company branches organized by geography. A company might also create subdomains for different business units, such as widgets. csmtech.local and publishing.csmtech.local.

When you create a subdomain, you must consider a few questions before beginning:

- *What server will be the first DC for the new domain?* You can use an existing server or put a new computer into service. If you use an existing server that's currently a member of the forest root domain or a stand-alone server, you can just install the Active Directory Domain Services (AD DS) role and promote the server to a DC. If you use an existing DC, you must demote it and promote it again as the first DC in a new domain.
- *What are the names of the subdomain and the new DC?* You should have a naming convention established so that this question is easy to answer.
- *What Active Directory–related roles will the new DC fill?* Will the DC be a global catalog server, a DNS server, or another type?
- *In which site will the new DC be located?* Do you need to create a new site or add this DC to an existing site? Be sure the DC's IP addressing matches the site location.
- *Are you going to install a second DC for the subdomain immediately?* Remember that each domain should have a minimum of two DCs for fault tolerance and load balancing. In addition, you might want to offload FSMO roles to a second DC.
- *Who will administer the new domain?* Each domain or subdomain has a Domain Admins global group. Aside from the local administrator account, what other users should be a member of this group, if any?

These are some of the questions you should answer before you create a subdomain, and there might be others, depending on the circumstances.

Adding a Tree to an Existing Forest

Recall that an Active Directory tree is a grouping of domains sharing a common naming structure. A tree can consist of a single domain or a parent domain and child domains, which can have child domains of their own. An Active Directory tree is said to have a contiguous namespace because all domains in the tree share at least the second-level and top-level domain names. For example, csmtech.local has a second-level domain name of csmtech and a top-level domain name of local.

Organizations operating under a single name internally and publicly are probably best served by an Active Directory forest with only one tree. However, when two companies merge or a large company splits into separate business units that would benefit from having their own identities, a multiple tree structure makes sense. There's no functional difference between domains and subdomains in the same tree or domains in different trees as long as they're part of the same forest. The only operational difference is the necessity of maintaining multiple DNS zones. Figure 7-1 shows a forest with two trees, each with two subdomains.

Adding a tree to an existing Active Directory forest isn't much different from adding a subdomain to an existing tree. Most of the same questions you should answer for adding a subdomain apply to adding a new tree except that you need a name for the new tree that includes the top-level and second-level domain names.

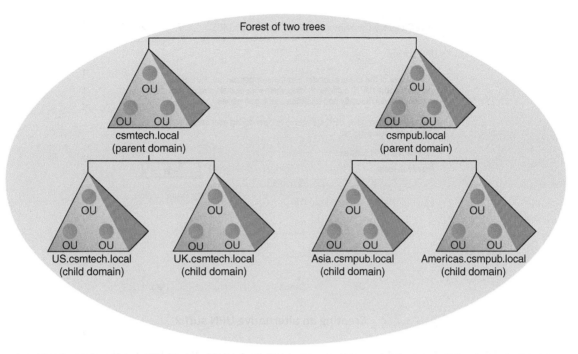

Figure 7-1 A forest with two trees

Configuring an Alternative UPN Suffix

When a user is created in a domain, the account is assigned a **UPN suffix** that's the same as the domain name. The UPN suffix is the part of the user principal name (UPN) that comes after the @. For example, in the UPN jsmith@csmtech.local, csmtech.local is the UPN suffix. In a multidomain environment, you might want to configure multiple UPN suffixes to make logons easier. For example, suppose you have a domain structure with multiple levels of subdomains, such as csmtech.local, development.csmtech.local, and us.development.csmtech.local. A user named jsmith in us.development.csmtech.local would have to enter jsmith@us.development.csmtech.local whenever the full UPN was required for authentication. To simplify logons, an alternative UPN suffix, such as csmtech.local, can be created and assigned to the jsmith account.

Note

A user account assigned an alternative UPN suffix can still use the original domain name when entering credentials. So even though jsmith is assigned the csmtech.local UPN suffix, jsmith can enter credentials by using jsmith@us.development.csmtech.local or jsmith@csmtech.local.

To create alternative UPN suffixes, follow these steps:

1. Sign in to the domain controller where you want to create the alternative suffix with enterprise administrator credentials. The account you sign in with must be a member of Enterprise Admins.

2. In Server Manager, open Active Directory Domains and Trusts.

3. Right-click Active Directory Domains and Trusts [*server name*] and click Properties to open the dialog box shown in Figure 7-2.

4. Type the suffix in the Alternative UPN suffixes text box, click Add, and then click OK. Close Active Directory Domains and Trusts.

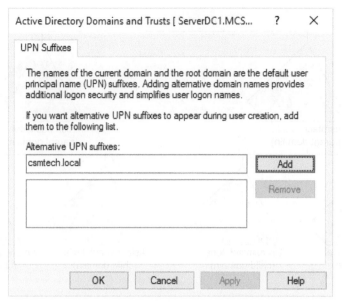

Figure 7-2 Creating an alternative UPN suffix

5. In Active Directory Users and Computers, open the Properties dialog box for the user to which you want to assign the UPN suffix and click the Account tab. Click the User logon name list arrow, and click the UPN suffix you want this user to use (see Figure 7-3). You can also assign a UPN suffix when you create a user.

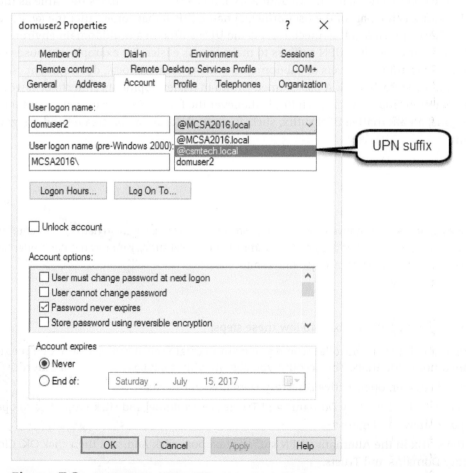

Figure 7-3 Assigning a UPN suffix to a user account

The UPN suffix doesn't need to have the same domain-naming structure as the account's actual domain. Although you should follow DNS naming rules when creating an alternative UPN suffix, the suffix name isn't required to be an actual DNS domain name. For example, you could create a single-level suffix named csm so that users assigned this suffix enter their user names as *username*@csm.

Activity 7-1: Resetting Your Virtual Environment

Time Required: 5 minutes

Objective: Reset your virtual environment by applying the InitialConfig checkpoint or snapshot.

Required Tools and Equipment: ServerDC1, ServerSA1

Description: Apply the InitialConfig checkpoint or snapshot to ServerDC1 and ServerSA1.

1. Be sure all servers are shut down. In your virtualization program, apply the InitialConfig checkpoint or snapshot to ServerDC1 and ServerSA1.
2. When the snapshot or checkpoint has finished being applied, continue to the next activity.

Activity 7-2: Installing a Subdomain

Time Required: 25 minutes or longer

Objective: Install a subdomain in an existing forest.

Required Tools and Equipment: ServerDC1, ServerSA1

Description: In this activity, you install the AD DS role on ServerSA1 and promote ServerSA1 to a domain controller, creating a subdomain named SubA.MCSA2016.local in the MCSA2016.local forest.

Note

It's important that ServerSA1's IP address settings are correct. In particular, the Preferred DNS Server option must be set to 192.168.0.1 (the address of ServerDC1).

1. Start ServerDC1. Start ServerSA1, and sign in as **Administrator** with the password **Password01**.
2. On ServerSA1, you'll install the Active Directory Domain Services role. Open a PowerShell window, type **Add-WindowsFeature AD-Domain-Services –IncludeManagementTools**, and press **Enter**.
3. After the role is installed, you need to promote the server to a domain controller. You will add a new domain named SubA to the MCSA2016.local domain. Type **Install-ADDSDomain –Credential (Get-Credential mcsa2016\administrator) –NewDomainName SubA -ParentDomainName mcsa2016.local -DomainType ChildDomain** and press **Enter**.
4. When prompted for your credentials, type **Password01** in the Password text box. When prompted for the SafeModeAdministratorPassword, type **Password01**, type it again, and press **Enter** to confirm it. Press **Enter** to confirm the operation. You will see a few warnings that you can safely ignore as long as there are no errors.
5. After the installation is finished, the server restarts automatically. After the server restarts, sign in as **Administrator**. (*Note*: You're now signing in to the SubA.MCSA2016.local domain.) In Server Manager, click **Local Server** and verify the domain information shown under Computer name (see Figure 7-4).
6. Click **Tools, Active Directory Domains and Trusts** from the menu. In the left pane, click to expand **MCSA2016.local**. You see the new subdomain. Right-click **MCSA2016.local** and click **Properties**. Click the **Trusts** tab. You see an outgoing and incoming trust with SubA.MCSA2016.local. Trusts are discussed later in the section "Configuring Active Directory Trusts." Click **Cancel**, and close Active Directory Domains and Trusts.

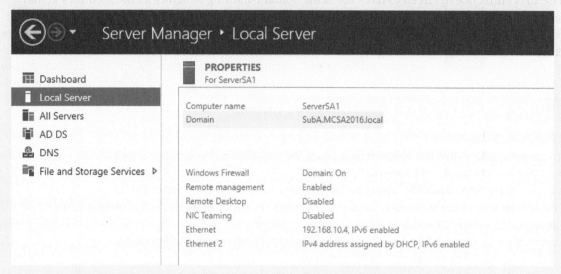

Figure 7-4 ServerSA1 is now in the SubA.MCSA2016.local domain

7. Click **Tools, DNS** to open DNS Manager (DNS was automatically installed when you installed Active Directory on ServerSA1). Click to expand **ServerSA1, Forward Lookup Zones**, and click **SubA.MCSA2016.local** to see the records that were created automatically, which include an A record for ServerSA1 and the folders holding Active Directory–related records.

8. On ServerDC1, in Server Manager, click **Tools, DNS**. In DNS Manager, click to expand **ServerDC1, Forward Lookup Zones**, and **MCSA2016.local**. The SubA folder is grayed out because the zone was automatically delegated to ServerSA1 when ServerSA1 was promoted to a DC for the SubA subdomain. Click **SubA** to see that there is only an NS record pointing to ServerSA1, which means that ServerSA1 will handle queries for the SubA subdomain. Close DNS Manager.

9. Continue to the next activity.

Activity 7-3: Removing a Subdomain and Creating a New Tree

Time Required: 15 minutes

Objective: Remove a subdomain.

Required Tools and Equipment: ServerDC1, ServerSA1

Description: In this activity, you demote ServerSA1, which removes the SubA subdomain. Note that you aren't uninstalling the Active Directory Domain Services role because you'll need it again to create a new tree. Next, you create a new domain tree in the MCSA2016.local forest. You will use PowerShell to demote ServerSA1 and then use the GUI to promote it as a DC for a new tree.

1. On ServerSA1, open a PowerShell window. Type **Uninstall-ADDSDomainController -LastDomainControllerInDomain -RemoveApplicationPartitions -Credential (get-credential)** and press **Enter**. The -RemoveApplicationPartitions parameter is needed to confirm that you want to delete the DNS data for the SubA subdomain. Note that the DNS Server role is still installed, but the zone data will be deleted.

2. In the Enter your credentials dialog box, type **MCSA2016\administrator** in the User name text box and **Password01** in the Password text box, and then click **OK**. Because you're removing a domain from the forest, you must enter the forest root administrator's credentials.

3. When prompted for the local administrator password, type **Password01**, press **Enter**, then type it again, and press **Enter** to confirm it. This sets the local administrator account password because this server will no longer be a domain controller.

4. When you're prompted to continue the operation, press **Enter**. After the operation is complete, the server restarts. At this point, the Active Directory Domain Services role files aren't actually uninstalled, so if you want it to be a DC again, you just need to promote this server.

5. Sign in to ServerSA1 as **Administrator**. Before you can add a new tree to the forest, you need to configure DNS properly on both servers. First, you create a conditional forwarder on ServerSA1 to point to the MCSA2016.local domain.

6. Open DNS Manager. Click to expand **ServerSA1** and then click **Conditional Forwarders**. Right-click **Conditional Forwarders** and click **New Conditional Forwarder**.

7. In the New Conditional Forwarder dialog box, type **MCSA2016.local** in the DNS Domain box. Then click in the **IP addresses of the master servers** text box and type **192.168.0.1** and press **Enter**. Click **OK**. Close DNS Manager.

8. On ServerDC1, open DNS Manager and create a conditional forwarder for the NewTree.local domain you are about to create following Steps 6 and 7 but using **NewTree.local** for the domain name and **192.168.0.4** for the IP address of the master server. When you are finished, close DNS Manager.

9. On ServerSA1, in Server Manager, click the notifications flag and then click **Promote this server to a domain controller**. The Active Directory Domain Services Configuration Wizard starts.

10. In the Deployment Configuration window, click the **Add a new domain to an existing forest** option button. In the Select domain type list box, click **Tree Domain**. Type **MCSA2016.local** in the Forest name text box and **NewTree.local** in the New domain name text box (see Figure 7-5).

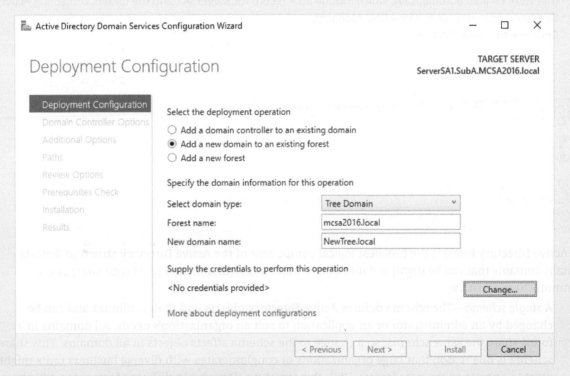

Figure 7-5   Adding a tree to an existing forest

11. Click **Change** to enter credentials. In the Windows Security dialog box, type **MCSA2016\Administrator** for the user name and **Password01** for the password, and then click **OK**. Click **Next**.

12. In the Domain Controller Options window, verify that the domain functional level is set to **Windows Server 2016**. In the Specify domain controller capabilities and site information section, leave the **Domain Name System (DNS) server** and **Global Catalog (GC)** check boxes selected. You should have a DNS server in each domain tree in the forest. Configuring this DC as a global catalog server is optional.

13. In the Directory Services Restore Mode (DSRM) password section, type **Password01** in the Password and Confirm password text boxes, and then click **Next**.

14. In the DNS Options window, you see a warning message about DNS delegation. This is okay and expected. Click **Next**.

15. In the Additional Options window, leave the default NetBIOS domain name, and then click **Next**.

16. In the Paths window, leave the default settings, and then click **Next**.

17. Review your choices in the Review Options window, and go back and make changes if necessary. When you're finished, click **Next**.

18. In the Prerequisites Check window, verify that all prerequisites have been met. You might see some warning messages, which is okay as long as there are no error messages. Click **Install**.

19. Watch the progress message at the top of the window to see the tasks being performed to install Active Directory. After the installation is finished, your computer restarts automatically. After the server restarts, sign in as **Administrator**. (*Note*: You're now signing in to the NewTree.local domain, which is part of the MCSA2016.local forest.)

20. In Server Manager, click **Tools**, **Active Directory Domains and Trusts** from the menu. In the left pane, you see both MCSA2016.local and NewTree.local. Right-click **MCSA2016.local** and click **Properties**. Click the **Trusts** tab. You see an outgoing and incoming trust with NewTree.local. Click **Cancel**. Right-click **NewTree.local** and click **Properties**. Click the **Trusts** tab. You see an outgoing and incoming trust with MCSA2016.local. Click **Cancel**. Close Active Directory Domains and Trusts.

21. In Server Manager, click **Tools, DNS** to open DNS Manager.

22. In DNS Manager, click to expand **Forward Lookup Zones**, and click **NewTree.local**. You see the records that were created automatically, which include an A record for ServerSA1 and the folders containing Active Directory–related records. Close DNS Manager.

23. Continue to the next activity.

Configuring Multiforest Environments

- **70-742 – Manage and maintain AD DS:**
  Configure Active Directory in a complex enterprise environment

An Active Directory forest is the broadest logical component of the Active Directory structure. Forests contain domains that can be organized into one or more trees. All domains in a forest share some common characteristics:

- *A single schema*—The schema defines Active Directory objects and their attributes and can be changed by an administrator or an application to suit an organization's needs. All domains in a forest share the same schema, so a change to the schema affects objects in all domains. This shared schema is one reason that large organizations or conglomerates with diverse business units might want to operate as separate forests. With this structure, domains in different forests can still share information through trust relationships, but changes to the schema—perhaps from installing an Active Directory–integrated application, such as Microsoft Exchange—don't affect the schema of domains in a different forest.

- *Forest-wide administrative accounts*—Each forest has two groups with unique rights to perform operations that can affect the entire forest: Schema Admins and Enterprise Admins. Members of Schema Admins are the only users who can make changes to the schema. Members of Enterprise Admins can add or remove domains from the forest and have administrative access to every domain in the forest. By default, only the Administrator account for the first domain created in the forest (referred to as the *forest root domain*) is a member of these two groups.

- *Operations masters*—As discussed, certain forest-wide operations can be performed only by a DC designated as the operations master. Both the schema master and the domain naming master are forest-wide operations masters, meaning that only one DC in the forest can perform these roles.
- *Global catalog*—There's only one global catalog per forest, but unlike operations masters, multiple DCs can be designated as global catalog servers. Because the global catalog contains information about all objects in the forest, it's used to speed searching for objects across domains in the forest and to allow users to log on to any domain in the forest.
- *Trusts between domains*—These trusts allow users to log on to their home domains (where their accounts are created) and access resources in domains throughout the forest without having to authenticate to each domain.
- *Replication between domains*—The forest structure facilitates replicating important information among DCs throughout the forest. Forest-wide replication includes information stored in the global catalog, schema directory, and configuration partitions.

With the preceding concepts in mind, you might need an additional forest for the following reasons:

- *Schema changes*—Business units in a large organization might require different schemas because of language or cultural differences or application differences. The schema controls the objects you can create in Active Directory and the attributes of these objects. If a new object or object attribute needs to be defined for language or cultural reasons, the schema must be changed. Likewise, an Active Directory–integrated application can make schema changes to accommodate its needs. Creating a separate forest isolates schema changes to the business unit requiring them.
- *Security*—Many industries and government entities have strict security requirements for access to resources. Domains in the same forest have a built-in trust, and members of the Enterprise Admins group have access to all domains, so the only way to have a true security boundary is with separate forests. Administrators in each forest can develop their own forest-wide security policies to ensure the degree of security suitable for the forest's assets. If necessary, a trust can be created between the forests to allow users in one forest to access resources in the other.
- *Corporate mergers*—Each of two businesses that merge might have its own established Active Directory forests and forest administrators. When the forests have different schemas or different security policies, merging them could be difficult or undesirable. Maintaining separate forests with trusts for cross-forest access is sometimes the best approach.

To create a forest, you simply choose the option to create a domain in a new forest when promoting a server to a domain controller. After the forest is created, you can choose whether to allow accounts in one forest to access resources in the other forest. You do that by creating a trust relationship, discussed next.

Activity 7-4: Creating a New Forest

Time Required: 25 minutes or longer
Objective: Create a new forest.
Required Tools and Equipment: ServerDC1, ServerSA1
Description: In this activity, you create a new forest, using ServerSA1 as the DC for the new forest root. First, you demote ServerSA1, and then you promote it, choosing the option to add a new forest. You name the new forest NewForest.local.

1. On ServerSA1 in Server Manager, click **Manage**, **Remove Roles and Features** from the menu to start the Remove Roles and Features Wizard.
2. In the Before You Begin window, click **Next**. In the Server Selection window, click **Next**.
3. In the Server Roles window, click to clear **Active Directory Domain Services**, and then click **Remove Features**. The Validation Results message box states that you must first demote the domain controller. Click **Demote this domain controller**.

4. In the Credentials window, you must enter enterprise administrator credentials. Click **Change**. In the Windows Security dialog box, type **MCSA2016\Administrator** in the User name text box and **Password01** in the Password text box. Click **OK**.

5. Click the **Last domain controller in the domain** check box, and then click **Next**. In the Warnings window, click the **Proceed with removal** check box, and then click **Next**.

6. In the Removal Options window, click the **Remove this DNS zone (this is the last DNS server that hosts the zone)** check box, and then click **Next**.

7. Type **Password01** in the Password and Confirm password text boxes. (It's the password for the local Administrator account when the server is no longer a DC.) Click **Next**.

8. In the Review Options window, click **Demote**. When the demotion is finished, the server restarts.

9. After ServerSA1 restarts, sign in as **Administrator**.

10. You need to ensure that all metadata is cleaned up after the demotion of ServerSA1. On ServerDC1, from Server Manager, open Active Directory Sites and Services. Navigate to **Sites\Default-First-Site-Name\Servers**. If ServerSA1 is listed, right-click it and click **Delete**. Click **Yes** to confirm. Close Active Directory Sites and Services.

11. On ServerSA1, in Server Manager, click the notifications flag, and then click **Promote this server to a domain controller**. The Active Directory Domain Services Configuration Wizard starts.

12. In the Deployment Configuration window, click the **Add a new forest** option button. Type **NewForest.local** in the Root domain name text box, and then click **Next**.

13. In the Domain Controller Options window, type **Password01** in the Password and Confirm password boxes. Click **Next**.

14. In the DNS Options window, click **Next**. In the Additional Options window, click **Next**.

15. In the Paths window, click **Next**. In the Review Options window, click **Next** and then click **Install**. The server will restart.

16. After the server restarts, sign in and verify the installation.

17. Continue to the next activity.

Active Directory Trusts

 **Certification**

- **70-742 – Manage and maintain AD DS:**
  Configure Active Directory in a complex enterprise environment

In Active Directory, a **trust relationship** (or simply "trust") defines whether and how security principals from one domain can access network resources in another domain. Active Directory trust relationships are established automatically between all domains in a forest. Therefore, when a user authenticates to one domain, the other domains in the forest accept, or trust, the authentication. Because all domains in a forest automatically have trust relationships with one another, trusts must be configured only when an Active Directory environment includes two or more forests or when you want to integrate with other OSs.

 Note

Don't confuse trusts with permissions. Permissions are required to access resources even if a trust relationship exists.

Active Directory trusts can exist between domains and between forests. With a trust relationship between domains in the same forest or in different forests, users can access resources across domains without having to sign in more than once. Moreover, a user account needs to exist in only one domain, which simplifies user management.

To say that Domain A trusts Domain B means that users in Domain B can be given permission to access resources in Domain A. Domain A is referred to as the *trusting domain*, and Domain B is referred to as the *trusted domain*. In Active Directory design documentation, a trust relationship is drawn with an arrow pointing from the trusting domain to the trusted domain as shown in Figure 7-6. Trust relationship types are explained in the following sections.

Note

Although configuring trusts in a single-forest environment might not be necessary, it can be a benefit in some configurations as you see later in the section "Shortcut Trusts."

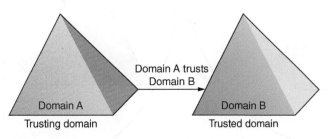

Figure 7-6   A trust relationship

One-Way and Two-Way Trusts

A **one-way trust** exists when one domain trusts another, but the reverse is not true as shown in Figure 7-6. Domain A trusts Domain B, but Domain B doesn't trust Domain A. This means Domain B's users can be given access to Domain A's resources, but Domain A's users can't be given access to Domain B's resources. More common is the **two-way trust**, in which users from both domains can be given access to resources in the other domain. The automatic trusts configured between domains in an Active Directory forest are two-way trusts. Both one-way and two-way trusts can be transitive or nontransitive, depending on the type of trust being created.

Transitive Trusts

A **transitive trust** is named after the transitive rule of equality in mathematics: If $A = B$ and $B = C$, then $A = C$. When applied to domains, if Domain A trusts Domain B and Domain B trusts Domain C, then Domain A trusts Domain C. The automatic trust relationships created between domains in a forest are transitive two-way trusts. These trusts follow the domain parent–child relationship in a tree and flow from the forest root domain to form the trust relationship between trees. Figure 7-7 shows two-way transitive trusts between all domains in a forest. The trust relationship between branches of the tree (US.csmtech.local and UK.csmtech.local) and between trees flows through the forest root domain.

Referring to Figure 7-7, the transitive nature of these trust relationships means that R&D.us.csmtech.local trusts Asia.csmpub.local because R&D.us.csmtech.local trusts US.csmtech.local, which trusts

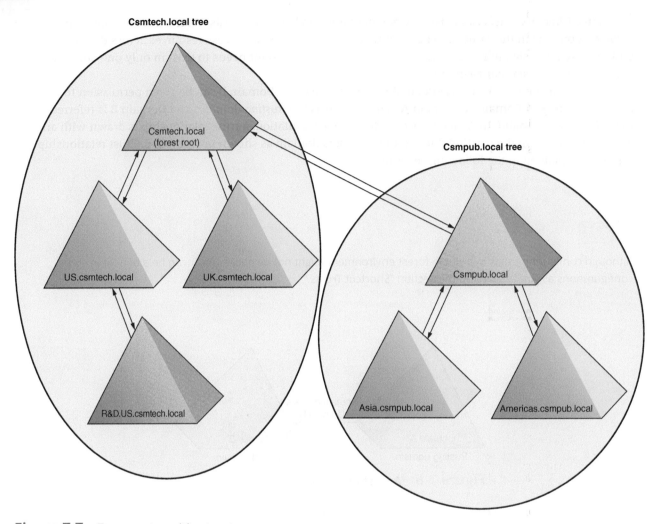

Figure 7-7 Two-way transitive trusts

csmtech.local, which trusts csmpub.local, which trusts Asia.csmpub.local. Because the trusts are two-way, the reverse is also true.

Note that for Asia.csmpub.local to authenticate a user account in the R&D.us.csmtech.local domain, the authentication must be referred to a DC in each domain in the path from R&D.us.csmtech.local to Asia.csmpub.local. A **referral** is the process of a DC in one domain informing a DC in another domain that it doesn't have information about a requested object. The DC requesting the information is then referred to a DC in another domain and on through the chain of domains until it reaches the domain that is holding the object. This referral process can cause substantial delays when a user wants to access resources in a domain that's several referrals away. Fortunately, you can reduce the delays caused by the referral process by implementing a shortcut trust.

Shortcut Trusts

A **shortcut trust** is configured manually between domains in the same forest to bypass the normal referral process. Figure 7-8 shows the same forest as Figure 7-7 but with a manually configured two-way shortcut trust between R&D.us.csmtech.local and Asia.csmpub.local.

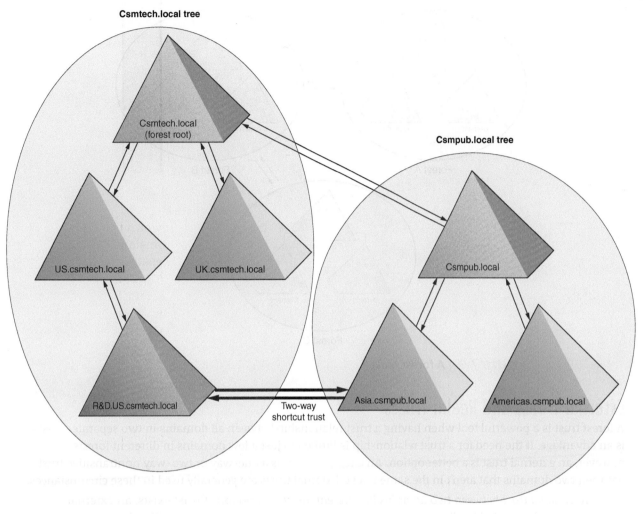

Figure 7-8   A shortcut trust

Shortcut trusts are transitive and can be configured as one-way or two-way trusts. Generally, they're configured when user accounts often need to access resources in domains that are several referrals away. Shortcut trusts can be used only between domains in the same forest. If users need access to resources in a different forest, you use a forest trust or an external trust.

Forest Trusts

A **forest trust** provides a one-way or two-way trust between forests that allows security principals in one forest to access resources in any domain in another forest. A forest trust is created between the forest root domains of Active Directory forests running Windows Server 2003 or later. Forest trusts aren't possible in Windows 2000 forests. A forest trust is transitive to the extent that all domains in one forest trust all domains in the other forest. However, the trust isn't transitive from one forest to another. For example, if a forest trust is created between Forest A and Forest B, all domains in Forest A trust all domains in Forest B. If there's a third forest, Forest C, and Forest B trusts Forest C, a trust relationship isn't established automatically between Forest A and Forest C. A separate trust must be configured manually between these two forests. In Figure 7-9, a two-way trust exists between Forest A and Forest B and between Forest B and Forest C, but there's no trust between Forest A and Forest C.

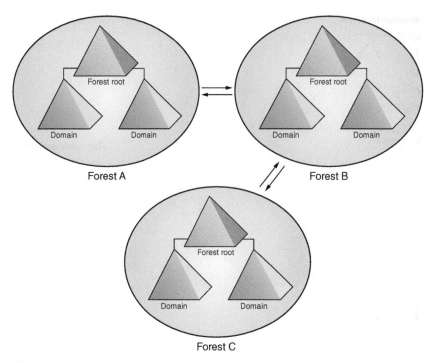

Figure 7-9 A forest trust

External Trusts and Realm Trusts

A forest trust is a powerful tool when having a trust relationship between all domains in two separate forests is an advantage. If the need for a trust relationship is limited to just a few domains in different forests, however, an external trust is a better option. An **external trust** is a one-way or two-way nontransitive trust between two domains that aren't in the same forest. External trusts are generally used in these circumstances:

- *To create a trust between two domains in different forests*—If no forest trust exists, an external trust can be created to allow users in one domain to access resources in another domain in a different forest. If a forest trust does exist, an external trust can still be used to create a direct trust relationship between two domains. This option can be more efficient than a forest trust when access between domains is frequent, much like a shortcut trust is used within a forest.
- *To create a trust with a Windows 2000 or Windows NT domain*—You probably won't run across many Windows 2000 or Windows NT domains, but if you do, an external trust is needed to create the trust relationship between a Windows Server 2003 and later forest and these older domains.

Networks are often composed of systems running different OSs, such as Windows, Linux, UNIX, and macOS. A **realm trust** can be used to integrate users of other OSs into a Windows domain or forest. It requires the OS to be running the Kerberos v5 or later authentication system that Active Directory uses.

Configuring Active Directory Trusts

 **Certification**

- **70-742 – Manage and maintain AD DS:**
  Configure Active Directory in a complex enterprise environment

One important requirement before creating any trust is that DNS must be configured so that the fully qualified domain names (FQDNs) of all participating domains can be resolved. DNS configuration might require Active Directory–integrated forest-wide replication of zones, conditional forwarders, or stub zones, depending on the type of trust being created and the OSs involved. Before you attempt to create a trust, make sure you can resolve the FQDNs of both domains from both domains by using `nslookup` or a similar tool.

Configuring Shortcut Trusts

You usually create a shortcut trust between subdomains of two domain trees. To create a shortcut trust, open Active Directory Domains and Trusts, and then open the Properties dialog box of the domain node. Follow these steps:

1. In the Trusts tab, click the New Trust button to start the New Trust Wizard, and then click Next.

2. In the Trust Name window, type the DNS name of the target domain, and then click Next.

3. In the Direction of Trust window, leave the default setting, Two-way, selected, and then click Next.

4. In the Sides of Trust window, specify whether to create the trust only in the local domain or in both the local domain and the target domain specified in Step 2. If you choose the latter, you must have the credentials to create a trust in the target domain. If you choose to create the trust only in the local domain, an administrator in the target domain must create the other side of the trust. Click Next.

5. In the User Name and Password window, if you choose to create the trust in both domains, you're prompted for credentials for an account in the target domain that can create the trust. You must be an administrator in the target domain and enter your credentials with the *username@domain* or *domain\username* syntax. If you're creating only the local side of the trust, you're prompted to enter a trust password. This password must also be used when creating the other side of the trust, so it must be communicated to the administrator who creates the trust in the other domain.

6. In the Trust Selections Complete window, you can review your choices. This window is the only place in the wizard where you actually see the word "shortcut" describing the trust type. After reviewing your choices, click Next to create the trust.

7. The next window shows the status of the created trust and summarizes the trust settings again. After reviewing the information, click Next.

8. Next, you can confirm the trust, which you should do if you created both sides of the trust.

After the wizard is finished, the Trusts tab shows the trust relationship and trust type. In Figure 7-10, the Trusts tab for the Sub1.ForestRoot.local domain shows an automatic parent trust with ForestRoot.local

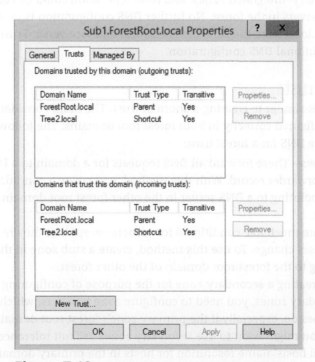

Figure 7-10   Reviewing a trust relationship

and a shortcut trust with Tree2.local, a domain in another tree in the forest. Figure 7-11 shows the entire forest and its trust relationships.

The forest in Figure 7-11 is a small forest of only two trees and three domains. The path between Sub1.ForestRoot.local and Tree2.local is only two referrals away, and normally you don't need to create a shortcut trust for such a small forest. However, if four or five other domains were along the path between these two domains, a shortcut trust makes sense if users from these domains access each other's resources frequently.

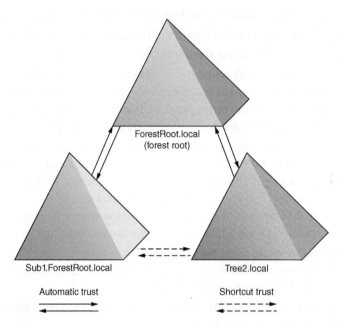

Figure 7-11   A forest with automatic trusts and a shortcut trust

In the preceding example, all the domains are in the same forest, so the DNS domains could be configured as Active Directory–integrated zones, and zone replication could be configured so that zones are replicated to all DNS servers in the forest. No further DNS configuration is necessary because the DNS servers in ForestRoot.local store the zone for Tree2.local and vice versa. Trusts between forests and external trusts require additional DNS configuration.

Configuring Forest Trusts

Configuring a forest trust is similar to creating a shortcut trust. The main consideration before you begin is making sure DNS is configured correctly in both forest root domains. The following are the three most common ways to configure DNS for a forest trust:

- *Conditional forwarders*—These forward all DNS requests for a domain to a DNS server specified in the conditional forwarder record. With this method, you create a conditional forwarder in the forest root domain pointing to a DNS server in the other forest root domain. Do this in both forests involved in the trust.
- *Stub zones*—These are much like conditional forwarders except that they're updated dynamically if DNS servers' addresses change. To use this method, create a stub zone in the forest root domain of both forests pointing to the forest root domain of the other forest.
- *Secondary zones*—Creating a secondary zone for the purpose of configuring forest trusts is probably overkill. With secondary zones, you need to configure zone transfers, which causes more network traffic than stub zones do, especially if the primary zone's forest root domain contains many records. However, you might want to use secondary zones as fault tolerance for the primary zone and to facilitate local hosts' name resolution for hosts in the primary domain.

You can also configure a DNS server to act as the root server for the DNS namespaces of both forests. On the root server, you must delegate the namespaces for each forest and then configure root hints on DNS servers in the two forests to point to the root server.

After DNS is configured and you can resolve the forest root domain of both forests from both forests, you're ready to create the forest trust. This procedure is very similar to creating a shortcut trust, but there are a few important differences. You must initiate the forest trust in Active Directory Domains and Trusts from the forest root domain by following these steps:

1. In Active Directory Domains and Trusts, right-click the forest root domain and click Properties. In the root domain's Properties dialog box, click the Trusts tab. In this example, you'll create a two-way forest trust between one forest root domain named Forest1.local and another named Forest2.local.

2. Click the New Trust button to start the New Trust Wizard, and then click Next.

3. In the Trust Name window, specify the forest root domain of the target forest, which is Forest2.local.

4. In the Trust Type window, Windows recognizes that the specified domain is a forest root domain and gives you the option to create an external trust or a forest trust, as shown in Figure 7-12. (*Note*: The forest trust option is available only from the forest root domain.) Click the Forest trust option button, and then click Next.

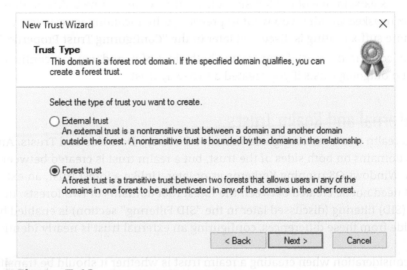

Figure 7-12 Selecting the trust type

5. In the Direction of Trust window, select Two-way, One-way: incoming or One-way: outgoing based on whether you need a two-way trust or just a one-way trust.

6. In the Sides of Trust window, specify whether you're creating the trust for the local domain only or for both domains. You need enterprise administrator credentials in both forests if you want to create both sides of the trust. If you create the trust for both domains, you're prompted for credentials for the other forest in the next window. Click Next.

7. In the Outgoing Trust Authentication Level window, the choices are forest-wide authentication or selective authentication (see Figure 7-13). **Forest-wide authentication** means that Windows should authenticate all users in the specified forest for all resources in the local forest. With **selective authentication**, you can choose which local forest resources that users in the specified forest can be authenticated to. Authenticating a user for a resource doesn't grant the user access; permissions must also be set. Microsoft recommends forest-wide authentication when both forests belong to the same company and selective authentication when the forests belong to different organizations. Select the authentication level, and then click Next. If you're creating both sides of the trust, you're prompted to specify the trust authentication level for the other forest.

Figure 7-13 Selecting the trust authentication level

8. If multiple trees exist in one of the forests, you see the Routed Name Suffixes—Specified forest window. You're asked whether you want to prevent authentication requests from any of the name suffixes. Name suffix routing is discussed later in the "Configuring Trust Properties" section.

9. Last, you can confirm the trust if you created both sides of it, and you can confirm both the incoming and outgoing trusts if you created a two-way trust.

Configuring External and Realm Trusts

External trusts and realm trusts are configured in Active Directory Domains and Trusts. An external trust involves Windows domains on both sides of the trust, but a realm trust is created between a Windows domain and a non-Windows OS running Kerberos v5 or later. Unlike a forest trust, an external trust isn't transitive and need not be created between the forest root domains of two forests. In addition, security identifier (SID) filtering (discussed later in the "SID Filtering" section) is enabled by default for external trusts. Aside from these differences, configuring an external trust is nearly identical to creating a forest trust.

The only real consideration when creating a realm trust is whether it should be transitive. If it's transitive, the trust extends to all child domains and child realms. Otherwise, the procedure is much the same as configuring other trust types.

Configuring Trust Properties

After creating a trust, you might need to view or change its settings. To do this, in Active Directory Domains and Trusts, open the domain's Properties dialog box and click the Trusts tab. Select the trust you want to configure and click the Properties button. The Properties dialog box of a forest trust contains three tabs—General, Name Suffix Routing, and Authentication—discussed in the following sections.

Note

A trust's Properties dialog box varies depending on the type of trust you're configuring. For example, an automatic trust has only a General tab.

The General Tab

The General tab shown in Figure 7-14 contains the following fields and information:

- *This Domain*—The domain you're currently configuring.
- *Other Domain*—The domain with which a trust has been created.
- *Trust type*—The type of trust, such as shortcut, forest, external, and so forth.

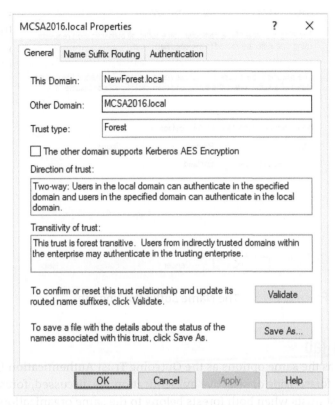

Figure 7-14   **The General tab of a trust's Properties dialog box**

- *The other domain supports Kerberos AES Encryption*—Kerberos AES encryption enhances authentication security and is supported by Windows Server 2008 and later. If the forest trust is between two Windows Server 2008 or later domains, you can select this option for better security.
- *Direction of trust*—This field is for informational purposes only. You can't change the trust direction without deleting and re-creating the trust.
- *Transitivity of trust*—This field is for informational purposes only. You can't change the transitivity without re-creating the trust. Some trusts, such as forest and shortcut trusts, are always transitive.
- *Validate*—Click this button to confirm the trust. It performs the same action as the confirmation process at the end of the New Trust Wizard. If you didn't create both sides of the trust with the wizard, you should validate the trust with this option after both sides have been created.
- *Save As*—Click this button to create a text file containing details of the trust.

The Name Suffix Routing Tab

In the Name Suffix Routing tab, you can control which name suffixes used by the trusted forest are routed for authentication. For example, the csmtech.local forest contains multiple trees—csmtech.local and csmpub.local—and csmtech.local is trusted by a second forest, csmAsia.local. Only users from the csmtech.local domain should have access to csmAsia.local resources, however. To do this, the csmAsia administrator can disable authentication requests containing the name suffix csmpub.local. The Name

Suffix Routing tab displays all available name suffixes in the trusted forest, and you can disable or enable them. In Figure 7-15, only one name suffix is listed because there's only one domain tree in MCSA2016.local.

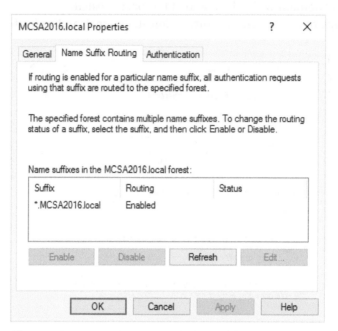

Figure 7-15 The Name Suffix Routing tab

The Authentication Tab

The Authentication tab has the same options as the Outgoing Trust Authentication Level window shown previously in Figure 7-13: forest-wide or selective authentication. As discussed, forest-wide authentication is recommended for forest trusts when both forests belong to the same organization. Selective authentication recommended for forests in different organizations enables you to specify users who can authenticate to selected resources in the trusting forest. After selecting this option, you add users and groups from the trusted forest to the discretionary access control list (DACL) of computer accounts in the trusting forest and assign the "Allowed to authenticate" permission to these computer accounts. When selective authentication is enabled, users from the trusted forest are prevented by default from authenticating to the trusting forest. If users try to authenticate to a computer in the trusting domain and haven't been granted authentication permission, they see an error message indicating a logon failure.

SID Filtering

Every account has an sIDHistory (meaning "SID history") attribute that's used when migrating accounts from one domain to another to determine the account's rights and permissions in both the new and old domains. This attribute can also be used for nefarious purposes to gain administrative privileges in a trusting forest. Suppose that ForestA is trusted by ForestB. An administrator in ForestA can edit the sIDHistory attribute of a user in ForestA to include the SID of a privileged account in ForestB. When this user logs on to a domain in ForestB, he or she has the same access as the privileged account.

To counter this security risk, Windows has a feature called **SID filtering** (also called *SID filter quarantining*) that's enabled by default on external trusts but is disabled on forest trusts. It causes the trusting domain to ignore any SIDs that aren't from the trusted domain. Essentially, the trusting domain ignores the contents of the sIDHistory attribute. SID filtering should be enabled or disabled from the trusting side of the domain and should be used only between forests or with external domains. It shouldn't be used between domains in the same forest because it would break Active Directory replication and automatic transitive trusts.

For Active Directory migration purposes, SID filtering can be disabled but should be re-enabled after the migration. To disable SID filtering, use the following command:

```
netdom trust TrustingDomainName /domain:TrustedDomainName
  /quarantine:No
```

To enable SID filtering, simply change the No to Yes. To check the status of SID filtering, omit the Yes or No at the end of the command.

Tip ⓘ

You can view and clear the contents of sIDHistory in Attribute Editor and ADSI Edit, but you can't add or change existing values. If you attempt to do so, you get an access denied error.

Activity 7-5: Testing Cross-Forest Access Without a Trust

Time Required: 10 minutes
Objective: Test access across forests before you create a forest trust.
Required Tools and Equipment: ServerDC1, ServerSA1
Description: In this activity, you see what happens when you try to access resources across forests before a trust is in place.

1. First, you need to create a conditional forwarder on ServerDC1 that points to the NewForest.local domain. On ServerDC1, open a PowerShell window and type **Add-DnsServerConditionalForwarderZone -Name "NewForest.local" -MasterServers 192.168.0.4** and press **Enter**. Close the PowerShell window. Because you have already created a conditional forwarder on ServerSA1 for mcsa2016.local, you don't need to do it again.
2. Right-click **Start** and click **Run**. Type **\\ServerSA1.NewForest.local** in the Open text box and press **Enter**.
3. You should see two shares that are created on all DCs by default: NETLOGON and SYSVOL. Double-click SYSVOL, and you will see the Enter network credentials dialog box asking for your username and password. Type **Administrator** and **Password01**, and then click **OK**. The attempt to sign in is unsuccessful. Without a trust between the two forests, you can't sign in to a domain in the other forest with your local credentials.
4. This time, in the Enter network credentials dialog box, type **NewForest\Administrator** and **Password01**, and then click **OK**. You're trying to sign in with credentials from the other forest. This sign in should be successful, and the contents of the SYSVOL share are displayed.
5. When no forest trust exists, you can still access a domain in another forest, but you need the logon credentials of a user in the other domain. The trust precludes the need for credentials in multiple domains as you will see in the next activity. Close File Explorer.
6. Sign out of both servers to clear the existing connection between the two domains.

Activity 7-6: Creating and Testing a Forest Trust

Time Required: 15 minutes
Objective: Create a forest trust.
Required Tools and Equipment: ServerDC1, ServerSA1
Description: In this activity, you create a forest trust between MCSA2016.local and NewForest.local. Then, you will test the trust by accessing resources in the NewForest.local domain from the MCSA2016.local domain, using credentials for the MCSA2016.local domain.

1. Sign in to ServerDC1 as **Administrator**, and from Server Manager, open Active Directory Domains and Trusts.

2. Right-click **MCSA2016.local** and click **Properties**.

3. Click the **Trusts** tab and click the **New Trust** button to start the New Trust Wizard. Click **Next** in the wizard's welcome window.

4. Type **NewForest.local** in the Name text box, and then click **Next**.

5. In the Trust Type window, click the **Forest trust** option button. (*Note:* You can create an external trust in this window, but an external trust creates a trust only between two domains whereas all domains in the forest are included in a forest trust.) Click **Next**.

6. In the Direction of Trust window, verify that the default **Two-way** option is selected, and then click **Next**.

7. In the Sides of Trust window, click **Both this domain and the specified domain**. If you're creating only one side of the trust, you're asked to enter a trust password, which must be used to create the second side of the trust. Click **Next**.

8. You need to specify credentials for the NewForest.local domain to create the other side of the trust. Type **Administrator** in the User name text box and **Password01** in the Password text box, and then click **Next**.

9. In the Outgoing Trust Authentication Level—Local Forest window, verify that **Forest-wide authentication** is selected for the authentication level, and then click **Next**.

10. In the Outgoing Trust Authentication Level—Specified Forest window, verify that **Forest-wide authentication** is selected, and then click **Next**.

11. Review your settings in the Trust Selections Complete window, and then click **Next**.

12. In the Trust Creation Complete window, the status of the trust creation and a summary of your choices are displayed. Click **Next**.

13. In the Confirm Outgoing Trust window, click **Yes, confirm the outgoing trust**, and then click **Next**.

14. In the Confirm Incoming Trust window, click **Yes, confirm the incoming trust**, and then click **Next**.

15. Click **Finish**. The Trusts tab should list NewForest.local in both the outgoing trusts and incoming trusts lists. Click **OK**, and close Active Directory Domains and Trusts.

16. Sign in to ServerSA1 as **Administrator**, and open Active Directory Domains and Trusts. Verify that the trust relationship with MCSA2016.local was created successfully, and then close Active Directory Domains and Trusts.

17. Now, you will set up a share on ServerSA1 and access that share from ServerDC1 to test the trust. On ServerSA1, open File Explorer. On the root of the C drive, create a folder named **Share1**. Right-click the **Share1** folder, click **Share with**, and click **Specific people**. Add **Everyone** with **Read/Write** permission. Click **Share**, and then click **Done**.

18. Repeat the previous step, this time creating a share named **Share2** and leaving the default sharing permissions as they are. (Don't add the Everyone group to the list of users who can access the share.) Close File Explorer.

19. On ServerDC1, right-click **Start**, click **Run**, type **\\ServerSA1.NewForest.local** in the Open text box, and press **Enter**. A File Explorer window opens and lists all shares on ServerSA1.

20. Double-click the **Share1** share to open it. Notice that you weren't prompted for credentials because a trust exists between the two forests. Create a text file named **doc1.txt** to show that you can write files to the share across the forest. Share1 has Read/Write permission assigned to the Everyone group, which includes authenticated users from other forests.

21. In File Explorer, click the **back arrow** to see the list of shared folders on ServerSA1. Double-click **Share2**. You see a "Windows cannot access" message. You can't access this share because you weren't given permission to do so. Click **Close**. Close File Explorer.

22. Stay signed in to both servers and continue to the next activity.

Upgrading Domains and Forests

- **70-742 – Manage and maintain AD DS:**
  Configure Active Directory in a complex enterprise environment

With each release of a Windows Server OS, features are added to make the Active Directory environment more capable and easier to manage. However, new features often aren't compatible with earlier releases. Instead of requiring administrators to upgrade servers before installing a new server OS, Windows enables administrators to configure functional levels on new domain controllers to maintain backward compatibility.

When you install the first domain controller in a forest root domain with Windows Server 2016, the forest and domain functional levels default to Windows Server 2016. These levels ensure the highest level of Active Directory functioning at least until the next version of Windows Server is released. Be aware that domain and forest functional levels are specific to domain controllers. Member servers and workstation computers don't have this setting and can be domain members of domains and forests running at any functional level. The following sections discuss the features and requirements of each forest and domain functional level.

> **Note** 🔗
>
> A functional level called "Windows 2000 mixed" provides backward compatibility with Windows NT domain controllers. This functional level was deprecated in Windows Server 2008, and Windows NT domain controllers are no longer supported in the same network as Windows Server 2008 and later domain controllers.

Forest Functional Levels

The **forest functional level** determines which features of Active Directory have forest-wide implications and which server OSs are supported on domain controllers in the forest. A Windows Server 2016 domain controller supports the following forest functional levels:

- Windows Server 2008
- Windows Server 2008 R2
- Windows Server 2012
- Windows Server 2012 R2
- Windows Server 2016

> **Note** 🔗
>
> The Windows Server 2003 forest and domain functional levels have been deprecated in Windows Server 2016. Before installing a Windows Server 2016 domain controller, all Windows Server 2003 domain controllers should be removed from the domain because they are no longer supported by Microsoft.

The forest functional level can be raised from an earlier version to a newer version, but it can't be changed from a newer version to an earlier version. In addition, a domain in a forest can't operate at a lower functional level than the forest functional level, but it can operate at a higher level.

The following sections describe the available features and supported OSs for each functional level. Windows 2000 functional level is included for completeness but isn't supported as of Windows Server 2012.

Windows 2000 Native

The Windows 2000 Native forest functional level supports all the default features of an Active Directory forest. Because Windows 2000 was the first server OS supporting Active Directory, this functional level is considered the baseline for forest operation. Some notable features not supported at this functional level include creating forest trusts and renaming a domain. This level supports domain controllers running Windows 2000 Server through Windows Server 2008.

Windows Server 2003

The Windows Server 2003 forest functional level requires all domain controllers in all domains to be running at least Windows Server 2003. This level supports all the forest-wide features of the Windows 2000 functional level and adds the following features:

- *Forest trusts*—This creates a trust relationship between forests.
- *Knowledge Consistency Checker (KCC) improvements*—Large networks with more sites are supported by the Intersite Topology Generator (ISTG), a function the KCC performs on a DC in each site.
- *Linked-value replication*—This replicates only changes to group membership instead of the entire group membership, which saves network and processor bandwidth.
- *Rename a domain*—Domains can be renamed by using the `rendom.exe` and `gpfixup.exe` command-line tools. This process is complex and should be attempted only after reviewing Microsoft documentation carefully.
- *Read only domain controller (RODC) deployment*—RODCs must be running Windows Server 2008 or later (because RODCs were introduced in Server 2008). In addition, a writeable Windows Server 2008 or later DC must be installed first to replicate with the RODC.
- *Additional features*—Other features related mostly to the Active Directory schema include creating the dynamic auxiliary class named `dynamicObject`, converting the `inetOrgPerson` object (used by some LDAP applications) to a user object and vice versa, creating new group types to support role-based authorization, and deactivating schema attributes and classes.

Windows Server 2008

No forest-wide features were added to this functional level. However, to operate at this forest functional level, all DCs must be running at the Windows Server 2008 domain functional level and therefore must be running Windows Server 2008 or later.

Windows Server 2008 R2

This forest functional level has all the features of the Windows Server 2003 forest functional level and adds the Active Directory Recycle Bin, which enables you to restore deleted Active Directory objects without taking Active Directory offline.

Windows Server 2012

No forest-wide features were added to this functional level. However, to operate at this forest functional level, all DCs must be running at the Windows Server 2012 domain functional level and therefore must be running Windows Server 2012 or later.

Windows Server 2012 R2

Again, no new forest-wide features were added at this functional level, but all DCs must be running at the Windows Server 2012 R2 domain functional level and therefore must be running Windows Server 2012 R2 or later.

Windows Server 2016

A significant feature added with the Windows Server 2016 forest functional level is **Privileged Access Management (PAM)**. One of the things you can do with PAM is use group membership expirations. Group membership expirations allow you to add an account to a group temporarily. For example, you can make a user a member of the Domain Admins group for a short period of time so the user can perform some task on her or his computer that requires that level of access. You must first enable the Privileged Access Management (PAM) feature before you can use group membership expirations. To enable PAM on the mcsa2016.local domain, use the following PowerShell cmdlet:

```
Enable-ADOptionalFeature 'Privileged Access Management Feature'
    -Scope ForestOrConfigurationSet -Target mcsa2016.com
```

After the feature is enabled, you can add an account to a group and assign an expiration using the `-MemberTimeToLive` parameter. The following cmdlet makes domuser1 a member of the Domain Admins group for 10 minutes:

```
Add-ADGroupMember -Identity "Domain Admins" -Members 'domuser1'
    -MemberTimeToLive (New-TimeSpan -Minutes 10)
```

> **Note**
>
> Like the Active Directory Recycle Bin feature, once PAM has been enabled, it cannot be disabled.

Domain Functional Levels

Windows Server 2016 supports five **domain functional levels** that have the same names as the forest functional levels. A domain controller can't be configured to run at a lower functional level than the functional level of the forest in which it's installed. Like forest functional levels, domain functional levels can be raised but not lowered. After a domain's functional level has been raised, no DCs running earlier versions of the OS can be installed in the domain. The following sections summarize the features available at each level.

Windows 2000 Native

The Windows 2000 native domain functional level includes all the original features given to domains by Active Directory. This functional level is supported only by Windows 2000 through Windows Server 2008 R2 but is described here for completeness. The following list of features can be thought of as upgrades to the Windows NT domain system:

- *Universal groups*—Allow administrators to assign rights and permissions to forest-wide resources to users from any domain
- *Group nesting*—Allows most group types to be members of most other group types
- *Group conversion*—Allows administrators to convert between security and distribution groups
- *Security identifier (SID) history*—Facilitates migrating user accounts from one domain to another (which changes users' SIDs). A user's original SID is kept in the sIDHistory attribute to determine the user's group memberships in the original domain and maintain the user's access to resources there.

Windows Server 2003

This level supports all the features in the Windows 2000 native domain functional level. All DCs must be running Windows Server 2003 or later. Added features for this functional level include the following:

- *Domain controller renaming*—The `netdom.exe` command-line tool makes renaming a domain controller possible without undue latency. Using the System Properties dialog box to rename a domain controller doesn't update DNS and Active Directory replication parameters completely, which could cause client authentication problems. `Netdom` does perform these updates.

- *Logon timestamp replication*—The lastLogonTimestamp user account attribute is updated with the time and date of a user's last logon. This attribute is replicated to all DCs in the domain.
- *Selective authentication*—With this feature, an administrator can specify users and groups from a trusted forest who can authenticate to servers in a trusting forest.
- *Users and Computers container redirection*—When creating users, groups, and computers with command-line tools that don't allow specifying a target OU (or if the location is omitted), these accounts are placed in the Users or Computers container. You can use the `redirusr` (for users and groups) and `redircmp` (for computers) commands to specify a different default location.
- *Additional features*—This level includes constrained delegation, Authorization Manager policy support, and the userPassword attribute set as the effective password on `inetOrgPerson` and user objects. These features are beyond the scope of this book, however.

Note

The Windows Server 2003 domain functional level has been deprecated in Windows Server 2016.

Windows Server 2008

This functional level supports all features in the Windows Server 2003 domain functional level with several additions, which are described in the following list. All DCs must be running Windows Server 2008 or later.

- *Distributed File System (DFS) replication*—DFS is used to replicate the contents of the SYSVOL share, which makes replication more reliable and efficient.
- *Fine-grained password policies*—This feature enables administrators to assign different password and account lockout policies for users and groups.
- *Interactive logon information*—Enabled through group policies, this option displays information about a user's most recent successful and unsuccessful logon attempts each time the user logs on. If you enable this policy in a domain with a functional level lower than Windows Server 2008, users who attempt to log on get a warning message explaining that the information couldn't be retrieved, and they can't log on.
- *Advanced Encryption Standard (AES) support*—AES 128 and AES 256 are supported encryption standards that can be used for Kerberos authentication to increase user logon security.

Windows Server 2008 R2

This functional level supports all features in the Windows Server 2008 domain functional level with the following additions. All DCs must be running Windows Server 2008 R2 or later.

- *Automatic Service Principal Name (SPN) management*—Includes automatic password management of service accounts and automatic DNS name changes if there's a name change on the computer where the service account is running.
- *Authentication mechanism assurance*—Simplifies authentication management when using a federated identity management structure. A federated identity is a person's electronic credentials that originate from a remote system, such as a nontrusted forest or a different operating system.

Windows Server 2012

This functional level supports all features in the Windows Server 2008 R2 domain functional level and adds Kerberos improvements in claims, compound authentication, and Key Distribution Center (KDC) armoring. All DCs must be running Windows Server 2012 or later.

Windows Server 2012 R2

This functional level supports all features in the Windows Server 2012 domain functional level with the following additions. All DCs must be running Windows Server 2012 or later.

- *Authentication improvements for Protected Users*—Older and less secure authentication methods can no longer be used by Protected Users, a security group introduced in Windows Server 2012 R2.
- *Authentication Policies*—Policies that define Kerberos properties for user, service, and computer accounts.
- *Authentication Policy silos*—New Active Directory containers to which authentication policies can be applied to restrict where high-privilege user accounts can be used in the domain.

Windows Server 2016

No new domain functional level features have been added in Windows Server 2016. All DCs must be running Windows Server 2016 or later.

Raising Domain and Forest Functional Levels

Functional levels can be set when a server is promoted to a DC, or they can be raised manually on the DC. Before you raise functional levels, make sure DCs meet the requirements for the functional level you want.

Note

Functional levels apply only to DCs. Member servers can run any version of Windows Server regardless of the domain or forest functional level.

Raising the Domain Functional Level

All DCs in the domain must be running the Windows version that supports the functional level you want. Raising the domain functional level affects all DCs in the domain. However, you need to raise the functional level on only one DC, and all other DCs reflect the change. To raise the domain functional level, right-click the domain node in Active Directory Domains and Trusts and click Raise Domain Functional Level. If the domain is already operating at the highest level, you can't change it. To raise the domain functional level using PowerShell, use the following cmdlet:

```
Set-ADDomainMode -Identity mcsa2016.local -DomainMode
    Windows2016Domain
```

Raising the Forest Functional Level

To raise the forest functional level, you must be a member of the Enterprise Admins group, and the Schema FSMO role must be available because the schema is changing. In addition, if you're raising both the forest and domain functional levels, you must first raise the domain functional level to at least the level to which you're raising the forest functional level. Remember that after a functional level is raised, it can't be changed back to a lower level, so be sure that your DCs meet the functional level's requirements. To change the forest functional level in Active Directory Domains and Trusts, right-click the Active Directory Domains and Trusts node and click Raise Forest Functional Level. If the forest is already at the highest level, you can't change it. To raise the forest functional level using PowerShell, use the following cmdlet:

```
Set-ADForestMode -Identity mcsa2016.local -ForestMode
    Windows2016Forest
```

To clear up any confusion about which configurations for forest and domain functional levels are valid, examine Figure 7-16. The first forest is set at the Windows Server 2016 level with domains at the Windows Server 2012 and Windows Server 2008 levels. This configuration isn't valid because domain functional levels must be equal to or higher than forest functional levels. The second forest is set at the

Windows Server 2012 level with domains at the Windows Server 2012 R2 and Windows Server 2016 levels, which is a valid configuration.

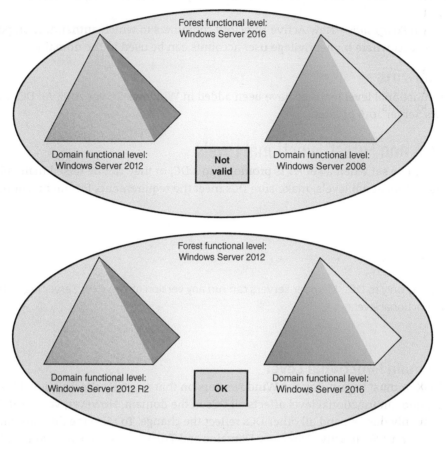

Figure 7-16 Valid and invalid configurations for forest and domain functional levels

Adding Domain Controllers to an Existing Domain

When you're installing Windows Server 2016 DCs in a new forest, the process is straightforward as you've seen. However, installing new Windows Server 2016 DCs in existing Windows Server 2012 R2 or Windows Server 2012 domains and forests also is common. With each version of Windows Server, new features are added, and the schema changes with new objects and object attributes. Before you can install a DC running a newer Windows Server version in an existing forest with a lower functional level, you must prepare existing DCs. Forest and domain preparation are done with the `adprep.exe` command-line program. It's built into the Windows Server 2012/R2 and later Active Directory Domain Services role installation process, so there's no need to run it manually when adding a Windows Server 2016 server to an existing domain or forest. However, you can run it manually if you want to prepare the environment before installation or extend the existing schema to support new features. `Adprep.exe` is in the \Support\Adprep folder on the Windows installation disc.

Note

Versions of Windows Server before Windows Server 2012 require running `adprep.exe` manually before adding a DC to a domain or forest with a functional level older than the OS version you're installing.

Configuring Sites

 **Certification**

- **70-742 – Manage and maintain AD DS:**
  Configure Active Directory in a complex enterprise environment

- **70-742 – Install and configure Active Directory Domain Services:**
  Install and configure domain controllers

In Chapter 6, you learned about basic site components and the reasons for creating additional sites and how to create subnets in preparation for creating new sites. You also learned about the components of intersite replication. This section covers the following topics about sites:

- Registering SRV records
- Working with automatic site coverage
- Moving DCs between sites

Registering SRV Records

Domain controllers advertise themselves by registering service (SRV) records with DNS servers so that clients can find DCs that offer services related to Active Directory. When a client needs the services of a DC (for example, to authenticate to the domain or join a domain), it queries a DNS server for SRV records for all DCs. It also queries for SRV records for DCs in its own site and uses these records first if they exist so that authentication and other procedures don't travel across a WAN.

The Netlogon service on the DC handles registration of SRV records for the Lightweight Directory Access Protocol (LDAP) and Kerberos services. These records are stored on the DNS server in folders in a subdomain named _msdcs located in the zone for the DC's domain. A folder for each site is maintained to make it easier to determine which sites offer these services. For example, a DC in the Headquarters site for domain MCSA2016.local registers SRV records under Forward Lookup Zones in _msdcs. MCSA2016.local\dc_sites\Headquarters_tcp and _msdcs.MCSA2016.local\dc_tcp (see Figure 7-17).

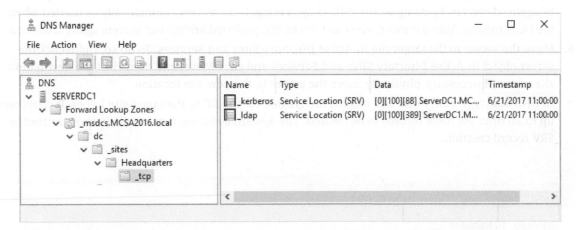

Figure 7-17 SRV records in DNS

If a DC fails to register its SRV records, you can force it to attempt to register the records by stopping and starting the Netlogon service in the Services MMC or with one of the following commands:

- At a command prompt: Type `net stop netlogon` and press Enter, and then type `net start netlogon` and press Enter.
- At a PowerShell prompt: Type `Restart-Service -Name netlogon` and press Enter.

Working with Automatic Site Coverage

Having a DC in each site is usually preferable so that authentication of clients occurs on the local LAN instead of having to traverse the WAN. However, having a DC at each site isn't always necessary or practical if you have a remote site with few users, an environment that isn't secure enough, or inadequate environmental controls for a DC.

When a site doesn't have a DC, other DCs in other sites in the domain can provide the services clients need. **Automatic site coverage** is a feature in which each DC advertises itself by registering SRV records in DNS in sites that don't have a DC if the advertising DC has the lowest cost connection to the site. When a client in the site attempts to contact a DC for authentication and other purposes, it performs a DNS lookup to request the closest DC. The SRV record for the advertising DC is returned. This process prevents clients from using DCs located across higher cost links. Generally, you want automatic site coverage enabled for efficient domain operation.

Moving DCs between Sites

When a Windows server is first promoted to a DC, it's assigned to a site based on its IP address settings, or you can choose the site to install the DC during the promotion process. If there's only one site, the DC is placed in it. If you later change a DC's IP subnet address or change subnet assignments for sites, the affected DCs aren't moved to a different site automatically. You need to move DCs to new sites manually if changes in your site design or IP addressing warrant it. Here's the basic procedure for moving a DC to a new site:

1. Verify that the target site has been created and has the right subnets assigned to it.
2. Change the DC's IP address, subnet mask, and default gateway as needed for the target site. If necessary, change the DC's DNS server addresses.
3. If the DC is used as a DNS forwarder, make the necessary changes in the forwarder configuration on other DNS servers.
4. If the DC hosts a delegated DNS zone, update the NS record in the parent domain's DNS zone to the new IP address of the DC.
5. If the DC being moved is a preferred bridgehead server, you must make the necessary adjustments in both the current site and the target site. In most cases, it's better to configure the DC so that it's not a preferred bridgehead server and ensure that no DCs in the current and target site are configured as bridgehead servers. By doing so, the ISTG assigns bridgehead servers automatically as needed when the DC is moved. After the move, you can then assign preferred bridgehead servers again, if necessary.
6. Move the server to the target site in Active Directory Sites and Services. To do so, right-click the server object in Active Directory Sites and Services and click Move, and then click the destination site name. If necessary, physically move the server to the new site location.
7. In DNS Manager, verify that SRV records are created for the DC in the target site folder. It could take up to an hour for these records to be created. The System event log contains any errors related to SRV record creation.

Activity 7-7: Creating a Subnet and a Site

Time Required: 10 minutes

Objective: Create a new subnet and site.

Required Tools and Equipment: ServerDC1, ServerSA1

Description: In this activity, you create a new subnet and site.

1. On ServerDC1, open Active Directory Sites and Services and click to expand the **Sites** folder, if necessary. You should see a Subnets folder, an Inter-Site Transports folder, and the Default-First-Site-Name site object.
2. Right-click **Subnets** and click **New Subnet**. In the Prefix text box, type **192.168.0.0/24** (assuming you're following the IP address scheme used in this book; otherwise, ask your instructor what to enter).
3. In the Select a site object for this prefix list box, click **Default-First-Site-Name**, and then click **OK**.

4. Right-click **Default-First-Site-Name** and click **Rename**. Type **Headquarters** and press **Enter**.

5. Right-click the **Sites** folder and click **New Site**. In the New Object - Site dialog box, type **BranchOffice** in the Name text box. Notice that you're prompted to select a site link object for the site. Click **DEFAULTIPSITELINK**, and then click **OK**.

6. You should see a message from Active Directory Domain Services stating that more steps are needed to finish configuring the site: making sure site links are suitable, adding subnets for the site in the Subnets folder, and adding a domain controller to the site. Click **OK**.

7. Close Active Directory Sites and Services, and continue to the next activity.

Activity 7-8: Adding a DC to the MCSA2016 Domain

Time Required: 20 minutes

Objective: Add a DC to the MCSA2016 domain.

Required Tools and Equipment: ServerDC1, ServerSA1

Description: In this activity, first you delete the trust between MCSA2016.local and NewForest.local. Then, you demote ServerSA1 to have the NewForest.local forest removed. Finally, you promote ServerSA1 as an additional DC in the MCSA2016.local domain.

1. On ServerDC1, open Server Manager, if necessary, and click **Tools**, **Active Directory Domains and Trusts** from the menu. Right-click **MCSA2016.local** and click **Properties**. Click the **Trusts** tab.

2. Click **NewForest.local** in the Domains trusted by this domain list box, and click **Remove**. In the Active Directory Domain Services dialog box, click **Yes, remove the trust from both the local domain and other domain**. In the User name text box, type **NewForest\administrator**, and in the Password text box, type **Password01**. Click **OK**, and click **Yes** to confirm.

3. Repeat Step 2 for the incoming trust. You don't need to re-enter the credentials for NewForest. Click **OK**.

4. On ServerSA1, from Server Manager, click **Manage, Remove Roles and Features** to start the Remove Roles and Features Wizard.

5. In the Before You Begin window, click **Next**. In the Server Selection window, click **Next**.

6. In the Server Roles window, click to clear **Active Directory Domain Services**. Click **Remove Features**. The Validation Results message box states that you must demote the domain controller first. Click **Demote this domain controller**.

7. In the Credentials window, click the **Last domain controller in the domain** check box, and then click **Next**. In the Warnings window, click **Proceed with removal**, and then click **Next**.

8. In the Removal Options window, click **Remove this DNS zone** and **Remove application partitions**, and then click **Next**.

9. In the New Administrator Password window, type **Password01** in both the Password and Confirm password text boxes, and then click **Next**.

10. In the Review Options window, click **Demote**. After a while, the server restarts.

11. After ServerSA1 restarts, sign in as **Administrator** with the password **Password01**. Before you promote this server to a DC, change the Preferred DNS server address in the TCP/IPv4 Properties dialog box to **192.168.0.1** (the address of ServerDC1). Also, set the TCP/IPv6 DNS server to **Obtain DNS server address automatically**.

12. Open Server Manager, if necessary, and click the notifications flag. Next, click **Promote this server to a domain controller**. In the Deployment Configuration window, accept the default deployment operation, **Add a domain controller to an existing domain**, and type **MCSA2016.local** in the Domain text box.

13. Click the **Change** button, and type **MCSA2016\administrator** for the username and **Password01** for the password. Click **OK**, and then click **Next**.

14. In the Domain Controller Options window, accept the default settings for domain controller capabilities and site information, and type **Password01** in the Password and Confirm password text boxes for the DSRM password. Click **Next**.

15. In the DNS Options window, click **Next**. In the Additional Options window, click **Next**.
16. In the Paths window, accept the default settings, and then click **Next**.
17. In the Review Options window, click **Next**. In the Prerequisites Check window, click **Install**.
18. Active Directory is installed, and the server restarts. After the server restarts, sign in as **Administrator** with the password **Password01** (click Other user if the sign in defaults to NewForest\administrator). Note that you're now logging on to the MCSA2016.local domain.
19. Open Active Directory Users and Computers, and verify that ServerDC1 and ServerSA1 are in the Domain Controllers OU. Notice that the Site column shows that both servers are in HeadQuarters. Close Active Directory Users and Computers, and continue to the next activity.

Active Directory Replication

- **70-742 – Manage and maintain AD DS:**
  Maintain Active Directory

Timely and reliable replication of data between domain controllers is paramount to a functioning Active Directory domain and forest. Active Directory replication includes the following types of information:

- Active Directory objects, such as OUs, user, group, and computer accounts
- Changes to data held in partitions maintained by FSMO role holders
- Trust relationships
- Global catalog data
- Group policy information
- Files located in SYSVOL, such as group policy templates and scripts

Most replication data is generated by changes to Active Directory objects and group policies. Active Directory replication occurs within sites (called *intrasite replication*) and between sites (called *intersite replication*). The following sections cover managing both types of replication along with RODC replication and SYSVOL replication as well as tools to help you monitor and troubleshoot replication.

Active Directory Intrasite Replication

Efficient and accurate replication of changes made to the Active Directory database is critical in a Windows domain. Intrasite and intersite replication use the same basic processes to replicate Active Directory data; the main goal is to balance replication timeliness and efficiency. To that end, the replication strategy between DCs within a site (intrasite) is optimized for high-speed, low-latency LAN links. Intersite replication involves two main components—the KCC and connection objects—and is optimized to take slower WAN links into account. It can be initiated in one of two ways:

- *Notification*—When a change is made to the Active Directory database, the DC on which the change was made notifies its replication partners. The partners then request replication from the notifying DC.
- *Periodic replication*—To account for missed updates, DCs request replication from their partners periodically. The interval can be configured in the connection object's Properties dialog box (explained later in "Connection Objects").

Knowledge Consistency Checker

For intrasite replication, the Knowledge Consistency Checker (KCC) builds a replication topology for DCs in a site and establishes replication partners. As shown in Figure 7-18, each DC in a site has one or more replication partners. For example, DC3 is partners with DC2, DC4, and DC5. The topology is designed to ensure that no more than two DCs lie in the replication path between two domain controllers. To put it another way, data in a replication transfer doesn't have to travel more than three hops to reach its destination DC. For example, if Active Directory data on DC1 changes, the changes have to hop through DC4 and DC6 to reach DC7. A domain controller waits 15 seconds after an Active Directory change before replicating with its partners with a 3-second delay between partners. This arrangement guarantees that all DCs in a site receive changes in less than 1 minute.

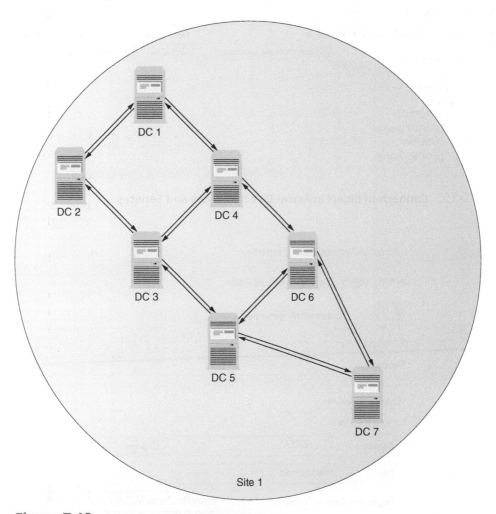

Figure 7-18   Intrasite replication partners

The KCC on each DC uses data stored in the forest-wide configuration directory partition to create the replication topology. The configuration directory partition is replicated to all DCs in the forest, so the KCCs don't need to communicate with one another. Because they all run the same algorithm on the same data, the KCCs on domain controllers create the same replication topology. The KCC recalculates the replication topology every 15 minutes by default to make sure that the topology accurately reflects DCs that come online or go offline. If necessary, the replication topology can be recalculated manually in Active Directory Sites and Services. You might need to do this after you have added, changed, or removed connection objects, for example. To do so, right-click the NTDS Settings node under a domain controller, point to All Tasks, and click Check Replication Topology. The partnership between DCs is controlled by a connection object, which the KCC creates automatically for intrasite replication.

Connection Objects

A **connection object** defines the connection parameters between two replication partners. The KCC generates these parameters automatically between intrasite DCs. Generally, you don't need to make changes to intrasite connection objects, but if you do, you can change them in Active Directory Sites and

Services. Figure 7-19 shows a connection object in Active Directory Sites and Services, and Figure 7-20 shows the Properties dialog box for one of the objects.

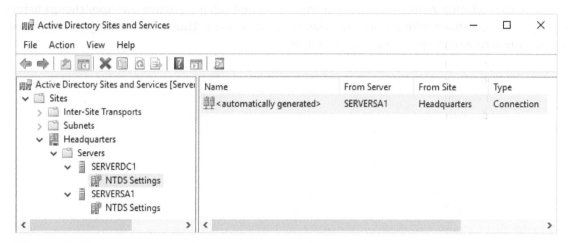

Figure 7-19 Connection object in Active Directory Sites and Services

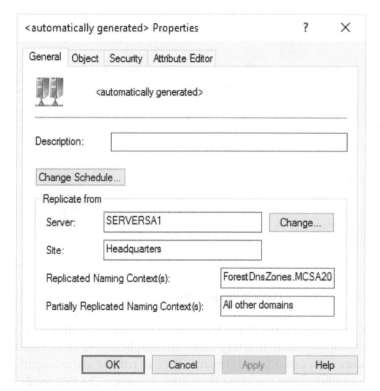

Figure 7-20 The Properties dialog box for a connection object

The General tab in the Properties dialog box is the only one of interest for connection objects; the other three tabs are the same for all Active Directory objects. The General tab contains the following options:

- *Change Schedule*—Click this button to view and change the KCC's default schedule (once per hour) for periodic replication. Periodic replication occurs in addition to triggered replication, which occurs after changes to Active Directory have been made. If you attempt to change the schedule on a KCC-generated connection object, Windows warns you that changes are overwritten by Active Directory unless you mark the object as not automatically generated.

- *Replicate from Server*—Replication is a pull process, whereby a DC requests replication from its partners after being notified of changes and at the periodic replication interval. The name of the connection object's replication partner is specified in this field; to change it, click the Change button. For intrasite replication in which the KCC creates the connection object, changing the server isn't recommended. As with the replication schedule, Windows warns you if you attempt to change the server name.
- *Replicate from Site*—The name of the site where the replication partner can be found. When only one site exists, this name is Default-First-Site-Name unless you rename it.
- *Replicated Naming Context(s)*—This specifies which partitions are replicated and from where. You might not see the full list because the text box isn't very wide. In Figure 7-20, several partitions are replicated, including the forest-wide and domain-wide DNS partitions, the domain partition, the schema partition, and the configuration partition.
- *Partially Replicated Naming Context(s)*—If the DC you're configuring is a global catalog server, you see a list of other domains from which partial Active Directory data is replicated or you see "All other domains" if there are no additional domains in the forest. This text box is usually empty if the DC isn't a global catalog server.

Creating Connection Objects

You can create connection objects for intrasite replication if you want to alter the replication topology manually. You might want to alter the topology if a site includes WAN links that could benefit from a different replication schedule. To do so, right-click NTDS Settings under the applicable server and click New Active Directory Domain Services Connection. You're asked to select a DC as a replication partner, and the connection object is named after this server by default. By default, the schedule for a new connection object is set to every 15 minutes, but you can change this value.

Creating a connection object is usually unnecessary, but it can be useful for troubleshooting replication problems or for creating special replication schedules between DCs. The KCC uses a new connection object in its topology calculations and might alter the topology as a result. You must be sure of what you're doing before making manual changes to the intrasite replication topology, or you could break replication.

If you do make changes, right-click the NTDS Settings node, point to All Tasks, and click Check Replication Topology to run the KCC algorithm. If you created a connection manually to a server that already exists, the KCC deletes the automatically generated connection and leaves the manually created connection. If you remove the manually created connection, the KCC generally re-creates the original topology.

Special Replication Scenarios

Some changes to Active Directory objects require special handling called **urgent replication**. This event triggers immediate notification that a change has occurred instead of waiting for the normal 15-second interval before replication partners are notified. Urgent replication events include the following:

- Account lockout changes sent immediately to the primary domain controller (PDC) emulator, which then replicates the event to other DCs
- Changes to the account lockout policy
- Changes to the password policy
- Changes to a local security authority secret, such as a trust relationship password
- Password changes to DC computer accounts
- Changes to the relative identifier (RID) master role holder

Password changes are handled slightly differently than other urgent replication events. When a password change occurs, the DC handling the change immediately transmits the new password to the PDC emulator, and the PDC emulator uses normal intrasite replication procedures. If a user attempts to log on to a DC with an incorrect password, the DC contacts the PDC emulator to see whether a password change has occurred before denying the authentication attempt. This process allows users to log on immediately after a password change even if not all DCs have been updated with the change.

Checking Replication Status

You can use Active Directory Sites and Services to force the KCC to check the replication topology, but if you want to view detailed information about connections and replication status, use the command-line program `repadmin.exe`. Many arguments can be used with this command, but to view replication status, use `repadmin /showrepl`. Figure 7-21 shows the output of this command in a domain with two DCs. Each replication partner is listed.

```
C:\Users\Administrator>repadmin /showrepl

Repadmin: running command /showrepl against full DC localhost
Headquarters\SERVERDC1
DSA Options: IS_GC
Site Options: (none)
DSA object GUID: dec5e365-816b-4e21-8fe4-987a8cb42ecb
DSA invocationID: 25b7298f-22e4-4d18-835a-773078156183

==== INBOUND NEIGHBORS ======================================

DC=MCSA2016,DC=local
    Headquarters\SERVERSA1 via RPC
        DSA object GUID: b2902817-a4e5-4aea-ac28-c53a81a186d3
        Last attempt @ 2017-06-21 13:49:18 was successful.

CN=Configuration,DC=MCSA2016,DC=local
    Headquarters\SERVERSA1 via RPC
        DSA object GUID: b2902817-a4e5-4aea-ac28-c53a81a186d3
        Last attempt @ 2017-06-21 13:49:18 was successful.

CN=Schema,CN=Configuration,DC=MCSA2016,DC=local
    Headquarters\SERVERSA1 via RPC
        DSA object GUID: b2902817-a4e5-4aea-ac28-c53a81a186d3
        Last attempt @ 2017-06-21 13:49:18 was successful.

DC=DomainDnsZones,DC=MCSA2016,DC=local
    Headquarters\SERVERSA1 via RPC
        DSA object GUID: b2902817-a4e5-4aea-ac28-c53a81a186d3
        Last attempt @ 2017-06-21 13:56:34 was successful.

DC=ForestDnsZones,DC=MCSA2016,DC=local
    Headquarters\SERVERSA1 via RPC
        DSA object GUID: b2902817-a4e5-4aea-ac28-c53a81a186d3
        Last attempt @ 2017-06-21 13:49:18 was successful.
```

Figure 7-21 Output of the `repadmin /showrepl` command

Each section of the output lists a directory partition followed by the DCs from which the partition is replicated. For example, the first line under INBOUND NEIGHBORS specifies the domain partition, and the second line shows that the ServerSA1 domain controller in site Headquarters is a replication partner for this partition. The next two lines show the connection object's globally unique ID (GUID) and the status of the last replication attempt. Each replication partner is listed along with the status of the last replication attempt. Other partitions are represented in the subsequent lines of output. You can also use `repadmin` to show the partitions being replicated by each connection object, force replication to occur, force the KCC to recalculate the topology, and take other actions.

Tip

Entering `repadmin /?` doesn't show all available parameters. To learn more about this command and see the full list of parameters, visit *http://technet.microsoft.com/en-us/library/cc736571.aspx*.

Active Directory Intersite Replication

You've learned that intrasite replication occurs among several domain controllers after the KCC creates the topology. Intersite replication, however, occurs between bridgehead servers. When the KCC detects that replication must occur between sites, one DC in each site is designated as the ISTG, which assigns a bridgehead server to handle replication for each directory partition. Because bridgehead servers perform such a vital function in multisite networks, and this function can consume considerable server resources, the administrator can override automatic assignment of a bridgehead server and assign the role to a specific DC.

You might need to designate bridgehead servers manually. Perhaps you've identified a DC in a site that's less burdened by other server tasks and is better able to handle the task than the server that the ISTG identified. You can use the `repadmin /bridgeheads` command to list which DCs in a site are acting as bridgehead servers to other sites.

After determining which DCs are currently acting as bridgehead servers, you can designate preferred bridgehead servers in Active Directory Sites and Services. Find the server in the Servers folder under the site, right-click the server object, and click Properties. Select the intersite transport protocol on the left (see Figure 7-22), and add it to the *This server is a preferred bridgehead server for the following transports* list box. You need to make sure that all directory partitions in the site are contained on the bridgehead servers you configure. If you don't, Windows warns you about which partitions the configured bridgehead servers won't replicate. Replication still takes place for these partitions because Windows configures the necessary bridgehead servers automatically, but relying on this automatic configuration defeats the purpose of assigning bridgehead servers manually.

Figure 7-22   Configuring a bridgehead server

Caution

If a manually configured bridgehead server fails, replication for the partitions it contains stops. The ISTG doesn't configure a new bridgehead server automatically for a failed manually configured one. However, if the ISTG assigns a bridgehead server and it fails, the ISTG attempts to assign a new one automatically.

Intersite Transport Protocols

Two protocols can be used to replicate between sites: IP and SMTP. By default, IP is used in the DEFAULTIPSITELINK site link and is recommended in most cases. To be precise, when you choose IP as the intersite transport protocol, you're choosing Remote Procedure Call (RPC) over IP. RPC over IP uses synchronous communication, which requires a reliable network connection with low latency. With synchronous communication, when a request is made, a reply is expected immediately, and the entire process of replication with one DC finishes before the process can begin with another DC.

If your network connections don't lend themselves to RPC over IP, you can use SMTP, which is used primarily for email. It's an asynchronous protocol that works well for slower, less reliable, or intermittent connections. The advantage of SMTP is that a DC can send multiple replication requests simultaneously without waiting for a reply; the reply can occur sometime later. So if you think of SMTP as an email conversation, you can liken RPC over IP to a chat session.

SMTP requires fairly complex configuration, and the administrative effort is rarely worth it, particularly with today's fast and reliable WAN connections. In addition, SMTP can't be used to replicate domain directory partitions, so it can't be used in domains spanning multiple sites. It can be used only to replicate the schema, global catalog, and configuration partitions. In a nutshell, here are the requirements for the bridgehead servers on both ends of an SMTP-configured site link:

- The SMTP feature must be installed on both servers.
- An enterprise certification authority must be configured on the network.
- The site link path must have a lower cost than an RPC over IP site link.
- You can't have DCs from the same domain in both sites.
- DCs must be configured to receive email.

Note

RPC over IP is the only replication protocol used in intrasite replication.

Site Link Bridges

As mentioned, site link bridging is a property of a site link that makes the link transitive. Site link bridging is enabled by default; however, in some circumstances, you don't want all site links to be transitive as when some WAN links are slow or available only sporadically (with a dial-up connection, for example). To change the transitive behavior of site links, turn off site link bridging and create site link bridges manually, which enables you to manage replication traffic between sites more efficiently with some network topologies.

Figure 7-23 shows a network with a hub-and-spoke WAN topology. Because of the transitive nature of site links, Site1 replicates with bridgehead servers in Site2 and can replicate with bridgehead servers in Site2A, Site2B, and Site2C. If WAN connections between all sites are fast and reliable with plenty of bandwidth for replication traffic, this default behavior works well.

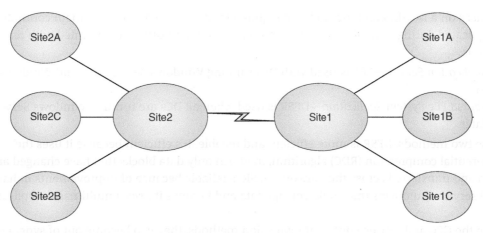

Figure 7-23   A hub-and-spoke topology

Keep in mind, however, that the same replication traffic is crossing WAN links four times, one for each site. On slower or heavily used WAN links between Site1 and Site2, this extra traffic could be excessive. To control the flow of replication traffic better, disable automatic site link bridging and create site link bridges between Site1 and Site2 and between Site2 and its satellites. Replication traffic still flows between Site1 and Site2, but Site2 distributes the traffic to satellite sites so that replication traffic crosses the Site1–Site2 WAN link only one time. You would probably want to create site link bridges in the opposite direction, too.

Other reasons to create site link bridges manually include the following:

1. *Control traffic through firewalls*—You might want to limit which DCs can communicate with one another directly through firewalls. You can configure firewalls to allow traffic between DCs at specific sites and create site link bridges as needed.

2. *Accommodate partially routed networks*—Normally, the KCC considers all possible connections when determining the replication topology. If sites are connected only intermittently, you can configure site link bridges between only the sites that map to full-time network connections, which bypasses intermittent links.

3. *Reduce confusion of the KCC*—A complex network involving many alternative paths between sites can cause confusion when the KCC and ISTG create the replication topology. You can force what kind of topology is created by using custom site link bridges and disabling transitivity.

To disable transitivity of site links, right-click the IP or SMTP folder under Inter-Site Transports and click Properties, and then click to clear the *Bridge all site links* check box. To create a site link bridge, right-click the IP or SMTP folder and click New Site Link Bridge. Give a descriptive name to the site link bridge, and then add at least two site links to it.

SYSVOL Replication

Not all Active Directory–related data is stored on Active Directory partitions. Some crucial information for domain operation is stored as files in the SYSVOL share on domain controllers, including group policy template files, the ADMX central store, and logon scripts. SYSVOL replication uses the same replication service as DFS, called Distributed File System Replication (DFSR). Versions of Windows Server before Windows Server 2008 used File Replication Service (FRS).

Group Policy Replication

A Group Policy object (GPO) is composed of a group policy template (GPT) and a group policy container (GPC). A GPC is an Active Directory object stored in the Active Directory domain partition, and a GPT is a collection of files stored in the SYSVOL share. Because these two components are stored in different places on a DC, different methods are required to replicate GPOs to all domain controllers. GPCs are replicated during normal Active Directory replication, and GPTs are replicated with one of these methods:

- *File Replication Service*—FRS is used with DCs running Windows Server 2003 and Windows 2000 Server.
- *Distributed File System Replication*—DFSR is used when all DCs are running Windows Server 2008 and later.

Of these two methods, DFSR is more efficient and reliable. It's efficient because it uses the remote differential compression (RDC) algorithm, in which only data blocks that have changed are compressed and transferred across the network. DFSR is reliable because of improvements in handling unexpected service shutdowns that could corrupt data and because it uses a multimaster replication scheme.

Because the GPC and GPT use different replication methods, they can become out of sync. As mentioned, GPCs are replicated when Active Directory replication occurs. Between DCs in the same site, the replication interval is about 15 seconds after a change occurs. Between DCs in different sites, the interval is usually much longer—minutes or even hours. Replication of the SYSVOL share (and therefore the GPT) occurs immediately after a change is made. Strange and unpredictable results could occur when a client computer attempts to apply a GPO when the GPC and GPT aren't synchronized. However, starting with Windows XP, the client computer checks the version number of both components before applying GPO settings.

As long as replication services are running correctly, the most likely problem with GPO replication is a delay in clients receiving changes in policy settings. This problem usually occurs when multiple sites are involved. Replication problems can be diagnosed with the Group Policy Management console (GPMC) by selecting the GPO in the left pane, clicking the Status tab in the right pane, and clicking the Detect Now button (see Figure 7-24).

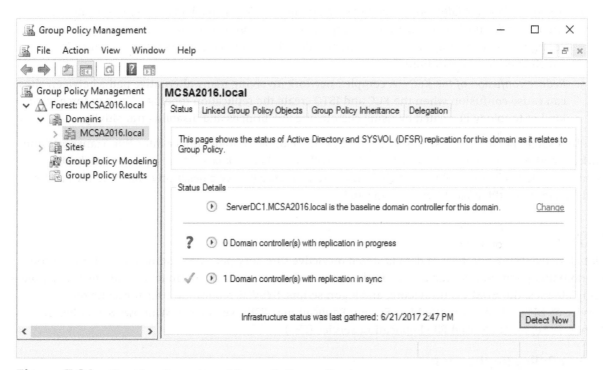

Figure 7-24 Checking the status of Group Policy replication

Upgrading to DFSR

If your domain includes Windows Server 2003 or older DCs, it's using FRS to replicate SYSVOL, and you should migrate to the more reliable DFSR as soon as possible. Even if you have upgraded all servers to Windows Server 2008 and later, FRS might still be running if your domain once contained older DCs and you haven't migrated to DFSR. Before migrating from FRS to DFSR, you need to understand the four phases of migration, referred to as *migration states*:

- *State 0: Start*—The C:\Windows\SYSVOL folder is present and mapped to the SYSVOL share and is being replicated with FRS.
- *State 1: Prepared*—The SYSVOL share continues to be replicated with FRS. A new folder named SYSVOL_DFSR has been created; it contains a copy of the SYSVOL share and is being replicated with DFSR.
- *State 2: Redirected*—The SYSVOL_DFSR folder is mapped to the SYSVOL share and is being replicated with DFSR. FRS continues to replicate the old C:\Windows\SYSVOL folder, which is no longer mapped to the SYSVOL share.
- *State 3: Eliminated*—The SYSVOL_DFSR folder is mapped to the SYSVOL share and continues to be replicated with DFSR. The original C:\Windows\SYSVOL folder is deleted, and FRS replication no longer occurs.

> **Tip** ⓘ
>
> You can use `dfsrmig /getmigrationstate` to see whether you need to perform DFSR migration. If you don't, you see the message "All domain controllers have migrated successfully to the Global state ('Eliminated'). Migration has reached a consistent state on all domain controllers."

Migrating from FRS to DFSR is done with the `dfsrmig` command-line tool on a writeable DC (not an RODC). Before beginning, do a system state backup on domain controllers with the command `wbadmin start systemstatebackup`. The steps for FRS-to-DFSR migration are as follows:

1. To verify that all DCs are operating in at least the Windows Server 2008 functional level, open Active Directory Domains and Trusts, right-click the domain, and then click Raise domain functional level. The current domain functional level is shown. Raise it to at least Windows Server 2008, if necessary.

2. To migrate the domain to the Prepared state, open a command prompt window, type `dfsrmig /setglobalstate 1`, and press Enter. To verify that all DCs have migrated to the Prepared state, type `dfsrmig /getmigrationstate` and press Enter. You see output similar to the following:

```
All Domain Controllers have migrated successfully to Global state
  ('Prepared').
Migration has reached a consistent state on all Domain Controllers.
Succeeded.
```

3. To migrate the domain to the Redirected state, type `dfsrmig /setglobalstate 2` and press Enter. To verify that all DCs have migrated to the Redirected state, type `dfsrmig /getmigrationstate` and press Enter. You see output similar to the following:

```
All Domain Controllers have migrated successfully to Global state
  ('Redirected').
Migration has reached a consistent state on all Domain Controllers.
Succeeded.
```

4. Before migrating the domain to the Eliminated state, verify that replication is working correctly by typing `repadmin /replsum` and pressing Enter. No errors should be reported. After this final step, you can't revert to FRS replication. Type `dfsrmig /setglobalstate 3` and press Enter. To verify that all DCs have migrated to the Eliminated state, type `dfsrmig /getmigrationstate` and press Enter. You see output similar to the following:

```
All Domain Controllers have migrated successfully to Global state
   ('Eliminated').
Migration has reached a consistent state on all Domain Controllers.
Succeeded.
```

5. To verify the migration, type `net share` and press Enter on all DCs. The NETLOGON share should be mapped to the C:\Windows\SYSVOL_DFSR\sysvol*DomainName*\SCRIPTS folder, and the SYSVOL share should be mapped to the C:\Windows\SYSVOL_DFSR\sysvol folder.

6. Unless you're using FRS for some other purpose, stop and disable the service by typing `sc stop ntfrs`, pressing Enter on each DC, and then typing `sc config ntfrs start=disabled` and pressing Enter on each DC.

Managing Replication

Active Directory and SYSVOL replication usually work fine with the built-in scheduling and processes. However, you might want to force replication to occur for troubleshooting or testing purposes or just so that you don't have to wait for the normal replication schedule between sites. The main tool for controlling Active Directory replication is the `repadmin` command-line program. Some commonly used variations of the `repadmin` command are shown in the following list:

- `repadmin /replicate`—This command causes replication of a specified partition from one DC to another. For example, to replicate the domain directory partition from ServerDC1 to ServerSA1, use the following command. Note that the destination DC (the DC you're replicating to) is listed first followed by the source DC (the DC you're replicating from).

```
repadmin /replicate ServerSA1 ServerDC1 dc=MCSA2016,dc=local
```

If one of the servers is an RODC, add the `/readonly` switch to the end of the command.

- `repadmin /syncall`—This command forces replication to occur between the specified DC and all its replication partners. All partitions are synchronized unless you specify a partition. For example, the following command synchronizes all partitions on ServerDC1 with all its replication partners:

```
repadmin /syncall ServerDC1
```

- `repadmin /kcc`—This command causes the KCC to check the replication topology and update it, if necessary. You should use it if you have recently made changes to the domain or forest, such as adding or removing domains or domain controllers, or if you have recently upgraded older DCs to Windows Server 2012/R2.

Managing Replication with Active Directory Sites and Services

With Active Directory Sites and Services, you can force replication to occur and force the KCC to check the replication topology. To cause replication to occur, expand the site node where the server on which you want to force replication is located. Expand the Servers node, click the target DC, and then click the NTDS Settings object. Right-click the connection object connecting the server on which you want to force replication and click Replicate Now (see Figure 7-25). In the figure, ServerDC1 replicates immediately with ServerSA1.

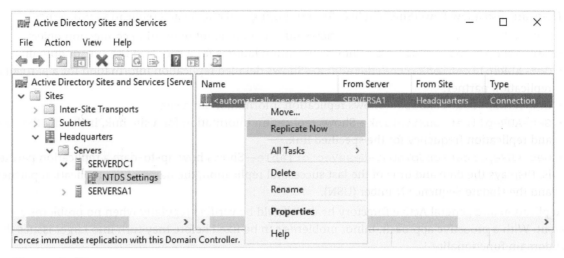

Figure 7-25   Forcing replication in Active Directory Sites and Services

To force the KCC to check the replication topology, right-click the NTDS Settings object under a DC, point to All Tasks, and click Check Replication Topology.

Note

The `Sync-ADObject` PowerShell cmdlet forces replication of a single specified Active Directory object between two specified DCs.

Monitoring Replication

There are several tools for monitoring Active Directory replication. You can use Performance Monitor to collect Active Directory replication statistics by using the predefined Active Directory Diagnostics data collector set, and you can monitor DFSR counters. In addition, you can use these command-line tools to get detailed replication status information:

- `repadmin`—Reports the replication status on each DC, allowing you to spot potential problems before they affect operations adversely. You can display replication partners for a DC with the `repadmin /showrepl` command, which informs you if a partner isn't available or communication problems are occurring. You can also display detailed information about connection objects with the `repadmin /showconn` command and view object replication information with the `repadmin /showobjmeta` command. For a less detailed summary of replication status, use the `repadmin /replsum` command. Repadmin can also be used to manage certain aspects of replication, as described earlier in the section "Managing Replication." For syntax help, type `repadmin /?`.

- `dcdiag`—Analyzes the status and overall health of Active Directory, performs replication security checks, and checks for correct DNS configuration and operation. Examples of some tests you can run include the following:
  - `dcdiag /test:Advertising`: Ensures that all DC roles are advertised so that client computers are aware of available services.
  - `dcdiag /test:Intersite`: Tests for failures in intersite replication.
  - `dcdiag /test:Replications`: Tests for timely and error-free replication.
  - `dcdiag /test:CheckSecurityError`: Verifies replication health, specifically its security.

There are also a few PowerShell cmdlets for monitoring and diagnosing replication problems:

- `Get-ADReplicationConnection`—Shows information about replication connection objects.
- `Get-ADReplicationFailure`—Shows replication failures for a specified DC, site, or domain.
- `Get-ADReplicationPartnerMetadata`—Shows detailed replication information for a particular replication partner.
- `Get-ADReplicationSite`—Shows replication information for a site.
- `Get-ADReplicationSiteLink`—Shows replication information for a site link, including the cost and replication frequency for the specified link.
- `Get-ADReplicationUpToDateNessVectorTable`—Shows how up-to-date a replication partner is. Displays the date and time of the last successful replication, the name of the replication partner, and the Update Sequence Number (USN).

Replication and general Active Directory health should be verified regularly when no problems are apparent. With a proactive approach, minor problems can be fixed before they turn into larger issues that affect domain functionality.

Activity 7-9: Working with Connection Objects

Time Required: 15 minutes

Objective: View and change properties of connection objects.

Required Tools and Equipment: ServerDC1, ServerSA1

Description: In this activity, you explore the properties of NTDS Site Settings, server NTDS Settings, and connection objects.

1. On ServerDC1, open **Active Directory Sites and Services**.
2. Click to expand **Sites**, and then click **Headquarters**. Two objects are displayed in the right pane: the Servers folder, which lists the DCs in the site, and NTDS Site Settings.
3. In the right pane, double-click to expand the **Servers** folder and then double-click **ServerDC1**. Right-click **NTDS Settings** and click **Properties** to open the dialog box shown in Figure 7-26. (Notice that NTDS Settings are associated with server objects and site objects.)
4. In the General tab, you can configure the server as a global catalog server. Click the **Connections** tab. You should see ServerSA1 in both the Replicate From and Replicate To text boxes. Click **Cancel**.

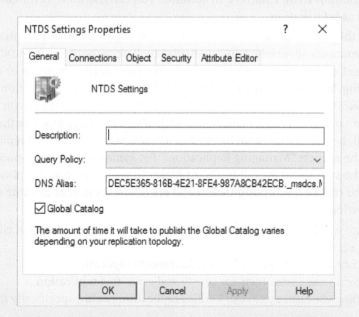

Figure 7-26   The NTDS Settings Properties dialog box

5. In the right pane, double-click to expand **NTDS Settings**. Right-click the connection object for ServerSA1. Notice that Replicate Now is an option, which you can use to force replication to occur immediately. Click **Properties**.

6. Click the **Change Schedule** button. The regular schedule for intrasite replication is once per hour. Click **Cancel**, and then click **Cancel** again.

7. In the left pane, click **Headquarters**. In the right pane, right-click **NTDS Site Settings** and click **Properties**.

8. In the Site Settings tab, click **Change Schedule**. In the Schedule for NTDS Site Settings dialog box, click **All**, and then click the **Four Times per Hour** option button. Changing the replication schedule here changes it for all automatically generated connections in the site. Click **OK** twice.

9. To verify that the schedule has changed, click **NTDS Settings** under ServerDC1 again. Double-click the connection object to open its Properties dialog box, and click the **Change Schedule** button. (The schedule change might take a while to occur under each server. Eventually, the change at the site level overwrites the server settings.) Click the **All** button at the upper left of the day/time table, click the **Once per Hour** option button, and then click **OK**.

10. Click **Apply**. You see a message indicating that changes to the connection will be overwritten because the connection object is generated automatically. When prompted to mark the connection as not automatically generated, click **Yes**, which changes the replication schedule for this connection only. Any other connections have their schedules set in NTDS Site Settings. Click **OK**. Notice that the connection object's name changes to a numeric GUID instead of "<automatically generated>."

11. Continue to the next activity.

Activity 7-10: Creating a Site Link

Time Required: 10 minutes

Objective: Create a site link.

Required Tools and Equipment: ServerDC1, ServerSA1

Description: In this activity, you create a site link to configure replication between sites Headquarters and BranchOffice.

1. On ServerDC1, in Active Directory Sites and Services, click to expand **Sites** and **Inter-Site Transports**, if necessary. Click the **IP** folder.

2. Right-click the **IP** folder and click **New Site Link**. In the Properties dialog box, type **SiteLinkHQ-BO** in the Name text box.

3. Because only two sites are defined and a site link must contain at least two sites, both Site12 and Site20 are added to the Sites in this site link list box. If there were more than two sites, you would choose two or more sites to include in the site link. Click **OK**.

4. In the right pane of Active Directory Sites and Services, right-click **SiteLinkHQ-BO** and click **Properties**. Click the **Change Schedule** button. Notice that replication takes place all day every day, which is the default setting for site links.

5. Drag to form a box around Monday through Friday from 8 a.m. to 3 p.m., and then click **Replication Not Available**. Now Headquarters and BranchOffice won't attempt to replicate during these times. Click **OK**.

6. Click in the Cost text box and type **200**. Recall that the higher the cost of the link, the less attractive it is when the topology is generated. If there are multiple paths between destinations, the lower cost path is selected. In this case, DEFAULTIPSITELINK also contains Headquarters and BranchOffice and has a cost of 100, so it's the preferred site link. Click **OK**.

7. Continue to the next activity.

Activity 7-11: Managing Replication

Time Required: 10 minutes

Objective: Manage replication with Active Directory Sites and Services and with the command line.

Required Tools and Equipment: ServerDC1, ServerSA1

Description: In this activity, you see how to force replication to occur and how to check the replication topology by using Active Directory Sites and Services and command-line tools.

1. On ServerDC1, in Active Directory Sites and Services, navigate to ServerDC1 under Headquarters. Click to expand **ServerDC1** and click **NTDS Settings** in the left pane.

2. In the right pane, right-click the connection object connecting ServerDC1 to ServerSA1 and click **Replicate Now**. Click **OK** in the message box.

3. Open a command prompt window, type **repadmin /showrepl**, and press **Enter**. You see detailed information about partitions that were replicated and the date and time of the last attempt and whether it was successful. You should see that the last attempt just occurred and was successful.

4. Type **repadmin /replsum** and press **Enter**. You see a less detailed summary of the most recent replication (see Figure 7-27). There are two parts to the display: Source DSA and Destination DSA. The Source DSA indicates the server from which data is being transferred, and the Destination DSA indicates the server to which data is being transferred. The "largest delta" column shows the last time replication occurred. Notice that for ServerSA1, under Source DSA, the time shows just a few seconds or minutes, and under Destination DSA, the times are reversed.

```
C:\Users\Administrator>repadmin /replsum
Replication Summary Start Time: 2017-06-21 18:19:52

Beginning data collection for replication summary, this may take awhile:
  .....


Source DSA          largest delta    fails/total %%   error
  SERVERDC1                29m:24s    0 /   5   0
  SERVERSA1                   :34s    0 /   5   0


Destination DSA     largest delta    fails/total %%   error
  SERVERDC1                   :34s    0 /   5   0
  SERVERSA1                29m:24s    0 /   5   0
```

Figure 7-27   Output of `repadmin /replsum`

5. In Active Directory Sites and Services, right-click the **NTDS Settings** object under ServerDC1, point to **All Tasks**, and click **Check Replication Topology**. Read the message. Click **OK** in the message box. Because no changes have been made to the domain, the topology won't change.

6. On ServerDC1 at the command prompt, type **repadmin /replicate ServerDC1 ServerSA1 dc=MCSA2016,dc=local**, and press **Enter**. You see a message stating that the sync was completed successfully. In this command, the source DC is ServerSA1, and the destination DC is ServerDC1. Recall that this command replicates only the domain partition unless additional partitions are specified.

7. Type **repadmin /replsum** and press **Enter**. You'll probably see that the replication doesn't seem to have happened because the timers weren't reset. However, `repadmin /replicate` replicates only changes; if no changes occurred since the last replication, no replication takes place.

8. Type **repadmin /syncall** and press **Enter**. This command replicates all partitions as needed.

9. Type **repadmin /showrepl** and press **Enter**. The most likely partition to have changed that requires replication is the Configuration partition.

10. Type **dcdiag /test:replications** and press **Enter**. The output indicates whether a connection can be made and the results of tests run on each Active Directory partition. Any replication errors are shown in the output.

11. Shut down ServerSA1. After ServerSA1 is shut down, on ServerDC1, type **dcdiag /test:replications** and press **Enter**. Because ServerSA1 was shut down, the command takes a while to time out. The output indicates that replication failed.

12. Type **repadmin /replicate ServerDC1 ServerSA1 dc=MCSA2016,dc=local** and press **Enter**. Because ServerSA1 was shut down, the command takes a while to time out. After it does, type **repadmin /showrepl** and press **Enter**. You should see that there was an error replicating the domain partition because it's the partition you attempted to replicate.

13. Type **repadmin /replsum** and press **Enter**. The output indicates that errors occurred in replication. You see the message "The RPC server is unavailable."

14. Shut down ServerDC1.

Chapter Summary

- A domain is the primary identifying and administrative unit in Active Directory. A unique name is associated with each domain and is used to access network resources. A domain administrator account has full control over objects in the domain, and certain security policies apply to all accounts in a domain.

- Most small and medium businesses have a single domain, but using more than one domain makes sense when there's a need for differing account policies, different name identities, replication control, internal and external domains, and tighter security.

- Adding a subdomain is a common reason for expanding an Active Directory forest. A tree can consist of a single domain or a parent domain and child domains, which can have child domains of their own.

- When a user is created in a domain, the account is assigned a UPN suffix that's the same as the domain name. To simplify logons, an alternative UPN suffix can be created and assigned to user accounts.

- The Active Directory forest is the broadest logical component of the Active Directory structure. Forests contain domains that can be organized into one or more trees. All domains in a forest share some common characteristics: a single schema, forest-wide administrative accounts, operations masters, global catalogs, trusts between domains, and replication between all domains.

- A trust relationship defines whether and how security principals from one domain can access network resources in another domain. Trust relationship types include one-way and two-way trusts, transitive trusts, shortcut trusts, forest trusts, external trusts, and realm trusts. You configure trusts with Active Directory Domains and Trusts.

- The Properties dialog box for a forest trust has three tabs: General, Name Suffix Routing, and Authentication. In the Name Suffix Routing tab, you can control which name suffixes used by the trusted forest are routed for authentication. In the Authentication tab, you choose forest-wide or selective authentication. SID filtering, which is enabled by default on external trusts but disabled on forest trusts, causes the trusting domain to ignore any SIDs that aren't from the trusted domain.

- The forest functional level determines the features of Active Directory that have forest-wide implications and which server OSs are supported on domain controllers in the forest. The domain functional level determines the features that Active Directory supports in a domain.

- Forest and domain preparation are done with the adprep.exe command-line program, which is included in the Active Directory Domain Services role installation.

- Domain controllers advertise themselves by registering service (SRV) records with DNS servers so that clients can find DCs that offer services related to Active Directory. The Netlogon service on the DC handles registration of SRV records for the Lightweight Directory Access Protocol (LDAP) and Kerberos services.

- Having a DC in each site is usually preferable so that authentication of clients occurs on the local LAN instead of having to traverse the WAN. However, having a DC at each site isn't always necessary or practical. Automatic site coverage is a feature in which each DC advertises itself by registering SRV records in DNS in sites that don't have a DC if the advertising DC has the lowest cost connection to the site.

- Timely and reliable replication of data between domain controllers is paramount to a functioning Active Directory domain and forest. Active Directory replication information includes Active Directory objects, such as OUs, user, group, and computer accounts; changes to data held in partitions maintained by FSMO role holders; trust relationships; global catalog data; group policy information; and files located in SYSVOL, such as group policy templates and scripts.

- The Knowledge Consistency Checker (KCC) is a process that runs on every DC and for intrasite replication, builds a replication topology among DCs in a site and establishes replication partners.

- A connection object defines the connection parameters between two replication partners. The KCC generates these parameters automatically between intrasite DCs. You can create connection objects for intrasite replication if you want to alter the replication topology manually.

- Two protocols can be used to replicate between sites: IP and SMTP. By default, IP is used in the DEFAULTIPSITELINK site link and is recommended in most cases.

- Group policy templates (GPTs) are replicated by using File Replication Service (FRS) or Distributed File System Replication (DFSR). Of these two methods, DFSR is the more efficient and reliable. If your domain includes Windows Server 2003 or older DCs, it uses the older FRS to replicate SYSVOL, and you should migrate to the more reliable DFSR as soon as possible.

- There are several tools for monitoring Active Directory replication. You can use Performance Monitor to collect Active Directory replication statistics by using the predefined Active Directory Diagnostics data collector set, and you can monitor DFSR counters. In addition, the command-line tools `repadmin` and `dcdiag` can give you detailed replication status information.

Key Terms

automatic site coverage	one-way trust	SID filtering
connection object	Privileged Access Management	transitive trust
domain functional levels	(PAM)	trust relationship
external trust	realm trust	two-way trust
forest functional level	referral	UPN suffix
forest trust	selective authentication	urgent replication
forest-wide authentication	shortcut trust	

Review Questions

1. Which of the following is *not* associated with an Active Directory tree?
   a. A group of domains
   b. A container object
   c. A common naming structure
   d. Parent and child domains

2. Which of the following best describes the first domain installed in a forest?
   a. Forest root
   b. Global catalog
   c. Master domain
   d. Primary tree

3. Which is responsible for facilitating forest-wide Active Directory searches?
   a. Knowledge Consistency Checker
   b. Infrastructure master
   c. Domain naming master
   d. Global catalog server

4. In intrasite replication, which of the following is responsible for building a replication topology for DCs in a site and establishing replication partners?
   a. GPO   c. RID
   b. PDC   d. KCC

5. Your company has merged with another company that also uses Windows Server 2016 and Active Directory. You want to give the other company's users access to your company's forest resources and vice versa without duplicating account information and with the least administrative effort. How can you achieve this goal?

   a. Transfer your global catalog to one of the other company's servers.
   b. Create a two-way forest trust.
   c. Configure an external trust.
   d. Configure selective authentication.

6. All domains in a forest have which of the following in common? (Choose all that apply.)
   a. The same domain name
   b. The same schema
   c. The same user accounts
   d. The same global catalog

7. Users of a new network subnet have been complaining that logons and other services are taking much longer than they did before being moved to the new subnet. You discover that many logon requests from workstations in the new subnet are being handled by domain controllers in a remote site instead of local domain controllers. What should you do to solve this problem?
   a. Create a new subnet and add it to the site that maps to the physical location of workstations.
   b. Enable automatic site coverage on the DCs in the site where users are having the problem.
   c. Create a new connection object between the DCs in the site where users are having a problem and the main site.
   d. Move the users' computer accounts to a new site and turn on automatic site coverage on the DCs in the old site.

8. You have three sites: Boston, Chicago, and Los Angeles. You have created site links between Boston and Chicago and between Chicago and Los Angeles with the default site link settings. What do you need to do to make sure that replication occurs between Boston and Los Angeles?
   a. Do nothing because replication will occur between Boston and Los Angeles with the current configuration.
   b. Create a new connection object between Boston and Los Angeles.
   c. Create a site link bridge between Boston and Los Angeles.
   d. Configure a site link between Boston and Los Angeles with SMTP.

9. Which of the following is a valid reason for using multiple forests?
   a. Centralized management
   b. Need for different schemas
   c. Ease of access to all domain resources
   d. Need for a single global catalog

10. What can you do to reduce the delay caused by authentication referral?
   a. Create a forest trust.
   b. Create an external trust.
   c. Create a shortcut trust.
   d. Create a transitive trust.

11. What can you do to integrate user authentication between Linux and Active Directory?
   a. Create a realm trust.
   b. Create an external trust.
   c. Create a one-way trust.
   d. Create a transitive trust.

12. Which of the following are reasons to use multiple domains? (Choose all that apply.)
   a. Need for different name identities
   b. Replication control
   c. Need for differing account policies
   d. Ease of access to resources

13. Your network is configured in a hub-and-spoke topology. You want to control the flow of replication traffic between sites, specifically reducing the traffic across network links between hub sites to reach satellite sites. What should you configure?
   a. Connection objects between domain controllers in each site
   b. Intersite transports
   c. Site link bridges
   d. NTDS settings

14. Bob is an administrator in a trusted forest, and you have some concerns about his trustworthiness. You want to be sure he can't gain privileged access to resources in your forest while masquerading as a user in his forest who doesn't normally have privileged access in your forest. What should you configure in the forest trust?
   a. SID filtering
   b. Trust transitivity
   c. Selective authentication
   d. One-way trust

15. Which of the following should you configure if you want users in a trusted forest to have access only to certain resources in your forest regardless of permission settings on these resources?
   a. SID filtering
   b. Trust transitivity
   c. Selective authentication
   d. One-way trust

16. You want to change the replication schedule between two domain controllers in the same site—and only these two domain controllers—to occur four times per hour. The KCC has generated all your intrasite connection objects. What's the best way to make this change?

    a. In the General tab of the connection object's Properties dialog box, click Change Schedule, and change the replication schedule to four times per hour. Make sure the object is marked as automatically generated.

    b. Create a new connection object for the two domain controllers, and set the schedule to four times per hour. Tell the KCC to check the replication topology.

    c. In the Site Settings tab of the NTDS Site Settings Properties dialog box, click Change Schedule, and set the schedule to four times per hour.

    d. In the Schedule tab of the server's Properties dialog box, click Change Schedule, and set the schedule to four times per hour.

17. Which of the following are true about using SMTP in site links? (Choose all that apply.)

    a. A certification authority must be configured.

    b. Domains can span the sites included in the site link.

    c. It's best used on slow or unreliable network links.

    d. It's the preferred transport protocol for intersite links.

18. A partition stored on a domain controller in SiteA isn't being replicated to other sites, but all other partitions on domain controllers in SiteA are being replicated. The problem partition is stored on multiple domain controllers in SiteA. What should you investigate as the source of the problem?

    a. An automatically configured bridgehead server

    b. A manually configured bridgehead server

    c. A failed site link bridge

    d. A failed ISTG

19. Which of the following is the default forest functional level for a Windows Server 2016 domain controller installed in a new forest?

    a. Windows Server 2012 R2

    b. Windows Server 2016

    c. Windows Server 2008

    d. Windows Server 2012

20. Which of the following are true about forests running at the Windows Server 2016 functional level? (Choose all that apply.)

    a. You can group membership expirations.

    b. You can create a forest trust with a Windows 2000 forest.

    c. RODCs can be part of the forest.

    d. Windows 2000 domain controllers can be part of the forest.

21. A user calls the help desk to change her forgotten password. A minute later, she attempts to log on with the new password but gets a logon failed message. She verifies that she's entering the correct password. She tries logging on again about 30 minutes later and is successful. What's the most likely cause of the delay in her ability to log on?

    a. The domain controller where the password was changed was in a different site, and normal replication between sites caused the delay.

    b. The domain controller that authenticated the user must have gone down and didn't receive the password change until it was brought back online.

    c. The domain controller holding the PDC emulator role wasn't contacted by the domain controller that authenticated the user.

    d. The intrasite replication schedule is set for 30 minutes instead of 15 seconds.

22. Which of the following is a new feature introduced with the Windows Server 2016 forest functional level?

    a. AES support

    b. Fine-grained password policies

    c. Domain controller renaming

    d. Privileged Access Management

23. Where is a GPT stored?

    a. In the SYSVOL share

    b. In Active Directory

    c. In GPMC

    d. In GPME

24. Several months ago, you installed a new forest with domain controllers running Windows Server 2016. You're noticing problems with GPT replication. What should you check?

    a. Verify that Active Directory replication is working correctly.

    b. Verify that FRS is operating correctly.

    c. Verify that DFSR is operating correctly.

    d. Check the GPOReplication flag for the GPT in the Attribute Editor.

The following activities give you critical thinking challenges. Case Projects offer a scenario with a problem to solve and for which you supply a written solution.

Case Project 7-1: Working with Trusts

Examine the network in Figure 7-28. You need to configure this network to meet the following requirements:

- *Requirement 1*—All users in the csmtech.local forest should be authenticated to all resources in the csmasia. local forest.
- *Requirement 2*—Selected users in the csmasia.local domains should be authenticated to selected resources in the csmtech.local forest.
- *Requirement 3*—No users in the csmchina.local domain tree should be authenticated to the csmtech.local forest.
- *Requirement 4*—Users in the bj.csmchina.local domain access resources in the phx.usa.csmtech.local domain frequently. Latency should be kept to a minimum.
- *Requirement 5*—Users in the phx.usa.csmtech.local domain access resources in the gb.uk.csmtech.local domain frequently. Latency should be kept to a minimum.
- *Requirement 6*—Users in the Linux network need to access resources in the csmasia.local forest frequently.

Given the preceding requirements, write a report describing how to configure trust relationships and listing configuration options, such as one way or two way, transitivity, authentication, and so forth.

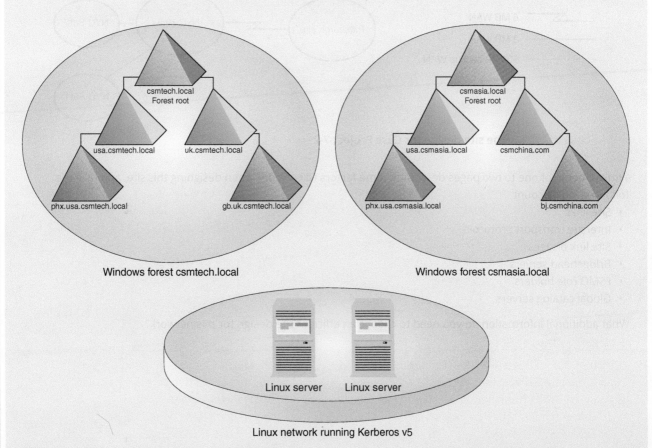

Figure 7-28   **The network for Case Project 7-1**

Case Project 7-2: Designing Sites

You're called in as a consultant to create a site design. The company has a network consisting of four hub sites and six satellite sites (see Figure 7-29). There are four domains, one for each city. Note the following facts about the company's site requirements:

- The satellite sites are in the same domain as the city to which they're connected.
- No sites contain domain controllers from outside their domain.
- Each hub site has 750 to 1000 users and 10 to 15 domain controllers.
- Each satellite site has 50 to 100 users and 2 to 4 domain controllers.

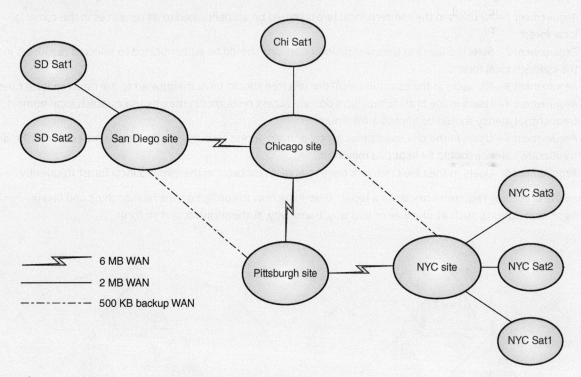

Figure 7-29   The site design for Case Project 7-2

Write a memo of one to two pages describing some factors to consider when designing this site, and take the following into account:

- Site links
- Intersite transport protocols
- Site link bridges
- Bridgehead servers
- FSMO role holders
- Global catalog servers

What additional information do you need to choose an efficient site design for this network?

CHAPTER **8**

IMPLEMENTING ACTIVE DIRECTORY CERTIFICATE SERVICES

After reading this chapter and completing the exercises, you will be able to:

Describe the components of a PKI system

Deploy the Active Directory Certificate Services role

Configure a certification authority

Maintain and manage a PKI

It's a matter of trust. Whether you're shopping on a website, engaging in online banking, or even reading an email, you must have a certain level of trust that the entity you're exchanging information with is actually who it says it is. Unfortunately, digital fraud and scams have become all too common. Fortunately, there are ways to protect yourself and your organization in the form of digital certificates.

Microsoft Active Directory Certificate Services provides the infrastructure for issuing and validating digital certificates in a corporate environment. With digital certificates, users can provide proof of their identities to corporate resources and confirm the identity of resources they access. Active Directory Certificate Services is Microsoft's implementation of a public key infrastructure (PKI), which secures information transfer and identity management and verification. This chapter describes how a PKI works and defines the terms used to discuss a PKI and Active Directory Certificate Services. You learn how to install and configure the Active Directory Certificate Services role and how to configure and manage key elements of this role, such as certification authorities and certificate enrollments and revocations.

321

Table 8-1 lists what you need for the hands-on activities in this chapter.

Table 8-1   Activity requirements

Activity	Requirements	Notes
Activity 8-1: Resetting Your Virtual Environment	ServerDC1, ServerDM1, ServerDM2, ServerSA1	
Activity 8-2: Installing the AD CS Role	ServerDC1, ServerDM1	
Activity 8-3: Creating an EFS Certificate Template	ServerDC1, ServerDM1	
Activity 8-4: Configuring EFS Certificate Autoenrollment	ServerDC1, ServerDM1	
Activity 8-5: Testing EFS Certificate Autoenrollment	ServerDC1, ServerDM1	
Activity 8-6: Installing the Web Enrollment Role Service	ServerDC1, ServerDM1	
Activity 8-7: Configuring an OCSP Response Signing Certificate Template	ServerDC1, ServerDM1	
Activity 8-8: Requesting the OCSP Response Signing Certificate	ServerDC1, ServerDM1	
Activity 8-9: Creating a Revocation Configuration for the OR	ServerDC1, ServerDM1	
Activity 8-10: Backing Up the CA Server and Archiving a Key	ServerDC1, ServerDM1	
Activity 8-11: Recovering a Lost Key	ServerDC1, ServerDM1	

Introducing Active Directory Certificate Services

 **Certification**

- **70-742 – Implement Active Directory Certificate Services (AD CS):**
  Install and configure AD CS

Active Directory Certificate Services (AD CS) is a server role in Windows Server 2016 that provides services for creating a public key infrastructure that administrators can use to issue and manage public key certificates. With AD CS, you can add security for a variety of applications, including email, wireless networks, virtual private networks (VPNs), Encrypting File System (EFS), smart cards for user logons, Secure Sockets Layer/Transport Layer Security (SSL/TLS), and others. This section describes the basic components of a PKI and defines several terms used in implementing PKIs and AD CS.

Public Key Infrastructure Overview

A **public key infrastructure (PKI)** is a security system that binds the identity of a user or device to a cryptographic key that secures data transfer with encryption and ensures data authenticity with digital certificates. PKI provides the following services to a network:

- *Confidentiality*—Protects data and communications by encryption algorithms, allowing only the authorized parties to access information
- *Integrity*—Ensures that data received is the same as data sent
- *Nonrepudiation*—Ensures that a party in a communication can't dispute the validity of the transaction, much like a signature on a letter or contract is used to verify that the signatory wrote the letter
- *Authentication*—Verifies the identity of a person or system involved in a transaction

Before going into the details of a PKI, you need to understand why this service is necessary. Suppose you want to do some online banking, a transaction that you want to be confidential. You open your web browser and go to *www.mybank.com*. You enter your sign-in information and proceed with your transaction. Without some type of security system in place, a number of things can go wrong with this procedure as in the following examples:

- DNS servers could be compromised, replacing the IP address of *www.mybank.com* with the IP address of a fraudulent site. All of your sign in information, including, perhaps, your account number, is actually being sent to the fraudulent website and could be used to access your real account. Without some type of security system in place, you can't be sure of the authenticity of the server with which you're communicating.
- Someone could be electronically eavesdropping on your conversation. You might actually be communicating with *www.mybank.com*, but someone could be "listening" to the conversation with a packet-capturing program, which means that your transaction is not confidential. The packets can be examined to find your sign-in information and account information for later use.

A public key security system, such as your web browser using HTTPS instead of HTTP in a URL, can thwart both of the preceding situations. In the first example, using digital certificates can authenticate the website's identity. If your browser is directed to a fraudulent site, the digital certificate doesn't match the site's URL. In the second example, encryption can ensure confidentiality and prevent an eavesdropper from interpreting information in captured packets.

Of course, for the security system to work, users have the responsibility to check that the web browser is using secure communication (usually indicated by a padlock icon in the browser). In addition, users must be vigilant in heeding warning messages about websites' certificate validity. PKI is commonly used in many other situations, but whenever a secure transaction is necessary between two parties that don't know each other, PKI is likely to be part of the transaction.

PKI Terminology

Before you delve into PKI transactions, review the following list of components of a PKI:

- *Plaintext*—Data that has been unaltered; as used in cryptography, this term defines the state of information before it's encrypted or after it has been decrypted.
- *Ciphertext*—Data that has been encrypted; it's the result you get when plaintext is transformed by an encryption algorithm.
- *Key*—In encryption, a numeric value used by a cryptographic algorithm to change plaintext into ciphertext (encrypt) and ciphertext back to plaintext (decrypt).
- *Secret key*—A key used to both encrypt and decrypt data in a secure transaction. The secret key must be known by both parties because it's used at both ends of the cryptography process. The terms *symmetric key* and *shared secret key* are also used. Secret keys are used in symmetric cryptography, defined later in this list, and provide a lower overhead secure transaction than using a public/private key pair.
- *Private key*—A key that's held by a person or system and is unknown to anyone else. A private key is part of a key pair used in asymmetric cryptography (defined later in this list) and is most often used by the owner to decrypt data that has been encrypted with the corresponding public key.
- *Public key*—A key owned by a person or system that's distributed to whoever wants to have a secure communication session with the key owner. The public key, part of the key pair used in asymmetric cryptography, is used to encrypt data, which can then be decrypted only by using the owner's private key. A public key is also used to verify a digital signature.
- *Symmetric cryptography*—An encryption/decryption process that uses a single secret key to encrypt and decrypt a message (also called *private key cryptography* or *secret key cryptography*). The key is often referred to as a *shared secret* because both parties involved in the communication must have the same key. Symmetric cryptography is vulnerable to attack because the shared secret must be transmitted to both parties, and the key used in the encryption algorithm tends to be easier to crack than those used in asymmetric cryptography.

Note @

Although symmetric cryptography is sometimes referred to as private key cryptography or private key encryption, these terms are somewhat imprecise. A private key is used as part of a pair in asymmetric cryptography and should never be shared with another party.

- *Asymmetric cryptography*—An encryption/decryption process used in a PKI system that uses both a public key and a private key. Asymmetric cryptography is more complex and requires more computing resources than symmetric cryptography, but it's also more secure. Because of its higher resource requirements, asymmetric cryptography is often used with symmetric cryptography. It's used to exchange secret keys, which are then used symmetrically for the bulk of data encryption and decryption.
- *Digital certificate*—A digital document that contains identifying information about a person or system; it's a central component of a PKI. Information in the certificate typically includes a person's or organization's name or a system's URL and IP address as well as the holder's public key, an expiration date, and the digital signature of the certification authority that issued the certificate. The certificate also defines the purpose for which it is used.
- *Digital signature*—A numeric string created by a cryptographic algorithm, called a *hash* (discussed later in "Installing the AD CS Role"), that's used to validate the authenticity of a message or document. The signature is verified by an algorithm that uses the stated owner of the signature's public key to accept or reject the signature as authentic. In a PKI, a certification authority's digital signature is used to verify the authenticity of digital certificates and other documents.
- *Certification authority (CA)*—An entity that issues and manages digital certificates and associated public keys and is an integral part of a PKI. Windows Server with the Active Directory Certificate Services role installed can be a CA for an enterprise network. Well-known companies, such as VeriSign, Comodo, and GlobalSign, are examples of universally trusted public CAs that issue certificates to people and systems needing to engage in secure communication with the public.

Now that you understand a few terms, take another look at an online banking session. The following steps are general because an actual secure web session involves many variables, but these steps are the basic framework for most secure web transactions (see Figure 8-1):

- Request secure transaction →
- ← Here's my certificate
- Certificate verified; here is the encrypted session key →
- ← Data can be transferred securely by using the session key

SSL client   SSL web server

Figure 8-1   Steps of a secure web transaction

1. The web browser requests a secure transaction with *www.mybank.com* using HTTPS. HTTPS is a secure form of HTTP that uses Secure Sockets Layer (SSL) or Transport Layer Security (TLS), both of which use a PKI.
2. The web server sends information about the encryption protocols it will use and its certificate containing its public key.
3. The web client verifies the certificate and extracts the CA's public key to verify the digital signature of the issuing CA. If the CA is trusted and the signature is verified, the web client sends additional parameters to the server that are encrypted with the server's public key. One parameter is a session key, which is a shared secret key used to encrypt and decrypt data transferred during the rest of the communication session.

4. The web server decrypts the session key with its private key. The session key is then used to encrypt and decrypt information communicated between the parties.

Notice that in the preceding steps, both asymmetric and symmetric encryptions are used. Asymmetric encryption is used in the beginning of the conversation to transmit several parameters, including the session key. After that point, symmetric encryption is used. So why not use asymmetric encryption throughout the conversation? Doing so requires both the client and the server to have a public/private key pair, and assuming that every client has one might be unreasonable. Also, the additional processing asymmetric encryption requires slows communication. Because the shared secret key (session key) is exchanged by using more secure asymmetric encryption, the transaction remains highly secure.

The online banking transaction example is used because of its familiarity to most people. A Windows network with Active Directory Certificate Services installed is typically used to add an extra layer of security to enterprise network communication. AD CS not only ensures confidential communication but also can protect users and resources by providing data integrity and authenticity.

Note

Don't confuse a PKI in which publicly trusted CAs are used to secure public transactions with a PKI used in a private organization. The fact that you set up a CA in your company doesn't mean that certificates issued by your CA are trusted by the outside world.

AD CS Terminology

Now that you have a general understanding of a PKI, review some terms used with AD CS to give you an overview of this server role:

- *Certificate revocation list*—A **certificate revocation list (CRL)** is a list of certificates that the CA administrator has invalidated before their expiration dates. Reasons for certificate revocation include the fact or suspicion that a private key has been compromised or a certificate is deemed no longer necessary as when an employee leaves the company that issued the certificate.
- *Certificate template*—A **certificate template** is a shell or model of a certificate that is used to create new certificates. Certificate templates define certificate characteristics, such as the intended use and expiration date. In Windows Server, AD CS includes more than 30 predefined certificate templates named for their intended purposes, such as Web Server for authenticating the identity of web servers and Smart Card Logon, which enables users to authenticate by using smart cards. You can also create custom certificate templates.
- *CRL distribution point*—A **CRL distribution point (CDP)** is an attribute of a certificate that identifies where the CRL for a CA can be retrieved and can include URLs for HTTP, FILE, FTP, and LDAP locations.
- *Delta CRL*—This is a list of certificates revoked since the last base, or complete, CRL was published. Using Delta CRLs reduces the traffic created when downloading CRLs.
- *Enterprise CA*—This is a CA installation on Windows Server that's integrated with Active Directory.
- *Standalone CA*—This is a CA installation that isn't integrated with Active Directory.
- *Enrollment agent*—This is a user authorized to enroll for smart cards on behalf of other users. A **restricted enrollment agent** limits the agent to enrolling only specific users or security groups; it's available only with an enterprise CA.
- *CA hierarchy*—The first CA installed in a Windows network is called the *root CA*. Its certificate is self-signed and distributed to Windows clients that automatically trust the root CA. Additional CAs, called *subordinate CAs*, can be installed. Their certificates are signed by the root CA, and because Windows clients trust the root CA, by extension, they trust subordinate CAs.

- *Online responder*—This is a server that supports Online Certificate Status Protocol (OCSP). This protocol is an alternative to having clients download CRLs periodically to check certificate status. Clients can instead query an online responder for a certificate's status.
- *Certificate enrollment*—This is the process of issuing a certificate to a client. AD CS supports a number of enrollment methods, including autoenrollment, web enrollment, smart card enrollment, and manual enrollment. In addition, AD CS supports Network Device Enrollment Service (NDES), which allows network devices to get certificates.
- *Key management*—This involves functions to restore, recover, or back up keys. Users' private keys are stored in their profiles. If a private key is lost or corrupted, it might need to be restored. Key archival provides a method for storing a backup of a private key, and key recovery is the process of restoring a private key.
- *Authority Information Access (AIA)*—The AIA is a path configured on a CA server that specifies where to find the certificate for a CA.

Deploying the Active Directory Certificate Services Role

 Certification

- **70-742 – Implement Active Directory Certificate Services (AD CS):**
  Install and configure AD CS

Before you decide to deploy AD CS on your network, you should have a clear understanding of how it will be used in your network and the options for implementing it. For example, if your reason for issuing certificates to employees is to give them secure access to external resources, such as web servers and Internet email, you should probably use a well-known external third-party CA. After all, outside entities are unlikely to trust a certificate that your internal CA issues. However, if your goal is to enhance the security of internal communication, that's the primary purpose of AD CS. All your internal clients and resources can be configured to trust the internal CA.

 Note

It's possible to have a third-party CA as part of your PKI. In this case, the third-party CA acts as a root CA and issues certificates to your internal subordinate CAs. With this setup, your client computers can access external resources securely because the third-party CA is a point of common trust between internal computers and external entities.

Some AD CS options you should be aware of before deploying this server role include the following:
- Standalone and enterprise CAs
- Online and offline CAs
- CA hierarchy
- Certificate practice statements

Standalone and Enterprise CAs

An **enterprise CA** is a server running Windows Server with the AD CS role installed. Enterprise CAs integrate with Active Directory and offer several advantages for a PKI running in a domain environment. A **standalone CA** is a server running Windows Server with the AD CS role installed, but it has little Active

Directory integration. If you're issuing certificates only to domain member users and computers, you can install all enterprise CAs. If your network consists of non-Windows devices, you need at least one standalone CA. Although standalone CAs can be integrated with Active Directory somewhat for storing configuration information, the CA certificate, and CRL data, the integration must be done manually. Table 8-2 compares standalone and enterprise CAs.

Table 8-2   Standalone and enterprise CAs

Standalone CA server	Enterprise CA server
Active Directory not required	Active Directory required; server must be a member server (preferred) or domain controller
Can operate offline	Must operate online
Certificate requests required to be approved manually	Requests approved manually or automatically by using Active Directory information
No certificate templates available	Certificate templates available
Certificates not published in Active Directory	Certificates published in Active Directory
Requirement that requester enter identifying information in certificate manually	Identifying information taken from Active Directory
CA's certificate distributed to clients manually	CA's certificate distributed to clients automatically
CRL optionally published to Active Directory	CRL published automatically to Active Directory

Online and Offline CAs

A CA server is a critical component in a network's security. If a CA is compromised, all certificates the CA has issued are also compromised and must be revoked immediately. Given the critical nature of servers acting as CAs, running one or more servers in the CA hierarchy in offline mode is a common practice.

An offline CA isn't connected to the network, which makes it less vulnerable to attacks. However, all certificates and CRLs must be distributed with removable media. In a small network, using removable media to process certificate transactions works well, but in a large network, depending on an offline CA for all certificate needs isn't practical. Typically, when a hierarchy of CAs is necessary, a mix of offline and online CAs is used.

The root CA is the most critical and is the server typically configured for offline operation. An offline CA must also be a standalone CA. The root CA issues certificates only to CAs in the next level of the hierarchy that can be accommodated by using removable media. The next section discusses this concept in more detail.

CA Hierarchy

A small organization might require only a root CA if certificate requirements are modest. Large organizations, however, might want to create a hierarchy of CAs consisting of a root CA, intermediate CAs, and issuing CAs. A CA hierarchy distributes the load placed on CA servers and augments security.

The **root CA** is the first CA installed in a network. If it's an enterprise CA, its certificate is distributed to clients automatically via group policies. If it's a standalone CA, manual configuration of group policies is required to distribute its certificate. In either case, after clients are configured to trust the root CA's certificate, they also trust the certificate of any CA that's subordinate to the root. Administrators can use this fact to create a hierarchy that insulates the root CA from network exposure. This hierarchical arrangement is how you can operate a root CA in offline mode. The root CA needs to grant issuing certificates only to subordinate CAs, which are trusted by the clients to which they issue access certificates.

Depending on an organization's needs, a CA hierarchy can be single-level, consisting of only the root CA; two-level, consisting of the root CA and one or more issuing CAs; or three-level, consisting of the root CA, one or more intermediate CAs, and one or more issuing CAs. Figure 8-2 shows two-level and three-level hierarchies.

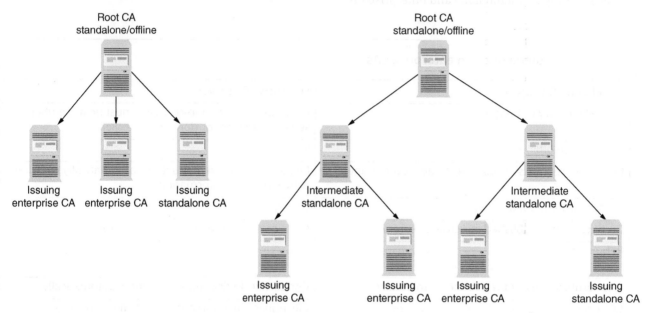

Figure 8-2 Two-level and three-level CA hierarchies

In the two-level hierarchy, the root CA issues certificates to subordinate CAs and then is usually taken offline for security. The subordinate CAs are referred to as **issuing CAs** because they interact with clients to field certificate requests and maintain the CRL. Because the root CA issues certificates to issuing CAs and the clients trust the root CA, clients also trust the issuing CAs. Issuing CAs are generally enterprise CAs or can be a combination of enterprise and standalone if the network includes non-Windows clients.

The three-level hierarchy is a common configuration and offers the strongest security because the issuing CAs, where user certificate requests are made, is farther from the root CA. In this arrangement, the root CA issues certificates to **intermediate CAs** (sometimes called *policy CAs*), authorizing them to issue certificates to other CAs. Intermediate CAs issue certificates to issuing CAs, which respond to user and device certificate requests. The root CA and intermediate CAs can be standalone and operate in offline mode. Issuing CAs can be a mix of enterprise and standalone CAs and operate in online mode.

Multilevel CA hierarchies are often used to distribute the certificate-issuing load in organizations with multiple locations. Each intermediate CA is responsible for one or more issuing CA in each location. In Figure 8-2, for example, one intermediate CA and its subordinate issuing CAs might handle certificate management for the U.S. location, and the other intermediate and issuing CAs handle certificates for the Europe location.

Certificate Practice Statements

A **certificate practice statement (CPS)** is a document describing how a CA issues certificates. A CPS isn't a required component of a PKI, but it should be developed as part of the planning process when an organization is designing its PKI. The document is usually published on the Internet, and every certificate that the CA issues has a URL pointing to the CPS so that people examining the certificate can read the statement. Because the CPS describes the process used to issue certificates, it can be used as a guide when deploying a CA design. A CPS usually contains the following elements:

- Identification of the CA
- Security practices for maintaining CA integrity

- Types of certificates issued
- Policies and procedures for issuing, revoking, recovering, and renewing certificates
- Cryptographic algorithms used
- Certificate lifetimes
- CRL-related policies, including the location of CRL distribution points
- Renewal policy of the CA's certificate

The CPS is installed by creating a `CAPolicy.inf` file and placing the file in the CA server's *%systemroot%* directory before the AD CS role is installed. For more on creating this file, see *http://technet.microsoft.com/en-us/library/jj125373.aspx*.

Installing the AD CS Role

Best practices dictate that the AD CS role shouldn't be installed on a domain controller. In fact, for optimum security, AD CS should probably be the only role installed on the server. If you're installing a standalone CA, the server can be a member server if you want to take advantage of the limited Active Directory integration possible with standalone CAs. An enterprise CA must be installed on a member server running Windows Server Standard or Datacenter Edition.

AD CS is installed in Server Manager by adding the AD CS role. During installation, you have the option to install several role services, including the following:

- *Certification Authority (selected by default)*—The CA component that issues, validates, and revokes certificates
- *Certificate Enrollment Policy Web Service*—Enables users to get certificate enrollment policies via a web browser
- *Certificate Enrollment Web Service*—Allows users and computers to perform certificate enrollment via HTTPS; works with Certificate Enrollment Policy Web Service to allow policy-based automated certificate enrollment for nondomain members; supports Windows 7/Windows Server 2008 R2 and later.
- *Certification Authority Web Enrollment*—Allows users to request certificates, submit certificate requests by using a file, and retrieve the CRL via a web browser; supports a wide variety of OSs.
- *Network Device Enrollment Service*—Used to issue certificates to network devices, such as routers and switches.
- *Online Responder*—Allows clients to check a certificate's revocation status without having to download the CRL periodically.

Your selections of role services depend on how the CA will be used in your network. Will users enroll in certificates by using a web browser? Will the CA issue certificates only to users and computers, or will certificates be issued to network devices, such as access points and routers? Will you use an online responder to automate CRL distribution?

Activity 8-1: Resetting Your Virtual Environment

Time Required: 5 minutes
Objective: Reset your virtual environment by applying the InitialConfig checkpoint or snapshot.
Required Tools and Equipment: ServerDC1, ServerDM1, ServerDM2, ServerSA1
Description: Apply the InitialConfig checkpoint or snapshot to ServerDC1, ServerDM1, ServerDM2, and ServerSA1.

1. Be sure all servers are shut down. In your virtualization program, apply the InitialConfig checkpoint or snapshot to ServerDC1, ServerDM1, ServerDM2, and ServerSA1.
2. When the snapshot or checkpoint has finished being applied, continue to the next activity.

Time Required: 20 minutes

Objective: Install the AD CS role.

Required Tools and Equipment: ServerDC1, ServerDM1

Description: You want to set up a PKI on your network to augment security, so in this activity, you install AD CS on ServerDM1, a member server, and configure it as an enterprise CA.

1. Start ServerDC1, if necessary. Start ServerDM1, and sign in to the domain as **Administrator**.
2. In Server Manager, click **Manage, Add Roles and Features** to start the Add Roles and Features Wizard. Click **Next** until you get to the Server Roles window.
3. In the Server Roles window, click the **Active Directory Certificate Services** check box. Click **Add Features**, and then click **Next**. In the Features window, click **Next** again.
4. In the AD CS window, read the description and the paragraph under "Things to note." In particular, notice that you can't change the computer name, join a different domain, or promote the server to a domain controller after the role is installed. Click **Next**.
5. In the Role Services window, the Certification Authority option is selected by default. Click **Certification Authority Web Enrollment**, and then click **Add Features**. Click **Online Responder**, click **Add Features**, and then click **Next**. In the Web Server Role (IIS) window, click **Next**. In the Role Services window, click **Next**. In the Confirmation window, click **Install**. Click **Close** when the installation is finished.
6. In Server Manager, click the notifications flag, and then click the **Configure Active Directory Certificate Services on the destination server** link to start the AD CS Configuration Wizard. In the Credentials window, accept the default credentials **MCSA2016\Administrator** and click **Next**.
7. In the Role Services window, click **Certification Authority**. (You configure the other role services later.) Click **Next**.
8. In the Setup Type window, accept the default **Enterprise CA**, and then click **Next**.
9. In the CA Type window, accept the default **Root CA**, and then click **Next**.
10. In the Private Key window, accept the default option **Create a new private** key (see Figure 8-3). If this CA were replacing a failed CA or you had an existing certificate you wanted to use, you would click "Use existing private key." Click **Next**.
11. In the Cryptography window, accept the default selections (described after this activity), and then click **Next**.
12. The CA Name window requests a name for the CA (see Figure 8-4). By default, the name is generated automatically to include the domain name and server name followed by CA. You can also enter the distinguished name suffix, but for most situations, the default is okay. Click **Next**.
13. In the Validity Period window, you can set the validity period of the certificate issued to this CA. The validity period should be specified in the certificate practice statement. The period you choose depends on how this CA is used and the types of certificates it will issue. If the certificate expires, the CA and any certificates it has issued are no longer valid. The validity period of the CA's certificate should be longer than that of the certificates it will issue. Certificates can be renewed as needed. Accept the default **5 Years**, and then click **Next**.
14. In the Certificate Database window, you can choose where certificates and the certificate log should be stored. If the CA will be used heavily, these two databases should be stored on separate drives and shouldn't be placed on the same drive as the Windows folder. For testing purposes, you can use the default location C:\Windows\system32\CertLog for both databases. Click **Next**.
15. Click **Configure** in the Confirmation window. When the configuration is finished, click **Close**. If prompted to configure additional role services, click **No**.
16. Open a command prompt window. Type **certutil-viewstore** and press **Enter**. The View Certificate Store dialog box opens, listing all certificates currently published in Active Directory. Click **More choices** to see all the certificates. Scroll down until you see MCSA2016-SERVERDM1-CA (see Figure 8-5). Click the **MCSA2016-ServerDM1-CA** certificate, and then click the **Click here to view certificate properties** link.

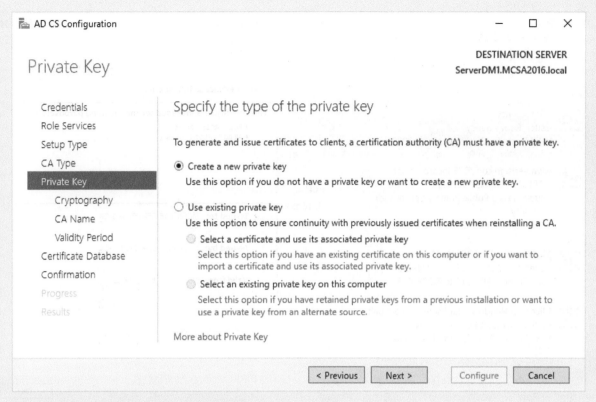

Figure 8-3   Specifying the private key

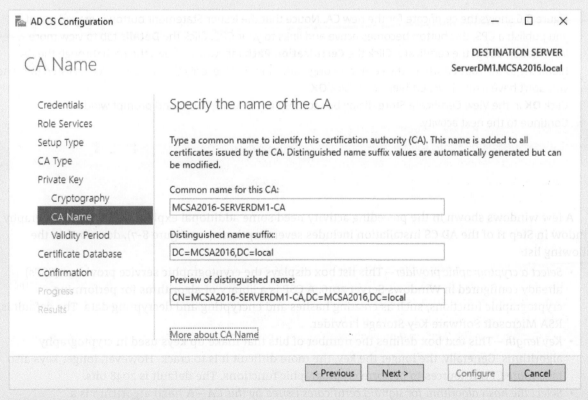

Figure 8-4   Specifying the CA name

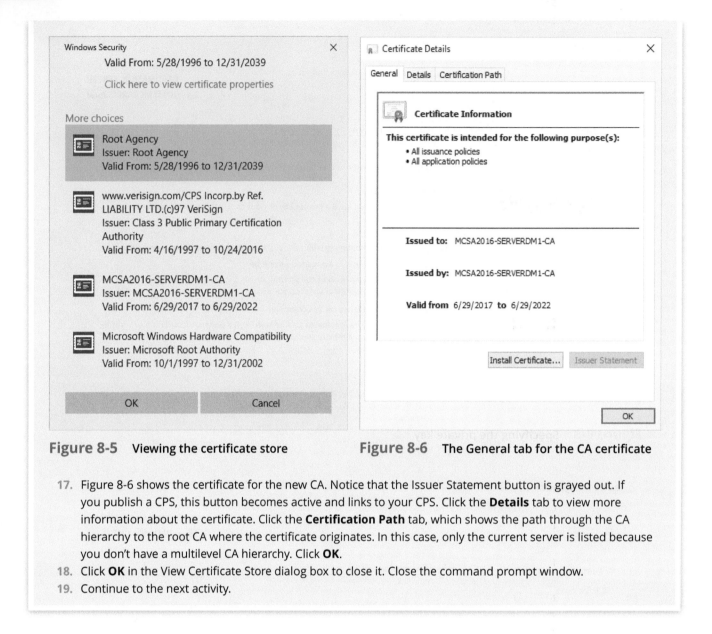

Figure 8-5 Viewing the certificate store

Figure 8-6 The General tab for the CA certificate

17. Figure 8-6 shows the certificate for the new CA. Notice that the Issuer Statement button is grayed out. If you publish a CPS, this button becomes active and links to your CPS. Click the **Details** tab to view more information about the certificate. Click the **Certification Path** tab, which shows the path through the CA hierarchy to the root CA where the certificate originates. In this case, only the current server is listed because you don't have a multilevel CA hierarchy. Click **OK**.

18. Click **OK** in the View Certificate Store dialog box to close it. Close the command prompt window.

19. Continue to the next activity.

A few windows shown in the preceding activity need some additional explanation. The Cryptography window in Step 11 of the AD CS installation includes several options (see Figure 8-7), described in the following list:

- *Select a cryptographic provider*—This list box displays the cryptographic service providers (CSPs) already configured in Windows Server 2016. A CSP is a library of algorithms for performing cryptographic functions, such as creating hashes and encrypting and decrypting data. The default is RSA Microsoft Software Key Storage Provider.
- *Key length*—This text box defines the number of bits that make up keys used in cryptography algorithms. Generally, the longer the key, the more difficult it is to crack. However, longer keys also take more CPU resources to perform cryptographic functions. The default is 2048 bits.
- *Select the hash algorithm for signing certificates issued by this CA*—A hash algorithm is a mathematical function that takes a string of data as input and produces a fixed-size value as output. Hash values are used to verify that the original data hasn't been changed and to sign the CA certificate and certificates issued by the CA. The default is SHA256.

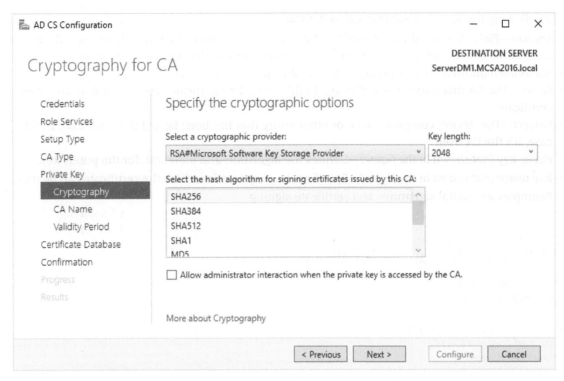

Figure 8-7   Options in the Cryptography window

- *Allow administrator interaction when the private key is accessed by the CA*—If this check box is selected, cryptographic operations require the administrator to enter a password, which helps prevent unauthorized use of the CA and its private key.

The Details tab you viewed in Step 17 of Activity 8-2 contains considerable information (see Figure 8-8).

Figure 8-8   The Details tab for a certificate

The following list describes some items in this tab:

- *Version*—Field that specifies the version of the X.509 standard that the certificate uses. X.509 is an international standard that defines many aspects of a PKI, including certificate formats.
- *Signature algorithm*—The hash algorithm used to sign the certificate.
- *Issuer*—The CA that issued the certificate. In this case, the certificate is self-signed as are all root CA certificates.
- *Subject*—The device, computer, user, or other entity that has been issued the certificate; in this case, it's the CA itself.
- *Public key (not shown in the figure)*—Defines the algorithm and bit length for the public key.
- *Key usage (not shown in the figure)*—Specifies the purposes for which the certificate can be used. Examples are digital signatures and certificate signing.

Configuring a Certification Authority

 Certification

- **70-742 – Implement Active Directory Certificate Services (AD CS):**
  Install and configure AD CS
  Manage certificates

After installing AD CS on a server, you must perform several configuration tasks, including the following, before using a new CA:

- Configure certificate templates
- Configure enrollment options
- Configure the online responder
- Create a revocation configuration

Configuring Certificate Templates

If you install an enterprise CA, some predefined certificate templates can be configured to generate certificates. Windows Server 2016 supports four versions of certificate templates:

- *Version 1 templates*—Provide backward compatibility; Windows Server 2003 Standard Edition and Windows 2000 Server support only version 1 templates. These templates can't be modified or removed, and autoenrollment is not an option. Windows Server 2016 includes several version 1 templates. You can duplicate these templates, and then they're converted to version 2 or 3 templates, which can be modified.
- *Version 2 templates*—Allow customization of most certificate settings and permit autoenrollment. They're supported by Windows Server 2003 Enterprise Edition and later.
- *Version 3 templates*—Provide advanced cryptographic functions; they can be issued only from Windows Server 2008 and later enterprise CAs and can be used only on Windows Server 2008/ Windows Vista and later clients.
- *Version 4 templates*—Can only be used only on Windows Server 2012 and Vista and later clients. Support cryptographic service providers and key service providers and enforcement of renewal with the same key. On Windows Server 2012 R2 and Windows 8.1 and later clients, Version 4 templates support Trusted Platform Module (TPM) key attestation, which lets the CA verify that the private key is protected by a hardware TPM.

Certificate templates are created and modified in the Certificate Templates snap-in (see Figure 8-9), which you can add to an MMC or open in the Certification Authority console via the Tools menu in Server Manager. Templates shown with Schema Version 1 must be duplicated before they can be modified. Each template type has different properties and a different number of tabs in the template Properties dialog boxes.

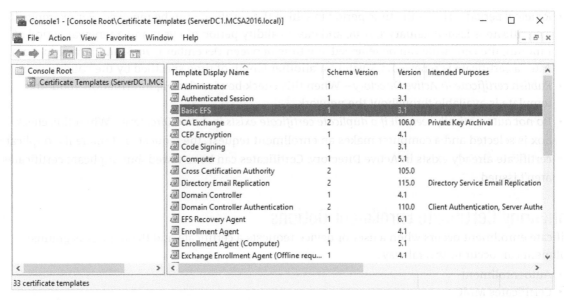

Figure 8-9   The Certificate Templates snap-in

A common certificate type is one used for EFS, which allows users to encrypt and decrypt files on a hard drive. The Basic EFS template is used to issue certificates to users so that they can protect files with EFS. The EFS Recovery Agent template is used to issue certificates to users who are designated as recovery agents so that EFS-encrypted files can be recovered if a user's EFS certificate becomes unusable for some reason.

The following list describes some options in the General tab for certificate templates (see Figure 8-10):

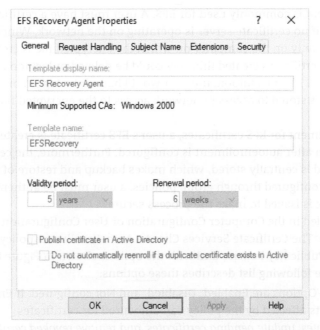

Figure 8-10   The General tab of a certificate template

- *Template display name and Template name*—By default, these two fields have the same value, but they can be different. However, after the template has been created, you can't change either name.
- *Validity period*—This is the length of time that the certificate is valid if it's not renewed. If the period elapses, the certificate expires, is invalid, and can no longer be renewed. You can specify the validity period in units of years, months, weeks, or days.

- *Renewal period*—This is the time period in which the certificate can be renewed. For example, if a certificate is issued January 1, 2018, and has a validity period of 1 year and a renewal period of 1 month, the certificate can be renewed any time between December 1, 2018, and January 1, 2019. After a certificate is renewed, it's valid for another length of time specified by the validity period.
- *Publish certificate in Active Directory*—When this check box is selected, information about the template is available throughout the network.
- *Do not automatically reenroll if a duplicate certificate exists in Active Directory*—When this check box is selected and a computer makes an enrollment request, the request isn't made if a duplicate certificate already exists in Active Directory. Certificates can be renewed, but duplicate certificates aren't issued.

Configuring Certificate Enrollment Options

Certificate enrollment occurs when a user or device requests a certificate and the request is granted. Enrollment can occur in several ways:

- Autoenrollment
- Certificates MMC
- Web enrollment
- Network Device Enrollment Service
- Smart card enrollment

Configuring Certificate Autoenrollment

When autoenrollment is configured, users and devices don't have to make an explicit request to be issued a certificate. Autoenrollment options are configured through group policies and the certificate template. In addition, the CA must be configured to allow autoenrollment, which is an option only on enterprise CAs.

Certificate autoenrollment is commonly used for EFS. A user must have a certificate to encrypt and decrypt a file with EFS. If no certificate server is operating on the network, Windows creates the certificate automatically but only on the computer on which the encrypted file is created. Without a central store of certificates, certificates created this way could be deleted or lost too easily, resulting in loss of access to the encrypted file. In addition, the user would have to be logged on to the computer on which the encrypted file is stored to access it; network access to the encrypted file wouldn't be possible.

By setting up autoenrollment for EFS certificates, a user's EFS certificate is created the first time he or she logs on to the domain after autoenrollment is configured. Furthermore, the certificate is available anywhere in the domain and is centrally stored, which makes backup and restore of the certificate easier. Because autoenrollment is configured through group policies, a user must be authenticated by a domain controller before a certificate is issued to make the process secure.

Autoenrollment is enabled in the Computer Configuration or User Configuration node of the Group Policy Management console. The Certificate Services Client - Auto-Enrollment policy, under Windows Settings, Security Settings, Public Key Policies and with the options shown in Figure 8-11, controls autoenrollment settings. The following list describes these options:

- *Configuration Model*—Options are Enabled, Disabled, and Not configured. If Enabled is selected, the Active Directory objects affected by the policy can autoenroll for certificates.
- *Renew expired certificates, update pending certificates, and remove revoked certificates*—When this check box is selected, autoenrollment is extended so that certificates are renewed, updated, and removed (for revoked certificates) automatically.
- *Update certificates that use certificate templates*—When this check box is selected, certificates created with a certificate template can be updated through autoenrollment if the template changes.
- *Log expiry events and show expiry notifications when the percentage of remaining certificate lifetime is*—This determines how much time can be left on a certificate's lifetime before a notification is issued and an event is logged.

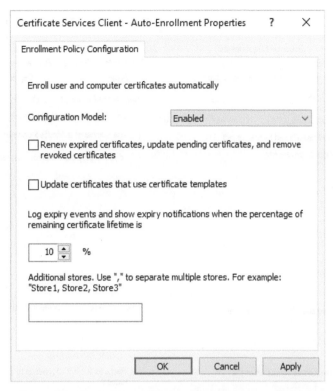

Figure 8-11   Options for the Autoenrollment policy

- *Additional stores*—This specifies additional certificate stores that should be monitored for certificate expiration. By default, the CurrentUser\My and LocalMachine\My stores are monitored.

Autoenrollment is configured for certificate templates in the Request Handling, Issuance Requirements, and Security tabs of a template's Properties dialog box. In the Request Handling tab (see Figure 8-12), you can configure the amount of user interaction required during autoenrollment with the following options:

- *Enroll subject without requiring any user input*—This option is required for autoenrollment of computers and services. You can also select it if you want user autoenrollment to occur in the background without user interaction.
- *Prompt the user during enrollment*—Users must respond to prompts during autoenrollment.
- *Prompt the user during enrollment and require user input when the private key is used*—Users must enter a password during autoenrollment and each time their private keys are used. This option is the most secure but least user friendly.

The Issuance Requirements tab has options for specifying enrollment requirements for certificates issued from the template (see Figure 8-13):

- *CA certificate manager approval*—If checked, a CA manager must approve the certificate request before it's issued.
- *This number of authorized signatures*—If checked and the number of signatures is more than zero, certificate enrollment requests must be signed with a digital signature. If more than one signature is required, autoenrollment is disabled.
- *Require the following for reenrollment*—Two options are available. If *Same criteria as for enrollment* is selected, the same process must be used for renewal that's required for initial enrollment. If *Valid existing certificate* is selected, renewal is automatic as long as the current certificate is valid.

The Security tab of a certificate template is similar to the Security tab of most Active Directory objects. By default, Domain Users group members have the Enroll permission. The Autoenroll permission must be set for users in the domain to autoenroll in the certificate.

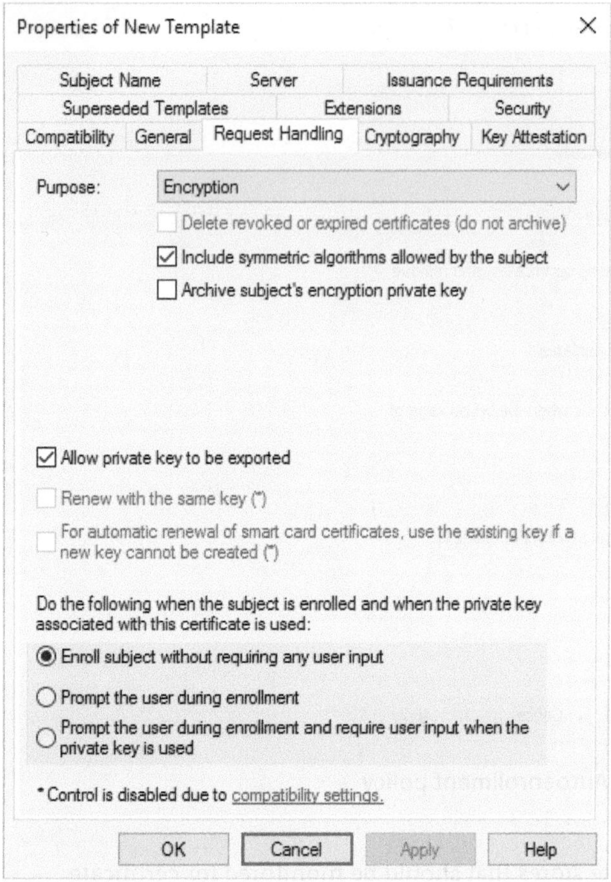

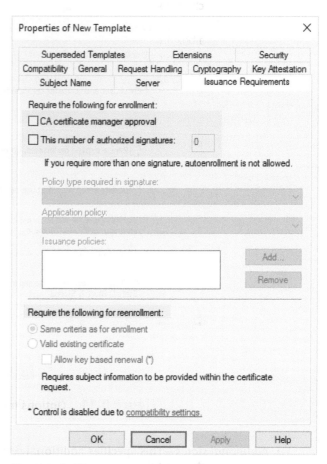

Figure 8-12 Request Handling tab on a certificate template

Figure 8-13 Issuance Requirements tab on a certificate template

The CA must be set to allow autoenrollment by configuring request-handling options (see Figure 8-14). To open this dialog box, click Properties in the Policy Module tab of a CA's Properties dialog box. The default option is *Follow the settings in the certificate template, if applicable. Otherwise, automatically issue the certificate.* This option enables the CA to autoenroll applicable templates, so normally there's no need to change it unless you want to disallow autoenrollment. The *Set the certificate request status to pending* option accepts certificate requests but requires an administrator to issue the certificate manually in the Certificates MMC.

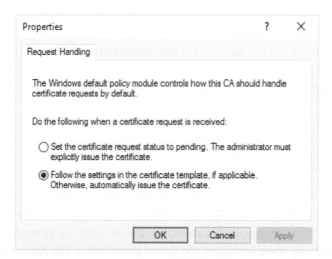

Figure 8-14 Request-handling options

The following list summarizes the steps for configuring autoenrollment after you have installed an issuing CA:

1. Create a certificate template.
2. Set options as needed in the Issuance Requirements and Request Handling tabs of the Properties dialog box.
3. Configure the template to allow autoenrollment by setting the Autoenroll permission for the users or groups who should autoenroll for the certificate.
4. Configure the Certificate Services Client - Auto-Enrollment policy.
5. Make sure the CA's request-handling options are configured to allow autoenrollment.
6. Add the template to the Certificate Templates folder under the CA server node.

Requesting a Certificate with the Certificates Snap-in

Users can request certificates that aren't configured for autoenrollment by using the Certificates snap-in. To do so, make sure you're signed in to the domain. Then right-click the Certificates folder under the Personal folder, point to All Tasks, and click Request New Certificate to start the Certificate Enrollment Wizard.

The Request Certificates window (shown in Figure 8-15) lists the certificates available for this method. If you click the *Show all templates* check box, other templates are listed but have the status Unavailable. Select the certificates you want to enroll in, and click Details to see the certificate's validity period and how the certificate key can be used. This method for requesting certificates can be used only with enterprise CAs.

Figure 8-15   Using the Certificate Enrollment Wizard

In most cases, autoenrollment is preferred over manual requests. If you want users to know their certificate information or you have specialized templates that only a few users require, you might want to use manual requests.

Configuring Web Enrollment

After autoenrollment, the most common certificate request method is web enrollment, which requires installing the Certification Authority Web Enrollment role service in Server Manager. This role service enables users to request and renew certificates, retrieve CRLs, and enroll for smart card certificates via their web browsers. Web enrollment is the main method for accessing CA services on a standalone CA because, as mentioned, autoenrollment and the Certificates snap-in can be used only with enterprise CAs.

To access the Certification Authority Web Enrollment role service, users simply open a browser and go to *http://CAServer.domain/certsrv*; *CAServer* is the name of the CA server, and *domain* is the domain name. The server with the Web Enrollment role service installed can be, but need not be, the CA server. A server configured for web enrollment is called a **registration authority** or a *CA web proxy*.

Using the Network Device Enrollment Service

The **Network Device Enrollment Service (NDES)** allows network devices, such as routers and switches, to get certificates by using Simple Certificate Enrollment Protocol (SCEP), a Cisco proprietary protocol. With this protocol, Cisco internetworking devices can request and get certificates to run IPsec even if they don't have domain credentials. The procedure for installing and configuring NDES involves the following steps:

1. Create a user for NDES and add it to the IIS_USRS group.
2. Configure a certificate template with Enroll permission assigned to the NDES user.
3. Install the NDES role service.
4. Create a public/private key pair, using the network device's OS to enroll.
5. Forward the key pair to the registration authority on the server hosting NDES.
6. Submit a certificate request from the device to the NDES server.

Tip ⓘ

For more information on using NDES, see *http://aka.ms/ndes*.

Using Smart Card Enrollment

Smart card enrollment is not so much an enrollment method as a specialized type of certificate template. It takes place through web enrollment at a smart card station. After a user supplies credentials to request the smart card certificate and presents his or her card, the certificate information is embedded in the card.

Smart cards are used to enhance security. Users can sign in to a network by presenting the card to a station with a card reader and entering a PIN, much like using an ATM card. A user designated as an enrollment agent can enroll smart card certificates on behalf of users to simplify the process. However, enrollment agents can enroll on behalf of any user, including administrators, which could pose a security risk. After a smart card is created for a user, the card can be used to sign in as that user. Enrollment agents must be issued an Enrollment Agent certificate to perform this task, but considering the power that an enrollment agent has, these people must be highly trusted in the organization.

To mitigate security concerns, AD CS offers restricted enrollment agents. With this feature, administrators can configure smart card certificate templates to specify which users or groups an enrollment agent can enroll in the certificate. To do this, use the *Restrict enrollment agents* option in the Enrollment Agents tab of the CA server's Properties dialog box. By default, enrollment agents are not restricted.

Configuring the Online Responder

An **online responder (OR)** enables clients to check a certificate's revocation status without having to download the CRL. To use an OR, you install the Online Responder role service. You can install this role service on the same server as the CA role or a different server, and it requires the Web Server role service. After the OR role service is installed, it must be configured with these steps:

1. Configure an OCSP Response Signing certificate template, which is used to sign the response that the OR provides to certificate revocation queries. (OCSP stands for Online Certificate Status Protocol.)

2. Configure the CA to support the online responder. An Authority Information Access (AIA) extension is configured on a CA to indicate the OR's location.

3. Add the OCSP Response Signing Certificate template to the CA, and enroll the OR with this certificate.

4. Configure revocation for the OR, including the settings required for the OR to reply to certificate status requests.

Creating a Revocation Configuration

A revocation configuration tells the CA what methods are available for clients to access CRLs. To create one, you use the Active Directory Certificate Services snap-in under the Roles node in Server Manager. The steps are described later in Activity 8-10.

To configure the CRL distribution schedule, right-click the Revoked Certificates folder in the Certification Authority console and click Properties to open the Revoked Certificates Properties dialog box (see Figure 8-16). The default CRL publication interval is 1 week, and the default publication interval for delta CRLs is 1 day. You can change the publication interval for the CRL from as little as 1 hour to as many as 999 years and the delta CRL from 30 minutes to 999 years. In addition, you can right-click the Revoked Certificates folder, point to All Tasks, and click Publish to publish the CRL immediately.

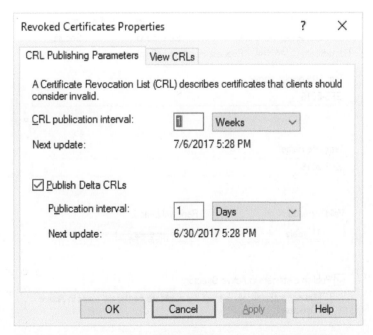

Figure 8-16 Configuring the CRL publishing schedule

One way to test the OR's configuration is to issue and then revoke some certificates. You can revoke certificates in the Certification Authority console by clicking Issued Certificates, right-clicking a certificate, pointing to All Tasks, and clicking Revoke Certificate. Then open a web browser and go to *http://ServerDM1.MCSA2016.local/CertEnroll/MCSA2016-ServerDM1-CA.crl*. After you download this CRL file, open it. The Revocation List tab lists serial numbers and revocation dates for revoked certificates.

Activity 8-3: Creating an EFS Certificate Template

Time Required: 10 minutes

Objective: Create an EFS certificate template.

Required Tools and Equipment: ServerDC1, ServerDM1

Description: You want to issue certificates to employees so that they can use EFS throughout the domain. In this activity, you duplicate the version 1 Basic EFS template and create a version 3 EFS template for use on Windows 10 and Windows Server 2016 clients.

1. On ServerDM1 from Server Manager, click **Tools, Certification Authority**. Click to expand the server node. Right-click **Certificate Templates** and click **Manage** to open the Certificate Templates console.

2. Right-click **Basic EFS** in the right pane and click **Properties**. Notice that all options are grayed out because you must duplicate the version 1 template to make changes. Click **Cancel**.

3. Right-click **Basic EFS** and click **Duplicate Template**. In the Properties of New Template dialog box, you can select the minimum version of Windows Server with which you want the certificate to be compatible. In the Certification Authority list box, click **Windows Server 2016**. Click **OK** in the Resulting changes dialog box. In the Certificate recipient list box, click **Windows 10/Windows Server 2016**. Click **OK** in the Resulting changes dialog box.

4. Click the **General** tab, and type **EFS-2016** in the Template display name text box (see Figure 8-17). Notice that the certificate is set to publish in Active Directory automatically.

Figure 8-17 Changing the display name on a new template

5. Click the **Request Handling** tab. Click the **Purpose** list arrow to view the options for certificates created with this template. Leave **Encryption** as the selected purpose. Review the other options in this tab.
6. Click the **Superseded Templates** tab. Click **Add**, click **Basic EFS** in the Certificate templates list box, and then click **OK.** Now when a request for an EFS certificate is made, only the new EFS-2016 certificate is used.
7. Browse through the options in other tabs to see the configuration settings available for this template, and click **OK** when you're finished. Close the Certificate Templates console and Certification Authority console.
8. Continue to the next activity.

Activity 8-4: Configuring EFS Certificate Autoenrollment

Time Required: 20 minutes
Objective: Configure autoenrollment for users to use EFS.
Required Tools and Equipment: ServerDC1, ServerDM1
Description: In this activity, you configure autoenrollment by configuring group policies and certificate template properties.

1. On ServerDC1, open the Group Policy Management console. Click to select the **Group Policy Objects** folder.
2. Right-click the **Group Policy Objects** folder and click **New**. Type **CertAutoEnroll** in the Name text box, and then click **OK**.
3. Right-click **CertAutoEnroll** and click **Edit**. In the Group Policy Management Editor, click to expand **User Configuration, Policies, Windows Settings, Security Settings**, and **Public Key Policies**. Click to select **Public Key Policies**. In the right pane, double-click **Certificate Services Client - Auto-Enrollment**. (*Note*: Make sure that you configure the policy in the User Configuration section of the GPO, not the Computer Configuration section.)
4. In the Enrollment Policy Configuration tab, click the **Configuration Model** list arrow and click **Enabled**. Click the **Renew expired certificates, update pending certificates, and remove revoked certificates** check box and the **Update certificates that use certificate templates** check box. Click **OK**. Close the Group Policy Management Editor.
5. In the Group Policy Management console, right-click the domain node and click **Link an Existing GPO.** In the Select GPO list box, click **CertAutoEnroll**, and then click **OK**. Close the Group Policy Management console.
6. On ServerDM1, in Server Manager click **Tools, Certification Authority**. Click to expand the server node. Right-click **Certificate Templates** and click **Manage** to open the Certificate Templates console.
7. Double-click **EFS-2016** to open its Properties dialog box, and then click the **Security** tab. Click **Domain Users**, click the **Autoenroll** permission in the Allow column, and then click **OK**. Close the Certificate Templates console.
8. In the left pane of the Certification Authority console, right-click the CA server node **(MCSA2016-ServerDM1-CA)** and click **Properties**.
9. Click the **Policy Module** tab, and then click **Properties**. Verify that the **Follow the settings in the certificate template, if applicable. Otherwise, automatically issue the certificate** option button is selected, and then click **Cancel** twice.
10. In the Certification Authority console, click the **Certificate Templates** folder. The listed templates represent the certificates that this CA can issue. Right-click the **Certificate Templates** folder, point to **New**, and click **Certificate Template to Issue**.
11. In the Enable Certificate Templates dialog box, click **EFS-2016**, and then click **OK**. Your CA is now ready to issue EFS certificates through autoenrollment. (*Note*: If you do not see the EFS-2016 template right away, close the Certification Authority console, wait a few minutes, and try Steps 8–11 again.)
12. Sign out of ServerDM1 and continue to the next activity.

Activity 8-5: Testing EFS Certificate Autoenrollment

Time Required: 20 minutes

Objective: Test EFS certificate autoenrollment.

Required Tools and Equipment: ServerDC1, ServerDM1

Description: You have configured a certificate template to autoenroll members of the Domain Users group with an EFS certificate. You test the configuration by signing in to the domain from ServerDM1 using a test user account and verifying that a new certificate has been issued.

1. On ServerDM1 sign in to the domain as **domuser1** with password **Password01**.
2. When you sign in, autoenrollment of user certificates takes place. To verify that the EFS-2016 certificate has been issued, you can view your certificates. Right-click **Start**, click **Run**, type **MMC** in the Open text box, and press **Enter**.
3. Click **File, Add/Remove Snap-in** from the MMC menu. In the Available snap-ins list box, click **Certificates**, and then click **Add**. Click **OK**.
4. In the left pane, click to expand **Certificates - Current User** and **Personal**, and then click **Certificates**. The issued EFS-2016 certificate is displayed in the right pane (see Figure 8-18). Note that the Intended Purposes column shows Encrypting File System. (*Note:* If you don't see the certificate, you might need to run gpupdate from a command prompt on ServerDM1, sign out, sign in again as domuser1, and then repeat this step.)

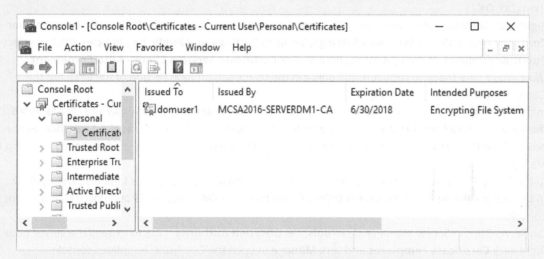

Figure 8-18 Viewing issued certificates

5. In the left pane, click to expand **Trusted Root Certification Authorities**, and click the **Certificates** folder to view certificates of CAs your computer trusts. MCSA2016-ServerDM1-CA should be listed near the top. Close the MMC. When prompted to save the console, click **No**. Sign out of ServerDM1 and sign in again as the domain administrator (remember to sign in using mcsa2016\administrator as the user name).
6. On ServerDM1, open the Certification Authority console and click the **Issued Certificates** folder. The EFS-2016 certificate for domuser1 and administrator are listed (the administrator account was issued a certificate when you signed in as administrator in the previous step). You will also see one or more certificates issued to ServerDC1.
7. Close the Certification Authority console. Continue to the next activity.

Activity 8-6: Installing the Web Enrollment Role Service

Time Required: 20 minutes

Objective: Install the Web Enrollment role service.

Required Tools and Equipment: ServerDC1, ServerDM1

Description: In this activity, you install the Certification Authority Web Enrollment role service with PowerShell and test it by requesting a certificate from ServerDM1. (If you want to test the configuration from your CA server or domain controller, you must enable IE to run ActiveX controls.)

1. On ServerDM1, in Server Manager, click the notifications flag, and then click the **Configure Active Directory Certificate Services on the destination server** link. The AD CS Configuration Wizard starts. In the Credentials window, click **Next**.

2. In the Role Services window, click **Certification Authority Web Enrollment**, and then click **Next**. In the Confirmation window, click **Configure**. Click **Close**. If you're prompted to configure additional role services, click **No**.

3. IIS must have a Web Server Certificate. To request one, click **Tools, Internet Information Services (IIS) Manager** from the Server Manager menu.

4. In the left pane of IIS Manager, click the **ServerDM1** node. In the middle pane, double-click **Server Certificates**.

5. In the Actions pane, click **Create Domain Certificate** to start the Create Certificate Wizard. In the Distinguished Name Properties window shown in Figure 8-19, fill in the following information:
   - Common name: **ServerDM1.MCSA2016.local**
   - Organization: **Server 2016 Class**
   - Organizational unit: *Your name*
   - City/locality: *Your city*
   - State/province: *Your state or province*
   - Country/region: *Your country*

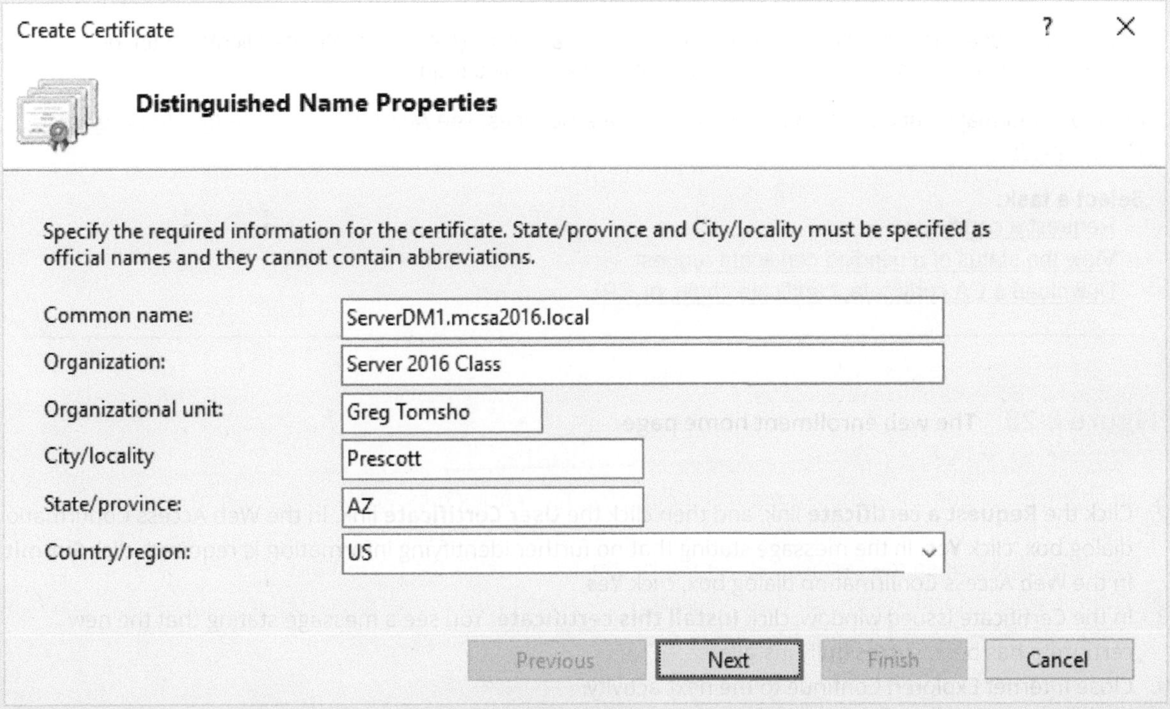

Figure 8-19   Entering distinguished name information

6. Click **Next**. In the Online Certification Authority window, click **Select**, click **MCSA2016-ServerDM1-CA**, and then click **OK**. In the Friendly name text box, type **ServerDM1.MCSA2016.local**, and then click **Finish**.

7. In the left pane of IIS Manager, click the **Sites** node. Right-click **Default Web Site** and click **Bindings**.

8. In the Site Bindings dialog box, click **Add**. In the Add Site Binding dialog box, click the **Type** list arrow and click **https**. Click the **SSL certificate** list arrow, click **ServerDM1.MCSA2016.local**, and then click **OK**. Click **Close**.

9. In the left pane of IIS Manager, click to expand **Default Web Site**, and then click **CertSrv**. In the middle pane, double-click **SSL Settings**. In the SSL Settings dialog box, click **Require SSL**. Notice the options under Client certificates. You can have the Web server ignore, accept, or require client certificates. If you want client computers to connect to the Web server to verify their identity, you would select Require. For now, leave the default **Ignore** selected. Click **Apply** in the Actions pane, and then close IIS Manager.

10. To test your configuration, first you need to turn off IE enhanced security. On ServerDC1, from Server Manager, click **Local Server**. Click the link next to **IE Enhanced Security Configuration**. Click the **Off** option button for both Administrators and Users and click **OK**.

11. Open **Internet Explorer**, type **https://ServerDM1.MCSA2016.local/certsrv** in the Address box, and press **Enter**. (If you see a Security Alert dialog box, click the check box and then click **OK**). When prompted for a user name and password, sign in as **domuser1** with **Password01** and click **OK**. The web enrollment home page opens (see Figure 8-20).

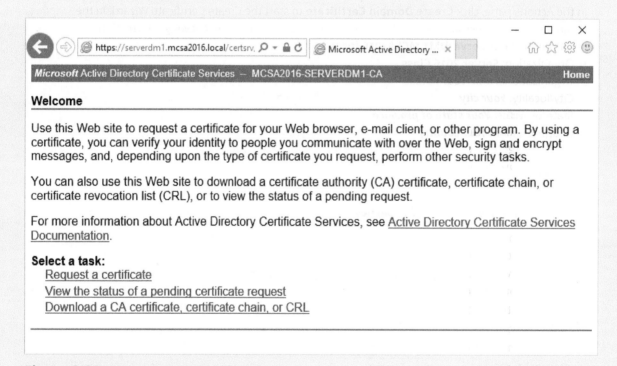

Figure 8-20 The web enrollment home page

12. Click the **Request a certificate** link, and then click the **User Certificate** link. In the Web Access Confirmation dialog box, click **Yes**. In the message stating that no further identifying information is required, click **Submit**. In the Web Access Confirmation dialog box, click **Yes**.

13. In the Certificate Issued window, click **Install this certificate.** You see a message stating that the new certificate has been successfully installed.

14. Close Internet Explorer. Continue to the next activity.

Activity 8-7: Configuring an OCSP Response Signing Certificate Template

Time Required: 20 minutes

Objective: Configure an OCSP Response Signing Certificate template.

Required Tools and Equipment: ServerDC1, ServerDM1

Description: In this activity, you configure an online responder to field certificate status requests instead of requiring clients to download the CRL. You have already installed the Online Responder role service. Now you need to configure it.

1. On ServerDM1, in Server Manager, click the notifications flag, and click the **Configure Active Directory Certificate Services on the destination server** link. The AD CS Configuration Wizard starts. In the Credentials window, click **Next**.

2. In the Role Services window, click **Online Responder**, and then click **Next**. In the Confirmation window, click **Configure**. Click **Close**.

3. Open the Certification Authority console. Click to expand the server node. Right-click **Certificate Templates** and click **Manage**. In the right pane of the Certificate Templates console, right-click the **OCSP Response Signing** template and click **Duplicate Template**.

4. In the Properties of New Template dialog box, click the **General** tab, type **OCSP-2016** in the Template display name text box, and then click the **Publish certificate in Active Directory** check box.

5. Click the **Security** tab, and then click the **Add** button. In the Select Users, Computers, Service Accounts, or Groups dialog box, click **Object Types**. Click the **Computers** check box, and then click **OK**. Type **ServerDM1** and click **Check Names**. Click **OK**.

6. Click the **Enroll** and **Autoenroll** permissions in the Allow column, and then click **OK**. Close the Certificate Templates console.

7. The next step is to add the template to the CA. In the Certification Authority console, right-click **Certificate Templates**, point to **New**, and click **Certificate Template to Issue**.

8. In the Enable Certificate Templates list box, click **OCSP-2016**, and then click **OK**.

9. Next, you must inform the CA of the online responder's location. Right-click the CA server node and click **Properties**. Click the **Extensions** tab. Click the **Select extension** list arrow, and then click **Authority Information Access (AIA)**.

10. In the *Specify locations from which users can obtain the certificate for this CA* list box, click the entry starting with **http**. Click the **Include in the online certificate status protocol (OCSP) extension** check box (see Figure 8-21), and then click **OK**.

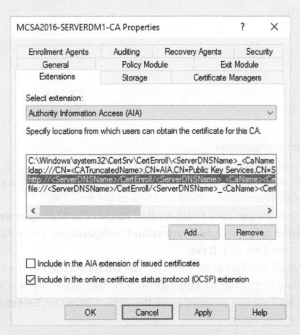

Figure 8-21 The Extensions tab

11. When you're prompted to restart Active Directory Certificate Services, click **Yes**.

12. Now the OR server (ServerDM1 in this case) must enroll in the signing certificate you configured earlier in this activity. You can do this by restarting the server or requesting it manually. The next activity goes through the steps to request the certificate manually so that the server doesn't have to be restarted. Continue to the next activity.

Activity 8-8: Requesting the OCSP Response Signing Certificate

Time Required: 10 minutes

Objective: Request the OCSP Response Signing certificate.

Required Tools and Equipment: ServerDC1, ServerDM1

Description: In this activity, to avoid restarting the OR server, you request the OCSP Response Signing certificate in the Certificates snap-in.

1. On ServerDM1, right-click **Start**, click **Run**, type **MMC** in the Open text box, and press **Enter**. Click **File, Add/Remove Snap-in** from the MMC menu.

2. Click **Certificates**, and then click the **Add** button. In the Certificates snap-in dialog box, click the **Computer account** option button, and then click **Next**. In the Select Computer dialog box, leave the default selection **Local computer**, click **Finish**, and then click **OK**.

3. In the left pane, click to expand the **Certificates** node and the **Personal** folder, and then click **Certificates**. Notice that two certificates are issued to this computer.

4. Right-click the **Certificates** folder, point to **All Tasks**, and click **Request New Certificate** to start the Certificate Enrollment Wizard. Click **Next** twice.

5. In the Request Certificates window, click the **OCSP-2016** check box, click the **Enroll** button, and then click **Finish**.

6. Click the **Certificates** folder again. You should see the new OCSP-2016 certificate in the list (scroll to the right to see the template from which the certificate was created).

7. The last step is configuring the certificate. Right-click the **OCSP Signing** certificate, point to **All Tasks**, and click **Manage Private Keys**.

8. In the Security tab, click **Add**. In the *Enter the object names to select* text box, type **Network Service**, click **Check Names**, and then click **OK**. Click **OK**, and then close the MMC. Click **No** when prompted to save the console.

9. Continue to the next activity.

Activity 8-9: Creating a Revocation Configuration for the OR

Time Required: 10 minutes

Objective: Create a revocation configuration.

Required Tools and Equipment: ServerDC1, ServerDM1

Description: You're almost finished configuring the online responder. The last task is creating the revocation configuration so that the CA can direct clients where and how to get their CRL.

1. On ServerDM1, in Server Manager, click **Tools, Online Responder Management** from the menu. Right-click **Revocation Configuration** and click **Add Revocation Configuration**. In the Add Revocation Configuration Wizard's Getting started window, click **Next**.

2. In the Name the Revocation Configuration window, type **ORServerDM1** in the Name text box. The name should describe the online responder function and include the server name. Click **Next**.

3. In the Select CA Certificate Location window, leave the default selection **Select a certificate for an Existing enterprise CA**, and then click **Next**.

4. In the Choose CA Certificate window, click **Browse** next to the *Browse CA certificates published in Active Directory* text box. The Select Certification Authority message box opens. Because there's only one choice, click **OK**. The Online Responder Signing certificate is loaded automatically. Click **Next**.

5. In the Select Signing Certificate window (see Figure 8-22), accept the defaults, and then click **Next**.

Figure 8-22   The Select Signing Certificate window

6. In the Revocation Provider window, click the **Provider** button, and then click **Add**. Type **http://ServerDM1.MCSA2016.local/CertEnroll/MCSA2016-ServerDM1-CA.crl**, and click **OK**.

7. Under the Delta CRLs text box, click **Add**. In the Add/Edit URL text box, type **http://ServerDM1.MCSA2016.local/CertEnroll/MCSA2016-ServerDM1-CA.crl**, and then click **OK** twice. In the wizard's final window, click **Finish**.

8. Read the information on the Online Responder Configuration window, close all open windows, and continue to the next activity.

Maintaining and Managing a PKI

 **Certification**

- **70-742 – Implement Active Directory Certificate Services (AD CS):**
  Install and configure AD CS
  Manage certificates

CA servers, issued certificates, and associated private keys are critical components of a network that depends on a public key infrastructure, so these components must be maintained and protected against disasters. In addition, key CA administrative roles must be assigned to responsible, trusted users to carry out the numerous tasks in maintaining a PKI environment.

Windows Server includes CA role-based administration, which limits the PKI tasks that a domain administrator account can perform. By default, administrators can perform all tasks on a CA server. However, after roles have been assigned, administrators can perform only tasks related to their assigned roles. Whether you use role-based administration or not, four key roles must be filled to administer a CA and its components:

- *CA Administrator*—Configures and maintains CA servers. This role can assign all other CA roles and renew the CA certificate. To assign this role, give the selected user the Manage CA permission in the Security tab of the CA server's Properties dialog box.
- *Certificate Manager*—Approves requests for certificate enrollment and revocation. To assign this role, give the selected user the Issue and Manage Certificates permission in the Security tab of the CA server's Properties dialog box.
- *Backup Operator*—Is not so much a CA role as an OS right. Members of the local Backup Operators group or a user who has been assigned the *Back up files and directories* and *Restore files and directories* rights can perform this role.
- *Auditor*—Manages auditing logs. Assigning the *Manage auditing and security log* right confers this role on a user.

CA Backup and Restore

Regular backup of all servers in a network is mandatory. When a full backup or system state backup is performed on a CA server, the certificate store is backed up along with other data. You might also want to back up the certificate database on each CA separately. The Certification Authority console includes a simple wizard-based backup utility you can use to perform backups with the following options:

- *Private key and CA certificate*—Backs up only the local CA's certificate and private key.
- *Certificate database and certificate database log*—Backs up the certificates issued by this CA. If your certificate database is large, you can choose to perform incremental backups, which back up only the changes to the database since the last full or incremental backup.

You can also use the `certutil` command-line program to back up the CA, and you can automate the process by using the command in a batch file or script and use Windows Task Scheduler to do periodic backups of the CA database.

Like backups, CA restores can be done with the Active Directory Certificate Services snap-in or the `certutil` command. Before you can restore the CA database, however, the CA service must be stopped. When you start the CA Restore Wizard, you're prompted to stop the service.

Key and Certificate Archival and Recovery

If a user's private key is lost or damaged, he or she might lose access to systems or documents. If the key has been used for authentication to a system, a new certificate and key can be issued. However, if the key was used for applications such as EFS, the user loses access to encrypted documents. If a data recovery agent has been assigned to the user's documents, they can be recovered, but data recovery agents should be used only when there's no hope of the document owner regaining access to the files. By using **key archival**, private keys can be locked away and then restored if the user's private key is lost. Private keys can be lost if a user's profile is lost or corrupted or a smart card holding the private key is lost or damaged.

There are two methods for archiving private keys. Manual archival requires users to export their keys to a file by using the Certificates snap-in. The file is password protected, and the password must be entered to import the key. The certificate to which the private key is related must allow the private key to be exported. The default setting for private key export depends on the type of certificate template. For example, the default setting on an EFS or a User certificate template is to allow exportation. The default setting on a Computer or an IPsec template is not to allow the private key to be exported.

The procedure for exporting the private key for a certificate is straightforward:

1. Open the Certificates snap-in in an MMC.
2. Locate the certificate for the key that you want to export. Right-click the certificate, point to All Tasks, and click Export.
3. The Certificate Export Wizard walks you through the process.

The Certificate Export Wizard exports the certificate and can export the private key if allowed. You're prompted to select the format for the certificate export (see Figure 8-23). However, the only format supported for exporting the private key along with the certificate is Personal Information Exchange. If only the certificate is exported, other formats are enabled. You might want to export the certificate without the private key if the certificate is to be used on another computer or OS or for later recovery if the certificate is lost. To import a certificate and/or the private key, in the Certificates snap-in, simply right-click the folder where you want to import the key, point to All Tasks, and click Import. You're asked to supply the password used when the certificate was exported.

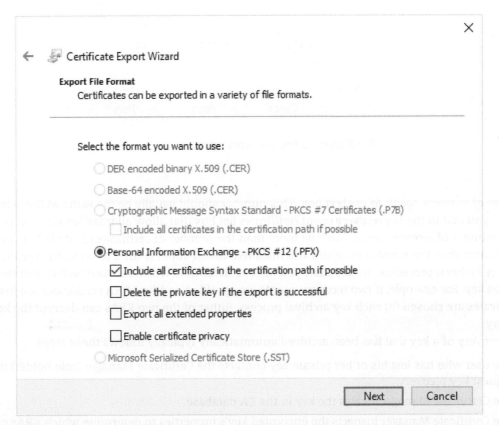

Figure 8-23   Selecting an export format for a certificate

Manual key archival is fine for a network with few users and keys to manage. However, Windows Server offers automatic key archival when manual key archival isn't adequate. Automatic key archival uses a **key recovery agent (KRA)**, which is a designated user with the right to recover archived keys. A KRA has a lot of power, so the user should be chosen carefully. The designated user must enroll for a Key Recovery Certificate after the Key Recovery Agent template has been configured to allow the designated user to enroll. The Key Recovery Agent certificate is then added to the Recovery Agent tab of the CA server's Properties dialog box (see Figure 8-24).

After a KRA is assigned, the key for each certificate issued from a certificate template with key export enabled is archived automatically. Multiple KRAs can be assigned to a certificate by entering a value in

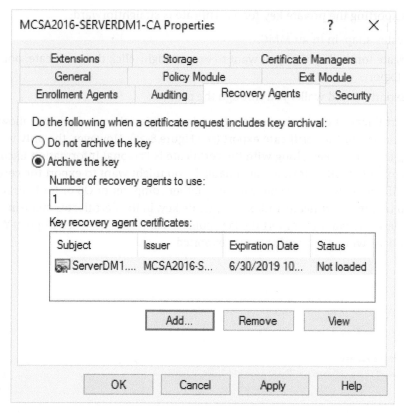

Figure 8-24   Configuring a key recovery agent

the *Number of recovery agents to use* text box. This number should usually be the same as the number of certificates you add to the *Key recovery agent certificates* list box that allow all installed KRAs to recover keys. The number of recovery agents can't be more than the number of certificates installed. If you specify a number lower than the number of certificates installed, round-robin is used to select the certificates for each key archival procedure. In this case, you have to determine which recovery agents can recover an archived key. For example, if two recovery agents are specified and four KRA certificates are installed, two certificates are chosen for each key archival process. Either of the two KRAs can decrypt the key for recovery.

The recovery of a key that has been archived automatically typically follows these steps:

1. The user who has lost his or her private key contacts the Certificate Manager (role holder) to request key recovery.
2. The Certificate Manager locates the key in the CA database.
3. The Certificate Manager inspects the encrypted key's properties to determine which KRAs can recover the key. The Certificate Manager can copy the key from the CA database but can't decrypt the key unless he or she is also a designated KRA.
4. The key is sent to a KRA for decryption.
5. The KRA decrypts the key and sends it to the user in a password-protected file.
6. The user imports the key using the password supplied by the KRA.

Using Windows PowerShell to Manage AD CS

Table 8-3 lists some PowerShell cmdlets for managing AD CS. To see the full list of cmdlets for AD CS administration, type `Get-Command -Module AdcsAdministration`. To see the full list of cmdlets for AD CS deployment, type `Get-Command -Module AdcsDeployment`.

Table 8-3   PowerShell cmdlets for AD CS

Cmdlet	Description
Add-CACrlDistributionPoint	Adds a CRL distribution point path indicating where the CA publishes certification revocations
Add-CATemplate	Adds a certificate template to the CA
Backup-CARoleService	Backs up the CA database and all private key data
Get-CACrlDistributionPoint	Gets all the locations set on the CRL
Get-CATemplate	Gets the list of templates the CA can use to issue certificates
Remove-CACrlDistributionPoint	Removes the CRL distribution point
Remove-CATemplate	Removes the templates the CA can use to issue certificates
Restore-CARoleService	Restores the CA database and all private key data
Install-AdcsCertificationAuthority	Configures the Certification Authority role service
Install-AdcsNetworkDeviceEnrollmentService	Configures the Network Device Enrollment Service
Install-AdcsOnlineResponder	Configures the Online Responder role service
Install-AdcsWebEnrollment	Configures the Certification Authority Web Enrollment role service

Activity 8-10: Backing Up the CA Server and Archiving a Key

Time Required: 10 minutes
Objective: Back up the CA server and archive a private key.
Required Tools and Equipment: ServerDC1, ServerDM1
Description: In this activity, you perform a backup of the CA certificate, private key, and certificate database. Then, you archive a private key.

1. First, you need to create a folder for storing the backup. Normally, this folder is on another server or removable media. For this activity, on ServerDM1, create a folder named **CABack** in the root of the C drive.
2. Open the Certification Authority console. Right-click the CA server node, point to **All Tasks**, and click **Back up CA** to start the Certification Authority Backup Wizard. Click **Next** in the welcome window.
3. In the Items to Back Up window, click **Private key and CA certificate** and **Certificate database and certificate database log**.
4. Click the **Browse** button next to the *Back up to this location* text box. In the Browse For Folder dialog box, navigate to and click the **CABack** folder you just created, and click **OK**. Click **Next**.
5. In the Password and Confirm password text boxes, type **Password01**, and then click **Next**. In the Completing the Certification Authority Backup Wizard window, click **Finish**. The backup begins.
6. When the backup is finished, close the Certification Authority console. Next, you'll archive a private key using the Certificates snap-in.
7. Open an MMC and add the **Certificates** snap-in to it using the default options. In the left pane, click to expand the Certificates node and the **Personal** folder, and then click the **Certificates** folder.
8. Right-click the certificate, point to **All Tasks**, and click **Export**. In the Certificate Export Wizard's welcome window, click **Next**.
9. Click the **Yes, export the private key** option button, and then click **Next**.
10. In the Export File Format window, leave the **Personal Information Exchange - PKCS 12 (.PFX)** option button selected, and then click **Next**.

11. In the Security window, click the **Password** check box, type **Password01** in the Password text box and the Confirm password text box, and then click **Next**.

12. In the File to Export window, click **Browse**. Note which folder is selected as the destination folder (by default, it is the Documents folder). Type **EFSCert** in the File name text box, and click **Save**. Click **Next**.

13. In the Completing the Certificate Export Wizard window, click **Finish**. Click **OK** in the success message. Leave the Certificates snap-in open and continue to the next activity.

Activity 8-11: Recovering a Lost Key

Time Required: 15 minutes

Objective: Recover a lost key.

Required Tools and Equipment: ServerDC1, ServerDM1

Description: In this activity, you recover your private key from an archived backup.

1. First, you delete your existing certificate and key. On ServerDM1, in the left pane of the Certificates snap-in, click the **Certificates** folder, if necessary. Right-click the **EFS-2016 certificate** and click **Delete**.

2. In the message box explaining that you can't decrypt data encrypted with this certificate, click **Yes**.

3. Right-click the **Certificates** folder, point to **All Tasks**, and click **Import**. (Note that you can request a new certificate, but it can't decrypt data encrypted with the deleted certificate.)

4. The Certificate Import Wizard starts. Click **Next**.

5. In the File to Import window, click **Browse**. In the File types list box, click **Personal Information Exchange**. Click the **EFSCert** certificate that you exported in the previous activity, and then click **Open**. Click **Next**.

6. In the Private key protection window, type **Password01** in the Password text box, and then click the **Mark this key as exportable** check box. If you don't select this check box, you can't export the key again. Click **Next**.

7. In the Certificate Store window, accept the default **Personal** option, and then click **Next**.

8. In the Completing the Certificate Import Wizard window, click **Finish**. In the success message box, click **OK**. You see your EFS-2016 certificate displayed in the Certificates folder.

9. Shut down all computers.

Chapter Summary

- Active Directory Certificate Services (AD CS) provides services for creating a PKI in a Windows Server 2016 environment. A PKI enables administrators to issue and manage certificates, which can add a level of security to a network.

- A PKI binds the identity of a user or device to a cryptographic key. The main services that a PKI provides are confidentiality, integrity, nonrepudiation, and authentication.

- Some key terms for describing a PKI and AD CS include private and public keys, digital signature, certification authority, certificate revocation list, online responder, and certificate enrollment.

- An enterprise CA integrates with Active Directory; a standalone CA does not. Windows Server 2016 Enterprise Edition must be installed to install an enterprise CA. For non-Windows devices or users, you need to install a standalone CA.

- A CA can be online or offline. An offline CA is more secure and usually is used in a CA hierarchy with one or more online issuing CAs. An issuing CA issues a certificate to users and devices. A CA hierarchy is usually two or three levels. The first level is the root CA, and each level created is subordinate to the level above it.

- The AD CS role shouldn't be installed on a domain controller. An enterprise CA must be installed on a domain member server, but a standalone CA can be installed on a member server or a standalone server.

- Configuring a CA involves configuring certificate templates, enrollment options, and an online responder and creating a revocation configuration. There are four template versions, with the Version 1 templates provided for backward compatibility, and the Version 4 templates used only with Windows Server 2012/R2 and later.

- Certificate enrollment occurs when a user or device requests a certificate, and the certificate is granted. Enrollment can occur with autoenrollment, the Certificates MMC, web enrollment, NDES, and smart cards.

- An online responder allows clients to check a certificate's revocation status without having

to download the CRL periodic
Responder role service requir
Server role service, too.

- Role-based administration li
a domain administrator acco
key roles must be filled to ad
components: CA Administrator, Certificate Manager, Backup Operator, and Auditor.

- When a full backup or system state backup is performed on a CA server, the certificate store is backed up along with other data. You use the Active Directory Certificate Services snap-in to back up the certificate database and database log.

- When users' private keys are lost or damaged, they could lose access to systems or documents. Keys can be archived manually with the Certificates snap-in or automatically on enterprise CAs by assigning users as key recovery agents.

Key Terms

Active Directory Certificate
  Services (AD CS)
certificate practice statement (CPS)
certificate revocation list (CRL)
certificate template
CRL distribution point (CDP)
enterprise CA

hash algorithm
intermediate CA
issuing CA
key archival
key recovery agent (KRA)
Network Device Enrollment Service
  (NDES)

online responder (OR)
public key infrastructure
  (PKI)
registration authority
restricted enrollment agent
root CA
standalone CA

Review Questions

1. Which of the following are services provided by a PKI? (Choose all that apply.)
   a. Confidentiality   c. Authorization
   b. Nonrepudiation   d. Antivirus

2. Which of the following is used at both ends of the cryptography process (encryption and decryption) and must be known by both parties?
   a. Public key   c. Secret key
   b. Private key   d. Digital signature

3. A PKI is based on symmetric cryptography. True or False?

4. If you want the most security, which of the following should you use?
   a. Symmetric cryptography only
   b. Asymmetric cryptography only
   c. A combination of symmetric and asymmetric cryptography
   d. Secret key cryptography

5. Camille and Sophie want to engage in secure communication. Both hold a public/private key pair. Camille wants to send an encrypted message to Sophie. Which of the following happens first?
   a. Camille encrypts the message with her public key.
   b. Camille sends Sophie her private key.
   c. Sophie sends Camille her public key.
   d. Camille encrypts the message with her private key.

6. You have installed your root CA and will be taking it offline. The root CA must be which type of CA?
   a. Standalone
   b. Enterprise
   c. Intermediate
   d. Online

three-level CA hierarchy, the middle-level servers are referred to as which type of CA?
   a. Standalone
   c. Intermediate
   b. Enterprise
   d. Online

8. Which of the following identifies the CA and describes the CA's certificate renewal policy?
   a. Root CA
   c. CRL
   b. Online responder
   d. CPS

9. You're installing AD CS in your network. You need a secure environment and want to require the CA administrator to enter a password each time the CA performs cryptographic operations. Which option should you enable during installation?
   a. Select the hash algorithm for signing certificates issued by this CA.
   b. Select a cryptographic service provider (CSP).
   c. Use strong private key protection features provided by the CSP.
   d. Change the key length.

10. Version 1 templates can't be modified, but they can be duplicated and then modified. True or False?

11. A certificate is issued on July 1, 2018. Its validity period is 2 years, and its renewal period is 2 months. When can the certificate first be renewed?
   a. September 1, 2018
   c. September 1, 2020
   b. May 1, 2020
   d. May 1, 2019

12. Which of the following is *not* a necessary step to configure autoenrollment?
   a. Configure a KRA.
   b. Configure a certificate template.
   c. Configure a group policy.
   d. Add the template to the CA.

13. You want to prevent tampering on your internetworking devices by issuing these devices certificates to run IPsec. What should you install?
   a. Online responder
   c. Intermediate CA
   b. NDES role service
   d. CDP

14. Which of the following steps are necessary to configure an online responder? (Choose all that apply.)
   a. Configure an OCSP Response Signing certificate template.
   b. Enroll the OR with the OCSP Response Signing certificate.
   c. Configure the OR enrollment agent.
   d. Configure revocation for the OR.

15. Which role can renew the CA certificate?
   a. CA Administrator
   b. Certificate Manager
   c. Backup Operator
   d. Auditor

16. You want to create a separate backup for the certificate store and make sure the backup occurs every Friday at 11:00 p.m. How should you do this?
   a. Use Windows Backup to schedule a CA database backup weekly on Fridays at 11:00 p.m.
   b. Hire a technician to work Friday nights and instruct her how to use the AD CS snap-in to back up the certificate store.
   c. Use `certutil` and Windows Task Scheduler.
   d. Use the AD CS snap-in to schedule the backup.

17. To reduce the amount of traffic generated when clients download the CRL, which of the following should you use?
   a. AIA
   c. CDP
   b. Delta CRL
   d. SCEP

18. You want to begin using smart cards for user logon. The number of enrollment stations you have is limited, so you want to assign department administrators to enroll only other users in their departments in smart card certificates. How should you go about this?
   a. Issue the designated department administrators an Enrollment Agent certificate. Publish the smart card certificate template. Have the designated enrollment agents use the Certificates snap-in to enroll departmental users in the smart card certificates.
   b. Issue the designated department administrators an Enrollment Agent certificate. Configure the smart card certificate templates with the list of users each enrollment agent can enroll. Have the designated enrollment agents use web enrollment to enroll departmental users in the smart card certificates.
   c. Issue the designated department administrators an Enrollment Agent certificate. Configure the CA server's properties to restrict enrollment agents. Publish the smart card certificate template. Have the designated enrollment agents use web enrollment to enroll departmental users in the smart card certificates.
   d. Configure Enrollment Agent Certificate templates with the list of users that agents can enroll. Issue the designated department administrators an Enrollment Agent certificate. Publish the smart card certificate template. Have the designated enrollment agents use web enrollment to enroll departmental users in the smart card certificates.

19. Your company runs a commercial website that enables your business partners to purchase products and manage their accounts. You want to increase the site's security by issuing certificates to business partners to augment logon security and protect data transmissions with encryption. What should you install?

a. An online enterprise CA
b. An online standalone CA
c. An offline root CA
d. An intermediate CA

20. Which of the following is *not* a step in the recovery process for a key that has been archived automatically?

a. The key is sent to a KRA for decryption.
b. The KRA decrypts the key and sends it to the user in a password-protected file.
c. The user encrypts the password-protected file using the KRA's public key.
d. The user imports the key by using the password supplied by the KRA.

Critical Thinking

The following activities give you critical thinking challenges. Case Projects offer a scenario with a problem to solve and for which you supply a written solution.

Case Project 8-1: Designing a PKI and CA Hierarchy

You're called in as a consultant to create a CA hierarchy for a company. The company has three locations: one in the United States, one in South America, and one in Europe. Each location has approximately 1000 users who need certificates. About 75% of the users in each location are domain members running Windows 8.1 and Windows 10. The others are running a non-Windows OS and aren't domain members. Some features of the PKI should include the following:

- Web enrollment
- Autoenrollment
- Smart card enrollment in which designated users can enroll other users
- EFS
- Automatic key archival
- Network device certificates
- Real-time query for certificate revocation status

Design the CA hierarchy, and label each CA according to its function and status (standalone, enterprise, root, intermediate, issuing, online, offline). The design should include a drawing showing the hierarchy as well as a detailed description, including how users and clients interact with the systems you selected. In addition, list the role services that need to be installed and the certificate template types that must be configured.

CHAPTER 9

IMPLEMENTING IDENTITY SOLUTIONS

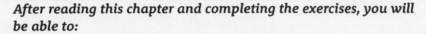

After reading this chapter and completing the exercises, you will be able to:

Deploy Active Directory Federation Services

Implement Active Directory Rights Management

Implement Web Application Proxy

Active Directory Domain Services (AD DS) is the foundation on which a Windows Server network is built. By now, you should have enough knowledge to install and set up a secure, reliable domain-based network. However, although AD DS is the core technology in a Windows Server domain, some complementary technologies installed as server roles can augment AD DS features and flexibility.

This chapter discusses three server roles: Active Directory Federation Services, Active Directory Rights Management Services, and Web Application Proxy. These roles use or integrate with AD DS technology to give users flexible, secure access to applications and network resources.

Table 9-1 lists what you need for the hands-on activities in this chapter.

Table 9-1   Activity requirements

Activity	Requirements	Notes
Activity 9-1: Resetting Your Virtual Environment	ServerDC1, ServerDM1, ServerDM2, ServerSA1	
Activity 9-2: Preparing for AD FS Deployment	ServerDC1	
Activity 9-3: Installing the AD FS Role	ServerDC1	
Activity 9-4: Installing the AD RMS Role	ServerDC1, ServerDM1	
Activity 9-5: Creating a Rights Policy Template	ServerDC1, ServerDM1	
Activity 9-6: Exploring the Active Directory Rights Management Services Console	ServerDC1, ServerDM1	

Active Directory Federation Services

 **Certification**

- **70-742 – Implement identity federation and access solutions:**
  Install and configure Active Directory Federation Services (AD FS)

The **Active Directory Federation Services (AD FS)** server role allows single sign-on access to web-based resources even when resources are in a different forest or a different network belonging to another organization. A typical situation is a user in Company A who needs to access resources in partner Company B with a web browser, so Company B sets up a secondary account for the Company A user. The user is prompted for credentials when attempting resource access. If the number of users involved in this type of transaction is low, the extra work required to maintain users is minimal. The inconvenience of having to enter credentials each time the resource is accessed might not be a major burden. However, if many users must be maintained or users must communicate with many external companies, a single sign-on might be warranted. AD FS is designed for just this situation.

AD FS Overview

AD FS provides functions similar to a one-way forest trust except that in a forest trust, domain controllers in each forest must be able to communicate directly with one another without interruption of service. As a result, when forests are hosted on separate organizations' networks, firewalls on the networks must be configured to allow Active Directory communication, which raises security concerns. AD FS is designed to work over the public Internet with a web browser interface. Its main purpose is to allow secure business-to-business transactions over the Internet; users need to sign in only to their local networks. AD FS servers and AD FS–enabled web servers then manage authentication and access to resources on partner networks without additional user sign-ins.

Like most OS technologies, AD FS has its own terms for describing its components. The next sections discuss some terms and components used by AD FS.

Federation Trusts

A **federation trust**, like other types of trust relationships, involves a trusting party and trusted party. Because AD FS is designed to facilitate business partnerships, the term *partner* is used instead of *party*. A federation trust is inherently a one-way trust, but a two-way trust could be formed simply by creating a trust in both directions.

A typical business partner relationship involves users on one company network accessing resources on another company network. For example, with a supplier of goods and a wholesale purchaser of those goods, the supplier is likely to be the trusting partner, and the purchaser is the trusted partner. Users at the purchasing (trusted) company might access order entry, inventory, and order status applications and databases at the supplier (trusting) company. In AD FS terminology, the trusted company is referred to as the **account partner**, and the trusting company is called the **resource partner**. In the trust relationship in Figure 9-1, the arrow points from the trusting (resource) partner to the trusted (account) partner. Users in the account partner organization are said to have a federated identity, which describes the agreed-on standards for sharing user identity information among two or more parties. This shared identity information is used to grant users privileges and permissions to resources across organizations.

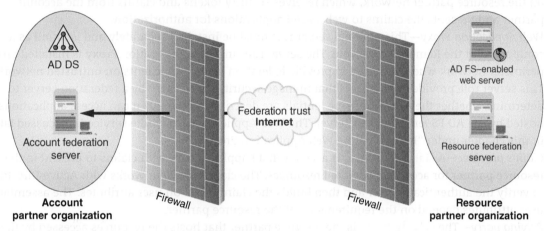

Figure 9-1   A federation trust relationship

Account Partners and Resource Partners

User accounts in the account partner can be Active Directory or Active Directory Lightweight Directory Service (AD LDS) user accounts. The resource partner organization hosts applications and other resources that are accessible to account partner users. When a user in the account partner organization wants to access these resources, a federation server in the account partner's network presents a security token representing the user's credentials to web resources in the resource partner's network. Based on the security token, the federation server in the resource partner's network grants or denies access.

Claims-Aware Applications

In AD FS parlance, the user credentials packaged in a security token are called *claims*. A **claim** is an agreed-on set of user attributes that both parties in a federation trust use to determine a user's credentials, which specify the user's permissions to resources in the partner's network. Claims typically include a user's logon name and group memberships and can include other attributes, such as department, title, and so forth. A claims-aware application is an ASP.NET application that makes user authorization decisions based on claims packaged in AD FS security tokens.

Windows NT Token Applications

Applications that aren't claims aware can still participate in AD FS. These applications rely on Windows NT-style access tokens to determine user authorization. These tokens contain traditional user and group security principal security IDs (SIDs), and access control lists (ACLs) are used to determine user permissions to a resource. An NT token-based application is an Internet Information Services (IIS) application that relies on standard Windows authentication methods rather than claims. This type of application might be developed by using a legacy scripting language, such as Perl or an older version of ASP that doesn't use the .NET programming interfaces.

AD FS Components

In Windows Server, a functional AD FS implementation requires the following components:

- *Active Directory Domain Services (AD DS)*—AD FS relies on the services of Active Directory, so the AD DS role must be installed in a network that is deploying AD FS, and the AD FS servers must be members of the domain. As part of the Active Directory implementation, DNS must be running to provide name services.
- *Federation server*—When you install the Active Directory Federation Services role, the server becomes a **federation server**. The function of the federation server depends on whether the network where it's installed is acting as an account partner or a resource partner. When used in an account partner network, the federation server's function is to gather user credentials into claims and package them into a security token. The security token is then passed to the federation service on the resource partner network, which receives security tokens and claims from the account partner and presents the claims to web-based applications for authorization.
- *Web Application Proxy*—This optional server role must be installed separately and is found as a component of the Remote Access role. The server running Web Application Proxy is installed on the perimeter network when you need to provide federation services to clients on untrusted networks. This server role provides web agents that manage security tokens sent by a federation server to determine whether the user whose credentials are described in the token can access applications hosted by the AD FS–enabled web server. The Web Application Proxy role service is discussed later in this chapter under "Implementing Web Application Proxy."
- *Claims provider*—A **claims provider** is a server that supplies a user with claims to present to the resource partner for access to federated resources. The claims provider works with Active Directory to verify the authenticated user and then builds the claim based on user attributes. The assembled user attributes depend on the requirements of the resource partner.
- *Relying party*—The **relying party** is the resource partner that hosts the resources accessed by the account partner. It processes and validates claims issued by the claims provider and presents a token that grants access to a resource.
- *Relying party trust*—A **relying party trust** is an AD FS trust created on the AD FS server that acts as the claims provider in an AD FS deployment. This trust causes the claims provider to "trust" the relying party for which claims are being made.
- *Claims provider trust*—A **claims provider trust** is a trust created on the AD FS server that acts as the relying party or resource partner. This trust causes the relying party (resource partner) to "trust" the claims provider so that claims supplied by the claims provider are considered reliable.
- *Claim rules*—**Claim rules** are conditions that determine what attributes are required in a claim and how claims are processed by the federation server. There are two types of claim rules: Relying party trust claim rules and claims provider trust claim rules.
- *Certificates*—Certificates are used to identify AD FS server components for security purposes. Certificates can be self-signed or issued by a Windows Server certification authority (CA) running Active Directory Certificate Services or an external CA. All parties must be configured to trust the CA. An AD FS deployment between two separate organizations typically uses an external CA whereas an AD FS deployment within a single organization used to facilitate remote access to web applications can use a Windows Server enterprise CA.
- *Attribute store*—The **attribute store** is an LDAP–compatible database that stores the values in claims. Active Directory is used by default and is the most commonly used attribute store, but other LDAP databases and Microsoft SQL Server can also be used.

AD FS Design Concepts

AD FS can be deployed in several situations. Depending on the situation, you might use a combination of AD FS role services to address an organization's federated identity needs. The AD FS designs discussed in the following sections cover the federated identity needs of most organizations.

Web SSO

The simplest of the AD FS designs, the **web SSO** provides single sign-on access to multiple web applications for users external to the organization's network. This design is most often used in consumer-to-business relationships. There's no federation trust between federation servers as there is with other AD FS designs because this design has only one federation server. Usually, it consists of a federation server inside the organization's firewall and a Web Application Proxy connected to the internal network as well as an Internet-accessible perimeter network. In addition, it contains one or more AD FS–enabled web servers, also Internet accessible, that are connected to the organization's network. Clients requiring access to web applications need to sign in only once. A user name and password must be created for each user in Active Directory. Credentials are presented to the federation proxy server, which forwards them to the internal federation server, which then issues a security token after successful authentication. Web SSO is an ideal design to for using Active Directory Certificate Services to deploy certificates using Group Policy. Figure 9-2 shows the following process for authenticating to an AD FS–enabled web application:

> **Note**
>
> The perimeter network in the figure is sometimes referred to as a *DMZ (demilitarized zone)*, and there's a firewall (not shown) between the perimeter network and the internal network.

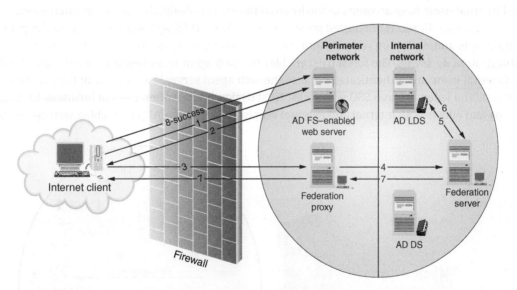

Figure 9-2   Web SSO authentication and authorization

1. A user attempts to access an application on the AD FS–enabled web server.
2. The AD FS–enabled web server refuses access and redirects the browser to the federation proxy server's sign-in page.
3. The user's browser requests the sign-in page from the federation proxy server.
4. The user enters sign-in credentials, and the federation proxy server passes them to the federation server in the internal network.
5. The federation server validates the credentials with a directory service, such as AD LDS.
6. The federation server receives credential information from the directory service and creates the security token.

7. The security token is passed back to the client with the URL of the application on the AD FS–enabled web server.

8. The client presents the security token to the web server and accesses the application.

Federated Web SSO

The **federated web SSO** design is similar to Figure 9-1 in which a trust relationship is established between the resource partner and the account partner. A federation server is running on both networks. Although not shown in the figure, federation proxy servers are often used in this design to enhance security. The web SSO design is inherent in this design where Internet users who aren't part of the trust can still access web applications in the resource partner network. In this situation, the account partner users request web services from the resource partner. The resource partner doesn't authenticate the user locally but redirects the user back to the federation server in the account partner network. The account federation server validates the credentials and creates a security token for the client to present to the resource federation server. The federation server creates a security token for the client to present to the AD FS–enabled web server, and the client requests the application. The federated web SSO design supports business-to-business relationships for collaboration or commerce purposes.

Federated Web SSO with Forest Trust

The **federated web SSO with forest trust** design involves a network with two Active Directory forests. One forest, which is in the perimeter network, is considered the resource partner. The second forest, which is in the internal network, is the account partner. A forest trust is established between domain controllers in both forests. In this design (see Figure 9-3), internal forest users and external users have access to AD FS–enabled web applications in the perimeter network. External users have Active Directory accounts in the perimeter forest, and internal users have accounts in the internal forest. This design is used most often when Windows NT token applications are hosted on web servers. The AD FS web agent running in the perimeter network intercepts authentication requests and creates the NT security tokens that web applications need to make authorization decisions. The forest trust enables the web agent to authenticate users from the internal network. External users are authenticated because the web agent server is a member of the perimeter network forest. The federated web SSO with forest trust design is most often used in business-to-employee relationships and allows both internal and external employees to access AD FS–enabled web applications.

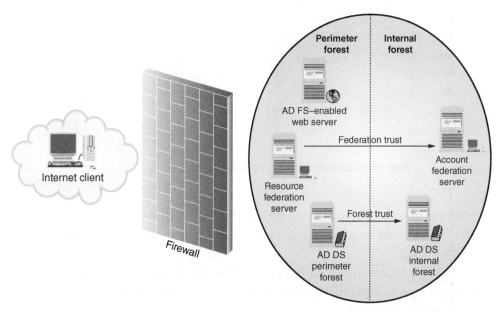

Figure 9-3   The federated web SSO with forest trust design

Preparing to Deploy AD FS

After you have decided on a federation design, there are a few other requirements to consider:

- You can use Federation Proxy or Web Application Proxy. If your servers are Windows Server 2012 R2 or later, use Web Application Proxy. To use Federation Proxy, install AD FS on the server to be used as a proxy and configure AD FS for proxy mode.
- Federation servers, federation proxy servers, and web servers hosting AD FS web agents must be configured with Transport Layer Security/Secure Sockets Layer (TLS/SSL), which is used by the HTTPS protocol. Firewalls must permit HTTPS traffic.
- Web browsers on client computers must have JScript and cookies enabled.
- One or more account stores, such as AD DS or AD LDS, must be running on the network. However, running AD DS on the same server as any AD FS roles isn't recommended.
- Certificates are required by federation servers, federation server proxies, Web Application Proxy servers, and AD FS–enabled web servers. Certificates can be requested from a public CA or internally from an Active Directory Certificate Services certification authority (AD CS CA). Optionally, you can self-sign certificates, which works well for testing environments.

As you have seen in the figures of AD FS designs, installing and testing AD FS require a complex network environment and several computers. Setting up and testing AD FS with the simplest design, web SSO, require at least four computers. Other designs could require up to eight computers if proxies are used. Following is an overview of the steps for implementing a web SSO design using Web Application Proxy:

1. Create a service account to be used by the AD FS role.
2. Install a Web Server certificate.
3. Install the AD FS role on a server in the internal network.
4. Install the Web Application Proxy role service on a server in the perimeter network (optional).
5. Install the Web Server role service on the AD FS–enabled web server.
6. Install AD DS or AD LDS to maintain the account store (the database containing user accounts).
7. Install the claims-aware or Windows NT token-based application on the web server.

Most of these steps involve several substeps, such as issuing certificates, configuring DNS, and so forth. Activities 9-2 and 9-3 later in the chapter walk you through the first steps of configuring an AD FS deployment. The Microsoft Technet website describes a thorough step-by-step procedure for deploying each AD FS design at *http://technet.microsoft.com/en-us/library/dn486820.aspx*.

> **Note** 📎
>
> You don't configure a full AD FS deployment in this chapter. A full AD FS deployment requires a claims-aware web application, a web server to host the claims-aware application, an AD FS server, a domain controller, and a client machine at minimum. However, this chapter guides you through installing the AD FS role and discusses some configuration options that should be enough to get you started with AD FS and prepare you for the 70-742 certification exam.

Configuring a Relying Party Trust

Recall that the relying party is the resource partner that accepts claims from the account partner to make authentication and authorization decisions. A relying party trust sets up the trust relationship between the claims provider and the relying party (resource partner). You configure the relying party trust on the AD FS server that issues claims (usually the account partner), which in effect causes the claims provider to "trust" the relying party. To configure the relying party trust, right-click the Relying Party Trusts folder in the AD FS console and click Add Relying Party Trust to start the Add Relying Party Trust Wizard. In the Welcome window, click Start. Then provide the following information:

- *Select Data Source*—In this window, you specify how the wizard gets information about the relying party. This information is the metadata that the relying party needs to create the trust, including the SSL certificate. It's usually published by the claims-aware application that users will access via federation services. Select from the following options (shown in Figure 9-4):
  - Import data about the relying party published online or on a local network: With this option, you import data from a server, usually by supplying the URL of the relying party's published application metadata.
  - Import data about the relying party from a file: Use this option if the relying party can't be contacted directly and has exported the metadata to a file. The location can be a local path or a UNC path.
  - Enter data about the relying party manually: This option requires entering a display name, choosing an AD FS configuration profile (the AD FS compatibility version), configuring a certificate, selecting authentication options, setting authorization rules, and so forth. Choose this option if the relying party application can't publish or export its federation metadata.
- *Choose Access Control Policy*—You configure an access control policy with a number of options as shown in Figure 9-5. Several of the configurations require multi-factor authentication (MFA).
- *Ready to Add Trust*—On this screen, you can review the relying party trust information.

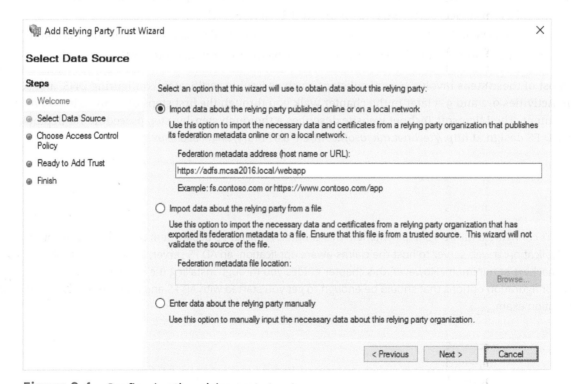

Figure 9-4   Configuring the relying party trust

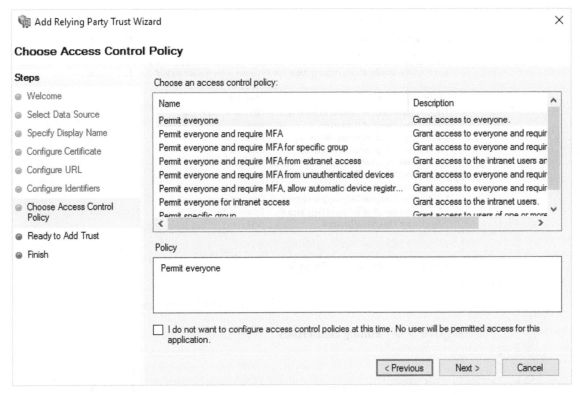

Figure 9-5   Choosing an access control policy

Configuring a Claims Provider Trust

You configure a claims provider trust on the AD FS server that acts as the relying party (resource partner). Doing so configures the relying party to trust the claims issued by the claims provider (account partner). To configure a claims provider trust, right-click the Claims Provider Trusts folder in the AD FS console and click Add Claims Provider Trust to start the Add Claims Provider Trust Wizard. In the Welcome window, click Start. The Select Data Source window has the same options as in the Add Relying Party Trust Wizard. That's all the information you need to enter to set up this trust.

Configuring Claims Provider Claim Rules

A claims provider claim rule determines what claims AD FS issues. Claim rules are configured on the attribute store, which by default is Active Directory. Another term for claims provider rules is *acceptance transform rules*. A claim rule can pass a claim through to the relying party, or it can perform a transformation on the rule if certain attributes from the claims provider must be mapped to attributes that the relying party can accept. For example, the claims provider can use the attribute Group to define a type of user, and the relying party can use the attribute Role. A claim rule can transform the claim by changing the Group attribute to Role so that it's accepted by the relying party.

To configure a claim rule for Active Directory, click the Claims Provider Trusts folder in the AD FS console, and in the middle pane, right-click Active Directory and click Edit Claim Rules. In the Edit Claim Rules for Active Directory dialog box, you see a list of predefined rules. You can add new rules, edit existing rules, or remove rules (see Figure 9-6). You can also change the order in which claim rules are processed by selecting a rule and clicking the up or down arrow.

If you need to transform a claim, you click Add Rule and then click Transform an Incoming Claim. The Add Transform Claim Rule Wizard walks you through the process as shown in Figure 9-7.

Figure 9-6   Editing claim rules

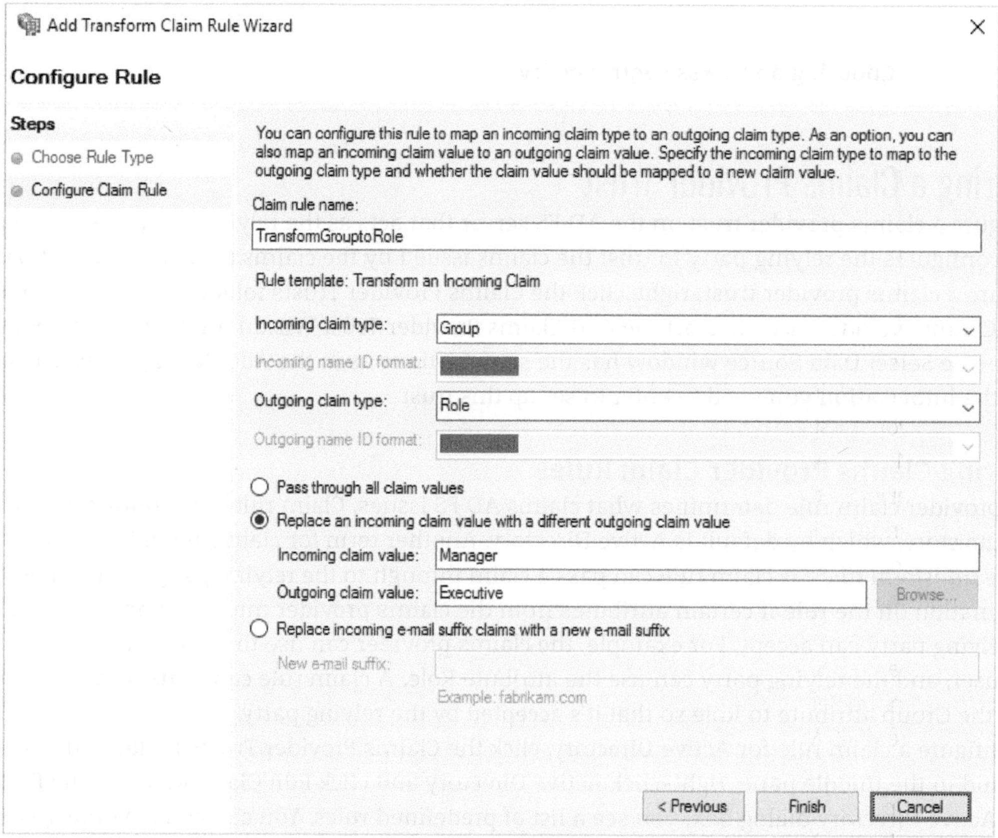

Figure 9-7   Creating a transform rule

Configuring Authentication Policies

Authentication policies enable you to determine what type of authentication is required in the AD FS system. You configure authentication policies in the AD FS console by clicking the Service folder and then clicking the Authentication Methods folder (see Figure 9-8). There are two types of authentication policies:

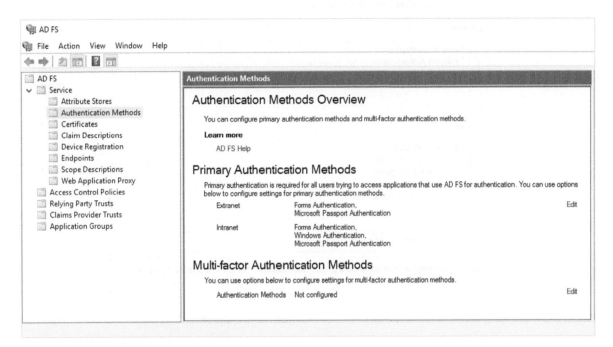

Figure 9-8 **Authentication methods**

- *Primary authentication*—This is required for all users who access applications that use AD FS. Primary authentication can be configured globally or on a custom basis for each relying party. You configure primary authentication based on whether the user is accessing the application from the intranet or extranet. By default, extranet access uses forms authentication (the user enters credentials on a web form) and Microsoft Passport Authentication. If both options are selected, the user can choose the authentication method at sign-in. Intranet access uses Windows authentication, Forms Authentication, and Microsoft Passport Authentication by default, and you can enable certificate authentication (see Figure 9-9). In addition, you can enable device authentication. You also can use Azure multi-factor authentication if you have configured an Azure Active Directory tenant.
- *Multi-factor authentication*—**Multi-factor authentication (MFA)** means that users must authenticate with more than one method, such as with a user name and password as well as a digital certificate or a smart card. MFA can be configured to use Certificate Authentication or Azure MFA (see Figure 9-10).

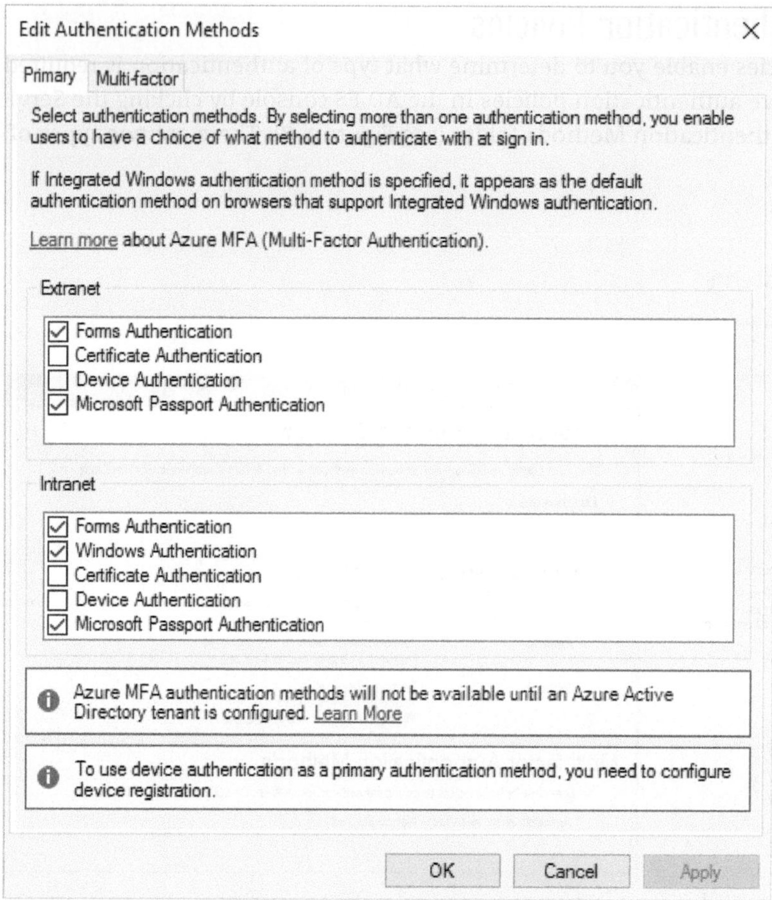

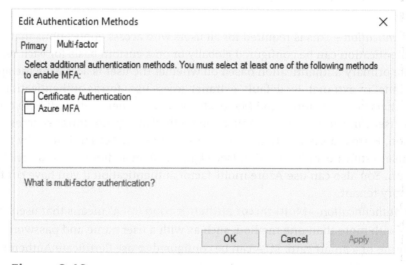

Figure 9-9   Configuring primary authentication

Figure 9-10   Configuring multi-factor authentication

Device Registration

Device registration is a feature that allows nondomain-joined devices to access claims-based resources securely. You can use this feature to cope with the "bring your own device (BYOD)" revolution; it enables you to permit users with smartphones and tablets to access domain resources without creating a security risk. Using device registration also makes things easier for BYOD users because they can enjoy the benefits of SSO.

The mobile device used to perform a device registration must trust the SSL certificate installed on the AD FS server. This is usually done by installing the CA certificate on the mobile device. In addition, you must configure the device registration service on the AD FS server. To do so, use the following PowerShell cmdlets:

- `Initialize-ADDeviceRegistration`—When prompted, enter the name of the service account you created for use with AD FS, being sure to add a dollar sign ($) at the end of the name, as in `mcsa2016\ADFSsvc$`. When prompted that the command prepares Active Directory to host Device Registration Service, press Enter to confirm.
- `Enable-AdfsDeviceRegistration`—After the command runs, open the AD FS console, click the Authentication Policies folder, click Edit in the Primary Authentication section, and click the *Enable device authentication* check box.

You can also use the AD FS console by clicking Service, Device Registration and then clicking the Configure device registration link.

Next, you need to make sure that an alias (CNAME) record named "enterpriseregistration" exists on the DNS server that points to the AD FS server. This alias name is used by devices to find the AD FS server to perform the device registration.

In addition, you need to install the claims-aware application that devices will access by installing the Web Server (IIS) role and the Windows Identity Foundation feature on another member server (separate from the AD FS server). Finally, you create a relying party trust on the AD FS server. Depending on your AD FS design, you might also want to install the Web Application Proxy role service. Here are the steps for allowing third-party devices to perform device registration to access domain resources from the Internet:

1. Install a certificate from a third-party CA. A third-party CA, such as VeriSign, is needed when the devices performing the device registration don't have access to the domain's internal public key infrastructure (PKI).
2. Install and configure AD FS.
3. Initialize and enable the device registration service.
4. Add DNS records for the AD FS server and the device registration alias, if necessary.
5. Install and configure the web server and a claims-aware application.

Upgrading AD FS to Windows Server 2016

AD FS has been a feature in Windows Server since Windows Server 2003 R2, so it's possible that you have an existing deployment you might want to upgrade to enjoy some of the new features added since then. AD FS in Windows Server 2016 adds the following features to AD FS compared to AD FS in Windows Server 2012:

- *Multi-factor authentication sign in with Azure*—You can use Azure MFA for both intranet and extranet access.
- *Enhanced device registration*—Users can gain access to AD FS protected resources based on the credentials of the device they are using.
- *Microsoft Passport support*—Windows 10 Hello for Business can be enabled to replace passwords with device-bound biometric credentials.
- *Support for LDAPv3 compliant directories*—AD LDS and non-Windows LDAP implementations are supported.

Note

You can add a Windows Server 2016 AD FS server to an existing Windows Server 2012 R2 AD FS farm, but you cannot use the new features available in Windows Server 2016 AD FS. In addition, you cannot simply upgrade a Windows Server 2012 R2 AD FS server to Windows Server 2016; you must install a new Windows Server 2016 AD FS server and decommission the old servers to use the new features found in Windows Server 2016.

To upgrade an existing AD FS deployment that uses a WID database, follow these steps:

1. Install AD FS on a new Windows Server 2016 server and add the server to the existing Windows Server 2012 R2 AD FS farm. The new server will be considered a secondary server and any AD FS configuration changes must be made on the primary server.

2. On the Windows Server 2016 AD FS server, run the following PowerShell cmdlet to make the new server the primary server: `Set-AdfsSyncProperties -Role PrimaryComputer`.

3. On the original primary server that is running Windows Server 2012 R2, run the following PowerShell cmdlet to make the original server a secondary server: `Set-AdfsSyncProperties -Role SecondaryComputer PrimaryComputerName` *ADFS2016Computer* where *ADFS2016Computer* is the name of the server you promoted as the primary server.

4. Now you must upgrade the forest and domain schema by running `adprep /forestprep` and then `adprep /domainprep` from an elevated command prompt.

5. Finally, on the Windows Server 2016 AD FS server, run the following cmdlet to enable AD FS 2016 functionality: `Invoke-AdfsFarmBehaviorLevelRaise`.

To see the current AD FS farm level, run the following cmdlet: `Get-AdfsFarmInformation`. The cmdlet returns a value of 3 to indicate AD FS 2016 farm functionality. The Windows Server 2012 R2 AD FS servers should be removed from the deployment.

Activity 9-1: Resetting Your Virtual Environment

Time Required: 5 minutes
Objective: Reset your virtual environment by applying the InitialConfig checkpoint or snapshot.
Required Tools and Equipment: ServerDC1, ServerDM1, ServerDM2, ServerSA1
Description: Apply the InitialConfig checkpoint or snapshot to ServerDC1, ServerDM1, ServerDM2, and ServerSA1.

1. Be sure all servers are shut down. In your virtualization program, apply the InitialConfig checkpoint or snapshot to ServerDC1, ServerDM1, ServerDM2, and ServerSA1.

2. When the snapshot or checkpoint has finished being applied, continue to the next activity.

Activity 9-2: Preparing for AD FS Deployment

Time Required: 20 minutes
Objective: Prepare for AD FS deployment.
Required Tools and Equipment: ServerDC1
Description: In this activity, you create a service account and install a self-signed certificate for use with AD FS.

1. Start ServerDC1, if necessary, and sign in as **Administrator**.

2. On ServerDC1, open a PowerShell window. Type **Add-KdsRootKey -EffectiveTime (Get-Date).AddHours(-10)** and press **Enter**. This key is used to generate Managed Service Account passwords.

3. Next, type **New-ADServiceAccount ADFSsvc -DNSHostName ServerDC1.mcsa2016.local -ServicePrincipalNames http://ServerDC1.mcsa2016.local** and press **Enter**.

4. Next, create a self-signed certificate. Because this deployment is only for testing purposes, you can use a self-signed certificate, but for an actual deployment, you need to use a CA. Open a PowerShell window and type **New-SelfSignedCertificate -CertStoreLocation cert:\localmachine\my -dnsname adfs.mcsa2016. local, enterpriseregistration.mcsa2016.local** and press **Enter**. The "enterpriseregistration" alternative DNS name is needed for device registration for Workplace Joins if you want to use this feature. Close the PowerShell window.

5. Continue to the next activity.

Activity 9-3: Installing the AD FS Role

Time Required: 20 minutes
Objective: Install the AD FS role.
Required Tools and Equipment: ServerDC1
Description: In this activity, you install the AD FS role on ServerDC1. Typically, you would choose a server other than a DC, but because this is only for demonstration purposes, you can install AD FS on a DC.

1. On ServerDC1, in Server Manager, click **Manage**, **Add Roles and Features** to start the Add Roles and Features Wizard. Click **Next** until you get to the Server Roles window.
2. In the Server Roles window, click **Active Directory Federation Services**, and then click **Next** until you get to the Confirmation window. Click **Install**, and when the installation is finished, click **Close**.
3. In Server Manager, click the **notifications flag**, and click the **Configure the federation service on this server** link to start the Active Directory Federation Services Configuration Wizard. In the Welcome window, read the information, accept the default option **Create the first federation server in a federation server farm**, and then click **Next**.
4. In the Connect to AD DS window, accept the default credentials, and click **Next**.
5. In the Specify Service Properties window, you need to specify the SSL certificate. Click the **SSL Certificate** list arrow, and click **adfs.mcsa2016.local**. The Federation Service Name text box is filled in with the name on the certificate. In the Federation Service Display Name text box, type **FS mcsa2016** (see Figure 9-11), and then click **Next**.

Figure 9-11   Specifying service properties

6. In the Specify Service Account window, type **ADFSsvc** (the service account you created in the previous activity) in the Account Name text box, and then click **Next**.
7. In the Specify Database window, accept the default **Create a database on this server using Windows Internal Database**. (If you have an SQL server available, you could use it instead.) Click **Next**.
8. In the Review Options window, review the selections, and click **Next**. (If you were going to do similar installations on additional servers, you could click the View script button to see the PowerShell script that performs the installation and use it on other servers.)
9. In the Pre-requisite Checks window, verify that all prerequisites were met, and then click **Configure**. You might see a warning about group Managed Service Account. You can ignore this warning.
10. When the configuration is finished, on the Results page, click **Close**. In Server Manager, click **Tools**, **AD FS Management**. You are now ready to configure AD FS. At this point, you should explore the AD FS console and practice some of the configuration tasks described in the previous sections.
11. Continue to the next activity.

Integrating AD FS with Additional Services

Q Certification

- **70-742 – Implement identity federation and access solutions:**
  Install and configure Active Directory Federation Services (AD FS)

You've seen how AD FS can be used to provide authentication services between two organizations and to provide remote access to web applications using single sign on. AD FS can also be integrated with other authentication services and online applications. This section discusses the following AD FS integration scenarios:

- Integrating AD FS with Microsoft Passport
- Integrating AD FS for use with Microsoft Azure and Office 365
- Configuring AD FS to work with LDAP directories

Integrating AD FS with Microsoft Passport

Microsoft Passport is an authentication service that provides multi-factor authentication combining a PIN or biometric sign-in with encrypted keys on a user device. Microsoft Passport uses Windows Hello on Windows 10 for biometric authentication using either face recognition or a fingerprint scan.

To integrate AD FS with Microsoft Passport, you must be running the Windows Server 2016 forest functional level and perform these three steps:

1. Enable device registration in AD FS as described in the previous section.
2. Configure a group policy to automatically register domain-joined computers as devices.
3. Configure a group policy to enable Windows Hello for Business.

To perform the second step, create a new GPO in Group Policy Management, and open the policy in Group Policy Management Editor. Then, navigate to this policy: Computer Configuration\Policies\Administrative Templates\Windows Components\Device Registration (see Figure 9-12). Double-click the *Register domain joined computers as devices* policy and click Enabled.

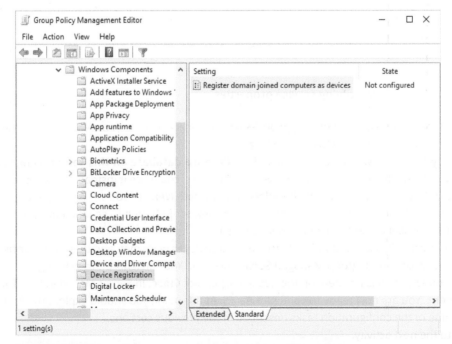

Figure 9-12 Configuring automatic device registration

Next, navigate to Computer Configuration\Policies\Administrative Templates\Windows Components\ Windows Hello for Business. Double-click the Use Windows Hello for Business policy and click Enabled.

Finally, link the GPO to the domain or OU that contains the computer accounts you wish to automatically register and that should use Microsoft Passport for authentication. You should also configure Active Directory Certificate Services and request a Kerberos Authentication certificate on each Domain Controller.

> **Note**
>
> Microsoft has changed the branding of Microsoft Passport and now calls it Microsoft Hello for Business. The 70-742 exam objectives still reference Microsoft Passport as of this writing, and some of the AD FS authentication-related dialog boxes still reference Microsoft Passport, but this could change.

Integrating AD FS with Microsoft Azure and Office 365

If your organization is using Microsoft Azure or Office 365, you can use integrate them with AD FS so that your users can seamlessly use these online services with a single sign on. This discussion assumes that your AD FS deployment is within the intranet. Although you can deploy AD FS in Microsoft Azure, that scenario is beyond the scope of this book. The general steps for configuring AD FS for use with Azure and Office 365 are as follows:

1. Install a certificate from a public CA; you can't use an internal CA for use with Azure and Office 365.
2. Install and Configure Web Application Proxy to provide access to the federation server from the Internet. Web Application Proxy installation is discussed later in this chapter.
3. Install the Microsoft Azure Active Directory module in PowerShell. You can find it at *http://connect .microsoft.com/site1164/Downloads/DownloadDetails.aspx?DownloadID=59185*.
4. Create a trust between Azure AD and AD FS.
5. Configure directory synchronization between Azure AD and your Active Directory domain using Azure AD Connect, which you can find on the Microsoft Download Center. By synchronizing your local Active Directory domain with Azure AD, you can access Office 365 and any Azure application with a single sign in through your local domain controllers.

These steps provide a high-level overview of integrating AD FS with Microsoft Azure and Office 365. If you want to learn more, try the following links:

- *https://blogs.technet.microsoft.com/rmilne/2017/04/28/how-to-install-ad-fs-2016-for-office-365/*
- *https://docs.microsoft.com/en-us/azure/active-directory/connect/active-directory-aadconnect*

Configuring AD FS to Work with LDAP Directories

AD FS is designed to work with LDAP-compliant directories. Active Directory is LDAP compliant, but other OSs and applications could use another directory service, such as OpenLDAP for Linux and Unix, for storing user authentication information. Windows Server 2016 provides Active Directory Lightweight Directory Service (AD LDS) for use with applications that require an LDAP directory but don't integrate well with Active Directory. AD FS can integrate with any LDAP v3–compliant directory service.

AD FS authenticates users stored in an LDAP directory by creating a claims provider trust between AD FS and the LDAP service. To create a claims provider trust, right-click the Claims Provider Trust folder in the AD FS console and click Add Claims Provider Trust. Specify a URL to the claims provider metadata, if available, or enter claims trust data manually (see Figure 9-13).

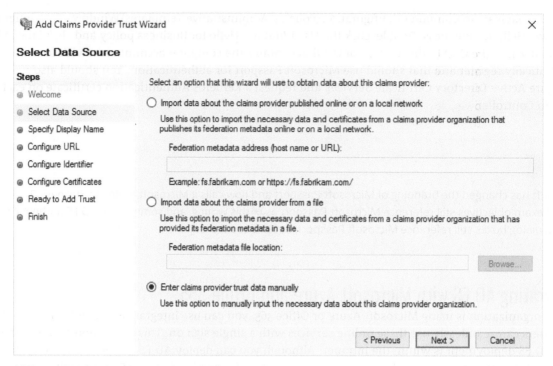

Figure 9-13   Configuring a claims provider trust

If the LDAP service does not publish its claims data, you must enter it manually by specifying the following information:

- The Display Name, which is a friendly name for the provider
- The URL to the claims provider
- An identifier, which defaults to the claims provider URL
- Configuration of certificates to verify the digital signature on claims sent by the provider

After you have configured a Claims Provider Trust, configure an Attribute Store that consists of a display name, the type of store, and the URL of the LDAP service. To do so, click Service, right-click Attribute Stores, and click Add Attribute Store. Enter a display name, select LDAP for the attribute store type and enter the connection string. A typical connection string might look like ldap://ldap.mydomain.com:389/cn=users,dc=mydomain,dc=com (see Figure 9-14).

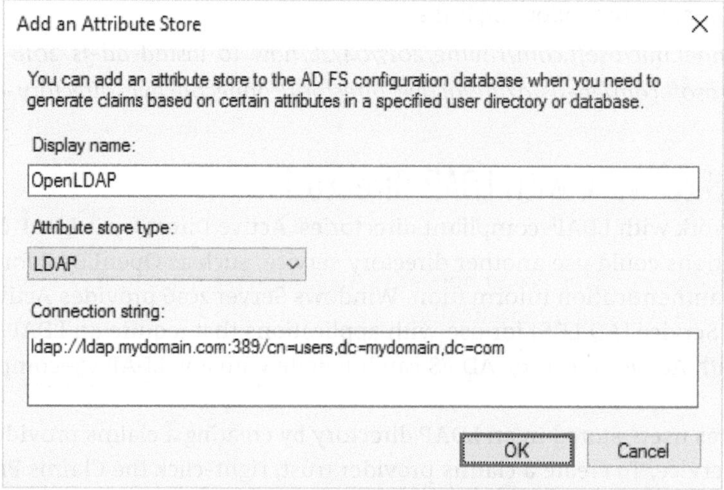

Figure 9-14   Configuring an attribute store for LDAP

Active Directory Rights Management Service

 **Certification**

- **70-742 – Implement identity federation and access solutions:**
  Install and configure Active Directory Rights Management Services (AD RMS)

You have learned methods for allowing some users to access information while disallowing other users. Access to digital information stored on computers can be allowed and disallowed by controlling who can authenticate to the servers, assigning permissions to files and folders with NTFS permissions, and using encryption methods, such as EFS. However, what users can do with data after being granted access to it hasn't been discussed.

Active Directory Rights Management Service (AD RMS) helps administrators get a handle on this critical step in securing data. Whether protecting trade secrets, customer account information, or intellectual property, many organizations struggle with this important facet of network security. With AD RMS, an administrator can create policies that define how a document can be used after a user accesses it. Actions such as copying, saving, forwarding, and even printing documents can be restricted. For example, suppose you send an "eyes-only" email to another employee. With AD RMS, you can restrict the recipient from printing the message or forwarding it to someone else.

To be effective, AD RMS requires AD RMS–enabled client or server applications, such as Microsoft Office, Microsoft Exchange, and Microsoft SharePoint. Developers can also create AD RMS–enabled applications by using the AD RMS Software Development Kit (SDK), available on the Microsoft website (*https://www.microsoft.com/en-us/download/details.aspx?id=38397*).

AD RMS Key Features

AD RMS is a server role in Windows Server, but it requires each AD RMS client to have a client access license. Some key features of the AD RMS server role include the following:

- *AD FS integration*—AD RMS can be integrated with AD FS to set up a federated trust between organizations. With AD FS, the benefits of AD RMS can be extended outside the organization's network to ensure document security in business-to-business relationships.
- *AD RMS Server self-enrollment*—An RMS server must connect to the Microsoft Enrollment Service over the Internet to acquire a certificate, which allows the RMS server to issue client licenses and certificates to access protected content. With AD RMS, the server can self-enroll in this certificate, so there's no need to contact Microsoft servers.
- *Support for mobile devices*—AD RMS supports mobile devices and Mac computers when you install the mobile device extension.
- *Administrator role delegation*—AD RMS enables network administrators to delegate AD RMS responsibilities to different users. There are four AD RMS administrator roles:
  - AD RMS Enterprise Administrator: This role has full administrative authority over an AD RMS installation.
  - AD RMS Service Group: This group holds the AD RMS service account. The service account is added to this administrative role automatically.
  - AD RMS Auditor: This role can view RMS-related logs and reports.
  - AD RMS Template Administrator: This role can create and manage AD RMS templates.

AD RMS Components

An AD RMS environment, like an AD FS environment, consists of several components, usually set up as separate servers:

- *AD RMS server*—The AD RMS server role can be installed on one or more servers. Whether it's installed on one server or multiple servers, the installation is referred to as an **AD RMS root cluster**. Multiple servers can be used for redundancy and load balancing. Only one AD RMS root cluster can be installed in an Active Directory forest. The AD RMS server self-signs a server licensor certificate (SLC), which allows the server to issue AD RMS client licenses and certificates. When the AD RMS role is installed, some web server roles are also installed.

> **Note** 📎
>
> Don't confuse the term *cluster* used to describe an AD RMS deployment with a failover cluster or a network load balancing (NLB) cluster. Neither cluster service is required to install AD RMS.

- *AD RMS database server*—AD RMS uses a database to store AD RMS configuration data and Active Directory group membership information. An SQL database installed on a separate server is recommended for production environments, but you can use the Windows internal database for test environments.
- *Active Directory domain controller*—Servers running the AD RMS server role must be domain members, and users who use or publish AD RMS–enabled content must be in Active Directory with a valid email address.
- *AD RMS-enabled client computer*—AD RMS client software is included with Windows Vista and Windows Server 2008 and later OSs, so there is no need to install any client software.

The AD RMS process consists of two distinct actions: publication of AD RMS–protected documents and access to these documents by an AD RMS client. Publication requires the user authoring the document to acquire a rights account certificate (RAC) and a client licensor certificate (CLC). With these certificates, the user can publish AD RMS–protected content, which involves the following steps.

1. A document with an AD RMS–enabled application must be created and rights must be specified for the document. A publishing document with use policies is created.
2. The document is encrypted by the AD RMS application, and the publishing certificate is bound to the document. The AD RMS server cluster is the only entity that can issue licenses to decrypt the file.
3. The document author can then distribute the application for users to access it.

A user accesses an AD RMS–protected document with the following steps:

1. A user attempts to access the document by using an AD RMS–enabled application.
2. The AD RMS client reads the publishing license.
3. The AD RMS server specified in the publishing license is contacted to request a use license.
4. After verifying that the user is authorized to access the document, the AD RMS server issues a use license to the client.
5. The document is decrypted, and the user can use it according to the rights granted.

AD RMS Deployment

Before installing the AD RMS role, you must address the following requirements:

- Prepare a domain member server for the AD RMS role; its users should be people who will be using AD RMS–protected content.
- Create a service account, which must be a regular domain account because it interacts with other services and computers. The account should have a strong password and shouldn't be a member of any groups except Domain Users; no additional rights should be granted to this account. The AD RMS configuration wizard assigns the account the necessary rights.
- Make sure the user account for installing AD RMS has the right to create databases on the SQL server if you use an external database.
- If an external database is used, install the database server before installing AD RMS.
- Create a DNS CNAME record for the AD RMS cluster's URL; this record is used to access the AD RMS service.

When you're ready to install AD RMS, install the role and the required role services in Server Manager with the Add Roles and Features Wizard. Activity 9-5 walks you through this process, but many of the selections are described in the following steps:

1. In the Server Roles window, click Active Directory Rights Management Services. In the Role Services window, you have options to install the following role services:

   - Active Directory Rights Management Server: This is the main role service required to protect documents from unauthorized use. It is required and selected by default on the first AD RMS server.
   - Identity Federation Support: Select this option if you're integrating AD RMS with AD FS to extend document protection outside the organization's network to federated business partners.

2. You're prompted to install the Web Server Role (IIS) and several of its role services. Accept the default choices.

3. After the role is installed, click the notifications flag in Server Manager, and then click the *Perform additional configuration* link to start the AD RMS configuration wizard. In the AD RMS window, read the information, and click Next.

4. In the AD RMS Cluster window, you have the option to create an AD RMS root cluster or join an existing AD RMS cluster. For the first AD RMS server, select the default option *Create a new AD RMS root cluster*. A root cluster supports certification and licensing. After a root cluster is set up, you can install additional licensing-only clusters if needed. Click Next.

5. In the Configuration Database window, specify where the required database will be hosted:

   - Specify a database server and a database instance: If you select this option, you must enter the name of an SQL server and a database instance.
   - Use Windows Internal Database on this server: The Windows internal database can be used for test environments or for single-server cluster configurations. If more than one server will participate in the cluster, this option can't be selected.

6. After selecting the database configuration, click Next. In the Service Account window, click Specify, enter the username and password for the account you created to serve as the AD RMS service account, and click Next.

7. In the Cryptographic Mode window, you have the following options:

   - Cryptographic Mode 2: This mode provides RSA encryption using 2048-bit keys for signature and encryption and SHA-256 hashes for signature. This mode is recommended because it's more secure than Mode 1. Mode 2 is supported in Windows Server 2008 R2 with Service Pack 1 and later. Mode 2 provides regulatory compliance with the security standards set by the National Institute of Standards and Technology (NIST) in 2011.

- Cryptographic Mode 1: Provides RSA 1024-bit keys and SHA-1 hashes. Use this mode for backward compatibility with earlier versions of AD RMS that don't support Mode 2.

8. In the Cluster Key Storage window, you decide how the AD RMS cluster key should be stored:

   - Use AD RMS centrally managed key storage: This option requires specifying a password to protect an encrypted key, which is shared by all servers in the AD RMS cluster automatically.

   - Use CSP key storage: This option requires selecting a cryptographic service provider to store the cluster key. If you select this option, the cluster key must be distributed to other servers manually.

9. After selecting a key storage option, click Next. In the Cluster Key Password window, enter the cluster key password or select a CSP, depending on your selection on the previous window, and click Next.

10. The Cluster Web Site window prompts you to select an IIS website to create the virtual directory for hosting AD RMS. If you set up a virtual directory before starting the AD RMS installation, you select it here; otherwise, the Default Web Site directory is used.

11. In the Cluster Address window (see Figure 9-15), enter the address of the AD RMS that website clients use to access the AD RMS service, which is usually hosted on the AD RMS server. You're prompted to choose an SSL-encrypted or unencrypted connection type. If you choose an unencrypted connection (via HTTP instead of HTTPS), you're warned that identity federation support can't be added. Note also that you can't change the URL or port number after AD RMS configuration is finished. If you choose an SSL-encrypted connection, you're prompted to specify the server certificate in the next window.

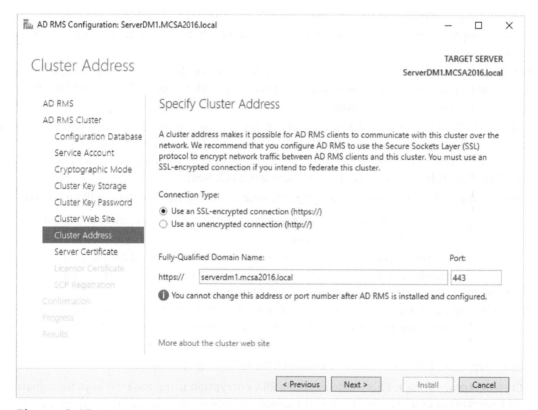

Figure 9-15   The Cluster Address window

12. In the Server Certificate window (which isn't shown if you selected an unencrypted connection in Step 11), specify the certificate for SSL encryption or create a self-signed certificate. A self-signed certificate can be used for test deployments, but you should choose a certificate from a CA for production deployments. Click Next.

13. In the Licensor Certificate window, enter a descriptive name for the certificate used to establish the cluster's identity to clients. For example, you could use mcsa2016ADRMS.You should create a backup of this certificate after the AD RMS configuration has finished because without this certificate, clients can't connect to the AD RMS server. Click Next.

14. In the SCP Registration window, you can register the **service connection point (SCP)** now or later. You must be signed in to the domain as a member of Enterprise Admins to register the SCP. The SCP provides clients with URLs for the AD RMS cluster, which must be registered before clients can access the cluster. Click Next, and then click Install in the Confirmation window. The AD RMS portion of the installation is finished. Next, you install the additional IIS role services and confirm the installation.

As you can see, setting up AD RMS takes considerable planning and several pre-installation tasks. The complexity of this server role and AD FS reflects businesses' growing need to give users and partners secure, flexible access to network resources.

Note

The server roles discussed in this chapter are often installed as the only role on a Windows Server 2016 server, so they lend themselves particularly well to virtualization. If you're using AD FS or AD RMS, consider installing these roles as virtual machines in Hyper-V.

AD RMS Certificate Types

AD RMS uses four types of certificates to identify servers that are used in the AD RMS cluster, identify client computers that access AD RMS–enabled applications, and verify the identity of users and computers accessing AD RMS content. Following is a description of each certificate type:

- *Server licensor certificate*—The **server licensor certificate (SLC)** contains the public key of the AD RMS server and identifies the AD RMS cluster. The private key of this self-signed certificate is used to sign other certificates used in AD RMS. The certificate has a 250-year validity period so that it can protect archived rights management data for a long time.
- *Rights account certificate*—The **rights account certificate (RAC)** identifies users of AD RMS content. Users are issued an RAC when they first attempt to open a protected document. A standard RAC has a validity period of 365 days. A temporary RAC, issued to users who access content from a device that isn't trusted, has a validity period of 15 minutes.
- *Client licensor certificate*—The **client licensor certificate (CLC)** is issued to clients when they're connected to the AD RMS network and grants them the right to publish protected content. The certificate contains the client licensor's public and private keys. The private key is encrypted by the user's public key. It also contains the public and private keys of the cluster that issued the CLC.
- *Machine certificates*—A **machine certificate** is created on a client computer when it first uses an AD RMS application. The certificate is issued by the root cluster and contains the computer's public key. The private key for the certificate is stored in a "lockbox" on the computer that's associated with the currently logged-on user.

AD RMS License Types

A license is actually a specific type of certificate used to determine the rights a user has to publish or access protected documents. There are two types of AD RMS licenses:

- *Publishing license*—A **publishing license** is tied to a rights-protected document and is created when a client publishes the document. It contains a list of users, identified by email address, and specifies what the users can do with the document. For example, a publishing license might specify that a user can view and edit a document but not copy it.

- *Use license*—A **use license** is issued to certain users when they authenticate to an AD RMS server and request access to a rights-protected document. This license contains the key to decrypt the document.

Configuring the AD RMS Service Connection Point

The AD RMS service connection point (SCP) is defined during installation of the AD RMS root cluster and allows domain members to discover the AD RMS cluster automatically. You can perform the following SCP management tasks in the SCP tab of the Properties dialog box of the AD RMS server (see Figure 9-16):

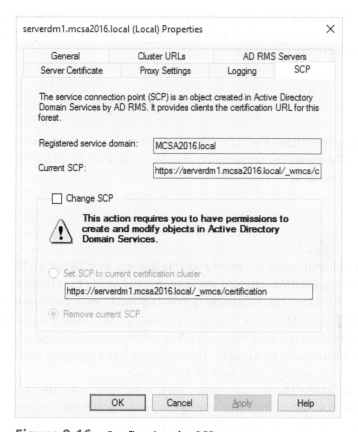

Figure 9-16   Configuring the SCP

- *Change SCP*—You might need to change the SCP if the URL of the AD RMS server has changed.
- *Set SCP to current certification cluster*—You need to set the SCP if you didn't do so during the initial AD RMS configuration. The SCP must be set before clients can discover and access the AD RMS cluster.
- *Remove current SCP*—You might need to remove the current SCP if you're planning to uninstall AD RMS and reinstall it on the same server. You can't reinstall AD RMS if an existing SCP is found during the installation, and uninstalling AD RMS doesn't remove the SCP.

If you uninstall AD RMS before removing the SCP and need to install it again, you can remove the SCP by using the `ADscpRegister.exe` command-line tool, which is available only in the RMS Administration Toolkit from the Microsoft Download Center.

The SCP is stored in Active Directory, and only domain member clients have access to it. If you want a nondomain member client to access the AD RMS cluster, you must modify the Registry on the client computer. Create a key named Activation in HKEY_Local_Machine\Software\Microsoft\MSDRM\ServiceLocation on the client and enter the value of the SCP. You can view the SCP's current value in the SCP tab shown previously in Figure 9-16.

Working with Rights Policy Templates

A **rights policy template** enables you to configure policies for determining who can access a rights-protected document and what actions can be taken with the document. When a document is published, a template can be applied to the document that specifies the rights the recipients have to the document. File Server Resource Manager (FSRM) can be used to scan documents and apply rights policy templates automatically based on resource properties or the contents of the document.

To create rights policy templates, open the Active Directory Rights Management Services console, scroll down the middle pane, and click the *Manage rights policy templates* link in the Tasks section. In the Distributed Rights Policy Templates window, click *Create distributed rights policy template*, and then specify the following information:

- *Add Template Identification Information*—Give a descriptive name to the template and a description that specifies what rights are assigned.
- *Add User Rights*—Add users and groups (see Figure 9-17). You can select users or groups from Active Directory, but the account you select must have an email address assigned in its properties. Alternatively, you can specify ANYONE to include all users in the organization. You can assign rights from a predefined list or create custom rights. Most of the predefined rights are self-explanatory, but a few warrant explanation:

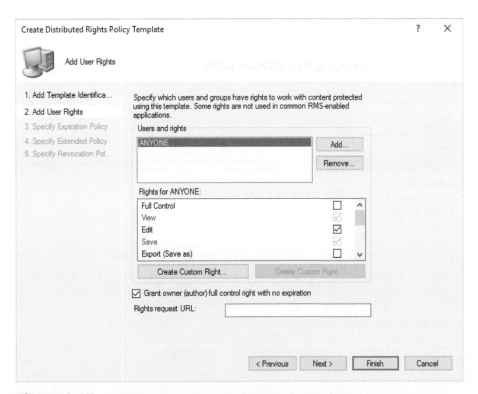

Figure 9-17   Adding user rights to a rights policy template

- Export: Allows a user to use the Save As option when saving a document.
- Forward, Reply, Reply All: These rights are used with protected messages created with Microsoft Exchange.
- Extract: This lets a user copy content from a document.
- *Specify Expiration Policy*—Determine whether the published document availability expires. You can specify expiration parameters for content availability and for the use license. If the use license expires, the document is no longer available to users, and users must get another license to access the content (see Figure 9-18).

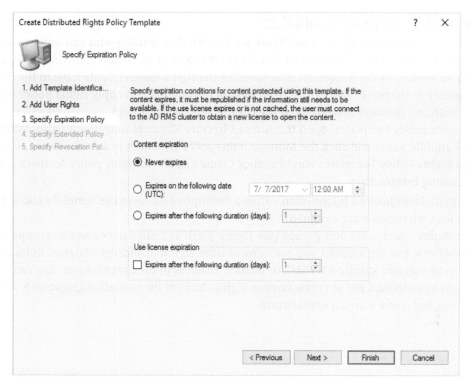

Figure 9-18   Specifying an expiration policy

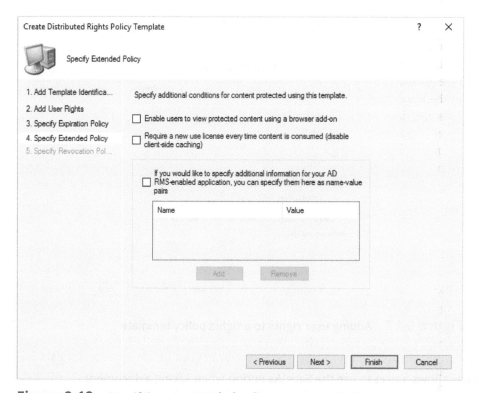

Figure 9-19   Specifying an extended policy

- *Specify Extended Policy*—Configure additional content protection options (see Figure 9-19):
  - Enable users to view protected content by using a browser add-on.
  - Require a new use license every time content is consumed (disable client-side caching): If users shouldn't be able to open protected content when they're disconnected from the network, you should enable this option.

- Application-specific options: You can specify additional policies with values that are specific to the application.
- *Specify Revocation Policy*—You use these settings (see Figure 9-20) to specify that content can be revoked, which disallows access to content based on the content ID, user, or application. If you enable revocation, specify the URL of the revocation list.

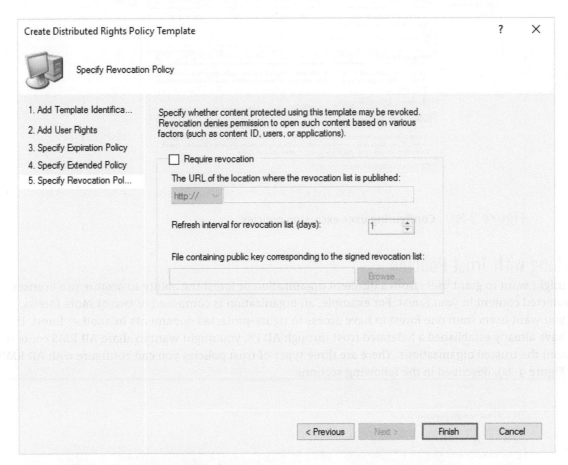

Figure 9-20   **Specifying a revocation policy**

Configuring Exclusion Policies

Exclusion policies enable an administrator to prevent specific users, AD RMS client versions, and applications from interacting with AD RMS content. Exclusions are configured in the Active Directory Rights Management Services console by clicking the Exclusion Policies node in the left pane (see Figure 9-21). Exclusion policies can be configured as follows:

- *User Exclusion*—Prevents user accounts (based on their email addresses) from acquiring use licenses for protected content. When you add a user, you must enable use exclusion before you can add the account to the exclusion list, which you do by clicking the *Manage AD RMS user exclusion list* link and then clicking *Enable User Exclusion* in the Tasks pane. You add domain users by specifying their Active Directory user account names. Specify nondomain users by entering their public key strings.
- *Application Exclusion*—Enable application exclusion, and then add an application to the exclusion list by entering the application's file name and its minimum and maximum version level.
- *Lockbox Version Exclusion*—This exclusion policy allows you to specify the minimum AD RMS client version that can acquire use licenses from AD RMS. If the AD RMS client version is less than the specified minimum, the client can't acquire use licenses.

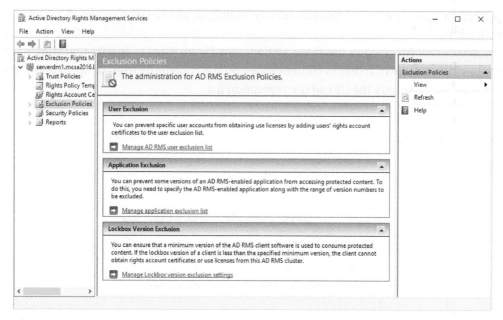

Figure 9-21   Configuring user exclusion policies

Working with Trust Policies

You might want to grant users from a different organization or forest the ability to acquire use licenses to protected content in your forest. For example, an organization is composed of two or more forests, and you want users from one forest to have access to rights-protected documents in another forest. If you have already established a federated trust through AD FS, you might want to share AD RMS content between the trusted organizations. There are three types of trust policies you can configure with AD RMS (see Figure 9-22), described in the following sections.

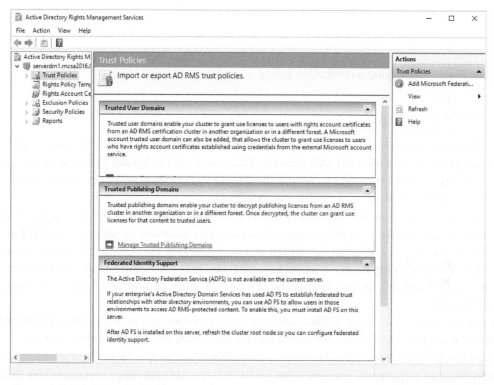

Figure 9-22   Trust policies

Trusted User Domains

A **trusted user domain (TUD)** establishes a trust between AD RMS clusters in separate forests so that users in the trusted forest can access AD RMS content in the trusting forest. A TUD enables the trusting AD RMS cluster to accept rights account certificates from the trusted cluster and grants use licenses to its users. A TUD is a one-way trust, meaning that if you have two forests, you need to establish two trusts for users in both forests to access AD RMS content in both forests. Each time a user accesses content protected by the remote AD RMS cluster, the user receives the use license from the remote cluster, so connectivity between clusters must exist.

Although a TUD doesn't require an Active Directory forest trust between forests, such a trust makes it easier to work with groups of users from the partner organization because group membership data is available between trusted forests. The process of establishing a TUD has two steps:

1. *Export the trusted user domain file on the trusted AD RMS cluster*—The TUD file contains the SLC but doesn't contain the private key. In the Active Directory Rights Management Services console, click Trust Policies in the left pane, and then click the Manage Trusted User Domains link in the Trusted User Domains section in the middle pane. Then click Export Trusted User Domain in the Actions pane.

2. *Import the trusted user domain file on the trusting AD RMS cluster*—First, copy the exported TUD file to a location accessible to a server in the trusting AD RMS cluster. In the Active Directory Rights Management Services console, click Trust Policies in the left pane, and then click the Manage Trusted User Domains link in the Trusted User Domains section in the middle pane. Then click Import Trusted User Domain in the Actions pane. Browse to the location of the exported TUD file, and enter a descriptive name for the certificate.

After a trust is established, the following process occurs when a user from the trusting partner publishes protected content, and a user from the trusted partner attempts to access the content:

1. A user from the trusting partner publishes protected content, which is sent to the user from the trusted partner.

2. The user from the trusted partner acquires an RAC from his or her local AD RMS server.

3. The RAC is sent to the trusting partner's AD RMS cluster to request a use license.

4. The RAC is validated by the trusting partner, and a use license is issued to the user.

Trusted Publishing Domains

A **trusted publishing domain (TPD)** allows an AD RMS cluster to issue use licenses for content published by another AD RMS cluster. With a TPD, the private key and rights policy templates are exported from the trusted domain, so after the trust is established and content is published, there's no need for the trusted cluster to have connectivity with the trusting cluster. However, because the private key of the trusting cluster is exported along with the SLC, a high degree of trust between organizations must exist. Not all organizations allow their private keys to be shared with other organizations. TPDs make working with groups of users much easier because all authentication takes place at the trusted cluster, but because of the security risks of sharing private keys, they're usually used only when the two forests are in the same organization. The steps for establishing a TPD are similar to those for establishing a TUD except that you start with the trusting domain:

1. *Export the trusted publishing domain file on the trusting AD RMS cluster*—The TPD file contains the SLC, private key, and rights policy templates. In the Active Directory Rights Management Services console, click Trust Policies in the left pane, and then click the Manage Trusted Publishing Domains link in the Trusted Publishing Domains section in the middle pane. Then click Export Trusted Publishing Domain in the Actions pane. You must enter a password used to encrypt the TPD file. This password is used when the TPD file is imported on the trusted cluster.

2. *Import the trusted publishing domain file on the trusted AD RMS cluster*—Copy the exported TPD file to a location accessible to a server in the trusted AD RMS cluster. In the Active Directory Rights Management Services console, click Trust Policies in the left pane, and click the Manage Trusted Publishing Domains link in the Trusted Publishing Domains section in the middle pane. Then click Import Trusted Publishing Domain in the Actions pane. Browse to the location of the exported TPD file, enter the password entered in Step 1, and enter a descriptive name for the certificate.

After a trust is established, the following process takes place when a user from the trusting partner publishes protected content, and a user from the trusted partner attempts to access the content:

1. A user from the trusting partner publishes protected content, which is sent to the user from the trusted partner.

2. A user from the trusted partner attempts to open the protected content and requests a use license from its AD RMS cluster.

3. The AD RMS server uses the private key imported from the trusting partner to create the use license and issues it to the user.

Federated Identity Support

If AD FS is installed on your AD RMS servers, you can use the trusts established with AD FS to share rights-protected content without having to create additional AD RMS trusts. The following process occurs when a user in an AD RMS cluster publishes protected content for a user in a partner organization where an AD FS trust has been established:

1. A user from the publishing AD RMS cluster publishes protected content, which is sent to the user in the partner organization.

2. The user from the partner organization attempts to open the protected content.

3. An AD RMS server in the publishing cluster is contacted.

4. The request to the AD RMS server is redirected to a federation server in the publishing organization.

5. The federation server requests identity confirmation from a federation server in the partner organization.

6. The user contacts his or her home federation server, and the client is authenticated by Active Directory.

7. The federation server confirms the user's identity, and the user contacts the AD RMS server in the publishing organization with proof of identity.

8. The AD RMS server in the publishing organization issues a use certificate to the user.

Backing Up and Restoring AD RMS

Configuring AD RMS can be a complex undertaking, so backing up the configuration is paramount. The backup of AD RMS involves the following procedures:

- *Back up the AD RMS databases*—There are three databases: the configuration database, the directory services database, and the logging database. The configuration database is the most important because it contains the data needed to manage account certification and licensing. The directory services database contains cached content from Active Directory, including users, group memberships, and security IDs (SIDs). The logging database contains log files about issued licenses and client activity. If you're using SQL Server to host these databases, use the SQL Server Backup tool. If you're using the Windows internal database, you must use SQL Server Management Studio Express.

- *Export the trusted publishing domain file*—The steps for this procedure were described earlier in "Working with Trust Policies."

- *Store the cluster key password in a safe place*—If you don't know the password, you can change it first in the AD RMS console by clicking Security Policies, Cluster Key Password in the left pane, and then clicking the *Change cluster key password* link in the middle pane. If you do change the password, you must do so on all AD RMS servers in the cluster.

To restore an AD RMS configuration after a server failure, restore the databases and redeploy the AD RMS role. During installation, choose the option to join an existing AD RMS cluster. When you select this option, you must supply the location of the AD RMS configuration database and the cluster key password. After the installation is finished, import the trusted publishing domain file that you exported during the backup process.

Activity 9-4: Installing the AD RMS Role

Time Required: 20 minutes
Objective: Install the AD RMS role.
Required Tools and Equipment: ServerDC1, ServerDM1
Description: In this activity, you install the AD RMS role on ServerDM1. ServerDC1 must be running.

1. On ServerDM1 in Server Manager, click **Manage**, **Add Roles and Features** to start the Add Roles and Features Wizard. Click **Next** until you come to the Server Roles window.
2. In the Server Roles window, click **Active Directory Rights Management Services**, and then click **Add Features**. Click **Next** twice. In the AD RMS window, read the description and the *Things to note* section, and then click **Next**.
3. In the Role Services window, accept the default selection **Active Directory Rights Management Server**, and click **Next**. In the Web Server Role (IIS) window, click **Next**.
4. In the Role Services window, accept the default selections, and click **Next**. In the Confirmation window, click **Install**. When the installation is finished, click **Close**.
5. In Server Manager, click the notifications flag, and click the **Perform additional configuration** link to start the AD RMS Configuration Wizard. In the AD RMS window, read the information, and then click **Next**.
6. In the AD RMS Cluster window, accept the default option **Create a new AD RMS root cluster** and click **Next**.
7. In the Configuration Database window, click the **Use Windows Internal Database on this server** option button, and then click **Next**.
8. In the Service Account window, click **Specify**. In the Windows Security dialog box, type **domuser1** in the User name text box and **Password01** in the Password text box. In an actual deployment of AD RMS, you would create a new user specifically for the AD RMS service account. Click **OK**, and then click **Next**.
9. In the Cryptographic Mode window, accept the default option **Cryptographic Mode 2** and click **Next**.
10. In the Cluster Key Storage window, accept the default option **Use AD RMS centrally managed key storage** and click **Next**.
11. In the Cluster Key Password window, type **Password01** in the Password and Confirm Password text boxes, and then click **Next**.
12. In the Cluster Web Site window, click **Next**. In the Cluster Address window, accept the default option **Use an SSL-encrypted connection**, type **ServerDM1.mcsa2016.local** in the Fully-Qualified Domain Name text box, and then click **Next**.
13. In the Server Certificate window, accept the default option **Create a self-signed certificate for SSL encryption**, and then click **Next**. In an actual deployment of AD RMS, you would create a certificate for SSL encryption using Active Directory Certificate Services or use a certificate issued from a public CA.
14. In the Licensor Certificate window, type **mcsa2016ADRMS** in the Name text box, and then click **Next**.
15. In the SCP Registration window, accept the default option **Register the SCP now** and click **Next**.
16. In the Confirmation window, click **Install**. Your selections should look like Figure 9-23. When the installation is finished, click **Close**.

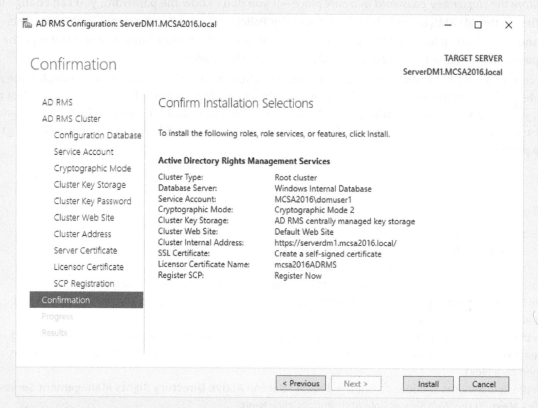

Figure 9-23   Confirming installation selections

17. Sign out of ServerDM1 and sign in again as **Administrator** to update the security token so that you can access the AD RMS console (if you don't sign out first, you will get an error when you try to open the AD RMS console). Verify that you can access the AD RMS console by clicking **Tools**, **Active Directory Rights Management Services** from the Server Manager menu.

18. Continue to the next activity.

Activity 9-5: Creating a Rights Policy Template

Time Required: 10 minutes

Objective: Create a rights policy template.

Required Tools and Equipment: ServerDC1, ServerDM1

Description: In this activity, you create a rights policy template in preparation for publishing rights-protected content. This template gives anyone view, edit, and save rights to published content.

1. On ServerDM1, open the **Active Directory Rights Management Services** console, if necessary.

2. In the left pane, click to expand the AD RMS server node, and then click **Rights Policy Templates**.

3. In the middle pane, click the **Create distributed rights policy template** link to start the Create Distributed Rights Policy Template Wizard.

4. In the Add Template Identification Information window, click **Add**. In the Add New Template Identification Information dialog box, type **TestTemplate** in the Name text box and **Test Rights Policy Template** in the Description text box. Click **Add**, and then click **Next**.

5. In the Add User Rights window, click the **Add** button. In the Add User or Group dialog box, click the **Anyone** option button, and then click **OK**.

6. Scroll through the Rights for ANYONE list box to see the predefined rights you can assign. Click the **Edit** check box (notice that the View and Save check boxes are selected automatically), and then click **Next**.

7. In the Specify Expiration Policy window, click the **Expires on the following date** option button in the *Content expiration* section, and then click a date and time in the corresponding list boxes.

8. In the Use license expiration section, click the **Expires after the following duration (days)** check box, type **10** in the text box, and then click **Next**.

9. In the Specify Extended Policy window, click the **Require a new use license every time content is consumed (disable client-side caching)** check box. Enabling this option means that users must have a network connection to the AD RMS cluster each time a protected document is opened. Click **Next**.

10. In the Specify Revocation Policy window, read the description of this policy option, and then click **Finish**. In the middle pane of the Active Directory Rights Management Services console, you see the new template. Leave this console open.

11. Continue to the next activity.

Activity 9-6: Exploring the Active Directory Rights Management Services Console

Time Required: 10 minutes
Objective: Explore the Active Directory Rights Management Services console.
Required Tools and Equipment: ServerDC1, ServerDM1
Description: In this activity, you review some of the options in the Active Directory Rights Management Services console.

1. On ServerDM1, open the **Active Directory Rights Management Services** console, if necessary.

2. In the left pane, click **Trust Policies**. Click the **Manage Trusted User Domains** link in the Trusted User Domains section of the middle pane. Read the information about trusted user domains.

3. Click **Export Trusted User Domain** in the Actions pane. Type **TUDmcsa2016** in the File Name text box and click **Save**. Notice that the file is saved in the Documents folder of the current user by default.

4. Click **Import Trusted User Domain** in the Actions pane. Read the information about importing a trusted user domain, and then click **Cancel**.

5. In the left pane of the Active Directory Rights Management Services console, click **Trusted Publishing Domains**. Notice that the mcsa2016ADRMS domain is trusted by default. Click **Export Trusted Publishing Domain** in the Actions pane. (This step is part of the AD RMS backup procedure.)

6. Click the **Save As** button. Type **TPDmcsa2016** in the File name text box and click **Save**.

7. In the Password and Confirm Password text boxes, type **Password01**, and then click **Finish**.

8. In the Actions pane, click **Import Trusted Publishing Domain**. Read the information about importing a TPD, and then click **Cancel**.

9. In the left pane, click **Exclusion Policies**. Click the **Manage AD RMS user exclusion list** link in the User Exclusion section in the middle pane.

10. In the Actions pane, click **Enable User Exclusion** and then click **Exclude RAC**. Read the information about excluding a user, and then click **Cancel**. Repeat this procedure for applications and lockbox exclusions.

11. In the left pane, click **Security Policies**. In the middle pane, click **Reset password**. This is where you can reset the cluster key password if you don't have the current one. You need it to restore AD RMS. Close the Active Directory Rights Management Services console.

12. Shut down all running servers.

Implementing Web Application Proxy

- 70-742 – Implement identity federation and access solutions:
  Implement Web Application Proxy (WAP)

Web Application Proxy (WAP) is a Routing and Remote Access role service that allows remote users to access network applications from any device that supports a web browser. Applications made available to users with this method are said to be *published applications*. Published applications can also be accessed from an Office client or a Windows store app. Web Application Proxy works with AD FS to enable features such as single sign-on.

Some requirements for configuring Web Application Proxy include the following:

- A functioning AD FS deployment on the network
- Two NICs installed on the Web Application Proxy server with one NIC accessible to the Internet and the other connected to the private network
- A certificate in the Personal certificate store issued by a CA that covers the federation service name and one that covers the address of the web application you publish

Here are the basic steps for configuring Web Application Proxy:

1. Install the Remote Access server role and the Web Application Proxy role service.
2. Open the Remote Access Management console from the Tools menu in Server Manager and click Web Application Proxy in the left pane (see Figure 9-24).

Figure 9-24 The Remote Access Management console

3. Click the Run the Web Application Proxy Configuration Wizard link, and then click Next in the Welcome window.
4. In the Federation Server window, enter the fully qualified domain name (FQDN) of the server running AD FS, and enter the credentials of the local administrator account on the federation servers (see Figure 9-25). Click Next.
5. In the AD FS Proxy Certificate window, select the certificate to be used by the AD FS proxy. The certificate must have already been installed in the server's Trusted Root Certification Authorities store. Usually, this is the same certificate used by the AD FS server to which you import the WAP server. Click Next.
6. Click Configure in the Confirmation window.

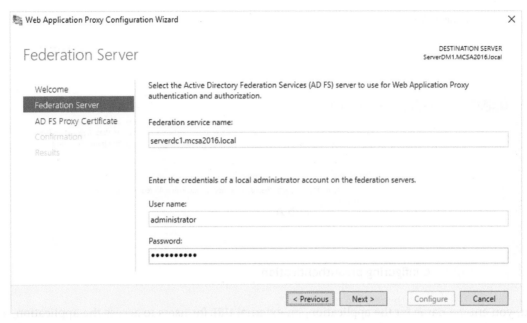

Figure 9-25   Specifying the AD FS server

Publishing Web Apps with WAP

After WAP is configured, you can begin publishing applications. To do so, in the Remote Access Management console, click Web Application Proxy, and click Publish in the Tasks pane (see Figure 9-26) to start the Publish New Application Wizard, which guides you through the process.

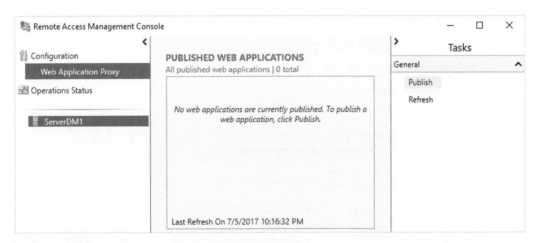

Figure 9-26   Publishing an application with WAP

When publishing a web application, you have two options for preauthentication (see Figure 9-27):

- *AD FS preauthentication*—With this option, client requests for the application are redirected to the federation server. If AD FS authenticates the user successfully, the request is forwarded to the application server. This option configures WAP as a proxy for AD FS because client requests must first go through the WAP server.
- *Pass-through preauthentication*—With this option, client requests for the application are sent directly to the application server.

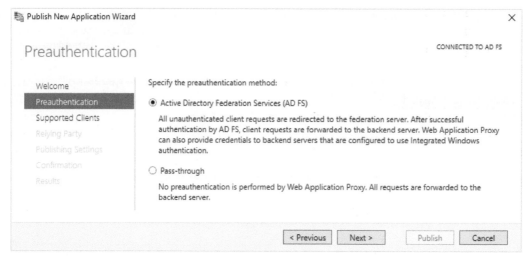

Figure 9-27 Configuring preauthentication

Next, you enter a name for the application, an external URL for users to access the application, a certificate for the application, and the URL of a backend server (if it's different from the external URL) as shown in Figure 9-28. The external and backend server URLs must be able to be resolved through DNS to the IP address of the Web Application Proxy server's external interface. Optionally, you can click Enable HTTP to HTTPS redirection so that all URLs entered using HTTP will be automatically changed to HTTPS. This option ensures that users can still access the application even if they omit the S in HTTPS for secure transactions.

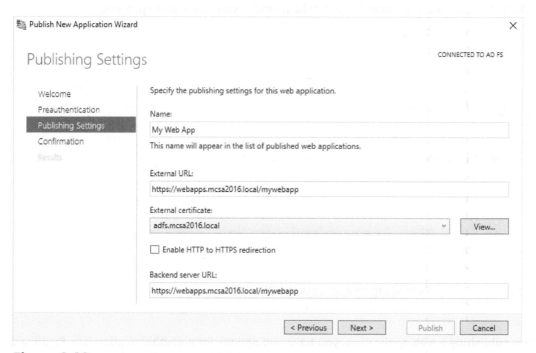

Figure 9-28 Web application publishing settings

Publishing Remote Desktop Gateway Applications

Remote Desktop (RD) Gateway applications are convenient ways for organizations to make applications available to users without having to install the application on each user's computer. In addition, RD Gateway allows users to access applications with a web browser interface. However, RD Gateway doesn't provide sufficient security by itself to allow users to access the applications remotely. You can use WAP as a front end to RD Gateway using either pass-through preauthentication or by using AD FS preauthentication. If you use pass-through authentication, you can simply publish the application as described in the previous section, choose pass-through preauthentication, and then specify the URL of the RD web server as the External URL.

To use AD FS preauthentication for RD Gateway, you must also create a Relying Party Trust on the AD FS server and specify the URL of the RD Gateway server as the Relying Party Trust identifier. Then, on the WAP server, publish the application, choose AD FS preauthentication, and follow the wizard. When prompted for the Relying Party, specify the relying party trust that you created on the AD FS server (see Figure 9-29).

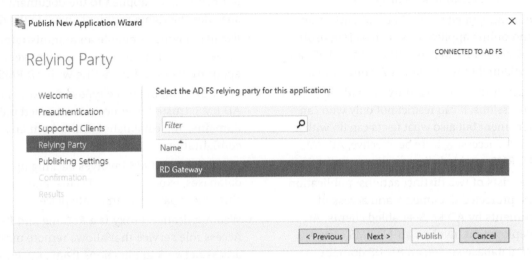

Figure 9-29   Specifying the RD gateway as the relying party for an RD Gateway app

Chapter Summary

- AD FS allows single sign-on access to web-based resources between business partners and in other situations when a single sign-on to diverse web-based resources is needed. Most business-to-business AD FS environments involve a federation trust between an account partner and a resource partner.

- An AD FS installation in Windows Server 2016 involves three role services: Active Directory Federation Services, Active Directory Rights Management Services, and Web Application Proxy. These roles use or integrate with AD DS technology to give users flexible, secure access to applications and network resources.

- AD FS deployment includes the following components: claims provider(s), relying party, relying party trust, claims provider trust, claim rules, certificates, and the attribute store.

- AD FS can be deployed in several situations. Depending on the situation, you might use a combination of AD FS role services to address an organization's federated identity needs. AD FS designs include web SSO, federated web SSO, and federated web SSO with forest trust.

- A relying party is the resource partner that accepts claims from the account partner to make authentication and authorization decisions. A relying party trust sets up the trust relationship between the claims provider and the relying party (resource partner).

- You configure a claims provider trust on the AD FS server that acts as the relying party (resource partner). This trust configures the relying party to trust the claims issued by the claims provider (account partner).

- Authentication policies enable you to determine what type of authentication is required in the AD FS system. There are two types of authentication policies: primary authentication and multi-factor authentication.

- Device registration is a feature that allows nondomain-joined devices to access claims-based resources securely; it enables you to permit users with smartphones and tablets to access domain resources without creating a security risk.

- AD FS can be integrated with other authentication services and online applications such as Microsoft Passport, Microsoft Azure, and Office 365. AD FS can also be configured to work with LDAP directories.

- AD RMS extends document security beyond file system permissions. It can restrict not only who can access a document but also what users can do with a document after accessing it. To be effective, AD RMS requires AD RMS–enabled client or server applications.

- AD RMS consists of two distinct actions: publication of AD RMS–protected documents and access of these documents by AD RMS–enabled clients. An AD RMS deployment involves an AD RMS server, an AD RMS database server, an AD DS domain controller, and an AD RMS–enabled client computer. AD RMS takes considerable planning and several pre-installation tasks.

- AD RMS uses four types of certificates to identify servers used in the AD RMS cluster, identify client computers that access AD RMS–enabled applications, and verify the identity of users and computers accessing AD RMS content.

- A license is a specific type of certificate for determining the rights a user has to publish or access protected documents. There are two types of AD RMS licenses: publishing and use. A publishing license is tied to a rights-protected document and is created when a client publishes the document. A use license is issued to certain users when they

authenticate to an AD RMS server and request access to a rights-protected document.

- The AD RMS service connection point (SCP) is defined during installation of the AD RMS root cluster and allows domain members to discover the AD RMS cluster automatically.

- Rights policy templates enable you to configure rights policies that are applied to rights-protected documents. When a document is published, a template can be applied to the document that specifies the rights recipients have to the document.

- Exclusion policies enable an administrator to prevent specific users, AD RMS client versions, or applications from interacting with AD RMS content.

- You can configure three types of trust policies with AD RMS: trusted user domains, trusted publishing domains, and established trusts from an AD FS configuration.

- Backing up AD RMS involves backing up the AD RMS databases, exporting the TPD file, and storing the cluster key password in a safe place.

- Web Application Proxy is a Routing and Remote Access role service that allows remote users to access network applications from any device that supports a web browser. Web Application Proxy works with AD FS to enable features such as single sign-on.

- After Web Application Proxy is configured, you can begin publishing applications. To do so, use the Remote Access Management console. When publishing a web application, you have two options for preauthentication: AD FS preauthentication or AD FS pass-through preauthentication.

- Remote Desktop (RD) Gateway applications make applications available to users without having to install the application on each user's computer. RD Gateway doesn't provide sufficient security by itself to allow users to access the applications remotely. You can use WAP as a front end to RD.

Key Terms

account partner
Active Directory Federation
   Services (AD FS)
Active Directory Rights
   Management Service (AD RMS)
AD RMS root cluster
attribute store
claim

claim rules
claims provider
claims provider trust
client licensor certificate (CLC)
device registration
federated web SSO
federated web SSO with forest
   trust

federation server
federation trust
machine certificate
Microsoft Passport
multi-factor authentication
   (MFA)
publishing license
relying party

relying party trust	server licensor certificate (SLC)	use license
resource partner	service connection point (SCP)	Web Application Proxy (WAP)
rights account certificate (RAC)	trusted publishing domain (TPD)	web SSO
rights policy template	trusted user domain (TUD)	

Review Questions

1. In a federation trust, the company whose users are accessing resources is referred to as which of the following?
   a. Account partner
   b. Claims provider
   c. Resource partner
   d. Federated server

2. What is the term for an agreed-on set of user attributes that both parties in a federation trust use to determine a user's credentials?
   a. Token
   b. Policy
   c. Claim
   d. Exclusion

3. What AD FS server role must be installed separately on a perimeter network to provide federation services to clients on untrusted networks?
   a. Web Application Proxy
   b. AD FS web agents
   c. Online responders
   d. Federated Web SSO with forest trust

4. You have several web applications that you want trusted Internet clients to be able to access with a single sign-on. The Internet clients aren't from a single company; they can be from anywhere on the Internet. Which AD DS design should you use?
   a. Web SSO
   b. Federated web SSO
   c. Federated web SSO with forest trust
   d. AD FS claims-aware web agents

5. Which of the following role services is the resource partner that hosts the resources accessed by the account partner and validates claims issued by the claims provider?
   a. Web agent
   b. AD Certificate Services
   c. Relying party
   d. Web Application Proxy

6. Which of the following is *not* part of a typical AD FS deployment?
   a. Web browser
   b. Certificate
   c. Account store
   d. DHCP

7. Which of the following should be installed to prevent employees from printing security-sensitive emails?
   a. AD LDS
   b. AD FS
   c. AD RMS
   d. AD DS

8. What should you configure in AD FS when you want the claims provider to trust the relying party from which claims are made?
   a. Claims provider trust
   b. Relying party trust
   c. Trusted user domains
   d. Trusted publishing domains

9. Which of the following is the storage location for the values used in claims?
   a. Claim directory
   b. Federation proxy
   c. Federation server
   d. Attribute store

10. What is the first step when configuring a relying party trust?
    a. Configure multi-factor authentication
    b. Choose issuance authorization rules
    c. Select the data source
    d. Configure a TPD

11. What should you configure if certain attributes from the claims provider must be mapped to attributes the relying party can accept?
    a. Acceptance transform rule
    b. Claims provider trust
    c. Authentication policies
    d. AD device registration

12. You and another company are engaging in a joint operation to develop a new product. Both companies must access certain web-based applications in this collaborative effort. Communication between the companies must remain secure, and use of exchanged documents and emails must be tightly controlled. What should you use?
    a. AD CS and AD LDS
    b. AD RMS and AD DS
    c. AD FS and AD RMS
    d. AD LDS and AD RMS

13. Which of the following is *not* part of a typical AD RMS installation in a production environment?
    a. AD RMS database server
    b. Active Directory domain controller
    c. Client certificate
    d. Microsoft Enrollment Service

14. You need to delegate AD RMS responsibilities to a junior administrator. You don't want to give the administrator more permissions than required to allow her to view RMS-related logs and reports. What should you do?
    a. Add the user to the Server Operators group on the AD RMS server.
    b. Delegate the AD RMS Template Administrator role.
    c. Delegate the AD RMS Auditor role.
    d. Add the user to the AD RMS Service group on the AD RMS server.

15. Which of the following is true about an AD RMS deployment?
    a. The service account must be a regular domain user.
    b. The AD RMS role must be installed on a domain controller.
    c. The database must be hosted by an external SQL server.
    d. The AD RMS role must be installed on a standalone server.

16. Which of the following is true about AD RMS installation and configuration?
    a. The SCP must be registered by a member of Domain Admins.
    b. You must use an unencrypted connection to support identity federation.
    c. A self-signed certificate can be used for the server certificate.
    d. The cluster key password can't be changed by the administrator.

17. Which of the following contains the public key of the AD RMS server?
    a. Use license
    b. Rights account certificate
    c. Publishing license
    d. Server licensor certificate

18. Which of the following is created when a client publishes a rights-protected document?
    a. Server licensor certificate
    b. Rights account certificate
    c. Publishing license
    d. Use license

19. Which of the following should you configure if you want to exclude certain application versions from accessing a rights-protected document?
    a. Exclusion policy
    b. Revocation policy
    c. Rights policy template
    d. Trusted publishing domain

20. Which of the following AD FS features should you configure if you want a user to gain access to AD FS–protected resources based on the credentials of the device they are using?
    a. Microsoft Passport support
    b. Support for LDAPv3
    c. Enhanced device registration
    d. Trusted publishing

21. What installation procedure must be followed to allow all the new AD FS features in Windows Server 2016 AD FS to be available when changing a Windows Server 2012 R2 AD FS server to a Windows Server 2016 AD FS server?
    a. Upgrade your Windows Server 2012 R2 AD FS server to Windows Server 2016.
    b. Install a new Windows Server 2016 AD FS server and decommission the old a Windows Server 2012 R2 server.
    c. Install the new Windows Server 2016 AD FS server and use a configuration template.
    d. Create a new GPO in Group Policy Management and link the GPO to the OU that contains the previous computer account.

22. Which of the following are requirements for configuring the Web Application Proxy role service on a Windows Server 2016 server? (Choose all that apply.)
    a. A database hosted by an external SQL server
    b. A functioning AD FS deployment on the network
    c. Two NICs, one NIC for the Internet and the other connected to the private network
    d. The installation of the Web Application Proxy on a standalone server

23. Which of the following preauthentication methods for publishing a web application with Web Application Proxy configures WAP as a proxy for AD FS because client requests must first go through the WAP server?
    a. AD FS pass-through preauthentication
    b. AD FS remote preauthentication
    c. AD FS preauthentication
    d. AD FS direct preauthentication

24. When using AD FS preauthentication for Remote Desktop, what type of trust must be used on the AD FS server?
    a. Claims provider trust
    b. Two-way trust
    c. AD FS trust
    d. Relying party trust

Critical Thinking

The following activities give you critical thinking challenges. Case Projects offer a scenario with a problem to solve and for which you supply a written solution.

Case Project 9-1: Illustrating a Federated Web SSO Design

This project can be completed in groups. Designs should be presented to the class with discussion concerning their implementation details.

You have been asked to consult with a publishing company, WebBooks, to develop an AD FS design. WebBooks wants its largest business partners, which are several booksellers, to be able to access purchasing and inventory web applications running on the WebBooks web servers.

WebBooks has a Windows Server 2016 network with Active Directory. It has a web server that's publicly accessible through the perimeter (DMZ) network and plans to add a web server to host the purchasing and inventory web applications. The applications are directory enabled.

Develop an AD FS design with an accompanying diagram that WebBooks can use to achieve its goal of giving business partners single sign-on access to its web-based applications. For clarity, include only one partner bookseller. You should include the following items in your design:

- A diagram with the account partner and resource partner labeled showing servers and server roles to run at both WebBooks and the bookseller location
- An explanation of the role that each server plays in the process
- A description of how authentication and authorization to web applications take place

Case Project 9-2: Devising an AD DS Design with AD FS and AD RMS

This project can be completed in groups. Designs should be presented to the class with discussion concerning implementation details.

Create a fictitious multilocation company that uses Windows Server 2016 Active Directory as its primary directory service. Describe the company's business and explain why it will benefit from using the following roles and how they will be used:

- AD DS, including RODCs
- AD FS
- AD RMS
- DNS

Keep in mind that the main goal of this project is to create a company in which these roles should be used. Create a diagram showing where servers will be located and indicating which roles will be installed on the servers. Include information about sites. Write documentation explaining why each role service is needed, and include information such as which servers will be global catalog servers and which servers will perform FSMO roles.

Present your project to the class, along with a detailed diagram showing sites, servers, role services, and so forth.

MCSA EXAM 70-742 OBJECTIVES

The table in this Appendix maps the exam objectives for Microsoft Certified Solutions Associate (MCSA) Exam 70-742, Identity with Windows Server 2016, to the corresponding chapter and section title where the objectives are covered in this book. After each main objective, the percentage of the exam that includes the objective is shown in parentheses.

MCSA Exam 70-742: Skill Measured	Chapter	Section
Install and configure Active Directory Domain Services (AD DS) (20–25%)		
Install and configure domain controllers	1, 6, 7	
• Install a new forest	1	Installing Active Directory
		Working with Forests, Trees, and Domains
• Add or remove a domain controller from a domain	1	Installing Active Directory
• Upgrade a domain controller	7	Upgrading Domains and Forests
• Install AD DS on a Server Core installation	1	Installing Active Directory
• Install a domain controller from Install from Media (IFM)	1	Installing Active Directory
• Resolve DNS SRV record registration issues	7	Configuring Sites/SRV Record Registration
• Configure a global catalog server	6	Understanding and Configuring Sites
• Transfer and seize operations master roles	6	Working with Operations Master Roles
• Install and configure a read-only domain controller (RODC)	6	Configuring Read-Only Domain Controllers
• Configure domain controller cloning	6	Cloning a Virtual Domain Controller
Create and manage Active Directory users and computers	2, 4	
• Automate the creation of Active Directory accounts	2	Automating Account Management
• Create, copy, configure, and delete users and computers	2	Managing User Accounts
		Working with Computer Accounts
• Configure templates	2	Managing User Accounts
• Perform bulk Active Directory operations	2	Automating Account Management
• Configure user rights	4	Security Settings
• Implement offline domain join	2	Working with Computer Accounts
• Manage inactive and disabled accounts	2	Managing User Accounts

MCSA Exam 70-742: Skill Measured	Chapter	Section
• Automate unlocking of disabled accounts using Windows PowerShell	2	Automating Account Management
• Automate password resets using Windows PowerShell	2	Automating Account Management
Create and manage Active Directory groups and organizational units (OUs)	1, 2, 4	
• Configure group nesting	2	Managing Group Accounts
• Convert groups, including security, distribution, universal, domain local, and domain global	2	Managing Group Accounts
• Manage group membership using Group Policy	4	Security Settings
• Enumerate group membership	2	Managing Group Accounts
• Automate group membership management using Windows PowerShell	2	Automating Account Management
• Delegate the creation and management of Active Directory groups and OUs	2	Working with Organizational Units
• Manage default Active Directory containers	1	What's Inside Active Directory?
• Create, copy, configure, and delete groups and OUs	2	Working with Organizational Units / Managing Group Accounts
Manage and maintain AD DS (15–20%)		
Configure service authentication and account policies	3	
• Create and configure Service Accounts	3	Managing Service Accounts
• Create and configure Group Managed Service Accounts (gMSAs)	3	Managing Service Accounts/Working with Managed Service Accounts
• Configure Kerberos Constrained Delegation (KCD)	3	Managing Service Accounts/Kerberos Delegation
• Manage Service Principal Names (SPNs)	3	Managing Service Accounts/Working with Service Accounts
• Configure virtual accounts	3	Managing Service Accounts/Working with Managed Service Accounts
• Configure domain and local user password policy settings	3	Configuring Account Policies
• Configure and apply Password Settings Objects (PSOs)	3	Configuring Password Settings Objects
• Delegate password settings management	3	Configuring Account Policies
• Configure account lockout policy settings	3	Configuring Account Policies
• Configure Kerberos policy settings within Group Policy	3	Configuring Account Policies/Kerberos Policy Settings
Maintain Active Directory	1, 6, 7	
• Back up Active Directory and SYSVOL	6	Maintaining Active Directory
• Manage Active Directory offline	6	Maintaining Active Directory
• Perform offline defragmentation of an Active Directory database	6	Maintaining Active Directory
• Clean up metadata	6	Maintaining Active Directory
• Configure Active Directory snapshots	6	Maintaining Active Directory

MCSA Exam 70-742: Skill Measured	Chapter	Section
• Perform object- and container-level recovery	6	Maintaining Active Directory
• Perform Active Directory restore	6	Maintaining Active Directory
• Configure and restore objects by using the Active Directory Recycle Bin	1	What's Inside Active Directory?/Recovering Objects with the Active Directory Recycle Bin
• Configure replication to Read-Only Domain Controllers (RODCs)	7	Active Directory Replication
• Configure Password Replication Policy (PRP) for RODC	7	Active Directory Replication
• Monitor and manage replication	7	Active Directory Replication
• Upgrade SYSVOL replication to Distributed File System Replication (DFSR)	7	Active Directory Replication
Configure Active Directory in a complex enterprise environment	1, 7	
• Configure a multi-domain and multiforest Active Directory infrastructure	1	Working with Forests, Trees, and Domains/ Understanding Domains and Trees
	7	Configuring Multidomain Environments
		Configuring Multiforest Environments
• Deploy Windows Server 2016 domain controllers within a pre-existing Active Directory environment	7	Upgrading Domains and Forests
• Upgrade existing domains and forests	7	Upgrading Domains and Forests
• Configure domain and forest functional levels	7	Upgrading Domains and Forests
• Configure multiple user principal name (UPN) suffixes	7	Configuring Multidomain Environments/ Configuring an Alternative UPN Suffix
• Configure external, forest, shortcut, and realm trusts	7	Active Directory Trusts
		Configuring Active Directory Trusts
• Configure trust authentication	7	Configuring Active Directory Trusts/Configuring Trust Properties
• Configure SID filtering	7	Configuring Active Directory Trusts/Configuring Trust Properties
• Configure name suffix routing	7	Configuring Active Directory Trusts/Configuring Trust Properties
• Configure sites and subnets	7	Configuring Sites
• Create and configure site links	7	Configuring Sites
• Manage site coverage	7	Configuring Sites
• Manage registration of SRV records	7	Configuring Sites
• Move domain controllers between sites	7	Configuring Sites
Create and manage Group Policy (25–30%)		
Create and manage Group Policy Objects (GPOs)	4, 5	
• Configure a central store	4	Working with Administrative Templates
• Manage starter GPOs	4	Group Policy Objects
• Configure GPO links	4	Group Policy Objects
	5	Configuring Group Policy Processing/Managing GPO Status and Link Status

MCSA Exam 70-742: Skill Measured	Chapter	Section
• Configure multiple local Group Policies	4	Group Policy Objects
• Back up, import, copy, and restore GPOs	5	Managing GPOs
• Create and configure a migration table	5	Managing GPOs
• Reset default GPOs	5	Managing GPOs
• Delegate Group Policy management	5	Managing GPOs
• Detect health issues using the Group Policy Infrastructure Status dashboard	4	Group Policy Objects/Group Policy Replication
Configure Group Policy processing	5	
• Configure processing order and precedence	5	Configuring Group Policy Processing/GPO Scope and Precedence
• Configure blocking of inheritance	5	Configuring Group Policy Processing/Group Policy Inheritance
• Configure enforced policies	5	Configuring Group Policy Processing/Group Policy Inheritance
• Configure security filtering and Windows Management Instrumentation (WMI) filtering	5	Configuring Group Policy Processing/GPO Filtering
• Configure loopback processing	5	Configuring Group Policy Processing/Loopback Policy Processing
• Configure and manage slow-link processing and Group Policy caching	5	Configuring Group Policy Client Processing
• Configure client-side extension (CSE) behavior	5	Configuring Group Policy Client Processing
• Force a Group Policy update	5	Configuring Group Policy Client Processing
Configure Group Policy settings	4	
• Configure software installation	4	Group Policy Settings
• Configure folder redirection	4	Group Policy Settings
• Configure scripts	4	Group Policy Settings
• Configure administrative templates	4	Working with Administrative Templates
• Import security templates	4	Working with Security Templates
• Import a custom administrative template file	4	Working with Administrative Templates
• Configure property filters for administrative templates	4	Working with Administrative Templates
Configure Group Policy preferences	4	
• Configure printer preferences	4	Configuring Group Policy Preferences
• Define network drive mappings	4	Configuring Group Policy Preferences
• Configure power options	4	Configuring Group Policy Preferences
• Configure custom registry settings	4	Configuring Group Policy Preferences
• Configure Control Panel settings	4	Configuring Group Policy Preferences
• Configure Internet Explorer settings	4	Configuring Group Policy Preferences
• Configure file and folder deployment	4	Configuring Group Policy Preferences
• Configure shortcut deployment	4	Configuring Group Policy Preferences
• Configure item-level targeting	4	Configuring Group Policy Preferences

MCSA Exam 70-742: Skill Measured	Chapter	Section
Implement Active Directory Certificate Services (AD CS) (10–15%)		
Install and configure AD CS	8	
• Install Active Directory Integrated Enterprise Certificate Authority (CA)	8	Deploying the Active Directory Certificate Services Role
• Install offline root and subordinate CAs	8	Deploying the Active Directory Certificate Services Role
• Install standalone CAs	8	Deploying the Active Directory Certificate Services Role
• Configure Certificate Revocation List (CRL) distribution points	8	Configuring a Certificate Authority
• Install and configure Online Responder	8	Configuring a Certificate Authority
• Implement administrative role separation	8	Maintaining and Managing a PKI
• Configure CA backup and recovery	8	Maintaining and Managing a PKI
Manage certificates	8	
• Manage certificate templates	8	Configuring a Certificate Authority
• Implement and manage certificate deployment, validation, and revocation	8	Configuring a Certificate Authority
• Manage certificate renewal	8	Configuring a Certificate Authority
• Manage certificate enrollment and renewal for computers and users using Group Policies	8	Configuring a Certificate Authority
• Configure and manage key archival and recovery	8	Maintaining and Managing a PKI
Implement identity federation and access solutions (15–20%)		
Install and configure Active Directory Federation Services (AD FS)	9	
• Upgrade and migrate previous AD FS workloads to Windows Server 2016	9	Active Directory Federation Services
• Implement claims-based authentication, including Relying Party Trusts	9	Active Directory Federation Services
• Configure authentication policies	9	Active Directory Federation Services
• Configure multi-factor authentication	9	Active Directory Federation Services
• Implement and configure device registration	9	Active Directory Federation Services
• Integrate AD FS with Microsoft Passport	9	Integrating AD FS with Additional Services
• Configure for use with Microsoft Azure and Office 365	9	Integrating AD FS with Additional Services
• Configure AD FS to enable authentication of users stored in LDAP directories	9	Integrating AD FS with Additional Services
Implement Web Application Proxy (WAP)	9	
• Install and configure WAP	9	Implementing Web Application Proxy
• Implement WAP in pass-through mode	9	Implementing Web Application Proxy
• Implement WAP as AD FS proxy	9	Implementing Web Application Proxy
• Integrate WAP with AD FS	9	Implementing Web Application Proxy
• Configure AD FS requirements	9	Implementing Web Application Proxy

MCSA Exam 70-742: Skill Measured	Chapter	Section
• Publish web apps via WAP	9	Implementing Web Application Proxy
• Publish Remote Desktop Gateway applications	9	Implementing Web Application Proxy
• Configure HTTP to HTTPS redirects	9	Implementing Web Application Proxy
• Configure internal and external Fully Qualified Domain Names (FQDNs)	9	Implementing Web Application Proxy
Install and configure Active Directory Rights Management Services (AD RMS)	9	
• Install a licensor certificate AD RMS server	9	Active Directory Rights Management Service
• Manage AD RMS Service Connection Point (SCP)	9	Active Directory Rights Management Service
• Manage AD RMS templates	9	Active Directory Rights Management Service
• Configure Exclusion Policies	9	Active Directory Rights Management Service
• Back up and restore AD RMS	9	Active Directory Rights Management Service

GLOSSARY

A

account partner In a federation trust, it's the trusted company whose users will be accessing resources of the trusting company (resource partner). *See also* resource partner.

Active Directory The Windows directory service that enables administrators to create and manage users and groups, set networkwide user and computer policies, manage security, and organize network resources.

Active Directory Administrative Center (ADAC) A GUI tool for managing Active Directory objects and accounts that is built on top of Windows PowerShell.

Active Directory Certificate Services (AD CS) A server role in Windows Server 2016 that provides services for creating a public key infrastructure that administrators can use to issue and manage public key certificates.

Active Directory Federation Services (AD FS) A Windows server role that allows single sign-on access to web-based resources across different forests or organizations.

Active Directory metadata Data that describes the Active Directory database, not the actual Active Directory data. Metadata can be left over if a DC had to be removed forcibly from the domain.

Active Directory replication The transfer of information between and among all domain controllers to make sure they have consistent and up-to-date information.

Active Directory Rights Management Service (AD RMS) A Windows Server role that enables administrators to create use policies to define how a document can be used after a user accesses it.

Active Directory snapshot An exact replica of the Active Directory database at a specific moment.

Active Directory Users and Computers (ADUC) A GUI tool for managing Active Directory objects and accounts.

AD RMS root cluster One or more servers configured with the AD RMS server role. Multiple servers can be used for redundancy and load balancing. *See also* Active Directory Rights Management Service (AD RMS).

administrative template files XML-formatted text files (with an .admx extension) that define policies in the Administrative Templates folder in a Group Policy Object (GPO). Custom ADMX files can also be created.

ADMX central store A centralized location for maintaining ADMX files so that when an ADMX file is modified from one domain controller, all DCs receive the updated file.

application directory partition An Active Directory partition that applications and services use to store information that benefits from automatic Active Directory replication and security.

assigned application An application package made available to users via Group Policy and places a shortcut to the application in the Start screen. The application is installed automatically if a user tries to run it or opens a document associated with it. If the assigned application applies to a computer account, the application is installed the next time Windows boots.

asynchronous processing A type of group policy processing that allows a user to sign in and see the desktop while policies are still being processed.

attribute store An LDAP–compatible database that stores the values used in AD FS claims. *See also* claim.

attribute value Information stored in each attribute. *See also* schema attributes.

authentication A process that confirms a user's identity, and the account is assigned permissions and rights that authorize the user to access resources and perform certain tasks on the computer or domain.

authoritative restore   A method of restoring Active Directory data from a backup to ensure that restored objects aren't overwritten by changes from other domain controllers through replication.

automatic site coverage   A feature in which each domain controller advertises itself by registering SRV records in DNS in sites that don't have a DC if the advertising DC has the lowest cost connection to the site.

B

background processing   Periodic group policy processing that occurs after a computer is running or a user is signed in.

batch file   A text file with the `.bat` extension that's used to enter a command or series of commands normally typed at the command prompt.

bridgehead server   A DC at a site that the Inter-Site Topology Generator designates to replicate a directory partition with other sites.

built-in user account   One of two user accounts created by Windows automatically during installation.

C

certificate practice statement (CPS)   A document describing how a certificate authority (CA) issues certificates containing the CA identity, security practices used to maintain CA integrity, types of certificates issued, the renewal policy, and so forth.

certificate revocation list (CRL)   A list of certificates that the CA administrator has invalidated before their expiration dates.

certificate template   A shell or model of a certificate that is used to create new certificates; defines characteristics of the certificate, such as the intended use and expiration date.

child domain   Domain that shares at least the top-level and second-level domain name structure as an existing domain in the forest; also called *subdomain*.

claim   An agreed-on set of user attributes that both parties in a federation trust use to determine a user's credentials. *See also* federation trust.

claim rules   Conditions that determine what attributes are required in an AD FS claim and how claims are processed by the federation server. *See also* federation server.

claims provider   A server that provides a user with claims to present to the resource partner for access to federated resources. *See also* claim *and* resource partner.

claims provider trust   A trust created on the AD FS server that act as the relying party or resource partner. *See also* relying party *and* resource partner.

client licensor certificate (CLC)   A certificate used in AD RMS that's issued to clients when they're connected to the AD RMS network; it grants them the right to publish protected content.

client-side extension (CSE)   An extension to the standard Group Policy client that applies specific types of group policy settings to client computers.

configuration partition   An Active Directory partition that stores configuration information that can affect the entire forest, such as details on how domain controllers should replicate with one another.

connection object   An Active Directory object created in Active Directory Sites and Services that defines the connection parameters between two replication partners.

constrained delegation   A type of delegation that limits the delegation to specific services running on specific computers. *See also* Kerberos delegation.

contact   An Active Directory object that usually represents a person for informational purposes only, much like an address book entry.

CRL distribution point (CDP)   An attribute of a certificate that identifies where the CRL for a CA can be retrieved and can include URLs for HTTP, FILE, FTP, and LDAP locations. *See also* certificate revocation list (CRL).

D

DC clone   A replica of an existing domain controller (DC).

delegated administrator account   A user account that has local administrative rights and permissions to the RODC, similar to members of the local Administrators group on a member computer or standalone computer.

delegation of control   In the context of Active Directory, the process by which a user with higher security privileges assigns authority to perform certain tasks to a user with lesser security privileges; usually used to give a user administrative permission for an OU.

device registration   A feature that allows nondomain-joined devices to access claims-based resources securely.

directory partition   A section of an Active Directory database stored on a domain controller's hard drive. These sections are managed by different processes and replicated to other domain controllers in an Active Directory network.

directory service   A database that stores information about a computer network and includes features for retrieving and managing that information.

Directory Services Restore Mode (DSRM)   A boot mode used to perform restore operations on Active Directory if it becomes corrupted or parts of it are deleted accidentally.

distribution group   A group type used when you want to group users together, mainly for sending emails to several people at once with an Active Directory-integrated email application, such as Microsoft Exchange.

domain   The core structural unit of Active Directory; contains OUs and represents administrative, security, and policy boundaries.

domain controller (DC)   A Windows server that has Active Directory installed and is responsible for allowing client computers access to domain resources.

domain directory partition   An Active Directory partition that contains all objects in a domain, including users, groups, computers, OUs, and so forth.

domain functional levels   Properties of domains that determine which features of Active Directory have domain-wide implications and which server OSs are supported on domain controllers.

domain GPO   Group Policy object stored in Active Directory on domain controllers. It can be linked to a site, a domain, or an OU and affect users and computers whose accounts are stored in these containers.

domain local group   A group scope that's the main security principal recommended for assigning rights and permissions to domain resources.

domain naming master   A forest-wide FSMO role that manages adding, removing, and renaming domains in the forest.

domain user account   A user account created in Active Directory that provides a single logon for users to access all resources in the domain for which they have been authorized.

downlevel user logon name   The user logon name field defined in a user account object that's used for backward-compatibility with OSs and applications that don't recognize the UPN format.

E

elevation   A process that occurs when a user attempts to perform an action requiring administrative rights and is prompted to enter credentials.

enterprise CA   A server running Windows Server with the AD CS role installed which integrate with Active Directory.

extension   An item in a Group Policy Object (GPO) that allows an administrator to configure a policy setting.

external trust   A one-way or two-way nontransitive trust between two domains that aren't in the same forest.

F

federated web SSO   An AD FS design in which a trust relationship is established between the resource partner and the account partner. *See also* account partner *and* resource partner.

federated web SSO with forest trust   An AD FS design that involves a trust between two Active Directory forests. One forest, which is in the perimeter network, is considered the resource partner. The second forest, which is in the internal network, is the account partner. *See also* account partner *and* resource partner.

federation server   A server configured to run the Federation Service role service. When used in an account partner network, its function is to gather user credentials into claims and package them into a security token. When used on the resource partner network, it receives security tokens and claims from the account partner and presents the claims to web-based applications for authorization.

federation trust   A trust between two networks using AD FS; one side of the trust is considered the account partner, and the other side is the resource partner. *See also* account partner *and* resource partner.

filtered attribute set   A collection of attribute data configured on the schema master; used to specify domain objects that aren't replicated to RODCs, thereby increasing the security of sensitive information.

Flexible Single Master Operation (FSMO) role   A specialized domain controller task that handles operations that can affect the entire domain or forest. Only one domain controller can be assigned a particular FSMO role.

Flexible Single Master Operation (FSMO) roles   Specialized domain controller tasks that handle operations that can affect the entire domain or forest. Only one domain controller can be assigned a particular FSMO.

folder redirection   A Group Policy feature that allows an administrator to set policies that redirect one or more folders in a user's profile directory.

foreground processing   Group policy processing that occurs when the system boots or a user signs in.

forest   A collection of one or more Active Directory trees. A forest can consist of a single tree with a single domain, or it can contain several trees, each with a hierarchy of parent and child domains.

forest functional level   A property of a forest that determines which features of Active Directory have forest-wide implications and which server OSs are supported on domain controllers.

forest root domain   The first domain created in a new forest.

forest trust   A trust that provides a one-way or two-way transitive trust between forests, which enables security principals in one forest to access resources in any domain in another forest.

forest-wide authentication   A property of a forest trust for granting users in a trusted forest access to the trusting forest.

fully qualified domain name (FQDN)   A domain name that includes all parts of the name, including the top-level domain.

G

global catalog (GC) server   A DC configured to hold the global catalog. Every forest must have at least one GC server. GCs facilitate domain-wide and forest-wide searches and logons across domains, and they hold universal group membership information.

global catalog partition   An Active Directory partition that stores the global catalog, which is a partial replica of all objects in the forest. It contains the most commonly accessed object attributes to facilitate object searches and user logons across domains.

global group   A group scope used mainly to group users from the same domain who have similar access

and rights requirements. A global group's members can be user accounts and other global groups from the same domain. *See also* group scope.

GPO enforcement   A setting on a GPO that forces inheritance of settings on all child objects in the GPO's scope, even if a GPO with conflicting settings is linked to a container at a deeper level.

GPO filtering   A method used to change the default inheritance settings of a GPO.

GPO scope   A combination of GPO linking, inheritance, and filtering that defines which objects are affected by the settings in a GPO.

group managed service account (gMSA)   A specially configured managed service account that provides the same functions as an MSA but can be managed across multiple servers. *See also* managed service account (MSA).

Group Policy caching   A client-side feature that loads policy information from a cache on the local computer instead of having to always download it from a domain controller.

Group Policy Container (GPC)   A GPO component that's an Active Directory object stored in the System\Policies folder. The GPC stores GPO properties and status information but no actual policy settings.

Group Policy Object (GPO)   A list of settings that administrators use to configure user and computer operating environments remotely through Active Directory.

Group Policy preferences   A feature of Group Policy that contains settings organized into categories and enables administrators to set up a baseline computing environment yet still allows users to make changes to configured settings.

Group Policy Template (GPT)   A GPO component that's stored as a set of files in the SYSVOL share. It contains all the policy settings that make up a GPO as well as related files, such as scripts.

group scope   A property of a group that determines the reach of a group's application in a domain or a forest, for example, which security principals in a forest can be group members and to which forest resources a group can be assigned rights or permissions.

group type   A property of a group that defines it as a security group or a distribution group.

H

hash algorithm   A mathematical function that takes a string of data as input and produces a fixed-size value as output; used to verify that the original data hasn't been changed and to sign CA certificates and certificates issued by the CA.

I

infrastructure master   A domain-wide FSMO role that's responsible for making sure changes made to object names in one domain are updated in references to these objects in other domains.

Install from Media (IFM)   An option when installing a DC in an existing domain; much of the Active Directory database contents are copied to the new DC from media created from an existing DC.

intermediate CA   A CA in a multilevel CA hierarchy that issues certificates to issuing CAs, which respond to user and device certificate requests; sometimes called a *policy CA*.

intersite replication   Active Directory replication that occurs between two or more sites.

intrasite replication   Active Directory replication between domain controllers in the same site.

issuing CA   A CA that interacts with clients to field certificate requests and maintain the CRL. *See also* certificate revocation list (CRL).

item-level targeting   A feature of group policy preferences that allows an administrator to target specific users or computers based on specified criteria.

K

Kerberos   The authentication protocol used in a Windows domain environment to authenticate logons and grant accounts access to domain resources; also the basis for authorization to network resources in a Windows domain.

Kerberos delegation   A feature of the Kerberos authentication protocol that allows a service to "impersonate" a client, relieving the client from having to authenticate to more than one service.

key archival   A method of backing up private keys and restoring them if users' private keys are lost.

Key Distribution Center (KDC)   A component of Kerberos that uses the Active Directory

database to store keys for encrypting and decrypting data in the authentication process. *See also* Kerberos.

key recovery agent (KRA)   A designated user with the right to recover archived keys.

Knowledge Consistency Checker (KCC)   A process that runs on every domain controller to determine the replication topology.

L

leaf object   A type of Active Directory object that doesn't contain other objects and usually represents a security account, network resource, or GPO.

Lightweight Directory Access Protocol (LDAP)   A protocol that runs over TCP/IP and is designed to facilitate access to directory services and directory objects. It's based on a suite of protocols called *X.500* developed by the International Telecommunications Union.

local GPO   Group Policy Object stored on local computers that can be edited by the Group Policy Object Editor snap-in.

local group   A group created in the local SAM database on a member server, workstation, or standalone computer.

local user account   A user account defined on a local computer that's authorized to access resources only on that computer. Local user accounts are mainly used on standalone computers or in a workgroup network with computers that aren't part of an Active Directory domain.

loopback policy processing   A Group Policy setting that applies user settings based on the GPO whose scope into which the logon computer (the one the user is signing in to) falls.

M

machine certificate   A certificate used in AD RMS that's created on a client computer the first time it uses an AD RMS application.

managed policy setting   A type of group policy setting by which the setting on the user or computer account reverts to its original state when the object is no longer in the scope of the GPO containing the setting.

managed service account (MSA)   A service account that enables administrators to manage rights and permissions for services with password management handled automatically.

Microsoft Passport An authentication service that provides multi-factor authentication combining a PIN or biometric sign-in with encrypted keys on a user device.

Microsoft Software Installation (MSI) file A collection of files gathered into a package with an `.msi` extension that contains the instructions regarding what Windows Installer needs to install an application.

migration table A list of security principals and UNC paths in a GPO that can be mapped to the security principals and UNC paths in a destination domain to which a GPO is being copied.

multi-factor authentication (MFA) An authentication process whereby users must authenticate with more than one method, such as with a username and password as well as a digital certificate or smart card.

multimaster replication The process for replicating Active Directory objects; changes to the database can occur on any domain controller and are propagated, or replicated, to all other domain controllers.

mutual authentication A type of authentication in which the identities of both the client and server are verified.

N

Network Device Enrollment Service (NDES) A service that allows network devices, such as routers and switches, to get certificates by using Simple Certificate Enrollment Protocol (SCEP), a Cisco proprietary protocol.

nonauthoritative restore A method of restoring Active Directory data from a backup that restores the database, or portions of it, and allows the data to be updated through replication by other domain controllers.

O

object In Active Directory, a group of information that describes a network resource, such as a shared printer, or an organizing structure, such as a domain or OU.

offline defragmentation Defragmentation of the Active Directory database that also compacts the database to improve performance. The Active Directory service must be stopped before offline defragmentation can occur.

offline domain join A feature that allows a running computer or offline virtual disk to join a domain without contacting a domain controller.

one-way trust A trust relationship in which one domain trusts another, but the reverse is not true.

online defragmentation Defragmentation of the Active Directory database that removes deleted objects and frees up space in the database but doesn't compact the database. Online defragmentation occurs automatically when Active Directory performs garbage collection.

online responder (OR) A role service that enables clients to check a certificate's revocation status without having to download the CRL. *See also* certificate revocation list (CRL).

operations master An Active Directory domain controller with sole responsibility for certain domain or forestwide functions.

organizational unit (OU) An Active Directory container used to organize a network's users and resources into logical administrative units.

P

password settings object (PSO) An Active Directory object that enables an administrator to configure password settings for users or groups that are different from those defined in a GPO linked to the domain.

PDC emulator A domain-wide FSMO role that processes password changes for older Windows clients (Windows 9x and NT) and is used during logon authentication.

permissions Settings that define which resources users can access and what level of access they have to resources.

piping Sending the output of one command as input to another command.

Privileged Access Management (PAM) A feature added with the Windows Server 2016 forest functional level that allows adding an account to a group temporarily.

public key infrastructure (PKI) A security system that binds the identity of a user or device to a cryptographic key that secures data transfers with encryption and ensures data authenticity with digital certificates.

published application An application package made available via Group Policy for users to install by using Programs and Features in Control Panel. The application is installed automatically if a user tries to run it or opens a document associated with it.

publishing license   A type of certificate used in AD RMS that's tied to a rights-protected document and is created when a client publishes the document.

R

read only domain controllers (RODC)   A DC that stores a read-only copy of the Active Directory database but no password information. Changes to the domain must be made on a writeable DC and then replicated to an RODC, which is called *unidirectional replication.*

realm trust   A trust used to integrate users of other OSs into a Windows domain or forest; requires the OS to be running Kerberos V5 or later authentication system that Active Directory uses.

referral   The process of sending a request for information about an object to DCs in other domains until the information is found.

registration authority   A server configured with the Web enrollment role service; also called a CA web proxy.

relative identifier (RID)   The part of a SID that's unique for each Active Directory object. *See also* security identifier (SID).

relying party   The AD FS resource partner that hosts the resources accessed by the account partner. *See also* account partner *and* resource partner.

relying party trust   An AD FS trust created on the AD FS server that acts as the claims provider in an AD FS deployment.

replication partner   A domain controller configured to replicate another domain controller.

resource partner   In a federation trust, it's the trusting company whose resources are accessed by the trusted company (account partner). *See also* account partner.

restartable Active Directory   A feature introduced in Windows Server 2008 that makes it possible to take Active Directory offline to perform maintenance operations instead of requiring a server restart in DSRM.

restricted enrollment agent   An enrollment agent that's limited to enrolling only specific users or security groups; available only with an enterprise CA.

RID master   A domainwide FSMO role that's responsible for issuing unique pools of RIDs to each

DC, thereby guaranteeing unique SIDs throughout the domain.

right   A setting that specifies what types of actions a user can perform on a computer or network.

rights account certificate (RAC)   A certificate used in AD RMS for identifying users of AD RMS content.

rights policy template   A component of AD RMS that enables you to configure policies for determining who can access a rights-protected document and what actions can be taken with the document.

root CA   The first certificate authority (CA) installed in a network. Clients are configured to trust the root CA's certificate and then implicitly trust the certificate of any CA that's subordinate to the root.

S

schema   Information that defines the type, organization, and structure of data stored in the Active Directory database.

schema attribute   A category of schema information that defines what type of information is stored in each object.

schema class   A category of schema information that defines the types of objects that can be stored in Active Directory, such as user or computer accounts.

schema directory partition   A directory partition containing the information needed to define Active Directory objects and object attributes for all domains in the forest.

schema master   A forestwide FSMO role that's responsible for replicating the schema directory partition to all other domain controllers in the forest when changes occur.

script   A series of commands that have been saved in a text file to be repeated easily at any time.

Security Accounts Manager (SAM) database   A database on domain member and workgroup computers that holds the users and groups defined on the local computer.

security filtering   A type of GPO filtering that uses permissions to restrict objects from accessing a GPO.

security group   A group type that's the main Active Directory object administrators use to manage network resource access and grant rights to users. *See also* group type.

security identifier (SID)   A numeric value assigned to each object in a domain that uniquely identifies the object; composed of a domain identifier, which is the same for all objects in a domain, and an RID. *See also* relative identifier (RID).

security templates   Text files with an `.inf` extension that contain information for defining policy settings in the Computer Configuration, Policies, Windows Settings, and Security Settings node of a local or domain GPO.

selective authentication   A property of a forest trust that enables administrators to specify users who can be granted access to selected resources in the trusting forest.

server licensor certificate (SLC)   A certificate used in AD RMS that contains the AD RMS server's public key and identifies the AD RMS cluster.

service account   A user account that Windows services use to log on to a computer or domain with a specific set of rights and permissions.

service connection point (SCP)   An AD RMS component that provides clients with URLs for the AD RMS cluster, which must be registered before clients can access the cluster.

service principal name (SPN)   A name that uniquely identifies a service instance to a client.

service ticket   A digital message used by Kerberos that is requested by an account when it wants to access a network resource, such as a shared folder. *See also* Kerberos.

shortcut trust   A manually configured trust between domains in the same forest for the purpose of bypassing the normal referral process. *See also* referral.

SID filtering   An option that causes a trusting domain to ignore any SIDs that aren't from the trusted domain.

site   In Active Directory, a physical location in which domain controllers communicate and replicate information regularly.

site link   A component of a site that is needed to connect two or more sites for replication purposes.

special identity group   A group whose membership is controlled dynamically by Windows and doesn't appear as an object in Active Directory Users and Computers or Active Directory Administrative Center; can be assigned permissions by adding it to resources' DACLs.

staged installation   An RODC installation method that doesn't require domain administrator credentials; a regular user at a branch office can perform the installation. Called *delegated installation* in Windows Server 2008.

standalone CA   A server running Windows Server with the AD CS role installed, but it has little Active Directory integration.

Starter GPO   A GPO template that can be used as a baseline for creating new GPOs much like user account templates.

synchronous processing   A type of group policy processing that forces the processing to finish before certain other system tasks can be performed.

SYSVOL folder   A shared folder that stores information from Active Directory that's replicated to other domain controllers.

T

ticket-granting ticket (TGT)   A digital message used by Kerberos; grants an account access to the issuing domain controller and is used to request a service ticket without having to authenticate again. *See also* Kerberos.

timestamp   A record of the time a message is sent; used in Kerberos authentication. *See also* Kerberos.

tombstone lifetime   A period of time in which deleted Active Directory objects are marked for deletion but left in the database. When the tombstone lifetime expires, the object is removed during garbage collection.

transitive trust   A trust relationship based on the transitive rule of mathematics; therefore, if Domain A trusts Domain B and Domain B trusts Domain C, then Domain A trusts Domain C.

tree   A grouping of domains that share a common naming structure.

trust relationship   An arrangement that defines whether and how security principals from one domain can access network resources in another domain.

trusted publishing domain (TPD)   A trust between AD RMS clusters in separate forests that allows an AD RMS cluster to issue use licenses for content published by another AD RMS cluster.

trusted user domain (TUD)   A trust between AD RMS clusters in separate forests that allows users in the trusted forest to access AD RMS content in the trusting forest.

two-way trust   A trust in which both domains in the relationship trust each other, so users from both domains can access resources in the other domain.

U

unidirectional replication   A replication method used with RODCs in which Active Directory data is replicated to the RODC, but the RODC doesn't replicate the data to other domain controllers.

universal group   A group scope that can contain users from any domain in the forest and be assigned permission to resources in any domain in the forest. *See also* group scope.

universal group membership caching   This feature stores universal group membership information retrieved from a global catalog server so that the global catalog server doesn't have to be contacted for each user logon.

unmanaged policy setting   A type of group policy setting that persists on the user or computer account, meaning that it remains even after the computer or user object falls out of the GPO's scope.

UPN suffix   The part of the user principal name (UPN) that comes after the @.

urgent replication   An event triggering immediate notification that a change has occurred instead of waiting for the normal 15-second interval before replication partners are notified.

use license   A type of certificate used in AD RMS that's issued to particular users when they authenticate to an AD RMS server and request access to a rights-protected document.

User Account Control Policies   Policies that determine what happens on a computer when a user attempts to perform an action that requires elevation. *See also* elevation.

user principal name (UPN)   A user logon name that follows the format *username@domain*. Users can use UPNs to sign in to their own domain from a computer that's a member of a different domain.

user template   A user account that's copied to create users with common attributes.

V

virtual account   A simple type of service account that doesn't need to be created, deleted, or managed by an administrator.

W

Web Application Proxy (WAP)   A Routing and Remote Access role service that allows remote users to access network applications from any device that supports a web browser. Applications made available to users with this method are said to be "published applications."

web SSO   An AD FS design that provides single sign-in access to multiple web applications for users external to an organization's network.

WMI filtering   A type of GPO filtering that uses queries to select a group of computers based on certain attributes, and then applies or doesn't apply policies based on the query's results.

INDEX